HANDBOOK OF NORTH AMERICAN BIRDS

Sponsored by the Smithsonian Institution

Peregrine (*Falco peregrinus*)

HANDBOOK OF

NORTH AMERICAN BIRDS

VOLUME 5

Family ACCIPITRIDAE (concluded)
Buteos
Golden Eagle

Family FALCONIDAE
Crested Caracara
Falcons

EDITED BY RALPH S. PALMER

Yale University Press   New Haven and London

Published with assistance from the foundation
established in memory of Philip Hamilton McMillan
of the Class of 1894, Yale College.

Set in Caledonia types by The Composing Room of Michigan, Inc. and
printed in the United States of America by
Vail-Ballou Press, Binghamton, New York.

Library of Congress Cataloging-in-Publication Data
   (Revised for vols. 4 & 5)

Palmer, Ralph S. (Ralph Simon), 1914–   ed.
   Handbook of North American birds.

   Vols. 1–3   "Sponsored by the American Ornithologists' Union
and New York State Museum and Science Service."
   Vols. 4–5   sponsored by the Smithsonian
Institution.
   Includes bibliographies and indexes.
   Contents: v. 1. Loons through flamingos.—
v. 2–3. Waterfowl.—v. 4–5. Diurnal raptors.
   1. Birds—North America—Collected works. I. Title.
QL681.P35   598.297   62–8259
ISBN 0–300–04060–1 (v. 5)
ISBN 0–300–04062–8 (v. 4 & 5 set)

*The paper in this book meets the guidelines for
permanence and durability of the Committee on
Production Guidelines for Book Longevity of the
Council on Library Resources.*

10   9   8   7   6   5   4   3   2   1

CONTENTS

Family Accipitridae (concluded)   1
    Broad-winged Hawk *Buteo platypterus*   3
    Short-tailed Hawk *Buteo brachyurus*   34
    Swainson's Hawk *Buteo swainsoni*   48
    White-tailed Hawk *Buteo albicaudatus*   74
    Zone-tailed Hawk *Buteo albonotatus*   85
    Red-tailed Hawk *Buteo jamaicensis*   96
    [Common Buzzard *Buteo buteo*]   134
    Ferruginous Hawk *Buteo regalis*   135
    Rough-legged Hawk *Buteo lagopus*   152
    Golden Eagle *Aquila chrysaetos*   180

Family Falconidae   233
    Crested Caracara *Polyborus plancus*   235
    Eurasian Kestrel *Falco tinnunculus*   250
    American Kestrel *Falco sparverius*   253
    Merlin *Falco columbarius*   291
    Aplomado Falcon *Falco femoralis*   315
    Northern Hobby *Falco subbuteo*   323
    Peregrine *Falco peregrinus*   324
    Gyrfalcon *Falco rusticolus*   381
    Prairie Falcon *Falco mexicanus*   407

Literature Cited in Volumes 4 and 5   425

Index to Volumes 4 and 5   461

Family ACCIPITRIDAE (concluded)
    Osprey
    Kites
    Bald Eagle and allies
    Harrier
    Accipiters
    Buteo allies

dorsal

BROAD-WINGED HAWK

Buteo platypterus

Rather small, stoutish buteo. Middle toe minus talon shorter than front of tarsus. Wings rather short and broad, the tip of the folded primaries reaching only to middle of tail; 3 outer primaries emarginated on inner web. Conspicuous alternating black and white tail bars; in Basic Plumage (dorsal view) typically 2 wide black and 2 narrower whitish ones are visible; in Juv., the bars narrower and number greater. **Color phases:** almost all individuals are "normal," or light; melanistic individuals are few and reported only in mainland birds.

"**Normal**" Basic Plumages: much of head, the dorsum, and upper wing coverts variably quite darkish; narrow black "mustache" mark; underparts white to whitish buff with transverse rusty barring that sometimes nearly supplants the ground color (except n. Caribbean birds, streaked longitudinally). Juvenal Plumage: darkish dorsal feathers margined palish brown; head tends to be streaked light and dark, with thin "mustache"; white or whitish venter with individually varying amount (nearly absent to heavy) of dark longitudinal streaking and more (usually 7, but to 9) narrower dark tail bars than in Basic. **Dark phases:** the "normal" pattern may be seen dimly in birds in any feathered stage, or it may be obscured except in the tail.

Mainland birds: sexes essentially similar in appearance, the ♀ larger; they overlap considerably in linear meas., but only slightly in wt. Sexes combined: length 13¼–17 in. (34–43.9 cm.), wingspread 34–39¾ (86–100), tail 5½–7 (14–18); wt. 9⅓–19 ¾ oz. (265–560 gm.)—dividing line between the sexes in summer adults is 13⅗ oz. with slight overlap.

One mainland and 5 Caribbean subspecies (Friedmann 1950).

DESCRIPTION *B. p. platypterus*. One Plumage/cycle with Basic I earliest definitive.

3

▶ ♂ Def. Basic Plumage (entire feathering), acquired by prolonged molting that begins in SPRING; retained a year. "**Normal**" phase: **Beak** blackish, grading proximally to grayish blue; cere pale yellowish to orange-yellow; **iris** varies from cinnamon grading downward to buffy brown, to somewhat brownish yellow, but pale gray to pearly gray of early life may persist for unknown length of time. **Dorsal coloring** from head to tail varies from a muted chestnut toward blackish brown, the darker individuals with more tawny feather margins; a sheen on new feathering; white feather bases in occipital region (common to many raptors); side of head mostly dark with light streaking and, on lower cheek, a narrow black "mustache" mark (rictal stripe); chin and throat whitish to white, often streaked blackish (sometimes heavily). **Underparts** dark streaks on shafts of white feathers are variously widened—to bars or diamonds—on upper breast, varying from muted brownish to variably brownish red and sometimes so extensive as to appear a solid color; they become transverse bars on lower breast; lower abdomen to tail white, in some with dark markings on under tail coverts; elongated "flags" (tibial feathers) have medium to light brownish red to tawny bars on pale background. Legs and **feet** some variant of yellow, talons black.

Tail (dorsal view) narrowly tipped whitish (may wear off); black subterminal bar generally wide, the next one very pale or white; the next proximal black one usually narrower than the distal one, and the dark-light alternation continues proximally. Outer tail feather has 3–4 wide blackish bars, and the intervening light bars usually continue as distinct across the outer web.

Wing outer webs of primaries vary with individual from barred blackish to evenly brownish black, inner webs typically whitish with 5–6 dark bands, which are more or less incomplete on the distal 4–5 primaries. Secondaries brown with distinct dark barring on the inner white webs, and tips muted brownish. Upper coverts essentially as dorsum. Wing lining usually white with some dark brownish markings, occasionally plain. **Dark phase:** see above.

▶ ♀ Def. Basic Plumage. Friedmann (1950) noted **1** that ♀♀ av. slightly darker than ♂♂ but that "extremes" were similar in the sexes, and **2** that the dorsal coloration varied with the individual from dusky with little rufous or brownish in feather margins through a continuous range of intermediates to darker with muted brownish feather edges and venter so heavily barred as to almost obscure any white. **Dark phase** individuals vary to some extent in all flying ages—at least in Basics to so dark that indication of "normal" pattern can only be discerned in tail.

AT HATCHING   Beak nearly black, cere very pale yellow and later more vivid, edge of gape flesh color, eyes blue-black (Burns 1911) or gray to bluish gray (J. Mosher). Known natal downs are as follows: A white down (Burns), also described as "short, dirty white" (D. and K. Wetherbee 1961) with eyes closed at first and talons gray. Some days later another down appears; it is white and soon much longer.

▶ ♂ ♀ Juv. Plumage (entire feathering) develops during the nestling period and is retained nearly a year. Primaries and secondaries begin to emerge at age 9–11 days posthatching. followed, in order of emergence of feathering, by the caudal, humeral, spinal, ventral, and capital tracts (Lyons 1983). Burns (1911) described feather development in detail; growth data for some body parts and wts. of growing nestlings were given by Fitch (1974), Lyons (1983), and Lyons and Mosher (1983). In general, growth of body parts precedes development of feathering, which is complete at 45–51 days.

Size is not a dependable character for determining sex; based on 16 morphological variables of 17 wild young between 1 and 46 days old, Lyons and Mosher (1983) worked out an age-estimation regression model for predicting age from these known data. In the Adirondacks of N.Y., according to Matray (1974), by the time the young leave the nest they have reached "adult" wt.: ♂ av. 380 gm. and ♀ 450.

"Normal" phase Beak and cere as in Basics; **iris** gray at time of nest leaving, gradually becoming 2-toned and variably brownish later. Top of **head** and nape dark, although much more basal white shows than in Basic; indistinct pale superciliary line; sides of head white streaked dark, the latter concentrated ("mustache mark") along sides of chin; chin and throat white or palish tan, often with dark midline, sometimes streaked. **Upperparts** much as in Basic, but wider buffy brown feather margins give a patterned effect, and basal white of some feathers are visible. **Underparts** whitish to light buffy yellowish or even pale brownish red, with elongated dark markings astride the feather shafts; these markings typically are larger, broader, and variable in shape on sides and flanks (they are sparse and mostly lateral on some individuals, and this apparently correlates with unmarked wing lining); lower abdomen to tail white. Tibial "flags" with heart-shaped tawny to reddish brown markings. Legs and **feet** pale yellow, talons black.

Tail Feathers av. longer and are narrower, with more rounded ends, than in Basic (when more squarish); 6–9 (usually 7) dark bars against a light background, the feathers basally white. Dorsal view: very tip of tail light; distal dark band usually widest; dark bars on inner vanes of feathers (outer vanes darkish, plain, or with faint indication of light barring); proximal barring uneven (pattern of adjoining feathers unaligned). Outer tail feather has very narrow dark bars on inner vane, the distal one sometimes 2-shaded; outer vane evenly dark (Burns 1911, D. Brinker).

Wing Essentially as Basic, except inner webs of outer 3 or 4 primaries mostly white; wing lining white or toward pale brownish red, lighter than in Basics and usually more sparingly marked, occasionally plain.

♂ ♀ **Dark phase** As "normal," but feathers margined rufous, especially on breast (B. H. Bailey 1917). Confirmation needed.

NOTE Prebasic I molting (out of Juv.) does not invariably yield a typical Basic tail pattern. In some individuals, inner feathers tend to have light areas more or less mottled dark. The outer feathers may be quite Juv.-like, intermediate (in shape, number of bars, etc.), or typically Basic. Occasionally, left and right outermost feathers of the same individual differ greatly—one being "retarded" (toward Juv.), the other "advanced" (toward Basic)—hormonal influence apparently having altered during molting. Thus birds with atypical tails presumably are in Basic I Plumage.

Molting As in various raptors, it is typical for active nests to contain some molted feathers (of the ♀) and down, to have down adhering to the outside of the nest, and to have feathers and down scattered on the ground below.

In Pa., according to Burns (1911), Prebasic I molt (out of Juv.) in calendar year after hatching occurs somewhat earlier than succeeding Prebasics. Evidently it also begins a few days earlier in the ♀ than in the ♂. Prebasic I molting lasted 81 days in a captive ♂ and ♀, the latter bird, especially, being reported on in great detail. Primaries are dropped in descending order (inner to outer), each with its upper covert, and some scapular feathers and the alula soon drop. [Contrary to standard procedure, Burns numbered the primaries from outer to inner and stated, erroneously, that they are renewed in that sequence.] The secondaries begin soon afterward, over a considerable span of time that overlaps primary molting, and from 3 molt centers and with some variation in feather sequence. In all Prebasic molts the tail feathers are usually dropped thus: central pair, outer pair, 3d from central, 2d from central, next to central, and next to outer; the last 4 pairs, however, vary in sequence. Tail molting begins fairly early during primary molting, as does head–body molting.

Individual variation in molting sequence is considerable. Furthermore, molting is seldom complete, except sometimes Prebasic I; some secondaries may be retained for more than 1 cycle. Molting of flight feathers is rarely bilaterally symmetrical (D. Brinker).

In Wis., 4 birds in Juv. feathering examined in May of calendar year after hatching (earliest, May 9) had begun molting primaries. Of 70 birds in Basic, only 4 (2 ♂ and 2 ♀) had dropped primaries (earliest, May 12). Thirty-seven breeding birds examined in July had replaced approximately 25% (range 5–70%) of wing flight feathers. On Sept. 26, a ♀ still was molting, with 5 rectrices in various stages of growth (T. Erdman). In the 37 nesting adults, in early July the most frequently observed new rectrices were: central pair 59%, outer pair 39%, 2d from central 23%, next to central 20%, 3d from central 11%, and next to outer 4%. With exception of central and outer pairs, rectrices may be dropped in a very short time (D. Brinker).

It is difficult to reconcile the above information with Skutch's (1945b) statement that migrant Broadwings in Mar.–Apr. in Costa Rica were "still molting"—clearly showed gaps in their wings and tails. Yearling (Juv.) migrants in late spring (late May–early June) near Rochester, N.Y., show onset of Prebasic I molting—1 or 2 feathers missing in the middle of each wing and, frequently, 2 central tail feathers missing (L. and N. Moon 1985).

Color phases Individual variation in the "normal" phase is considerable, as indicated above. Beyond this range of lighter to darker is a discontinuity separating the rather rare melanistic individuals. The focus of these in summer is in Alta., but in various seasons records exist at least for Man., Calif., Ariz., N.D., Wis., and Iowa (*B. p. "iowensis"* of B. H. Bailey 1917) and as far se. as s. Fla. For some further details on dark birds, see Friedmann (1950) and N. Johnson and Peeters (1963).

More or less **albinistic** individuals are known.

Measurements *B. p. platypterus*. See Friedmann (1950) and N. Snyder and Wiley (1976) for WING across chord, with some duplication of specimens measured.

N.Y. Nine ♂ WING across chord 262–278 mm., av. 268, TAIL 142–156, av. 150; and 10 ♀ WING across chord 274–292 mm., av. 285, and TAIL 155–178, av. 166 (Mosher and Matray 1974).

MD. Four ♂ WING across chord 264–270, av. 266 mm.; and 13 ♀ 271–281 mm., av. 275 (J. Mosher).

WIS. Breeding individuals, WING flattened: 14 ♂ WING 272–288 mm., av. 280, TAIL 149–161, av. 155; and 23 ♀ WING 275–300 mm., av. 292, and TAIL 156–169, av. 163 (D. Brinker). "Adults," Apr.–May: 40 ♂ WING 260–293 mm., av. 276, TAIL 143–165, av. 155; and 37 ♀ WING 271–304 mm., av. 288, and TAIL 151–172, av. 162 (D. Brinker, T. Erdman). Migrant birds in 1st fall (Juv.), mostly Aug.–Sept.: 11 ♂ WING

6

265–289 mm., av. 278, TAIL 156–172, av. 164; and 5 ♀ WING 281–302 mm., av. 291, and TAIL 162–182, av. 173 (D. Brinker, T. Erdman). Juvenal migrants in Apr.–May of calendar year after hatching: 3 ♂ WING 257–276 mm., av. 274, TAIL 154–169, av. 159; and 6 ♀ WING 279–298 mm., av. 289, and TAIL 162–176, av. 170 (D. Brinker, T. Erdman).

MINN. At Hawk Ridge near Duluth: 147 1st-fall birds (Juv.), sexes not distinguished, WING flattened 255–301 mm., av. 276, and tail 151–180, av. 165 (D. Evans).

From the above it is evident that the TAIL in both sexes av. about 10 mm. longer in Juv. than in Basic Plumages.

Although the larger av. dimensions of the ♀ are apparent, overlap in WING and TAIL meas. are sufficiently broad (flattened WING 25%, TAIL 30%) that these meas. should not be relied on to distinguish sex in Broadwings (D. Brinker).

Weight Breeding individuals: N.Y.—9 ♂ 310–400 gm., av. 357, and 10 ♀ 389–460, av. 440 (Mosher and Matray 1974). Md.—4 ♂ 325–355 gm., av. 343, and 13 ♀ 410–520, av. 454 (J. Mosher). Wis.—14 ♂ 328–368 gm., av. 351, and 23 ♀ 398–506, av. 453 (D. Brinker); in Apr.–May 40 ♂ 325–384 gm., av. 361, and 37 ♀ 394–559, av. 443 (D. Brinker, T. Erdman).

Juvenal birds: In Wis., mostly in Aug.–Sept. at Little Suamico, 11 ♂ 325–380 gm., av. 347, and 5 ♀ 385–430, av. 409; and individuals elsewhere in Wis. when nearing a year old in Apr.–May, 3 ♂ 321–324 gm., av. 323, and 5 ♀ 387–476, av. 433 (D. Brinker, T. Erdman).

First-fall birds at Hawk Ridge, Minn., sexes not distinguished, 142 weighed 265–502 gm., av. 373 (D. Evans).

Based on analysis of 37 known-sex Wis. breeders, wt. is a reliable indicator of sex—there is less than 3% overlap between ♂ ♂ and ♀ ♀. Also in Wis., spring wts. of over 70 "adults" of unknown sex fall into 2 size groups not significantly different from those of the 37 sexed birds weighed in July. Therefore, in Wis., approximately 99.2% of "adult" ♂ Broadwings weigh less than 385 gm., and 98.5% of ♀ ♀ exceed this figure (D. Brinker, T. Erdman).

Hybrids None reported.

Geographical variation Rather slight in size, based on extant data (see Subspecies). There is some variation in color saturation; in addition, mainland birds have a blackish phase with focus northwesterly, and in birds of Cuba and Isla de la Juventud [Isle of Pines] the longitudinally streaked venter of the Juv. stage is repeated thereafter throughout life. On av., mainland birds lay smaller clutches southerly. They are also highly migratory, while those of Caribbean is. are resident. At least one is. subspecies reportedly lays unmarked eggs.

Affinities No useful information.   RALPH S. PALMER AND JAMES A. MOSHER

SUBSPECIES Some is. races have been described from such scant material that some adjustment—even possibly elimination of names—may be advisable if and when more material is available. There is a possible problem as to whether some sightings and/or specimens in Cuba of birds with longitudinally streaked underparts are of young individuals that have managed to get there from the mainland. (Various Cuban specimens were collected in Sept. and Oct.) This approach might be expanded to postulate that is. populations result from fall vagrants from Fla. at one end and spring vagrants from Venezuela at the other and that established populations were (are?) augmented by occasional birds from the mainland. For meas. of a few is. specimens, see Friedmann (1950).

In our area   *platypterus* (Vieillot)—descr. and meas. given above. Dimorphic. Large breeding range in temperate N. Am. Highly migratory. In winter, some in Fla., but principally in s. Cent. Am. and the nw. ⅓ of S. Am.

Nominate *platypterus* has been taken on Trinidad. A "kettle" of some 500 Broadwings was seen on Tobago on Mar. 17, 1977 (Rowlett 1980), which must also have been nominate *platypterus*. It is unlikely that they succeeded in a northbound water crossing in spring, just as Broadwings rarely succeed in continuing southbound beyond the Fla. Keys in fall.

Extralimital   The following, all resident, are listed in clockwise sequence around the Caribbean perimeter. The 1st 2, although smaller than mainland birds, are the largest Caribbean birds.

cubanensis Burns—underparts in Basic Plumages continue the Juv. pattern—longitudinal streaking. Friedmann measured only 2 ♂ and 3 ♀, which av. smaller than mainland birds. Cuba and Isla de la Juventud [Isle of Pines]. Nowhere common. A mounted bird from Dominica (Hispaniola) is suspected of having been taken in Cuba (J. Bond 1980).

brunnescens Danforth and Smyth—reportedly (and excepting dark-phase mainland birds) a dark form, judging from Friedmann, who described a ♂ in Basic and a Juv. bird. Slightly smaller than mainland birds; heavily barred a muted brownish. Puerto Rico. This bird was not recorded during a span of 30 years in this century. H. and J. Recher (1966) suggested that it is only a migrant from N. Am., but J. Bond (1978) stated that the Broadwing breeds there and reported its occurrence at 6 localities. Historical data to 1977 were summarized by W. B. King (1981).

insulicola Riley—reportedly palest and smallest of the insular birds, based on scant material. Basic Plumage: underparts barred, spotted, and streaked. Antigua. Friedmann examined a ♂.

rivierei Verrill—reportedly slightly darker than the next-following; breast markings without ochraceous tinge, according to Friedmann, who measured a ♂ and ♀. Dominica, Martinique, St. Lucia.

antillarum Clark—av. smaller than mainland birds, and chin and throat more heavily streaked, judging from "adults" (4 ♂ and 3 ♀) (Friedmann); iris said to be yellowish white (Burns 1911). Barbados, St. Vincent, at least 5 of the Grenadines, Grenada, Tobago (common), Trinidad (occasional) (last 2 localities—Herklots 1961).

RALPH S. PALMER

FIELD IDENTIFICATION   A small, crow-sized, stoutish woodland buteo. **In our area,** usual or "normal" phase in Basic Plumage: underparts with variable amount— usually much—rusty reddish transverse barring; plain dark dorsum; contrasting tail pattern—a few alternating wide black-and-white bars. When flying or soaring, almost all of underwing appears white. The larger Red-shouldered Hawk has brownish red "shoulders" and narrower, hence more, alternating black-and-white tail bars (former substantially wider than latter); in flight shows rusty wing lining and conspicuous checkered black-and-white pattern in wing flight feathers. Cooper's Hawk has no white in its fairly long tail. (For important data on field identification of migrants, see Swainson's Hawk, below.)

As migrant and winterer, the Broadwing can be confused with the Roadside Hawk, which is very similar but has wider gray or rufous light tail bars and narrower black ones; in flight the underwing shows considerable conspicuous reddish brown. Also in this volume, see Gray Hawk (gray body and wing lining) and Short-tailed Hawk in light phase (white underparts).

Juvenal hawks pose considerable problems, even misidentified in hand by the novice. Some diagnostic features of the Broadwing are given at beginning of this species account. Young Broadwings have a variable amount of light streaking on the head; whitish or white underparts vary from sparsely to (usually) heavily streaked dark longitudinally, and dark markings on the white underwing apparently vary correspondingly; the tail has numerous narrow bands, alternating dark (usually 7) and light. In the Juv. Redshoulder ventral streaking is more concentrated anteriorly, there is a hint of red in the "shoulder," wing lining is toward rusty, and flight feathers of wing and tail have a checkered dark and light pattern (and unmarked tibial "flags" in most subspecies). Young Cooper's have dark markings throughout the light wing lining (as do some Broadwings) and a very contrasting pattern of barring in flight feathers of wing and tail, the latter with about the same number of dark bars as young Broadwing.

Dark phase at any age tends to show, though more or less obscurely, the pattern of the "normal" phase; even in darkest individuals the "normal" tail pattern is evident. Dark Redtails differ in pattern and are much larger. In Fla., the dark-phase Broadwing (very rare there) might be confused with a dark Short-tailed—see account of that species.

South of the border   Confusing species are principally 3 mentioned above; Roadside, Short-tailed, and Gray Hawks, all discussed elsewhere in this volume.

DAVID F. BRINKER

VOICE   The Broadwing's usual call has been described in numerous ways and by many persons. Much of the apparent variation may be accounted for by extent of alarm and difference in voice between the sexes plus differences among observers and in reporting. See compilation in Burns (1911). The usual call is a relatively pure-toned whistle of 2 recognizable notes; the 1st is short and is of a slightly higher pitch than the 2d, an extended plaintive note. It is described most often as *Kill-e-e-e* or *Pee-we-e-ee* (somewhat Killdeer-like), heard when an intruder approaches a nest or from a bird circling over a nesting territory. According to the practiced ear of the late A. A. Saunders (MS), the call is a prolonged high-pitched scream, all on one pitch or slurring slightly upward at beginning or end. There is variation in loudness. Pitch is "exceedingly high for a bird of its size—range A_6 to D_7, a tone higher than the highest note of the piano."

When both sexes are heard calling at the same time, they are distinguishable; the ♂'s voice is approximately an octave higher (Burns 1911, D. Brinker). Recordings of breeding Broadwings reacting to a Great Horned Owl used as a decoy near the hawk nest are not distinguishable to the human ear from the characteristic call (J. Mosher).

Three vocalizations were recorded and described by Matray (1974), including the call described above. The others: "transfer call" and "dismissal call." He described the former as "a series of whining sounds heard when the male gives food to the female" and the latter as "similar to the typical whistle, but somewhat more plaintive." His several sonagrams are much alike and also closely match the one of the characteristic call on the "Eastern Birds" recording produced to accompany R. T. Peterson's *Field Guide to Birds East of the Rockies*. Nonetheless, the calls are recognizably distinct to the human ear.

One other adult vocalization is reported. Shelley (in Bent 1937) 1st described it, based on observations of copulating birds in the wild, as a "wheezy whistle, with an intake of breath and then its expulsion, thus giving a 2-toned call that has a rather musical sound, as *whee-oou*." It was uttered each time the ♂ lowered his tail. Subsequently, Mueller (1970) described apparently the same call, made by a 2-year-old captive bird as it attempted to copulate on a gloved hand.

Nestlings A "peeping cry" when just out of the shell. A ♀ aged 29 days uttered a repeated *Chic-chic-chic* as it fought its human captor. A week or 2 past age 46 days and when hungry, a ♀ uttered a prolonged shrill *Che-e-e-e-the-e* (Burns 1911).

DAVID F. BRINKER

HABITAT **In our area** During the **breeding season** the Broadwing is a forest bird, generally perching under or in the tree canopy and foraging at openings, edges, and wet areas but also within woodland.

It nests in patches of a few acres in size to within large expanses of deciduous and mixed forest (in one area even in pine plantations), where it is usually the most common diurnal raptor. Nesting is associated regularly with wet areas relatively close by. Burns (1911) provided the 1st review of nesting habitat, giving information on nest tree species, height of nest in trees, and placement. Later studies: Rusch and Doerr (1972)—5 nests in 4-year period in Alta.; Fitch (1974)—3 nests in Kans.; Matray (1974)—14 nests in n. N.Y.; Bush and Gehlbach (1978)—1 site in Tex.; Keran (1978)—29 nests in Minn. and Wis.; Titus and Mosher (1981)—24 nests in w. Md.; Rosenfield (1984)—72 nestings in Wis. in 1976–1981; and Crocoll (1984)—18 nestings in w. N.Y. Full citations of most of these, plus other relevant papers, were given by Rosenfield.

The gist of various studies (of well over 500 nestings) is that the nest generally is 25–40 ft. up (range 8–70), primarily in the 1st main crotch of a moderate- to large-sized tree and in the bottom ⅓ of the forest canopy. Over 40 tree species are recorded, with various aspens, oaks, birches, pines, and larch preponderant. Burns stated that the "most abundant and characteristic species of the locality is apt to be the favorite." He noted that a preferred tree in ne. U.S. in his day was the chestnut (*Castanea dentata*), which, due to disease has been scarce in the wild in recent decades. Cantwell (1888) stated that in Minn. this hawk always nests in the immediate vicinity of a lake or marsh and less than 30 ft. aboveground. Keran's sites in Minn., in oak-aspen stands aged 35 years or older, were within 408 ft. (124 m.) of a forest opening and 468 ft. (143 m.) of a wet area. Also in Minn., ½ of Rosenfield's sites were in aspen and nearly a ⅓ were in white birch; like others, he reported a propensity for nesting near water and where habitat types were interspersed. Only Crocoll's (1984) study in w. N.Y. recorded nesting in pine plantations. Yet the Broadwing preferred larch for nesting (the Red-shoulder preferred beech), tended to nest on slopes (the Redshoulder on level terrain) less than 1 km. from a wet area, and built on a platform of horizontal branches against the trunk (the Redshoulder nested higher, in the 1st substantial crotch from the top).

Many authors have indicated that nearness to forest openings, edges, and woodland roads is important—these being foraging areas. Titus and Mosher demonstrated that while Broadwings place the nest closer to water and to a forest opening than would be expected nest sites otherwise are similar to randomly selected forest plots with regard to forest structure.

In migrations Concentrated as indicated on the maps in this volume. Favorable updrafts are a requisite; foraging is, at most, a very minor activity of any of the thousands of birds during passage.

Winter, in our area In s. Fla., Tabb (1973) noted that Broadwings and Redshoulders often use the same hunting areas. Most (of both species) are 1st-winter birds. Unlike Redshoulders, the Broadwings tend to occupy small areas for an extended time. There is stratification—Redshoulders use treetops, while Broadwings use the lower tiers of branches and tend to stay in the shade. The Broadwings have winter feeding territories from which Am. Kestrels have tried, usually unsuccessfully, to evict them.

Cent. and S. Am. Little useful information. In Costa Rica, migrant Broadwings prefer medium heights, seldom settling in the tops of trees (Slud 1964). For lack of information, Caribbean birds are not covered here.   JAMES A. MOSHER

DISTRIBUTION See spring and fall migration maps, which indicate most of occurrence in N. Am.; for resident Caribbean birds, see Subspecies, above. The following supplements the maps.

Spring Occurrences in coterminous U.S. in the 1980s extend to the Pacific coast, where they are few and irregular. In warmer months, occasionally seen n. of known breeding limits, as in extreme nw. Sask. Beyond, reportedly sighted May 14, 1983, at Ft. St. John, Yukon Terr. (1983 *Am. Birds* 37 891).

Breeding range Currently extends w. to cent. Alta., somewhere in the Dakotas or beyond, and to Okla. and e. Tex.; thence e. and s. to include the Gulf states and n. Fla. West of the longitude of the Dakotas, numbers thin drastically, but recent spread and/or increase in N.Mex., Ariz., Colo., Wyo., se. Idaho, and Mont. may indicate additional breeding range. May be expected occasionally in this season in Mexico and Cent. Am., presumably birds too debilitated to complete a migration.

Fall Occurs w. to the Pacific; now fairly regular in Utah and Nev.; small numbers regular in Calif. Dry Tortugas—1st recorded by W. E. D. Scott (1890); the birds are trapped there by lack of thermals (see Migration, below). There is no solid evidence that any birds from Fla. reach Cuba (where birds are resident) at present; see J. Bond (1973) for remote possibility. Almost no records from Yucatan (1st: Dec. 1958) and around the Gulf of Honduras, which are e. of lines of travel in Cent. Am.

Winter Occasionally a bird begins the season even to lat. 40° N but probably does not survive until spring. Rare in s. Calif. Very rare in e. Tex. Almost no Mexican records. A considerable number (at least 80% are Juv.) winter in Fla., almost all of them in areas approximately from Miami s. to Key West (commonest winter buteo on the keys). A ♀ banded Jan. 25 on Key Largo was found dead exactly 1 year later in Chiapas, Mexico (Tabb 1973). In Cent. Am., occurs s. from Guatemala—principally in S. Am. with s. limits approximately in n. Bolivia and s. Brazil.

Recorded as **fossil** from the Pleistocene of Va. (1 site) and Fla. (3) and from 1 **prehistoric** site each in Iowa, Ill., W.Va. (identification uncertain), Puerto Rico, and Martinique. (From Brodkorb 1964, with 2 additions.)   RALPH S. PALMER

MIGRATION   *B. p. platypterus*. The migrations of the Broadwing are more interesting than might be expected of a bird rather inconspicuous at other seasons of the year. Its travels are widely extended, are accomplished with minimum expenditure of energy, and follow routes that at some points are so geographically restricted as to concentrate spectacular numbers of individuals. These 3 circumstances combine in a method and outward form of migration that is shared with Swainson's Hawk and in part by the Turkey Vulture and several of the kites but is not duplicated by any other bird species of the W. Hemisphere.

Extent of migration   Readily apparent from the maps; distances from the n. fringe of summer range to s. edge of range in the austral summer, skirting the Gulf of Mexico, approach 5,500 mi. and from the weighted center of boreal summer range, somewhere in sw. Que. or se. Ont., to center of "wintering" in Colombia in S. Am., some 4,800 mi. Such distances, 10,000–11,000 mi. round-trip, are well into the upper brackets of travel for any diurnal raptor in N. Am.

The strategy of Broadwing migration is so unusual that a rather detailed description is needed to understand it. Briefly, it is based on exploitation of rising air currents to gain altitude, followed by gliding on set wings in the general direction of travel. The supporting updrafts and favoring winds are associated with weather patterns that recur at intervals of several days or more during the seasons of migration, and since these patterns typically cover a broad front, they set off waves of Broadwing movement simultaneously over wide areas, thus contributing to the great numbers seen together at points of geographical restriction. Down the ages, Broadwings and other soaring raptors have evolved a singular ability to ride favorable weather systems with the least possible effort. A mechanical factor in this skill is the configuration of wings and tail for aerodynamic efficiency. In gaining or maintaining altitude, both are spread to fullest extent, primaries separated; in gliding, wing shape is changed by slight retraction of the "elbow," slight advance of the "wrist," and partial folding of primaries to produce pointed tips, angled backward, and the tail is narrowed. An added behavioral factor is freedom from flock attachment, which allows each bird to adjust itself to changes in the currents of air on which it moves. By deft use of rising air for lift, Broadwings accomplish major parts of their travels with very little flapping flight and thus, except for adjustments of wing and tail surfaces for balance, with little energy expenditure.

Updrafts used in migration may be divided into 4 general types: 1 In hilly country even a slight wind blowing up a slope at an angle to the trend of a ridge acquires an upward component that, at the crest and for an appreciable distance to leeward, will support a gliding hawk. Where the ridge tops are rough and broken, shifting air currents may cause lower birds to alternate their glides with short bursts of flapping; higher birds sail more steadily. **2** In flatter country, thermals rising from fields and other open spaces on a sunny day supply not only initial lift for a circling hawk but under favorable conditions carry it to a height from which the following glide covers many miles; in the whole sequence, except for 2 or 3 quick wingbeats to gain speed in passing from circling to gliding, there is virtually no flapping flight. **3** In a springtime weather pattern common across the Mississippi basin, a moderate to gentle flow of warm air from the sw. is displaced upward as it overrides retreating cool air to the ne.; hawks sail on the rising air behind the front for miles with little wing motion. **4** Where the land borders a large body of water, a temperature differential between the two may set up a sheet of rising warm air on which again hawks may glide in a quartering direction for long distances with minimal effort. Currently, it appears that every substantial movement of Broadwings is based on one of these 4 types of rising airflow or on a combination of thermals with any of the other 3. In simplest terms, the migration is a process of locating updrafts sufficient to support forward motion and, when none can be found, of putting down into the nearest woods or trees to await more favorable conditions.

While such a method is economical, it has limitations. Two simple examples are apparent to an observer: for ridge migration in hilly country the wind must come from a rearward angle to the direction of flight, and for thermals in flatter country the sun must be well above the horizon—that is, in the seasons of migration, from 0800–0900 hrs. to 1600–1700 hrs. A 3d limitation, not clearly revealed until its results are plotted on maps, is nevertheless a major determinant of routes traveled. While a land surface reflects the sun's heat in thermals, a water surface absorbs and diffuses it. Over water, Broadwings apparently find no usable thermals. Thus, they very rarely will attempt any water crossing that cannot be accomplished by gliding from the height to which the last land-based updrafts have lifted them. In turn, this means that all Broadwings traveling from or to extensive nesting grounds n. and ne. of the Great Lakes—at a rough estimate ½ or more of the total population—are funneled into 4 relatively narrow corridors around or between the lakes. It also explains why very nearly the whole migration, both fall and spring, goes around the Gulf of Mexico over land—not by the shorter distance across the water. And from this, again, comes the broad pattern of migration in Canada and the U.S.: in the center, 4 travel lanes controlled by the Great Lakes corridors; on the e. side, a wide lane using chiefly the updrafts of the Appalachian ridges; and on the w. side, another wide pathway between the Mississippi R. and the edge of the High Plains; all converge on s. Tex. in fall, diverging thence in spring. Except on the Appalachian route, the spectacular passages of Broadwings that arouse such interest among observers are caused by avoidance of watercrossings.

The constrictions imposed by the Great Lakes and the Gulf of Mexico are rigid, but elsewhere the routes followed by migrating Broadwings are regularly modified by local weather conditions and are, therefore, essentially fortuitous. Once Broadwings are in the air, the most constant weather-related influence on the routes they follow during the day is downwind drift. It operates to some extent in all circumstances but has greatest effect and is most readily demonstrated from birds migrating on thermals. A

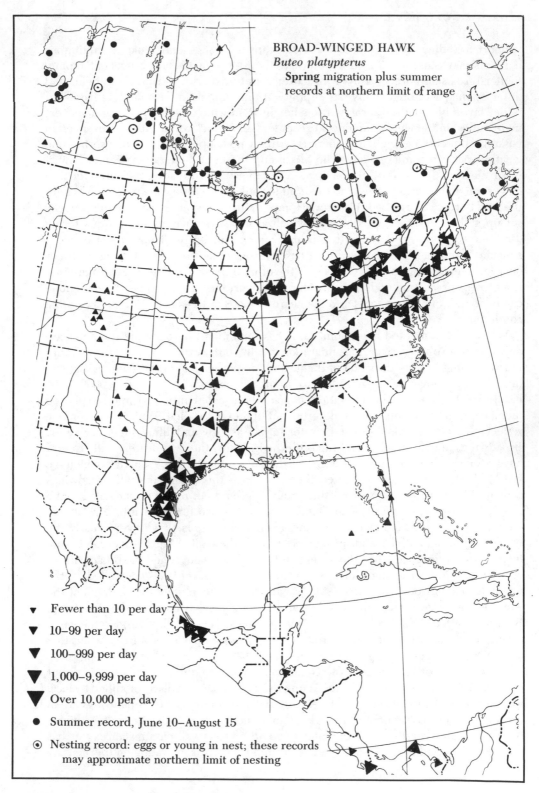

BROAD-WINGED HAWK
Buteo platypterus
Spring migration plus summer
records at northern limit of range

▼ Fewer than 10 per day

▼ 10–99 per day

▼ 100–999 per day

▼ 1,000–9,999 per day

▼ Over 10,000 per day

● Summer record, June 10–August 15

⊙ Nesting record: eggs or young in nest; these records
  may approximate northern limit of nesting

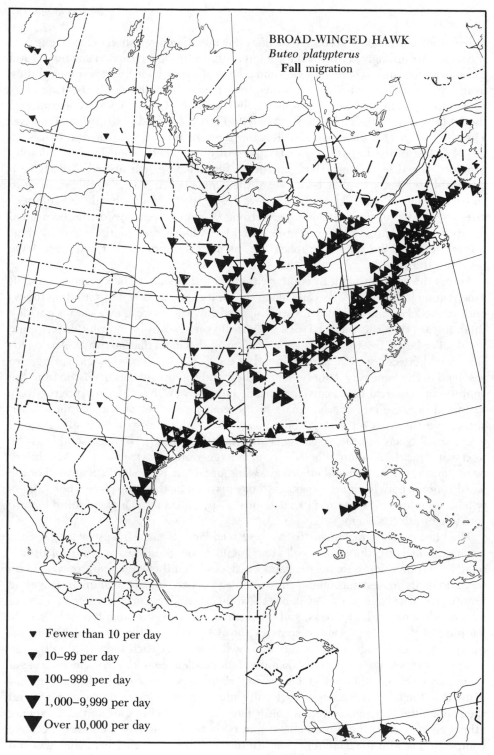

BROAD-WINGED HAWK
Buteo platypterus
Fall migration

▼ Fewer than 10 per day

▼ 10–99 per day

▼ 100–999 per day

▼ 1,000–9,999 per day

▼ Over 10,000 per day

thermal column is rarely vertical; it inclines downwind in proportion to the strength of the wind. Accordingly, a Broadwing circling within a thermal is carried downwind and toward the top, unless wind direction and course of travel coincide. It resumes gliding from a point to leeward of its original course. It may then change the bearing of its course to rejoin the old course at some further point, or it may hold to its bearing and then will be following a new course parallel to but downwind of the original course. The general effect of uncorrected drift is to widen the front of a movement, that is, to disperse the birds, but this result is apparently less likely when local topography provides visual lead lines. Thus, on the e. flight lane in fall drifted birds have a noticeable tendency to glide back toward the connected Appalachian ridges, even to an isolated monadnock like Mt. Wachusett, Mass.; the minority that do not compensate, especially on days of moderately strong w. winds, account for the occasional flights directly along the upper Atlantic coast. Even these birds continue to work their way w. and, by the time they reach Va., as appears from the autumn map, have regained the ridges.

Across the midcontinent, by contrast, there is little evidence of correction for drift except among the Great Lakes and along the Gulf coast. Broadwings rounding the w. ends of the lakes, most notably L. Erie, on a fall day when a fresh nw. wind is pushing them toward the water, may be seen to extricate themselves by intermittent flapping flight, at or below treetop level, over much longer distances than are usual. Analogous situations between w. Fla. and the bend of the Tex. coast, both fall and spring, are resolved in the same way. Otherwise, the thousands of Broadwings that issue from the confines of the Great Lakes corridors in fall, and of s. Tex. in spring, are progressively scattered because individuals remain in thermals for shorter or longer times, leave successive thermals on slightly different courses, and otherwise take advantage of every small change in the air currents on which they travel. They reassemble at the next water barrier, but until then are seen in large groups less frequently. Whether e. or w., one result of drift and other local weather factors is an elastic definition of the word *route;* where birds are in passage today may not be the same place where others will be seen tomorrow, or on a like date next year, unless some topographical feature restricts or attracts them.

The behavioral characteristic that allows Broadwings to make full use of local weather conditions is freedom from flock attachment. Many published accounts of Broadwing migration refer to their gatherings as "flocks," but the word is appropriate in no more than its loosest meaning—an assemblage of any bird or mammal. Traveling groups, small or large, do not evidence the tight internal organization seen in flocks of waterfowl, shorebirds, starlings, and other birds that move through the air by steady flapping of their wings. On the contrary, at every stage of the circle-soar-glide sequence of Broadwings, close observation will show that each individual, although aware of others in the group, is following an independent course. Thus, any number of them may circle in a thermal, giving the superficial appearance of a flock, but each has come in at the bottom as a single, each will glide out at the top as a single, and, beyond the probability that some incoming birds have been guided to the "kettle" by seeing others already in it, there is no observable tie between any 2 of them. A suggestive comparison is with the Sandhill Crane. In the corridor between Lakes Michigan and

Superior a flock of cranes, flying in formation, will sometimes enter the lower part of a thermal in which Broadwings are circling. As they do so, their formation dissolves and each crane circles and rises independently. At the top, however, as they leave the thermal, they immediately resume flock form and flapping flight. It appears, then, that the Sandhills must flap to maintain formation, while the hawks, without flock attachment, are free to exploit with greater efficiency the air currents upon which they ride.

The same independence of movement is manifest during later parts of the glide phase. A common example occurs when a number of Broadwings have recently come off the top of a thermal on some warm still day in Sept. and are now sailing across the sky in loose ranks and long swaying lines. To an observer on the ground, and therefore without reliable perception of the relative levels of different birds, it may appear that they are maintaining some sort of formation. The illusion is produced by the fact that the air is relatively quiet and they are all riding the same gentle currents. If presently, however, they encounter even mild turbulence in the air, from whatever cause, each bird adjusts to its own surroundings, and the apparent formation slowly changes shape or dissolves. Again, as they near the ends of their glides and a new kettle begins to form ahead or to one side, the nearer birds may join while those farther away or higher in the air sail on until they come across another updraft, of which there will be many on a favorable day.

The end result of freedom from flock attachment, which cannot be explained otherwise, is the gradual dispersal that takes place as Broadwings issue from restricted corridors and move out across the midcontinent flatlands. Traveling waterfowl hold tenaciously to their formations; Broadwings do not. They may be gathered by weather patterns into what seem like flocks, but in fact they are as individually free to use the air currents around them as are Red-tailed Hawks or eagles, which are never described as flocking birds. In sum, it appears that freedom from flock attachment is a key element in the ability of the Broadwing to make long migrations with the least possible effort.

Favorable weather patterns for Broadwing migration in Canada and the coterminous U.S. are, as might be expected, seasonally different. In fall, 80% or more of all movement is on days with wind between wnw. and nne., surface wind speed below 12 mph, atmospheric pressure rising, and 24-hr. temperature dropping (Currie et al., in Harwood 1985) These conditions characteristically follow the e. departure of a low pressure system succeeded closely by a high pressure system; a flight is likely to begin as soon as the cold front passes and wind speed drops into the required range. In spring, virtually all movement is on s. winds on the se. side of a low pressure system moving e. ahead of a cold front. South of the U.S. there is less information available on flight weather; presumably the same patterns are involved, with the added factor of trade winds at some times and places.

Initial phases of daily flight routine Best observed from some vantage point high enough to look down into the trees on a wooded slope, facing e., where a considerable number of Broadwings put down the previous afternoon. Soon after the sun is up next morning, single birds may be picked out here and there perched quietly on open branches, apparently warming themselves after the cool of the night. One or 2 hrs. go by, the chill lessens, and now they are increasingly restless, 1 or 2 perhaps changing position to sunnier branches. Suddenly, far up the slope where the sun has lain

17

longest, 1 is in the air, flapping heavily as it rises above the trees. In a moment it seems to catch a bit of support beneath its wings and circles once before flapping again. Now another is up—2 more—several at once—in quick succession many others. The 2d bird has now found a stronger updraft over an opening in the woods and is circling steadily. One by one, the others change course to join it, some from several hundred yds. away, and within another 1–2 mins. a kettle has formed, from the top of which each hawk soon will be gliding away on a course between s. and sw. if it is fall, ne. and n. if it is spring. A day's travel has begun, not only here but at countless other places along the flight lanes where weather is favorable. Details will vary with topography and the available roosting trees, but whether the birds are leaving a forested slope in the Appalachians, a farm woodlot in the midlands, or a grapefruit grove in s. Tex., the pattern is similar—the initial heavy flapping to rise above the treetops, the casting about by individual birds for updrafts, and the quick convergence by others on the bird that begins to circle most steadily.

As the air warms on **a flight day,** thermals become stronger and rise higher, and with them go the hawks, until by early afternoon many appear to be moving near the limits of human vision. A great kettle of Broadwings, revolving lazily against lofty white clouds, soon raises the question, "How high?" For serious watchers, the answer bears on the further question of how many passing Broadwings are seen from a given lookout and how many go by undetected. Given the nature of Broadwing migration, it is reasonable to suppose that birds would remain in a thermal as long as they find lift, and no longer. Initial answers to these questions were based on systematic ground observation, which soon revealed that an available-time factor biased the data. When watching for hawks from the ground one constantly sweeps the sky overhead for the telltale shape on which to focus one's vision. With the unaided eye this field of vision is relatively wide; with an optical aid it is narrowed in reverse proportion to the gain of visual range. Compared with other observers, one's acuity of vision may be greater or less, but the general rule, derived from many trials, is that the sharpest unaided eye will not regularly pick up a single Broadwing more than 1 mi. away. In effect, then, the area under unaided visual search will be an inverted bowl shape, with limits at about 1,600 yds. in every direction. To scan this area with the unaided eye requires an appreciable length of time; with binoculars, a longer time. Assuming an av. glide speed of 40 mph for a Broadwing, one has 1½ min. to locate a bird approaching on a course to pass directly overhead and at moderate height above one's own level, and another 1½ min. as it goes away; with the bird at 800 yds. one has only slightly less time, *but at 1,600 yds. only the briefest moment.* Visibility of birds passing to 1 side of an observer is further reduced in proportion to the angle between line of sight and the perpendicular. A figure illustrates these situations at a glance. Although a kettle of birds will be picked up more readily than a single, the conclusion was reached that the percentage of passing Broadwings seen from a ground station diminished rapidly if they were above 800 yds. and approached 0 at about 1,600 yds. directly overhead. As to how much higher birds might pass, experienced watchers noticed that when detected near the limits of unaided vision and watched through binoculars, thus increasing the range of observer vision, still higher birds were rarely seen.

In recent years, particularly in New Eng., hawk watchers using radar, advanced optical instruments, and a motor glider capable of traveling with birds, have collected

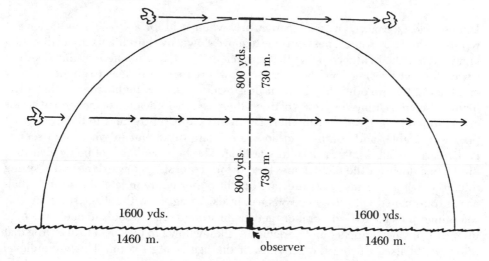

800 yds.
730 m.

800 yds.
730 m.

1600 yds.   1600 yds.

1460 m.   1460 m.

observer

data that seem to confirm the limits of **high-level migration** at not much over 1 mi. On flight days in Canada and most of the U.S., afternoon thermals, although variable, usually rise 1,300–1,800 yds., and in the Gulf states probably higher, before reaching a layer of cooler air, where they condense into cumulus cloud. As expected, Broadwings tend to stay in a thermal while the air is clear, most birds of a kettle beginning to glide just below the cloud cap, but a relative few actually enter the cloud and have been observed coming out of it again at a distance. Birds have even been seen to emerge from the top of a cloud cap. Those in clouds are lost to sight by observers on the ground but may still be able to see the ground, if but dimly. On emergence, their glide courses do not differ greatly from those of birds below the cap, which indicates some ability to maintain direction in clouds. To summarize, there is no current evidence, even by radar, of Broadwing migration much above 2,000 yds.

Closing phases of a day's flight   Subject to as many variables as other parts of the routine, although uncommonly seen by ground observers because they may take place wherever lift declines and roosting cover exists. When weather deteriorates during the day, individuals drop out so gradually as to attract little attention. By contrast, on a fine afternoon birds stay up until they sense a loss of lift in the air, either because the sun is too low for thermals or the wind is dying away, as it usually does toward sundown. In hilly country, the occasional favorable opportunity for observation is provided when a loose group of gliding Broadwings happens to be approaching a watchpoint as lift gives out. Abruptly, 1 bird half folds its wings and pitches down into the trees, followed by another and another, until all those at lower levels have disappeared while some still high in air sail on a bit further. The down birds are now scattered through the woods and will not be seen above the canopy until morning. In the flatter country of the midlands, where Broadwings are more widely dispersed and travel on high thermals, only by chance will an observer be at hand to catch sight of their precipitate afternoon descent when, with wings closed, they plunge down headfirst at speeds that blur their shapes to the eye.

Once down, Broadwings again become quiet woodland hawks, difficult to observe.

19

Under a closed canopy of trees, particularly when held for a day or 2 by inclement weather, they may sometimes continue to move slowly by short flights in the direction of migration, the evidence being that a watch on the 1st favorable morning does not always find birds rising from the same woods where they were seen to put down a day or 2 before. On the other hand, when Broadwings in the w. flight lanes settle for the night in isolated clumps or groves of trees, there is little indication of movement across open ground from 1 wood to another. Down birds apparently hunt to the extent that prey is available, and continue to do so until late dusk, but in what often seems, particularly in fall, a rather desultory fashion. The best evidence of how much they hunt when down for the night comes from the n. tier of states toward the end of spring migration when, for instance, they are caught rather easily in late afternoon by bal-chatri traps baited with live mice or small birds. Or again, with foliage still thin, it is sometimes possible to find 1 or more at twilight around some woodland pool, watching intently from low branches and periodically gliding down to pick up a toad or frog that has exposed itself during the activities of the egg-laying season. This groundlevel hunting terminates just before full dark, when the hawks slip away through the shadows to find night perches, as is their habit, on open branches at low and moderate heights. In fall, with foliage still thick and the woods dry, hunting activities are hard to find and watch. On the mornings of flight days, more often in fall than spring, they pick up prey when opportunity offers—a bird is occasionally seen carrying a small snake or frog in its talons as it passes a watchpoint. Again, it is not unusual to see a bird in flight diverge slightly to pick up a dragonfly or other large insect and tear it apart on the wing to eat the body, but this carries no suggestion of serious hunting. Unlike falcons and the larger buteos, relatively few passage Broadwings show full crops. By and large, available data indicate that migration, both fall and spring, is accomplished on a very meager intake of food. Considering the great numbers of them which flood through Tex. and the Cent. Am. countries, it hardly could be otherwise.

Fall migration   With its dependence on weather cycles, fall migration tends to be leisurely and variable. The nesting season ends in late July and early Aug. when the young attain flight and breeders are molting. Shortly after the young birds begin a gradual dispersal, which at first is probably random in direction but by late Aug. tends increasingly s. At the same season, total population includes a floating segment of prebreeders, young of the previous year, which apparently scatter after completing their spring migration and are thus virtually indistinguishable during the summer. These birds may be presumed, by analogy with other hawks more easily observed, to complete their molting earlier than breeders and begin to wander by early Aug., along with the young of the year. The movements of the 2 age classes (cohorts), intermixed, are revealed chiefly by the occasional occurrence of "flights" along the upper Atlantic coast, sw. N.S. to Cape May, N.J., in middle and late Aug., which are typical results of downwind drift after periods of brisk w. winds. These gatherings may run to many hundreds of birds and are more than likely to be made up of 60–70% of individuals in Juv. feathering, with many of the remainder probably a year older. At the same time a thin s. movement with a more normal ratio of 1-fall birds to breeders is getting under way across the interior n. portions of Broadwing range. This movement builds in numbers with each successive period of favorable weather until observation points in

20

the n. tier of states see their peaks Sept. 12–25, with thousands of birds passing on flight days. South of the Great Lakes and beyond the Appalachian ridges, dispersal over flat country reduces the wave effect, but presently it reappears in Tex., where the great flight days, with counts running into the tens of thousands, commonly occur during the last week of Sept. and 1st week of Oct. South of the Mexican border there are few fall data short of Costa Rica and Panama, where strong movements begin in mid-Oct. and continue into Nov., with major arrivals on the wintering grounds in Nov. Meanwhile, late stragglers linger in the n. states well into Oct., with occasional small groups in passage even at the end of Oct. Apparently these attract no attention in Tex. or beyond, where they are anticlimactic. Assuming, however, that some continue into S. Am. over the same time periods as earlier migrants, they may still be on the move in Dec., thus rounding out the span of fall migration at upwards of 4 months.

Spring movement From the wintering range movement begins slowly in mid-Feb. and gathers full volume in Panama by Mar. 12–22, in Mexico w. of Veracruz city by Mar. 20–Apr. 1, and in s. Tex. by Mar. 25–Apr. 12. Arrival of breeding adults across the n. tier of states begins about Apr. 18 and is largely complete by May 10, but the youngest cohort (hatched the previous year and still recognizable by streaked underparts) continues to pass the major watchpoints until at least June 10.

Spring migration produces 2 examples of Broadwing travel on the updraft caused by temperature difference between a large body of water and its bordering landmass. The 1st is above the coastal plain of e. Mexico between Veracruz state and the U.S. border, some 500 mi. Throughout this distance, at the time of peak movement in late Mar., the usual weather pattern includes a process that sustains migration: the spring sun beating down on the plain warms the air rapidly in the morning, and from about 0800 hrs. on cooler air from the ne. tradewind over the gulf is drawn inshore, gathers strength, and pushes inland, its leading edge underrunning and quickening the upward and w. flow of heated air over the plain. In due course this warm air, having risen several thousand ft., meets cool upper air above the foothills of the Sierra Madre Oriental and condenses into a long narrow band of white cloud, more or less continuous from s. to n. for long distances. As the tradewind freshens during the day, the cloud cap moves inland and higher, but wherever it is at a given time, the bulk of the migrating raptors will be not far to the e.—on a good day thousands and tens of thousands of Broadwings, Swainson's Hawks, and Turkey Vultures sail n. in what may be called, quite soberly, broad sheets of spaced-out individuals. The 2 hawks sometimes mix, the vultures almost never, and as a rule the 3 appear to be stratified at different levels, which may reflect subtle variations in their aerodynamic efficiency. In a sheet of Broadwings each bird, while heading a bit e. with wings spread wide to catch the lift of rising air, is also sliding off n. at an angle to its heading, covering mile after mile without flapping or circling. This is, without question, the most spectacular concentration of Broadwings to be found anywhere along their routes of travel, for not only does it involve nearly the entire migratory population but as they round the sw. edge of the Gulf of Campeche, the flight lane is narrowed to some 35 mi. by the foothills to the w., here at their closest approach to the coast. The Cordoba-Veracruz highway, transecting this corridor at right angles, supplies convenient watchpoints under the width of each day's flight. On Mar. 26, 1962, systematic counts back and forth under a major movement, at fixed

21

intervals of time and distance, gave a count-estimate of 8,200 Broadwings actually seen; extrapolated for noncount time and width of passage, the calculated probable number crossing the road northbound from 0800 to 1700 hrs. was 145,000 (Hagar).

The 2d instance of an air-temperature differential is found along the s. shores of the Great Lakes. The physical basis for the situation is that a body of water, because of more active vertical heat-cold exchange, cools more slowly in fall and warms more slowly in spring than the adjacent land. In Apr.–May each of the Great Lakes is blanketed by a plano-convex lens of cool air, its greatest thickness over the deepest and therefore coldest water. Warm s. winds, on which hawks arrive, ride up and over the relatively sluggish lake air below but soon begin to lose both heat and forward velocity. Hawks of all kinds circle in the last land-based thermals and at the top glide off across the water toward Canada but soon find the buoyancy of the air decreasing. Most species—accipiters, Rough-legged Hawks, and N. Harriers, all of the falcons—tend to complete the crossing by flapping flight when the lift and push are gone, but Broadwings invariably reverse course when their support drops below a critical level and return to land. For a large group of gliding birds, the reversal often is so abrupt and concerted as to suggest the presence of an invisible wall that bars further passage. The return may or may not be to the point of departure, according to the configuration of the shore. At Whitefish Point, upper Mich., where the crossing is some 18 mi. over open water, the birds come back again and again to the point itself, where most of them circle in thermals and presently try again; the remainder, a small but fairly constant fraction after each return, head off se. by quartering to the wind around Whitefish Bay and eventually cross into Canada s. of Sault Ste. Marie. At the Bass Is. in the sw. corner of Lake Erie, the end result is similar but is achieved by diverging routes. This would be, if completed, a stepping-stone crossing—from Catawba Point on the mainland to South Bass I. is some 2½ mi. (4 km.), across Middle Bass to N. Bass 2 short water-jumps, thence to Pelee I. 5 mi. (8 km.) or so, and to Point Pelee on the n. shore an additional 8 mi. (12.8 km.). Broadwings readily cross to the Bass Is. but there is no current evidence that they ever reach either Pelee I. or Point Pelee. Instead, after circling as high as possible in thermals over S. Bass, they glide off sse. at an angle to the wind and may be found regaining the s. shore at Cedar Point or beyond, a distance of 9–10 mi. e. of Catawba Point. Here they turn ne. and become the most w. units of the swelling stream of hawks, constantly increased by new arrivals from the sw., which travel up the L. Erie shoreline, cross overland to L. Ontario just w. of Rochester, and at last cut across the se. corner of the lake from Derby Hill to Pulaski, N.Y., where they are free to disperse toward the ne. nesting grounds. The whole stretch is about 400 mi.; some birds gain altitude in thermals from time to time, but many glide for miles, sustained by the warm sw. wind riding up and over the cooler lake air.

One problem of more than local interest remains to be considered: what becomes of **wind-drifted birds** that **in fall** regularly find themselves facing formidable water barriers at Brier I., N.S. (35 mi. to Grand Manan, 50 mi. to nearest point on the Maine coast); Cape May, N.J. (16 mi. to Cape Henlopen); Cape Charles, Va. (15 mi. to Cape Henry); and, in particular, Key West, Fla. (90 mi. to Cuba)? The shortest of these barriers exceeds, by 3 times, the L. Erie crossings at which Broadwings balk. Each of the upper Atlantic coast watchpoints is at the end of a long peninsula running sw. or s.

and bordered to the w. by wide water. Reports from the 3 stations share several recurring themes: most birds are in their 1st autumn of life, they circle to "great heights" in thermals, and they disappear from sight over the water on courses that, it is assumed, will take them across, but yet there are collateral observations of retrograde movement, rather straggling in form, up the w. sides of the peninsulas. A negative clue, quite striking on the plotted map, is lack of evidence that birds arrive on shores opposite the supposed departure points—no records at all for Capes Henlopen and Henry or the coast of Maine, and from Grand Manan a record of 2 small kettles totaling 75 birds, which are more likely to have been wind-drifted from the mainland, 9 mi. w., than to have come against the prevailing winds 35 mi. from N.S. In light of the limitations of ground observation previously discussed, it is probable that the birds that seem to leave over water do, in fact, turn back unseen when the thermals lose their lift, regain the shores n. of the departure points, and eventually work their way around the broad waters to their n. narrowings. In further support of this alternative, substantial numbers of passage Broadwings are seen on the mainland side of the Delaware R. n. of Cape May at Port Penn, Del., and of Chesapeake Bay n. of Cape Charles near Annapolis, Md., both places requiring water crossings of less than 4 miles.

The situation in the Fla. Keys is on a larger scale than those just discussed; it has attracted considerable attention because it suggests use of secondary routes to and from winter range by way of Cuba (90 mi.) and either Yucatan (a further 120 mi.) or the long chain of Leeward and Windward Is. (not less than 13 water crossings of 30–80 mi. each). Any solid evidence for the use of such routes is almost wholly confined to the keys. Here, variable numbers of Broadwings, estimated in different years at totals of 5,000–10,000, and 90% or more of them said to be 1st-fall birds, pass down the chain by thermaling high enough over 1 is. to reach the next by gliding and thus arrive at Key West. Numbers reported along the way are relatively small, rarely exceeding a 100–200, but apparently they accumulate at Key West to occasional totals of 1000s. On some days they seem reluctant to go further, circling in thermals to considerable heights but presently returning to mill about over the land before trying again. There are also numerous records of Broadwings moving back up the keys toward the mainland, but not in numbers to equal the Key West gatherings. Ultimately, despite false starts and retrograde movements, credible observers report the periodic formation of large kettles circling high over Key West and appearing to depart s–sw. over the water; they are not seen to return.

The unanswered questions about Fla. Broadwings begin with their source. Rather surprisingly, the plotted fall map shows, with the exception of 1 bird at Hilton Head I., S.C., a complete absence of Broadwing migration in autumn over the coastal plain and piedmont of the se. Atlantic states from Va. to the vicinity of Palm Beach, Fla. This directs attention to another possible origin. As 1000s of passage birds come off the end of the Appalachian ridges in n. Ga. and ne. Ala. and disperse on thermals over the flatter lands to the sw., some of them, largely inexperienced 1st-fall birds, are wind drifted se. until they reach the Gulf coast of the Fla. panhandle. Here they divide, part known to turn w. along a minor but well-documented flight lane past Pensacola and part continuing to drift se. into the Fla. peninsula. There are few records of the latter

23

after they round Apalachee Bay, but this could result from their being too widely scattered through the broader parts of the peninsula to be noticed until they are brought together by its abrupt narrowing at the s. end. That all s. Fla. birds are off course, wandering aimlessly, is suggested by the observed lateness of their movements; there are records of sizable numbers passing watchpoints in Broward and Dade cos. through Nov. into Dec. Notwithstanding scarcity of specific data across n. and cent. Fla., the s. end of the Appalachians is the likely source of the Key West gatherings.

As for the further travels of the Broadwings seen to leave Key West, existing evidence from the Caribbean region, both fall and spring, is meager. (See Subspecies, above, for resident birds on some is. of the Caribbean perimeter.) Definite fall records of nonresident birds arriving in w. Cuba, departing thence toward Yucatan, arriving or moving s. in Yucatan, or moving e. from Cuba seem to be wholly lacking. In the season of n. migration there are reports of kettling birds from Tobago and Little Tobago, near the S. Am. coast, and from Puerto Rico, but none from Cuba. The whole of peninsular Fla. supplies no indication of regular spring migration—in some years but not others a few scattered reports of single birds, occasionally 10–12 in a day, along the se. coast from Plantation Key to the vicinity of Cape Merritt, but none farther n. across e. Ga. and S.C.

An added difficulty in accounting for Broadwings leaving Key West in fall is scarcity of information about relevant weather patterns over the Strait of Fla. In the broad picture of mainstream migration across the U.S. the basic requirement, very clearly, is rising air to carry the birds to heights from which, with following winds, they can glide in the seasonal direction of travel. Woodcock (1942), watching gull behavior from shipboard, hypothesized autumn thermals over the inshore waters of the se. Atlantic states that enable the birds to forage 100 mi. at sea and return to land at will, but there is no evidence of valid application to hawks over the Strait of Fla. The factors identified by Woodcock are cool nw. winds from the land blowing at moderate to strong velocities over warm ocean water. At Key West a nw. wind in fall would be not cool but already warmed by blowing across the ne. corner of the Gulf of Mexico, and in direction would tend to drift hawks down the Bahama Channel parallel to the Cuban coast, thus lengthening the crossing. Darrow (1983) discussed weather conditions over the middle keys on a flight day but, except for an occasional citation of Woodcock, no Key West observer has described or suggested a weather system that—beyond the last land— might supply lift for a successful crossing.

The most consistent clue to the fate of Broadwings over the strait comes from the Dry Tortugas, some 60 mi. w. of Key West. Here, small numbers (once, 58 in a day) are reported quite regularly in fall and no less regularly by 1s and 2s in spring. At the Tortugas they are not on a direct course to any nearby landfall and are, therefore, by definition, vagrant. W. B. Robertson, Jr., who has frequently visited the Tortugas, regards raptors there as trapped, repeatedly rising on updrafts and gliding off over the water toward the mainland, only to come flapping back a few min. later; he suspects they are effectively marooned and ultimately starve. If stragglers from over the strait can reach the Tortugas, it is possible that others, by some fortunate combination of circumstances, accomplish the crossing to Cuba, but on present evidence they, too, must be considered vagrants, not travelers along an established route of migration. In any case, the Key West Broadwings, taking the most optimistic estimate of their number for comparison with the scores of 1000s passing back and forth through s. Tex., are too small a fraction to be very significant.   JOSEPH A. HAGAR

POSTSCRIPT   For decades, Hagar has used the **visual search diagram** reproduced herein (see fig. on p. 18); thus it long predates a comparable diagram in Welch 1979 *Newsletter of Hawk Migr. Assoc. of N. Am.* **5**, no. 2: 11–12.

Dry Tortugas as a **death trap**—in mid-Nov., about 1978, an observer saw a scattering of Broadwings there, mostly dead, a few alive but weak, possibly 20 birds altogether.   RALPH S. PALMER

BANDING STATUS   *B. p. platypterus.* As of Aug. 1981, total number banded was 3,569 and there were 115 recoveries (3.1%) (Clapp et al. 1982). Unlike some buteos, obviously the Broadwing is not banded in large numbers. Main places of banding: Wis., Minn., Pa., Mass., Mich., N.J., and Ont. Other bandings are scattered from the Canadian prairies to Mexico and Panama.   RALPH S. PALMER

REPRODUCTION   *B. p. platypterus.* In utility and completeness, no single recent study matches the early monograph by Burns (1911). There is much of value in Matray (1974), based on work in the Adirondacks of N.Y. Both are cited below frequently, by author's name only. Most recent studies have concentrated on defining nesting habitat; other facets of the breeding cycle are relatively unknown.

First breeds   Usually when in definitive feathering, that is, when at least 2 years old. Burns stated that a few breed in "immature plumage" (as yearlings), noting that a ♀ laid a clutch at that age. Yearling (Juv.) ♂ ♂ were found breeding in w. N.Y. in 1979, and there was no significant difference between adult/adult and adult/Juv. pairs except that the former hatched more eggs (Crocoll 1984). From all studies, it may be inferred that there is a large summer population of nonbreeding yearlings.

Pair bond   Although Burns believed that mates remained mated as long as both survived, it is probable that they go their separate ways part of the year and then meet again on their territory, where the bond is renewed for the season. The best evidence is Matray's—2 of 4 returning birds in 1972 were mates of the previous year and again paired, nesting 471 m. from their 1971 location.

Displays   Birds aged 2 years and older arrive back 1st in spring, some up to several weeks ahead of yearlings, and so have most breeding areas for their activities exclusively during early phases of the reproductive cycle. HIGH-CIRCLING advertising display begins immediately on arrival; the birds are conspicuous and noisy, uttering the far-carrying Killdeer-like call, and now and again 1 (♂?) dives or sideslips downward until very close to or touching another (♀?). In the SKY-DANCE a bird leaves its perch, flapping upward in widening circles, calling; then, "with spread wings and tail it soars lightly back and forth, still trending upward" until nearly lost from sight, then "descends with long sweeps and curves, terminating with a long horizontal dash" (J. Preston). In TUMBLING a circling bird dips earthward "with a momentum truly wonderful," checking its headlong course just before it reaches the ground (Gentry). Evidently, like the circling seen on warm sunny days, this display can also occur in another season. In Sept. in Ont., a gathering of Broadwings was sailing; every few min. 1 closed its wings and shot down sharply nearly to the treetops; when checking its descent, it produced a noise "almost like an explosion," then it swooped upward again. This information, given at somewhat greater length by Burns, comprises almost everything recorded about Broadwing displays.

Territory Within the seasonal home range the area defended until, or perhaps until briefly after, the young can fly is that to which the adults that survive return in subsequent years, although they typically nest in a different part each year and the young do not return to it (there may be exceptions). Ideally it contains both forested and open areas, the latter including wetlands and/or water, for hunting from nearby perches and for territorial interactions. In Minn. and Wis., 29 nests were within 408 ft. (128 m.) of an opening and within 468 ft. (143 m.) of a wet area (Keran 1978). Also in Wis., Rosenfield (1984) considered a "nesting area" reoccupied if, in subsequent years, a nest in use was found within 250 m. of 1 previously used, or if the previous 1 was reused. With these criteria, he found a reoccupancy rate of 0.60. In w. N.Y. there was a breeding pair per 171 ha. of forest, and Broadwing and Redshoulder nested nearer to each other than to other pairs of their own species (Corcoll 1984). In Kans., Fitch (1958) noted that Broadwings will fly well beyond the limits of "territorial boundaries," which makes defining such boundaries especially difficult.

Although Broadwings defend nesting territory against Redtails, Redshoulders, N. Harriers, and undoubtedly other species, Burns mentioned them nesting in proximity of nesting Cooper's and Sharp-shinned Hawks. In w. Md. (Mosher) they have nested within sight of active Redtail and Cooper's Hawk nests. In these associations, avoidance minimizes conflict. However, a pair of Broadwings joined a Redshoulder in endeavoring to defend the latter's nest from an "intruder" (Burns).

Three Broadwings were radio tracked in Minn. by Fuller (1979). Considerable activity consisted merely of preening, feeding, shifts in posture, and flight-intention movements and was not associated with changes in location. The activities of a breeding pair declined after they lost their brood and then were about the same as of a nonbreeding ♂. On 10 occasions the hawks were detected in flight after dark.

Nest Location and height were discussed under Habitat above. A new nest may be built, or an existing one—of Broadwings, some other raptor, crow, or squirrel—may have material added and be used. Occupancy of other than a new nest of their own is energy saving and the equivalent of refurbishing their own nest of a former year. In Mass., Broadwings successfully used a Cooper's Hawk nest of the previous year (V. Armstrong 1944). In 10 new and 5 refurbished Broadwing nests in w. N.Y., the birds seemed to do better reproductively in the newly constructed ones, and reuse of a nest never occurred until at least 2 years after original construction (Crocoll 1984).

At about lat. 38°–40° N, construction or refurbishing is reported as continuing over 3–5 weeks (Riley 1902) or 2–4 weeks (Mosher) or perhaps 3 weeks (Crocoll 1984). So far as reported, the birds spend little time working on it on days when active and may cease construction entirely for days at a time. Perhaps unobserved nests may be readied more rapidly; too much curiosity on the part of the observer "leads to the desertion of the location," and no time for duration of construction can be given (Burns). Both parents fetch material, but Matray reported that the ♀ did most of this

26

(mainly dead sticks and twigs), transporting larger items in the feet, smaller ones in the beak. Generally speaking, the nest seems rather small; no measurements are given here. It is "carelessly built" and is smaller than the well-built Redshoulder nest (Bent 1937). It is also smaller than the nest of Cooper's Hawk and is made of larger items collected from the ground (Cooper's breaks smaller branches from standing trees to build a bulkier structure) (J. Norris 1888a). Cantwell (1888) saw Broadwings collecting sticks from the ground, but twigs are also broken from trees.

After the bulk of the structure is completed, the ♀ begins bringing chips of bark to line the nest bowl; these are her "total responsibility," and such delivery continues during incubation (Matray). All 29 nests in Keran's (1978) study had bark chips in the cavity. Other materials incorporated in the lining have included bits of moss, corn husks, pine needles, and stringy outer bark of wild grape.

The presence of fresh **greenery** is typical of completed Broadwing nests (Burns, Matray), and its delivery continues during incubation and (see below) at least until well into the rearing period. Rosenfield (1982) saw a bird break twigs from the lower halves of deciduous trees, using the beak also to transport them.

Copulation Described by Shelley (in Bent 1937). Male and ♀ faced in the same direction, perched on limbs. He gave a whining call 6 times, flew to and alighted on the ♀, and remained a full min., continually calling and balancing with his wings. His 2-toned call was a rather musical wheezy whistling, uttered at each lowering of his tail. Mueller's (1970) captive ♂ alighted on him gently, the toes flexed ("balled into fists"), and the bird rested on the entire length of its tarsi.

One **egg** each from 20 clutches (Conn. 5, Pa. 12, N.H. 2, Mich. 1) **size** length 49.04 ± 1.90 mm., breadth 39.17 ± 1.19, and radii of curvature of ends 16.23 ± 0.97 and 12.17 ± 0.97; **shape** usually short elliptical (but varies from shorter to longer), elongation 1.24 ± 0.046, bicone −0.087, and asymmetry +0.131 (F. W. Preston). Fifty-one eggs av. 48.9 × 39.3 mm. (Bent 1937), and there seems very little, if any, geographical variation in egg size (within the mainland subspecies). The largest Broadwing eggs are larger than the smallest Redshoulder eggs, and both Burns and Bent were inclined to the view that many purported Broadwing clutches were of eggs of the other species—a viewpoint dating back at least to J. Norris (1887).

The shell is granulated, without luster; from 100 clutches, Burns selected and described 15 clutches that showed "every type of coloration known." There is great variation. Ground **color** of fresh eggs is white, very pale creamy, or slightly bluish; markings are more or less in 2 layers, each varying from large patches to tiny dots. Markings are mostly of various browns, the underlying (and sometimes only) ones tending toward palish ultramarine-violet (variants of lavender). Rarely is an egg plain or nearly so. Coloring has been characterized as "subdued" (only palish ground color) and same overlaid with blotches, and so forth; both "types" may be found in the same clutch (J. Norris 1888a). [St. Vincent, W. Indies: 6 clutches "dull bluish white, unspotted" (A. H. Clark 1905a).]

A fresh egg weighs about 42–43 gm.

Only the ♀ has an incubation patch (Matray). She sits for short periods during the several days before onset of laying (Burns), and the interval between eggs is 2 days (sometimes less), judging from spread in known hatching dates.

Clutch size   Usually 2–3 (range of 1–4, possibly 5). Data on 406 clutches: 15 (of 1), 183 (2), 190 (3), and 18 (4) (Burns). Bent stated that he had found twice as many sets of 2 as of 3 (geographical area[s] unstated). Poling (in Bendire 1892) reported that clutches of 4 were not unusual in Ill. and that he knew of 1 of 5; Burns thought this possible, but believed it more likely that the large clutch was of misidentified Redshoulder eggs. In w. N.Y., clutch size was statistically significantly larger in 1979 (when prey was more plentiful) than in 1978 (Crocoll 1984).

Burns stated that there is an increase in av. clutch size going from s. to n., and the following analysis confirms this. The data are largely from Burns, who used the life zone terminology of C. H. Merriam et al., each "zone" being defined loosely here in brackets and with number of clutches in parentheses. Going n.: Lower Austral Zone [s. states] 1–3, av. 2.1 eggs (16); Upper Austral Zone [middle states] 1–4, av. 2.4 (157); Transition Zone [much of n. states, extending s. in highlands] 1–4, av. 2.6 (174), and (Janik and Mosher 1982) in Md. av. 2.7 (15); Canadian Zone [coniferous forest primarily] 1–4, av. 2.7 (59), and in Alta. (Rusch and Doerr 1972) 2–3, av. 2.4, but only 5 clutches).

In Minn. in 1886 the majority of clutches taken were of 3 eggs, and in 1887 of 2 with few exceptions; when years were combined, the majority were of 3 (J. Norris 1888a).

Egg dates   The Broadwing lays late, about the time that deciduous trees begin leafing out (Burns). Dates when presumably viable eggs have been taken, from Bent (1937), are: New Eng. and N.Y.—72 records, Apr. 19–June 28 (includes 36, May 16–31); N.J. to Md.—57 records, Apr. 13–June 14 (29, May 11–25); S.D. to Alta. and Sask.—45 records, May 15–June 27 (22, May 23–June 5); Ohio to Minn.—8 records, May 2–21; and Ga. to Fla. and Mo.—5 records, Apr. 15–May 26 (3, May 2–17). There is about a month's spread between completion of clutches s. and n., with corresponding w. dates perhaps slightly later than e. ones.

Incubation   By the ♀. The food-carrying ♂ flies toward the nest uttering his food transfer call and is met away from it by the ♀ (Matray, Fuller 1979). While she eats, the ♂ may continue on to the nest and cover the eggs briefly. If the ♀ returns there, he departs immediately. After a ♀ was shot from the nest, her presumed mate finished incubation and reared a nestling to near flight age (Burns).

The incubating ♀ is alert, occasionally standing to preen or stretch, or she may turn the eggs with her beak. Burns cited Audubon's account of a broody ♀ being lifted from her nest, but in general she takes wing and can sometimes be quite aggressive—even striking with swift, stooping blows (Burns, Rosenfield 1978). In the case cited by Rosenfield, the bird also attacked the observation blind. In over 150 visits to nests, Mosher was struck on the head by 3 different adults on several occasions, but usually the sitter took wing as the nest tree was climbed and remained nearby, perched or circling overhead, calling in alarm.

Incubation period   Longer than formerly stated. It is not less than 28 days (Matray); the 31 days of Bush and Gehlbach (1978) is probably close to the correct figure.

Since incubation begins with the 1st egg, **hatching** occurs over a span of time—6 days for a clutch of 4 in Md. (Mosher)—and the shells disappear; presumably they are transported elsewhere. In w. N.Y., the hatching interval in any sized clutch was 1.4 ± 1.0 days, they hatched a day apart in 2-egg clutches (Crocoll 1984).

Rearing period The ♀ broods almost continually for a week or longer; then she begins hunting, and her attentiveness declines; she continues to brood at night until the young are 21–24 days old (Matray). The ♂ provides food for the ♀ and growing young, but when he delivers directly to the nest his visits are brief; feathered prey is more or less plucked beforehand, and furred prey is usually decapitated. If he delivers during his mate's absence, he places the food on the nest and departs immediately; if he lingers and she returns, she discourages his presence. Especially during the breeding season, food not consumed may be cached for future use (Matray, Lyons and Mosher 1982).

Only the ♀ dismantles prey and feeds the brood. This lasts 2–50 min., depending on hunger of nestlings, kind of prey, and number of prey items (Matray). In 19 full days of observation at 3 nests, the av. energy value of prey delivered to each nestling was estimated at 137 kcal./day (Mosher and Matray 1974). Later, when the young become able to feed themselves, either parent remains only long enough to deposit food. In Mass. in 78 hours of observation at a nest with a single young, adults brought 11 "mice" (voles), 8 snakes, 5 frogs, a Blue Jay, and 2 unidentified birds. Most of the "mice" were delivered minus heads but otherwise quite intact, the snakes were half-eaten, as were the frogs, and the birds were almost invariably plucked beyond recognition. When the nestling was fully fed, the ♀ would pick up the prey and depart with it (J. B. Holt 1959).

Again the subject of **greenery.** In Mass., the adult Broadwings were quiet at 0600–0900 hrs. Around 0900 hrs. a chipping sound in the forest would announce the ♂'s arrival with food; the ♀ would depart to meet him, fetch the food to the nest, feed the single nestling, and then would depart, after which a quiet period ensued. The listener in the observation blind would hear strange tugging noises in the surrounding tree-tops—the ♀ "pruning" neighboring trees. She delivered the branchlets to the nest, depositing them on top of her nestling; this "garnishing" ceased when the nestling was about 2 weeks old (J. B. Holt 1959). Greenery fetched in the Adirondacks: sprigs of sugar maple, yellow birch, hemlock, balsam fir, n. white cedar, aspen, black cherry, and ash—in 12 nests examined (Matray). In Minn., nests found late in the season contain a large amount of green leaves, hence resemble squirrel nests (Cantwell 1888). At a Tex. nest the material delivered was red mulberry (*Morus rubra*), 1st seen when the nestlings were partly grown (Bush and Gehlbach 1978).

An unusual activity for raptors is for some Broadwing adults to nibble the excreta of nestlings from the branches supporting the nest (Rosenfield et al. 1982, Mosher); apparently they consume it.

Nestling behavior and development Described by Burns, Matray, and Lyons (1983). Very small young spend most of the time lying and sleeping, being active only during feeding bouts and when defecating. In performing the latter they crawl or (when older) walk backward, then forcibly eject excrement over the rim of the nest. This is not always accomplished at 1st; in w. Md., 10 nest bowls were soiled by the young when aged 1–3 days. In early sleeping posture the head droops forward in contact with the nest. At 14–15 days the head is rotated to face posteriorly, then rests on the back or is tucked between wing and back (adult sleeping posture). As feathers emerge and grow, preening increases. In early life the nestlings depend on the parent for tearing up and presenting food; at 16–20 days they nibble at carcasses held down by the parent during feeding bouts; at 18–20 days they begin to tear up prey, grasped in their own talons, while standing but do not perform this effectively until 10 days later. There are about 4–16 deliveries of food per day, depending on weather, number of young and their ages, and kinds of prey (Matray). "Mantling" over food 1st was seen at 21–26 days.

Brood reduction Nestlings begin to fight over food during their 4th week, and Matray thought that this might be the age when 1 might kill another. In Crocoll's (1984) study, also in N.Y., broods of 3 and 4, but not of 2, decreased in size; that is, some young may starve when food is scarce. Judging from Heintzelman (1966) and Lyons and Mosher (1982), a dead nestling may be eaten by others, but there is no evidence of fratricide.

Brancher stage Young Broadwings venture out onto limbs of the nest tree at 29–31 days (or perhaps older in undisturbed nests). They spend progressively less time at the nest, returning only to consume food brought there by the parents. They are capable of sustained horizontal flight at 5–6 weeks (Crocoll 1984). At about 6 weeks they begin intercepting parents away from the nest, and as soon as a food transfer is made the parent leaves. In their 6th week they become able fliers (Matray).

In captivity a 39-day-old Broadwing struck at live House Sparrows with its right foot—its 1st kill and "attempt to pluck feathers before eating" (Burns).

Breeding success In w. Md. in the nestling period, mortality was greater during the 1st 3 weeks; 31 (86%) of 36 active nests produced 59 young to flight age, an av. of 1.7 young/successful nest (Janik and Mosher 1982). Seventy active nests in Wis.: mean clutch size was 2.4 eggs, of which 1.8 hatched, and 1.5 young/nest attained flight (Rosenfield 1984). In the latter study, main factors reducing productivity occurred before hatching. In Crocoll's (1984) study in w. N.Y., over ½ the nesting attempts "suffered some form of mortality," mostly during laying and incubation; ½ of the losses were due to predation by the Great Horned Owl. There are few definite records of mammals destroying Broadwing nests, yet it seems quite remarkable that the raccoon has not been clearly implicated as a predator.

Flight to independence At first the parents assist by fetching food, but the young begin hunting almost immediately and can capture small prey by age 54 days. They have been found within 600 m. of the nest to age 8 weeks (Matray), which may be an indication of duration of family bond; in other instances, they have departed when younger.

Departure Although conspicuous and noisy in the spring, Broadwings in autumn before migrating do less soaring and are relatively quiet; time of departure is thus difficult to determine (Fitch 1958). JAMES A. MOSHER

SURVIVAL In discussing man-caused and natural mortality, the av. life span in 37 records was given by Keran (1981) as 1 year—a high mortality in early life. There is little other information on survival. The oldest bird reported by Clapp et al. (1982) was aged 14 years, 4 months. RALPH S. PALMER

HABITS *B. p. platypterus*. **Hunting methods** Usually the Broadwing hunts from a perch, such as a tree limb, utility pole, or overhead utility wire above the roadwide, watching for potential prey. Although perch-and-wait occurs beneath the forest canopy, typically it occurs at clearings, along woodland roads, forest edges, and at margins of seasonal and permanent waters. In brief, this hawk is an edge feeder.

The usual hunting pattern everywhere and in all seasons undoubtedly is similar to what Tabb (1973) observed in winter in Fla. when trapping Broadwings to band them. A bird's response to a baited snare set on the ground is predictable. It stands erect, with arched neck, bobbing the head sideways; then it launches quickly from its perch. Its flight path to the trap is flat, the initial wingbeats rapid and then a glide with heavy impact. Sometimes, if the bird has fed recently, its 1st response is to defecate and then quickly flutter its tail laterally; the attack that follows is remarkably swift and direct. The strike may be likened to that of the Red-tailed Hawk as described by Goslow (1973). Before the Broadwing becomes aware that it is snared, it "mantles" over the bait (live mouse), body erect, wings forward and out, and tail braced on the ground. It may stand thus for several min., surveying its surroundings. Then it assumes a standing posture and begins to "foot" the mouse—a killing action. "Adults" are always more deliberate than Juv. birds, hence more difficult to trap. (An "adult" usually carries its prey to a perch and feeds on it.)

Hunting methods used much less frequently or in special situations are as follows: 1 Search from flight, generally below treetop level—presumably a method of locating slow-moving prey among terrestrial or aquatic vegetation, as amphibians and snakes; Insects are taken both during flight and while perch-and-wait hunting. 2 Stooping from soaring flight—apparently rare; and 3 Although newly arrived spring migrants are in good physical condition, evidently ♀ ♀ at least may feed avidly in preparation for egg laying. Great numbers of amphibians are breeding at this time at temporary pools and at the margins of permanent waters, and the hawks hunt them from the closest perches, occasionally from the air, and sometimes even afoot.

Summer habits Persons driving along woodland roads in summer and early fall often see Broadwings perched solitarily on utility poles and wires. Their tameness is reason for their having been described as sluggish and lazy (as in Bent 1937), even "dumpy" (Tabb 1973), but their mode of life conforms to their preferred hunting method. Furthermore, the Broadwing can be an efficient opportunist. An E. Bluebird was in a nest box mounted on a pole; the hawk struck the pole with its wings, setting it aquiver, and the bluebird stayed inside briefly with the hawk perched on the box. When the bluebird's head appeared, the hawk seized it and pulled her from the entrance (Shelley, in Bent).

Broadwings soar in spirals on warm sunny days (J. Norris 1888a).

Food consumption rates Measured experimentally for 2 captive ♂ ♂; increased from 3.5–5.5% of body wt. (about 14–23 gm.) after 5–15 hrs. of deprivation to 8.5–14% (about 35–38 gm.) after 20–45 hrs. of deprivation (Mueller 1973a). Mean values for digestive efficiency for 7 captives ranged 72.3–79.1% on a diet of lean venison (Mosher and Matray 1974). Using field data, for example, amount of prey delivered to ♀/day, estimated caloric value of prey, and ♀ body wt., plus experimentally determined digestive efficiency rates, Mosher and Matray estimated the per gm. metabolic rate of incubating ♀ ♀ to be 0.236 kcal./gm./day.

Winter habits Individuals are solitary, each having its feeding territory—in se. Fla. (Tabb 1973), Costa Rica (Slud 1964), and Venezuela (W. Beebe 1947, others). At

31

Key West, Fla., several spend the winter within city limits; they are tame, perching in trees in yards, on television aerials, and so forth, rarely moving until approached closely. American Kestrels harass them noisily, and the Broadwings respond with a "high-pitched whistle which sounds shrill and complaining" (Hundley and Hames 1960). Many hunt along heavily traveled Fla. highways, and substantial numbers are killed by fast-moving vehicles (Tabb 1973).

Austral summer In S. Am., Broadwings presumably are territorial; this needs investigation.

Status In former times, at places where passage birds concentrated within shotgun range, large numbers of these little hawks were slaughtered. A very minor episode, from T. S. Roberts (1932): in mid-Sept. in Minn., toward end of a day's flight, several hundred Broadwings alighted in trees at a game farm where the superintendent and his assistant shot 102 in about 4 hrs.

Today, the Broadwing may be at least as numerous as it was before Caucasian settlement. Pesticides do not accumulate in its food chain—at least not in significant amounts. Decline in agriculture in much of the Broadwing's continental summer range and consequent growth of discontinuous woodlands has created much suitable habitat. In S. Am., destruction of primeval forest surely has resulted in the fragmented cover Broadwings prefer. Finally, hawk shooting on any scale is a rare practice today. This combination of factors bodes well for the future of the Broadwing.

JAMES A. MOSHER AND RALPH S. PALMER

FOOD *B. p. platypterus* **spring–fall** Small mammals and birds, reptiles and amphibians, occasionally fishes, and a wide assortment of invertebrates.

Many data are from stomach analyses, but recently there has been considerable information from findings at nests and from direct observation. Omitting incidental reports, the bulk of the data are in the following sources and in references they cite; listing is in chronological order. A. K. Fisher (1893)—compilation; Burns (1911)—much compilation, some original data; L. Snyder (1932)—Ont.; McAtee (1935)—145 stomach analyses; May (1935)—compilation, 254 digestive tracts; Mendall (1944)—Maine, 58 stomachs; McDowell (1949b)—Pa., 51 stomachs; Rusch and Doerr (1972)—Alta., food fed to 4 young; Fitch (1974)—Kans., 138 prey items; Mosher and Matray (1974)—N.Y., 333 prey items brought to nests; Sherrod (1978)—8 studies summarized, 1 previously unpublished; Janik and Mosher (1982)—w. Md., 31 items brought to nests; Crocoll (1984)—w. N.Y., food brought to nests; and Rosenfield et al. (1984)—Wis., food brought to a nest. A condensation follows.

Mammals Over 30 species. Squirrels (red preponderant), chipmunks, voles, mice, an occasional rat. Young hares and rabbits. A long-tailed weasel, moles (2 or more species), shrews (4 or more species), and bats (1 each of 2 species).

Birds At least 25 species recorded. In general, from N. Flicker and Blue Jay-size down to include wood warblers, with many intermediate (sparrow-size). Larger birds are taken occasionally when young—6 (of 7) Ruffed Grouse under 9 weeks old (Rusch and Doerr). Poultry is seldom attacked, rarely with success. Pileated Woodpecker listed without details. Saw-whet Owl (Rosenfield 1979). There are reports in Burns (1911) that young birds, still in the nest or recently out, are taken; in the Adirondacks of

N.Y. almost 80% of birds captured were "fledglings or nestlings" (Matray 1976); taking young birds also is reported in Wis. (Rosenfield et al.) and Kans. (Fitch).

Reptiles At least 11 species of snakes, 4 of lizards, and very young snapping turtles.

Amphibians At least 5 species; 3 aquatic frogs, a tree frog (*Hyla*), and numerous toads (*Bufo americanus*). Probably frogs are taken far more often than recorded, since their digestion is rapid and complete. Toads are especially vulnerable when mating.

Fishes In May in Conn. a ♂ with fish in talons perched near an active nest, presumably having brought it for the ♀ (Beers, in Burns).

Invertebrates At least 30 species. Partial listing: cicadas, grasshoppers, locusts, crickets, dragonflies, moth larvae, caterpillars, and earthworms. Also centipedes. Crayfish in Pa. and N.Y.; fiddler crabs in New Eng.

Winter foods Fla.—the locally abundant cotton rat (*Sigmodon*) and cotton mice (*Peromyscus gossypinus*). Evidence of having eaten Gray Catbird (*Dumetella*) and ground dove (*Columbina*). Fence lizards (*Anolis*) probably a minor food. (From Tabb 1973.) Panama—where the Broadwing is a bird of passage and "winter" visitor: large orthoptera extensively eaten and lizards to some degree; Chapman mentioned an immature ani (*Crotophaga*); not seen to show any interest in the abundant small birds. (From Wetmore 1965.) S. Am. in austral summer (recent sources not checked): Venezuela—large grasshoppers, spiders. Ecuador—Lepidoptera, cricket fragments, fish scales, locusts, beetles, and remains of frogs in digestive tracts. (Authors in Burns 1911.)

Prey availability The Broadwing exploits its opportunities, as the following examples indicate. Lake Umbagog, Maine-N.H.—seemingly a preference for toads (Brewster 1925); and Wis.—although not the bulk of the diet, toads were the item most frequently delivered to the nest (Rosenfield et al. 1984). Cent. Alta.—the only study in which young Ruffed Grouse (see above) and young snowshoe hares were significant. Okla.—29 young snapping turtles (Voelker, in Sherrod 1978). W. Md.—many chipmunks (*Tamias*) (Janik and Mosher). N.Y. (cent. Adirondacks)—predominantly mammals and amphibians, both in number and weight (biomass) (Mosher and Matray). Location unstated, but probably D.C. area—in May, after a shower, 1 had gorged on large earthworms (A. K. Fisher).

Interesting data on other subspecies Cuba—a creek dried to only shallow puddles, alive with small minnows; a ♀ Broadwing shot nearby contained 16 whole ones ½–1½ in. long (Ramsden 1911). St. Vincent (Lesser Antilles)—although regarded as a plague to poultry raisers, the Broadwing feeds largely on a significant agricultural pest, the mole-cricket, and 18 were found in 1 bird (A. H. Clark 1905b).

JAMES A. MOSHER AND RALPH S. PALMER

light phase

dorsal

SHORT-TAILED HAWK

Buteo brachyurus

Smallish buteo, about crow-sized, with short broad tail and fairly long rounded wings. Two **color phases,** each variable and, in relative numbers, varying geographically. The ♀ is larger (sexes overlap in size and wt.). Sexes combined: length 15–17 in. (38–43 cm.), wingspread to 35 (89 cm.), wt. 12¾–18¼ oz. (365–520 gm.).

DESCRIPTION This diagnosis fits *B. b. fuliginosus* of our area (Fla.), where the dark phase is numerically preponderant. **Light phase** definitive: **beak** black grading to bluish distally, cere yellow, **iris** very dark brown. Some white around top base of beak; most of **head** and **upperparts** very dark (toward chocolate), feathers white basally on occiput (concealed spot), rarely some rufous on neck (more frequent in Mexico than Fla.); **underparts** white from chin to tail; **tail** ventrally palish with 3–4 dark bars (distal bar most conspicuous and much the widest); **wing** primaries and secondaries somewhat palish and narrowly barred dark, ends of primaries blackish, and wing lining white. Juv. quite similar; some dorsal feathers edged palish, underparts more or less buffy, tail with many (7 or more) rather obscure narrow dark bars, distal bar wide. In all flying ages, legs and **feet** yellow, talons black.

Dark phase soft parts as above; white usually concealed around top base of beak and in occipital spot; most of head and upperparts some variant of dark brownish; tail and wing much as light phase. Color photo: 1977 *Audubon* **79** (4). Juv. has underparts marked or mottled dark on light (not white) and otherwise is much as Juv. light phase.

Downy stages—see Reproduction, below.

♂ ♀ Juv. Plumage—see Field Identification, below.

Color phases In FLA. the dark phase is more prevalent (Brandt 1924, J. Moore et al. 1953). From approximately 70 observations in Everglades Natl. Park between 1966 and 1973, J. Ogden (1973) estimated a color ratio of 4 dark : 1 light. Mated pairs have consisted of dark ♂ ♂ mated to light ♀ ♀, both members of the pair dark, and both light

(W. Scott 1889, Brandt 1924, A. Howell 1932, Ogden). The dark/light combination appears to be much more common in Fla. than either dark/dark or light/light. Of 11 known pairings in Fla. where both birds were seen, 7 were dark/light, 3 dark/dark, and 1 light/light. Twelve ♂ specimens from Fla. are all dark, while 11 ♀ are 8 light and 3 dark (Natl. Mus. Nat. Hist., Am. Mus. Nat. Hist., Mus. Comp. Zool., Field Mus., U. of Miami, and Fla. State Mus.). A dark/light pair in Everglades Natl. Park produced a dark young, while nestings by 2 different dark/dark pairs produced dark nestlings and a light/light pair in 2 nestings produced light nestlings.

MEXICO   Dark phase appears to be most common in Chiapas (M. del Toro), also in Colima, Veracruz, and Tabasco (Ogden). Several nesting pairs in cent. Veracruz each consisted of a light and a dark bird; in some cases the ♂ was light, in others the ♀ (L. Wolfe). A pair collected in cent. Veracruz were dark ♂ /light ♀ (Am. Mus. Nat. Hist.).

CENTRAL PANAMA   Light/dark and light/light pairings; the light phase generally predominates (N. Smith). Most Short-tails from S. Am. are light, although dark birds have been taken in Colombia (Rand 1960).

Measurements   ♂ 8 BEAK from cere 18–20 mm., av. 18.7, WING flattened 265–310, av. 284.7; and 7 ♀ BEAK from cere 19–22 mm., av. 20.7, and WING flattened 295–335, av. 322.2 (E. R. Blake 1977). For additional meas., see sources cited by Blake.

Weight   Few data. Dark ♀ "adult," Jan. 1968 near Homestead, Fla.—520 gm.; dark "imm." ♂ Jan. 1956, Dade Co., Fla.—417; dark ♀ from Colombia—425 (A. H. Miller 1952); and 2 from San Luis Potosi, Mexico—♂ 363 and ♀ 457 (R. Newman). Suriname—♂ ♂ 450–470, ♀ 530 (Haverschmidt 1968).

Hybrids   None.

Geographical variation   Condensed from Rand (1960). Essentially no size variation, or possibly slight amount in tail length (judging from small series). The Cent. Am. and Andean birds are more similar morphologically than are the latter to those in n. S. Am. There is intergradation from Cent. to S. Am.

FLA. AND CENT. AM.   Light phase definitive—upperparts chocolate, usually with brownish rufous on sides of neck, underparts and wing lining usually unmarked white. Juv.—dark streaking on sides of neck tends to extend onto buffy breast, thighs toward buff. Dark phase definitive—chocolate, paler on underside of barred tail and flight feathers of wing. Juv.—underparts, including thighs, buffy with clear-cut heavy pattern of reddish brown or neutral dark.

NORTHERN TWO-THIRDS OF S. AM.   Light phase definitive—upperparts slaty blackish, usually also sides of neck, underparts and wing lining usually plain white. Juv.—underparts buffy, unpatterned. Dark phase (rare)—blackish slate. ANDES MTS. definitive—upperparts dark brownish, sides of neck reddish brown, underparts white with reddish brown extending from sides of neck onto flanks, thighs barred reddish brown, white wing lining heavily marked reddish brown. Juv.—sides of head and neck streaked white, underparts white tinged brownish buff, thighs and wing lining with dark brown markings. No dark phase known.

Affinities   No useful information.   JOHN C. OGDEN

SUBSPECIES   Rand (1960) and E. R. Blake (1977) are followed here, not Stresemann (1959) or Lehmann and Haffer (1960), who regarded *albigula* as a separate species.

In our area *fuliginosus* Sclater—Fla., parts of Mexico including Cozumel I., and s. to Panama. Migratory, at least in Fla. and Mexico. Described above.

Elsewhere, *brachyurus* Vieillot—n. ⅔ of S. Am. at lower elevations, also Trinidad and Tobago. For diagnosis, meas., and details of distribution, see Rand (1960) and especially E. R. Blake (1977).

albigula Philippi—Andean highlands, at lower elevations to the south. Measurements and so forth in Rand and in Blake.   JOHN C. OGDEN

FIELD IDENTIFICATION   **In our area**   Generally similar in size to the small Fla. Red-shouldered Hawks, but differs in having proportionately longer, broader wings and shorter tail. Short-tails are much more often seen soaring than perched. When soaring, the wings are held flat except for a decided upturn to the outer primaries, thus presenting a different flight silhouette than that of the more completely flat-winged soaring of the Redshoulder and the smaller Broad-winged Hawk or the dihedral posture of Swainson's Hawk (J. Ogden 1973). The distinctive practice of Short-tails, uncommon among other soaring hawks in Fla., of capturing prey by swift vertical dives from great heights is seen often enough to be useful for identification.

The 2 color phases, dark much more common in Fla., were mentioned above. The dark-phase adult, quite unlike any other soaring hawk regularly seen there, appears black at a distance, with vivid yellow cere, legs, and feet. Undersides of flight feathers of the wing are thinly barred on a dull grayish background, which lightens (almost to white) at base of primaries. Undertail is pale grayish with a thin, dark subterminal band and about 2 thinner dark bands anterior to the subterminal.

The light phase is uniformly dark brown dorsally and pure white on most of the ventral surface, including wing lining. The head appears hooded, a good field mark— the dark extends down solidly to the narrow white chin and throat (J. Moore et al. 1953). The lower edge of the dark border across the white breast may be slightly reddish on some individuals. Undersides of primaries, secondaries, and tail are similar to dark phase, but less distinctly barred on the wings and usually showing only the single, sometimes obscure, subterminal tail band. Strong sunlight shining through the spread tail of a high soaring bird may cause the tail to appear reddish.

Juvenal feathering   Birds in both color phases, when seen at a distance, do not differ recognizably from adults. At close range, dark birds show varying amounts of mottling, almost always more dark than light, on chin, upper throat, belly, and wing lining that contrast with an entirely dark chest. Light ones have some light streaking on sides of head, particularly in auricular area, varying amounts of buffy or orange-buffy on all of venter, which is white in later life, and generally inconspicuous dark shaft streaks on sides of breast. The buffy areas seem to fade so that birds aged 6 months to 1 year may appear white below. Heavily streaked "immature plumages" as illustrated in some field guides (Pough 1951, Robbins et al. 1966) are incorrect.

Juv. birds of both phases have heavier and more numerous tail bands than in later life, about 5 show on dark and 3 on light birds (includes broader subterminal band), but total number is greater.

The only similarly marked buteos in Fla. are occasional wintering Redtails having pure white underparts (Olson 1965) and the rare dark phase of the Broadwing. The former is much larger than the Short-tail, less solidly dark on the head and with a different tail pattern. The dark Broadwing is much smaller than the Short-tail and has broader and darker tail bands. Broadwings behave differently than Short-tails, including the Broadwing's habit of perching on telephone cables along Fla. Keys roads, where the dark Broadwings are sometimes seen in winter (W. B. Robertson, Jr.).

Mexico and Cent. Am. Short-tails appear and behave as do Fla. birds; those in Mexico have darker, more prominent, tail bands than those in Fla. (Rand 1960).

JOHN C. OGDEN

VOICE Generally silent except on nesting territory, where sometimes fairly noisy. Calls variously described as a scream resembling that of the Red-shouldered Hawk, "but finer and not so prolonged" (Pennock 1890); "uttering a few cackling notes, somewhat like the Red-shouldered Hawk" and "a single high pitched squeal, not unlike the alarm note of the Broad-winged Hawk, but a little bit harsher" (Brandt 1924); "screaming in a slightly different but almost identical way to Red-tailed Hawks" (Nicholson 1951); and "quite unlike that of the Red-shouldered Hawk but somewhat resembling the high notes of the Osprey or the squeal of the Red-tailed" (A. Howell 1932). Nicholson reported it calling on moonlit nights.

The following is based on study of 3 pairs on nesting territories in Fla. (Ogden). In general, calls are quite different from those of other Fla. raptors, being higher-pitched than any except the Broadwing, but not the pure whistle of that species.

Keeeea high-pitched squeal, slightly dropping at end, often much drawn out. By either sex, but ♂'s rendition is higher-pitched than ♀'s and sometimes quavering. The ♂'s version has more of the long-*e* sound; at a distance may resemble *jay* call of Blue Jay. Most often heard when hawk is in presence of an intruder—someone near the nest or another raptor in nesting territory.

Keee shorter, less intense version of above, without drop at end; sometimes in series of 2–4 calls on same pitch. Mostly given by ♂ when approaching nest, as when delivering food to ♀. Once heard from a ♀ perched near a nest when ♂ flew over the site. A variation is *Kleee* given by ♂ approaching nest.

Keee, Keee-e, or *Kleee-e* perhaps corresponds to call immediately above; given almost entirely by ♀ while perched near nest or circling low over nest site, occasionally while incubating. Sometimes in series of 2 or 3 and, as with other ♀ calls, with less of the long-*e* tone than in ♂ calls.

Keek seems to be a more intense squeal given by ♀♀ in response to *Keee* of incoming ♂ at nest site. Often the ♀ responds quickly to calls of approaching ♂ by giving several *Keee* or *Keeek* calls, either remaining perched or flying to meet the ♂. The ♀ may continue to call until the 2 birds meet.

A series of 4–6 rather spaced high-pitched *Keee* or *Klee* calls, each note usually slightly higher than preceding note. At times resembles similar call of ♂ Osprey. Only heard from ♂♂, most often when perched alone in woods. On numerous occasions this call was heard at a densely wooded roost site, given at spaced intervals before the bird departed from roost in morning or after it arrived in evening.

Squeee or *Skleee* a prolonged squeally call given by either sex, perhaps more often by the ♀, immediately before or during copulation, or by ♀ about to receive food from mate.

Newly hatched nestlings give often-repeated soft or loud *chip* calls, as single notes or in short series of 2–4. By age 4 days a nestling may give a weak quavering squeal, inaudible to human ear at more than 150 ft. At this age, squeals often precede feedings and chips precede brooding. Older nestlings utter a high thin squeal *eee*.

Reports from outside Fla. are almost nonexistent. A Short-tail in Michoacan, Mexico, gave a "clear two-syllabled whistle" (J. Davis 1953). From Costa Rica, Slud (1964) described a long-drawn-out nasal *Keeer*.   JOHN C. OGDEN

HABITAT   FLA.   A bird of mixed woodland and savanna (J. Ogden 1974b). Nesting and roosting are in patches or stands of mature woodland that are encompassed by, or adjacent to, expanses of open country. A variety of woodland types are used, including cypress (Brandt 1924, Nicholson 1951), pinelands (Pennock 1890, J. Ogden 1974b), swamp hardwoods (W. Scott 1889, Brandt 1924), and mangroves (A. Howell 1932, Sprunt, Jr., 1939). Nesting sites consist of dense or open stands of tall trees in either flooded or upland locations (Brandt 1924, Ogden). Nests are in tall straight trees near the edge of or at small clearings in woodlands or near the tops of trees that are taller than the surrounding canopy. Because in many regions of Fla. the most common type of woodland consisting of tall straight trees of the type used by Short-tails for nesting is swamp forest, in early accounts this hawk is described as a swampland species (Brandt 1924, A. Howell 1932, Bent 1937). Subsequent observations in other regions of Fla. (J. Moore et al. 1953, J. Ogden 1974b) indicate broader habitat use.

The juxtaposition of a lengthy woodland edge with a distinctly open-country terrain is an important feature of most hunting ranges (J. Ogden 1974b). Examples are belts of tall cypress along creek borders that finger through native Fla. prairie, large "islands" of pinelands or cypress "domes" surrounded by broad marshes or rough pastures, and dense forest of mangroves mixed with everglades or coastal marshes. Most known hunting ranges in Fla. contain more open and brushy country than woodland. In such areas, hunting occurs over forest canopy, along woodland edges, and well out over adjacent marshes, rough pastures, or prairies.

MEXICO   The Short-tail seems to be widespread primarily in lowlands of both coasts and in a variety of open country and wooded habitats. It has been recorded from pinelands in Michoacan (J. Davis 1953), coastal arid thorn forest (L. Binford), pine-oak hill country in Oaxaca (A. Phillips), regions mixed with thorn scrub, large agricultural fields and remnants of tropical deciduous forest in Colima (Schaldach 1963, Ogden), remnants of humid lowland forest and deciduous woodlands heavily invaded by agriculture in coastal Veracruz and Campeche (Ogden), open brushlands with few large trees in cent. Veracruz (L. Wolfe), and fields near edges of big forests in Chiapas (M. del Toro). Possibly a less characteristic location is from 6,300 ft. elevation in cold, dry country in w. San Luis Potosi (R. Newman).

ELSEWHERE   Similar diversity of habitats—primarily open country with a mixture of woodlands—appear characteristic in other tropical countries. Short-tails are reported from open and semi-open lowlands in Honduras (Monroe 1968); in Panama, from open lands and from a gallery forest (Wetmore 1965), and mixed grasslands and forest in a hilly region near Panama City (N. Smith). Also tropical and subtropical zones in Venezuela (W. Phelps and Phelps 1958), over open country and hill forests in Trinidad (ffrench 1973), tropical forest and savanna in Ecuador (Chapman 1926), and scattered scrub in Colombia (A. H. Miller 1952).   JOHN C. OGDEN

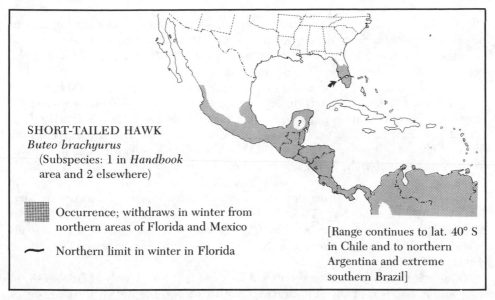

SHORT-TAILED HAWK
Buteo brachyurus
(Subspecies: 1 in *Handbook*
area and 2 elsewhere)

Occurrence; withdraws in winter from
northern areas of Florida and Mexico

— Northern limit in winter in Florida

[Range continues to lat. 40° S
in Chile and to northern
Argentina and extreme
southern Brazil]

DISTRIBUTION (See map.)   FLA.   Short-tails regularly **summer** from the region of the lower Suwanee R. on the Gulf coast (Dixie Co.) and the upper St. Johns R. in the interior (Brevard Co.) s. to Everglades Natl. Park. They are much rarer and irregular n. in coastal regions to Bay Co. and s. into the Fla. Keys (J. Ogden 1974b and in Kale 1978). Short-tail nests have been found in Wakulla, Putnam, Pinellas, Polk, Highlands, Glades, Collier, Dade, and mainland Monroe cos. (A. Howell 1932, J. Ogden 1974b). In **winter,** early Nov.–early Feb., most Short-tails occur from s. of L. Okeechobee to the Fla. Keys, primarily in the Big Cypress Swamp region and Everglades Natl. Park. Northernmost midwinter records are from s. Okeechobee and Highlands cos. (A. Howell 1932, Davidson 1951).

In MEXICO apparently of year-round occurrence in s. lowlands, including much of Yucatan Pen. and coastal plains as far n. as s. Sinaloa on the Pacific and region of Tampico on the gulf (Friedmann et al. 1950, A. Phillips). Early Feb. records near Tuxpan, Veracruz (Ogden). High-elevation records are a May specimen from near 1,900 m. in w. San Luis Potosi, mentioned above, and a dark adult at 1,200 m. near Comitan, Chiapas (Ogden).

Elsewhere   CENT. AM.   lowlands on both coasts, up to 1,400 m. in Honduras (Monroe 1968) and in cent. highlands of Costa Rica (Slud 1964).

S. AM.   Occurs in tropical and subtropical regions, mainly below 2,500 m. in the n. ½ of its range (Meyer de Schauensee 1966, E. R. Blake 1977). Range poorly known in much of interior, but generally it occurs w. of the Andes in Colombia and Ecuador, and e. of the Andes it is reported in w. and n. Venezuela, Trinidad, Guyana, French Guiana, and Suriname, s. to s. Peru, Bolivia, Paraguay, n. Argentina, and the Rio Grande do Sul in se. Brazil.   JOHN C. OGDEN

MIGRATION   In Fla., present all year but shows distinct seasonal changes in distribution and local numbers (J. Ogden 1974b). Pairs nesting in s. Fla. from about L.

Okeechobee s. appear to be resident, while those that summer in the cent. and n. peninsula disappear from these regions during winter and total numbers increase correspondingly in s. Fla. in winter. Although movements of Short-tails within the peninsula are seasonally predictable and appear to be true migration rather than dispersal, distances between summer and winter ranges are only 250–600 km.

Spring and fall flights Rarely detected, and may typically consist of movements by only 1 or a few birds traveling at a time rather than sizable assemblies. No spring data, except that Short-tails disappear from regular wintering sites in Everglades Natl. Park during Feb.–Mar. Between 1966 and 1971 the latest date for a nonresident definitive-feathered Short-tail in the Everglades was Feb. 16; for a young bird it was Mar. 22 (J. Ogden 1974b).

Fall movements occur during Oct. and early Nov. Small flocks in fall were 8 on Nov. 1, 1967, in Everglades Natl. Park (J. Ogden 1974b) and 11 mixed with a flight of Broadwings over Key West on Oct. 31, 1955 (Hundley and Hames 1960). First arrivals of wintering Short-tails in Everglades Natl. Park during 4 years occurred Oct. 10–18 (J. Ogden 1974b).

Nothing is known of migration routes, if any, in Fla. Most go only as far s. as the s. mainland in fall, principally to Everglades Natl. Park and the Big Cypress region. A few continue on to the Fla. Keys, usually mixed with flights of other raptors, and some may winter in the Keys (Greene 1944, Hundley and Hames 1960). None have been reported from Cuba (J. Bond 1971), and it is doubtful that this hawk makes the water crossing to points s. of Fla.

The picture is unclear in Mexico, where Short-tails seem to be resident on the Pacific coast (A. Phillips); they have been seen in winter as far n. as Tuxpan, Veracruz, on the Gulf coast (Ogden). Apparently also migratory in parts of Mexico, with suspected autumn flights reported from s. Veracruz (Anderle 1967); a Mar. flight at headwaters of the Usamacenta R., Chiapas (A. Phillips). In Cent. Am., Short-tails that seemed to be migrating have been seen in Honduras in mid-Feb. (Monroe 1968) and in Costa Rica during both spring and fall (Slud 1964). In Panama, N. Smith has observed Short-tails all months of the year without detecting any evidence that they migrate.

JOHN C. OGDEN

BANDING STATUS   To 1980, 1 had been banded in Fla. in 1967; later data, if any, are not at hand.   RALPH S. PALMER

REPRODUCTION   Florida data mainly, primarily from unpublished field notes (Ogden). Age when **1st breeds** unknown. A newly formed pair in s. Fla. consisted of an established resident ♂ joined by a new dark ♀ still showing distinct traces of pre-definitive mottled feathering. The new ♀, presumably 1 year old, participated in construction of a completed nest but did not lay. The same pair did produce eggs the next year but failed to rear young.

Displays By the ♂, high over nesting areas in s. Fla., most commonly Feb.–May. They peak in Mar., but some flights are seen as late as Aug. In HIGH-CIRCLING the ♀ usually perches in a treetop near the nest site and occasionally soars below the ♂. The ♂ SKY-DANCE includes variants of shallow roller coaster-like undulating soaring with

40

exaggerated full flapping on the upswing or in level flight and tightly closed wings on the downswoops. Undulations at times are interspersed with swift, downward dives or undulating downward spirals with wings alternately spread and closed. The entire display may end in TUMBLING—a steep headfirst dive. The ♂ may carry nesting material or prey and may end the flight with a dive to a perch near the ♀, where presentation of prey may occur. The ♂'s flight often covers considerable expanses of sky, undulations continuing for up to 350 m. Once a lone ♀ was seen to perform shallow, undulating flight low over a nesting area.

In Panama 2 birds grasped talons and tumbled earthward (N. Smith).

Copulation In 2 or 3 instances in s. Fla. in late Mar.: the ♂ either slowly dropped from the sky on spread wings and landed directly on the back of the perched ♀ or 1st alighted alongside her. In the latter, he leaned toward the ♀ and uttered a series of squeally 2-note calls; almost immediately the ♀ lowered her head and flattened her back. The ♂ mounted, resting on his tarsi, continuing to give the same calls. In all 3 instances, squeally calls were heard, and copulation lasted 5–7 sec. before the ♂ jumped to an adjacent branch.

Nest building In s. Fla. occurs primarily early Feb.–mid-Mar.; most pairs complete nests by mid- to late Mar. (A. Howell 1932, Sprunt, Jr., 1939, Ogden). A Short-tail flushed from a palm containing a nest of unknown status on Jan. 20, 1938, is earliest record (A. Sprunt, Jr., 1939). In n. Fla., where Short-tails are absent in winter, a nest was in early stages of construction on Mar. 16, another was near completion on Apr. 8, and a Short-tail was seen carrying nesting material near Orlando in Apr. (W. Scott 1889, Pennock 1890, A. Howell 1932).

At one s. Fla. site an identifiable ♂ had 2 different mates within a 3-year period; the ♂ collected almost all woody material for nests. Construction occurred primarily during the morning, before 0900 hrs.; only once were sticks added later in the day when the ♂ made 2 quick trips carrying sticks to a partially completed nest at about 1645 hrs. after having returned to a nearby roost for the evening. Most often the ♂ collected nest material from low trees or woody shrubs within 100 m. of the nest tree. Typically he flew low and direct to a woody perch in the understory, walked out toward the end of a thin branch, and broke off the outer portion with his beak. This often required considerable balancing with half-spread wings. Live and dead branches were taken almost equally. They were transported in talons or beak, most often the former. The pace of construction increased as the nest neared completion. For example, during 2 mornings in early Mar. 1967, the ♂ made 5 trips with material in 76 min. By late Mar., the same ♂ carried branches to the nest on 20 trips in 117 min. After dropping material at the nest, the ♂ either remained to work at construction or, more frequently, flew immediately to collect more material.

At the same 3 s. Fla. nests, ♀♀ did most of the actual construction. Typically the ♀ returned to the nest following each visit by the ♂ to work the latest stick into the structure. Once that task was completed, the ♀ remained either at the nest or close by to await the next delivery by the ♂. Only occasionally did the ♀ collect sticks from the surrounding vegetation. Both sexes gave short calls at fairly frequent intervals during construction. From the time the nest was completed until the 1st egg was laid, and beyond that time, both birds, but primarily the ♀, carried leafy **green branches** to the nest on an almost daily basis. Often they were dropped unceremoniously into the nest bowl during the days before laying.

Nests At L. Istokpoga, Fla., and in Everglades Natl. Park were bulky, measuring 2–3 ft. diam. and nearly 1 ft. in depth (Brandt 1924, Ogden). By contrast, some s. Fla. nests built on large air plants or containing much Spanish moss (a lichen) may be especially shallow—1 such meas. less than 5 in. depth (N. Snyder). Nests in Fla. have been constructed of cypress twigs (Brandt 1924), small sticks mixed with Spanish moss (Ralph, in Brandt), cypress twigs and "moss" (D. Nicholson), or a mixture of branchlets of live oak, red bay, wax myrtle, slash pine, and assorted other understory hardwood shrubs (Ogden). A pair that nested near Fisheating Creek, Fla., constructed a nest in the top of a great mass of hanging Spanish moss in 1968 and, in the same swamp in 1979, constructed a nest of sticks mixed with Spanish moss on top of a large air plant (*Tillandsia*). Sticks in 2 nests in Everglades Natl. Park meas. 7–20 in. long and ⅛–⅜ in. diam. with a few thicker ones for the outside frame. Leafy green nest lining material has consisted of cypress branchlets (Brandt 1924, Nicholson's notes, Pennock 1890), gum and oak leaves (Nicholson), swamp magnolia leaves (Brandt 1924), wild tamarind (*Lysiloma*) (Ogden), and leaves of mangrove, willow, wax myrtle, and eugenia (Sprunt, Jr., 1955).

Location of nests Usually at forks along the major trunk or larger lateral branches near the tops of tall, straight-trunked trees. Several nests have been placed just below the crown. Heights for Fla. nests have been 40 ft. above ground in a gum tree (W. Scott 1889), 44–65 ft. in pines (Pennock 1890, Ogden), 30–95 ft. in cypress (Brandt 1924, Nicholson 1951, Ogden), 58 ft. in a swamp magnolia (Brandt), 25 ft. in a red mangrove (A. Howell 1932, Sprunt, Jr., 1939), and 28 ft. in a cabbage palm (Sprunt, Jr., 1939). A nest only 8 ft. aboveground (Sprunt, Jr., 1939) in a small cypress, if correctly identified, is certainly the lowest and is atypical in several respects.

In Everglades Natl. Park over 4 years (1966–1969) a ♂ had 2 different mates and constructed 1–3 preliminary nests in both 1967 and 1968 before constructing a final nest each year. Preliminary nests were worked on early, mainly early Feb.–early Mar., and were located in less than typical situations. One was 25 ft. above ground in a crotch of a spreading gumbo-limbo tree at the edge between herbaceous marsh and a low dense hardwood thicket. Three other preliminary nests were 20–35 ft. up in large spreading live oaks within dense stands of similar oaks. Preliminary nests were constructed much as final nests; both adults participated, except for a few days when no ♀ was present. Work on preliminary nests was sporadic, and although each received considerable material, no nest appeared to be complete when the site was abandoned either to begin work on another preliminary nest or the final nest. Preliminary nests were located within 250 m. of final nests.

Pairs either build new nests annually or, less often, reuse a nest 2 or more consecutive years (Swann, in Brandt 1924; Ogden). New nests are often constructed in close proximity to a previously used one. In n. Fla. a nest was built on an old heron nest (Pennock 1890).

A completed nest located on Mar. 20 in Everglades Natl. Park was laid in on Apr. 8. Here, and at 2 other s. Fla. nests, ♀♀ spent most of each day before egg laying perched quietly near the nests and were provided food by their mates.

Outside of Fla. few nests have been found. One on Chacachacare I., Trinidad, was "in a tree on the thickly wooded, steep hillside" (Herklots 1961). In Panama a nest was 30–40 ft. up, built over the inflorescence of a coconut palm in open country; another was in an unidentified palm located in hilly, mixed, forest-savanna country (N. Smith). In e.-cent. Veracruz, L. Wolfe found nests 30–50 ft. up "and well towards the top or outer branches of large isolated trees in open brushland." One Veracruz pair was in the same nesting territory for 3 successive years, another for 2 years. Eggs collected at Altillo, Mexico, by J. A. Weber (J. Ogden 1974b) were from a nest 30 ft. above ground in a dense swamp.

Laying dates For Fla., early Mar. (Nicholson 1951) to late May (H. Snyder), with most eggs laid mid-Mar.–mid-Apr. (various sources). In Trinidad an active nest was on Chacachacare I. in Mar., 1942, and 2 eggs were collected from a different nest by Smooker on May 20, 1938 (Herklots 1961, L. Wolfe). Of 2 recent nests found in Panama, 1 was active during mid-Apr. and the other contained eggs during Oct. (N. Smith). It has been found nesting in Chiapas, Mexico, during Mar. (M. del Toro); in Veracruz, a set of eggs collected Feb. 12 and several records of eggs in early Apr. (L. Wolfe).

Clutch size In Fla., 1–3, usually 2 (A. Howell 1932, Bent 1937, Ogden); 3 is very rare (W. Scott 1889), once reportedly in Sprunt, Jr. (1939). Wolfe considered 2 to be the usual clutch size in Veracruz.

One **egg** each from 18 clutches (Fla. 12, Mexico 6) **size** length 52.48 ± 2.31 mm., breadth 42.38 ± 1.61, radii of curvature of ends 17.89 ± 1.22 and 14.38 ± 1.15; **shape** usually short elliptical, elongation 1.23 ± 0.056, bicone −0.053, and asymmetry +0.103 (F. W. Preston). Twenty-seven range in length 48.6–57.5 mm., breadth 40.3–45.5, and av. 53.4 × 42.8 (Bent 1937). **Color** dull white or very pale bluish or greenish, unmarked or sparingly marked with small brownish spots around the large end. The spots are reddish brown (Chapman 1916, H. Bailey 1925), dark brown, chestnut brown, and warm sepia (Bent 1937). Apparently less commonly, eggs may be more heavily marked with dark brown blotches around either end (Bent).

Incubation All by the ♀ at 9 s. Fla. nestings. During 38 hrs., 15 min., of observations over 4 different days at 1 nest, the ♀ left the nest 16 times, for a total absence of 3 hrs., 46 min. (absences of 5–28 min., mean 14.1). The ♀ perched quietly near the nest 5 times, preened nearby 4 times, left the nest 3 times each to receive food brought by the ♂ and to fly low over the surrounding canopy, and left once to collect a green branchlet for the nest bowl. Calling by the approaching ♂, carrying food, prompted the ♀ to fly from the nest and intercept him at a nearby perch.

Incubation period At 2 s. Fla. nests, approximately 34 days. At 1, the ♀ began "sitting tight" on Apr. 8, and an egg hatched on May 12 (the 2d egg failed). In the other—unusually late nesting—the ♀ began incubating on May 21, and a single young hatched on June 29 (Ogden, N. and H. Snyder).

Development of young A day-old nestling in Fla. weighed 35 gm.; it had a white downy head, creamy-white downy body, black beak, blackish brown eyes, and yellow cere, base of beak, legs, and feet. At age 9 days, the yellow soft parts had become greenish yellow and the nestling weighed 90 gm. The same nestling at 2½ weeks weighed 165 gm. and was showing emergence of gray woolly 2d layer of down on upperparts and emergent primaries up to 9 mm. long and still sheathed. At age 3 weeks—and following several days of uninterrupted rain when few feedings occurred—wt. 200 gm., primaries to 25 mm. including sheath, and solid layer of gray down dorsally. At another s. Fla. nest a pair of nestlings estimated at less than a full day old and between 1 and 2 days old weighed 22 and 55 gm.; the former died soon after, and the latter weighed 320 gm. at 2 weeks. At a 3d nest, 2 nestlings estimated at 3⅓ weeks old weighed 370 and 390 gm.

Nestlings are generally fed 2–3 times/day. During 40 hrs. of observation on 6 different days at 3 successful nests, each containing a single young, nestlings were fed 12 times (1 feeding/3.3 hrs.). At an unsuccessful nest with a single nestling, feedings occurred at a rate of once every 7.9 hrs. during 63 hrs. of observation on 9 different days.

During 2 feedings of a 4-day-old bird, the ♀ passed 101 small bits of food to the nestling and, somewhat alternating with feeding the nestling, consumed 87 bits herself.

At 4 Fla. nests containing downy young, the ♀ remained perched on or near the nest during most of the day. The ♀ carried leafy green branchlets to the nest 1–2 times daily during this period. Food was brought by the ♂ and passed to the ♀ either on the nest or at some nearby perch. All feedings of nestlings were by ♀ ♀. A 4-day-old young was brooded or shaded by the ♀ most of the day, whereas a 15-day-old and a 28-day-old nestling were covered in daytime only during brief rain showers.

At a nest containing a large, feathered nestling both adults were away hunting most of each day, and both delivered food to the nest. The young bird fed unaided. No green branchlets were brought to the nest and it showed no sign that any had been added recently.

Age at first flight Unknown; a s. Fla. nest on June 16 contained a single, fully feathered young, which perched on an adjacent horizontal branch part of the day.

Breeding success Although most Fla. nests evidently received 2-egg clutches, the same nests, if successful, more often than not reared a single young to flight age. Of 6 Fla. nests observed during the nestling period, 5 contained 1 young and 1 contained 2. Two of the nests with single young were known to have had 2-egg clutches; in 1, an egg failed to hatch, while in the other, a nestling died within a day after hatching.

JOHN C. OGDEN

SURVIVAL   No information.

HABITS   Almost all data here are from unpublished field notes (Ogden), mainly from Fla. An inconspicuous species that spends much of each day soaring at medium to great heights.

Daily routine Bird usually perches quietly and inconspicuously within woods for 1–2 hrs. after sunrise, occasionally preening, sometimes actively looking about, but rarely if ever flying. Birds frequently perch on horizontal branches in the upper ⅓ of large trees or in the leafy crown of a tree with only its upper body and head showing. It is also known to roost on the stiffer, horizontal leaves of large royal palms (*Roystonea*) in

s. Fla. Flight begins once breezes or thermals develop sufficiently to allow relatively effortless soaring. First flight by a nonbreeding adult in Everglades Natl. Park often coincides closely with the arrival of the 1st soaring vultures. Once a Short-tail takes wing it may be in the air with few interruptions for much of the remainder of the day. Aerial activity ceases 1–2 hrs. before sunset, when the bird returns to roost in woodland.

During flight birds primarily search for prey. Short-tails hunt over relatively large areas, as much as 2–2.5 km. in diam. Most hunting ranges in s. Fla. are 2–3 times larger in diam. than those maintained by Red-shouldered Hawks in the same region. The Short-tail hunts during long periods of relatively effortless soaring, usually at heights of 250–750 m.

Hunting techniques Short-tails often actively search the ground below from a nearly stationary position in **midair,** hanging seemingly motionless on spread wings. This works especially well where upward-deflected air currents are created along ridge tops (as in Trinidad—Ogden) or where a lengthy woodland edge interfaces with a broad expanse of open country. They also search for prey while soaring slowly into the wind in a rather straight-line direction. A Short-tail may repeat a hunting pass over an area by turning with the wind and sailing swiftly back over its previous course for several hundred m., then back into the wind to resume hunting. Hunting **from a perch** seems to be rare.

Capture of prey The bird makes swift, closed-wing dives initiated from the soaring or hanging positions (J. Ogden 1974b). Dives are either uninterrupted from high up down to the intended prey or may include 1 or more midair "holds" when the hawk spreads its wings to halt its descent briefly. Dives may be resumed from a midair hold, or the capture attempt may then terminate and the hawk will soar to regain altitude. Dives consist of nearly vertical, headfirst plummeting with wing tips folded against the tail or of shallow, angled, swift sails on bowed wings. Most dives are directed toward avian prey in the tops of shrubs or trees in open country, along woodland edges, or in forest canopy. Dives are directed less often to prey on the ground and rarely toward low-flying birds (e.g., Tree Swallows over a marsh). The element of surprise may be important to capture success, as most dives consist of a single pass at the intended prey and are not followed by additional pursuit if the 1st effort fails.

Prey may be partially or wholly eaten at a perch near the capture site. Otherwise the hawk circles upward with prey in talons and soars to some regular woodland perch or delivers the quarry to its mate or nest. Prey may be partially plucked or eaten in the air, the slow-soaring hawk swinging its talons forward and reaching down and under with its beak.

Most capture attempts directed toward avian prey are unsuccessful. Two nonbreeding adults watched in s. Fla. during 30 hrs. of uninterrupted hunting on 17 different days attempted 107 stoops on prey, of which 64 were carried to completion; 12 resulted in successful captures, for a rate of 1 capture/2.5 hrs. of hunting (J. Ogden 1974b). Adult ♂ ♂ at several active Fla. nesting sites brought only 1–3 prey items to a nest per day, even though they seemed to be devoting most of the day to hunting.

On nesting territories the ♂ takes the lead role in defending the full **hunting range,** while the ♀ is most energetic in defending the immediate area of the nest tree. Males vigorously chase or escort intruding Short-tails from their hunting range and often make diving passes at other broad-winged species of raptors—other buteos or the Bald Eagle. In Panama, resident Short-tails chase migrating Broad-winged and Swainson's Hawks (N. Smith). Swallow-tailed Kites, the N. Harrier, or vultures flying quite close to an active Short-tail nest are usually ignored. In turn, Short-tails flying low over marshes or fields may be mobbed or chased by Red-winged Blackbirds or Loggerhead Shrikes.

Female Short-tails often seem quite **tame** when on nests and may allow close approach by humans before flushing (Brandt 1924, Ogden). A ♀ usually responds to a human climbing to a nest by circling low overhead, calling frequently, and occasionally stooping swiftly at the intruder (Brandt 1924, Nicholson 1951, L. Wolfe). One ♀ in Everglades Natl. Park often struck a climber during repeated visits to a nest containing a small nestling (Ogden).

Nesting Short-tails and Redshoulders in Fla. are often involved in **interspecific conflict** where they occupy the same woods. The more aggressive Short-tail ♂ may dive upon a flying Redshoulder near the former's nest; both may join in tight circling flight with much calling, mainly by the noisier Redshoulder. Conflict between these species may be lessened in some situations due to difference in timing of nesting—the Redshoulder starts 4–6 weeks earlier. Redshoulders also often hunt most actively early and late in the day, times when Short-tails are at their roosts. A Short-tail may also ignore a Redshoulder that is perched below the canopy in solid woods, even when quite close to the former's nest.

Two or more Short-tails of unknown relationship may circle together or hunt within sight of one another in winter in s. Fla. without aggression. Short-tails are generally quiet except near active nests.

Numbers   Short-tails are usually quite scarce throughout s. Fla. and often are overlooked where they do occur. In s. Fla. they are much less numerous than the other 2 nesting hawks—Redtail and Redshoulder. The state population may total fewer than 500. Important habitats have been destroyed, notably the swamps around L. Istokpoga (Brandt 1924, Nicholson 1951), but this hawk still seems to occupy the same total range as was historically described by A. Howell (1932) and Bent (1937). Although Sprunt, Jr. (1939), feared that the species had declined considerably in the early decades of this century, the blocks of years in the past when few Short-tails have been seen could just as well be due to reduced observer effort. No information exists to suggest strongly that the total population in Fla. has changed greatly.

Little information exists on numbers or history elsewhere, although the bird is nowhere common. Short-tails seem more numerous in parts of Mexico than anywhere in Fla., and there is some evidence that the species has spread n. along both Pacific and gulf coasts in recent decades (A. Phillips). Certainly opening the forest would seem to favor the bird in most of its range. In 1968, L. Wolfe (letter) considered the ratio of Roadside Hawks (*A. magnirostris*) to Short-tails in the coastal plain between Tampico and Veracruz city to be about 30 : 1, while A. Phillips (letter) considered the Short-tail to be the most common *Buteo* in a pine-oak region in the lower mountains of sw. Oaxaca.   JOHN C. OGDEN

46

FOOD **Fla.** A specialized hunter of small birds, as it is elsewhere. The Short-tail has relatively heavy feet and long talons for its size; this is likely an adaptation for capturing birds (Rand 1960).

At 8 active nests in Fla. prey remains of 73 birds of 17 identifiable species ranged in size from gnatcatchers and wood warblers to Bobwhite and Mourning Dove (J. Ogden 1974b, N. and H. Snyder). An additional list of prey, determined by watching hunting Short-tails in Everglades Natl. Park mainly during winter, were 29 birds of 9 species and 3 small rodents (J. Ogden 1974b). In both lists, open-terrain species of birds, especially E. Meadowlarks and Red-winged Blackbirds, predominated; woodland and understory species were relatively scarce. Small birds that are exposed at territorial perches located either in the canopy of woodlands or in isolated shrubs in open country may be especially vulnerable to capture. Nestling birds are not known to be taken. Older reports from Fla. also show birds as primary prey (5 records), including a Sharp-shinned Hawk (Cottam and Knappen 1939), but also 2 rodents (*Sigmodon?*) and a small snake (J. Moore 1954, Sprunt, Jr., 1955, J. Ogden 1974b).

Elsewhere Food may be more varied in more tropical parts of the species' range, although birds predominate. Avian prey included a small bird in Michoacan, Mexico (J. Davis 1953), small birds in Veracruz, Mexico (L. Wolfe), thrush-sized birds in Costa Rica (Slud 1964), and in Panama a thrush (*Turdus*) (A. Wetmore 1965), a small bird (Hallinan 1924), and a mockingbird (*Mimus*) (N. Smith). In Trinidad it has been seen stooping at a Ground Dove (Herklots 1961) and a Dickcissel (ffrench 1973). A Guyana specimen (U. of Miami) contained a small bird.

Nonavian prey includes 2 14-in. ground lizards (Hallinan 1924) and an *Ameiva* lizard (N. Smith), both in Panama. Snakes, tree frogs, and insects in Suriname (Haverschmidt 1968). Capturing insects suggests a hunting technique other than the usual soar and stoop. JOHN C. OGDEN

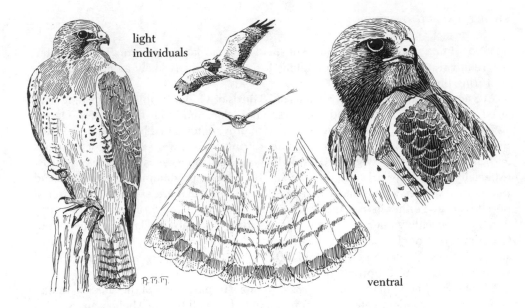

light
individuals

ventral

SWAINSON'S HAWK

Buteo swainsoni Bonaparte

A fairly large open-country buteo; approximates the Red-tailed Hawk in size but is more trim. The wings are narrow distally, and only 3 outer primaries are emarginated ("notched") along their trailing edges. Feet rather weak and delicate; tarsus much less than ½ as long as tail and almost entirely unfeathered.

Basic Plumage remarkably variable, hence often described as having color phases, but, instead of disjunct categories, there are all degree of intermediates from light to dark individuals. All have dark upperparts and tail gray ventrally with subterminal dusky band and narrow, less conspicuous barring proximally. Underparts vary from white (may have dark markings, concentrated laterally) with wide dark "bib" from lower throat down onto upper breast, to rufescent with bib prominent to indistinct, to almost totally blackish or slaty. Juv. birds vary more or less correspondingly; feathers of upperparts conspicuously margined with light browns, underparts streaked or blotched dark (or possibly solid dark in some).

Sexes similar in appearance. The ♀ is larger; sexes overlap greatly in meas. (nearly complete in beak, although averages differ) but very little in wt. The ♂ length is about 19–20 in. (48–51 cm.), wingspread to 49 in. (124 cm.); ♀ length 20–22 (51–56), wingspread to 54 (137). On av., the ♂ weighs about 1¾ lb. (800 gm.) and the ♀ 10 oz. more (1,100 gm.); practically all birds under 33 oz. are ♂♂.

No subspecies.

DESCRIPTION One Plumage/cycle with Basic I earliest definitive. The birds are here divided arbitrarily into 3 categories: belly light/intermediate/dark, caused by several genes. In each, the dorsum is much alike. Full description of complete range of variation would fill many pages. Dark birds, very much in the minority anywhere, apparently are more frequent n. in breeding range (useful information is lacking).

48

▶ ♂ ♀ Def. Basic Plumage (entire feathering), acquired by molting from spring into fall, sometimes with pause during fall migration and then completed.

LIGHT **Beak** black, cere variably yellow; **head** dark dusky browns or even toward slaty, except pale (to white) area across forehead, often some white between cere and eye, and white chin; **iris** dark brownish, but occasionally the Juv. gray persists into later life; feathers at rear of head white basally. **Dorsum** variable, usually muted dark browns, the feathers frequently with narrow lighter margins that wear off. **Underparts** throat onto upper breast ("bib") a solid warm brown or darker, sharply defined, but in some reduced to dark spots, and in others the dorsal coloring (it may be slaty) extends to include this area; lower breast to tail white or toward buffy, individuals varying from unmarked to quite heavily barred browns or blackish (densest on thighs). Some white (inconspicuous at times) in lateral upper tail coverts. **Legs** and **feet** yellow, talons black. **Tail** ventrally palish gray, terminally white (may wear off) with dusky subterminal bar (width 8–18 mm., usually about 12), then 9–12 (usually 10) openly spaced, very narrow, darkish bars. **Wing** dark dorsally, brown feather margins on coverts in fresh feathering most conspicuous near leading edge toward body; flight feathers appear blackish dorsally and ventrally are distally black, then lighter (medium gray or gray-brown) with fine narrow dark barring and wing lining almost all white except a small carpal patch ("thumb mark")—a narrow black crescent or bar composed of ends of most distal underwing coverts.

INTERMEDIATE (reddish brown venter) Main differences from above: forehead stripe poorly indicated or absent, concealed bases of feathers on rear of head usually buffy, upperparts various dark browns, underparts brownish reds (highly variable) with more or less darker (to blackish) barring, and wing lining variably tawny with some dark markings in addition to carpal patch.

DARK (venter more or less blackish) Most of feathering nearly black, with some palish edging on dorsum; often a white chin patch and sometimes some light on sides of abdomen, or same barred dark; some off-white in under tail coverts, which are barred and/or blotched dark; the tail has the usual pattern and both ventrally and dorsally appears lighter proximally; narrow dusky tail bars are wider than in the light-bellied category.

Molting (Prebasic II and later) All feathering is usually renewed through SPRING– EARLY FALL but is sometimes completed later after a pause. The primaries and their greater coverts molt from inner to outer (descendantly); secondaries have molt centers at #1, #5, and #12; and tail feathers tend to drop from central pair outward (the outward sequence often irregular). Wing molting summarized from A. H. Miller (1941): orderly replacement of primaries and corresponding greater coverts; 3 molt centers in secondary series; early replacement of greater secondary coverts; and outward progression in renewal of the 4 principal tertial feathers.

Primary molting may sometimes be suspended during fall migration and then would presumably be completed on "winter" range. Skutch (1945b) stated that some spring migrants had gaps in wings and tail, but whether this relates to a previous molt or to the beginning of a new molt is unclear. Occasionally, at least the outermost primary is retained through 1 cycle and then dropped at beginning of the next.

NOTES Friedmann (1950), who gave very detailed descriptions, stated that ♀ ♀ have a darker forehead stripe than ♂ ♂, when present, that their dorsal feathers have reduced brown edging, and that their "shoulder" area feathers are darker. Many breeding ♀ ♀, however, have both a light forehead and chin.

The palest birds, which are rare, have head, "shoulders," and all of venter white or nearly so—very striking when seen afield. Some particularly handsome individuals are bicolored: the bluish slaty dark areas contrast greatly with the sharply delineated white of underparts. In the dark category some individuals are bluish slaty overall, that is, not blackish. Cameron (1908b) stated that, in "bluish ash" ♂ ♂, the iris is "brownish yellow," while in ♀ ♀ and "immatures" it is "pale hazel."

Past authors have tried to account for great individual variation by fitting the birds into a sequence of recognizably different Basic Plumages: 2 (Coues 1874a); 4 (Cameron 1913); and 3 or 4, based on Cameron (Bent 1937).

AT HATCHING Down-A is white, slightly tinged yellowish, and becomes "whiter with advancing age"—that is, incoming down-B (Bent 1937).

▶ ♂ ♀ Juv. Plumage (entire feathering), completed about at end of nest life, retained through WINTER, then succeeded by Basic I beginning in SPRING.

Beak slaty, iris gray or blue-gray at first, gradually altering (timing unknown) to a palish brown in most individuals. Feathering so variable that no concise description will serve; it parallels the variation in later life. **Head** tends to be streaked dark on light; feathers on dorsum have wide lighter margins (brownish or buffy); **underparts** (at least of many) a yellowish brown marked with elongated dark blotches; **tail** has narrower subterminal bar and more very narrow dark bars than later in definitive. **Wing lining** buffy to brownish, generally with dark markings. Reddish birds show more reddish brown above and below. The underparts of blackish birds tend to have a somewhat broken pattern, very dark blotches on somewhat lighter background.

Molting (Prebasic I) of captives, BEGINNING IN SPRING. In a ♂ this began at end of Apr., the 3d primary (from inner) dropped 1st, and soon some secondaries and upper wing coverts; on June 8 the tail started with central pair of feathers. Molting lasted about 6 months, and primary #10 (outer) was the last feather dropped (Cameron 1913). Two others began molting in Mar.–Apr.; in 1, molt began with loss of contour feathers and an innermost primary (M. Bechard).

Color phases do not exist as discrete entities; there is a continuum from lightest to darkest individuals. Dark birds are uncommon in Wyo., Man., and Sask., but "become more abundant" in Calif and Wash. (references in H. Munro and Reid 1982). Relative numbers of the different categories in different areas remain unknown. Several authors who have watched migrants in Cent. Am. have given rough figures of 90% light-bellied and 10% variably dark.

Measurements Twenty ♂ BEAK from cere 20.5–24.9 mm., av. 22.1, WING across chord 362–406, av. 383.6, MIDDLE TOE minus talon 36.7–44.4, av. 39.5; and 38 ♀ BEAK from cere 20.5–25.7 mm., av. 23.7, WING across chord 375–427, av. 404.6, and MIDDLE TOE minus talon 38.3–46.5, av. 42.1 (Friedmann 1950). (In this sample, the ♀ WING chord may include wrongly sexed ♂ birds. In Alta.: WING flattened 67 ♂ 375–410 mm. and 48 ♀ 403–440 [J. Schmutz].)

TAIL (right center feather) of breeding birds in Alta.: 61 ♂ 170–198 mm., mean 126, and 43 ♀ 124–221, mean 205 (J. Schmutz). This feather often is 3–5 mm. shorter than the tail because it covers the others and wears faster. Presumably the tail is longer in Juv. than in Basic Plumages, but no data.

50

Weight   Breeders (corrected for wt. of crop contents) in summer in Alta.: 69 ♂ 683–936 gm., mean 808, and 50 ♀ 937–1,367, mean 1,109 (J. Schmutz).

Mean figures: 5 ♂ 908 gm., and 7 ♀ 1,068 (N. Snyder and Wiley 1976).

First-winter (Juv.) birds in Fla.: ♂ 958 gm., and 2 ♀ 849 and 785 (D. R. Paulson).

Hybrids   None; Swainson's has fostered Prairie Falcons.

Geographical variation   Evidently none, although some shift in light/dark ratio in the breeding range may be discovered.

Affinities   Ancestral *Buteo* probably originated in S. Am., which is still austral range of Swainson's and Broad-winged Hawks. Swainson's (New World) and Common Buzzard *B. buteo* (Old World) were formerly thought to comprise a single species, but polymorphism is their main common characteristic at the species level.

Ralph S. Palmer

FIELD IDENTIFICATION   **In our area** primarily. In open country. Wingspread to over 4 ft. (122 cm.) but somewhat trimmer, with narrower, more pointed, wings than the Red-tailed Hawk. Three emarginated outer primaries (but 4 in the Redtail, Ferruginous Hawk, and Rough-legged Hawk). Tail neutral (appears lighter gray proximally), barring mostly thin, seldom noticeable. Most importantly, Swainson's soars with upward-angled wings (dihedral), and, although it is capable of fast action, it can appear to be leisurely or (especially when taking wing) even sluggish. At times it hovers. Some nesters allow humans to approach closely before flushing.

In all feathered stages and color categories there is usually some white on upper sides of rump (may be more or less barred browns); it appears white at a distance, is smaller and differently located than the centered white on rump of the N. Harrier, and is a good recognition mark. Under tail coverts are at least partially white. All have dark backs. Some comparisons follow.

Basic feathering   LIGHT birds in flight show a dark "bib," sharply delineated (except during molting), not a bellyband (as in Redtail and some Roughlegs), and usually pale forehead and chin. In a soaring bird, white of underwing extends clear to the leading edge next to the body (a sort of inverted V) and the dark "thumb mark" is small and more or less of a bar; flight feathers of wing are mixed dark and light. The thumb mark is much more prominent in the light underwing of the Ferruginous. The much smaller Broad-winged Hawk has inconspicuous thumb mark and dark trailing edge.

INTERMEDIATES show great variation in pattern and coloring. For example, many have rusty underparts, barred dark, and 2-toned underwing (coverts lighter but seldom, if ever, white).

DARK Swainson's cause the most problems, being easily confused with other dark buteos. Winglinings are dark, and remainder of underwing patterned. Often there is some white at chin, almost invariably some on sides of rump, also in under tail coverts.

Undersurface of **tail:** 1 Swainson's—grayish (not colored), lightest proximally, distal darkish band, white in under tail coverts; 2 dark Broadwings—a few wide, conspicuous bars, alternating white and nearly black; 3 dark Redtails—some reddish in tail (it may be muted), also usually some fine dark barring, and subterminal dark band varies from merely indicated to prominent; 4 dark Ferruginous—tail light to dark overall (as viewed from below) without discernible pattern, white area basally in primaries much as in the Roughleg; and **5** Roughleg—tail variable, from dusky with indistinct darker barring to light except for wide dark subterminal band, light area basally in primaries. (Overlap of occurrence of Roughleg and Swainson's is almost entirely in migration.)

Downies   Best identified by parentage. The tarsus is: **1** almost naked in Swainson's, **2** feathered well down in the Redtail, and **3** feathered all the way down in the Ferruginous.

Juvenal Plumage   Light Swainson's have underwing about as in Basic (and young Redtail); the bib area is heavily streaked dark (not solid), and any whitish laterally on lower rump is diagnostic. Intermediate and dark birds vary so much that they present real problems—sometimes even in hand until it is ascertained that only 3 of the primaries are notched (as in the much smaller Broadwing) and that tarsi are feathered for less than ½ their length. Example: Juv. "Swainson's" collected in B.C. turned out to be dark Redtails (A. Brooks 1927a).

When perched   Swainson's is a limb-, post-, and pole-sitter, like other buteos. It also perches on the ground—but less readily in summer than the Ferruginous—and often on a "gopher" mound, hillock, or other slight eminence. Folded wings extend beyond the tail. Lighter birds show dark bib; dark birds are difficult to identify unless some light on sides of rump is visible. If flushed, they may soar with diagnostic dihedral. Dark Redtails tend to have mottled or patchy dorsum; it is evenly dark in Swainson's. Many Swainson's, when low on the nest (incubating), can be identified instantly if they show a white or pale area across the forehead.

Migrant Swainsons v. Broadwings   The circumstances in which these species can be distinguished in the air are too variable for useful definition. The principal factors involved are light conditions, height of the birds above ground, and angular relation of birds to observer. At distances of a few hundred yds. the 2 species are separable by color and pattern, the 3 wide, white tail bands of "adult" Broadwings being particularly diagnostic. At somewhat longer range, with birds in silhouette overhead, an experienced observer will still be able to pick up subtle differences in shape—the tail of Swainson's is longer, and its wings are longer, more pointed, proportionately narrower, and join the body nearer the base of the tail. Beyond an indeterminate limit of perhaps 700–800 yds., identification becomes questionable. In terms of daily flight routine, sure identification is most likely in early morning, when birds are rising, and late afternoon, when they are coming down for the night. At midday most birds are too high for determination. Anyone watching hawks on a good flight day in s. Mexico or the Cent. Am. corridor can expect to see 100s, perhaps 1,000s, that are near enough to be identified to species and 10 times as many so high or so far to 1 side that they are no more than black dots moving across the sky. To meet this difficulty many observers, and some of the best, have fallen back on the expedient of making sample counts of birds within range of identification and extrapolating the ratios to distant birds, assuming they will be similar. This device is subject not only to small errors but also to a major flaw from the different roosting habits of the 2 migrants.

Swainson's (although a tree nester) typically roosts at night on bare ground with scattered trees, the Broadwing in closed-canopy woods and thickets. Where such habitats are somewhat separated, the 2 hawks put down for the night in separate areas, each to its own liking; they then rise in the morning and tend to maintain this separation during the day. A theoretical example would be a wide valley of fields and pastures, bound laterally by wooded hills, the whole lying athwart a migration route. In late afternoon, Swainson's would put down in pastureland, Broadwings on the ridges. In the morning, an observer on the hills would see many Broadwings rising but few Swainson's; an observer on the valley floor would experience the opposite, many Swainson's but few Broadwings—Broadwings that had spent the night to windward would already be too high in the air to identify. Count ratios from the valley would have no valid application to the distant birds, which could as well be 1 species as the other.

From experience in the Terraba Valley, Skutch drew the conclusion that the "innumerable hosts of Swainson's Hawk" far outnumbered the passing Broadwings in Costa Rica. Present-day counts from s. Tex. indicate fairly equal numbers, with any preponderance on the Broadwing side. Since Skutch was writing of 1936–1945, approximately the time observers in w. U.S. began to report a decrease in Swainson's, it is possible that the latter was indeed more abundant in that period. Yet it seems quite as possible that he saw more Swainson's than Broadwings only because of his location. Careful reading of his paper shows that descriptions of his surroundings and the circumstances under which he counted hawks agree in every substantial detail with those of the valley observer in the theoretical example above.

Boreal winter   As to purported sightings of Swainson's in N. Am. outside their usual range, or anywhere in our area in winter, beware especially of dark Redtails and of Roughlegs.   JOSEPH A. HAGAR AND RALPH S. PALMER

VOICE   Reported to be silent except in the nesting-rearing season.

The usual call is a shrill, rather plaintive *kreeeee*, weaker than the Redtail's; quite like the Roughleg's, but terminates in clear-cut fashion; also like the Broadwing's, but shorter, less plaintive. Sometimes followed by series of whistled syllables *tsip tsip* . . . (W. Taylor and Shaw 1927). Uttered in flight or when perched. The ♀'s call is "shorter and lower-pitched" than the ♂'s (Dunkle 1977).

After much experience with this hawk, Bendire (1892) wrote that it uttered a "peculiar gurgling sound" while "diving through the air" (Sky-dance) and that its voice could otherwise be described as *"pi-tick pi-tick* frequently repeated."

Cameron (1913) raised a captive ♂. Its voice at first resembled that of a kitten, but at 7 weeks it became loud and shrill, like a gull but more piercing. At 8 weeks the bird made a musical cry of 4 notes "insistently repeated." At about 12 weeks it became silent, but soon after its ordinary call was a "very soft low whistle," not a scream except when guarding food. Coues (1874a) had 2 young of different age; they uttered a "peculiarly plaintive whistle to signify hunger or a sense of loneliness, a note that was almost musical in intonation."   RALPH S. PALMER

HABITAT   **Summer**   Semiopen to open terrain from extreme nw. Canada down into Mexico; drier terrain to the s., including deserts; greatest density, however, probably on the prairies and intermountain area of U.S. To some extent the ecological counterpart of Roughleg, although much of the year it feeds largely on smaller prey—large insects (F. Beebe 1974).

On the prairies, shelterbelts and other plantings have made trees more widely available than formerly. This plus reduction of fires has produced a man-altered habitat for 3 breeding buteos—Ferruginous in open, drier landscapes, Redtail in woodlands, and Swainson's in the interfaces of trees and shrubs. They coexist where these inter-digitate, which has not greatly altered the general breeding range of the Ferruginous and Swainson's. The breeding range of the latter on the Canadian prairies approximates that of Richardson's ground squirrel (*Spermophilus richardsonii*), a major prey species. Swainson's nests near human habitations; for example, 15 of 68 nests were within 0.5 km. of a farmyard (based mainly on Schmutz 1980 and Schmutz et al. 1984.) In Colo., a tree on an abandoned farmstead or at a reservoir is as good a nesting place as sparse forest along a dry creek (Olendorff 1975). In Wash., telemetered ♂ ♂ did little hunting on cultivated land, favoring sparsely vegetated areas even though they supported fewer, if more visible, prey (Bechard 1982). In nw. Mexico (s. Chihuahuan desert), Swainson's occupied the lowlands, Redtails the highlands; they overlapped in contact zones, and the entire area was divided into territories (Thiollay 1981).

Migrations Over any terrain where updrafts provide needed buoyancy for soaring; typically, Swainson's perches at night on the ground, spaced apart, not feeding. (Occasionally they feed during initial and terminal stages of migration.)

Boreal winter A few in open areas in s. Fla. and during **austral summer** in S. Am. on such open terrain as the pampas. RALPH S. PALMER

DISTRIBUTION (See map.) **Boreal summer** Known to have bred in e.-cent. Alaska e. into Yukon Terr. and extreme nw. Mackenzie Dist.; evidently a hiatus in the heavily forested regions to the s. until again breeding on the Canadian prairies.

In coterminous U.S., not many occur w. of the Cascades (apparently absent from w. Wash.), and in Calif. numbers are now greatly reduced (may no longer breed in s. part of the state), the decline continuing in mid-1980s. Eastern breeding limits have been unstable. Said to have reoccupied the periphery of former breeding range near Winnipeg since 1951 (H. Munro and Reid 1982). At times has bred e. into Ill. (see Keir and Wilde 1976), Mo., and Ark., and apparently more often in Iowa. Southern breeding limits are somewhere in n. Mexico—here tentatively placed in n. Durango, s. Coahuila, Nuevo León, and Tamaulipas. It seems probable that in Mexico more pairs breed in Chihuahua e. of the Sierra Madre than anywhere else. No longer known to breed in Baja Calif. To generalize, the vast majority presently breed from the Canadian prairies to beyond the Mexican boundary and from the e. foothills of the Rockies e. nearly to the Mississippi.

Migration Over the breeding range plus fairly regular occurrence e. toward the Atlantic—records from Ont. and Que. s. over many years—and a few in some years to extreme s. mainland Fla. and the Fla. Keys. An increase in reported e. sightings in N. Am. reflects more observers (and some questionable reports?). For passage through Cent. Am., see Migration, below. Probably absent from the Yucatan Pen.

Boreal winter Occurred in some numbers in s. Fla. beginning probably in the early 1960s, but has now apparently reverted to earlier status of a few birds and perhaps none some winters. There is evidently an occasional migration dropout in states on the U.S. side of the Mexican border.

54

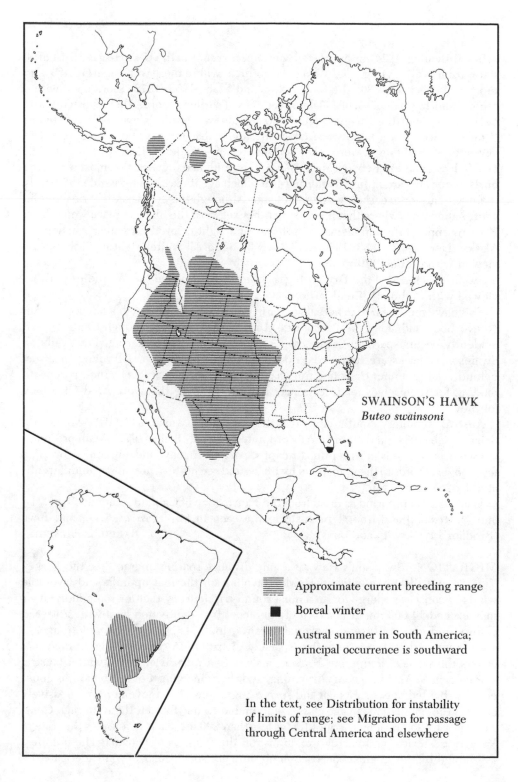

SWAINSON'S HAWK
Buteo swainsoni

▤ Approximate current breeding range

■ Boreal winter

▥ Austral summer in South America;
principal occurrence is southward

In the text, see Distribution for instability
of limits of range; see Migration for passage
through Central America and elsewhere

See Browning (1974) for purported winter occurrence in the U.S. He gave a list of 20 states from Wash., Oreg., and Wyo., and Nebr. s. where there were sightings (39) and reports of specimens (30) "between" Nov. and Mar., 1968–1972. Florida led with 4 reports and 15 specimens; of 4 Colo. specimens of earlier history, 3 have subsequently been reexamined (the 4th unavailable) and are not Swainson's. Eleven of 18 specimens Browning listed in a table were taken in Nov.—that is, may have been very late migrants. In addition, 2 were taken in Dec. (Calif.—"adult," La.), 4 in Jan. (Calif., Tex. 2, Fla.), and 1 in Feb. (N.Mex.—"adult"). Evidence suggests that most wintering birds in our area are in Juv. feathering—at which age it may be impossible to identify them with absolute certainty except in hand. Although this species might be found in winter almost anywhere that it occurs in other seasons, the likeliest place would be s. Fla. An apparently outrageous report was of a light-colored bird near Anchorage, Alaska, Dec. 4–25, 1983 (1984 *Am. Birds* **38** 348). All winter sightings "should be viewed with caution" (Browning).

Swainson's reached the Dry Tortugas. Alleged sightings in the W. Indies must be viewed with caution (J. Bond 1978).

This hawk must be rare in boreal winter in upper Mexico, although it has occurred in Nuevo León and along the Pacific side. In s. Mexico and on through Cent. Am., it evidently occurs sparingly, again, at least mostly in Juv. feathering. Practically all Swainson's Hawks are funneled through Panama into S. Am. Of young that stay behind, a late summer transition from having been fed vertebrates by their parents to fending for themselves for insects may not always leave them prepared for a long journey.

Austral summer South Am. distribution, from Amadon (1964), Meyer de Schauensee (1964), and others are incorporated in E. R. Blake (1977). Main presently known occurrence is in Argentina (except s. part), Uruguay, and adjacent s. Brazil; a few known records to the n. mapped by Blake (and see his text) are mostly undifferentiated by season.

Swainson's is reported as **fossil** from the Pleistocene of Calif. (3 locations), Nev. (1), and N.Mex. (2) and from 1 **prehistoric site** each in Calif., Ariz., S.D., and Iowa (Brodkorb 1964, with additions). RALPH S. PALMER

MIGRATION Swainson's Hawk is a long-distance soaring migrant like the Turkey Vulture and the Broad-winged Hawk, traveling on thermal updrafts and favorable winds to conserve energy for an annual round-trip journey that for some individuals may exceed 14,000 mi. It is a bird of open country—cultivated land with scattered clumps and groves of trees, shortgrass prairie, high plains, and dry cattle range. It spends upward of 4 months rather sparsely distributed over a breeding range that covers the w. ½ of temperate N. Am., a short 3–4 months of the n. winter (austral summer) in S. Am. s. to cent. Argentina, and the remaining 4 or more months about equally divided between its fall and spring migrations. Fall movement progressively collects the population (all age classes) and in due course funnels them through Cent. Am. via a 1,500-mi.-long corridor that is less than 200 mi. wide as it leaves the state of Veracruz, Mexico, and narrows to 45 mi. on the Isthmus of Panama. The numbers assembled by this gradual constriction of route are spectacular beyond adequate description. In the Canal Zone during the fall almost the entire species is said to pass over Ancon Hill, Balboa (N. Smith 1973). Spring migration repeats the process in reverse: the gathering from the boreal winter range, the extreme concentration, and the eventual dispersion over the widespread nesting range. Skutch (1945b) said of spring passage through Costa Rica that only among the bird is. of Peru had he seen more impressive mass movements of birds.

Although the restrictions of the Cent. Am. corridor would, in time, gather migrating Swainson's Hawks into great mass flights, the process begins while they still are on the broader reaches of their boreal and austral summer ranges. This is a reflection of the weather conditions that permit and support migration on thermal updrafts. While variable in local detail, the requisites are clear or partly clear sky and gentle to moderate winds in the general direction of seasonal travel. On a favorable morning, when the sun has risen to a height where the angle between its rays and ground level approaches 60°, its heat reflecting from the surface warms the overlying air, which then begins to rise. Above an e.-facing slope the air warms earlier in the day than above level ground in proportion to the angle of the slope. When soaring conditions are established over any area where migrating birds have spent the night, they depart. In rising air they spread their wings fully, the outer primaries separated like fingers, tails at least half-open, and spiral upward. If more than a few birds are involved, they draw together behind the bird that rises fastest to form a "kettle," some circling clockwise, some counterclockwise, or again all in 1 direction. The air cools in rising, and as its buoyancy diminishes, the kettle begins to dissolve at the top. One after another, the higher birds fold their primaries so that they come to a point rearward, close their tails, and begin to glide downward at a low angle, exchanging altitude for distance. Others follow in their turn, until presently the traveling group is strung across the sky in loose ranks and lines. So they continue until 1 of the leading birds comes across another ascending air current and begins to wheel upward as it feels lift beneath its wings. Succeeding birds join in, some of them changing course slightly to reach the thermal, and soon another kettle has formed, with latecomers feeding in at the bottom as the 1st ones rise higher. Thus the group proceeds on its way, going from thermal to thermal so long as they can be found, and then putting down for the night to wait for another day.

From the inception of fall migration in N. Am., small original groups of Swainson's Hawks are constantly enlarged and their fronts broadened as more and more converge on the approaches to the Cent. Am. corridor. This results, while they still are in the sw. U.S., in the assemblies described by watchers as stretching from side to side across the sky and requiring several hrs. to pass. It has been customary, as with Broadwings, to refer to these gatherings as "flocks," but the term is inaccurate if it implies a binding internal organization, such as in goose flocks. On the contrary, observation will show that each hawk is acting individually in adjusting its course to the air currents around it. This is particularly evident at the top of a thermal as different birds begin to glide at different levels and frequently in slightly different directions. It appears again when members of a group of birds are nearing the ends of their glides and a new kettle is forming; those a bit to 1 side or the other deflect to join, while those farther off do not. Several of the more detailed accounts of broad-front Swainson's Hawk flights (Skutch 1945b; R. P. Fox 1956) refer indirectly to this absence of lateral movement when they

57

describe all birds as gliding in the same general direction on roughly parallel courses. A weather pattern favorable to migration provides so many thermals and ridge updrafts that few birds need turn aside in search of lift.

Swainson's is closely associated with its near relative, the Broadwing, in the seasons when both migrate through Cent. Am. but is almost entirely separated from it during the nesting season, the former mostly to the w. of the 95th meridian in N. Am., the latter to the e. The axis of Swainson's Hawk migration, broadly speaking, is se.-nw., and its fall routes across the width of Mexico are not finally brought together until they enter the Isthmus of Tehuantepec in the states of Veracruz and Oaxaca. In contrast, the Broadwing axis is sw.-ne., and Broadwing routes, in getting around the Gulf of Mexico, are joined before they leave s. Tex. A glance at a map of N. Am. will suggest that the difference is substantial. One result of the separation in the U.S., of no effect on the birds but bearing strongly on the analysis of their migrations, is that Broadwings move across country where hawk watching has been practiced actively for 50 years—Hawk Mt., Pa., C. May, N.J., Hawk Cliff, Ont., other points on the Great Lakes, and s. Tex.—while Swainson's passes over wide areas where observers, even casual, are few and far between. The published record of Broadwing migration amply indicates its pattern; equivalent data for Swainson's are so few that only parts of an outline can be sketched. The following attempts this by citing a cross-section of representative N. Am. migration records for fall, spring, and early summer to show both the substance and limitations of available information. [NOTE: *Audubon Field Notes* and its successor, *American Birds*, are cited herein as *AFN* and *AB*, respectively.]

Fall Departure from nesting territories appears to be so gradual and unobtrusive that it attracts little attention. Bent (1937) listed late departure dates for upward of 30 localities in Alaska, Canada, and the n. tier of states, but no numbers are given. Records of even small gatherings in the prairie provinces seem to be lacking. N.D. Bismarck, Aug. 9, 1980—90 "kettling" over the city (1981 *AB* **35** 197). S.D. Kimball, Sept. 28, 1980—100 "on the ground" and White River, Sept. 28, 1980—100 (1981 *AB* **35** 197); Chester Co., Sept. 23, 1981—100 "rested on fence posts and a stony hillside" (1982 *AB* **36** 191). Nw. IOWA Oct. 5, 1940—at least 200 (N. Williams 1941). NEBR. Hyannis, Sept. 24, 1980—200+ "fed in stubblefield" (1981 *AB* **35** 199); Belleview, Sept. 24, 1982—30 (1981 *AB* **37** 197). MONT. Great Falls, Sept. 17, 1980—75+ (1981 *AB* **35** 197). WYO. Buffalo, Sept. 24, 1982—75 (1983 *AB* **37** 205). OREG. Umatilla Co., Aug. 20, 1888—at least 200 "hopping about catching grasshoppers"; they hunted until dark, roosted in poplars along the Umatilla R., and returned to feed in the next day (A. K. Fisher 1893). COLO. Limon, Sept. 4, 1892—150 (1983 *AB* **37** 205). KANS. Hutchinson, Oct. 2, 1936—a large early morning flight that continued intermittently into the afternoon; a count that began a ½-hr. after start and continued 1½ hrs. tallied 3,400+, and "as the sun rose the birds rose to a higher altitude until after 11 o'clock one just arriving in the area would have been ignorant of a hawk migration for the birds were now mere specks, visible to the naked eye only after careful scrutiny" (A. Cruickshank 1937). TEX. Dalhart, Sept. 27, 1980—118 "rested in a stubble field" (1981 *AB* **35** 199); Parmer Co., Oct. 3-6, 1969—"assembly fed on an infestation of fall armyworms and roosted ½ mi. away on a bare hillside" (Littlefield 1973); San Angelo, Oct. 5, 1980—est. 1,000 (1981 *AB* **35** 199); Eldorado, Oct. 3,

1978—400 (1979 *AB* **33** 192); Austin, Oct. 9, 1982—a daylong flight; intermittent counts tallied 2,700+ Swainson's, 1,300 unidentified buteos, presumably Swainson's; 483 Swainson's passed in 5 min. at 1000 hrs. (1983 *AB* **37** 200); 10 mi. w. of San Antonio, Oct. 6, 1953—very great flight in clear weather following a cold-front rain the previous day; total est. from systematic sample counts as possibly reaching "several hundred thousand"; comments on behavioral aspects are among the best, and description of observer's counting methods is detailed (R. P. Fox 1956); Del Rio, Oct. 6, 1953—2,000 (Fox); Rockport, Oct. 1–7, 1953—"large numbers approached from a little east of north and left to the southwest" (Fox) (note that the 3 citations immediately preceding are for, or include, 1 date, indicating that a single weather pattern was supporting mass migration on a front of roughly 230 mi. e. to w.); Wilson Co., Sept. 1982—"deluged" with Swainson's Hawks feeding on locusts that infested coastal bermuda pastures (1983 *AB* **37** 200); Laredo and Falcon, Oct. 10–12, 1984—early afternoon of Oct. 10 "continuous thick cloud of Swainson's Hawks 13 mi. w. of Laredo, headed s., by conservative estimate 30,000 in 1½ hrs.; at Falcon State Park 10,000 put down to roost; on the 11th, 15 mi. ne. of Falcon, a continuous flight overhead, while 3,000 fed on 'caterpillars' in 2 large fields; these feeding birds left by 2 P.M. Oct. 12; estimated total seen in 3 days, 50,000" (1985 *AB* **39** 76). CALIF. Los Angeles Co., Aug. 1887, flock remained during the month feeding on extremely abundant grasshoppers; a hawk shot had eaten 105 of them before 0900 hrs. (A. K. Fisher 1893); Kern Co., Oct. 13–15, 1982—170+, "far more than reported in recent years . . . along the coast . . . now considered casual" (1983 *AB* **37** 223). MEXICO No useful information at hand on any fall movement w. of the Sierra Madre Oriental.

Spring As n. migration leaves the Mexican states of Veracruz and Oaxaca, it is released from the confines of the Cent. Am. corridor and might be expected to broaden its front w. The evidence, however, seems to include only a few suggestive records from Mexico and not many more from the w. U.S. VERACRUZ Spring migration "spectacular, especially inland" (Purdue et al. 1972); Alvacado, Apr. 24, 1958—3,000 (1958 *AFN* **12** 327); Jalapa, Apr. 18, 1939—4,200, and Las Vigas, Apr. 5, 1939—200+ (Loetscher 1955). TAMAULIPAS Gomez Ferias, Mar. 25, 27–28, Apr. 1, 3, 1941—great flocks seen high in air, and ♀ shot from large flock had "insect remains" in her stomach (G. Sutton and Pettingill 1942). TEX. Santa Ana Natl. Wildl. Refuge, Apr. 9, 1957—2,000+ (1957 *AFN* **11** 362); Apr. 4, 1958—several thousand, the next day 600 (1958 *AFN* **12** 368); Apr. 2, 1962—est. 3,000 (1962 *AFN* **16** 431); San Benito, Apr. 10, 1961—1,000 (1961 *AFN* **15** 425); Laguna Atascosa Natl. Wildl. Refuge, Mar. 25, 1957—200, and Apr. 16—750 (1957 *AFN* **11** 362); Edinburg, Mar. 28, 1966—450 (1966 *AFN* **20** 530) and Mar. 28, 1978—300+ "roosted in a ploughed field" (1978 *AB* **32** 1,029); Falfurias-Riviera, Apr. 4, 1968—3,000+ (1968 *AFN* **22** 559); Falfurias-Hebronville, Apr. 2, 1972—"scores perched on fence posts or standing on the ground in the morning, apparently having spent the night" (1972 *AB* **26** 781); Austin, Apr. 4, 1962—175 "following the plough" (1962 *AFN* **16** 431). OKLA. Oklahoma City, Apr. 16, 1980—41 fed in plowed field (1980 *AB* **34** 792). NEBR. Dawes Co., Apr. 28, 1983—31, and Sioux Co., Apr. 23, 1983—17 (1983 *AB* **37** 806). S.D. Lacreek Natl. Wildl. Refuge, Apr. 24–25, 1958—"heavy migration" (1958 *AFN* **12** 364); S. Hermosa, Apr. 24, 1979—128 in migrating flock of 88 on ground and 40 in air (1979 *AB* **33** 783).

N.D.   Tewauken Natl. Wildl. Refuge at Forman, last ½ of Apr. 1956—"fairly common" (1956 *AFN* **10** 342). COLO.   Campo, Apr. 22, 1979—35, of which "25 sat in freshly ploughed field" (1979 *AB* **33** 793); in sw. Colo., Apr. 27, 1982, along an 80-mi. stretch of highway—100 migrating (1982 *AB* **36** 878). WYO.   Sheridan, Apr. 24, 1979—several hundred circling in large groups and gliding n. into Mont., taking 40 min. to pass (1979 *AB* **33** 793). MONT.   Custer Co.. afternoon in April 1890—some 2,000 came from a sw. direction and put down for the night on a ranch at the Powder R. where a fenced pasture joined the buildings; when all had arrived, the trees in the pasture "were simply black" with them and the ground below was "covered with them sitting in rows among the cattle" (Cameron 1907); Fort Peck Dam, Apr. 27, 1975—50 passed in 15 min. but, on the whole, "still very low in numbers" (1975 **AB** 29 863). ARIZ.   Willcox, chiefly in Apr. 1978—67 in migration (1978 *AB* **32** 1,040). CALIF. Los Angeles Co., San Gabriel Mts. in 1951: Apr. 3—520, Apr. 4—470, Apr. 7—51 (1951 *AFN* **5** 275); e. San Luis Obisbo Co., Apr. 5, 1958—small numbers, in past years 1,000s in late Apr.–early May (1958 *AFN* **12** 385); Escondido, Apr. 4, 1961—75 "came to roost in eucalyptus grove" (1961 *AFN* **15** 439); Riverside Co., 1972—numbers migrating through s. Calif. "have declined drastically during the past ten years" (1972 *AB* **26** 808); Los Angeles Co., Borrego Springs, 1975: Mar. 30—10, Apr. 8—15, Apr. 10—110, appeared to be attracted by abundance of large caterpillars feeding on desert flowers, because "most were on the ground among the flowers" (1975 *AB* **29** 908); Los Angeles Co., Apr. 8, 1981—5, "far cry" from "hundreds" seen migrating 30 years ago (1981 *AB* **35** 863); s. Calif., 1984—"continue to decline" (1984 *AB* **38** 960). OREG.   Malheur Natl. Wildl. Refuge, 1963—records show Swainson's less common than 25 years ago (1963 *AFN* **17** 422).

Late spring–early summer   COLO.   Unspecified locality, July 10, 1889—500+ "feeding on a locally abundant cricket" (in A. K. Fisher 1893); Erie, July 26, 1980—116 (1980 *AB* **34** 915). SASK.   Locality? June 14, 1980—groups of 20 and 52 mixed Redtails and Swainson's, chiefly the latter and mostly "immatures" (1980 *AB* **36** 1006). NEV.   Boulder City, May 20, 1952—16 soaring over the city (1952 *AB* **6** 261). CALIF. Los Angeles Co., Aug. 1887—see Fall, above.

Probable N. Am. routes   The foregoing sampling of the records, while tedious reading, brings out the main points of what currently is known about Swainson's Hawk migration in N. Am. The listed citations comprise about ⅔ of those available, which is enough to demonstrate their uneven distribution. A large proportion of the remainder are from Tex. and Calif., increasing an imbalance that is still more striking when all the data are plotted on a map. North and w. of the s. plains states, fall movement appears to have gone almost unnoticed in the 40 years here reviewed, for nowhere do the numbers seen suggest the origin and routes of the great flights of 1936 at Hutchinson, Kans., of 1953 in the vicinity of San Antonio, Tex., and of 1984 between Laredo and Falcon Dam on the U.S.-Mexican border. Note, too, the gaps of 17 and 31 years between the flights when no comparable numbers were reported. There can be no question here of the identity of the birds making up these flights, because the 3 localities are n. and w. of the routes followed by any substantial numbers of Broadwings. From the information at hand we may surmise that in most years the fall movement is widely dispersed over the w. states of the U.S. and Mexico because isolated lead lines and such water barriers as the Great Lakes are lacking; in occasional years it may be that stronger than usual nw. winds increase the leeward drift associated with travel on thermals and bring about the great flights in Tex. The alternative is that in most years large flights in the s. plains states pass by unobserved. Only further fieldwork can resolve the question. The spring situation is similar: Swainson's is widely and regularly reported in s. Tex. where in recent years many observers have been watching Broadwing migration, but records anywhere n. and w. and from n. Mexico are few indeed.

Of the foregoing listed records, nearly a third make reference to the semiterrestrial behavior of migrating Swainson's—either their putting down for the night on bare ground of some sort or their gathering in large numbers to feed on grasshoppers and other insect infestations. That these habits attract attention is expectable; any observer whose previous experience has been with other buzzard-hawks is likely to be impressed by a 1st sight of scores, even 100s, of Swainson's standing about in a cattle pasture, loosely grouped like so many barnyard fowl. Their walking easily, running down insects, and resembling small turkeys, is cited below (see Habits). Eating insects during early fall and late spring contrasts with Broadwings, which do not seem to have any comparable food resource in fall. Swainson's must, however, accomplish long stretches of migration on stored reserves. It is probable that all summer gatherings of Swainson's on outbreaks of grasshoppers and crickets are made up in large part of individuals hatched the previous year, as suggested by the 1980 Sask. record.

A final point of interest in the cited records is repetition of the theme that Swainson's has decreased in numbers from the 1940s on. This appears most often in reports from s. Calif. but is supplemented by others from N.D., Mont., and w. Oreg. The decrease is substantial, but, rather oddly, there is no accompanying speculation about causes. An easy explanation is reduction of favorable habitat through changes in agricultural practice. There may be more specific reasons. Both grasshoppers and ground squirrels (another major seasonal food) are considered detrimental to agriculture and have been targets of widespread poisoning campaigns in the w. states during the general period when the hawk is said to have declined. Coincidence of timing suggests a possible connection. Whether biocides on austral summer range in S. Am. may be a factor is unknown.

Cent. Am. passage in fall Poorly documented; no more than a few scattered reports between se. Mexico and w. Panama plus a somewhat larger sampling from the Canal Zone. Coverage of spring return is no better except in s. Costa Rica. A. F. Skutch was resident there, 1936–1945; in all but 1 of these years he was able to watch the spring migration w. along the Pacific slope of the Cordillera Central at localities collectively described as the basin of El General and the upper part of the Tèrrabà Valley. His report (Skutch 1945b) of this relatively long-term study will repay separate reading for its careful observations and vivid descriptions of the passing hawks.

Reports from se. Mexico in fall are limited to the states of Veracruz on the Atlantic side (Anderle 1966) and Chiapas on the Pacific side (H. Wagner 1941). If Chiapas birds come from the w. part of the nesting range, no connecting records show the routes. Two citations from the Pacific slope of Guatemala are hearsay, without detail: Skutch, on a visit in 1935, "was told more than once of enormous flocks which pass southward during autumn," and he quoted A. W. Anthony (in Griscom 1932) as mentioning "a great flock of hawks, apparently Swainson's, which on the morning of Oct. 25, 1925, flew southward" over the plantation in the Dept. of San Marcos, but Anthony himself did not see them, being told of them only when he returned to the house at noon. Dickey and van Rossem (1938) supplied little more than a general statement for El Salvador. There seem to be no useful records from Honduras or Nicaragua. For Costa Rica, where Skutch spent the fall months of 6 years (4 of them in El General), he said: "I have never seen a single individual of either kind [Broadwing or Swainson's] traveling southward." He did quote Carriker (1910) as mentioning "an enormous flock" of hawks, "soaring at too great a height to be identified, which during the early autumn of 1906 passed from nw. to se. over El Hogar in the Caribbean lowlands." Worth (1939) reported that a plantation owner near Boquete, on the Pacific side of the Cordillera in w. Panama, was familiar with Swainson's Hawk as a regular spring transient, passing n. in 1,000s, but had never seen any s. migration in fall. From the Panama Canal Zone, references include Loftin and Olson (1963), Slud (1964), A Wetmore (1965), N. Smith (in Keast and Morton 1980), and others, but they deal for the most part with spectacular numbers rather than detailed observations of behavior. A photograph (in Keast and Morton 1980), taken at Panama City on Nov. 2, 1974, shows 889 Swainson's Hawks and some Turkey Vultures overhead.

From the above records, scanty as they are, it is conjectured that the principal fall route follows the Pacific slope of the Cordillera through Guatemala, Honduras, and El Salvador, crosses over to the Caribbean side above the lowlands of s. Nicaragua and n. Costa Rica, and recrosses to the Pacific side before reaching the Canal Zone. Over terrain that probably offers suitable soaring conditions on many alternative routes, this is the most direct and therefore the most economical of energy. It was 1st suggested by Skutch and is diagrammed by N. Smith (fig. 4, in Keast and Morton 1980), but Skutch added: "many more observations will be needed to firmly establish it."

Return passage through Cent. Am. in spring   T. Barbour observed 2 great flights rounding the Gulf of San Miguel, extreme e. Panama, in Apr. 1922 (Bangs and Barbour 1922). Griscom (1927) said of Panama observations: "In the late P.M. of March 7 [1927] an enormous flock of at least 1,000 came up from the east . . . at a great altitude . . . wheeling in a great cloud which gradually drifted westward. On the morning of March 8 a flock of 820 passed overhead with similar evolutions." In the Canal Zone, Loftin and Olson (1963) stated that in spring "a few" pass over the Pacific terminus of the canal, implying that the bulk migrate more inland, presumably traveling on the dry season tradewinds of the Caribbean slope. The same authors reported "great numbers" in extreme nw. Panama near Costa Rica. Worth (1939), cited earlier, indicated a return of the spring movement to the Pacific side of the Continental Divide; this agrees with Skutch's experience in Costa Rica, for which see below. There appear to be no spring records for Nicaragua or Honduras. For El Salvador, Dickey and van Rossem (1938) supplied a general statement of occurrence, as in fall, but added the note that Swainson's Hawks rest for the night on the lava fields of local volcanos and are said sometimes to leave an egg or 2 behind. From Guatemala there is a record of some 4,000 on Mar. 23 (year?) passing n. over the Pacific slope at L. Atitlan (Hundley 1967). Beyond this point there are only the records, already cited, in Veracruz, Mexico. As the migration leaves Guatemala it must cross Chiapas, and terrain suggests that birds headed for the w. parts of the nesting range may be looked for crossing cent. Oaxaca, but there are no confirmatory clues.

Again Costa Rica   The particular merit of Skutch's account is the perspective he acquired over many years. In successive years he saw "enormous flocks of big hawks streaming majestically across the sky, taking at times an hour to pass overhead." Swainson's and Broadwing "migrate in much the same manner . . . maximum of forward movement with a minimum of muscular exertion . . . journey only during the daytime while conditions are favorable for soaring . . . seem reluctant to make a single unnecessary wing-beat . . . pass without eating, and I believe without drinking . . . saving of energy is of the utmost importance." On Apr. 15, 1940, at the head of the Tèrrabà Valley, "countless thousands" stopped for the night on the opposite side of the Rio Pecuar, and he watched as they settled on the pasture slopes, some on the ground, some on stumps and logs, still others in the scattered trees. The next morning he watched their departure. When the last of the great "kettles" disappeared w., he searched for droppings and castings where they had spent the night but found none, confirming his previous observations that they traveled without hunting. On Apr. 11–12, 1941, he watched 2 massive flights of Swainson's Hawks passing "at a low elevation down the valley of the Rio Pejivalle . . . on the Caribbean slope of Costa Rica, separated from El General by a range of mountains 10,000 to 12,000 feet in height," which convinced him that spring passage followed both sides of the Cordillera and that a complete picture would require widely scattered cooperating observers.

On 1 point only does Skutch make statements that may vary from current information. His earlier notes referred to all the big hawks that migrate in flocks as Broadwings. Until 1940, his 5th year of watching, he failed to distinguish Swainson's, "but from subsequent observations I feel confident that the most spectacular flocks" were made up chiefly of Swainson's. Further on he stated: "Later in the day, the hawks usually pass overhead at heights far greater than . . . in the early morning. . . . At midday in fair weather [they] pass unnoticed because of the great height at which they travel." On Apr. 12, 1936, he saw a "single immense flock," apparently of Swainson's, but too high for positive identification. On Apr. 16, 1940: a few were still soaring by from the e. ridge, while far to the se. were "great circling swarms that had rested, apparently, among the distant hills." On Mar. 10, 1944: 3 great flocks, each containing "thousands," doubless of this species but too high for identification. The identity problem implicit in these quotations appears not only in Skutch but in many other records from places where Swainson's and Broadwing are loosely associated because they are migrating on the same weather pattern. For the special problems of identification that come up only during migration, see earlier Field Identification, above.

Boreal winter   FLA.   Like Broadwings, a relatively few Swainson's in fall drift se. from their normal routes to winter in s. Fla., where the species has been known since 1890 or earlier. They appear to be trapped there, unable to manage an overwater crossing to Cuba. There were 25 at Boca Chica, Nov. 7, 1947, and about 100 over Key West, Oct. 15, 1967 (1968 *AB* **22** 27; also see Hundley and Hames 1960 and Amadon 1964). L. Brown and Amadon (1968 **2**) and W. B. Robertson believed that most Fla. birds are in their 1st winter. Seven Fla. specimens 1940–1956 are all "immature." In the past few years, s. Fla. records of Swainson's Hawk in *AB* are few, and the species may have reverted to its former status there—not many, in some winters perhaps none. No evidence supports N. Smith's diagram (in Keast and Morton 1980) showing an overwater route to Cuba and thence perhaps to Yucatan. For Caribbean is. there is only a doubtful report from Jamaica.

Austral summer S. AM.   East of the Canal Zone and in all directions beyond in n. S. Am., the whereabouts of any number of Swainson's Hawks is a mystery. Amadon (1964) and other authors have listed some scattered records. Since the Andean Cordillera runs nearly n.-s. along the w. coast of Colombia, birds heading e. or s. must cross it. Going s., presumably they either traverse the great Amazon basin or skirt it along the e. slopes of the Andes. Now that parts of the Amazon basin have been deforested and opened to agriculture, it is possible that many Swainson's are scattered there during the boreal winter. It has long been supposed that the major "wintering" area was the pampas grasslands of Argentina, where the birds moved about in groups searching for food and roosting on the ground, but some who have sought them there have not found them; Olrog (1967; see N. Smith, in Keast and Morton 1980) stated that there are no Argentine records of "adult" Swainson's Hawks, "which is certainly peculiar." This suggests that the youngest cohort supplies most of those that continue s. to the pampas. For numerous earlier references pertaining to S. Am., see citations in Hellmayr and Conover (1949) and Friedmann (1950).

Migratory timetable Can be set up in only the most flexible terms, the great difficulty being that a nesting range some 3,000 mi. long, from e.-cent. Alaska to Baja Calif., Sonora, and Chihuahua, entails a wide disparity in dates of departure and arrival at its 2 extremes and in between. Other difficulties are the tendency of the species to gather in late summer on insect infestations, thus obscuring the real start of migration, and the uneven distribution of published records, so that much movement goes unnoticed. An abbreviated timetable covering chiefly sw. U.S. to Colombia is all that the actual data support. Peak migration clears the n. prairie states the last week of Sept. and 1st week of Oct., the s. plains states and s. Tex. the last few days of Sept. and 1st ½ of Oct., and Cent. Am. the last 3 weeks of Oct. to early Nov.; arrival in Argentina is said to be late Nov. Returning in spring, average dates are Panama in mid-Mar., Costa Rica in the last 3 weeks of Mar., state of Veracruz, Mexico, last ½ of Mar. and 1st week in Apr., and s. Tex. chiefly in early Apr. Formerly spring arrival in Calif. was said to have been Mar. 10–20, but this does not fit well with Cent. Am. dates and may represent earliest arrival or even (doubtful) wintering birds from nearby.

Some banding data One banded in Mont. on Sept. 19, 1916, was killed near Bogota, Colombia, Oct. 29, 1916 (Bent 1937). One banded as an "adult" in Okla., June 7, 1959, was shot Feb. 5, 1962, in w. Brazil (G. Sutton 1967). Birds banded in Sask. and recovered in coterminous U.S. are scattered in a wide, straight corridor down to include the e. ½ of Tex., "outsiders" being 1 each in Mich. and Ala. (Houston 1968). See also below.   JOSEPH A. HAGAR

BANDING STATUS To Aug. 1981, the total number banded was 6,068 with 245 (4%) recoveries (Clapp et al. 1982).

Much banding of nestlings has been done in Sask., Alta., and in n. and w. breeding range in coterminous U.S. For Sask., see Houston (1968) for earlier details and map of some recoveries; those recovered in the U.S. were mostly scattered in a corridor s. to include the e. ½ of Tex., "outsiders" being mentioned above. Later (Houston and Millar 1981) it was reported that Houston himself had banded 862 individuals. To Aug. 1985, his total was 1,634, and the 50 recoveries included: El Salvador 1, Panama 1, Colombia 2, Uruguay 1, and Argentina 9. The Argentine records include birds in Juv. and in Basic feathering. RALPH S. PALMER

REPRODUCTION Known to **first breed** when in Basic Plumage—that is, at least 2 years old. A ♀ "which had not reached her mature plumage" was collected in mid-Aug. at a nest containing half-grown nestlings (Coues 1874a); it is possible that she was a foster parent.

Swainson's arrives comparatively late and so must establish, or reestablish, a niche among earlier migrant and resident Red-tailed Hawks, Ferruginous Hawks, and the much earlier nesting Great Horned Owls.

Pair bond At least single-brood monogamy, but probably often renewed by mates returning to their previous territory (sustained monogamy). Early in the season, 2 birds sometimes roost or perch on the same branch less than 1 ft. apart. In se. Alta., Schmutz (1977) noted remating with another ♂ after removal of the mate within 1–4 days in 3 instances. A nesting survivor of either sex would probably remate quickly.

Displays The birds perform "spectacular aerial gymnastics" (Olendorff 1975)— rarely described. There is HIGH-CIRCLING over territory with underwing flashing in the sunlight and rather plaintive-sounding calling. In a SKY-DANCE 2 birds soared, spiraling upward; then the presumed ♂, starting from about 300 ft. above an old tree nest and with wings slightly bent, glided away, dropping about 200 ft. in ¾ mi. He then began a circling soar. Once, from over the nest, he flapped rapidly and then, with wings partly closed, went into a shallow (20–30 ft.) dive, then flapped vigorously on a circular course some 25 ft. in diam., climbed a few ft., stalled, and dived again, repeating this twice rapidly. After some horizontal flight in a tight circle, he made a 15-ft. near-vertical climb and stalled. This was followed by a long, fast dive on a parabolic course, terminating on the nest. Soon the ♀ alighted 5 ft. away. There was no posturing, calling, or copulation. Another observer of a Sky-dance noted that it did not end at the nest. (From Olendorff 1974a.) Undoubtedly the pattern varies, but tight circling, display of underwing plus light feathers at base of tail, and steep dives are probably typical.

Copulation Occurs repeatedly; has been observed in a tree and on fence posts (J. Schmutz).

Territory Swainson's Hawks must establish and maintain a nest site or reoccupy a traditional territory—in many areas among established coexisting buteos.

In n.-cent. Oreg. there was strong interspecific territoriality with Redtails, which showed much stability in their occupancy. Each year, some Redtail pairs lost portions of territory to later-coming Swainson's. There was contention at boundaries, but the end result was near-equilibrium with no detected effects on reproductive success of either species (Janes 1984a). On farmland near Calgary, Alta., conditions were near-optimal for both buteos—abundance both of nest sites and of Richardson's ground squirrels. Nearest-neighbor distance for each hawk species was about the same, with wider spacing of Swainson's relative to Redtails (more of the latter present). A territorial ♂ (either species) would fly, usually calling, toward any approaching interloper. The defender would strike at or swoop at the other buteo, then the 2 would circle upward until the intruder reached the vertical limit of defended territory. Females were rarely seen assisting ♂ ♂ in such defense. For details and compilation of nearest-neighbor distances, see Rothfels and Lein (1983).

In an area of se. Alta., nesting density of Swainson's and Ferruginous Hawks was high in 1975 and 1976—0.04 and 0.13/sq. km. for the former. Artificial nests were added, giving the hawks more choice of sites than before. The 2 species then nested farther apart. The density of Swainson's increased and decreased equally between experimental and control areas, suggesting that artificial sites had no augmenting effect but that density changed according to overall fluctuations in the area (Schmutz et al. 1984).

In cold desert habitat of s.-cent. Idaho, Thurow and White (1983) found that if an investigator approached the nest of either Swainson's or Ferruginous, in 19 instances a member of the other species appeared and called in alarm first. This may have alerted the absent pair earlier than it otherwise would have detected danger. Often both pairs arrived and concentrated their attention on the terrestrial invader. On the other hand, in se. Alta., if the 2 species nested too closely (under about 0.2 km. for Swainson's and 0.3 for the Ferruginous), competition for space resulted in lowered reproductive success (Schmutz et al. 1980). The closer the nests, the more aggression—with Swainson's often deserting. The diet of the 2 buteos greatly overlapped; both this and minimal space may have contributed to lower success (Thurow and White).

In creosote bush desert in Chihuahua, Mexico, an area was divided entirely into Swainson's and Redtail territories, the 2 differing but overlapping in habitat (Thiollay 1981).

In shortgrass prairie/riparian woodland, the struggle between Swainson's and the Great Horned Owl for control of small groves of trees is probably the most common raptor-raptor feud (Olendorff 1975). On the Laramie Plains, Wyo., they shared 5 groves, and all but 1 Swainson's nest was destroyed in the egg stage. Of 9 other Swainson's nests, probably in hunting areas of the owl, 3 failed; in 1 nest the 2 nestlings vanished when nearly ready to fly, and there were owl feathers at the site. The hawks attack the owl in daylight (Dunkle 1977). In Oreg. and Calif., presence of this owl may limit the numbers of breeding Swainson's (Littlefield et al. 1984).

Nest site Typically a solitary tree, bush, or small grove, the nest itself sometimes only 3–5 m. above ground. Many are built on old Black-billed Magpie nests. Generalized comparison: **1** Swainson's Hawk nests at any height but near the top, just within the crown (shaded) on smaller limbs, the nest often appearing flimsy or ragged; **2** the Ferruginous Hawk also nests at any height, more exposed (on or in the crown), as high up as there is solid support for its heavier structure, which tends to appear flat-topped; **3** the Redtail's nest is often in the tallest tree available, high up but within the crown, on solid support. In places where an aerial site is not available, Swainson's may nest on sloping ground, a ledge, or at edge of an eroded bank.

Sometimes Swainson's has a tree nest and a nearby bush nest, one more recent than the other, indicating reoccupation of the territory. In Calif. a banded bird was recaptured 4 years later and had mate and young only ¼ mi. from where it had been reared (Bloom 1980). A bird was found dead in Sask. some 15 km. from where it had hatched 16 years earlier (Houston and Millar 1981). The same nest may be refurbished and used another year, but, for example, in N.D., 50% of pairs built new nests each year (Gilmer and Stewart 1984). A disused nest in Mont. might remain practically intact after 7 or 8 years (Cameron 1908b). Yet many nests, in use or not, are blown down by high winds. (For renesting, see Replacement clutches, below.) The birds frequently select sites attributable to human activity, especially shelterbelts—44 of 45 nests on abandoned farmsteads in ne. Colo.—and, as previously noted, they also accept platforms provided for them. The nest should be shaded. In N.D., although shelterbelts are heavily favored, a variety of other sites are also used (Gilmer and Stewart). Forty-one nests in Ariz. were in mesquite, 3–15 ft. above ground (Bendire 1892). Like the Redtail, Swainson's builds in saguaros.

The span from arrival to laying evidently can extend for nearly a month in s. Canada and n. U.S. but often is much briefer. Near Laramie, Wyo., Dunkle (1977) noted that the birds were usually territorial as soon as they arrived; he also saw them arranging twigs in nests as early as 25 days, and sitting on the nest 13 days, before laying. According to Olendorff, nest building is "intense" and relatively brief.

Nest Materials used in construction are branches, twigs, and debris, with lining of such finer material as bark, forbs, even dry dung, and so forth. Exterior diam. is usually about 2 ft. (60 cm.) and, unless extensively refurbished, only about ½ as high. Mean height (depth) of 89 nests in se. Alta. was about 12½ in. (32 cm.) (Schmutz et al. 1980). The bowl is up to 8 in. (20 cm.) in diam. and perhaps ⅓ as deep initially, but later the activities of the preflight brood tends to flatten the top.

Greenery Swainson's and the Broadwing are said to be the most diligent carriers of green material to their nests (Olendorff 1975), but authors disagree. Most active Swainson's nests do have much of this material. In se. Alta. it is added more commonly early in the nestling period (J. Schmutz). In Wyo., 2 ♀♀ were seen to break off leafy twigs from their nest trees with their beaks and fly to the nest with them. Old nests near active ones often had such vegetation added, as did 1 or more nests of pairs that laid no eggs (Dunkle 1977). Near Winnipeg, 2 nests robbed by predators had fresh leaves and twigs added afterwards, but no greenery was added to nests that were deserted or from which the young departed normally (H. Munro and Reid 1982).

One **egg** each from 20 clutches (Calif. 6, Tex. 4, Okla. 1, Wyo. 1, N.D. 3, Idaho 1, Minn. 2, Man. 1, Sask. 1) **size** length 56.96 ± 2.84 mm., breadth 44.30 ± 1.94, radii of curvature of ends 17.89 ± 1.08 and 13.75 ± 1.30. **Shape** short elliptical to elliptical, elongation 1.28 ± 0.057, bicone −0.080, and asymmetry +0.120 (F. W. Preston). Measurements of 116 eggs in Natl. Mus. Nat. History are remarkably similar: length 50–62 mm., av. 56.5, and breadth 39.5–47.5, av. 44 (Bent 1937). For tabulation of meas. of 4 series (Bent included), see Bechard and Houston (1984); their table also provides a size comparison with eggs of Rough-legged (very similar), Red-tailed, and Ferruginous Hawks.

The shell is smooth, finely granulated, **color** white tinted bluish or greenish when fresh but soon a dull whitish. "Plain colorless eggs" are the exception in most buteos,

67

but "are here the rule" (Coues 1874b). About ⅕ are plain or nearly so; the others are irregularly and more or less sparsely spotted and lightly marked with various (mostly rather drab) browns. Some resemble those of the N. Harrier. Heavily marked eggs are unknown (L. R. Wolfe).

Clutch size Commonly 2 or 3, rarely 1 or 4. Single clutch of 4 in over 30 clutches (Bendire 1892). Near Winnipeg, 1 (of 2), 4 (3), and 3 (4)—but fewer elsewhere, 4 being rare in Mont. and Wash. and unknown in Wyo. and Calif. (H. Munro and Reid 1982). (On the contrary, 4-egg clutches do occur widely.) In 31 successful nests in Calif., clutch size was 1–4, av. 2.58 (Bloom 1980). In 33 nests in se. Wash., clutch size av. 2.66 ± 0.47 eggs (Bechard 1983).

Egg dates For presumably viable clutches, from s. to n., from Bent (1937), with dates for 50% or more in parentheses: Ariz.–Okla. and Tex.—38 records, Mar. 6–July 9 (Apr. 13–May 25). Calif. and Oreg.—68 records, Mar. 17–June 10 (Apr. 24–May 11), Iowa–Kans. and Colo.—May 10–July 14 (May 17–June 5), and Sask.–B.C.—May 10–June 18 (May 30–June 14). At any given latitude, laying, hence hatching, is much later than in the Redtail and Ferruginous Hawks.

Incubation By the ♀; food is supplied by her mate. The ♂ is on the eggs only exceptionally (Cameron 1913, Dunkle 1977). The ♀ has been seen "balling" her feet so as not to damage the eggs with widespread toes (Olendorff 1975). She may flush when an observer is at a distance or not until a person is near or starts to climb to the nest (Dunkle, others), and in the incubating phase the parents may defend vigorously (Olendorff 1975)—perhaps especially so if nesting on the ground (Woffinden and Mosher 1979). In brief, some sitters sit "tight." Redtails, on the other hand, readily flush when approached.

Egg losses This example, from the Laramie Plains, Wyo., in 1964, is fairly typical. Three clutches were lost to crows, 2 nests blew down, 1 was destroyed by man, 1 clutch was smashed (cause unknown), and the eggs disappeared from 8 other nests; thus 16 (33%) of 49 clutches were lost. In 33 successful nests, 15 (of 80) eggs were lost— 4 apparently infertile, dead embryos in 2, and 6 others disappeared; 3 (of the 4) infertile eggs were in clutches of 3 (Dunkle 1977).

Replacement clutches In Wyo., Dunkle found no evidence of relaying after clutches were destroyed. He did have evidence that, after a single egg was laid and lost, laying continued very soon ("continuation clutch" of 2 eggs) in another nest close by. One pair built 2 new nests after losing their clutch; another pair, not known to have laid any eggs, built a 2d nest. All 3 were very flimsy and built in the very tops of trees near the original nest trees. This aligns with the experience of C. S. Sharp (1902). An unmated ♀ laid a clutch, which was destroyed; she then built an unlined nest a few ft. higher in the same isolated tree (Dunkle). If a nest is blown out of a tree, relaying usually occurs elsewhere in 14–16 days (Olendorff 1975).

Unmated "adults" were believed to defend areas of the same size as those of paired breeders (Dunkle 1977). The many yearlings (prebreeders) by midsummer wander in search of food (primarily large insects) and occur in assemblies wherever they find an adequate source.

Associates The frequency with which birds, from the size of small passerines up to the Am. Kestrel and Mourning Dove, nest near active Swainson's Hawk nests has intrigued many observers—Coues (1874b), Bendire (1892), A. K. Fisher (1893), Dunkle (1977), and authors listed by Konrad and Gilmer (1982). Sometimes there are several species. The House Sparrow finds Swainson's nests very suitable structures within which to build. Kingbirds (*Tyrannus* spp.), although they may dispose of insects attracted to the hawks' food remains, can be a minor aggravation. Cameron saw a ♂ E. Kingbird alight on a ♀ Swainson's back and be "carried about for several seconds, while he vented his rage by pecking at her." Then the kingbird pursued the hawk as she mounted high in the air.

Incubation period   Per egg, 34–35 days (Fitzner 1978); the young hatch over a period of time, indicating a laying interval and incubation beginning not long after clutch initiation. Soon after hatching, the eggshells disappear. In ne. Colo., most hatch when young Lark Buntings (*Calamospiza melanocorys*) are abroad; they are captured easily. In late June, young birds recently out of the nest, ½ of them Lark Buntings, formed about ⅘ of the prey fed to nestling Swainson's (Olendorff 1975). In se. Alta., Swainson's Hawks hatch later than Ferruginous Hawks, at a time when prey is less abundant and less easily captured (Schmutz et al. 1980).

Nestling period   According to Dunkle (1977), the ♀ performs all nest duties until the young are about 20 days old and thereafter spends considerable time hunting. On July 20 in Okla., G. Sutton (1967) saw a food-pass in which prey of cotton rat (*Sigmodon*) size was transferred from 1 flying hawk to another. Several authors have commented that the growing young are very active and have large appetites, especially from about age 3 weeks. Olendorff was much impressed with the orchestration of predator-prey interactions through the seasons. So many young ground squirrels (*Spermophilus*) are abroad that Swainson's switches quickly from a diet of about 20% mammals in late June to about 70% in early July. He noted that young Swainson's reach flight age in the hottest part of the year, on a diet of about ½ mammals and ½ birds plus a few miscellaneous items. Even when food is available, evidently the parents can have difficulty in rearing more than 3 young, as determined experimentally by augmenting the number of nestlings above normal brood size (Schmutz et al. 1980). Although otherwise essentially insect eaters, the parents must switch largely to vertebrate prey seasonally to meet energy needs when the brood is growing. Prey remains are removed from the nest and dropped at a distance (Dunkle). The young move out on branches when they are strong enough, returning at night and on hot days to be shaded by a parent (Cameron 1913).

Brood reduction   In a 4-year study in se. Wash., of 87 nesting attempts (plus additional data), high nestling mortality occurred when the young were 15–30 (usually 20–25) days old. It was not always evident whether death of the youngest resulted from starvation or fratricide, but bloody heads of live birds indicated the latter as a common cause. Partially eaten chicks were found at 10 (of 16) nests in 1978 and 15 (of 26) in 1979. At 2 (of 4) nests the 1st year and 4 (of 10) the 2d year there was further reduction when a 2d nestling died. The ultimate cause was dearth of food. See Bechard (1983) for details and earlier literature.

Growth of young   Average wt. at hatching is 39.4 gm. (Olendorff 1974b). As a rough guide to aging, these are data (J. Parker 1974) on 2 wild nestlings: 3 days (49 gm.), 5 (72), 10 (226), 15 (328), 21 (530), 23 (595), and 32 (680). Length of posterior side of tarsus: 3 days (17.9 mm.), 5 (20,8), 10 (35.5), 15 (47.2), 21 (54.5), 23 (64.5), 32 (69.6), and 40 (75.4). Flight feathers of wing emerged at 9–11 days; the 7th primary grew thus: 10 days (1 mm.), 12 (6), 15 (20), 17 (35), 21 (63), 23 (83), 32 (111), 34 (169), and 40 (209). Tail feathers appeared at about 14–15 days; at 17 days (11 mm.), 21 (27), 23 (42), 32 (79), 34 (112), and 40 (133). There are additional growth data in Olendorff (1974b), Bechard (1980), and Schmutz et al. (1980). They **attain flight** in 42–44 days (Fitzner 1978).

Breeding success   On the Laramie Plains, Wyo., 49 pairs had active nests, 6 pairs were without eggs, and 5 were single nonbreeders (in "adult" feathering); thus 17 (14.8%) of 115 birds were not breeding. Forty-one active nests produced 109 or more eggs (mean clutch size 2.22 or more). Thirty-one "probably complete" clutches (2 or 3 eggs) had a total of 79 (mean size 2.55). The 31 pairs of hawks produced an av. of 2.06 young to flight age, or 1.24/pair for all 55 pairs present (Dunkle 1977). In 33 nests in se. Wash., 93% of the eggs hatched, and the number of young attaining flight in successful nests av. 1.11 ± 0.06 (for the high nestling mortality, see Brood reduction, above). This compares with 1.5–2.0 in 5 other studies (Bechard 1983). In se. Oreg., 15 (of 21) nests were successful with 26 young attaining flight—1.24/nesting attempt—this judged good to excellent (Henny et al. 1984a). In 26 successful nests in Calif. in 1979, the number of young attaining flight av. 2.27/nest (Bloom 1980).

In se. Colo. in 1973, fierce winds destroyed many nests, and only 50 young in 200 nests were reared to flight age; in 1974 the number attaining flight was 196 in 142 nests (1974 *Am. Birds* **28** 930). In Sask. in 1982, 35 of 71 nests in 3 areas produced 68 young (1982 *Am. Birds* **36** 982). In N.D., over 30% of nesting failures are due to wind and hail (Gilmer and Stewart 1984).

Dependency   Although nestlings are fed many vertebrates, after they are on the wing one may see them jumping through the grass, wings raised, in brisk pursuit of crickets and grasshoppers (Wheelock 1904). They are inexperienced and very inept. Olendorff (1975) saw them fly to tree limbs, lose their balance, and hang upside down until they dropped to the ground. In Wyo., evidently they remained on their parents' territories until fall departure; in 6 of 20 possible cases, 1 or more young circled and called with the parents (Dunkle 1977). Dependency lasts 4–4½ weeks (Fitzner 1978). The transition from having been fed vertebrates to getting an adequate diet of insects on their own must be stressful.   RALPH S. PALMER

SURVIVAL   Of 54 records of banded birds, already dead when recovered, av. age was 18.8 months and the oldest was 5 years, 2 months (Keran 1981). There is no published information on survival by age class. From Houston and Millar (1981): 1 banded as a nestling in Sask. was caught alive in Argentina at age 11 years, 5 months, and 13 days; another, also banded in Sask., was found freshly dead not far from where banded almost exactly 16 yrs. after calculated date of hatching. The latter record may indicate potential natural longevity. See Houston (1968) for some other records of shorter spans.   RALPH S. PALMER

HABITS   Swainson's can appear somewhat sluggish at times (it has been called indolent—Cameron 1913), but once well on the wing, it is strong, buoyant, and graceful. It is not a heavy bird for its overall size, and its feet are rather delicate; rarely can it manage prey larger than middle-sized "gophers" (ground squirrels—*Spermophilus*) or young hares (*Lepus*) and cottontails (*Sylvilagus*), being better suited for taking voles (*Microtus*), young birds, snakes, and quantities of large insects.

Hunting methods   The birds **soar** in open country, at times high in the air (Bent 1937), to hunt or to first locate other individuals that are hunting successfully. A bird can appear motionless, especially in a breeze. At times it courses low over the prairie, suggestive of the N. Harrier (May 1935); it is rarely observed to fly low at high speed— this is a trait of the Ferruginous Hawk (Schmutz et al. 1980). In capturing vertebrates, undoubtedly it has best success when hunting from a perch.

In the canyon of the Yellowstone, a number of these hawks hunted dobson flies (adult hellgrammites), catching them in their talons and eating them in flight (May 1935). Elsewhere, several flying hawks were seen to repeatedly extend their feet forward and apparently peck at them with their beaks. These flying hawks were catching flying insects in the kite manner, seizing them with a quick thrust of the foot and transferring them to the lowered beak (Crone, in Bent 1937). Other observers have also noted this. A hunting technique unsuited to the Red-tailed Hawk was used by Swainson's in catching free-tailed bats (*Tadarida*) in Okla. (Harden 1972). The hawks glided into the side of a stream of flying bats, and, without altering speed or course, one would snatch a bat in its talons. One hawk caught a bat, transferred it to its beak, then caught another in its talons, and flew off with both.

Using a beater   Swainson's has been seen during summer fallowing, following a tractor; it keeps close behind the harrows, watching for voles and "gophers" (J. W. Preston 1885). It hunts close to prairie fires in search of rodents, snakes, and large insects trying to escape the flames.

Perch-and-wait hunting   May be done from any height, as from a limb, or a pole or post, often from a slightly elevated spot on the ground. These are a stable base, but the birds also alight on telephone wires and clutch firmly "to control the wobble that overtakes them" (Olendorff 1975).

Terrestrial hunting   In the San Fernando Valley, Calif., toward dusk, at least a dozen Swainson's perched on mounds thrown up by ground squirrels (*Spermophilus beecheyi*) in a large colony. The hawks waited with patience to "snatch a supper"—a method also seen employed elsewhere (Henshaw, in A. K. Fisher 1893). In Mont., when irrigation ditches were dug, the dirt was piled to 1 side; the hawks perched on the high side, waiting to spot various prey, and a 28-in. garter snake "did in" its attacker (Cameron 1913).

This hawk "can walk quite easily and even run expertly," running down crickets, grasshoppers, and so forth. A gathering of hawks hunting in this fashion much resembles a flock of small turkeys (Skinner, in Bent 1937); a single bird might skip about "in an awkward way," looking as if rather ashamed to be seen in such low performance (Coues 1874a). For excellent accounts of large numbers of these hawks getting grasshoppers and crickets on the ground, see especially A. K. Fisher (1893). On catching a grasshopper, the hawk crushes it in *Buteo* fashion by "spasmodically clenching" its foot (Olendorff 1975). In Argentina during the austral summer, according to Olrog, Swainson's moves about in groups of 25–40 or more, foraging on local outbreaks of locusts (N. Smith, in Keast and Morton 1980). That is, in this season also, it hunts insects afoot.

Swainson's is known to eat traffic-killed carrion, such as cottontails and jackrabbits (Allan and Sime 1943b).

Tameness   Nesters vary from shy to unwary. Four young, taken as downies and reared in captivity, were very docile. On attaining flight they had complete liberty and never went far; they always returned after a short absence to be fed bits of meat and the skinned carcasses of birds. They pursued grasshoppers on the ground "by leaping after them, with wings extended." In between, they perched quietly on a fence (Ridgway 1877). Swainson's is easily trained to fly to the fist for food and soon becomes very tame (F. Beebe 1974).

An accident   In sw. Okla., in late afternoon of Oct. 5, 1951, there was a severe hailstorm with high winds and rain in an area of 110 sq. mi. Tree shelterbelts in full foliage were completely denuded. Three days later, in 1 shelterbelt, dead wildlife included 45 Swainson's Hawks (plus 4 with broken wings) and other dead raptors, crows, and so forth (G. Jones 1952).

Shooting   Currently, it is hard to envision the former attitude toward harmless hawks. In Merrick Co., Nebr., many migrant Swainson's roosted in a grove on September 26, 1938. Seven people, with 100 shotgun shells and 500 rifle cartridges, started shooting around 2100 hrs. The purported "chicken hawks" would flutter but did not fly away. Shooting continued with aid of flashlights until ammunition was exhausted. The next day the number of dead hawks was "placed at 225," and they were left where they fell (Swenk 1939).

Numbers   Swainson's Hawks have become far fewer in much of their breeding range. For a raptor, it was at one time literally abundant. Cameron (1908b) stated that Swainson's was the "worst sufferer of any" hawk, since it built conspicuously in scattered low trees and so was a target of ranchmen and others. Nests and young were destroyed and the parent birds shot if possible. Although this attitude has largely changed, the environment has been altered, more people are on (and off) roads, and many nests are vulnerable. Although Swainson's is regarded, by current standards, as doing very satisfactorily on the Canadian prairies, one must recall that population changes over the years and over much of the range have not been documented or addressed.

In Calif., basing his calculations on formerly available habitat, Bloom (1980) arrived at estimated former minimum and maximum numbers of breeding pairs in the state as 4,824 and 17,136. In comparison with the smaller figure, the 375 pairs of 1979 indicate a 91.2% statewide decline. The loss is not evenly spread, but about ½ of historic breeding range is now vacant. It seems most unlikely that such a drastic change has also occurred elsewhere.

Swainson's eats short-lived prey that do not accumulate biocides to any great extent (Henny et al. 1984a), yet a cumulative effect may occur and be undetected. In Tex. in Oct., migrants fed on the fall armyworm, even after these had been sprayed with parathion (Littlefield 1973). Especially now that biocides are banned or used sparingly in our area, the question arises as to whether their continued application in S. Am.—

for example, large-scale use for locust control in Argentina—may affect survival. The answer to this is currently unknown (Bloom 1980, Littlefield et al. 1984).

At a guess, the total number of Swainson's Hawks in autumn is of the order of 300,000 ± 50,000.   RALPH S. PALMER

FOOD   Vertebrates are preponderant during the breeding cycle and invertebrates at other times. Occasionally carrion, such as traffic victims. Many earlier data were summarized by McAtee (1935), a paper omitted from Sherrod (1978), who summarized 9 sources. To these add several authors listed below.

Breeding season   The older literature tabulated prey by species without seasonal breakdown. The more recent work, such as those by Olendorff (1975), Dunkle (1977), Schmutz et al. (1980), Gilmer and Stewart (1984), and others, indicate a heavy reliance in this season on mammals, especially young ground squirrels (*Spermophilus*), pocket gophers (*Thomomys*), and some microtines, in some localities small birds at times, and miscellaneous other vertebrates. In Wash., Fitzner (1978) found that snakes comprised 63.6% of food—86 yellow-bellied racers, 18 gopher snakes, and 2 striped whipsnakes. Reptiles are listed in almost all N. Am. studies, lizards increasing to the s.—mainly lizards and rodents in the Chihuahuan desert of Mexico (Thiollay 1981).

Perhaps Swainson's occasionally tackles prey too large to manage. Evidence of their having eaten Mallard, Sage Grouse, and large jackrabbits probably indicates injured or young individuals or carrion.

There is some evidence (Schmutz et al. 1980) that, in the nesting season, the smaller Swainson's takes larger young white-tailed jackrabbits than the larger Ferruginous Hawk—the probable explanation being that Swainson's nests later when the young hares have grown larger.

Some unusual items: fully grown Am. Kestrel (Ridgway 1877); Am. Kestrel and young Short-eared Owl (Gilmer and Stewart 1984); rattlesnake (Cameron 1913); tiger salamander (Dunkle 1977); 2 toads (Fitzner 1978) and apparently swimming toads (Sexton and Marion 1974); 5 white suckers (Dunkle); and part of a whitefish in a nest (Dall and Bannister 1869).

Other seasons   Although "energy considerations may dictate" reliance on vertebrates in the breeding season, at other times diet is over 90% invertebrates—especially large insects (N. Snyder and Wiley 1976). There are numerous reports of the taking of quantities of various grasshoppers and crickets, also small quantities of other insects. Example: "Those that I shot after midsummer all had their craws stuffed with grasshoppers" (Coues 1874a). Such food evidently is adequate for flying young and for adults as long as they are not feeding young. Olendorff (1975) made the general statement that, during late Aug. and Sept., each hawk eats 1,000s of grasshoppers and that there are small deposits of fat throughout the bodies of the hawks to sustain them during their long migration.

The few birds **wintering** in Fla. are said to forage preferably in plowed fields. In the **austral summer** in Argentina, they hunt "locusts," as mentioned above.

RALPH S. PALMER

lighter individuals

dorsal

WHITE-TAILED HAWK

Buteo albicaudatus

Medium-sized buteo with long wings and short tail (less than half as long as WING across chord), rounded, largely white with fine darkish bars and broad black subterminal one. Three outer primaries abruptly emarginated midway on inner webs—outer 2 to the extent that distal width is about half of proximal width. Said to have disjunct **color phases** in S. Am., but J. D. Webster (1973) stated "variation is continuous from dark to light" in the U.S. and Mexico. Darker birds are uncommon in the U.S. Much size overlap in the sexes, ♀ av. larger. The sexes combined: length 20–24 in. (51–61 cm.), wingspread 48–54 in. (122–137 cm.), wt. 2–3 lb. (900–1,360 gm.).

If subspecies are maintained, 1 (of 3) occurs in our area.

DESCRIPTION   *B. a. hypospodius.* In **lighter birds** in definitive feathering, there are some av. differences between sexes in coloring. A separate "plumage" (feather generation) between Juv. and Def. Basic has been suggested by some authors, labeled "immature" by Friedmann (1950); it may be a stage in Prebasic I molting.

▶ ♂ ♀ Def. Basic Plumage (entire feathering) ALL YEAR. **Lighter birds**   **Beak** black distally, bluish proximally; cere greenish yellow to bluish; **iris** dark brown. **Head** forehead white, crown and much of neck as upperparts, sides of head variably gray, chin white. **Upperparts** neutral to ashy gray with reddish brown to brownish barring, grading to white rump; **tail** dorsally white with about 9–10 fine reddish brown to grayish bars (prominent on outer webs), broad black subterminal bar, and very tip white. **Underparts** white (in some grayish) from chin to tail (in some with variably reddish brown to fine gray barring on abdomen, flanks, and thighs). Legs and **feet** yellow, talons black. **Wing** dorsally has prominent reddish brown area proximally and extending back from leading edge, including some adjoining scapulars; other coverts

74

much as dorsum; flight feathers mostly with indistinct grayish barring, becoming white on inner webs, with distal portions of outer primaries and trailing edge of wing black; wing lining white with fine reddish brown to gray barring.

Females are generally darker dorsally, have more extensive reddish brown "shoulder" patches, and are more heavily barred ventrally.

Darker birds The dark of dorsum (excluding white rump) extends downward to include most of underparts, with reddish brown and white barring on lower abdomen and flanks; tail essentially as lighter birds except proximal bars darker; wing lining as lighter birds.

Two breeding birds, trapped in late Apr. in Tex., had begun molting remiges (1 on each bird) and rectrices (4 on 1 bird).

AT HATCHING Nestlings are "very interesting and peculiar" (Sennett 1887). Beak and eyes dark, eyelids and surrounding area black (J. Stevenson and Meitzen 1946, photograph). Down-A is short; on the top of the head it is erect, hairlike, to ¾ in. (about 2 cm.) long, and dark grayish with light tips. Legs and feet flesh color, talons pale. Down-B is white, cottony, with muted brownish tipping; there is more brownish on head–neck—that is, the head sometimes appears quite brown. Birds in both natal downs have a white occipital spot (as throughout life).

▶ ♂ ♀ Juv. Plumage (entire feathering) evidently worn about a year and then may be molted gradually. Much individual variation. The following applies at least to birds that presumably are in the lighter category when older.

Head Forehead white and much of remainder nearly black, the feathers variably tipped reddish brown and with white bases; lighter streaking on darker background behind eyes or, in some, a prominent orange patch across side of head. **Upperparts** very dark, feathers white basally, and many are distally margined or tipped a deep reddish brown, which may wear off and leave a uniformly dark appearance. Darkness of dorsum is individually variable, as are extent and density of ventral streaking—the degree of which does not correlate with darkness of dorsum (J. D. Webster 1973). Lower back to tail mostly white with variably reddish brown and brownish barring. Most of **underparts** variably dark (feathers white basally); area of pale buff to bleached orange that extends from near the corners of the gape and on the throat down onto the breast is highly variable in width and is marked with some black; remainder of underparts including thighs mottled dark and light (feathers mostly black, basally white, tipped pale buff, often with fine lines of reddish brown). **Tail** pale gray with up to 11 narrow darker bars plus a wider and better defined subterminal dark bar; some variably reddish brown spotting along distal shafts. The tail pattern is more muted ventrally.

Wing Upper surface mostly dark, lesser coverts and some adjoining scapulars deep reddish brown (inconspicuous "shoulder" patch) and other coverts more or less tipped same; the primaries show progressively more dark (3 outer ones nearly black), the flight feathers otherwise barred (mottled appearance) and the wing is not noticeably darker at the trailing edge; wing lining mottled dark on buffy on whitish, the dark concentrated distally.

Molting From Juv. into Basic is evidently quite prolonged, in SPRING–SUMMER of 2d calendar year of life, or else some striking changes in appearance occur. The breast area becomes white, eventually including all of breast and upper sides, while belly and flanks still show much dark; the dorsum becomes a dark blue-gray (pearly gray in some), the "shoulder" patches larger and sharply defined. The white-breasted stage has been regarded by some authors as an additional "plumage" between Juv. and Def. Basic.

Color phases   In the species, mentioned by various authors, but whether disjunct entities or ends of a continuum is not always evident. For Mexico and Tex., see above. Evidently for S. Am., Voous (1968) mentioned "saturated" gray and brown "adults" as rarer than dark brown Juv. birds; other "saturated color types" included "mainly uniform grey" birds and an individual with blackish slaty anterior and remaining underparts dark brown.

Measurements   (Tex. birds)   Basic feathering: BEAK from cere of 5 ♂ 23.5–27.5 mm., av. 25, and 4 ♀ 25.5–28.5, av. 27.5; WING across chord 5 ♂ 404–430 mm., av. 416.4, and 4 ♀ 423–450, av. 438.8 (Friedmann 1950).

WING flattened 9 ♂ 410–447 mm., mean 424, and 6 ♀ 433–457, mean 447 (Voous 1968).

Juvenal Plumage: WING flattened 2 ♂ 414 and 426 mm., 1 ♀ 451 (Voous).

Voous stated that in this species the WING is the same length regardless of age but the Juv. TAIL is longer (see his tables). He gave for Tex.: Basic Plumage TAIL 7 ♂ 164–192 mm., mean 178, and 3 ♀ 182–188, mean 185; Juv.: 2 ♂ 204 and 209, a ♀ 215.

Whether in Juv. or Basic, there is much overlap in meas. of the sexes.

Weight   Tex. "adults," sexes not distinguished: 6 weighed 920–1,351 gm., av. 1,111 (Kopeny, J. Grier, F. and F. Hamerstrom).

Hybrids   None known.

Geographical variation   In the species; Voous (1968) pointed out that migratory behavior and breeding distribution are poorly known, that breeding range is interrupted with 3 widely separated centers, and that birds from the Tex. through Cent. Am. "do not differ at all" from those of subtropical S. Am. Northern migrants perhaps penetrate far into S. Am. and may be confused with presumably local birds there. Although the is. birds of Aruba, Curaçao, and Bonaire are "very small," so also are some from nearby Venezuela. In brief, although the birds seem to fit Bergmann's rule (tropical ones smaller), Voous held that available information did not warrant recognition of subspecies.

Affinities   The White-tailed is very closely related to red-backed birds of S. Am. currently listed as *B. polysoma* and *B. poecilochrous*. Whether the 3 are separate species may be debatable.   MARK KOPENY

SUBSPECIES   After examining 145 specimens, Voous (1968) argued against recognition of subspecies (see above); 3 were listed that same year by L. Brown and Amadon (1968 2) and a decade later by E. R. Blake (1977). They are tentatively listed here.

In our area   *hypospodius* Gurney—descr. and meas. of Tex. birds given above; parts of U.S.-Mexican border states down into Colombia and Venezuela.

Elsewhere   *colonus* Berlepsch—part of n. S. Am., including several adjacent Atlantic is. See Voous (1968) and E. R. Blake (1977).

albicaudatus Vieillot—somewhere in Brazil to s. Argentina. See Voous and Blake.
                                                                      MARK KOPENY

FIELD IDENTIFICATION **In our area** Among our buteos, has longest wings and shortest tail in proportion to its bulk—more so than Swainson's Hawk, which it most nearly resembles in proportions (A. Brooks, in May 1935). Very graceful flight. Hovers like the Rough-legged Hawk and kites.

Basic Plumage **Light** birds. When perched: folded wings project beyond end of tail, underparts white, tail white with conspicuous black band distally, reddish brown "shoulders" may be visible on dark dorsum. In flight overhead: underparts white; wing lining white, remainder mixed light and moderately dark, trailing edge and distal portion of primaries black; very conspicuous black band distally on white tail. In flight as viewed from behind or above; very dark, contrasting with white of lower back and most of tail. All our other buteos and allies have different tail pattern (and other differences). The Ferruginous Hawk has chestnut or reddish brown thighs, some of this color also on posterior venter, and tail darkens gradually toward tip. Not likely to be confused with the Osprey, which is white ventrally. **Dark** Whitetails have some light in underwing, the characteristic white rump, and light tail with heavy distal dark bar.

Juvenal Plumage Very dark dorsally and largely so ventrally (much individual variation in underparts), light and dark pattern of underwing extends to trailing edge, primaries dark distally, and tail moderately dark (inconspicuous narrow barring). Especially during molting, when with white breast and dark belly, might be mistaken for young Red-tailed Hawk. **Dark** birds: compare with various dark-phase buteos and note differences in underwing, tail pattern, and so forth.   MARK KOPENY

VOICE High-pitched, punctuated alarm call has been likened to voice of Laughing Gull (J. Stevenson and Meitzen 1946), of Cooper's Hawk except much higher-pitched and with tinkling musical sound (Burrows 1917), and much like bleating of a goat (Merrill 1879).

Distinct sexual differences in alarm calls are known from sonagram analysis (C. Farquhar): single tone (ascending in frequency for ♂♂, descending for ♀♀) followed by series of bisyllabic tones (♂♂ 3–6, ♀♀ 4–11); frequency of entire call is generally higher and with clearer tones for ♂♂ than ♀♀. Duration of call 1.5–3 sec., with ♀♀ tending to call longer; ♂ *aaaaAAAA ke-HAK ke-Hak ke-Hak* and ♀ *AAAAaaaa KUH-tuh HUH-tuh KUH-tuh*.

Breeders call at least from Feb. through July in s. Tex. They call throughout the year in Venezuela (Mader 1981), where they are resident.

Small nestlings have a catlike call and a sucking call (see Reproduction, below).   MARK KOPENY

HABITAT **In our area** Tex.—breeding areas are open or semiopen terrain; near the coast on prairies, cordgrass flats, and scrub-live oak communities; farther inland on prairies, mesquite and oak savannas and mixed savanna-chaparral. Generalizations concerning habitat requirements have limited birds to extensive prairie habitat and other open country, which is incorrect.

The likelihood that in the U.S. this hawk is at least seasonally restricted in habitat by the presence of competing raptors needs investigation.

Elsewhere Along the Caribbean coast of Venezuela—hot climate, rocky plateaus, low escarpments. Aruba, Curaçao, and Bonaire—particularly acacia- and cactus-deserts (Voous 1957). Argentina—open country, "but it is not a bird of the pampas, where it is replaced by *Buteo polysoma*" (Pereyra 1937). Voous (1968) found that habitat is "invariably described as dry open country," sparsely vegetated and with patches of bare soil, usually some thorny scrub or cacti. Later accounts (E. R. Blake 1977, T. Howell 1972, Mader 1981) and that of Meyer de Schauensee (1964) indicate greater latitude with respect to habitat requirements. For example, it nests in wet palm savanna—lush vegetation and ground-cover. Even so, reliable information is lacking from many areas where this species occurs. MARK KOPENY

DISTRIBUTION   (See map.)   **Breeding** season information is sparse for some areas and changes may be expected. TEX. uncommon to rare in upper and cent. coastal area; breeding and nonbreeding season observations have been increasing in recent years; greatest numbers reported in lower coastal area from Kleberg Co. to Willacy Co., where they are common (35 nests found in Kleberg Co., 1986, by Kopeny); uncommon to rare in lower Rio Grande Valley.

In **nonbreeding** season in Tex., and outside known breeding range, has occurred from Chambers Co. (n. coastal area), Bexar Co. (San Antonio area), Callahan Co. (Abilene area), Dallas Co., and Val Verde Co. (Big Bend area). Largest numbers per mi., reported on Audubon Christmas counts and averaged over recent years, are from Padre I., where there are no recent reports of nesting (M. Morrison 1978).

Historically, this hawk bred farther inland and n. into cent. Tex. (Medina Co. 1914, Comal Co. 1900, Taylor Co. 1896) and in ARIZ. between Florence and Red Rock in 1897 (OKLA. reports for 1905 and 1916 undoubtedly are based on misidentifications). Probably absent from Ariz. between 1899 (last specimen record) and winter of 1954–1955; sightings have since become more frequent. Absent from cent. and most of s. Tex. during approximately the same years—1890s–1950s.

Reduction in area occupied and changes in distribution have been attributed to the

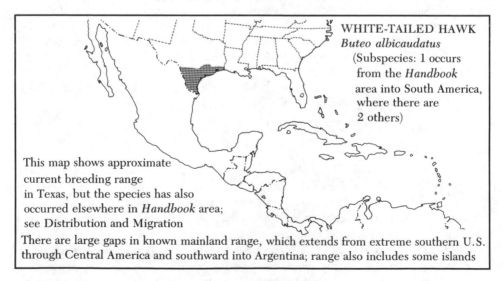

WHITE-TAILED HAWK
Buteo albicaudatus
(Subspecies: 1 occurs
   from the *Handbook*
   area into South America,
   where there are
   2 others)

This map shows approximate
current breeding range
in Texas, but the species has also
occurred elsewhere in *Handbook* area;
see Distribution and Migration

There are large gaps in known mainland range, which extends from extreme southern U.S. through Central America and southward into Argentina; range also includes some islands proliferation of woody vegetation, agricultural development, and also urban and industrial development (Oberholser and Kincaid 1974). M. Morrison (1978) found significant levels of eggshell thinning, which may explain the 1950–1970 decline and the subsequent 1971–1985 increase in number of Whitetails seen on Christmas counts in the gulf coastal area.

Recent information indicates that the Tex. population is growing and its range expanding—large increases in sightings in the lower coastal area from Kleberg to Willacy cos.; northerly, 6–7 breeding pairs established at the Attwater Prairie Chicken Natl. Wildl. Refuge (Colorado Co.) in recent years (C. Farquhar).

Sw. LA. Nov. 18, 1888. CALIF. hypothetical. ST. VINCENT (Windward Is. in Lesser Antilles) hypothetical (J. Bond 1976).

For the species overall there are several published maps, such as in L. Brown and Amadon (1968 2) and E. R. Blake (1977), but perhaps most useful is that in Voous (1968) showing very few records scattered over some very large areas and discontinuous known breeding distribution   MARK KOPENY

MIGRATION   Evidently resident in our area, seasonally dispersing more or less, yet some possibly (age?) are migratory. J. Stevenson and Meitzen (1946) reported increased numbers on the Aransas Refuge in autumn and winter; they cited evidence that Whitetails come to prairies of Colorado Co. about the last of Nov., remain until Jan. 1–20, then disperse to breed along timber edges bordered by scrub and live oaks. There are increased Whitetail densities along the gulf coast in winter.

Migratory or other movement in Cent. and S. Am. is inadequately known. Purported n. spring migration in Cent. Am. has been noted a few times; see Voous (1968). A. Wetmore (1943) observed birds moving n. near Tres Zapotes in s. Veracruz, Mexico, Mar. 30–Apr. 12—a few to 100 passing daily. This is the only such report from a well-studied Mexican state. One Whitetail with Turkey Vultures on Mar. 4 in El. Salvador was "most probably a northbound migrant" (Dickey and van Rossem 1938). In ne. Nicaragua considered resident all year (T. Howell 1972).

In S. Am. there is at least some seasonal shifting, but documentation is poor. W. H. Hudson (1920) observed spring and fall flocks on the Argentine pampas (where absent as breeder) near La Plata. He stated that flocks were typically of 30–100 birds but at times up to 2,000. Was his identification correct? There is no confirmation from other sources. At least in Paraguay, this hawk is probably a nonbreeding visitor (Voous 1968).

MARK KOPENY

BANDING STATUS   As of June 1986, approximate numbers banded, all in Tex.: Colorado Co., 35; San Patricio Co., 10; and Kleberg Co., 120. Almost all banding has been done in the 1980s.   MARK KOPENY

REPRODUCTION   Texas data unless otherwise stated. Age when **first breeds** probably usually 2 years—that is, in 3d calendar year of life, but Benners (1887) found a ♀ in what he considered 2d-calendar-year feathering breeding with a ♂ in "full plumage," and Kopeny found a pair, both similarly "immature," breeding in Kleberg Co. in 1986.

79

Territory   In the cent. gulf coast area breeders are paired and occupying territories by the 1st week in Jan., probably earlier. Some areas have high concentrations of wintering raptors—primarily Redtails and N. Harriers—until Feb. or early Mar.; their presence very close to Whitetail nests is generally tolerated, but the Whitetails do initiate some aggression.

Whitetails are most conspicuous late Jan.–early Apr. (most ♀ ♀ are on eggs by Apr.) when seen soaring over their territories. HIGH-CIRCLING is done by singles or pairs; if the latter, then often in tight circles with 1 bird directly above the other. No other display is yet known. An adult in Kleberg Co. was observed, before laying, soaring 50–100 ft. over nesting territory with a long stick in 1 foot; it transferred this to its beak, dropped it, and caught it in midair.

Nests   Usually built in low trees or shrubs. Most have been reported in various oaks, mesquite, huisache, and, near the coast, live oak is most common in Kleberg Co. and Macartney rose in Colorado Co. (C. Farquhar, M. Kopeny, M. Morrison 1978). Average nest height is about 3 m. (Kopeny). On Padre I., Benners (1887) found a nest 1.5 ft. from the ground in scrub oak growth—the only bush in sight—and a nest in Kleberg Co. was 1.1 m. above ground in a 1.7-m live oak (Kopeny). On the Aransas Refuge, most nests were 8–12 ft. up in the tops of solitary blackjack or live oaks. One in Brazoria Co. was in the topmost branches of a 40-ft. cottonwood (J. Stevenson and Meitzen 1946).

Old nests may be visited and refurbished (or new ones built) in Feb. or earlier, long before eggs are deposited (Stevenson and Meitzen, Kopeny), and work continues until clutches are laid (Morrison). Timing is presumably the same whether work is on a new or an old structure. Nests are generally in plain sight and command a wide view. They are particularly conspicuous in unleaved mesquite, with much snowy white down present, but those in such trees as live oak and ebony, or where there are grapevine tangles, are not readily visible (Morrison, Kopeny). Occasionally nests are taken over by Great Horned Owls, and then the hawks nest nearby (J. Stevenson and Meitzen 1946, Kopeny). Bay-winged Hawks and Caracaras also nest close by; in 1 instance Caracaras used a nest in granjeno that had been occupied 2 seasons earlier by Whitetails (Kopeny).

Most nests are quite bulky, built of sticks and dry vegetation and with recognizable successive layers from usage in previous years. One in Nueces Co. had an outside diam. of 33 × 26 in., and diam. of bowl was 11 in. (Brandt, in Bent 1937). Normally the nest is lined with dead grasses, some with roots attached, as 1st noted by Goss (in Bendire 1892).

Greenery   Goss (in Bendire 1892) mentioned a "few green twigs and leaves," and Benners (1887) stated that the clutch is sometimes covered with grass. Fresh sprigs are not uncommon in nests in Kleberg Co., and 2 pairs are known to have brought small pieces of cow dung (Kopeny).

Laying   Principally Feb.–May but has been recorded as early as Jan. 20 (Stevenson and Meitzen) and presumably viable eggs as late as Aug. 4 (Oberholser and Kincaid 1974). M. Morrison (1978) reported that the peak of egg laying was in the middle 3d of Mar. (based on museum data) and suggested that those laid from Apr. onward were replacement clutches, with (Nyc, in Morrison) a 10–15 day interval before relaying.

80

Estimated clutch initiation in Kleberg Co. for 28 nesting attempts in 1984 and 85 attempts in 1985 varied Mar. 11–May 12 and peaked in the last week of Mar. and 1st week of Apr. (13 nests). Laying began approximately 2 weeks later in 1985 than in 1984 (Kopeny).

In Venezuela this hawk is a dry-season nester, although replacement clutches extend the span into the rainy season; clutches found on dates as far apart as Feb. 14 and Aug. 19 (Mader 1981). Haverschmidt (1968) reported a nest in Suriname that contained young almost ready to fly by the end of the dry season.

In the Falfurrias area (s. Tex.) in 1969, a nest was "in continuous use as two broods of 2 young were raised" (F. S. Webster 1969)—possible evidence that this hawk is sometimes double-brooded.

Clutch size   Usually 2 eggs, sometimes 3, occasionally 1. The av. was 2.26 eggs in 139 nests (M. Morrison 1978). Both Morrison and Worcester (1905) reported 4-egg clutches. The av. was 1.8 for 10 nests in 1984 in Kleberg Co. (Kopeny). No data are available on rate of deposition.

One **egg** each from 20 Tex. clutches **size** length 58.94 ± 1.96 mm., breadth 46.13 ± 1.88, and radii of curvature of ends 19.16 ± 1.28 and 15.26 ± 1.56; **shape** short elliptical to nearly oval, elongation 1.27 ± 0.043, bicone −0.043, and asymmetry +0.108 (F. W. Preston). Fifty eggs (from Tex.?) av. 58.9 × 46.5 mm. (Bent 1937). They are nearly smooth, without sheen, **color** white or very pale bluish; perhaps a ⅓ are plain, the others sparingly and faintly spotted lavender overlaid with small spots of various buffs and browns.

Incubation period   Based on Data from about 20 nests in Colorado Co., 31 days (C. Farquhar). Most nesters are very shy, but an incubating ♀ dived silently behind a person inspecting a nest (Stevenson and Meitzen).

Nestling period   Few data. Young hatch about a day apart, with eyes open; 1 egg was still pipping 3–4 days after the 2 others in the clutch had hatched (Kopeny). By age 10–12 days nestlings peer skyward frequently and often utter a catlike *mee-ow* and a sucking *tsick* (J. Stevenson and Meitzen 1946). Ditto (1943) found that the larger of 2 nestlings was dominant when food was in limited supply; at about 14 days of age there were signs of dominance, but a size discrepancy was no longer noticeable. At about age 28 days, they fed themselves.

Breeding success   Highly variable among few available data. Poor on the Aransas Refuge (Stevenson and Meitzen); 2 of 8 nests (6 with 2 eggs, 2 with 3 eggs) raised young to flight age; Caracaras robbed 1 nest, and unknown predators destroyed 4 others. Six breeding pairs produced 13 eggs in Colorado Co. in 1983 and reared 13 young; similar high productivity was found there in 1984 and 1985 (C. Farquhar). In Kleberg Co., 44 nesting attempts (1984–1985) were successful, with 1.52 young attaining flight per successful attempt (Kopeny). Five nests in 1984 were built in pastures that were subsequently burned (presumably before egg laying). Three of the 5 nests were destroyed by fire, and 2 of these 3 pairs (unmarked birds) renested; 1 pair raised 1 young to flight age and the other pair failed on eggs twice. The 3d pair that lost its nest to fire remained on territory but was not known to renest.

Age at first flight   Averaged 54 days in 1 season and 57 another (C. Farquhar); 47 days at 1 nest (Stevenson and Meitzen).   MARK KOPENY

SURVIVAL   No data.

HABITS   **In our area** unless otherwise stated. The most commonly reported **hunting method** of the Whitetail is a low **soaring** search, usual altitude 50–150 ft., the bird cruising occasionally, then **hovering,** seemingly hanging in midair with outstretched wings that are motionless or moving in a very narrow arc, the feet occasionally lowered and raised. When the air is calm it will occasionally flap to maintain station. From searching flight the bird draws in its wings and descends swiftly on its prey. In se. Brazil, M. Mitchell (1957) described this hovering, noting that the alulae project from the leading edge of the wing in a very noticeable way.

Whitetails also use **perch-and-wait** hunting tactics on their territories and may even combine it with piracy. An "immature" in Dec. caused a Black-shouldered Kite to drop its prey (Heredia and Clark 1984). In an instance before egg laying, an "adult" remained perched near the nest while a N. Harrier coursed back and forth in the immediate area. The harrier evidently captured prey (or appeared to do so) in tall grass some 150 yds. from the Whitetail, which immediately flew directly to it and displaced it. A 2d "adult" Whitetail flew low over the 1st, then returned to its perch. In 2 other instances of pirating, a harrier and a Caracara (both were in flight) were attacked by "adult" Whitetails and forced to drop food items (Kopeny).

Stevenson and Meitzen observed a pair of Whitetails and a "full grown juvenal" attack a Red-tailed Hawk, successfully routing it.

In Tex. in early May a Whitetail struck and held onto a 6-day-old Wild Turkey; in 2–3 sec. a Bay-winged Hawk also hit the poult, and the raptors faced each other, both maintaining their grip until the turkey hen drove them off (Haucke 1971).

Using a beater   Whitetails appear to be tolerant of machinery and human activity away from the nest and take advantage of such in hunting situations. On the Aransas Refuge in Sept., 2 Whitetails were hovering over doveweeds (*Croton*) in the middle of a field that was being harrowed. They apparently spotted potential prey, because they flew to nearby fenceposts and remained perched for almost 2 hrs. until the circling tractor had nearly finished. When most of the weeds were cut, a jackrabbit flushed and was struck immediately by a Whitetail, which, unable to lift it, pinned it to the ground. The other hawk joined, and they proceeded to feed on it (J. Stevenson and Meitzen 1946). Similarly, a Whitetail pair remained in a low soar behind a tractor mowing the tall grass along the median strip of a Kleberg Co. highway. One dropped into the freshly mowed grass approximately 40 yds. behind the tractor, caught a small rodent, flew to a nearby fencepost to eat it, and was back in the air near the 1st bird within 2 min. (Kopeny, J. Grier).

In Jalisco, Mexico, in late June, 2 Whitetails were capturing and eating "large flying insects in midair, kitewise" (Zimmerman and Harry 1951).

Prairie Fires   Whitetails often congregate at fires. This has been observed in the Tex. gulf coast region (Tewes 1984, J. Stevenson and Meitzen 1946, Kopeny, F. and F. Hamerstrom) and in the lowland pine savannas of Nicaragua (T. Howell 1972). They appear to be well adapted to this form of opportunistic feeding and employ particular strategies depending on the stage of the fire and, presumably, the potential prey species. Other raptors tend fires, but these generally appear to be individuals in the area of the fire at its initiation, whereas the high number of Whitetails often in attendance suggests that many are attracted from mi. away. J. Stevenson and Meitzen (1946) counted 16 "adults" and 4 "immatures" at a fire. Based on their knowledge of the local hawk population, they felt that the fire had attracted nearly all "adult" Whitetails within a 10-mi. radius.

Apparently attracted by smoke, Whitetails begin arriving from several min. to an hr. or more after the fire is set (prescribed burns mainly). A single "immature" Whitetail arrived within 20 min. in the previously mentioned instance, and all 20 arrived within 2¼ hrs. One arrived 5 min. after a backfire was initiated at 2 adjacent 2-ha. burns (Tewes 1984).

The number of Whitetails attracted to fires is highly variable. Apparently the most important factor is their local numbers, but attendance also may be a seasonal matter (more "adults" will attend before incubating), visibility of the presumed cue (size of fire, scope of smoke column), and "competing" fires that may be attracting birds.

Two adjacent 2-ha. burns were conducted on Jan. 14, 1981, and another 2 the following day. These attracted 1 and 5 Whitetails, respectively. Four more 2-ha. burns conducted in the same general area on Feb. 22, 1981, did not attract any (Tewes 1984). A total of 14 were attracted to a 40-ha. burn in gulf cordgrass on Feb. 2, 1981, at the Aransas Refuge (Tewes). Upper limits of observed Whitetail attendance at several large burns in Kleberg Co. were 20–30 individuals (Kopeny, Grier).

Whitetails generally hover in and above the smoke column while the fire is in full blaze, pursuing such prey as grasshoppers wafted upward. Less often (at this stage of the fire) they course back and forth in front of the fire line, pursuing grasshoppers, small mammals, and other terrestrial life that is moving to keep ahead of heat and flames (see Stevenson and Meitzen, also Tewes 1984). T. Howell (1972) collected a ♀ in Feb. that was foraging at "the edge of a grassfire" in ne. Nicaragua. Her digestive tract contained remains of frogs, a snake, a lizard, and mammal hair.

Hunting strategy changes as the fire starts to subside—the birds begin to spend more time in a low soar or coursing over freshly burned areas, apparently seeking dead, injured, or disoriented prey. The birds will hunt from perches, if any are available near a fire. This may continue until dusk (often hrs. after the fire is out), and the birds, particularly "immatures" (Kopeny, Grier), may remain in the area for several days (Tewes 1984). MARK KOPENY

FOOD   In Tex. Mammals, birds, reptiles, amphibians, crustaceans, insects, and carrion. Small birds and snakes are common prey. The young of various prey species "bear the brunt" of predation in the nesting season of this hawk (J. Stevenson and Meitzen 1946); Stevenson and Meitzen also list prey taken in other seasons. The following is a condensation of information at hand:

Mammals   In size from jackrabbit down to pocket mice (*Perognathus*).

Birds   Blue-winged Teal (probably an injured individual) and large rails down to include Seaside Sparrow. The incidence of birds in the diet of nestling Whitetails is greater than the literature indicates (Stevenson and Meitzen).

Reptiles   Skink (*Eumeces*), fence lizard (*Sceloporus*), and at least 5 genera of snakes (*Ophisaurus, Pituophis, Thamnophis, Opheodrys, Coluber*). Horned "toad" (*Phrynosoma*).

Amphibians   Frogs (*Rana*).

Crustaceans Blue crab (*Callinectes sapidus*).

Insects Grasshoppers, crickets, large beetles, true bugs, larvae of dragonflies and butterflies, ants.

Carrion Cow, rattlesnake, probably any carcass in a burned area.

Among the more useful sources of data are May (1935), J. Stevenson and Meitzen (1946), and Sherrod's (1978) summary.

Elsewhere There are a few S. Am. data in Voous (1969) and Mader (1981)— snakes, lizards, small birds, small mammals, and so forth.

NOTE The above species account is based on preliminary work in 1983 supported by the Natl. Wildl. Federation; the Welder Wildl. Foundation (contribution #300) has provided all support thereafter.   MARK KOPENY

dorsal

ZONE-TAILED HAWK

Buteo albonotatus Kaup

Middle-sized, slender-bodied buteo with long wings and tail (quite like a harrier). Third and 4th primaries (counting from outer) about equal in length, the 4th very slightly longer, the 3d somewhat longer than the 5th; the 4 outermost deeply and about equally incised or emarginated for ½ the exposed length of inner webs.

Most of feathering sooty or blackish but with very pronounced gray bloom (lacking in museum specimens); lower forehead, lores, and narrow ring around eye white; feathers of much of head, neck, and breast white basally. Underside of tail tipped off-white, then a wide black band, then alternating white bands (3) and somewhat irregular black bands—the white ones, especially, progressively narrow toward the body, and the proximal band is largely concealed. In the underwing the lining is sooty or darker and the flight feathers grade to palish basally (lightest at bases of inner primaries), crossed with narrow dark bars; distal ⅓ of primaries sooty.

Juvenal somewhat more brownish overall than definitive, the lower forehead white, the dorsal feathers edged (not conspicuously) brown; on breast and sides a considerable number of variably shaped white spots and, on some individuals, a few on dorsum. Underside of tail grayish with dusky band close to tip (narrower than the black band of older birds), the remaining light area crossed with at least 4 or 5 exposed narrow dusky bars, progressively closer together proximally. On underside of wing the flight feath-

85

ers, especially primaries, paler than in later Plumages, with narrower and fewer dusky bars.

Sexes similar(?), but the ♀ larger; length (sexes combined) 17½–21¼ in. (45–54 cm.), wingspread 47–53 in. (119–134 cm.), mean wt. ♂ 22 oz. (628 gm.), ♀ 31 oz. (886 gm.).

DESCRIPTION   In sw. U.S.

▶ ♂ ♀ Def. Basic Plumage (entire feathering) ALL YEAR, as described above. **Beak** very dark distally, paling to light grayish at cere, which is yellow; **iris** dark brownish; **tarsi** and toes yellow, talons black. Color portrait: A. Brooks (1948). No data on molting except primaries and tail are renewed in Aug. in Ariz. (Baird et al. 1875); probably, as in other *Buteo*s, fairly prolonged molting begins early in breeding season.

According to E. A. Mearns (1886), a ♀ in mid-May in Ariz. had (compared to a ♂) an additional tail bar "plainly indicated above," the white bases of feathers exposed on the breast, the tail somewhat more rounded, and the "exposed tail-bar are tinged with brown." Another ♀ did "not differ appreciably" from this one. These matters should be checked further.

AT HATCHING   No information. In Venezuela a "rather large" nestling was "still covered with grayish down" (Friedmann and Smith 1955).

▶ ♂ ♀ Juv. Plumage (entire feathering), as described above. **Beak** blackish distally and lighter basally, cere yellow, **iris** dark brownish, **legs** and feet palish yellow. White bases of feathers of at least part of **head** and the **upper body** more or less exposed; upper side of **tail** brownish gray crossed with about 10 narrow blackish bars, the distal

♂ Juv.   ♀ Basic

J. Schmitt, del.

one much the widest; underside grayish with the barring dusky. **Wing** lining blackish, flight feathers grayish grading to white on inner webs (thus lighter than underside in definitive feathering), barred and spotted, except primaries dark distally. No data on molting. Although Friedmann (1950) indicated 2 predefinitive feather generations, only 1 is definitely known.

Color phases None. This hawk may represent a situation in which what may have been a melanistic phase in the past has come to include all individuals at present (L. Brown and Amadon 1968 **2**).

Measurements Birds from sw. U.S.: 7 ♂ BEAK from cere 21.5–22.3 mm., av. 21.9, WING across chord 380–393, av. 387.5; and 9 ♀ BEAK from cere 24.5–25 mm., av. 24.6, and WING across chord 409–438, av. 419.6 (Friedmann 1950). These show no overlap of the sexes, but note that the following, presumably including birds from farther s. (E. R. Blake 1977), overlap appreciably: 14 ♂ BEAK from cere 20.6–24 mm., av. 21.7, WING across chord 365–394, av. 383.1; and 18 ♀ BEAK from cere 23–25 mm., av. 24.2 and WING across chord 382–438, av. 410.9.

Mean meas. from H. Snyder and Wiley (1976): 16 ♂ BEAK from cere 21.4 mm., WING across chord (of 17) 392.2; and 14 ♀ BEAK from cere 24.1 mm., WING across chord 422.9.

Weight Mexico: 3 ♂ 607–667 gm., mean 628; 4 ♀ 845–937, mean 886 (Dunning 1984).

Hybrids None.

Geographical variation Slight, and only in size. The birds in S. Am. were once regarded possibly as migrants, or including migrants, from N. Am. Friedmann (1950) listed the birds of the Pearl Is. of Panama plus those of S. Am. as "somewhat smaller" and without slaty tinge. A. Wetmore (1965) discounted the latter. This hawk is resident on mainland S. Am. and some nearby is., which does not, of course, preclude occurrence of migrants.

Affinities No useful information.   RALPH S. PALMER

SUBSPECIES None currently recognized. On slim evidence, Van Tyne and Sutton (1937) thought that there was no justification for maintaining 2 subspecies. Friedmann (1950) listed 2—the s. birds as *abbreviatus* Cabanis. A. Wetmore (1965) gave meas. of a few s. birds and concluded, from the material he had seen, that recognition of a s. race was not clearly justified. L. Brown and Amadon (1968 **2**) and E. R. Blake (1977) recognized none, but both cited Friedmann's meas. for smaller birds.

RALPH S. PALMER

FIELD IDENTIFICATION **In our area** Quite harrierlike shape—trim body, long wings, and fairly long tail. Mostly black (with pronounced gray sheen), except for part of wing lining and black and white tail—usually shows only 1 or 2 white bands. At a distance, compared with the Turkey Vulture, very small-headed. Screaming voice.

On the wing, misleadingly like the Turkey Vulture (Stephens, in Brewster 1883; Swarth 1905; recent authors). "Often easily overlooked" because it resembles the vulture (P. and K. Meeth 1978) and often flies with it (see Habits, below). At times soars or sails with up-angled wings, the body rocking and unsteady, tail only partially spread. Often soars at high altitudes, but also cruises somewhat in the manner of a low-flying harrier. Both this hawk and the Turkey Vulture have light on underside of primaries; in the hawk it is much lighter all along, but palest about where primaries meet the secondaries. Also soars with wings nearly horizontal and tail fully spread. Flight photos: approaching bird (Bohl 1957, mislabeled) and departing bird (1979 *Am. Birds* 33 897).

Frequently confused with the Lesser [or Common] Black Hawk (see species account); it is stouter bodied and much broader winged, and underside of wing shows whitish only in part of the primaries (toward leading edge), and a single white band midway in the tail. Often it has a noticeable terminal white band as well. Perched birds of the 2 species can be difficult to distinguish.

Hardly to be confused with melanistic Swainson's Hawk, with its different configuration and tail pattern. In times and places where both Zone-tailed and Rough-legged Hawks occur, however, it is easily confused—especially at long range—with the dark phase of the latter. This may account for some reports of Zonetails beyond their usual area of occurrence (B. Millsap).

The Juv. Zonetail differs from older stages in having underside of flight feathers of wing lighter and underside of tail whitish with numerous narrow dusky bars (distal bar much the widest). An "immature" (Juv.) ♀, when perched, raised its neck feathers, showing the white basally; it thus had a white-headed appearance, and the collector was surprised to find the bird actually black headed (Huey 1933).

Outside our area Other identification problems, in Cent. Am. notably with the Black Hawk-Eagle (*Spizaetus tyrannus*), whose voice is very different.

RALPH S. PALMER

VOICE An exaggerated *meeeew*, almost catlike (B. Millsap). Loud "shrill whistle" when disturbed near nest (E. A. Mearns 1886); "loud querulous cry" not unlike Red-tailed Hawk (Bendire 1892); similar to Broad-winged Hawk's whistle, but not as high pitched and more piercing (Huber 1929); "incessant and somewhat peevish whistle" halfway between Redtail and Broadwing (Bent 1937).　　　RALPH S. PALMER

HABITAT **In our area** The following is based primarily on data from Ariz. (Millsap 1981, R. Glinski) and w. Tex. (Matteson and Riley 1981). The species occurs from near sea level (lower Colo. R. valley) to above 8,500 ft. but mostly in the Upper Sonoran Life Zone. It shows a preference for mountains, canyons, and other areas of steep topographic relief. Twenty-two (of 23) nest sites studied in w. Ariz. were located in solitary trees or small groves on canyon walls, in canyon bottoms adjacent to cliffs, or on steep mountain slopes. In w. Tex., found in similarly rugged terrain, usually adjacent to (or on) cliffs.

Nests Have been found in riparian deciduous forests and woodlands and in montane coniferous forest; less commonly in oak woodlands, rarely in paloverde-ironwood stands along desert washes. Of 29 nests in w. Ariz., 16 were in cottonwood, 7 in sycamore, 3 in Emory oak, 2 in ponderosa pine, and 1 in paloverde. Nine in w. Tex.: 6 in ponderosa pine, 1 in Emory oak, and 2 on cliffs. Other known nest trees include walnut, fir, cypress, and mesquite. The trees used are typically mature to senescent and very large; heights of trees in Ariz. ranged from 51 ft. (Emory oak) to 130 ft. (ponderosa pine). They are usually either in open groves or are lone trees near cliffs. Although many nests are near permanent streams, this is not a requisite; over ⅓ of Ariz. nests were more than 1 mi. from surface water. In the past, Zonetails may have nested more commonly in broad valleys in the Lower Sonoran Life Zone, particularly around Tucson, Ariz. (A. Phillips et al. 1964).

Zonetails forage widely over open to sparsely wooded uplands. In w. Ariz. this hawk was observed primarily over interior chaparral and desert grassland plant communities, but it also hunted over saguaro-paloverde desert scrub and open pinyon-juniper woodland. It prefers rugged terrain for foraging as well as for nesting. Both May (1935) and Willis (1963) described use of updrafts off cliffs and slopes by foraging Zonetails; typical foraging habitat in Ariz. consists of steep, rocky, shrub-covered slopes.

Elsewhere within the range of the species, habitat is at least as varied as in our area.

BRIAN A. MILLSAP

DISTRIBUTION **In our area** (see map.) Additionally, the species occurs s. through Mexico and Cent. Am. (sparse or absent in some or all seasons from large areas); in S. Am. a very considerable and apparently discontinuous, as well as local, distribution (Blake 1977, map); occurs in Trinidad and some other coastal is. From w. to e. in sw. U.S.:

CALIF. Perhaps 2 dozen records in 5 s. counties (San Diego Co. leading), including 6 in winter in coastal lowlands and 1 on Mt. Palomar. Seasonally earliest Calif. (and

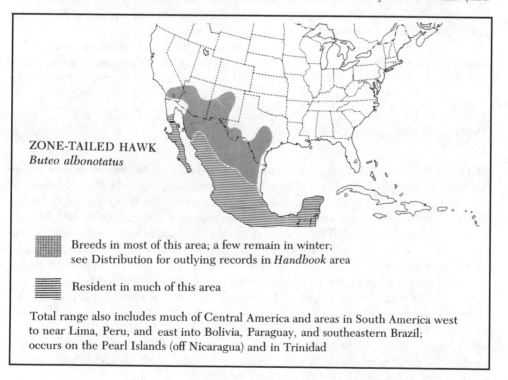

ZONE-TAILED HAWK
Buteo albonotatus

Breeds in most of this area; a few remain in winter; see Distribution for outlying records in *Handbook* area

Resident in much of this area

Total range also includes much of Central America and areas in South America west to near Lima, Peru, and east into Bolivia, Paraguay, and southeastern Brazil; occurs on the Pearl Islands (off Nicaragua) and in Trinidad

U.S.) record was for winter—1 "adult" collected Feb. 23, 1962. There are more recent Dec., Jan., and Feb. sightings (1986 *Am. Birds* **40** 334). Attempted unsuccessfully to nest annually 1978–1982 in Riverside Co.—2 eggs hatched in 1980 (1980 *Am. Birds* **34** 930).

NEV.   One, 13 km. se. of Las Vegas, Apr. 19, 1975 (Lawson 1977); probably others.

UTAH   One, Capitol Reef Nat. Park, June 3, 1984 (Behle et al. 1985).

ARIZ.   In area indicated on map; scattered nester; very few remain in winter.

N.MEX.   As mapped. Most regular in sw. part of state. Has nested in Guadalupe and Capitan mts., Gila R. valley, and n. as far as Los Alamos. Rare in winter.

TEX. As mapped; in sw. part has bred from sea level up to about 7,500 ft.; Glass and Chisos mts., Trans-Pecos Mts., Rio Grande valley, Edwards Plateau. Said (Oberholser and Kincaid 1974) not to breed by early 1970s on e. Edwards Plateau, but this unsubstantiated. At present evidently a very few in winter in lower Rio Grande valley. Records into early 1970s: text and map in Oberholser and Kincaid.

Elsewhere   See map caption.

NOTE   Through unknown circumstance, a Zone-tailed Hawk was present in Halifax Co., N.S., Sept. 24–Oct. 4, 1976 (I. McLaren and MacInnis 1977).

This species has no known fossil or prehistoric record.   RALPH S. PALMER

MIGRATION   **In our area   Spring** arrival at nesting areas, aside from a few winterers, is from mid-Mar. or earlier to some time in Apr. Early dates: Mar. 12 in Ariz. (B. Millsap), arrives early Apr. in N.Mex., and by mid-Mar. in Tex. (eggs Mar. 29). **Fall** departure is primarily in Sept. Latest: Oct. 3 in Ariz. (B. Millsap) and early Oct. in Tex. (These data were compiled from various sources.)

The sometimes-cited report by W. E. D. Scott (1886) that he twice saw flocks of at least 50 in early Sept. in Ariz. is highly suspect. Perhaps a few Zonetails were mixed in with Swainson's Hawks.   RALPH S. PALMER

BANDING STATUS   Fourteen were banded in Ariz. (1962–1967) and 1 in Tex. (1976); post-1980 figures are not at hand.   RALPH S. PALMER

REPRODUCTION   Data from our area. Age when **first breeds** unknown. There are few data on **displays.** HIGH-CIRCLING with occasional flapping and calling is common and conspicuous—2 or more birds usually high, perhaps on an updraft or thermal. Where present all winter, such circling can be expected even on warm days in that season. Hubbard (1971, 1974b) observed it on Feb. 3 in N.Mex.: 3 "adults" were soaring in huge circles, 2 birds higher than the 3d. Suddenly 1 of the higher birds swooped at the lower bird, which turned over, and they grasped talons and fell about 100 yds.; they separated, flapped back upward, and gradually circled away.

SKY-DANCE was observed in the Chisos Mts. of Tex. on May 27, 1901, by L. A. Fuertes, who illustrated it (see Oberholser and Kincaid 1974). The wings are depicted well out at the "wrist," the primaries in on the rump, the tail fully spread—an aerodynamic configuration for great speed. The bird is shown making a steep dive into a canyon. It goes nearly to earth with "amazing velocity," then remounts and repeats (Oberholser and Kincaid). It calls during this display.

Nest trees Deciduous and coniferous; listed under Habitat, above. Typically, the **site** is within and near the top of the crown, far up in a tall tree, and supported by secondary branches. Boquillas Canyon, Tex. on south-facing cliffs—on a ledge near the top, another in a hole in a cliff wall (Matteson and Riley 1981). The nest is loosely constructed of rather large sticks. Brandt (1951) described a nest as 20 in. high, 24 in. diam., with bowl 9 in. wide and 4 in. deep. It is lined with twigs bearing green leaves, or sometimes yucca fiber, and **greenery** is brought throughout the nesting cycle.

Long use of sites In a cottonwood in a canyon some 21–22 mi. e. of Tucson there was a nest, used for "many years," that had become "quite bulky through its annual accretion." This was in 1886. Earlier, in the spring of 1872, Bendire had climbed to this nest, about 40 ft. up, and while examining it he saw that he was being watched from behind a giant cactus by an Apache. In order to avoid "lingering death at the stake," Bendire pretended not to see the Indian, slowly descended, sprinted to his horse, and outdistanced about 30 Apaches (H. Brown 1901). At Fish Creek, Ariz., a nest tree reportedly (Swarth 1920) was used for some 70 years. At the mouth of Tornillo Creek, e. of the Chisos Mts. in Tex., on May 27, 1901, L. A. Fuertes shot 1 of a pair and was stranded temporarily on the cliff face while retrieving it. A pair, "probably nesters," still frequented this cliff in the summer of 1971 (Oberholser and Kincaid 1974).

Egg dates In 22 nests in w. Ariz., earliest was Apr. 19 and latest May 17; eggs were in 50% of nests by May 1 (Millsap 1981). In Tex., dates range Mar. 29–May 17. In Cent. Am., nesting begins in Nov.–Dec. Trinidad—breeds Feb.–Mar. (Herklots 1961).

Egg size of 37 length 52.4–63 mm. and breadth 38.9–49.6. av. 55.6 × 43.5 (Bent 1937). **Shape** approximately ovate. The shell is smooth or finely granulated, **color** white or very pale bluish when fresh, plain, occasionally faintly and sparingly spotted with pale lavenders and brownish yellows—not heavily marked like those of the Lesser Black Hawk. Fresh wt. about 60 gm.

Clutch size One to 3, usually 2. Mean clutch size was 2.0 in 16 nests in w. Tex. (Matteson and Riley 1981) and 2.1 in 22 nests in w. Ariz. (Millsap 1981). Ariz. nests had 19 clutches of 2 and 3 of 3.

Incubation Presumably usually by the ♀. Two days after a ♀ was shot at a nest a ♂ was incubating and was also shot (van Rossem 1936). According to Newton (1979), incubation **period** is 35 days.

Rearing period As with various hawks, the ♀ probably remains on or near the nest most of the time until the young are about 2 weeks old, and the ♂ does most of the foraging in this period. Both adults forage during later stages of the nesting cycle; in w. Ariz. they were seen hunting as far from the nest as 26 km. (Millsap 1981, R. Glinski). The young attain flight in 6–7 weeks (Millsap, Glinski).

Breeding success In w. Tex. in 1975, 7 nests contained 14 eggs, 12 hatched, and 8 young attained flight; in 1976, 9 nests held 18 eggs, 7 (in 4 nests) hatched, and 7 young attained flight (Matteson and Riley 1981). In 22 nests in w. Ariz. in 1979 and 1980, a total of 46 eggs were laid, 42 hatched, and 41 young attained flight (Millsap 1981). Young had flown from ½ the Ariz. nests by July 28, the latest by about Aug. 10.

Although renesting has been mentioned (Call 1978), presumably after failure of a 1st attempt, there is no satisfactory information on this topic.

BRIAN A. MILLSAP and RALPH S. PALMER

SURVIVAL   No information.

HABITS   **In our area** unless otherwise stated. **Hunting methods**   Unlike most buteos, the Zonetail does not ordinarily hunt from a perch, nor does it hover-hunt. Its usual method of foraging is to soar rapidly and widely over the ground at about 50–500 ft. altitude; apparently most strikes are initiated from the air. It is usually seen foraging in areas with at least light steady winds, such as in slightly sloping or level desert habitat and rocky canyons where solar heating of terrain creates thermal currents. It also uses updrafts along cliffs and forest edges (Willis 1963).

The Zonetail forages in habitats and at heights frequented by Turkey Vultures, to which it bears a remarkable resemblance in its hunting behavior. It soars on fixed wings that are tilted up at a slight angle in the manner of a vulture's, and it rocks in flight as does the Turkey Vulture. It rarely flaps except when leaving nest or roost, when defending the nest against other species or interacting with individuals of its own species, or when making a capture attempt.

In 10 years of field work in Zonetail habitat, H. Snyder had numerous scattered observations of them hunting for a total of 7.4 hrs. in which the birds were in sight. A minimum of 10 individuals made 56 capture attempts, of which 7 were successful and 49 were misses. In all cases, the Zonetail was in view before it appeared to have sighted its potential prey. Typical search pattern: the Zonetail, circling or moving in a straight line without flapping and wings held in a slight dihedral, soars at 50–200 ft. altitude, usually 75. Its head is bent nearly straight down and can be seen to be moving from side to side, actively searching the terrain. Once it appears to have spotted prey, the Zonetail's head stops moving and fixes on the animal while the bird continues to circle and move in the same way as before while dropping behind intervening cover. Once the hawk is out of sight of the prey, it swiftly turns, and in a low flat stoop it glides in and pounces on the prey. It appears to try to use cover within ½–2 m. of the prey as a screen for its approach.

Near-vertical stoops are a less common hunting technique. In these the bird plunges with amazing speed. In vertical-plunge hunting there probably is less opportunity for the diving hawk to make use of cover; sheer speed and surprise may be its main advantage.

In Colombia, a Zonetail soared rather low with up-angled wings, then half-folded its wings and went into a shallow dive toward a tree. It struck at the terminal leaves; after the strike, the legs were tucked up, and no prey was visible until the hawk was at least 150 m. away; it then extended its legs and began to pluck a small bird (Willis 1966). In late Nov., 2 were seen regularly, soaring together or apart, hunting low over thickets and along a river like the N. Harrier (P. and Meeth 1978).

In Ariz. in Mar., at the Rio Verde, a Zonetail moved on motionless wings out over the cottonwoods straight toward the observer, "scanning the water beneath with intent interest" and "moving its head with a restless side movement" (E. A. Mearns 1886). In Apr. at Tucson, F. Stephens was standing on a dam. What he supposed to be a vulture "attempted to catch some minnows in a shallow place, fluttering over the water and trying to snatch up the little fish with its feet." The bird, a Zonetail, was unsuccessful, and when it alighted on the dam it was shot (Brewster 1883).

92

The fall bird in Nova Scotia—far outside its normal range—twice was seen to make swift attacks on prey. Once it dropped like an Osprey into long grass; the other time it made a "rapid feint" at a small bird on the top of a tree. Another observer watched as it flapped along ridges, "in both directions, periodically flapping hard" to gain altitude, then soaring in "tight spirals" 50–100 m. above treetops. Twice it plunged from such a spiral, to "inspect or attack(?) something in the trees" (I. McLaren and MacInnes 1977).

With the exception of Turkey Vultures, Zonetails do not normally associate with other raptors (or even other Zonetails) except briefly when away from the nesting area. We suspect that reports of flocks of Zonetails are actually Swainson's Hawks—as in the observation of "hundreds" that came to feed on cotton rats and other rodents driven out by the heat of a fire in a marsh and canebrake 50 mi. s. of the Ariz. border (Price, in F. M. Bailey 1927), and of W. Scott's (1886) observation of flocks of at least 50 Zonetails in early Sept., the birds "evidently migrating and closely associated together."

Mimicry   Willis (1963) proposed the idea that the Zonetail is an aggressive mimic of the Turkey Vulture, using its physical and behavioral resemblance to the vulture to get closer to prey that would ordinarily react to the sight of a cruising raptor but that habituate to Turkey Vultures. In support of the hypothesis he cited: **1** it is the only N. Am. hawk that lacks a decidedly different Juv. Plumage; if appearance is important to hunting success, the young must either resemble the adults or hunt differently; **2** the Zonetail resembles the Turkey Vulture in shape; and **3** the Zonetail behaves like the Turkey Vulture. He pointed out that we need to learn what prey Zonetails take and whether the prey have the visual acuity and behavioral characteristics that would make the evolution of the mimicry feasible.

Zonetails take approximately 97% vertebrates, including birds, lizards, frogs, and diurnal rodents—all of which have well-developed visual predator-avoidance responses. Birds, at least, habituate to vultures; in a study of responses to predators by Marbled Godwits, Meretsky (in preparation) found that wintering Godwits in Humboldt Co., Calif., would flush to vultures high overhead when the vultures 1st returned to the area after several months' absence, but that godwits seemed to cease to respond to vultures overhead after several weeks' exposure.

The Zonetail often associates in an apparently deliberate way with Turkey Vultures. In Lincoln Co., N.Mex., in Apr. 1 was seen soaring with Turkey Vultures at 7,000 ft. (Huber 1929). In Cochise Co., Ariz., in Apr. 1970 a foraging Zonetail soared with 2 Turkey Vultures as they circled down the San Simon valley for a total distance of about 10 mi. (16 km.). The Zonetail left the vultures on 2 occasions to make a fast, shallow diving stoop at presumed prey; after each attempt it soared up and clearly made an effort to return to the group of vultures, which were proceeding at a steady rate down the valley (H. Snyder).

Willis (1963) reported watching Zonetails soar among Turkey Vultures in Colombia, Panama, Mexico, and se. Ariz. In early July near Silver City, N.Mex., a cruising Zonetail was twice seen to plunge earthward and miss its target. At the time of the 2d attempt there were several foraging Turkey Vultures in the area, and the hawk did not join them.

In N.C., Mueller (1976) saw 4 "incidents of vultures flying over the vicinity while

[Bobwhite] quail were feeding near my house. In all four cases the vulture was at least 70 m. from the quail, and I noted no reaction." One "immature" vulture, however, flew near the quail and initially caused them to freeze and watch, and then to flush and hide when it turned and flew straight toward them, low, flapping, in full view. From this observation, Mueller concluded that a Zonetail would not receive much benefit from resembling a vulture, because it would not be able to approach prey close enough to capture it once it had stopped acting like a vulture and had begun to attack. In most observed horizontal attacks, however, the Zonetail conceals its approach—it only begins a stoop after it is concealed by rocks or vegetation. Mueller's observations thus support the mimicry hypothesis, despite his conclusion to the contrary.

In Colombia, Purple Gallinules and swallows apparently ignored a Zonetail soaring overhead with Turkey Vultures, but when it plunged to earth nearby "as if shot," the gallinules scattered and the swallows mobbed it. The Zonetail climbed back up to soar again after apparently missing its prey, and both the swallows and the gallinules ignored the hawk from then on, although it continued to soar in the vicinity (Willis 1963).

These observations support the hypothesis that some vertebrates (birds) appear to ignore Turkey Vultures and Zonetails when they are soaring together or separately and that vertebrates will also give escape responses to vultures and Zonetails when they are not soaring in the usual vulturelike manner. Zimmerman (1976b) presented some observations of birds recognizing a Zonetail; Am. Kestrels ignored Turkey Vultures, but a kestrel chased a cruising Zonetail that appeared near its nesting area. Two W. Kingbirds mobbed the same Zonetail, but only as it came out of a hunting dive. R. Johnson (1961) reported an observation of a probable Zonetail that was attempting to catch Wild Turkey poults and that was itself attacked several times by adult turkey hens.

If the Zonetail's resemblance to the Turkey Vulture improves its chances of approaching prey without alarming it, then we might expect to see a higher percentage of successful prey-captures by Zonetails when they hunt in the presence of vultures than when they hunt away from them. H. Snyder (MS) attempted to test the hypothesis that the presence of Turkey Vultures improves the hunting success of Zonetails by putting out carcasses to attract the vultures in an area where several individual Zonetails were foraging separately and intermittently during the day. Over a 2-day period, Zonetails made 6 capture attempts in the presence of vultures and 14 attempts in their absence; of the 6, 2 were successful and 4 were not, while of the 14, 1 was successful and 13 not. These proportions suggest an effect, but the sample size is too low for them to be significant.

For its resemblance to vultures to be a hunting advantage to the Zonetail, the effect need not work all the time. If behavioral and physical resemblance to vultures does not cost the Zonetail anything in terms of hunting efficiency and is sometimes (but not always) a factor in its hunting success, it should be maintained and selected for.

One observation suggests that associating closely with vultures may at times involve a cost to the Zonetail. In 1977 H. Snyder observed a ♀ Zonetail that caught a Mourning Dove and carried it off into some mesquite brush. The hawk was followed closely by several Turkey Vultures that dived on her in an apparent effort to make her drop the prey—which eventually she did when a young Red-tailed Hawk joined the vultures in diving on the Zonetail. The Redtail made off with the food.

Status The greatest threat to the Zonetail in our area is loss of riparian nesting habitat. In sw. Tex. the presence of DDT in several river systems is a concern, since contamination of lizards by this insecticide is documented in these areas. Protection from gunners is a further concern. (From B. Millsap.) HELEN SNYDER

FOOD Lizards, small mammals, birds, frogs. For **our area** the older literature, based mostly on stomach analyses, is probably misleading because of frequent confusion of the Zonetail with the Lesser Black Hawk (*Buteogallus anthracinus*). Recent and more extensive findings, based on studies at nests by Glinski and Matteson et al. (summarized in Sherrod 1978) and by Millsap (1981) are probably more representative. In Ariz., Glinski found birds (80% of identified prey) and lizards (20%) to be principal items. In w. Ariz., of 88 prey items identified at nests by Millsap (1981), lizards (mostly colared lizards, *Crotaphytus collaris*) 42.1% by number, small mammals 31.8%, birds 14.8%, frogs 8%, centipedes 2.3%, and snakes 1%. In w. Tex., Matteson et al. identified 138 prey items: lizards dominated (all crevice spiny lizards. *Sceloporus poinsetti*) 70%, birds 27.5%, mammals 1.5%, and snakes 0.7%.

In general, size of prey taken is much smaller than would be expected based on size of the hawk (Millsap 1981).

Elsewhere In Chiapas, Mexico, it killed Roseate Spoonbill nestlings (Toro 1952). Stated to feed on beetles and locusts in Cent. Am. (Sclater and Salvin 1859); these probably only supplement the diet there. BRIAN A. MILLSAP

dorsal

RED-TAILED HAWK

Buteo jamaicensis

Large, stoutish, soaring buteo, in Basic feathering not always with reddish tail. The 4 outer primaries are emarginated (notched) on their trailing edge, and most primaries have some dark barring (but may be mottled, spotted, or even plain, especially northwesterly in N. Am.); TAIL exceeds ½ length of WING across chord; approximately ½ tarsus unfeathered; middle toe minus talon longer than bare front of tarsus.

In parts of the vast breeding range the birds tend to be homogeneous. The most widely occurring variant is dark (melanistic) individuals, which become numerically preponderant (but are not the only ones occurring) northwesterly. Pale individuals are more restricted, occurring primarily on both sides of the Canadian border from w. Ont. westward. Birds having all rufescent lighter areas are typical of some w. areas in U.S. and s. Canada. All these variants have been categorized as "**color phases**"—pale, "normal," reddish, and dark. They are not disjunct. From interbreeding, they are mongrelized, resulting in enormous individual variation. It is demonstrably great— even among siblings.

Sexes similar in appearance, with considerable overlap in size—the ♀ av. decidedly larger, as reflected (Latimer 1938) in the skull and long bones. The species: ♂ length about 18–22½ in. (46–56 cm.) and wingspread to 45 (114 cm.); ♀ length about 20½–25 in. (52–64 cm.) and wingspread to 48 in. (122 cm.) or possibly 54 in. Usual wt. with digestive tract empty: ♂ about 27½–39 oz. (780–1,000 gm.) and ♀ 32½–50 oz. (925– 1,415 gm.).

96

Twelve named subspecies are listed, although some are doubtfully recognizable. Our area has 5, plus part of the range is occupied more or less by color variants that are not labeled subspecifically here. There are 7 extralimital named populations.

DESCRIPTION One Plumage/cycle with Basic I earliest definitive; prolonged Prebasic molting begins in the breeding season and generally ends in early fall (northerly); a few feathers may be retained another year, rarely longer. The Juv. Plumage is retained nearly a year.

▶ *B. j. borealis* ♂ ♀ Def. Basic Plumage (entire feathering), acquired over a span of about 100 days in warmer months and retained a year. **Beak** blackish grading to bluish basally, cere and gape yellow. **iris** medium brownish with dark pupil. **Head** largely warm browns with blackish "mustache mark" usually indicated at sides of white chin; on lower rear of head (occiput) the feathers are white basally with blackish ends. **Upperparts** a mixture of browns and neutral shades with a scattering of white feather bases often visible. **Underparts** upper breast ("shield") to tail white or slightly buffy with variable amount of (usually considerable) dark markings ("belly band"); flanks unbarred. Legs and **feet** yellow, talons black. **Tail** rufous to deep reddish dorsally, usually with narrow black subterminal band and very tip nearly white; ventrally it is paler, "washed out," the band faintly evident. **Wing** dorsally as back, some coverts with lighter terminal margins; wing lining white to buffy with black concentrated inwardly along leading edge and in ends of distal greater coverts—prominent carpal patch ("thumb mark"). Primaries and secondaries variably dark with light barring and dark ends.

Molting Some tardy spring migrants in Basic feathering show missing primaries, presumably molted. Breeding ♀ ♀ begin dropping primaries approximately during egg laying and ♂ ♂ later while their mates are incubating. Lowe (1978) stated that as soon as they completed their clutches ♀ ♀ "rapidly began dropping feathers." Nonbreeders in Basic feathering probably begin molting somewhat earlier in any latitude. Although the sequence of molting in the wing has been termed irregular, the primaries and their greater coverts tend to be renewed in this order (counting from inner to outer): #1, #2, then #6 or #7 (either 1st), then (by no means invariably) #3, #4, #5, #8, #10 usually last (or sometimes retained). The secondaries and their greater coverts usually begin molting (inwardly) at #1, #5, and (outwardly) at #12. The larger tertials molt from inward to outward. Early during wing molting, the 2 central tail feathers ("deck feathers") usually drop, then the others in varying sequence (next to outermost pair often right after the deck feathers). Molting of flight feathers is seldom, if ever, bilaterally symmetrical. Body molting begins early during wing molting.

Bierregaard (1974) noted long retention of some primaries and secondaries in resident birds in Mass. and a color change in an individual (new remiges and some upper coverts were erythristic). H. Mueller, who livetrapped many Redtails, noted that some apparently had 3 generations of remiges; judging from fading and wear, some feathers appeared quite new, others about a year older, and an occasional badly worn and faded feather appeared to be even older.

Eye color In e. Redtails, at least, the iris is generally pale neutral or yellowish at time of attaining flight, becoming vivid yellow by some time in 1st winter. It continues to change, becoming a medium or darker warm brown; how long this takes is unreported. Lowe (1978) noted that some dark-phase young recently out of the nest had dark brown eyes and others pale yellow. On winter range in Okla. he saw 1st-year dark birds again having brown, and others yellow, eyes. In Alaska he reared 2 young (parentage: ♂ dark with white tail, ♀ light with tail barred and not red), and both had dark brown eyes at age about 3½ weeks; then, in a period of about 15 months they became very pale tan. A "Harlan's" (dark bird) nestling taken in Alaska in June 1981 had pale yellow eyes in Dec. 1982 (D. Mindell). Most *calurus* begin assuming a yellow eye at 4–5 months, and in 1st winter it is yellow, but a captive retained the Juv. eye color even when "adult" (Jollie 1947). A live trapped "adult" "Krider's" (pale bird) had vivid yellow eyes (H. Mueller).

AT HATCHING   Eastern chicks are largely covered with short white down-A; the later down-B is much longer and somewhat toward grayish or gray-brown. The white occipital spot is visible.

▶ Juv. Plumage (entire feathering) well developed at time of 1st flight (see cursory coverage of development under Reproduction, below), retained through winter into following spring, then succeeded by Basic I over about a 4-month period.

Differs from Basics in having much of head and upperparts darkish neutral color. **Iris** palish yellow at first; occipital spot (feathers whitish basally) present. "Mustache mark" absent or obscure. The **dorsum** often has a somewhat ragged appearance, because white (usually basal) portions of some feathers show. **Underparts** chin to tail white or near-white with an abdominal band of mostly elongated blackish markings, concentrated laterally. Others have more scattered smaller black markings, but the shield is typically white. Legs and **feet** yellow, talons black. **Tail** feathers grayed brown above, rather dingy below, with about 9 narrow dark transverse bars of approximately equal width, and the very tips whitish. **Wing** upper coverts as dorsum; flight feathers variably grayish (paler ventrally) with very dark bars; wing lining white with very dark markings scattered, not concentrated at leading edge near body and in carpal area. Thus the Juv. underwing does not have the conspicuous dark outline of Basic.

Prebasic I molting (out of Juv.). These are data on *borealis* trapped and examined in Wis. by Frances Hamerstrom (1971): Wing molting began in late Apr. or in early May, in some individuals later; tail molting began after the wings, was conspicuous in June, and continued through summer (in 1 individual to Oct.). In June there was a new cohort of Juv. birds recently out of the nest (not molting) plus yearlings (molting). The margin of the tail of the latter was uneven, the Juv. feathers being longer and narrower than incoming Basic I. In general, molting was more orderly in Prebasic I than subsequently.

Near Rochester, N.Y., many yearlings that are still migrating in May–June have missing flight feathers (L. and N. Moon 1985)—that is, they have begun molting.

Captives in Alaska, under a regimen possibly not as in the wild: the ♀ began Prebasic I 1st and required about 115 days, to July 6; the ♂ began later and required about 121 days, to Aug. 12 (Lowe 1978).

As in various raptors, if a Redtail in 1st winter or early spring (Juv.) loses a feather through accident, the replacement will have Basic characteristics. Thus a bird in Juv. feathering may acquire a more or less reddish tail feather (Basic character) or same with transverse barring (Basic plus Juv. characters). On attaining flight in Mont. a young *calurus* already had a red tail, its sibling a "normal" Juv. tail. The former was seen during the following 8 weeks, and the red faded considerably. Another Juv., photographed in Okla., had a vivid red tail. Both had dark transverse tail barring and lacked a broad subterminal band (Lowe 1978). A captive Juv. ♂ with damaged rectrices had Basic (reddish) ones spliced in; he suddenly became dominant over 2 large Juv. ♀♀ (Frances Hamerstrom).

"Color phases" Mostly melanistic birds; mentioned under various headings; no combination of characteristics is disjunct, because interbreeding occurs at random (is not assortative) in mixed populations. There seems no useful information on genetics of polymorphism in this highly variable bird.

Albinos More or less albinistic individuals are not rare in e. N. Am. but are scarcer to the w. All reported all-white individuals have dark eyes. In Ore. an "imperfect albino" ♂ (a hint of red in tail, a few dark feathers on head and body) was mated to a "normal" ♀ in 1977 and 1978; the young had "normal" feathering in both years. On several occasions the white ♂ chased an "immature" in "normal" feathering from the nesting area (Oakley and Eltzroth 1980). In N.Y., a white ♀ was mated to a "normal" ♂ (Devers 1982), and evidently the brood was "normal."

Measurements "Adult" (Basic) *B. j. borealis* from "all parts of the range" (Friedmann 1950): 35 ♂ BEAK from cere 23.5–28.5 mm., av. 25.5, WING across chord 337–396, av. 369.6, TAIL 197–240, av. 215.6; and 27 ♀ BEAK from cere 25.5–31.3 mm., av. 26.9, WING across chord 370–427, av. 388.8, and TAIL 214.5–254, av. 230.3. The sexes obviously overlap in size.

Eastern Redtails in Basic feathering and sexed internally, mean plus standard deviation: 8 ♂ WING across chord 385.5 ± 46.77 mm., TAIL 208.5 ± 7.96; and 6 ♀ WING across chord 391.67 ± 14.25, and TAIL 215 ± 8.02. Juv. 24 ♂ WING across chord 360 ± 9.03, TAIL 215.67 ± 6.66, and 42 ♀ WING across chord 393.4 ± 28.98, and TAIL (of 44) 229 ± 10.84. Sex for sex, the Juv. tail is longer than Basic. (Data from H. Mueller.)

In another series livetrapped in Wis. and not sexed internally, 29 Juv. had WING chord above or below a span of overlap—that is, birds may be sexed by this meas.: ♂ to 370 mm., overlap 370–395, and ♀ over 395 (Geller and Temple 1983).

Weight Mueller's birds (see above) in Wis., trapped except in Jan., Feb., and Apr., sexed internally and minus crop contents: Juv. 32 ♂ 698–1,296 gm., av. 945.3, and 24 ♀ 904–1,455, av. 1,222.4. Lighter and heavier birds were distributed quite evenly through the seasons. "Adults" 4 ♀ late Nov.–early Dec., 1,305–1,723 gm., av. 1,468, and a ♂ in Dec. 750 gm.

Averages of Redtails: 108 ♂ 1,028 gm. and 100 ♀ 1,224 (the Craigheads 1956)—evidently from specimen labels and subspecies not indicated (mostly *calurus* and *borealis?*).

Hybrids None reported. In Scotland an escaped ♂ mated with a ♀ *B. buteo* and produced fertile eggs (J. B. Murray 1970). At the Topeka, Kans., zoo a flying cage contained 3 Redtails and a ♂ Swainson's Hawk; a ♀ Redtail and the Swainson's displayed to each other (Wolhuter and Kish 1970). Presumably they formed a pair bond, since the ♀ frequently attacked an additional ♂ Redtail when it was put in the cage.

Fostering The Redtail has fostered the Prairie Falcon (Fyfe 1976), the Bay-winged Hawk, and others. A nestling Redtail was fed by a ♀ Goshawk; their nests were close (Gammon, in Shy 1982). Three young Redtails were reared by a Great Horned Owl (Hovingh and Ponshair 1951).

Individual identification in hand A study of captives has revealed that each bird is unique in dorsal scale pattern of middle toe, with differences even between siblings; furthermore, right and left toe differ on the same individual (Stauber 1984).

Geographical variation Moderate in the species, aside from occurrence of color phases and their proportionate numbers. Taverner (1927), for example, could find "no constant difference" in size to define the various named Canadian populations. Northerly birds tend to be larger, except for smaller (nonmigratory?) birds of the nw. N. Am. coast. Color saturation of "normal" phase birds correlates to some extent with temperature and humidity, the breeding birds of warm dry areas being somewhat paler. To the s. there are small birds on is. of the Caribbean perimeter. In N. Am. n. of Mexico some geographical variation in clutch size has been reported (see Reproduction, below).

Affinities Ancestral stock presumably evolved in S. Am., where there are presently many *Buteo* species. The genus, known from fossils in N. Am., spread from S. or N. Am. to the W. Indies, Galapagos, Hawaii, and the Old World. *B. jamaicensis* is a large generalized N. Am. representative. *B. ventralis* of s. S. Am. (which has been considered conspecific with the N. Am. bird) is so similar to it that Juv. birds of the 2 continents are indistinguishable. For some discussion, see Voous and de Vries (1978).

RALPH S. PALMER

SUBSPECIES Comparing individuals that fall within the range of what may be termed "normal" coloration and pattern, av. subspecific differences are slight. Comparing birds that include all individual variation, av. regional size differences seem to be minimal for a bird occupying diverse habitats in a vast breeding range. From Taverner (1927) and from examining the specimens he had plus many others, it is evident that large series (of which there are few) of regional populations include occasional small individuals. The spread of meas. in such series is much greater than in the few specimens available for most subspecies (including all except 1 outside the *Handbook* area).

Friedmann (1950) measured chord of unflattened WING (chord of arc) and Storer (1962) measured "wing (arc)," presumably over curve of unflattened wing; both are included in L. Brown and Amadon (1968 **2**). On basis of data at hand, WING across chord (not flattened) for the species collectively is approximately ♂ 335–400 mm. and ♀ 355–430. Entities listed below vary within these spans as averaging larger, medium-sized, and smaller birds, but coloration and pattern are crucial in attempting to assign "normal" individuals to most named populations.

The trinomials "*harlani*" and "*kriderii*" are not recognized here, the birds from certain areas that they purportedly designate being refered to vernacularly as "Harlan's" (dark) and "Krider's" (light) Redtails. This is a convenience. In the large genus *Buteo*, more than ½ of the species have dark individuals occurring among "normal" birds, and nomenclatural separation of them is not even considered. The exception has been the Redtail, which has a few dark birds in various regional popula-tions and, to the nw., melanistic birds nearly (but not exclusively) supplanting "nor-mal" individuals. That "Harlan's" has nearly exclusive occupation of an area does not equate it with a subspecies. Individuals identifiable as e. (*borealis*) and w. (*calurus*) Redtails occur even in Alaska. To the s., "Krider's" Redtails, which also must be reckoned with, seems to have sole occupation of little or no breeding range. Birds assignable to either "morph" can be sorted out, more or less, by coloring and tail pattern. Physical dimensions are not diagnostic. Some individuals in appearance are combinations between or among recognizable *calurus*/"Harlan's"/"Krider's"/*bor-ealis* birds and among these and/or their progeny. Differences can be demonstrably great, even among siblings.

On basis of extant information, it is prudent to refer to nw. variants vernacularly and leave open the question whether they might be included in expanded definitions of *calurus* or *borealis* or occupy an area of intergradation where both of these still occur. When dark, light, and mongrel nw. Redtails (plus dark ones from within what is currently mapped as *calurus* range) are lined up in museum trays adjacent to *calurus* and *borealis* as currently defined, they appear to rest comfortably.

In our area The sequence of treatment here is more or less from n. to s., but the "Harlan's" and "Krider's" birds are placed after the w. birds (*calurus*). For a graphic presentation of the entire species breeding range with areas labeled trinomially, see map 61 in L. Brown and Amadon (1968 2).

borealis (Gmelin)—descr. and meas. given above. Size variable but av. large. Spec-imens in Natl. Mus. Nat. Hist.: tails of nearly all have some dark barring on outermost feathers; those with plain inner feathers have faint barring on inner vane of outermost feather; those having faint black traces of bars on inner feathers have fairly well developed bars on outer feathers; extent of markings on underparts is not helpful in predicting tail pattern (M. R. Browning). In general, *borealis* birds might be thought of as *fuertesi* (see beyond) with added belly band.

Either darker individuals from elsewhere occasionally occur e. as breeders or else variation in e. birds occasionally includes very heavily marked or otherwise dark birds. A dark pair bred annually 1898–1902 in Iowa (Keyes 1907, or see N. A. Wood 1932); C. W. Townsend (1913) saw a "very dark" bird, its tail red dorsally, in s. Labrador (=Que.); Rand (1948b) reported a dark bird shot at its nest on Prince Edward I.

Breeds in e. N. Am. from somewhere in the boreal forest zone down into upper peninsular Fla. (presumably intergrading there with *umbrinus*) and w. to the gulf coast; it intergrades with *fuertesi* in a broad area about in the longitude of e. Tex.; in the nw. (as in Alta.), in typical form, it largely disappears in the jumble of birds that show tremendous variation in color and pattern. A few red-tailed birds having pre-dominantly *borealis* characters occur (some even in winter) in interior Alaska. Some n. birds, including all prebreeders, migrate long distances; well to the s., at least breeders are resident. Recorded in winter to s. Fla. and s.-cent. Mexico. Recorded in Bermuda.

[W. E. C. Todd (1950) named some quite heavily pigmented birds *abieticola*, but it is not a valid race and was not included in the 1957 A.O.U. *Check-list*.]

calurus Cassin—highly variable. In many the venter is some variant of buff, toward

101

rusty, some a deep reddish tan. Tibia heavily barred (usually). Some dark birds have more or less light in the wing lining. In definitive feathering, tail usually a somewhat grayed or diluted brownish or a reddish brown with multiple blackish barring. (Juv. Redtails have neutral-colored tails with numerous narrow, dark bars; barring persists into definitive stages in several populations, including this one, the bars then fewer and wider.) Both white and gray nestling down-B have been reported. From interbreeding, "color phases" are bridged by individual variation, from white-breasted palish brown birds through others having tan or rufescent ("red") venter to some that are largely blackish except for much of the tail. See Friedmann (1950) for further details.

Although there are satisfactory records of occurrence in interior Alaska, breeding range has usually been given as extending from interior (and s. coastal) B.C. and s. Alta. to w. Nebr. and s. into Mexico (Chihuahua, Sonora, all of Baja Calif.). Presumably it intergrades with adjoining populations (and n. limits may need adjustment depending on provenance of dark birds). The occasional e. breeding of dark birds was mentioned under the preceding subspecies. Many, especially n., birds are migratory. Occurs in winter in much of its breeding range; also spreads e. onto the Great Plains, being quite regular in fall as far e. as Wis. Recorded s. into Guatemala and n. Nicaragua. An "adult" was taken in Panama in 1870 (Hellmayr and Conover 1949). Stragglers reportedly into s. Ont., Ill., Pa., N.Y., N.J., Miss., and undoubtedly elsewhere.

Large in size "Adults" from "all parts" of range: 37 ♂ WING across chord 358–404 mm.. av. 387, TAIL 207–237, av. 223.4; and 45 ♀ WING ACROSS CHORD 386–428 MM., AV. 411.2, AND TAIL 220–249, av. 236.9 (Friedmann 1950).

Weight Idaho: 90 ♂ av. 957 gm. and 113 ♀ 1,154 (Steenhof 1983).

The following **color variants, designated by vernacular names only,** are placed here arbitrarily but could as well have been placed between the 2 subspecies treated above. Color photographs: Mindell (1985).

"Harlan's"—dark nw. Redtails. They were treated as a species at least from Audubon (1840) to G. Sutton (1967); as a subspecies of Redtail at least from Ridgway (1890) to Mindell (1985); and herein as melanistic individuals, undesignated as to subspecific name(s). Much has been written about which Redtails are a "color phase" of what—see Friedmann (1950), for example. Dark birds are greatly preponderant in interior Alaska/Yukon; s. in interior Canada, the proportion evidently diminishes and there is more interbreeding with birds having other characteristics. Even in interior Alaska, it was Lowe's (1978) experience that some individuals are so mixed in characteristics that they cannot be labeled subspecifically.

For mixed pairs of Redtails at Canadian locations, see Taverner (1927, 1936); for Alaska, Kessel and Springer (1966), Lowe (1978), and Mindell (1983a). North of Fairbanks, Lowe observed 285 "adult" Redtails, characterized as follows: *calurus* (tail "not typical") 7.9%, atypical *borealis* (basal part of tail variable, not reddish) 3%, atypical "Harlan's" 83.9%, and unassignable barred-tailed birds (light to melanistic, including 1 each with broad, dark subterminal tail-band as in *B. buteo* of Eurasia) 5.2%. Incidentally, there are 2 records of *borealis* from the Mackenzie Delta.

"Harlan's" breeds in interior Alaska, n. nearly to a line from s. of the Seward Pen. to the s. foothills of the Brooks Range and e. in Canada in Yukon Terr. or into the lower

Mackenzie drainage; and s. into interior B.C. or thereabouts, becoming largely mongrelized to the s. Recorded n. in Alaska to the Barrow region.

Some birds of breeding age remain all year on boreal range (on or near their territories), if food is available, but dark birds are also highly migratory, going s. in Sept.–late Nov. and n. in Apr.–early May. Although they are very widely scattered, principal winter occurrence is on the s. Great Plains from Kans. and Mo. down into Tex.—some thus having traveled long distances. In winter many are interspersed among resident *fuertesi* and migrant and resident *borealis* and *calurus;* see Habits, below.

Although the provenance of some birds is uncertain (is a melanistic bird of Calif. or Alaskan origin?), dark birds have been recorded in winter in all states w. of the Mississippi except (for lack of observers?) Nev. Southerly occurrences extend to n.- cent. Mexico. East of the Mississippi they have been reported (mostly in winter) in at least Wis., Mich., Ill., Ind., Ky., La., Miss., S.C., Va., Pa., and Mass.

Large in size Judging from meas. and wt. in N. A. Wood (1932); in winter, av. heavier than *borealis,* ♀♀ especially. "Adults" 30 ♂ (from Ark., N.D., Kans., Tex., and Man.) WING across chord 365–390 mm., av. 380.9, TAIL 203–224, av. 211.2; and 31 ♀ (Ark., Kans., N.D., Man., Alta., and Alaska) WING across chord 390–430 mm., av. 409.1, and TAIL 207.5–238, av. 226.2 (Friedmann 1950). Note that most of these are not from breeding range.

"Krider's"—very variable light (or pale) birds; dorsal coloring neutral (seldom any browns); underparts mostly (to all) white, often extending to include most of head; tail very variable, in many white with more or less of a subterminal dark bar plus frag- mented narrower bars, yet others have the tail some shade of gray (appears dirty) with or without white tip or subterminal darker bar, or with latter plus narrow bars.

Reportedly breeds in s. Canada from extreme w. Ont. w. into Alta. and in coter- minous U.S. from Minn. and w. Nebr. w. into Colo., Wyo., and Mont. Even far beyond in interior Alaska, however, a small percentage of individuals has predomi- nantly "Krider's" characteristics. In winter, some pale birds occur within breeding limits as here stated, but others have occurred s. as far as La., s. Tex., N.Mex., Ariz., and Mexico (Durango, Zacatecas). Probably in greatest numbers in upper Mississippi drainage—that is, in the flight path of dark Redtails (which are concentrated s. of light Redtails at this season). Light birds have occurred e. into at least Ill., Ky., S.C., and Ga.

Large in size "Adults" 8 ♂ WING across chord 352–400 mm., av. 379.5, TAIL 204– 232, av. 221.3; and 10 ♀ WING across chord 393–432 mm., av. 413, TAIL 219–248, av. 237.5 (Friedmann 1950).

alascensis Grinnell—dorsum very dark (as compared with "normal" *calurus*); ab- domen has reddish brown markings (reduced melanin); tail reddish with wavy crossbars. The few birds measured to date are notably **small**—largest ♀ smaller than almost all ♂♂ from elsewhere in Canada. Even so, Taverner (1936) gave it only "guarded acceptance" as a recognizable race. "Color phases": Taverner mentioned an erythromelanistic ♂ that he had figured earlier (1927, plate 2). Said to occur in coastal areas from Yakutat Bay, Alaska, to s. Vancouver I., B.C., but not known to nest s. of the Queen Charlottes. Probably not migratory; if so, records are lacking.

"Adults" 7 ♂ WING across chord 334–362 mm., av. 347.7, TAIL 193.6–243, av. 217.2; and 5 ♀ WING across chord 358–363 mm., av. 361.3, and TAIL 217.9–247, av. 228 (Friedmann 1950).

umbrinus Bangs—much like *borealis*, but tail has narrow and incomplete transverse dark bands in addition to the subterminal band. "Color phases" not reported. Breeds at present in s. ⅗ of peninsular Fla. (formerly also to San Mateo and Cedar Keys). The resident Redtails of the Bahamas (Grand Bahama, Abaco, and probably Andros I.) are also presumably of this subspecies (J. Bond 1980). Straggler to e. N.C.

Large in size "Adults" from Fla.: 4 ♂ WING across chord 398–400 mm., av. 398.8, TAIL 222.5–227, av. 224.9; and 6 ♀ WING across chord 373–432 mm., av. 409.7, and TAIL 218.5–242, av. 233.4 (Friedmann 1950).

Sightings, especially on other Bahamian is., may pertain to vagrant birds or (most unlikely) Swainson's Hawk.

fuertesi Sutton—in definitive feathering might be described as diluted *borealis* or as paler overall than most light examples of *calurus*. Abdominal band usually much reduced and consisting only of brownish markings laterally; tail reddish, varying from plain to having a broad subterminal dark band to having also several (generally incomplete) bars. Dark markings on primary under coverts reduced, in Juv. Plumage often lacking. The Juv. abdominal band varies but often extends over much area, rather densely marked dark. "Color phases" not reported. Evidently resident, perhaps with some seasonal dispersal. Intergrades with *borealis* about in e. Tex. and to the n. in a wide zone about in the latitude of Kans. and Mo.; to the w. it intergrades with *calurus*, probably in the longitude of w. Tex.; and s. in Mexico (Nuevo León-Chihuahua) presumably with *hadropus*. Recorded in Nov. in Sonora. Van Tyne and Sutton (1937) mentioned a ♂ apparently mated to a ♀ *calurus* in Tex.

Large in size "Adults" WING across chord 8 ♂ 385–402 mm., av. 393.2, and 4 ♀ 425–436, av. 430 (Friedmann 1950).

Extralimital Probably none of the following are migratory. They are listed in this sequence: Caribbean/Mexico and Cent Am./Pacific. Some trinomials may need reappraisal when material is available to encompass individual variation.

solitudinis Barbour—similar to *umbrinus* but smaller; not highly differentiated. "Color phases" not reported. Cuba and Isla de la Juventud [Isle of Pines]. (The Bahamian birds are assigned to *umbrinus;* see earlier.) **Medium-sized:** WING across chord 2 ♂ 357–382 mm. and 2 ♀ 397–412 (Friedmann 1950).

jamaicensis (Gmelin)—abdominal band largely dark (to black) rather than browns; tail deep reddish brown with subterminal blackish band. Jamaica, Hispaniola, Puerto Rico, and various smaller is. extending to include St. Kitts. "Color phases" not reported. **Small-sized** (about as *alascensis*): "adults" WING across chord of 5 ♂ 330–339 mm., av. 335.2, and 6 ♀ 350–371, av. 365.8 (Friedmann 1950).

The following 3 are compared in a photograph in Storer (1962):

hadropus Storer—quite like pale *calurus;* only moderately dark dorsally; abdominal band consists of well-defined transverse barring plus some dark longitudinal streaking, thus contrasting with white or nearly white of "shield" (upper breast). "Color phases": Storer (1962) examined a dark bird. Highlands of s. Mexico from Oaxaca n. and w. at least as far as Jalisco. **Medium in size:** WING meas. over curve of 20 ♂ 348–390 mm., mean 379, and 13 ♀ 377–420, mean 397 (Storer).

kemsiesi Oberholser—pale overall with abdominal band poorly indicated or lacking; flanks with pale rufous barring. "Color phases": Storer (1962) examined 2 dark specimens. Highlands of Chiapas (extreme s. Mexico), Guatemala, Honduras, El Salvador, and n. Nicaragua. **Medium in size:** WING meas. over curve of 8 ♂ 368–382 mm., mean 375, and 6 ♀ 377–420, mean 397 (Storer).

costaricensis Ridgway—heavily pigmented dorsally; white of breast contrasts with deep rufous abdominal band containing black streaks and spots; flanks unbarred deep rufous. "Color phases" not reported. Uplands of Costa Rica and w. Panama. **Medium in size:** WING meas. over curve: 6 ♂ 352–393 mm., mean 376, and 8 ♀ 376–408, mean 395 (Storer).

fumosus Nelson—similar to *socorroensis* (below), except head–neck plain sooty brownish; upperparts quite uniform dusky; venter washed cinnamon (is not white) with some black streaks, the sides and flanks more toward reddish brown. In "immature" (Juv., not Basic I) Plumage, is. birds differ from mainland ones in having the throat dark brown (P. R. Grant 1965). "Color phases" not reported. Tres Marias Is. off the coast of Nayarit, w. Mexico. **Medium in size:** WING across chord 2 ♂ 368–370 mm., 1 ♀ 395 (Friedmann 1950). Length of long tarsus diagnostic of sex; see P. R. Grant (1965) for further details.

socorroensis Ridgway—authors generally follow Friedmann (1950), who compared 3 specimens with pale *calurus*. In 1978 and 1981, Jehl and Parkes (1982) found the birds to be "highly variable but predominantly melanic." They were not distinguishable from *calurus* on basis of color, and it was suggested that validity must rest on their more robust legs and feet (precise data lacking). The birds feed partly on land crabs, as known earlier. Resident on Socorro I., over 230 mi. (370 km.) off the s. tip of Baja Calif., Mexico, at approximately lat. 19° N. Population estimated at 15–20 pairs (Jehl and Parkes). **Medium in size:** WING across chord 2 ♂ 368–385 mm., and 1 ♀ 415 (Friedmann 1950). WING chord of another ♀ 385 mm. and wt. 1,260 gm., little fat (Jehl and Parkes). RALPH S. PALMER

FIELD IDENTIFICATION In our area Large stoutish buteo; wings comparatively broad, distally rounded, span about 4 ft., with 4 notched primaries (same as in most confusing species). Any reddish in the tail identifies a bird as a Redtail (nearest is a warm tan in the Ferruginous Hawk)—but a great many individuals n. from the Canadian prairies and a few w. of there (which occur also as migrants or winterers elsewhere) have tails that vary from largely blackish through intermediates to white. They soar with wings nearly horizontal.

Basic Plumage EASTERN and many other birds have the diagnostic reddish tail, are dark dorsally, variably light ventrally, and an often incomplete dark abdominal band (markings concentrated laterally). Wing lining white or light with conspicuous black "thumb mark"; the entire underwing has a notably dark perimeter (leading edge, flight feathers distally). At a great distance some Redtails can still be identified by the squarish shape of the light "window" basally in the primaries as viewed in transmitted

105

light. Closer, when hovering motionless and viewed head-on, often some white is visible in the carpal area of leading edge of wing.

For other Redtails, see earlier pages here. The observer also should be familiar with other buteos and *Asturina* with which this species can be confused.

DARK BUTEOS (an arbitrary separation) often cannot be identified to species—and certainly not to place of origin—with any confidence under various field conditions. These terse guidelines, however, may be helpful: **1** Redtail—see above; wing lining variable to darker than bases of flight feathers; venter often darker than underside of tail; **2** Swainson's Hawk—comparatively narrow and pointed wings with 3 notched primaries; under tail coverts white; only species that soars with pronounced dihedral; **3** Ferruginous Hawk—underside of tail palish, adjoining black under tail coverts; hovers; **4** Rough-legged Hawk—if so dark as to have almost no visible pattern, bases of primaries and of tail light; buoyant flight; often hovers; **5** Broad-winged Hawk—if comparatively diminutive size does not eliminate it at a glance, the rare dark individuals have very few and wide alternating white and black tail-bars; and **6** Red-shouldered Hawk (not a *Buteo*)—no "dark phase" known; reddish venter; very broken and contrasty underwing pattern; in flight at long distance (when other details not evident), the light "window" basally in the primaries is crescent shaped. Juv. birds—see below.

There is every individual variation imaginable, however, from the darkest Redtails through those that might be grouped as intermediate in coloration (tail not necessarily red) and pattern to variably light individuals. The lightest of Canadian prairie birds have pale heads and almost entire undersurface white. Perhaps the most difficult to distinguish from light Redtails are: **1** Swainson's—only 3 primaries notched; white venter usually has some dark on throat and upper breast, underside of flight feathers of wing and tail finely barred dark; and **2** Ferruginous—much white ventrally, but with rich rusty flanks, dark "thumb mark" notably conspicuous on white wing lining, and underside of tail pale with more or less of a darkish distal bar.

Juvenal Plumage Tail color is neutral (no reddish) in young Redtails. Eastern birds and many others have a sort of gray or gray-brown tail with numerous, usually narrow, dark transverse bars; venter light with longitudinal dark streaking concentrated laterally on abdomen; underwing pattern not highly contrasting. Many others, especially w. and nw. (migrant to the s.), reflect the enormous variation in tail (blackish to white) and other parts of older birds. Even in hand, some have been mistaken for other *Buteo* species.

Perched Juv. Redtails may show a mottled or ragged dorsum (scattered light feather bases evident), which is lacking or greatly reduced in older birds. Soaring Juv. birds generally appear slimmer, and the perimeter of the wing is darker (but not contrastingly so) compared with birds in Basic feathering.

In brief, Redtails are a challenge, and any competent observer must list some sightings as of large buteos not certainly identified to species. Novices have enlarged the problem, for example, by mistaking an albinistic Redtail for a light Gyrfalcon.

In **nestling** Redtails the feathering usually extends at least halfway down on the tarsus (in Swainson's it is almost naked; in the Ferruginous it extends all the way down), but banders identify them by their parents. RALPH S. PALMER

VOICE   The usual call, when soaring or occasionally hunting, is a drawn-out downward slurred scream, hoarse and sibilant, of at least 2–3 sec. duration; an initial slight rise in pitch. Calls differ in pitch for various reasons, probably including a sex difference. Quite similar to scream of the Redshoulder. There also are variants. Unless otherwise indicated, the following is from Fitch et al. (1946b).

The scream, uttered from a perch and in flight, seems to be a territorial call. Possibly it may be used to startle quarry from cover.

A modification, a loud piercing chirp, *chwirk*, appears to express "excited and territorial assertion" and is heard most often when mates are in flight together, especially after a territorial encounter. A pair circled in N.Mex., the smaller bird carrying a snake; at least 1 bird uttered a loud, low, and raspy *hrrr* (in series), apparently the *chwirk* of Fitch et al.; it may represent some stage of "courtship feeding" (Hubbard 1974).

A "low grunting or quacking" *gank* with ducklike nasal quality, repeated several times. Little carrying power. Evidently conversational between mates, perched or flying; may be the Redtail's most common utterance.

"Adults" in Calif.: "hunger calls" like those heard from "fledglings" are sometimes heard in late winter; on Feb. 17 a ♀ was heard giving these calls, and the same pair was seen copulating the next day. In Alaska, incubating ♀♀ "beg" similarly for food from their mates (Lowe 1978).

Nestlings first have peeping notes of a "soft, sleepy quality" when moving about or aroused by a parent's arrival. Half-grown nestlings occasionally scream when disturbed—a soft whistle lacking the piercing quality of its adult counterpart. Different from it is the hunger call, a 2-syllabled *klee-uck* in series; this was not heard in Calif. until the young had flown (Fitch et al.), but in Alaska it was heard from about 11 days of age (Lowe).

A mechanical sound "not very unlike the rush of distant water" of a bird in rapid descent during Sky-dance (Warren, cited in Bent 1937).

The Redtail's scream is imitated (not exactly) by the Blue Jay and (better) by the Mockingbird; there is a recording of a mocker imitating a jay imitating a Redtail.

RALPH S. PALMER

HABITAT   **Nesting** Redtails prefer a tall tree—of any species—with good aerial access to the site (within the crown) plus a suitable nearby hunting area. This combination is employed in a great spectrum of environments extending from coniferous and other boreal forest, through mixed and deciduous woodland, to saguaros in hot desert and tropical rain forest. Some examples in our area include spruce forest in Alaska and Canada, aspen bluffs and wooded stream valleys on the prairies, trees in canyons, all habitats from sea level to 9,000 ft. in Calif., and mixed or deciduous forests, woodlots, and groves almost anywhere.

For New Eng. there is some information in Bent (1937) on expansion or shift in occupied habitat, mostly from supplanting the declining Redshoulder population as woodlands were reduced by cutting; see Reproduction, below. The following are other regional studies of change.

In s. Sask., the control of fires on the once-open prairies and the planting of trees and

107

shrubs has resulted in a semiopen tree-grassland mosaic and consequent great spread and increase of once-rare nesting Redtails. There is some indication that Redtail numbers peaked around 1970 and that subsequent destruction of trees has started a decline (Houston and Bechard 1983).

In an area e. of Syracuse, N.Y., William Minor has watched Redtails for nearly 40 years. The hawk has adapted to man and apparently now nests in every available niche, including suburbia and even urban areas to some extent if near enough to an open hunting area. The mowed and fenced lateral strips along main highways also create an "edge effect"—the hawks nest back in the trees and hunt in the open. Passing vehicles do not disturb them, and the fences limit human encroachment. A few nests are in trees standing in permanent water, a few others in wet woods. Nesting trees include white pine, hemlock, and deciduous species (and Redtail nests are convenient for the Great Horned Owl). Construction of major travel lanes, however, has fostered the spread of *Phragmites communis*, which effectively covers large areas of former Redtail hunting territory. For additional information, see W. and M. Minor (1981). In Mich., the Redtail nested 2 consecutive years each in suburban Detroit and Flint—in the latter city in a large white pine overhanging a residence (Hull 1980).

As a migrant and winterer The Redtail needs elevated perches and a food supply whether in wilderness or elsewhere. Winter density of these species (or with others interspersed) can be many times greater than on breeding range. It is widely noted that Juv. birds winter close to towns, because they are less fearful of people than they are of older Redtails, which dominate them in unsettled areas. In Calif., from loss of much habitat and from adapting to current conditions, foraging young Redtails especially are forced to hunt on grassy freeway medians and vacant lots. Space is at a premium, and tremendous numbers are concentrated in small areas. In the Los Angeles basin, for example, there were 100+ Redtails in an area of less than 4 sq. mi. in the fall of 1977. Such places are de facto wildlife refuges in a sea of houses and industrial developments (P. Bloom).

For habitat partitioning and coexistence with other raptors in spring–summer, see Reproduction, and, for other seasons, Habits, both below. Note also vertical stratification, as when Juv. Redtails avoid aggressive attacks of older ones by flying above the defended airspace of the latter.   RALPH S. PALMER

DISTRIBUTION   (See map, which omits arbitrary boundaries of subspecies or other units.)

Breeds   From w. interior Alaska into Mackenzie and e. in the forest belt to include part of Que. and possibly into Labrador, also Nfld.; thence s. more or less throughout N. and parts of Cent. Am. into w. Panama. Also is. including PACIFIC Tres Marias and Socorro and ATLANTIC Bahamas, some Greater and n. Lesser Antilles.

In other seasons   Found throughout much of breeding range, but many withdraw from n. areas, especially in severe seasons. For coterminous U.S. and a small portion of s. Canada, Bock and Lepthien (1976) diagrammed relative numbers, based on Christmas censuses. The only empty quadrant (lack of observers?) was w. of L. Superior. The birds were most plentiful in Pacific coastal and Mexican border states; there were

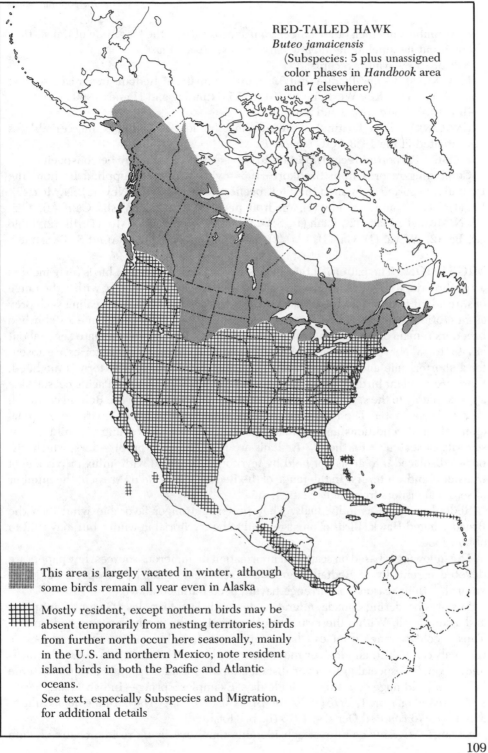

RED-TAILED HAWK
Buteo jamaicensis
(Subspecies: 5 plus unassigned
color phases in *Handbook* area
and 7 elsewhere)

This area is largely vacated in winter, although
some birds remain all year even in Alaska

Mostly resident, except northern birds may be
absent temporarily from nesting territories; birds
from further north occur here seasonally, mainly
in the U.S. and northern Mexico; note resident
island birds in both the Pacific and Atlantic
oceans.
See text, especially Subspecies and Migration,
for additional details

lesser numbers in much other range; from approximately the longitude of Kans., they thinned out ne. (including in New Eng.) and se. (Ga., Fla.).

NFLD.   Few winter records.

FLA. KEYS   Generally rare, but 32 "mostly immature" Redtails in a mixed soaring flock of raptors at Key West on Oct. 31, 1955 (Hundley and Hames 1960).

BERMUDA   rare spring and autumn.

ENGLAND   Alleged natural occurrence in 1850, long regarded as unacceptable, is perpetuated in the 1983 AOU *Check-list.*

S. AM.   Purported records pertain to *B. ventralis* (which may be conspecific).

Combining records from Brodkorb (1964) with later ones supplied by him, the Redtail is reported as **fossil** in the Pleistocene of Calif. (4 sites), Nev. (2), N.Mex. (2), Va. (1), Fla. (5), and Barbados (1), and from **prehistoric** sites in Wash., Calif. (3), Ariz. (2), N.Mex. (1), Idaho (2), Utah (1), S.D. (8), Ark. (1), Iowa (1), Mo. (1), Ill. (2), Ohio (1), Pa. (2), W.Va. (1), Ga. (1), Fla. (2), and Puerto Rico (1).   RALPH S. PALMER

MIGRATION   The pattern of the species is as follows: 1 Many n. birds (may include all prebreeders) migrate varied—often long—distances s., wintering within the range of s. resident Redtails. That is, where snow cover is long-lasting, concealing such prey as microtines, birds tend to have extended absences. Even so, some established breeders remain on or near their territories all year. 2 At an intermediate zone, about lat. 43° to 48° N, winter is shorter; here Redtails that vacate their territories are absent for a shorter time and evidently travel variable distances. The pattern is modified; there are resident birds (none at any age known to migrate) up the Pacific coastal side approximately to the s. border of Alaska, and on the Atlantic side the Redtail occurs all year in Nova Scotia. The location of this lat. zone thus varies both with av. regional climatological conditions and annually to some extent, depending on mildness or severity of season. 3 Farther s., Redtails are resident, with prebreeders (which disperse) displaced into areas not held by territorial birds and with influx or passage of transients and winterers. In the range of the Redtail s. beyond n. Mexico, the number of seasonal visitors from higher lats. is small.

Redtails migrate as individuals. They prefer a stronger favorable wind than the Broad-winged Hawk. Birds of any age tend to be territorial in winter but may shift to obtain food.

The following is based on scattered information in numerous sources; few papers are devoted essentially to Redtail migration. Treatment is not by subspecies or color "morph," their seasonal occurrence having been outlined above.

In states bordering Canada, migration generally lasts for at least 3 months in spring and again in fall. Within these spans peak periods show yearly variation and timing. Thus a cold weather front can hasten movement; inclement weather and lack of thermals can halt it; an ideal air movement, including thermals, can cause the birds (older cohorts especially) to cover distance rapidly. Under special conditions, some localities yield huge counts on a single day. Examples: spring—Indian Head, Sask., 1,000 passed on Apr. 1, 1976 (1976 *Am. Birds* **30** 856); fall—Hawk Ridge near Duluth, Minn., 1,376 counted Oct. 14, 1973 (P. B. Hofslund).

Spring   Migrants go n. over considerable time, overflying residents already into their breeding cycle. Early arrivals reach the n. states while the ground is still under snow, the weather is cold, and thermals for soaring are scarce. The birds travel at moderate height, usually under 200 ft. This movement is overlapped by the later span of yearling migration. Along the Canadian boundary in the Great Lakes region, these young (and some older birds) are still moving in late May, some even well into June; they continue to arrive while breeders are well into nesting and are believed to return near where they hatched and so must find room outside occupied territories.

There is migration in Feb.–Mar. in n. Mexico and up into the U.S. (residents have eggs in s. U.S. in Feb.); near Rochester, N.Y., however, arrival has been noted as early as Feb. 15. Very early n. dates may be for birds that wintered not far s.—that is, had vacated their territories rather briefly. For spring dates for many localities, see accounts of various populations in Bent (1937).

Fall More s. migrant young, having attained flight within a comparatively long warm season, have time for premigration dispersal—including n. and laterally. Farther n., the abbreviated warm season precludes this; see, for example, Luttich et al. (1971) for Alta. In Alaska, where there is heavy movement in early and mid-Sept., "adults" are said to migrate before "immatures" (Kessel and Springer 1966), which is the reverse of what is said to obtain elsewhere. Fall migration ends to the n. with arrival of snow cover. Across s. Canada and adjoining U.S., Juv. birds are moving in Aug.; then they go s. principally from mid-Sept. through the 1st 10 days of Oct.; on av., this cohort probably winters farther s. than older migrants. The latter, in these lats., begin moving in early Oct., with high numbers passing from well along in that month to past mid-Nov.; their migration usually ceases about mid-Dec. There are numerous fall migration dates in Bent (1937).

The above indicates separate peaks for numbers of migrant Juv. and older birds in spring and fall, a frequent bimodal pattern in raptors.

Geller and Temple (1983) suggested that Juv. early migrants in Wis. are from very n. areas, which would seem to agree with dates when melanistic (n.) migrants arrive in the Dakotas, then Ark. and Okla.

There have been 42 recoveries in Mexico of birds banded as nestlings in 9 w. U.S. states (Steenhof et al. 1984).

Some variables Some mature birds remain far n. on or near their territories all year, presumably preferring to remain if conditions are tolerable. Near Fairbanks, Alaska, a bird identifiable by some white primaries spent 3 consecutive winters in the same territory (Lowe 1978). In early autumn at least, Redtail movements can be influenced by a local abundance of easily obtained food. For example, there have been temporary w. concentrations in Aug. of wandering Juv. birds where ground squirrels were abundant. In s. Mich., Juv. Redtails remained in winter only when voles were abundant (the Craigheads 1956). On the other hand, when winter is long and harsh, as in 1983–1984, many more Redtails than usual were reported in ne. Mexico (A. R. Phillips).

Terrain and wind Topographic features like mts. and lakes funnel large numbers of Redtails through certain locations, such as along shores and around the ends of the Great Lakes. Redtails also find more updrafts for soaring along n.-s. trending ridges and mt. foothills. In autumn, migrants more or less fan out to the s.; this includes a tendency for some nw. birds to occur se., as Houston (1967) demonstrated from banding recoveries. Apparently they are drifted by prevailing winds; many are 1st-fall birds, but some are older, providing regular e. records of w. Redtails (*B. j. calurus*) in Minn., "Krider's" (almost all Juv.?) to Wis., and "Harlan's" to Minn.

Three regional studies Southwestern Idaho (Steenhof et al. 1984): The birds winter w. of those banded in Sask. by Houston (1967). The Idaho young remain there for 2 months after attaining flight, then travel long distances and with a strong directional bias; 9 of 12 distant recoveries were se. of the study area—6 in coastal lowlands in Mexico (Michoacan 3, Sinaloa 2) and Guatemala (1); also, toward the w. coast of Mexico (5) and sw. Guatemala (1) (this last 4,205 km. from sw. Idaho). Some Redtails returned to the Idaho study area early—3 were found after Jan. 15 within 100 km. of where they hatched. One Idaho bird nested 6 km. from where it had hatched. Redtails marked when in Basic feathering occupied the same territory for 1, 3, and 10 consecutive years.

California (data from P. Bloom): The Redtail not only nests in virtually all habitats up to 9,000 ft., but large numbers of transients and winterers are in Calif. Of 35 recoveries of birds banded as nestlings, 26 moved less than 50 mi. When a s. Calif. nestling later traveled over 100 mi., direction generally was n.; if banded as a nestling in n. Calif. and later moving over 100 mi., it went s. A s. Calif. bird went 740 mi. n. into Oreg. A Sierra bird moved 1,100 mi. s. into Sinaloa, Mexico. Fall migrants livetrapped in s. Calif. eventually returned as far n. as cent. Wash.; others trapped in ne. Calif. moved sw. into the Central Valley.

Wisconsin (Orians and Kuhlman 1956): A number of recoveries of birds banded as nestlings in Greene Co. showed none going long distances in the 1st few months after they were banded. In Dec. there was a recovery each in Ill., Iowa, Tex., La., and Fla. Compared with the number of "adults," Juv. birds were scarce in winter in the study area. RALPH S. PALMER

BANDING STATUS To Aug. 1981 the total number banded was 46,647, with 2,775 recoveries (6%) (Clapp et al. 1982).

Main places of banding: Calif., Sask., Idaho, Minn., Wis., Ont., and Pa.

Since the 1920s, many notes on recoveries have appeared in journals and field station reports. Intensive uses of banding data are mostly recent: longevity (E. L. Sumner 1940), dispersal of young (Orians and Kuhlman 1956), survival rates (Henny and Wight 1972), causes of mortality (Keran 1981), and regional analyses of recoveries and returns—Sask. (Houston 1967, 1970), Kittatinny Ridge of Pa. (J. B. Holt and Frock 1980), Ont. (S. Fowler 1981, D. and S. Fowler 1981), and Idaho (Steenhof et al. 1984). RALPH S. PALMER

REPRODUCTION Age when **first breeds** is commonly assumed to be 2 years. This is possibly the minimum for successful reproduction. Presumed yearlings twice have been reported breeding: in Alta., a ♀ with tail not reddish was a member of a pair that successfully reared a brood (Luttich et al. 1971); in Wis., a member of a breeding pair (sex unknown) had a brown tail (Gates 1972). Considering the geographical area, these birds possibly were "adults" without red tails. In w.-cent. Ariz., 2 pairs each contained a bird in "immature plumage," and eggs were not deposited in these territories (Millsap 1981). Widely scattered studies indicate that yearling prebreeders, as well as nonbreeding older birds (some mated, even holding territories and building nests), are present among established breeders. Their combined numbers in different studies have varied about 10–40% (av. about 20%). The reasons why some build yet do not lay are probably unrelated to capability of reproducing successfully. In areas where food is adequate and habitat is essentially saturated with established breeders, although younger birds are presumably capable of successful breeding when 2 years old, the territoriality and accompanying displays of breeders must surely inhibit some from entering the breeding population until older.

Sexual nexus Pair-bond form typically is **lifelong monogamy**—that is, maintained until death of a partner. There are exceptions. At least in nonmigratory birds, mates are closely associated all year. Marked birds in Wis.: the bond is maintained year-round; in winter, roosting patterns were "rigidly maintained" by location, cover, and mate association. Mates of a wintering pair moved independently to their roost before sunset and shortly after sunrise moved a short distance to a common location, where they remained until midmorning. In 1 instance a ♂ was apparently displaced by another during the breeding cycle, but other pairs maintained their bonds throughout the 1971–1975 study (Petersen 1979). In Alaska, rarely, migrant pairs displaced residents, generally when only 1 resident bird defended; lone ♂ ♂ were more susceptible to displacement than were ♀ ♀ (Lowe 1978).

At least in breeding season, acquisition of a new mate can occur rapidly. In Baja Calif., a ♀ was shot May 16 as she rose from the nest; on May 17 the pale ♂ mate was seen with another dark ♀, which was tending the brood (Anthony 1893).

In migrant Redtails, whether a bond may be maintained away from breeding territory is less evident. Some evidently travel in 2s, and such activities as High-circling on warm winter days and displays during spring migration may have a bond-maintenance function.

Trio bond Recorded by Wiley (1975b). At a nest in Calif., apparently the ♂ fetched food for the 2 ♀ that were observed to tend the 4 nestlings; the ♀ ♀ appeared to have separate hunting areas, and food for the young was plentiful. For different activities in the rearing season of a trio bond (♂ and 2 ♀) in Wis., see Santana C et al. (1986).

Displays Treatment here is cursory. They vary in location and context and so forth as between birds in Basic feathering, between Basic and Juv., between the latter, and somewhat seasonally. Perhaps there are differences in repertoire between long-distance migrants and residents, as was intimated by Lowe (1978).

HIGH-CIRCLING Has been seen in all seasons, occurs in various contexts, and is also often a forerunner of other aerial activities. On warm winter days, 1 or more Redtails may rise to a great height and soar in wide circles, drifting over the landscape. Frequently they are silent or beyond "earshot." Others are stimulated to join in, presumably rising from within their own defended airspace. The birds may remain aloft a long time, circling and sunning. Circling above terrestrial territory is also a prominent and integral early phase of the breeding cycle; Redtails then are noisy and conspicuous. Soaring in circles increases when spring migrants pass through, as territorial birds defend against possible takeovers. The spring circling of a pair evolves into a prelude to copulation. The ♂ assumes a station close behind and slightly above the ♀, frequently with dangling legs, and they may touch wings or the ♂ even may touch the back of the ♀ with his extended feet. Usually her reaction seems passive, but sometimes she turns over and presents her talons upward. Roles of the sexes were once seen reversed; both birds may also dangle their feet (Fitch et al. 1946b). In interior Alaska, when resident pairs thus displayed, migrant "adults" often joined in (Lowe 1978). A variant was described by Hubbard (1974). The presumed ♂ carried a snake, trailing it as the ♀ turned over to meet him, but she did not succeed in grasping it. At least 1 of them uttered a raspy call unlike the ordinary scream, as had been reported earlier by Fitch et al. This prelude to copulation thus included a food-pass. Soaring, at times by 1 bird, occurs at least until well along in the breeding cycle.

Two birds cartwheeling earthward with talons interlocked occasionally are seen in spring; usually 1 is evidently a territory holder and the other is an interloper. When they are about to crash, they disengage. B. H. Warren (1890) witnessed this behavior, the Sky-dance (described below), and other antics on a clear autumn day in Pa.; although not stated, migrants were evidently passing through territories of residents.

TILTING   Performed by migrating ♂ ♂ in spring. Wings are out anteriorly with tips held in as in Sky-dance, and the tail is partly spread, legs extended downward and talons spread. While circling slowly, he tilts from side to side so that 1 wing and then the other is uppermost. The ♂ may maintain this awkward posture for some time without loss of altitude. A ♀ is always nearby, but none perform this display. Lowe (1978), who saw it in Alaska, thought that it probably serves to reinforce the pair bond. Yet it is not performed on territory.

SKY-DANCE   Has been described by Skinner (in Bent 1937) and others. A bird rises to a high altitude and, with wings out anteriorly and in at the tips, dives steeply at tremendous speed, then checks its descent and shoots upward at an approximately equal angle. This is done in series, at times until the bird is out of sight. It varies from deep dives (tumbling) to a slower roller-coaster display. It designates territory limits and adjacent Redtails may respond by displaying similarly and sometimes on parallel course. Whether it is strictly ♂ behavior is unknown. It is more prevalent from some time before until late in incubation.

WHIRLING   While soaring on a light wind, a (♂?) Redtail quickly rotates 360° on a wing tip. This eye-catching action may serve as territorial advertisement or as a means of gaining a new vantage point for hunting. Usually, however, it is done by individuals soaring above normal hunting altitudes (Lowe 1978).

BOUNDARY-FLIGHTS   Performed by ♂ ♂, at least, near perches on the perimeter of the defended area. There are variants in mode of flight.

DROP-AND-CATCH   The birds toy with symbolic or substitute prey in midair. In *B. buteo* this was done by younger birds, "of low social status," sometimes in small groups and away from territories, in Sept.–Mar. (Weir and Picozzi 1975). Lowe listed it as a Redtail activity. Compare with N. Harrier and Golden Eagle.

HIGH-PERCHING   In any season, a bird advertises its presence, claim to a site, and social rank ("adults" perch higher than Juvs.). Postures vary in significant ways. For example, a bird may call and fluff out its breast feathers, expanding the white "shield" so that it looks quite different than an undisturbed individual.

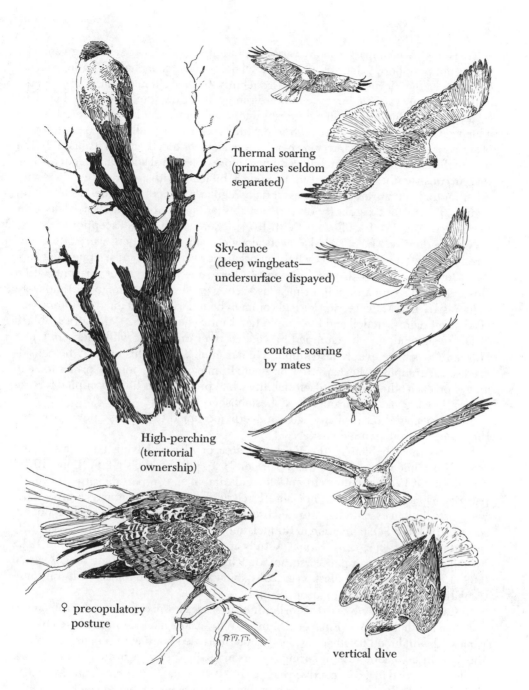

Thermal soaring
(primaries seldom
separated)

Sky-dance
(deep wingbeats—
undersurface dispayed)

contact-soaring
by mates

High-perching
(territorial
ownership)

♀ precopulatory
posture

vertical dive

Territory Encompasses many variables, but at least a concept can be given. The nest is not peripherally located, and the total defended area includes hunting area(s); collectively they form the territory—frequently termed "home range." Its overall outline is highly variable but tends toward roundish or oval; it may be partly bounded by a physiographic feature like a forest edge, road, or a ridge. Perchtrees, a few of which get the bulk of usage, are scattered within it. These are tall vantage points, easy of access and departure; a bird may perch there alone or together with its mate. In the heat of the day a bird may perch lower down, more or less in shade. One might assume that, in consistently suitable nesting-foraging habitat and with no serious conflicts with other raptors, territories would be essentially regularly spaced. This does occur—with a kind of persistent regularity of nest distribution and stable boundaries—as near Rochester. Alta. (McInvaille and Keith 1974). There are obvious exceptions.

Nesting density In sw. Alaska, nests along certain river sections were often clustered or aggregated, bordered by large unoccupied sections of similar-appearing habitat. Omitting the few distant lone nests, there was fairly regular spacing within clusters; 28 (of 33) measured inter-nest distances were less than 8 km. (5 mi.) and were as low as 1.7 km. Many territories had common boundaries maintained by interaction of adjacent pairs (Mindell and Dotson, in Ladd and Schempf 1982; Mindell 1983b). In N.D., nests tended to be clumped in wooded river drainages, while nests of Great Horned Owls were evenly distributed (Gilmer et al. 1983). Clusters may be considered social groupings. Perhaps they originate from pairs that evidently prefer to keep an eye on each other and approach stability when prebreeders fill in occupied territories as they are vacated through loss of established breeders.

Single or paired birds of any age can overfly occupied territories safely, provided they keep above defended airspace.

In suboptimal habitat in the Fairbanks area of Alaska, having both vacant and sparsely occupied areas, there was a pair per 18 sq. mi., or 46.6 sq. km. (Lowe 1978). To date about 15 other studies from Calif. and Alta. to N.Y. report densities down to a pair per 320 acres (½ sq. mi.) in Calif. (Fitch et al. 1946b), which may approach the lower size limit in essentially saturated breeding habitat. The av. is probably about 2.2 sq. mi. (5.5 km.). See tabulation in Rothfels and Lein (1983). An example of essentially saturated habitat: in s.-cent. Mont., a study area had 64 pairs in 1971 and 73 in 1972; overall density av. a pair per 3.1 sq. mi.; in 9 instances estimated home ranges varied 0.99–1.8 sq. mi.—the smallest on grazed habitat and the largest on agricultural country with 56% cropland (S. Johnson 1975).

In Calif., birds heavily used a smaller (nesting) area in spring, using the remainder less than in other seasons (Fitch et al.). In se. Wis., a 60% increase in used area by ♂ ♂ coincided with brood hatching, evidently from increased hunting to support the family; the ♀'s shrank about 40% in spring (Petersen 1979). Near Rochester, Alta., breeding density varied in 4 consecutive years: 2.1, 3.0, 3.2, and 3.3 sq. mi./pair (Luttich et al. 1971). Redtails reach highest nesting densities in habitat where prey is available, hunting perches are optimally distributed, and other diurnal raptors are not serious competitors. Possibly, highest densities will be found on some is. or in Cent. Am.

Coexistence and partitioning With minor exceptions, evidence indicates that buteo species have separate territories, or, where territories overlap, that the birds adjust their daily routines to minimize contact. In sw. Alaska there was much spatial overlap with the Rough-legged Hawk, which is both a cliff and a treenester; areas used by adjacent nesting pairs of the 2 species "are not necessarily mutually exclusive"— each seems to avoid the other, in part by being on somewhat different schedules. For details, see Mindell (in Ladd and Schempf 1982), also Mindell (1983b).

In comparing Redtail, Swainson's Hawk, and Ferruginous Hawk in se. Alta., it was evident that spatial separation of nests—not food supply—allowed them to coexist; when 2 species nested in proximity, reproductive success declined significantly (Schmutz et al. 1980). There is some segregation according to habitat preference. In n.-cent. Oreg., some Redtails (they are earlier nesters) lost part of their hunting areas to Swainson's (which arrive and reoccupy or acquire territories later); this apparently did not diminish Redtail breeding success (Janes 1984a). For important recent information on long occupancy and boundary stability of territories, see Janes (1984a, 1984b). Again in Alta., nearest neighbor tests demonstrated regular patterns of nest dispersion of Redtails and Swainson's; this was supported by observations of intra- and interspecific territorial defenses (Rothfels and Lein 1983). Far s., in the Chihuahuan desert of Mexico, an area was divided entirely into buteo territories, both Redtail and Swainson's having aggressive interactions among themsleves and toward each other. There was habitat segregation: Swainson's in lowlands, Redtails in uplands, and overlap in contact zones (Thiollay 1981).

The Red-shouldered Hawk and the Redtail are "competitive species, each intolerant of the other, antagonistic and occupying entirely separate [home] ranges" (Bent 1937). In Mass., nesting habitat differences: Redshoulder in mixed forest and hardwoods, Redtail in pitch pine and stunted oaks on C. Cod, and overlap elsewhere in white pine forest. As the Redshoulder became scarcer, the Redtail took over its haunts, even its old nests in 2 observed instances. The Redtail "seems to be dominant" over the Redshoulder (Bent); it is dominant (Fitch 1958).

Except for Golden Eagles "escorting" spring migrant Redtails across eagle territories, Olendorff (1975) noted very little interaction between these 2 species. On the other hand, resident Redtails in Calif. were "particularly hostile" to eagles. There was constant harassment, the eagles being attacked by 1 pair of hawks after another when passing through a succession of Redtail territories. Turkey Vultures were not molested (Fitch et al. 1946b).

The Redtail, by and large, is an aggressive bird, and some other raptors are loath to actively pursue it. Sharpshins often rise up and approach both migrating and soaring Redtails but are careful about how they do it.

Versus Great Horned Owl It requires no license to label the Redtail the sworn enemy of the owl; their recorded interactions have filled many pages and deserve space here. Where the Redtail is the preponderant, or even common, breeding buteo, the owl (which never builds a nest) is largely dependent on it for a nesting site. Thus these 2 raptors may be termed supplanting or replacing species whose areas and activities overlap. The owl nests earlier, thus preempting old Redtail (or other) nests. In warmer climates the owl may lay sufficiently early to have vacated before the Redtail begins occupancy. Where there is temporal overlap in reproductive cycles, the owl sometimes takes over an occupied Redtail nest, causing desertion. The hawk hunts by day, the owl in low light and at night, yet some prey species are common to both. The hawk has a constancy of occupation of areas and remains independent of fluctuations of

117

some prey by using others; the owl, which is stressed in at least nonbreeding seasons if preferred prey is scarce, fluctuates in numbers (hence breeding density) as a consequence. As a nester, it tends to be spread more evenly through different habitats than the Redtail. The owl apparently works over its hunting area quite often; the denser the owl population, the more likely it is to have contact with nesting Redtails. There is reasonable evidence that the owl preys occasionally on adult Redtails, yet obviously they coexist widely—a sort of balance between aggression and competition. Nestling Redtails, when old enough so that both of their parents are away from the nest at night, are common prey of the owl. It is probable that young owls developing their hunting skills find young Redtails to be easy prey at night. (Disappearance of many eggs and some nestlings is probably the work of the raccoon.)

Redtails in N.Y. harassed an owl incubating on a Redtail nest (Spofford 1958b). In Okla., an owl was twice knocked to the ground by a hawk without sustaining serious damage (P. Wilson and Grigsby 1980). In Calif., a Redtail dived at and struck an owl on the back (Sumner, in Bent 1937). Bent himself saw an owl feeding on a dead Redtail, which does not confirm that the owl captured it. Since Redtails have lower reproductive success or even desert their nests if close to nesting owls, one wonders if the owl's voice has an unsettling effect. The following are examples of hawk-owl interactions:

ALTA. (near Rochester)   Disappearance via predation of nestling Redtails over 4 years: 5%, 12%, 49%, and 36%. Increase in losses was accompanied by increase in nesting owl pairs: 1 (1966), 3 (1967), 8 (1968), and 9 (1969) (Luttich et al. 1971). In another study, interactions between nesting owls and Redtails did not cause reduction in the latter, even though owl densities more than trebled. As snowshoe hares increased over a period of years, the hawk took more of them, yet the hawk's numbers remained essentially stationary. Absence of a numerical response by the Redtail was "almost certainly" linked to its migratory status; it occurred seasonally when prey was plentiful, while the owl was resident year-round and was subject to winter stress (McInvaille and Keith 1974).

SASK.   In good habitat the owl and hawk often nested in the same 160 acres, even sharing (but at opposite ends of) the same 40-acre clump of aspens when other potential sites were available. Six inter-nest close distances varied 35–72 yds., and all owl but only 2 Redtail nests appeared to be successful (Houston 1975).

WIS. (Waterloo area)   Marked hawks and owls; considerable overlap in areas used by the 2 species. In Feb.–Mar., owls commonly hunted near a Redtail nest. In Apr.–June, the owls were "never located" in the woodlot occupied by nesting Redtails, and the latter avoided the woodlot where the owls nested—that is, competitive exclusion. (From Petersen 1979.)

OHIO (Delaware Co.)   Sixty-nine Redtail nests. As others have reported, breeding owls are limited by available nest sites (about ⅗ were Redtail nests). Diet of the 2 raptors overlapped in prey species, but temporal segregation and daily activity patterns minimized direct competition. It was believed that the further the hawk nested from an owl activity center, the higher the chance of Redtail nesting success. (From M. A. Springer and Kirkley 1978.)

CENT. N.Y.   Owls began to appropriate nests and incubate the last week in Feb. or

118

1st week in Mar., and its nestlings flew before the end of Apr. Redtails rarely laid earlier than the last week in Mar., and nestlings generally attained flight in late May–early June. There were overlapping hawk-owl territories, but if they attempted to nest closely, the hawks usually abandoned their nest. (From D. Hagar [1957].)

Nest site Requisites are isolation from disturbance, a commanding view, and unobstructed access. Nests typically are high up in the crown of a tree taller than those surrounding it, regardless of species. The chosen tree often is well up a slope or on a ridge or hilltop; it may be within extensive forest, a woodlot, grove, or clump of trees on farmland. Generally it is within view of several perch sites. Nearness to water is not a requisite. The Redtail seems to prefer trees with open crowns, while the Great Horned Owl prefers more sheltered sites within a closed canopy.

Reported sites vary greatly. A low tree will be used where others are lower or nonexistent, and nests may be almost on the ground in some desert areas. Redtails occupy large saguaros in which limbs project to provide a site against the trunk. Nests are, at most. a few yds. above ground in paloverde. Redtails use cliff ledges occasionally in Calif., S.D., w. Canada, and less elsewhere to rarely in e. N. Am.; such use is more frequent in arid areas where trees are scarce (Pinel and Wallis 1972). They occupy unused aeries of the Golden Eagle and nests of ravens, crows, various buteos; gray squirrel dreys serve as foundations. Other sites include cross arms of utility poles and towers, as well as such artifical sites as platforms installed for Golden Eagles and Ospreys.

In cent. N.Y., Great Horned Owls occupied Redtail nests in the season of their construction (D. Hagar 1957). Crows appropriate old Redtail nests, gray squirrels may build on them, and raccoons may take over inactive or active (robbed) ones for sleeping platforms. The most common small avian tenant within active nests is the House Sparrow.

Succession or heirarchy On such w. grasslands as in Colo., Redtails nest primarily in trees on abandoned farmsteads. At any 1 farmstead usually only a single raptor species is found. The early-nesting Great Horned Owl has precedence (using a buteo nest), followed by the Redtail, then Swainson's Hawk, and finally Am. Kestrel. The owl can use the site annually until the nest disintegrates or is blown down. Then, only a buteo builds a new nest (Olendorff and Stoddart 1974). In Mass.: a nest was occupied by the Redshoulder, 8 years later by the Broadwing, 1 year later by the Redtail, and then deserted; a Redshoulder nest was used by the Barred Owl, subsequently by the Redtail (Bent 1937). Resident birds in Tex.: the Great Horned Owl nests in early winter; in 3 seasons the owl used the nest 1st, then the Redtail (Singley 1886a).

Nest construction and refurbishing Since Redtail territories tend to be stable in dimension over the years and are reoccupied repeatedly unless the habitat is altered, a couple of old nests are often available at the onset of the breeding cycle. Greenery may be placed on one or more of these and not be used; the pair may use another old nest or build a new one. There is much on this in Bent (1937), confirmed by Vaughn (1943) and others. Some pairs evidently build a new nest each year for at least several years, reuse a nest during successive years, or leave 1 vacant for a year or longer and then reuse it— **alternative nest.** Redtails sometimes build but do not lay eggs there or presumably anywhere; it is thought that some pairs may have an incomplete breeding cycle in the year before a 1st complete cycle. If a new nest is built a distance from former nest(s), the pair may include a new ♀.

Building can proceed quite rapidly, both birds working at least for part of the morning; they are very sensitive if distrubed at this stage and readily abandon the site. In Wis. a pair usually builds in 4–7 days (Petersen 1979). Petersen stated that Redtails use their beak to break off and carry material to the site but that they break larger sticks from trees by downward pressure of their feet and then, if feasible, transfer the sticks to the beak while flying to the site. Although both sexes participate, the ♀ spends the greater portion of her time forming the nest and its bowl (Petersen). When finished, the typical diam. of a nest exceeds the length of the ♀, frequently being over 30 in. (76 cm.) across, over ½ as high as wide, and with a bowl to 4–5 in. (10–13 cm.) deep. Nests can become slightly more bulky if refurbished over several years. The lining is usually of strips of bark, some small twigs, *Usnea*, and the like. The top appears rather flat but becomes much more so when well trodden by the growing young.

In Wis., a tame ♂ courted and copulated with humans, built a nest, incubated chicken eggs, and reared young hawks provided by the keeper (F. and F. Hamerstrom 1971). In N.Y., a captive pair was given an old nest; the ♂ showed immediate interest, added material to it, and spent much time shaping the bowl; the ♀ showed no interest (H. Meng).

Greenery Placing conifer springs in the nest usually comes to mind when this subject is discussed, but more should be said. Deciduous twigs, once partly leaved, are also delivered. Other items have included corn cobs, husks, and pieces of stalk, willow and aspen catkins, an assortment of other plant materials, an oriole nest. and various rubbish (no preference at some nests)—see especially Bohm (1978). Delivery is known to occur weeks before laying (see Bent 1937), probably almost daily from some time during nest construction or refurbishing until late in incubation, when it then tapers off—yet it is known to have occurred shortly after the brood has departed. Occasionally it occurs in autumn (like the Golden Eagle). Numerous other theories notwithstanding, it appears to be a behavioral derivation of prey capture and delivery that serves to indicate active attachment to a site. A possible utilitarian function might be to advertise ownership to prebreeding and/or other Redtails (and other diurnal raptors) in temporary absence of the owner; presence of such materials in a nest may not occur invariably and is not a requisite of nesting success. The question may arise as to what is "intended" as "decoration" and what as "lining." In a Wis. study, corn husks were found in all nests and were referred to as "lining material" by Orians and Kuhlman (1956).

In Sweden, a *B. buteo* nestling that had fallen to the ground was surrounded by dead prey and fresh pine boughs; a week later it was 20 m. away, again surrounded by greenery (Johansson 1958).

Copulation In 8 Calif. records, the pair once perched beforehand, but otherwise the ♂ was in flight and alighted on the ♀'s back. It was not always preceded by posturing by the ♀ and once was not preceded by soaring. It lasted 5–12 sec., once 20 sec.; the birds then either perched quietly or else soared and performed aerial acrobatics (Fitch et al. 1946b). A pair rose on thermals and both made dives, barrel rolls, and ascents (Sky-dance?); coming out of independent dives, they locked talons and cartwheeled downward, then separated; they then attempted aerial copulation and then copulated in the nest tree (M. A. Springer 1979). The frequency and span of time over which copulation may occur is unrecorded. Artificial insemination has been successful.

Arrival to laying The span varied 14–21 days in interior Alaska in 5 instances (Lowe 1978); it was about 3 weeks in Alta. (Luttich et al. 1971).

Laying interval Ordinarily an egg is laid every other day, occasionally with an additional day skipped.

Clutch size In coterminous U.S. and s. Canada usually 2 or 3, not infrequently 4, but Bent (1937) twice found a bird incubating 1 egg. That clutch size is adjusted to major differences in prey availability has been suggested more than once but has not been clearly demonstrated. In an analysis of clutch sizes from the coterminous U.S. and s. parts of the 3 westernmost Canadian provinces, Henny and Wight (1972) found an increase from e. to w. and from s. to n.; smallest was Fla. (2.11) and largest Oreg. and Wash. (2.96), which is in general agreement with Bent (1937). See below for Alaska. Apparently there are no data for s. of the Mexican border. Several interesting reports follow:

CALIF. 302 clutches taken between 1885 and 1961 showed a mean of 3.05 ± 0.68, possibly biased by collectors taking larger clutches; 51 clutches in 1973: 22 (of 2), 26 (3), and 3 (4), the mean 2.53 ± 0.77 (J. Wiley 1975a). ARIZ. (Sonoran desert) 1969–1976, 1 egg (in 5 nests), 2 (31), 22 (3), and 1 (4), the mean being 2.32 for 137 eggs in 59 clutches (Mader 1978); there was some yearly variation. ALTA. (cent.) counts of young nestlings plus unhatched eggs in 68 nests, had a mean of 2.1, lower than Henny and Wight's figures from anywhere (Luttich et al. 1971); snowshoe hare numbers fluctuated greatly, but the Redtail does not rely on this prey. ALASKA (Fairbanks area) mean clutch size of 1.96 for 27 nests in years when snowshoe hares were scarce (Lowe 1978). MONT. (s.-cent.) in 1966 and 1967, 4 clutches (of 2), 15 (3), and 3 (4), averaging 2.9 ± 0.1 (Seiden-sticker and Reynolds 1971). N.Y. clutches of 3 quite regularly and 4 frequent, based on Bent (1937). NEW ENG. 42 sets (of 2) and 63 (3) (F. H. Carpenter 1887).

For e. Redtails, Bent stated that sets of 4 are not rare and 5 "have been found." For w. birds, high numbers were 4 "occasionally" and 5 or even 6 "recorded"—but no details. A cliff nest in s. Alta. had 4 young and a heavily incubated egg (Pinel and Wallis 1972). In Calif. in 1973, of three 4-egg clutches, only the polygamous nest (♂ and 2♀) produced 4 young to flight age (J. Wiley 1975b).

Replacement clutches Bent stated that a Redtail will lay again 3 or 4 weeks after a clutch has been taken, usually in another nest, rarely also a 3d set. Again no details, but it seems probable that egg removal from captives would at least result in double-clutching. When the infertile clutch of an unmated captive ♀ was removed, she laid 2 eggs 3 weeks later (H. Meng).

Eastern Redtail: 1 **egg** each from 20 clutches **size** length 60.66 ± 2.82 mm., breadth 46.66 ± 1.22, radii of curvature of ends 19.16 ± 0.88 and 14.59 ± 0.73; **shape** short elliptical, elongation 1.29 ± 0.07, bicone −0.057, and asymmetry +0.128 (F. W. Preston). This compares with Bent's av. of 59 × 47 mm. for 59 eggs.

Western Redtail: Preston's same av. 59.33 × 47.18 mm., and Bent's figure was 59.2 × 46.4 for 48 eggs.

For the species, see also comparison (plus original data) in Bechard and Houston

(1984): Redtail eggs are smaller than those of the Ferruginous Hawk, but considerably larger than both Rough-legged and Swainson's Hawk eggs; size differences are diagnostic. The eggs of a very old captive Redtail tended to be smaller and paler than normal (D. Bird and Tinker 1982).

Redtail eggs have been illustrated frequently. For a good recent color illus. plus comparison with other species, see C. J. O. Harrison (1984). The shell is smooth, **color** pale bluish to nearly white (and soon fades), overlaid with a mixture of dots, spots, and blotches of various browns; eggs vary from nearly unmarked to (usually) at least spotted to (rarely) heavily blotched. In Ill. a clutch of 2, light blue and unmarked (Cruttenden 1940). Bent maintained that clutches of a particular ♀ were usually consistent in shape, ground color, and markings; that is, if a decided change occurred, then the ♂ had another mate. He also stated that w. eggs may av. "a little more heavily marked."

Egg dates In at least some areas, the mean date for clutches varies considerably because of weather variation and may possibly be influenced by scarcity or abundance of prey. Full clutches may be expected in warmer parts of Calif., the states bordering Mexico, and across to include Fla. in Feb. and occasionally earlier; for much of coterminous U.S., Mar. is the month for fresh clutches; in n. states and s. Canada, from well along in Mar. into early May; in interior Alaska, from some time in Apr. to past mid-May.

Incubation Evidently begins before completion of the clutch; hence, laying is over a longer period than hatching. The sitter commonly rests her head on the rough nest edge, which "wears away the feathers and causes a rugose condition of the throat"—often prominent corrugations that are yellow-tipped and less apparent (except for thickened skin) in dried museum specimens (Taverner 1936). Marked birds in Wis.: the ♀ sits at night, and either sex (but ♀ mostly) sits in daytime. The ♂ sat regularly for periods of 15 min.–5 hrs. Typically, he sat for a time in the morning while the ♀ was absent hunting or perching, and his afternoon span was usually briefer. He was seen to bring food to the ♀, but she usually hunted for herself, and during the final week, his share of sitting diminished (Petersen 1979). In interior Alaska in 1975 (when snowshoe hares were scarce), adults were absent for periods of 15–30 min. or longer, incubating ♀♀ begged for food from their mates, 8 of 10 nests failed, and the birds vacated territories within 2 days (Lowe 1978).

Redtails must guard their eggs lest they be eaten by jays or ravens. The hawks become less liable to desert because of human disturbance as incubation progresses. Few e. Redtails show aggression toward a climber, but in w. N. Am. Redtails often attack persistently. In interior Alaska in 1976, territorial defense toward investigators was intense in some instances—they were attacked not only in nesting trees but also on the ground; some pairs were more aggressive than others (Lowe 1978). In brief, the Redtail is far more aggressive where it has had less exposure to Caucasians. (The same applies to the Goshawk.)

Incubation period Very close to 34 days per egg, as 1st indicated by Hegner (1906); Bent, and those quoting him, have given an incorrect shorter period. At least ordinarily, only a minute percentage of eggs fails to hatch.

Nestling period Hatching usually occurs over several days; the ♂ provides most of

3–5 days

13–15 days

25–27 days

30–33 days

123

the food for the ♀ and brood from the start. In Petersen's tagged birds, only the ♀ brooded the young, and, she was strongly attached to the nest until the young were about 5 weeks old, leaving only for brief hunts and exercise. As they approached this age, she was away more often and longer. The ♀ feeds the nestlings. Both parents deliver food directly to the nest; the ♂ also may deliver to the ♀ while she is guarding the nest from a perch, and both parents consume food while away from the nest.

In cent. Alta., McInvaille and Keith (1974) reported that an av. of 710 gm. of prey was brought daily to broods of 2 young, and an av. of 410 gm. to nests having a single nestling; during 5 years, adults brought an av. of 340–570 gm./day per nestling. An estimated 520 gm., reported from Wash. by Stinson (1980), was adequate for the lone survivor in a 2-young brood. Assuming that food is readily available, there is a question as to whether the amount delivered to the nest is adjusted to number and age(s) of the nestlings. At a Colo. nest 2 "hatchling" Redtails were surrounded by 20 ground squirrels, 7 small jackrabbits, and a "fledgling" meadowlark (Olendorff 1975). The food supply seems to have been adequate in some, but not all, studies of breeding Redtails.

Growth of young Weight increase of preflight Redtails, plotted as a curve, has a maximum below that of "adult" birds; the same applies to BEAK from cere. Body wt. correlates well with age early in nest life, but after about 23 days (when energy-allocation is channeled into feather development) WING and 4th primary lengths are much more reliable age-indicators (M. A. Springer and Osborne 1983). The smaller ♂ grows faster and attains full nestling size earlier than the ♀; the time required for ♀ ♀, especially, to reach full nestling size has varied in different studies. Sexual dimorphism (♀ larger) is evident by age 3 weeks. The reader will find much of value in Sumner (1929b), Fitch et al. (1946b), Olendorff (1974b), and M. A. Springer and Osborne (1983) on physical and behavioral development.

Moritsch (1983a) authored an illus. guide for estimating age of nestlings, and the nestling illus. in this book are based on his photographs. The following guidelines for aging at least approximately wild nestlings includes length of 4th primary (counting from inner) from Petersen and Thompson (1977), sexes of young combined. Age in days is in boldface. (See also Bechard et al. 1985.)

1 Beak black, iris dark; down-A short and whitish with some bare skin on femur; wt. at hatching about 57 gm (♂) or 58 (♀). **5–7** As above but larger; length about 5 in. (12.5 cm.). **9–11** Iris still dark, but darker pupil distinguishable; incoming down-ᴮ is longer, woolly, palish gray-brown, lighter on head and venter, with white spot evident on occiput; length about 8 in. (20.3 cm.). **13–15** Can sit up briefly; primaries begin breaking through their sheaths; length about 9 in. (23 cm.). **17–19** Dark wing tips (4th primary 30–40 mm. at 20 days); young are sitting up. **21–23** Iris has lightened appreciably; ear openings visible; scapulars show in dorsal down; tail feathers begin to emerge but are still down-tipped. **25–27** Fourth primary about 80 mm. at 25 days; dark brown Juv. feathers form small patch almost completely covering ear opening; Juv. feathers above the down on center of upper "shoulders," on scapulars, all of wing, and tail; length about 12–13 in. (30–33 cm.). **30** Fourth primary about 100 mm.; upper-parts appear largely feathered, but much of head still downy with dark feathering just visible on occiput; breast ½ feathered; legs beginning to feather; length about 14–16 in. (30–35 cm.). **35** Fourth primary about 135 mm.; rear of head now ½ feathered;

124

upperparts mostly free of any down; dark feathering extends across breast, is considerable on belly (sides especially), and extends down on flanks. **37–39** Fourth primary 170–180 mm.; iris has lightened to between light and medium gray with hint of yellowish, the dark pupil now conspicuous; white occipital spot evident basally in Juv. feathering; a small amount of down may persist on flanks.

Brood reduction In Man., during a scarcity of ground squirrels, the smallest nestling in a brood probably died of starvation—no indication of violence (Criddle 1917). At a nest in Wash. containing 2 young, the amount of food delivered was low, and by the time the young were 11–13 days old, there was violent aggression. Apparently the larger nestling was dominant. The ♀ parent fed the subordinate young only occasionally, frequently pecked it, and the young fought more frequently when she was present. About a week later there was a single nestling (Stinson 1980). It is quite possible that bad weather might deter the parents from hunting and that a weaker nestling would not survive. A parent killed one by trampling it (Orians and Kuhlman 1956). As for **cannibalism,** the eating of dead young in nests by the adults was noted in N.Y. (D. Hagar 1957). From Steffen's (1957) summary: an adult fed on an "immature" bird; in Calif. in Jan. an adult carried the remains of a smaller adult that had been partly eaten; buteo remains have been found in the pellets of nesting Redtails. (The Redtail has fed on other raptors, including the Redshoulder.) However dead young Redtails often disappear from nests, presumably having been removed (discarded) by a parent.

Breeding success This is Mader's (1982) compilation from various sources: 88% of 382 pairs laid eggs, av. clutch size was 2.79 eggs in 476 clutches, at least 1 egg hatched in 84.4% of 379 clutches, young reached flight age in 73% of 152 nests, and the av. number of young reared in 281 nesting attempts was 1.47. Hatchability of eggs is high, but nesting losses during incubation and rearing have varied greatly in different studies. About av. would be this study in the cent. Appalachians by Janik and Mosher (1982): of 15 active nests, 10 produced at least 1 young to flight age for a total of 22 nestlings, averaging 1.8 young/active nest and 1.4 attaining flight. The same authors summarized 15 additional sources (930 nests): 67% of nests produced young, for an av. of 1.35/nest attaining flight.

Age at first flight Young first leave the nest usually at 42–46 days; sexes differ (♂♂ earlier than ♀♀); the young may vacate the nest earlier if disturbed and later perhaps as a result of inadequate food.

Dependency The young are "branchers" for a time, remaining close to the nest, 1 or more may return to it to be fed or to roost at night. Typically branchers perch solitarily and inconspicuously, among lower branches or in brush, at times even on the ground. The adults fetch food, which may be delivered or dropped to them, and the entire brood may chase after a parent, begging noisily and persistently. Around 2 weeks out of the nest, when they are capable on the wing, they begin using higher perches. Generally they begin hunting solitarily, but Shelley (in Bent 1937) described a parent locating voles to aid its circling young in hunting and capturing techniques. In sw. Mont., 41 broods were studied by radio telemetry (S. Johnson 1973). Individuals stayed with parents 30–70 days, and broodmates left the territory up to 31 days apart. Some young made no movements until they departed permanently while others came and went up to 5 times. Most did not go far if they returned. Three migrated 34, 57, and 70 days after attaining flight. At 3 nests in interior Alaska (Lowe 1978), the parents abandoned their broods 13, 27, and 34 days after the latter could fly.

Tagged birds in Wis. (Petersen 1979): in the 18 days after 1st flying, the young usually remained within 150 m. of the nest—making short flights, exercising their wings while perched, and persistently begging for food. At about 9 weeks they moved away to the focal point of parental activity within overall range or actively followed the hunting adults. At 10 weeks, 2 consistently perched near hunting adults, and once an adult captured prey, the young would immediately alight nearby and beg. Some lone survivors of broods were more solitary, and adults delivered food to them. The 1st successful hunting attempt occurred when a Juv. was about 12 weeks old, and it was noted that birds of this age take less agile prey like frogs, toads, snakes, and some invertebrates. Yet they continue to beg at about age 15 weeks. Tagged young were "not capable of sustained, confident flights" until 9 weeks old and could probably not have survived when less than 15 weeks of age. With increasing confidence, their travels increased and the family bond was terminated. Petersen's study was of resident Redtails.

The Redtail has bred in captivity.   RALPH S. PALMER

SURVIVAL   Luttich et al. (1971) prepared a "composite life table and life equation," starting with a theoretical cohort of 1,000 eggs and small nestlings combined and continuing to age 28 years. Their calculation that a few yearlings do breed is suspect. The 1,000 had already dwindled to about 500 surviving to age 1 year, only 100 by age 6 years, 20 at 13 years, and a single bird at 25 years. From their calculations it appeared that Redtail numbers were declining slightly at Rochester, Alta., although they appeared to be stable throughout the continent. This raptor was not stressed by biocides.

Calculated from banding returns, the av. mortality rate from attaining flight to age 1 year is 54%, and mean annual mortality rate thereafter is 20% (Henny and Wight 1972). Populations in n. U.S. and part of adjacent Canada must produce between 1.33 and 1.38 young per breeding attempt to maintain a stable breeding population (Henny and Wight); these figures have led to comparisons when success has been low in short-term studies but Redtails appeared not to decrease numerically.

Having reached age 2 years, a Redtail may be expected to live 4–5 years longer—about ¼ maximum potential span of survival.

Earlier banding returns reported by Houston (1967) were mostly of birds that had been shot; Henny and Wight (1972) reported that the percentage of such recoveries had declined.

Several Redtails are known to have lived 20 years. A ♀ kept in captivity at Mill-brook, N.Y., was healthy at age 29½ years when reported to the author by F. Trevor.

RALPH S. PALMER

HABITS   **In our area.**   The Redtail is a large, solid raptor that spends a great deal of time perched high in relation to its surroundings. It commonly chooses an exposed limb or, elsewhere, such relatively high points as posts, utility poles, and saguaros. The greater the height, the less flapping and the faster the downward glide toward nearby prey. The bird perches in a more or less sentinel stance, guarding its territory and watching any movement within sight. It may shift from perch to perch frequently but tends to keep to a favored few day after day and so hunts the same areas repeatedly. Its profile varies, as when the crop is distended by a full meal or when the feathers are sleeked back and the hawk is trim and hungry. Various birds recognize this difference, and mob more frequently when the Redtail is about to hunt (F. Hamerstrom 1957). Well after sunrise a hawk may have a warm-up flight before beginning the day's activities (the Craigheads 1956). The Redtail is opportunistic, and its hunting methods are versatile.

Perch-and-wait　By far the commonest method of hunting, occupying to over ⅘ of daylight and yielding the highest reported percentages of successful strikes. The bird may be erect or lean forward. No stance indicates that an attack is imminent; hence attacks cannot be forecast. Close hunts are glides at a downward angle with few flaps. In Goslow's (1971) analysis of high-speed photographs, the hawk sets its wings in a gliding pattern some 10–15 ft. from the quarry and at about 10 ft. begins to extend the legs forward. The hawk watches its intended prey and can compensate successfully for its movements in milliseconds. It spreads its toes and usually strikes with 1 foot farther forward. On impact, while balancing with the wings, the bird drops down on its "heels." Relative strike impact is less than that of Cooper's Hawk and the Goshawk, even though the Redtail is heavier. If prey is farther from the perch, hence to be approached at a lesser angle, a few rapid wingbeats alternate with glides, as in the next method described.

Flap-glide　Often used in cruising for food; it has variants and is adaptable to circumstances. The bird generally maintains an altitude of under 200 ft., often much lower, and quarters over the terrain like a harrier to catch prey in the open before it can escape. The hawk may dodge among trees, taller bushes, and scattered rock outcrops, remaining concealed until coming on its quarry suddenly at close range. Although this method is less successful than perch hunting, it may be relatively useful for capturing small birds.

Soaring　The hawk circles overhead, sometimes high, occasionally with a few rapid wingbeats, probably advertising territory ownership while keeping a lookout for quarry. Presumably it is visible to at least some potential victims. It may dive steeply from high up but with little success.

Variant methods　At Ney Cave, Tex., free-tailed bats (*Tadarida*) depart in a stream beginning toward dusk. A Redtail would stoop with half-closed wings, quite falconlike, plowing through the stream and zooming upward, bat in talons; it would also fly parallel close to the stream, then veer sharply into it and seize a bat (Sprunt, Jr., 1950). In Uvalde, Tex., 6 Redtails patrolled a cave entrance, repeatedly catching bats (1984 *Am. Birds* 38 932). In Major Co., Okla, Redtails perched nearby just before the bat exodus began. Then they soared well above the bats and dropped rapidly, meeting the bats head-on and shooting right through the column. The bats banked and sideslipped, and the success rate of the persistent hawks was zero (Looney 1972).

Goss (1891) reported the Redtail, while "sailing," to catch flying "grasshoppers"— aerial foraging in a manner typical of Swainson's Hawk.

Accipiter method　This overlaps with flap-glide, above. In interior Alaska, not only did Redtails make hunting strikes from high perches but they also maneuvered through thick stands of spruce in a manner reminiscent of the Goshawk. All successful strikes witnessed were on or near the ground. Furthermore, the Redtail may actually run on the ground when attacking, especially if the prey is large (Lowe 1978). In other boreal regions with extensive areas of conifers, this may be an important Redtail hunting method.

Hunting afoot Common in Redtails, especially young birds in 1st fall and winter. One may see them from vehicular traffic on the medians between traffic lanes and on the mowed strips along highways. In a newly mowed field in N.H., Redtails bounded from prey to prey in pursuit of grasshoppers and crickets, momentarily touching the ground when seizing an insect—a maneuver that "resembled the floppings of a hen with its head cut off" (Shelley, in Bent 1937). Certainly some of the amphibians, fishes, crayfishes, and other invertebrates, in addition to large insects, which are known foods, are taken afoot. This might be termed a Swainson's or Broad-winged Hawk method.

A few birds have been captured with crop full of earthworms. After heavy rains, the water table in ne. Fla. was close to the surface, forcing worms (*Lumbricus?*) upward; as viewed from some distance, a young Redtail appeared to be working at extracting them from the soil (Helen Cruickshank).

Cooperative hunting Used to catch tree squirrels; the quarry can dodge if attacked by a single hawk but not if another is on the opposite side of the tree (Bent 1937). Since 2 Redtails, presumably mates, are occasionally flushed from dead prey of various sorts on the ground, this may indicate additional cooperative hunting.

Piracy In fall–spring occasionally a Redtail robs another in midair or causes it to drop its prey. The possibility that this transfer may occur between mates should not be overlooked. Redtails occasionally rob other species, as the Roughleg and N. Harrier. In one instance, however, the Roughleg was the pirate (Hogan 1983).

Carrion eating Dead wildlife, including fresh traffic victims, even the carcasses of large farm animals, is well known. This habit converges somewhat with that of vultures, although Redtails only eat fresh food.

Prey preferences and hunting ability Vary with individual; the former, at least, has been noted many times. A Redtail habitually hunts favorite spots, presumably for its preferred prey. Some individuals specialize in larger foods than others. Fitch et al. (1946b), for example, listed different pairs in Calif. that specialized in kangaroo rats, lizards, snakes, ground squirrels, or chipmunks. In an area where ground squirrels were abundant, a pair preyed on them least but compensated by taking pocket gophers.

Feeding Captured small prey is carried directly to a feeding perch, which is lower than a hunting perch. A vole is swallowed intact. Small birds are beheaded and carefully plucked. A larger mammal of transportable size may be beheaded; part of its fur is discarded, the hawk then feeds, and leftovers may be lodged in the tree or may fall below. Heavy quarry, which may struggle and crawl into brush or other cover when seized, may be dragged a short distance to a suitable spot. There the hawk plucks fur or feathers, feeds, and may then attempt to carry the remainder to an elevated perch. If it succeeds, it may continue feeding and then discard it.

Food requirements In experimental work, in fall–winter the av. wt. of food in-

128

alert

rousing

upright or
vertical

aggressive
(occipital feathers
raised)

R. M. Mengel

slant posture

aggressive or
preattack
(sleeked feathers)

full aggression on close approach

129

gested daily by ♂ ♂ (weighing an av. of 1,147 gm.) was 147 gm., or 10.2% of wt. of the bird; for ♀ ♀ (av. 1,218 gm.) it was 136 gm. (11.1%). The amount was less in spring–summer: ♂ ♂ (1,108 gm.) ingested 82 gm. (7.4%) and ♀ ♀ (1,210 gm.) ingested 85 gm. (7%) (the Craigheads 1956). Thus, on a daily basis, about 3 voles or their equivalent are required. (See also Reproduction, above.)

A caged adult in ne. Calif. ate on av. 140 gm./day, about ⅛ its wt. Sometimes it fasted. It ate more than a large nestling did and much more than the bird next mentioned. An unmated Juv. that was fairly tame was watched in late fall–winter. Its distended crop indicated when it had fed. Some days it did not eat, its longest period of fasting being 5 consecutive days. The hawk became restless, changed perches frequently, and hunted over several times as much terrain as otherwise. The food actually ingested was less than 100 gm./day—perhaps a minimum. The hawk may have ingested this much while an equal wt. of prey was discarded as waste (Fitch et al. 1946b).

Pellets Ejecta of undigested materials measure about $2 \times 1\frac{1}{2}$ in. (5×3 cm.); many are smaller; some taper at 1 end; often they are flat with a rounded side (shape of the bird's crop). When fed the usual foods gotten in the wild, a caged "adult" dropped a pellet on successive days; 1 pellet, however, may represent several meals over several days; 1 bird produced 21 pellets in 61 days (Fitch et al.). In experimental work, minimum time from feeding to ejecting a pellet was 17¾ hr., and it appeared that eating within 4 hrs. of dawn usually resulted in egestion from within 1 hr. before to 2 hrs. after the following dawn. See Fuller et al. (1979) for details.

Territory In marked resident birds in Wis., av. winter home ranges were nearly alike for the sexes (♂ 157 ha., ♀ 167), and monthly differences were minor. Boundaries followed roads, edges of woodlots containing perch trees, and so on. The birds seldom used the interiors of large woodlots, and large blocks of closed-canopy lowland hardwoods were apparently of little value to them. Although upland habitat of the sexes overlapped greatly, ♂ ♂ also used lowland pastures and ♀ ♀ lowland hardwoods (Petersen 1979). These were resident birds. Generally speaking, and perhaps aside from some forest populations, wintering Redtails need elevated perches and open landscape where quarry is available.

Behavior in winter As in summer, Redtails are seldom out of each other's sight, and they regularly interact. Population density is highly variable—perhaps 6 sq. mi. per pair under marginal conditions in interior Alaska, down to a pair per 2 sq. mi., which is about average in many places, to local concentrations of at least up to 10 birds per sq. mi. That is, an abundance of food (response to prey density) can override normal territoriality. There is a social aspect (birds attract more birds). as at winter roosts of some other raptors.

The birds hunt in good weather and often soar high when it is windy, but a very high wind drives them into the shelter of trees. After a full meal, or in various kinds of unfavorable weather, they spend time perched quietly. Juvenal birds seem to recognize that they are less likely to be persecuted in these circumstances and occasionally perch near an "adult" without eliciting attack. "Adults" perch high, advertising ownership; Juvs. perch low, as within a tree or even on the ground, do comparatively little soaring, and are relatively inconspicuous; an observer may miss sighting a perched Juv. until an older bird flushes it. An "adult" may perch erect (dominant), feathers of head, including nape, and breast ("shield") expanded, altering and enlarging the bird's outline. A Juv. keeps the head low and feathers sleeked. The "adult" watches every slightest movement and may lean forward, defecate, or maintain steady eye contact until the young bird takes wing. It is thought that larger Juv. birds are chased by "adults" less than smaller ones. A Juv. may occasionally displace another. A storm or prolonged cold weather with much snow may cause the birds to depart; typically, they reoccupy their winter territories when conditions improve.

In "adult" v. "adult" encounters, the owner raises its head, may shift position, and keeps a close eye on the other bird. If such concern does not discourage the interloper, the territory-holder advertises possession by various forms of flight, as by deep or "exaggerated" wingbeats, circling, and so forth, and the other individual generally withdraws. An "adult" tends to be cautious in approaching another; 1 yields and conflict is avoided. Occasionally 2 or even more pairs may become involved in a territorial dispute; there is much calling and circling, and a bird may close in on another; possibly ♂ defends against ♂. They maneuver, each trying to get the uppermost in order to launch a downward attack. Generally the intruder avoids contact by departing, but sometimes the low bird flips over and projects its outstretched feet toward its attacker.

Tails, ventral pattern and coloring, and iris color differ among "adult" Redtails, and these differ from the Juv. stage. It was Lowe's (1978) supposition that dark birds are more difficult to locate when perched and that they present other Redtails with "confusing" signals. It was his experience in Okla. that "adult" wintering "Harlan's" rarely were pursued by other Redtails. He noted gatherings or pockets of "Harlan's" in among other Redtails and that these groups persisted from year to year. Any interaction with white (albinistic) individuals in winter is unknown.

Partitioning of winter habitat The interrelationships of those species of diurnal raptors occurring in an area, a so-called guild, is too varied a subject for brief coverage. Each has its preferred places for hunting and perching. As a single example, Redtails are usually dominant over Roughlegs; the latter is more of an open-country bird and spends much more time in flight, so their contact is reduced. During spring migration in Okla., contacts between the 2 species were common and a Roughleg was quick to flee and able to dodge an oncoming Redtail (Lowe 1978). The 2 species were compared in some detail by G. Schnell (1968).

Versus prey populations First, 3 studies in cent. Alta.: In a 4-year study, primary prey was ground squirrels and snowshoe hares, together comprising about ½ the diet biomass; Ruffed Grouse were only 3%. Hawk numbers did not increase with high populations of primary prey. Redtails are spaced territorially and can change to alternative prey if needed; their numbers are not tied to any combination of prey species (Luttich et al. 1970). The Great Horned Owl, on the other hand, showed a marked response to increasing hares by an increase in nesting owls and an increase in hares in the diet (Rusch et al. 1972). The owl is tied to fluctuating primary prey. Again Alta., as hares increased, so did the number taken by Redtails, but magnitude of functional response did not match the increase in hare numbers. There was a comparable relation to changing vole numbers. There was a "buffering" of predation on Ruffed Grouse and probably some other prey species, which declined in the diet as hares increased. Redtail clutch size was largest with highest hare abundance (McInvaille and Keith 1974).

In cent. Wis., predation by Redtails and other raptors can depress the numbers of the introduced Ring-necked Pheasant. This occurs in spring, but in areas of greater snow depth elsewhere others have reported it in winter; details in Petersen (1979).

In the e. Great Basin in Utah, black-tailed jackrabbit numbers were low in 1966–1967, intermediate in 1968, and high in 1969. Redtail clutch size did not vary in synchrony with their density. Redtails may have partially adjusted their reproduction to prey numbers in a density-dependent fashion, but the matter is unclear (D. Smith and Murphy 1979).

Great fluctuations in numbers of some prey species of the Redtail appear to be more evident at higher latitudes; although fluctuations occur in warmer areas, there are also more potential prey species. Redtail spacing tends to result in approximate numerical stability maintained by shifts in prey selection. Clutch size possibly varies depending on the nature and amount of available food, but other unknown factors may need to be reckoned with, so current evidence is more suggestive than conclusive.

Temperature   Caged Redtails at air temperature were telemetered. Their body temperature fluctuated (as one would expect) with exertion and rest. But hawks that fasted in winter (food shortage plus thermal stress) had temperatures 3.2° C lower at night than in daytime—even though they rivaled the Great Horned Owl in excellence of insulation against cold. This may result in substantial energy savings (Chaplin et al. 1984). A captive ♀'s heart rate was telemetered outdoors for 10 days; it av. 202 beats/min. in daytime and 134 at night, and maxima occurred crepuscularly—just after sunrise and just before sunset (Busch 1984)—an unexpected bimodal pattern.

Flapping rate   Usually about 2.6/sec. (C. H. Blake).

Names   The Black Warrior of Audubon (1840) and Chief Black Hawk (leader of the Black Hawk War of 1832—see Hodge 1907) are based on the black, or "Harlan's," Redtail.

Falconry (or hawking)   The widely available Redtail is the raptor most often used in N. Am. It is easy to train, being of even temperament, and can be flown at game under almost any circumstance. Capable of taking sizable quarry, many trained birds can match the best European Goshawks in taking even the largest rabbits and hares (F. Beebe 1976).

Numbers   The Redtail is the most plentiful large raptor in much of N. Am. Although some fairly pronounced regional changes in numbers have occurred, both decrease and increase, in our area Redtails are believed to have increased slightly overall through the years. Although generally shy birds after early life, in a few instances Redtails become less wary where not persecuted. Prospects for more of this are favorable.

Literature   Well over 1,200 significant sources of Redtail data exist in journal articles, faunal reports, and so on. Of necessity, treatment in this volume consists more of examples than synthesis, although some 550 sources were at least scanned (and 135 cited).   RALPH S. PALMER

FOOD   Mammals form the bulk of the diet in both number taken and frequency in stomachs—to 80% or more in some studies; birds comprise much of the remainder; other items include reptiles, amphibians, fishes, various invertebrates, and some carrion.

So many regional studies have been done that there are compilations of these, notably May (1935), Bent (1937), N. Snyder and Wiley (1976), and Sherrod (1978). Since the Redtail can substitute 1 prey for another, depending on availability, and since what is available obviously varies in different regions and for many reasons, summaries and compilations mainly indicate relative quantities and diversity. For example, data on 754 stomachs in the sequence given by McAtee (1935) with frequent items starred: domestic fowl*, wild ducks, Ruffed Grouse, pheasants, quail (2 species), other grouse, (2 species), Gray Partridge, crows, Screech Owl, small birds*, squirrels*, rabbits* and hares*, shrews, moles, bats, voles*, mice, rats (various), pocket gophers, ground squirrels*, grasshoppers*, other insects and caterpillars, crayfishes, snakes*, frogs and toads, spiders, centipedes, lizards, salamanders, and turtles. It is highly probable that carrion was included, since dead poultry was used to bait pole traps set for raptors at game farms (whence came numerous specimens), and it is certain that the list has become longer.

Perhaps the dietary adaptability of the Redtail may be indicated by referring to some regional studies, scattered geographically, but see also Habits, above. Older studies were based on stomach contents. More recent studies are based on pellet analyses, on items found at nests and beneath perches, and on direct observation. Each method has biases, which will not be discussed here.

In PA., principally "mice," red squirrel, poultry (carrion?), insects, and cottontails (McDowell (1949a). One thinks of the Redtail as a vole catcher, but voles are often a subsistence food until larger prey can be captured. In an area in MICH., young Redtails took voles, but "adults" were diversified feeders (the Craigheads 1956). In an area in WIS. the introduced Ring-necked Pheasant was principal prey (Orians and Kuhlman 1956, Gates 1972), but where they were scarce the Redtails fed on mammals (Errington 1933). In KANS., the 6 most frequent items in pellets were vole, black rat snake, cottontail, "bird," cotton rat, and garter snake (Fitch and Bare 1978). In an area in UTAH, black-tailed jackrabbits comprised 98.5% of total biomass of nesting Redtails (D. Smith and Murphy 1979).

Various ALTA. studies emphasize the snowshoe hare and Richardson's ground squirrel. In interior ALASKA, 60% mammals (snowshoe hare most important even when its numbers were low); there were large numbers of breeding waterfowl, shorebirds, and passerines; the hawks took a surprising number of fully-grown birds, especially Mallards and Common Teal (Lowe 1978). Along the Columbia R. in n.-cent. WASH., there were no ground squirrels and few rabbits and hares; 4 kinds of snakes made up 40% of all prey items and 50% of the biomass (R. Knight and Erickson 1976); rattlers are included in this and various other studies. In a CALIF. study the diet was varied, but year-round staples were ground squirrels (by far the most important), cottontails, pocket gophers, and gopher snakes (Fitch et al. 1946b). In w.-cent. ARIZ., most food in breeding season was cottontails and jackrabbits; next were 2 ground squirrels; birds ranged from Starling to quail size; the desert spiny lizard was the most important of 13 reptiles recorded (Millsap 1981).

Most of the above prey might be termed primary species, which are few in any region; secondary species are more numerous in number and usually comprise a much smaller fraction of the diet except when primary species are scarce.

Cannibalism See Reproduction, above. The Redtail has been known to capture Cooper's Hawk, and in cent. Alta., 2 of these were found in the same Redtail nest (Meslow and Keith 1966). It has fed on, and probably captured, Screech and Burrowing Owls and has attacked the Long-eared Owl.

Surprises The number of pocket gophers reported in several studies, since they are so rarely seen on the surface of the ground, and crayfishes, which are aquatic and often somewhat hidden. Red squirrels are reported as food at least from New Eng. and Pa. to the Great Lakes states and to Alaska; one wonders how the hawk (or pair) gets these, if in thick conifers. Some are possibly captured on the ground. Although this hawk eats a considerable number of small birds, there may be only a single recorded observation of it catching one in flight.

Amphibians Undoubtedly taken fairly regularly; they are probably eaten immediately, as they evidently are rarely delivered to nests; it is also probable that their bones vanish quickly during digestion.

Carrion Few studies list traffic victims as food; it is eaten, as are dead and injured wild game. Carrion was important in s. Wis. (Errington 1933). Redtails in that state made off with dead chickens spread on fields with manure, carrying them to nests (Orians and Kuhlman 1956). In Calif., Redtail pellets contained evidence of cow, horse, sheep, bobcat, coyote, and skunk (Fitch et al. 1946b). Most fishes taken, including chum salmon in Wash., are dead; see summary by Stalmaster (1980).

Outside our area One or more subspecies hunts within the forest canopy, and 1 forages on land crabs.   RALPH S. PALMER

FOOTNOTE Common Buzzard *Buteo buteo* (Linnaeus)—**occurrence not substantiated.** Reported on Nizki in the Near Is. (outermost Aleutians), May 26, 1983 (1983 *Am. Birds* **37** 902). Nearest record in the Atlantic area is Nielsen's (1983)—1 found dead June 17, 1982, near Myvatn, Iceland.

FERRUGINOUS HAWK

Buteo regalis (Gray)

Sometimes called Ferruginous Roughleg. Our largest and heaviest buteo—at a distance sometimes confused with eagles or Osprey. Tarsi feathered down to the toes ("booted"). Two variable, disjunct **color phases,** yet they interbreed randomly.

Basic LIGHT Head very light, streaked sparingly chestnut; upperparts mixed blackish and rich browns, the latter concentrated on "shoulders" and rump; upper wing coverts with extensive browns; underparts white with some chestnut on flanks and belly, the thighs and tarsi vivid reddish browns barred black; tail (ventrally) variable, usually whitish basally grading into dusky with indistinct darker subterminal band; underside of wings largely white with black carpal patch, and upper surface of spread wing shows basal half of primaries palish. DARK Body and upper surface of wing dark browns (sepia and variants) or toward rufescent, some feathers edged paler; tail as light phase except lateral feathers darker; wing lining dark, contrasting with lighter undersurface of flight feathers.

Juv. LIGHT Quite like corresponding Basic except more neutral colored dorsally and venter white with few or no markings; tail whitish basally with darkish markings, grading to medium grayish and with indistinct darker subterminal band. DARK More or less as dark Basic, including tail.

Sexes overlap greatly, but ♀ av. larger within these spans: length 22–27 in. (56–69 cm.), wingspread 48–56 in. (122–142 cm.); wt.: ♂ av. about 39 oz. (1,100 gm.) and ♀ 44 (1,250 gm.).

No subspecies.

DESCRIPTION One Plumage cycle with Basic I earliest definitive. Any distinction between the sexes is slight and a matter of averages.

135

▶ ♂ Def. Basic Plumage (entire feathering) renewed from SPRING into FALL (but few data on molting). LIGHT   **beak** very dark, cere yellow to orange-yellow, **iris** palish yellow. **Head** usually appears rather pale, the feathers whitish to pale cinnamon with dark shaft streaks that combine to form longitudinal streaking (the dark preponderant in some individuals), throat white. **Upperparts** and extending out to include all small and median upper coverts of wing variably "ferruginous" (tawny-rufous or orange-cinnamon), the feathers with blackish centers. **Underparts** breast usually whitish grading into very pale reddish brown on belly and lower sides, the latter feathers with wavy dark transverse bars, variable in size and number; thighs and tarsi deep tawny-rufous with wavy black transverse bars; under tail coverts white. **Feet** yellow to orange-yellow, talons black. **Tail** (ventrally) varies with individual from nearly all white through various grays to tawny-rufous, the feathers paling at tips and occasionally with a dark spot toward end of outer pair. **Wing** upper surface as mantle except some coverts toward slaty; the secondaries at least with transverse blackish bars; undersurface mostly white, but usually some dark markings on the lining plus a conspicuous dark carpal patch ("thumb mark"); primaries darken in distal ⅓.

▶ ♀ as ♂ except (Friedmann 1950) dark areas in feathers of mantle and in reddish brown portion of wing "generally smaller." Tail variably brownish (probably none entirely neutral colored).

▶ ♂ ♀ DARK   Head and body commonly toward sooty, often with various feathers on anterior body margined reddish brown; tail more or less as light phase (in some, very light); wing has dark lining. Some individuals are largely dark reddish browns, except wing as in other dark birds and tail with much rufous brownish (not gray). These reddish birds are here included in the range of variation of dark birds rather than listed as a separate rufous (or erythristic) phase, as did Bent (1937), Friedmann (1950), and Thurow et al. (1980).

NOTE   Bent and Friedmann described an "immature" Plumage between Juv. and "adult," but Basic I is not separable. Descriptions of such birds should be incorporated in the range of individual variation occurring in any Basic Plumage. From Friedmann: ♂ ♀ LIGHT dorsum and upper wing coverts more reddish brown than later; underparts mostly white (no tawny "bib"), abdomen and sides tinged tawny; flanks white to tawny with very dark spotting; tail whitish, variably marked or washed with gray or with warm browns and without transverse barring. DARK upperparts dark neutral and underparts more colored, including heavy blackish barring on body and flanks.

AT HATCHING   Few details. Down-A is short and white except long and silky on crown and tinged gray on crown, wings, and rump. The later down-B is longer, thick, and white. (From Bent 1937.)

▶ ♂ ♀ Juv. Plumage (entire feathering), well developed by about age 44 days and retained through winter into following spring–summer. LIGHT   **Head** appears quite light, the forehead especially is white with very dark streaks. **Upperparts** dark with some white portions of feathers showing. **Underparts** tawny patch from throat onto breast, its borders and remainder of venter white with some dark spots on or across the abdomen and larger dark areas on sides; thighs spotted very dark on white. **Tail** medium grayish with about 4 transverse darker bands and a white tip. DARK young also reflect subsequent Basic pattern—white reduced or absent from forehead; **under-**

parts thighs mixed dark and light. **Tail** darkish overall, commonly rendering the blackish bars rather obscure. Excellent illus.: Olendorff (1975).

Molting In breeders, extends from about Apr. into early fall. Some flight feathers are dropped early, at least by nesting ♀♀.

Measurements Eight ♂ BEAK from cere 26.3–30.5 mm., av. 28, WING across chord 421–440, av. 431; and 4 ♀ BEAK from cere 27–30.5 mm., av. 29.5, and WING across chord 427–450, av. 432.2. Some of these birds, from Friedmann, were also probably measured by N. Snyder and Wiley (1976), who gave mean figures for WING across chord for 20 of each sex as ♂ 428 mm. and ♀ 444. Many birds cannot be sexed reliably by meas., since there is great overlap. DIAMETER OF HIND TOE of older nestlings is larger in the ♀ than in the ♂, with no overlap; see Reproduction, below.

Weight Mean figures from N. Snyder and Wiley: 15 ♂ 1,059 gm. and 4 ♀ 1,231. Average wt. of "adults" in Idaho: 20 ♂ 1,040 gm. and 13 ♀ 1,228 (Steenhof 1983). In se. Alta. in summer, 14 live-captured av. 1,676 gm. and were arbitrarily classified as ♂ if under 1,500 gm. and as ♀ if heavier (S. and J. Schmutz 1981). For some wts. of nestlings near flight age, see Reproduction, below.

Hybrids None reported; experimentally, the Prairie Falcon has fostered Ferruginous young, and the reverse has also occurred, as cited in Olendorff et al. (1980).

Geographical variation Apparently none except in proportions of light to dark individuals. In Wash., Bowles and Decker (1981) stated that only light birds occurred, but Fitzner et al. (1977) found 3 dark young in a nest. Summarizing 5 studies, S. and J. Schmutz (1981) reported these percentages of dark birds from within these areas: Alta. 9.4, S.D. 1.6, Idaho 3.9, Colo. 3.0, and Utah 3.4. In n. Utah and s. Idaho in 1972 and 1973, R. P. Howard (1975) observed 100 light and 4 dark birds; the latter all paired with light birds in these years. C. S. Houston estimated 30% dark in sw. Sask. (in Lokemoen and Duebbert 1976), and 40 years earlier Bent (1937) stated offhand that nearly ½ the birds his party saw in Sask. were melanistic.

In se. Alta. in 1976–1977, the colors of each "adult" (in 85 pairs) and each nestling (in 48 nests) were noted by S. and J. Schmutz (1981). Light and dark in all age-classes were disjunct, not bridged by intermediates. They suggested that dark is produced by a single dominant gene.

Affinities Our 2 hawks with "rough" legs (feathered, or "booted," tarsi) were placed in different subgenera and with another intervening by Friedmann (1950). The 2 species are in juxtaposition in the 1957 and 1983 AOU *Check-lists*. The smallish circumboreal Rough-legged Hawk of the tundra (*B. lagopus*) is a narrow-beaked, small-footed mouser; the much larger ferruginous plains bird (*B. regalis*) is wide-beaked, has large feet, and favors relatively heavy prey. Hubbard (1973) suggested that "during glacial intervals" the latter may have differentiated from the former.

RALPH S. PALMER

FIELD IDENTIFICATION Our largest buteo, a massive, chesty bird.

LIGHT birds: Even at a great distance on the plains, alighted or flying, the white underparts show like a beacon. Rusty back and part of wing, pale head, and white tail with some diluted rusty distally. The spread wing shows a white "window" basally in the primaries, the wing lining mostly white with dark carpal patch; the white of the venter contrasts with the mixed rusty and black of the thighs, or "leggings," which form a dark V—a unique character. In calm air the hawk may seem sluggish or cumbersome when taking flight, but it is graceful and buoyant once fully airborne. It flies swiftly, glides, soars, and circles with wings slightly up-angled. It often hovers when searching the terrain, as does the smaller Rough-legged Hawk.

Juvenal birds have some dark on the light flanks, but they do not contrast with the venter; the undersurface of the wings is essentially light from leading to trailing edge. and there is a "window" in the primaries; some at least show a few indistinct bars in the light tail. These birds might be confused with Juv. pale ("Krider's") Redtails, but the latter lack dark on the flanks and typically have multiple narrow, darkish tail barring.

Dark birds: Vary to mostly dark, including the wing lining; the flight feathers are paler, and the "window" is present; the tail is essentially white, becoming variably darkish distally. Juvenals have the pattern more broken; they might be confused with some Roughlegs (see species account), but usually the latter have a fairly well to clearly defined wide, dark distal tail band.

Nestlings As in the Roughleg, feathered to the toes. RALPH S. PALMER

VOICE Seldom mentioned by authors. Perhaps usually silent except when alarmed at its nest or probably during displays. In alarm, *kree-a* or *ke-a-h* or harsh *kaah, kaah* like one of the calls of the Herring Gull (Bent 1937). Also described as "screams" not unlike those of the Redtail (W. E. C. Todd 1947). RALPH S. PALMER

HABITAT Arid, semiarid, and grassland regions of w. N. Am. Level and rolling terrain and foothills. Avoids high elevations, forest interiors, narrow canyons, and cliff areas.

Breeding season Grasslands (natural and man-altered), sagebrush country, salt-bush-greasewood shrub growth, periphery of pinyon-juniper and other forest. Along watercourses in open country it nests in cottonwoods, willows, swamp oaks, and pines. Many nest on open terrain, even level ground, a boulder (or among boulders), creek banks, knolls, sides and summits of hills, low cliffs, and buttes. Some occupy hay-stacks, straw piles, roofs and chimneys of abandoned buildings, and power-line structures. See also various comparisons under Swainson's Hawk and Red-tailed Hawk.

In other seasons, open terrain from grassland to desert. The most common wintering buteo only on wide expanses of treeless terrain; where there are sizable trees and other high perches, the Redtail outnumbers it, as does the Roughleg to a lesser extent and in some seasons. In winter in w.-cent. Ariz., perch sites of the Ferr ginous had lowest mean vegetation height and canopy volume of any rapto; studied (Millsap 1984).

Habitat alterations Can only be touched on here; most of the prairies and high plains, for example, now are vastly man-altered. Control of fire on the prairies favors woody growth, which can affect the Ferruginous Hawk negatively while benefiting Swainson's and Redtail. Schmutz (1984) attributed a 40% decrease in Alta. breeding range directly to human disturbance and increased cultivation. Houston and Bechard (1984) reported a comparable decrease in Sask.—40% of former breeding range now vacant and another 40% used only sparsely, mostly caused by intensive agriculture plus human interference with nesting. In S.D., Lokemoen and Duebbert (1976) and Blair (1978) found that active sites were significantly farther from nearest human activity than were randomly selected points. Blair reported larger clutches and greater hatchability at more distant sites. Only 1 of 38 nesting attempts was on farmland, and it failed. In e. Oreg. a single nesting out of 46 was on farmland (Cottrell 1981). Such reports confirm what Bendire (1892) stated long ago, that the bird shuns settled regions. Yet in the Dakotas it has nested on haystacks and other sites, preferably where hayfields were unplowed native grasslands (Gilmer and Stewart 1983). Outside the nesting season, both natural and man-altered environment are used where prey is plentiful; pocket gophers, for example, may increase and be hunted on unplowed cropland (Wakeley 1978a). Livestock grazing, even some overgrazing, seems to increase the mammals on which the hawk feeds, but continued abuse of the land is as bad for the bird as it is for the livestock.   DWIGHT G. SMITH

DISTRIBUTION   (See map.) The Ferruginous Hawk has the smallest range of any buteo widely occurring n. of Mexico. Compare especially with Red-tailed and Swainson's Hawks, since the 3 species coexist in many areas. Although the Ferruginous is common in parts of its breeding range, other areas have seen a serious decline in numbers, and it is currently regarded as threatened or endangered in Canada and the U.S. Schmutz (1984) estimated a total of 3,000–4,000 breeding pairs, of which 500–

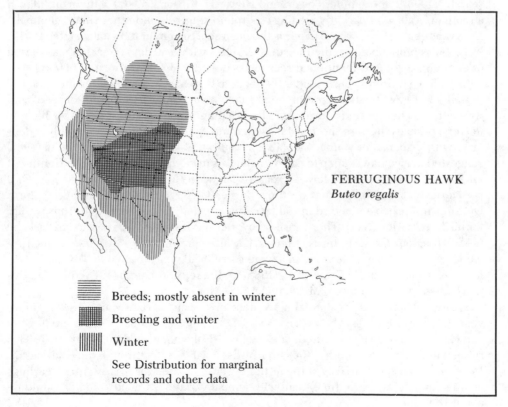

FERRUGINOUS HAWK
Buteo regalis

Breeds; mostly absent in winter

Breeding and winter

Winter

See Distribution for marginal records and other data

1,000 were in Canada. Some distributional changes in Canada are mentioned under Habitat, above. Various factors affecting distribution and numbers were discussed by Olendorff and Fish (1985), who cited the relevant literature.

Breeds A wide area from s. in the Canadian prairie provinces—s. Alta. e. of the Rockies, s. Sask., and a 1984 record for sw. Man. after a presumed absence for some 60 years. In the U.S.—e. perhaps into Minn. and in Kans. and w. Okla.; w. into e. Oreg., and e. Wash.; and s. into 3 U.S. states bordering Mexico; has occurred in summer in ne. Calif.

Winter Most birds withdraw from n. breeding range and occur s. well into Mexico. Recorded n. into Alta. and Sask. and in the 2 upper tiers of U.S. states from Wash. and Oreg. e. to the Dakotas and Nebr. The majority, however, occur primarily from Okla. and Tex. to Calif. and s. into Mexico (5 states, Durango southernmost, plus Baja Calif.).

Straggler Eastward in U.S. to Wis., Iowa (1 banded, 1963), Mich., Ill., N.J., Ark., La., Miss., Ala., Fla. (twice recently).

Reported as **fossil** from the Pleistocene of Calif. (4 sites) and from a **recent** site each in Calif., Ariz., Tex., and N.D. (references in Brodkorb 1964). Additional later reports of recent sites: Ariz. 1 and S.D. 4 (possibly 5).   RALPH S. PALMER

MIGRATION During a span after nesting, both parent and young birds disperse in search of food. For example, Powers and Howard (1973) saw 50–60 of them on 1 day in a montane valley, apparently feeding on ground squirrels and other small mammals. D. Evans et al. (1985), whose paper is the main source of migration data, stated that in N.D. birds probably leave their nesting localities within 40 days after the peak period of attaining flight and mentioned recoveries of young 350 km. nw. and 600 km. sw. within 55 days. Some young evidently begin to disperse very soon after they can fly.

Fall For most birds, migration begins in late Sept.–early Oct., with onset of cold weather and after ground squirrels are hibernating. Almost nothing is known about s. nesters; perhaps they are short-distance migrants; possibly they are essentially sedentary, with dispersal of young. Salt (1939), Thurow et al. (1980), and Harmata (1981) suggested that w. hawks keep to narrow corridors in foothills e. and w. of the Continental Divide. There are very few fall records far w. in the San Francisco region. Of 9 recoveries of birds banded as nestlings in ne. Colo., most were from Tex. plus a winterer in Mexico and a bird in Calif. (Harmata), and the recovery pattern is similar for birds from Alta. (Salt). There are 4 recoveries in Mexico of birds banded in Sask. by C. S. Houston. Easterly birds, from N.D., after premigratory dispersal (which includes n. into Sask.), migrate s. in a wide corridor to winter range in Tex. and Mexico—map and text of D. Evans et al. (1985). S. Russell and Lamm (1978) reported this hawk as frequent in Sonora, Mexico, Oct. 23–Mar. 2.

Spring There was substantial movement in w.-cent. Ariz., Mar. 15–Apr. 5 in 2 years (Millsap 1984). This hawk arrives in S.D. in late Mar. or early Apr., and in Utah and Colo. most return in late Feb. or early Mar. (Lokemoen and Duebbert 1976). This raises a question as to whether the latter birds remain locally through the cold season. In general, this hawk arrives in the n. tier of states in late Mar.–early Apr., yearlings coming later (May–early June), and with annual variation. Canadian dates would be about the same.

There have been recoveries in Calif. of individuals banded as nestlings in N.D., Idaho (2), Colo., and Alta. Presumably there is some lateral movement; also. an e. bird might winter in Mexico and then trend w. in spring.   DWIGHT G. SMITH

BANDING STATUS   To Aug. 1981 the number banded was 6,406 and there were 270 recoveries (Clapp et al. 1982). Main places of banding: Alta., N.D., Sask., Idaho, Colo., S.D., Utah, and Oreg.

It is of interest that much of the early banding of this hawk was done in Alta. by W. R. Salt and that in Sask., C. S. Houston had banded 850 nestlings to Aug. 1985. Recovery data have appeared in several papers, notably by D. Evans et al. (1985), who discussed changes in recovery rates.   RALPH S. PALMER

REPRODUCTION   Age when **first breeds** unknown; there is no evidence that year-lings breed.

This hawk is prone to desert its nest or eggs if disturbed, apparently more so in years of food scarcity. In former times, some collectors took whatever eggs they found on 1 visit, including incomplete clutches, since the birds were considered unlikely to return once the nest had been disturbed. In studying disturbance factors and their effect, White and Thurow (1985) reported a 33% desertion rate and significantly lowered productivity of eggs and young compared with control nests. Also of special interest is the great variation in some aspects of this raptor's biology, chiefly because it is so responsive to cyclic fluctuations in its primary prey.

Displays   On territory; both sexes engage in HIGH-CIRCLING with associated vo-calizing, neither adequately reported. In HIGH-PERCHING the ♂ occupies elevated or conspicuous sites, on or (if available) off the ground. L. Powers (1981) described the SKY-DANCE. The bird flies with slow, very deep, labored wingbeats and irregular yawing and pitching. This is stimulated by an intruder, being stronger toward other Ferruginous Hawks than toward other species, and may terminate in vertical dives. The FLUTTER-GLIDE (of Powers) may be a variant—a series of shallow, rapid wing-beats, interspersed with brief glides. HOVERING, as when hunting, may also have a display function, an aerial equivalent of High-perching, when it occurs over territory. In FOLLOW-SOAR. performed usually by the ♂, the hawk flies at a lower level than an intruder and "escorts" it out of the territory. It has been observed with intruding Golden Eagles, Rough-legged, Red-tailed, Swainson's, Cooper's, and Sharp-shinned Hawks. Powers noted that it sometimes occurred before or after more aggressive actions like attacking, talon-grasping, or chasing.

Pair bond   Once established, probably renewed annually (assuming it is not main-tained all year) as long as both mates survive, but the only evidence is circumstantial—an early and extremely high rate of reoccupation of territories by twos.

Copulation   Begins early, near a nest site of a former year, before new construction has begun. Olendorff (1973) stated that it increases in frequency to egg laying; it continues, at least sometimes, into incubation. Early in the cycle, a food pass (transfer of prey to the ♀) is likely to precede it, and L. Powers (1981) timed it at 4–18 sec. Angell (1969) saw it once, on the last day of Mar. on a cliff rim in Wash., within sight of an old nest that was reused.

Territory   This raptor is an early breeder, preceded in many localities only by

141

owls, the Golden Eagle, and perhaps the Redtail. In cent. Utah, both sexes are on territory by late Feb. or early Mar. In ne. Colo., Olendorff (1974b) found earliest occupation on Mar. 10 and most territories occupied by the end of the month. In Idaho, Powers heard territorial calling on Feb. 13, but most pairs arrived in the 1st week of March and were definitely territorial by midmonth.

Reoccupancy Approaches 90–100% in some areas and years. In s. Idaho, 39% of territories were reoccupied in 7 of 9 study years and 17% all 9 years. One nest site was used more or less continuously for about 30 years (Thurow et al. 1980).

In studies summarized by Olendorff and Fish (1985), **territory size** varied greatly in different areas and years with habitat, presence of other raptors, and availability of food. In 41 study years in 13 areas, Ferruginous density varied 8.8–123.5 sq. km. per pair and av. 32.5. In se. Alta., maximum density was 8.8 sq. km. (Schmutz et al. 1980) and in se. Oreg. 9.8 (Lardy 1980). In some areas, in years of food scarcity, many territories may be left vacant and some pairs that are territorial may fail to nest, but, generally speaking, nonnesting pairs do not maintain territory. A nonbreeding pair in Utah defended an area of 4.5 sq. km., and 3 singles av. 3.9 each. Prebreeders and nonbreeders are not observed (except sometimes as intruders) on defended territories. For details, see especially Woffinden and Murphy (1977).

In sagebrush desert in cent. Utah there was a pair per 20.7 sq. km. In Colo., 1 per 99.9 sq. km. on an area of 2,598 sq. km. (Olendorff 1973). In n. Utah and s. Idaho, av. densities were a pair per 40 sq. km. In n. S.D., Lokemoen and Duebbert (1976) found densities of a pair per 17.4 sq. km., while Blair and Schitoskey (1982) reported much lower densities in 1976 and 1977 in nw. S.D. In N.D., Gilmer and Stewart (1983) found densities of an active nest per 15.4 sq. km., and in se. Alta., Schmutz (1984) compared densities of a nest per 9.3 sq. km. to 1 per 66.7 sq. km. over a much wider area a few years later.

There are areas fully occupied by territories in desert shrub, along low hills and ridges, in pinyon-juniper country, grassland. and some types of agricultural areas. In N.D., Gilmer and Wiehe (1977) found 5 nests along 16 km. of power line, noting that they "tended to occur in clusters." Distances between nests in cent. Utah ranged 1.3–5.4 km., av. 2.48. In s. Idaho, Thurow et al. (1980) reported spacing along juniper-grassland ecotone av. 4.3 km. for 19 nests in 1978 and 3.8 for 38 nests in 1979.

Coexistence (See also Red-tailed Hawk, Reproduction.) In se. Alta., the Ferruginous, Swainson's, and Red-tailed Hawk each maintain a minimum distance between nests but often nest closer to 1 of the other species even when there was other opportunity (Schmutz et al. 1980). Thurow and White (1983) suggested that there was some benefit when the Ferruginous and Swainson's engaged in joint defense of their overlapping territories. In 9 study areas in the U.S., "nearest neighbor" distance between Ferruginous nests was 1.9–7.2 km., mean 3.2. In se. Alta., Schmutz et al. (1980) found lowered reproductive success where nests of different species were less than 0.3 km. apart, and Cottrell (1981) reported the same when buteo nests were visible to one another.

Territorial conficts With other species, such as the Great Horned and Short-eared Owls, N. Harrier, Red-tailed and Swainson's Hawks, Golden Eagle, accipiters, ravens, and magpies are reported. Being an early nester, the Ferruginous Hawk sometimes displaces ravens from or the later-nesting Swainson's Hawk from their sites. There are low-intensity reactions to intrusions by ♀ Ferruginous Hawks from adjacent territories (L. Powers 1981) but stronger ones, including dives and Follow-soars, to Great Horned Owls (several authors) and Golden Eagles, both of which may prey on Ferruginous adults and young. The most common interaction is with Swainson's Hawk; their territories (at least for foraging) commonly overlap, and the Ferruginous is dominant. The Ferruginous is outnumbered in some areas by Swainson's or the Redtail and, in the Snake R. area of Idaho, by several large raptors.

Nest site The Ferruginous Hawk shows "remarkable adaptability and flexibility" in site selection (Gilmer and Stewart 1983). In this respect it is a unique buteo. Depending on habitat, the site varies from trees to level ground and on man-made structures of various sorts. Terrestrial sites are more vulnerable to predation. Tree sites are more productive. Summarizing 19 studies in 8 states, for a total of 1,353 nesting attempts, Olendorff and Fish (1985) divided nesting substrates as follows: tree-shrub 796, rock or dirt outcrop 162, cliff 105, ground 121, utility structure 116, haystacks 48, and a few on buildings. Ground nests tend to be on slopes, knolls, and crests of ridges and are quite often on or lodged among boulders. A sharp reduction in use, or avoidance, of cultivated lands has been remarked on frequently. Examples of variation, in descending order of frequency of use for each location, follow: N.D.—ground, trees, boulders, hay and straw stacks. S.D.—clay buttes, ground. Great Basin desert—trees (mostly juniper, preferably the tallest lone or peripheral one), ground (desert shrub). Badlands and treeless areas—buttes, cutbanks, low cliffs, and ground. Wash.—rock outcrops, ledges on hills, and in some canyons. Southern Idaho and vicinity—wide variation from ground and desert shrub to (atypically) lower cliffs of Snake R. Canyon. Colo.—much variation includes such man-made structures as buildings and supports for powerlines. Artificial nest bases are accepted. In se. Alta., Schmutz (1984) reported preferential use of such platforms and better productivity on elevated bases than on ground sites. They should be shaded.

If a nest is in a tree (where it might be mistaken for a Swainson's or a Redtail nest), it is typically in an isolated one or in an isolated small cluster of trees in an exposed location. On power-line towers nests are exposed to high winds but are relatively free from predators. D. Smith and Murphy (1978, 1979) stated that Ferruginous Hawks choose to nest near a food supply; in some years, then, areas may contain many inactive old nests. In Colo., Olendorff (1973) thought that deterioration and destruction of traditional habitat from extensive cultivation and other usage resulted in a shift from ground to tree nesting. In se. Alta., the Ferruginous arrives early and regularly refurbishes and uses nests of previous years; Swainson's, arriving later, has fewer old nests to choose from and so often must build a new, hence shallower, one (Schmutz et al. 1980).

Many nest sites are traditionally used, while others are marginal and used only in years of favorable food supply. For example, since a major limiting factor in part of Alta. appeared to be lack of nest trees, baskets were placed where old nests had been destroyed—22 in former territories and 15 in grassland with adequate prey but no history of previous occupancy. The majority of those occupied were in former territories (Fyfe and Armbruster, in Chancellor 1977). In cent. Utah, reoccupancy of previously used sites is high, but tree sites are reused far more frequently (57.4%) compared to ground (18.5%) and ledge (14.2%) (D. Smith and Murphy 1978). Given a choice, at least in many areas, tree sites are selected over rock outcrops or ground locations. In n. Utah and se. Idaho, of 43 nests located in 1972, 30 were reoccupied in 1973 and 5 of the remaining 13 had been destroyed (R. P. Howard and Wolfe 1976). In N.D., when a brood fell or was blown from a tree, it was reared on the ground (Lokemoen and Duebbert 1976).

The only evidence to date that this hawk nests near where it was reared is Harmata's (1981) report of a 4½-year-old ♀ recovered 5 km. from her natal site and presumably breeding.

Nest building   L. Powers (1981) reported that there is first considerable perching near the site. Greenery may be delivered to several old nests before any construction or refurbishing begins. In Utah, an old nest was refurbished Mar. 6–11, and an adult was sitting on Mar. 12. Both sexes deliver materials, the ♂ more often. At 3 nests, ♂ ♂ brought about 51%, 68%, and 100% of construction materials (Powers); there was copulation during the building phase and "repair" was often begun on several alternative nests more or less simultaneously before one was selected for laying.

Material   Mostly debris from the ground, but D. Smith and Murphy (1979) and L. Powers (1981) observed the birds tugging at shrubs, attempting to uproot them. Several times Powers saw the ♀ stripping bark from trees and limbs to use as lining. He noted that ♂ ♂ carry most of the larger sticks, usually in the beak; ♀ ♀ delivered almost all of the smaller, softer materials used for lining. Males may assist in constructing the base, but ♀ ♀ line and mold the bowl.

Bendire (1892) reported nests made of bison bones and lined with bison wool, which had been known to occur much earlier. Cameron (1914) noted nests of cedar, soapwood, greasewood, ribs of bison and pronghorn, with grasses and cow dung in the lining. Bison dung was probably used commonly in presettlement times. In Mont., horse manure in 2 nests (Silloway 1903). In se. Wash., invariably some hard substance lying loose—"most often a ball of horse or cow droppings, often the size of 2 clenched fists and usually hardened by time." Such a ball was in many nests; the "dung disintegrated and formed a matted carpet over the nest surface as the nestlings grew" (Bowles and Decker 1931). Again e. Wash.: the lining mostly sage bark and "practically always" large, dried chunks of horse or cow dung and, when this was unobtainable, large dead roots (Bowles, in Bent 1937). Other items: paper, rubbish, various bones, barbed wire, cornstalks, plastic, and a piece of steel cable (C. Stone and Porter 1979). See also Woffinden and Murphy (1982). A nest is usually built, or an old one refurbished, in less than a week.

The nest seems disproportionately large for the size of the builders when compared, for example, with those of Swainson's Hawk, and Olendorff (1975) thought that constructing a bulky nest might be a stimulation to breed. Nests often measure well over 1 m. in both diam. and height, and they grow. especially in height, if refurbished in later years. In S.D., nests were layered: sunflower stalks, cottonwood, and so forth, in the bottom; sod, dung, and cattails in the middle; finer materials for the lining (Lokemoen and Duebbert 1976). They measured 0.9–1.5 m. in diam. and 0.72–1.45 m. high, with bowl 17–32 cm. deep. Nests on haystacks were lined with hay and the like, another example of using what is handy.

144

Alternative nests Common, especially 1 or 2 remaining from previous years; up to 8 on a territory have been reported. Some 87% of pairs have alternate nests in cent. Utah (D. Smith and Murphy 1978). In Alta. a nest on the buttress of a cliff had been occupied during a span of years, becoming a mass of material 12 or 15 ft. high (Taverner 1919).

Greenery Or possibly some substitute is typically found in nests, even though not reported from Utah desert by Woffinden and Murphy (1982). Green materials may be deposited in several nests beginning soon after the birds arrive, thus advertising ownership before 1 is singled out for laying. In se. Alta., Schmutz (1984) noted that such material was added to man-provided nesting platforms. Dawson and Bowles (1909) mentioned fresh fir twigs, Cameron (1914) observed a pair delivering green alfalfa, and L. Powers (1981) saw a ♀ delivering a leafy sprig in her beak to her nest containing young. That is, greenery is delivered through at least much of the time that the adults are territorial.

One **egg** each from 20 clutches (Alta. 1, Sask. 6, Mont. 2, N.D. 11) **size** length 62.39 ± 2.56 mm., breadth 48.48 ± 1.52, radii of curvature of ends 20.21 ± 0.89 and 14.81 ± 1.41; **shape** between spherical and elliptical, elongation 1.28 ± 0.040, bicone −0.065, and asymmetry +0.144 (F. W. Preston). These are very close to meas. of 53 eggs in Bent (1937). Size of eggs of this hawk plus the Redtail, Swainson's, and Roughleg are in this volume; see also comparative table in Bechard and Houston (1984). The shell is smooth, **color** creamy white or (at first) faintly bluish, blotched with pale to dark warm browns and buffs; occasionally there are few or almost no markings. Fresh eggs weigh about 80 gm.

Clutch size Large compared with our other buteos in similar latitudes. Clutches of 3–4 are common, but the number is said to range 1–8, in large measure varying with fluctuating food supply (D. Smith and Murphy 1978, D. Smith et al. 1981). Summarizing 10 U.S. sources, the av. was 3.44 eggs in 462 clutches (Olendorff and Fish 1985), which masks variation caused by changes in food supply. In n.-cent. N.D. in a year when Richardson's ground squirrels were plentiful, tree-nest clutches were significantly smaller than those in ground nests (Lokemoen and Duebbert 1976). When prey in general is scarce in an area, many hawks may not lay.

Egg dates Vary with lat., weather, and perhaps food supply. In cent. Utah in a mild winter, R. Bee and Hutchings (1942) found 2 eggs in a nest in Jan.—probably the earliest recorded laying. Some clutch dates follow. Utah—Mar. 17–Apr. 1; Colo.— Apr. 6 (early) and 16; S.D.—Apr. 12 and 17 in 1974 (Lokemoen and Duebbert 1976); and in nw. S.D. median dates were Apr. 21, 1976, and Apr. 15, 1977, with latest Apr. 28 and 22, respectively (Blair and Schitoskey 1982). Southern Wyo.—2d and 3d week in Apr. (B. Millsap). Mont.—laying mid-Apr.–mid–May.

Presumably viable clutches Dates from Bent (1937): Calif. to Colo. and Tex.—23 records Feb. 28–May 24 (12 were in the span Apr. 23–May 14); Oreg. and Wash. to the Dakotas—94 records Mar. 24–June 16 (48 in the span Apr. 16–May 10); and Canada—33 records Apr. 26–July 3 (16 were dated May 2–16). Olendorff and Fish (1985) gave laying dates between lat. 38° and 49° N as Mar. 20–May 1 and above lat. 50° N in Alta. as beginning 3 weeks later, with shorter spread.

Incubation Shared by the sexes, ordinarily with the ♀ on the nest much of the day and at night. She sits low when incubating. The ♂'s incubating spans diminish in length as time passes, with corresponding increase in sentinel perching and patrolling (L. Powers 1981). Rarely is a nest left unattended, although the ♀ may get off briefly to stretch, attack intruding birds, or receive food from her mate. She may return with nesting material, and occasionally there is copulation during these breaks. The ♂ hunts and keeps guard, and the sitting ♀ occasionally toys with nesting material. Neither sex defends the eggs against humans, but there is some defense after they hatch.

Incubation period   Thirty-two to 33 days. The 28 days of Bent (1937) is too short, the 32 of Weston (1968) is probably satisfactory, and up to 35 of some authors is too long per egg.

Hatching   In a season when vulnerable prey is plentiful. In Colo., for example, it occurs when the early broods of Horned Larks are just out of their nests—a common buteo adjusted to an abundant passerine. But Horned Larks are insufficient for the growing young, and so the Ferruginous shifts to young ground squirrels, cottontails, jackrabbits, and meadowlarks. Ground squirrels emerge during the 1st half of July. (From Olendorff 1975.) By nesting earlier than Swainson's Hawk, the Ferruginous may escape the consequences of summer drought.

Replacement clutches or renesting   Evidently rare. L. Powers (1981) reported a pair moving to an alternative nest 75 m. from a destroyed nest and succeeding at the new site. A late hatching date of July 1 in s. Idaho (Thurow et al.) might indicate relaying or renesting. When nests fail, pairs may continue for a time to occupy the territory and may engage in nest-defense behavior (Woffinden and Murphy 1977).

Nestling period   Wakeley (1978c) and L. Powers (1981) reported that ♀ ♀ tend the young, while ♂ ♂ hunt until well along in the preflight period, as usual with many raptors. In an exceptional case (Angell 1969), the ♂ did most of the brooding, while the ♀ hunted; either brooding bird was fed by the other, and both were on the nest at night. D. Smith and Murphy (1978) found that ♂ ♂ were the sole providers during incubation and 3 weeks of brooding, then ♀ ♀ resumed some hunting. The ♀'s detachment is gradual; as the young grow, she spends more time perching on the edge of the nest, then in a nearby tree or at some sentinel site, and in aggressive behavior toward interlopers. For a time, she may return to brood during inclement weather, especially on cold mornings (Powers). The prey brought by the ♂ is usually at least beheaded (especially mammals) before delivery, but the ♀ may consume the head at the nest. As the young grow, more prey is delivered, especially in early to midmorning. The ♀ at first presents small morsels to the beaks of her nestlings, and for 2–3 weeks mammals are dismembered and birds at least plucked before they are offered. She eats any dropped morsels. In Idaho a ♂ foraged actively all day, with peaks of activity in morning and evening; he hunted mostly from a perch and in low flight, but hunting from the ground resulted in more successful strikes (Wakeley 1974). As the young become able to feed themselves, food is brought and left for them; this includes items that the ♂ delivers to his mate at a favorite ground perch away from the nest.

In nest defense against humans, the ♂ is reportedly more aggressive. A ♀ who had a brood flew off and returned carrying a stone, which she dropped when turning up from a dive at the intruder (Blair 1981). This seems less remarkable when one recalls that clods of earth and balls of dung are delivered to nests.

146

Brood reduction Apparently there are no reports of a sibling causing the death of another, but there is some indication that surviving young have fed on starved dead brood mates. Some causes of nestling mortality were given by Woffinden and Murphy (1977).

Caching food Seldom reported near the nest. Angell (1969) found portions of 2 jackrabbits hidden in a tunnel under sage. In Alta., a hollow adjacent to a nest contained a bushel of dried bones and scraps of gophers (Taverner 1919).

Growth of young In captivity, 2 young at hatching weighed 47–53.6 gm., av. 51.6. Wing segments grew for 25 days, then slowed. Most leg segments grew earlier and ceased growth earlier (large feet are an early desideratum). Pinfeathers appeared at around 15 days. These young, as described by Olendorff (1974b), gained wt. slowly, and their development may not correspond with that of wild ones. R. P. Howard (1975) studied free-living nestlings, which gained wt. much more rapidly. His wt.-curves for presumed ♂♂ and ♀♀ show increasing divergence with time and essentially no overlap from about 30 days or earlier. By that age, mean wts. of 23 ♂ were 1,030 ± 22.2 gm. and 26 ♀ 1,477 ± 20.9; hind toe diam. was 13.9 ± 0.9 for ♂♂ and 17.5 ± 0.8 for the ♀♀. At 46 days, av. ♂ wt. was 1,060.5 gm. and ♀ wt. 1,354.

Behavioral development Data on wild young mostly from L. Powers (1981). Nestlings lie or sit for much of the 1st 2 weeks but may shuffle to seek shelter by 5–7 days. They stand at 18–21 days and walk soon after. They preen from 5–9 days onward, especially in early morning. They attempt to feed themselves by pecking at prey by 11–12 days and can feed on their own by 16–18 days (Angell 1969, Powers). Small prey is swallowed headfirst. At 22–23 days they seize food and "mantle" defensively over it. They wipe their beaks after feeding at 15–16 days and first cast pellets at 16–18 days. They are unsuccessful at dismantling prey until 4 weeks old. By age 23 or more days the young stand and flap their wings, and they are capable of vigorous flapping by 33–34 days, often making flap-jumps. Later they become "branchers," moving from tree nests out onto adjacent limbs; from ground nests, they hop, jump, and flap to find shade or a place to hide.

Thermoregulation Develops gradually, body temperatures being lower in early morning and late evening, with midday elevation of 4–5° C even when shaded by the ♀. The young are sensitive to higher ambient temperatures, panting, drooping their wings, and seeking shade. For details, see L. Powers (1981) and Tomback and Murphy (1981).

Initial movement out of the nest is often a response to heat stress, especially if the young are undernourished (Tomback and Murphy). Those in tree nests are shaded there by the ♀, while ground nesters seek shade nearby under sagebrush or any other concealment. One brood (Angell) sought shelter in a cave.

Age at initial flight For ♂♂, 38–40 days; the slower-developing, heavier ♀♀ fly about 10 days later (R. P. Howard and Powers 1973, L. Powers 1981).

Breeding success Jackrabbit population levels influence Ferruginous Hawk reproduction in this decreasing order of importance, as studied in the e. Great Basin desert: number of pairs that nest, failure of nesters to produce full clutches, number of young that attain flight, and number of young hatched. This can be mitigated somewhat by shifting to alternative prey if available; see R. P. Howard and Wolfe (1976), D.

Smith and Murphy (1979), and others. During a gradual decline in primary prey over a span of years there is a lag, but not a correspondingly great decrease, in number of young hawks reared to flight age; with an abrupt decline in prey, however, the decrease in number of young reared is also immediate and abrupt.

In cent. Utah, some 89% of pairs nested in high-prey years compared with 43% when it was low. Clutch size dropped from an av. of 3.8 to 2.1 eggs, and the av. number of young in successful nests from 2.9 to 0.7. Production of young to flight age was over 15 times as high as when prey was scarce (D. Smith et al. 1981). For a useful summary of nesting success, see Schmutz et al. (1984). Thurow et al. (1980) reported a loss of 23 (of 25) young that either disappeared or were found dead in nests in s. Idaho in 1980—a low jackrabbit year. Woffinden and Murphy (1977) reported av. nestling losses of 49.5% in the low jackrabbit years of 1973 and 1974 (there was evidence of starvation and possibly cannibalism) to 13.3% in the same area during 1967–1970.

High reproductive potential This allows rapid recovery of Ferruginous Hawk numbers when prey numbers increase. In Cedar Valley, Utah, however, even though jackrabbit numbers increased in 1984 after a severe decline, the hawks had not returned (Woffinden, in Olendorff and Fish 1985). This might be a lag preceding a recovery.

Olendorff and Fish summarized data in 20 sources, from 7 states for 1967–1984 inclusive. Averages: clutch size 3.44 eggs (462 clutches), brood size 2.32 young (377 broods) per nesting attempt, and an av. of 2.10 young attained flight when all nesting attempts (successful and failed: total 1,531) were included; for 1,071 successful nests, the av. was 2.93. They also compared 5 diurnal raptors as studied in 3 states: the Ferruginous has larger clutch size and av. more young per successful nest than the Redtail and Swainson's Hawks and Golden Eagle but fewer than the Prairie Falcon.

Dependency L. Powers (1981) reported that early movements of young were under 100 m. from the nest, then under 200 m. for a time. They perch in trees or on elevated places, calling to be fed. A young Ferruginous at age 52 days, and 4 days out of the nest, killed a 2-ft. bullsnake (Angell 1969). In nw. S.D., Blair and Schitoskey (1982) studied 6 radio-tagged young for 5 weeks. In less than 2 weeks the young were hunting within the parental home range, but no captures were observed. They ceased to return to the nest but were dependent on adults for up to 4 weeks. The area they covered increased from an av. of 60 ha. the 1st week to 488 ha. the 4th. One young each from 2 nests in cent. Utah were radio-tagged and their whereabouts checked for 3 weeks. Movements away from their nests av. 159 and 844 m. (maxima 1,300 and 2,800). Both departed about 28 days after 1st flying. Before leaving, adults and young were occasionally seen together in flight, but generally the young were in "loosely structured sibling groups" (Woffinden and Murphy 1983). In Colo., a young bird moved 21 km. in 8 days; that is, it began wandering immediately (Harmata 1981).

According to I. Newton (1979), this hawk has produced young in captivity.

DWIGHT G. SMITH

SURVIVAL Information is based on rather small numbers of recoveries, the most useful source being D. Evans et al. (1985). They found, as expected, that highest mortality is in 1st fall–winter; it was higher than expected in older birds. Shooting continues to be a problem, especially s. during the legal gamebird season, but leg-bands may be seldom reported because raptors are legally protected.

Maximum potential longevity is indicated by recovery of 2 individuals 20 years of age (Lloyd 1937, Houston 1984). Dwight G. Smith

HABITS **Flight** has been described principally by D. Smith and Murphy (1978), Wakeley (1978b), and L. Powers (1981). Apparently it varies depending on wind conditions. Soaring has special use as territorial advertisement but also occurs at other times and elsewhere. Other types of flight related to breeding territory are described under Reproduction, above.

In se. Idaho, the diets of nesting Red-tailed and Ferruginous Hawks were sampled before and after a decline in their principal prey. Species composition of their diets diverged during the shortage, being most pronounced in those individuals that did not share foraging ranges with their own species. The 2 species converged on similar-sized prey, and it was concluded that shifts in dietary overlap during shortages "do not necessarily imply that interspecific competition is occurring" (Steenhof and Kochert 1985). On winter range the Ferruginous and other buteos occur where food is abundant, seldom with evident conflict unless a bird attempts to rob prey from another.

Wakeley (1978a) noted that ♂ ♂ in n. Utah preferred to hunt bare-ground areas and pasture over grass-shrub, grain, old field, and juniper woodland. Males tended to rehunt areas in which they made their last successful kill. Woffinden and Murphy (1977) observed a ♀ hunting 5.2 km. from her nest in a low-prey year.

Hunting time Varies depending on prey size and abundance. When jackrabbits were abundant in cent. Utah, the 1st daily hunting period was from daybreak to midmorning, the 2d in late afternoon and evening. Wakeley (1974) found that ♂ ♂ primarily hunted ground squirrels and ♀ ♀ more varied prey throughout the day, but the data on strikes/hr. indicate a bimodal pattern of activity.

Hunting methods Include the following. **1** From a perch—a juniper, rock outcrop, or any elevated site—natural or man-made. **2** From low flight, especially along slopes and hillsides. Wakeley (1978b) reported a 16.6% success rate (about 1 strike/hr.) of hunting by 2 ♂; although low-flight hunting was most successful, they hunted mostly from perches and high flights. A special case: catching bats by patrolling a cave entrance in Tex. (1984 *Am. Birds* **38** 932). **3** From greater heights, including while soaring. Success rate is low. **4** From hovering, or this as a prelude to alighting to hunt. Powers stated that only ♂ ♂ performed this flight and only in wind above 20 km./hr. **5** From the ground, after aerial inspection. The hawk, with body nearly horizontal, awaits its opportunity near a rodent burrow. This variant is from Cameron (1914): Pocket gophers push up earthen piles while tunneling. The hawk flies slowly until it discovers a fresh damp pile. Then it alights and waits for a gopher to push close to the surface; then the hawk rises a few ft. in the air and comes down stiff-legged onto the loose earth to transfix the gopher, which then is brought out. Such capture of unseen prey is reminiscent of the Great Gray Owl, which, using auditory cues, pounces on snow to capture a mouse underneath. The hawk may eat the gopher or carry it away. In winter in Tex., at prairie dog towns, the hawks perch therein or on the perimeter, on shrubs or the ground. The "dogs" dive into their holes if a hawk circles overhead but

149

ignore those that are perched (1973 *Am. Birds* **27** 79). **6** Cooperative hunting by mates has been described by 5 authors, beginning with Cameron.

Wintering Ferruginous Hawks may exploit a favorable food supply and roost nearby, at times in association with Roughlegs or other raptors and without apparent aggression.

Using a beater In Union Co., N.Mex., in late Sept., a person was shooting prairie dogs for collection and a Ferruginous Hawk alighted nearby after several shots had been fired. Within 10 min. it was joined by 4 more spaced in a rough semicircle of 35 m. radius centered on the collector's vehicle. When a "dog" was shot in the general vicinity of a hawk, the bird ran to claim the kill, mantled over it, and threatened other hawks that approached. A bird with prey was reluctant to fly and could be approached closely. Three of the hawks followed when the vehicle moved elsewhere in the colony, attempting to claim a kill. The colony was often hunted for sport, and the hawks appeared regularly when shooting began, apparently associating gunfire with easily obtainable food (Chesser 1979).

A situation reminiscent of the famous tar pits of La Brea, Calif., was reported by R. P. Howard and Powers (1973). Where road tar was dumped in gravel pits, the hawks became entrapped while attempting to catch entangled kangaroo rats.

Nest mounds In desert n. of Knolls, Utah, there were scattered mounds to about 6 ft. high and 9 ft. in basal diam. These were former nesting sites, used for years, that formed by sand and salt blowing and filling the interstices of the accumulated materials (Behle et al. 1944).

Literature The most extensive recent coverage of this species is by Olendorff and Fish (1985). DWIGHT G. SMITH

FOOD Mainly small and medium-sized mammals, also some birds, cold-blooded vertebrates, and a few insects. Olendorff and Fish (1985) summarized principal food from 10 studies as follows: 85% mammals, 10.5% birds, 2.6% reptiles, occasional amphibians, and 1.7% insects. Since the early studies, which were based on stomach contents, almost all information has been from breeding range and in nesting season.

Based on food brought to nestlings, studies are as follows: In cent. and n. Utah and s. Idaho, black-tailed jackrabbits were the single most important item. It should be pointed out that most rabbits and hares taken are young individuals. In Colo., Oreg., Alta., and the Dakotas, ground squirrels are the most important, while in Wash. and s. Idaho pocket gophers rank 1st (Olendorff and Fish), but ground squirrels are important in high-prey years in s. Idaho (Steenhof and Kochert 1985). In cent. Utah, 25 species including 14 mammals, 7 birds, and 4 reptiles. Mammals composed 90.2% of prey items, birds 7.6%, and reptiles 2.2%. Bulk of prey was 3 species: black-tailed jackrabbits, Ord's kangaroo rat, and antelope ground squirrel. Others: cottontails, cricetid rodents, microtines, and long-tailed weasel. Of avian prey, only Horned Larks were recorded every year, averaging 6.1% frequency but only 0.2% biomass. Bull snakes were recorded in 4 of 5 study years. J. Platt (1971) found 12 prey species in nests in n. Utah, primarily black-tailed jackrabbits but also kangaroo rats and long-tailed weasels. He recorded 2 raptors as food: N. Harrier and Short-eared Owl.

In Idaho, Thurow et al. (1980) recorded 20 prey species, including 12 mammal and 8 birds. Black-tailed jackrabbits composed 36.6% of individuals taken = 83.5% of prey biomass. Also cottontails, ground squirrels. cricetids, and n. pocket gopher. Frequent avian prey were Horned Larks and W. Meadowlark. R. P. Howard and Wolfe (1976) found that black-tailed jackrabbits composed 88.7% and 79.4% of food by wt. in n. Utah and s. Idaho. Other food included cottontails, ground squirrels, kangaroo rats, cricetids, microtines, birds. and reptiles. In Colo., thirteen-lined ground squirrels replaced black-tailed jackrabbits in importance, composing 41% of prey individuals (Olendorff 1973). In S.D., 12 species: 8 mammal, 3 avian, and insects (Scarabaeidae). Richardson's ground squirrel was the most important food, 96% by frequency and 68% by biomass. Snowshoe hares were next important, with 17% of biomass and 5% frequency. Other mammals: pocket gophers, cricetids, microtines (including mud-krat), and cottontails. Birds: W. Meadowlark, Pheasant, and unidentified (*Anas*) ducks (Lokemoen and Duebbert 1976). In nw. S.D., most important were thirteen-lined ground squirrels, Horned Larks, and white-tailed jackrabbits (Blair and Schitoskey 1982). Schmutz et al. (1980) reported Richardson's ground squirrel as the most important food in se. Alta., annually comprising 89.7% frequency and 89.2% biomass. Fitzner et al. (1977) found 14 prey species in nests in Wash.: 6 mammal, 6 bird, 2 reptile, and 4 insect taxa. On a frequency basis, ground squirrels and pocket gophers were the most common mammal prey, but lagomorphs were important. Birds included: W. Meadowlark, Long-billed Curlew, Black-billed Magpie, and Burrowing Owl. Common reptiles were the yellow-bellied racer and bull snake. Insects: Carabidae, Tenebrionidae, Orthoptera, and Elateridae. Food in a nest in Mont. (Cameron 1914): 9 prairie dogs, 2 bull snakes, a Sharp-tailed Grouse, and a magpie.

In years of low prey abundance, Ferruginous Hawks will shift from primary to alternative prey. In cent. Utah these are mostly kangaroo rats and snakes plus various small birds. In s. Idaho, R. P. Howard and Wolfe (1976) noted a shift to pocket gophers and ground squirrels; in another study there (Steenhof and Kochert 1985), it was principally from ground squirrels to pocket gophers. R. P. Howard and Wolfe (1976) suggested that wheatgrass treatments (with chemicals) in various stages of reversion to original vegetation may increase the probability that hawks will produce young in years of low jackrabbit numbers, due to greater vulnerability of prey in these areas and elsewhere. DWIGHT G. SMITH

tail dorsal
common ♂ pattern

ROUGH-LEGGED HAWK

Buteo lagopus

Rather large buzzard hawk. Tarsus "booted" (densely feathered, except bare at back) to base of toes; feet small. Beak rather small with elliptical nostril and, as viewed from directly above, narrow at base—that is, much more narrowly wedge shaped than in the Ferruginous Hawk. In relation to size of head, the eye seems somewhat large as compared with other n. buteos. Wing long, the 4 outer primaries deeply incised or emarginated on their inner webs; counting from the outer, #1 is about ⅓ shorter than #2–4, with #3 slightly the longest. Tail slightly rounded. Feathering soft and lax. Pattern and amount of dark (melanin) extremely variable, in our area exceeded in individual variation only by the Redtail. Patchy, blotched, or streaked areas or combination of these; tail partly white or (in very dark individuals) light at least basally, the dark in distal ⅔ varying with age, sex, and individual; underwing has at least a dark

152

"thumb mark" (carpal patch), remainder of lining varying from white to mixed dark and white, to all dark.

Although the Roughleg is usually described as having color phases, to do so is to label a segment of each end of a continuum of variation from lightest to darkest birds. This is evident in the Juv. stage (and to some extent in downies)—even though color and pattern differ appreciably between Juv. and Basic—and light and dark birds interbreed.

The sexes differ appreciably in pattern in Basic Plumage in at least a high percentage of individuals but little if at all in Juv. (see below). The ♀ is larger, there being 75% or more of nonoverlap of the sexes in meas. The sexes combined: length 18½–20½ in. (47–52 cm.), wingspread 47–52 in. (119–131 cm.), wt. in N. Am. about 1 lb., 9 oz.–3 lb., 2 oz. (715–1,400 gm.). On av. in N. Am., definitive-feathered ♂ ♂ weigh about 800 gm. and ♀ ♀ 1,000 (very few ♂ ♂ weigh as much as 900 gm. and very few ♀ ♀ weigh so little; essentially no overlap in wt.). Sex for sex, birds in their 1st winter weigh considerably less than older ones. The largest Roughlegs are in Alaska and e. Asia.

Three subspecies are recognized here, of which 1 occurs across much of boreal N. Am.; another is claimed (unsatisfactorily) to reach nw. Alaska and presumably occurs in the Commander Is.

DESCRIPTION   Cade (1955b) is relied on here. Although Cade did not state this, he assumed that all museum specimens that he examined were labeled correctly as to sex—which is doubtful. Thus, in some instances Cade lists exceptions to a statement (see below) where possibly there are none.

If one were to equate the tremendous individual variation in color and pattern in the Redtail in the nw. quadrant of its breeding range with individual variation in the Roughleg in N. Am., the complexities of describing the latter would have some perspective. Although it is largely a matter of deposition of melanin, various areas on the Roughleg apparently vary independently so that each bird may be regarded as a kind of mosaic, although there are some common patterns. The following pertains to *B. l. s. johannis.*

▶ ♂ Def. Basic Plumage (entire feathering) ALL YEAR with principal molting of all feathering from early summer into fall. Basic I is earliest definitive.

Beak black, cere orange-yellow to orange, **iris** dark brownish. **Head** varies from nearly unmarked white through a long gradient of increasing width of dark (to black) markings along the shafts of most feathers until finally feathers all blackish (feathers at rear of crown white basally). **Upperparts** vary from feathers with wide white edges to others having much gray-brown, especially internally, to blotchy (feathers mostly very dark internally) to solid dark. **Breast** plain white to same variably streaked to solid dark, but a tendency to dark blotches laterally. **Belly** all white to blotchy to solid dark. Lower abdomen, sides, and under tail coverts white to same openly to densely marked or barred very dark to solid blackish. Undersurface of **tail** white, or at least pale, for basal half, more or less. Commonly 3–4 (distally) and rarely as many as 8 blackish bands, the terminal band widest and others progressively narrower toward base; very tip of tail white. In some, the distal ⅓ or more of dorsal side of tail is a bleached-appearing grayish brown, this area in others varying to medium brownish or to black-

153

ish, or the dark area variegated slightly (faint barring within it). In the darkest birds the tail still is palish, but only proximally, the lighter birds plain or (usually) barred. **Feet** yellow, talons black. The spread **wing** is variably dark above and lightest at bases of primaries (even in darkest individuals). On underside, the lining varies from nearly unmarked white with blackish carpal patch, with dark ends on the secondaries, and primaries very dark (to solid black) distally. The blackish near ends of the secondaries collectively forms a dark trailing edge of wing that extends to include the dark distal portions of the primaries. Others show progressively more dark within the features until, finally, the underwing in darkest birds is almost solid dark (to black) with bases of primaries whitish. The coverts at leading edge of wing are usually light with dark shaft streaks but in some are plain light and in others plain dark.

The different characteristics may be combined in many ways, although in general amount of deposition of melanin tends to have a certain consistency overall in the individual. For example, a ♂ may have a white breast and blackish belly, or just the opposite, or may have a dark dorsum and light venter, and so on.

The following are ♂ characters, although (assuming specimens were correctly sexed) not exclusively so; the 1st 2 characters are the most pronounced: **1** tail usually has 3–4 transverse dark bars on white; **2** belly usually white, varying through moderate to heavy dark barring; **3** coverts at leading edge of wing light with dark longitudinal shaft streaks in a large percentage of individuals; **4** head often lighter than dorsum; and **5** pattern of dorsal feathering tends to be more variegated than in the ♀.

Molting Begins in the breeding season, the ♂ beginning later than the ♀, and may terminate in late summer or fall or is sometimes interrupted by fall migration before it is completed. Molted flight and body feathers (and the down of nestlings) are often liberally scattered in and about a nest. Counting from the inner, the primaries molt from #4 outward, the "innermost 3 molting in sequence with the secondaries" (Cade), within which there are molt centers. The tail molts from the center outward. (Actually, all primaries molt in descendant mode, not always all in same year.)

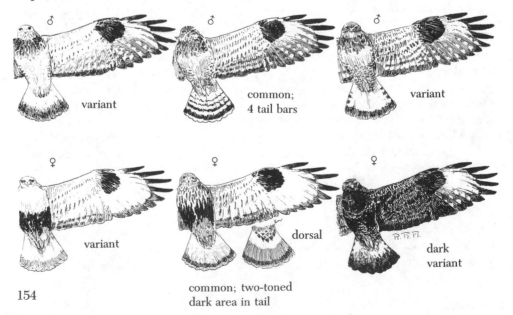

♂ variant

♂ common; 4 tail bars

♂ variant

♀ variant

♀ common; two-toned dark area in tail

♀ dorsal

♀ dark variant

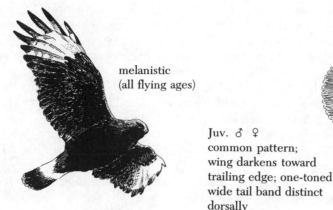

melanistic
(all flying ages)

Juv. ♂ ♀
common pattern;
wing darkens toward
trailing edge; one-toned
wide tail band distinct
dorsally

▶ ♀ Def. Basic Plumage (entire feathering) ALL YEAR with molting of all feathering starting earlier than in the ♂.

There is about the same amount of individual variation as in the ♂, but the following characteristics—especially the 1st 2—tend to be predominantly ♀: **1** tail usually with distal ⅖ or more brown, the distal ½ of the dark area markedly darker (2-toned dark area) and proximal area white (but some have barred tails), the very tip narrowly white; **2** belly usually heavily barred, laterally blotched, or with wide, solid, dark zone; **3** coverts at leading edge of wing often have subterminal wedge-shaped marks; **4** head feathers have dark shaft streaks, with head not distinctly lighter than dorsum; and **5** pattern of dorsal feathering is more uniformly dark than in ♂.

AT HATCHING There may be some variation in color of down-A, even within a brood. Older downies in sw. Alaska varied individually from light to dark gray; nestlings consistently had a prominent white patch, varying in shape from round to teardrop, on the occiput.

In captivity a light ♀ was mated to an overall dark ♂, and 4 (of 5) eggs hatched. Down-A of all nestlings was white. Down-B was whitish buff on 3 nestlings and dark gray on the 4th. Three of the young (1 ♂, 2 ♀) developed into birds of "medium" coloration of feathering, and the 1 with dark down was a blackish ♂ (Bird and Laguë 1976).

▶ ♂ ♀ Juv. Plumage (entire feathering) develops during nest life and is retained into following LATE SPRING, when molting into Basic I begins. The sexes are said to be similar in feathering (Cade), but Hamerstrom and Weaver (1968) stated that "rudimentary barring" near base of tail in ♂♂ is often sufficient to distinguish them from ♀♀. Juvenal characters: **1** cere greenish and iris (into 1st winter) light gray (Hamerstrom and Weaver); **2** tail ventrally has monochrome distal field of brown (not bands of 2 shades), only occasionally a faintly discernible darker distal portion—that is, it approximates the typical ♀ pattern; **3** coverts at leading edge of wing most frequently with longitudinal shaft streaks but are occasionally plain creamy (especially in Eurasia) and infrequently dark (in N. Am.); **4** shaft streaks on breast feathers are usually wide, medium brownish, with creamy margins (100% of Asiatic birds) or buffy or reddish

155

(90+% in N. Am.; and **5** the same holds for feathers on the dorsum. Coloring tends to be more blended—that is, dark areas less sharply defined, such as near trailing edge of underside of wing, in Juv. than in Basic.

In molting out of Juv. (Prebasic I), the primaries are probably renewed from inner to outer (V. and E. Stresemann 1960), that is, serially.

Color phases None in the strict sense; birds vary individually from relatively light through intermediate to black nearly overall. There are mixed light/dark mated and nesting pairs (Cade 1955, other authors) and broods. Captives: a "melanistic" ♂ and "medium phase" ♀ produced a brood of 2 "melanistic" and 3 "medium phase" young; a "medium-light" ♂ and "medium" ♀ produced "medium" young (M. Forness and D. Bird).

Measurements North Am., from Cade (1955b) unless otherwise indicated, giving spread and, in parentheses, mean and standard error:

ALEUTIANS and SW. ALASKA 12 ♂ BEAK from cere 33–38 (34.8 ± 0.36) mm., WING across chord 396–445 (418 ± 3.22); and ♀ BEAK from cere (of 12) 35–39 (36.8 ± 0.39) mm., and WING across chord (of 13) 430–461 (445 ± 4.42).

NW. ALASKA 13 ♂ BEAK from cere 33–38 (35.1 ± 0.43) mm., WING across chord (of 14) 394–444 (424 ± 4.36); and 12 ♀ BEAK from cere 35–39 (36.9 ± 0.38), and WING across chord 403–454 (435 ± 3.76).

W. CANADA 10 ♂ BEAK from cere 34–37 (35.1 ± 0.27) mm., WING across chord (of 12) 395–426 (411 ± 2.96); and 7 ♀ BEAK from cere 35–39 (37 ± 0.53), and WING across chord (of 8) 413–459 (436 ± 4.87). For some additional meas. of birds from the w. Canadian arctic, see Manning et al. (1956).

Migrant birds, all presumably from boreal N. Am., WING meas. across chord, averages: Basic feathering—2 ♂ WING 408 and TAIL 208.5, and 4 ♀ WING 433.7 and TAIL 223; in 1st winter (Juv.)—35 ♂ WING 402.8 and TAIL 215.7, and 41 ♀ WING 430.8 and TAIL 232.8 (D. Evans).

E. CANADA 11 ♂ BEAK from cere 32–38 (35 ± 0.49) mm., WING across chord (of 12) 392–412 (406.7 ± 1.71); and 14 ♀ BEAK from cere 34–39 (36.8 ± 0.39) mm., and WING across chord 416–450 (436 ± 2.59).

The considerable overlap of the sexes in linear meas. is evident; the tail is longer in Juv. than in Basic.

Weight Few N. Am. data; these are for summer birds: from the Colville R., Alaska: 4 ♂ 883–943 gm., av. 915, and 4 ♀ 1,033–1,400, av. 1,216; from Yukon Terr., 1 ♂ 840 and 1 ♀ 1,176 (Cade 1955).

From Adelaide Pen., NWT: 4 breeding ♂ 779–900 gm., av. 828, and 6 ♀ 1,055–1,227, av. 1,130; and young, almost all barely flying: 8 ♂ 701–869 gm., av. 815, and 4 ♀ 850–1,116, av. 1,001 (Macpherson and Manning 1959).

Averages for migrants livetrapped at Duluth, Minn.: Basic 2 ♂ 766 gm. and 4 ♀ 1,016; Juv. 35 ♂ 716 and 41 ♀ 910 (D. Evans).

Based on specimen labels, mean wt. 11 ♂ 1,027 gm. and 17 ♀ 1,278 (N. Snyder and Wiley 1976).

Hybrids None reliably recorded; Suchetet (1897) listed this species as having crossed with *Buteo buteo*.

Geographical variation In the species, discussed at length by Cade (1955b) and

156

can only be excerpted here. He examined 179 specimens, mostly from N. Am., and commented on the inadequacies of even so large a series.

The birds av. smaller in N. Am. than in Eurasia. Sexes tend to be less dimorphic in size from e. to w. in N. Am., excluding Aleutian-sw. Alaskan birds. WING varies from shorter in e. Canada to longer in nw. Alaska and Asia. There is greater individual variation in meas. and in characters of feathering in the Bering Sea region (excluding the Aleutians) than elsewhere in N. Am.

In ♂♂ a white tail with 3 or more blackish crossbars occurs in 62% of e. Canadian birds to less than 10% in Asia, with most abrupt change between w. Canada and nw. Alaska. A heavily barred belly occurs in 50% of e. Canadian birds to about 9% in e. Asia—an unbroken cline.

In mature ♀♀ the Juv. tail pattern (distal field uniformly brown) ranges from 78% in the Aleutians and sw. Alaska to 0% in e. Canada. Belly laterally blotched varies from 8% in the Aleutians and sw. Alaska to 58% in e. Canada, and belly with continuous dark band ranges from 8% in e. Canada to about 86% in Asia—an inverse relationship.

Definitive-feathered Asiatic ♂♂ differ from those in N. Am. in these characters of coverts of leading edge of wing: 1 higher frequency of individuals with light coverts with dark longitudinal shaft streaks; 2 a decidedly lower frequency with wedge-shaped marks; and 3 Asiatic birds have a uniformly light category (not reported in N. Am.), and N. Am. ♂♂ have a category of uniformly dark (not reported in Eurasia).

Outer web (leading edge) of primaries all to partially light in the Asiatic sample is the best criterion for distinguishing Asiatic birds in definitive feathering from those in N. Am.—about 80% of the former are different from about 90% of the latter, and 80% of Asiatic ones are different from about 83% of Alaskan birds. This lightness occurs in all Asiatic Juv. birds and in 62% of Am. ones (with differences in detail).

Breast feathers with narrow shaft streaks are more frequent going from e. to w. in N. Am., and the nw. Alaskan birds have it most often. The back shows the same trend.

There is some geographical variation in sexual dimorphism. For example, the difference in meas. between the sexes is greatest in N. Am. in the Aleutian-sw. Alaskan birds (the most consistent sexual divergence in size). There also are differences in feathering—that is, percentages of occurrence of various pattern details. Both sexes are more homogeneous in size and in tail pattern in Canada, less so in Alaska (with an exception), and still less so in Asia. This might indicate 2 parallel trends in gene frequency.

Occurrence of extreme melanism in the Roughleg correlates fairly well with relative humidity and Gloger's rule; however, it does occur at low frequency throughout the N. Am. breeding range. In the Colville drainage, Alaska, in the 1960s, there were clusters ("demes") of 6–10 pairs of melanistic birds (T. Cade, letter). On the Kuskokwim in sw. Alaska, in taiga, extreme melanism was seen rarely 1979–1983 (D. Mindell). There are few dark birds out on the Canadian barrens, but fairly dark birds have been noted occasionally even in the higharctic. In Ill. in 2 winters, 441 Roughlegs were divided arbitrarily into 52% light and 31% dark, the remainder intermediate (G. Schnell 1967a).

Cade (1955b) speculated on the effects of refugia during the last (Wisconsin) glaciation on present geographical variability in the Roughleg. More recent factors, how-

157

ever, may tend to reduce it. For example, Roughlegs evidently have a homing tendency to both nesting and wintering places; yet if hawks return n. and rodents are scarce, many birds apparently move in search of food or at least are not evident at nest sites. Extensive displacement and late breeding(?) would presumably result in a mixing of progeny (and of pair formation) of birds that had previously been reared or had bred in different areas. In fall, movement is diagonal se. from Alaska to interior coterminous U.S. and evidently to some extent diagonal sw. out of the Ungava Peninsula. This contributes to some mixing of birds in winter or, if any pairs are formed in winter–spring, all year. A tendency to wander (birds occur in the Aleutians seasonally, for example, even where they apparently do not nest [Byrd et al. 1974, Gibson 1981]) or displacement of some sort may account for the occasional very dark bird in Canada far beyond tree limit.

Affinities If the Roughleg and the Ferruginous Hawk share common ancestry, which is pure speculation, they must have gone their separate evolutionary ways much earlier than the Pleistocene.　　　　　　　　　　　　　　　　RALPH S. PALMER

SUBSPECIES Three, listed in Cade (1955b), Portenko (1972, trans. 1981) and Stresemann and Amadon (in Mayr and Cottrell 1979). They are weakly differentiated; av. differences in size are small, individual variation is great, and variable birds occupy large areas between those in which birds comfortably can be assigned a trinomial. Mensural data from various sources may not be strictly comparable—whether WING was meas. flat or across chord of arc is not always clearly indicated. From some regions, notably Kamchatka and around the Okhotsk Sea, analyses suffer from a dearth of specimens.

In our area *sanctijohannis* (Gmelin)—av. small in size and darkest overall; comparatively short-winged; highly polymorphic, especially in comparison with other subspecies. Description with meas. given above. Breeds in N. Am. from Nfld. w. across Canada into the Mackenzie drainage; beyond (in Alaska) individual variation becomes so great, in an apparent zone of intergradation between Am. and Asiatic birds, that trinomial designation is not recommended (Cade 1955b). The Aleutian-sw. Alaskan Roughlegs are more homogeneous in phenotype (this may have arisen independently) than are the w. Canadian and nw. Alaskan Roughlegs.

Marginally in our area In Eurasia a cline of increasing size extends from w. to e., and, at least on tundra, a cline of decreasing color saturation (reduction in melanin) runs in the same direction (Dementiev et al. 1951, Vaurie 1961). Disagreement remains as to whether breeding Roughlegs of the Okhotsk Sea perimeter differ sufficiently to warrant a separate subspecies as Dementiev (1931) designated. Stegmann (1937) and Portenko (1972, trans. 1981) consider Dementiev's *kamtschatkensis* as only a variant of the Siberian stock, based on examination of 3 (different?) specimens by each. Key characteristics of WING-length and color were judged to be within the range of variation of Siberian birds. Cade, Portenko, and Stresemann and Amadon (in Mayr and Cottrell) refrained from recognizing an Okhotsk Sea subspecies. The name *kamtschatkensis* supersedes *menzbieri* (Dementiev 1951, trans. 1966), since it has priority.

kamtschatkensis Dementiev—paler and av. slightly larger than nominate *lagopus*.

Breeds in n. Siberia from the lower Ob R. e. to the Pacific (Kamtchatka); Kuril Is. Winters s. to Turkestan, n. China, Korea, and Japan. For meas., see under *menzbieri* in Dementiev (1951) and Vaurie (1961c). Not satisfactorily recorded in Alaska, but Johansen (1961) listed it as winter and spring straggler to the Commander Is.

Extralimital *lagopus* (Pontoppidan)—av. dark and relatively uniformly colored dorsally, contrasting with pale head (Vaurie), but many are dark headed; av. somewhat smaller than *kamtschatkensis*. See especially Schüz (1942) for many descriptive data. Measurements from many sources were assembled by Glutz von Blotzheim et al. (1971). Eurasian tundra approximately from the Yamal Pen. w. and extending s. into the forest zone at least in Fennoscandia; to the e. it intergrades with *kamtschatkensis*.

David P. Mindell

FIELD IDENTIFICATION   In N. Am. A fairly large and comparatively broad-winged buteo. The long lax feathering adds bulk rather than wt., and this, accompanied with rather slow wing action, lends a buoyant character that sometimes seems to exaggerate actual size—roughly that of a Red-tailed or Swainson's Hawk. It soars and glides with wings flat out or in slight dihedral; the latter, plus a tendency to flap more frequently, can sometimes be used to distinguish Roughlegs from Redtails. It often hovers, kestrel-like. It tends to keep well out in the open, where it perches on elevated spots and in isolated trees.

When seen overhead, the tail is mainly white or pale for more than its basal half, and distally very dark; wing lining varies from white to blotched dark to mostly (even entirely) very dark; all except the darkest individuals have an obvious black "thumb mark" (carpal patch)—as in some other buteo hawks and the Short-eared Owl. Head varies from nearly white to nearly black; the body from predominantly light to patchy (often a dark breast shield, frequently a dark lower abdomen); various parts of the bird seem to vary independently; hence all manner of combinations of light, intermediates, and dark. The darkest birds appear blackish, relieved only by pale (to whitish) basal areas on some primaries and secondaries ("window" in wing) and basally in tail—about as in 1st-year Golden Eagles.

Lighter-colored Roughlegs are fairly easy to identify, but very dark ones, especially at some distance, may be confused with dark Red-tailed, Swainson's, and Ferruginous Hawks; each has its own profile and flight characteristics (see Field Identification for these species). The N. Harrier, which has a light rump and which overlaps the Roughleg in winter habitat, might possibly be confused with it. When dark Roughlegs occur in winter at unanticipated places, at a hasty glance they might be mistaken for Ravens or Crows. On the other hand, under favorable conditions, the sexes and 2 age-classes, at least of lighter individuals, may usually be recognized—see Description, above.

A hovering Roughleg, if preparing to stoop at prey, may dangle its feet. At close quarters the feathered tarsi may be discernible; they are, of course, positive identification of a bird in hand—with the exception of the larger and very differently patterned Ferruginous Hawk.

This is our only buteo regularly occurring n. of treeline. Territorial birds in summer, on sighting an observer or other intruder, leave the nest and fly toward the intruder, one or both uttering a rather petulant catlike call. They thus reveal their presence and nesting location. Occasionally, when nesting in proximity to Peregrine Falcons, Roughlegs will remain silent, perched on or near the nest while observers move past, apparently to avoid provoking the Peregrines.

Elevated spots on which Roughlegs (and Snowy Owls and Common Ravens) perch are generally marked by patches of orange-colored lichen, fertilized by their excreta. The same is evident at nesting sites. Disgorged pellets (1 × 3 in.) are often found at these places. DAVID P. MINDELL

VOICE North Am. data. Usually silent when away from breeding areas, but very noisy at times in spring–summer. Evidently has a varied vocabulary.

The usual alarm, heard over and over when an observer approaches a nesting place, is somewhat catlike—a drawn-out, descending, rather petulant, mellow or somewhat whistled *kee-eer*. Like escaping high-pressure steam (Brandt 1943). As the bird quiets down and calls are more spaced out, they trail off to nothing rather than ending abruptly. In the circumboreal literature on this bird there is contradiction as to which sex has the higher-pitched or louder voice—the ♀ higher (G. Sutton and Parmelee 1956); the ♂ higher (Hagen 1952a). It may depend on motivation, but in general the ♂ higher.

Captives (Bird and Laguë 1976.) A pair that did not breed: ♂ called as often as 100 times in 42 min.—soft *mews*, increasing to high-pitched whistling notes slurred downward, to a shrill scream. The ♂ chased the ♀, uttering *cheep* calls, and the ♀, "extremely nervous," chittered back at him. A pair that bred successfully: in copulation, the ♂ emitted high-pitched squeals and, as he dismounted, the ♀ uttered a "strangled squawk." After copulation and the birds often close together, the ♂ uttered downward-slurred whistling noises, and the ♀ gave a clucklike *nar-nar* call. After an egg was laid, with high-pitched cries similar to those made during copulation, the ♂ dropped a rat in front of the ♀ who was on the nest; she responded with a soft 2-syllabled clucking.

Captive young Rising, high-pitched whistle. When small, feeding occasionally could be stimulated by imitating this whistle. DAVID P. MINDELL

HABITAT A lowarctic-boreal species (Johansen 1956) of open country. These are data from N. Am.

Breeding Primarily a tundra breeder, avoiding mammalian predation at its nests by using sites high up on ledges or in niches in steep cliffs, escarpments, the faces of rock outcrops, and eroded riverbanks. Also on columnar rocks, hillocks of rock or dirt, and such man-made structures as cairns or "beacons" (Inuit *inukshook*). Very rarely on a slope or nearly level ground, occasionally on top of an escarpment. Also in trees (mostly near the top of spruces) in various places, notably in n. Yukon Terr., where treeline extends nearly to the Arctic Ocean.

In parts of forested Alaska, as also in n. Finland (Pasanen 1972), breeders hunt principally over open bogs and other clearings. More "buffer" species here—principally birds—assure that the Roughlegs can raise their young in seasons of low microtine numbers.

Habitat partitioning in arctic Alaska by several cliff nesters, as indicated by their physical dimensions, was discussed by White and Cade (1971), in part as follows:

Gyrfalcons have a 31% size overlap with Roughlegs; both capture ptarmigan and, especially, microtines but differ in how they get them. There is 4.9% overlap between large ♀ Gyrs and small ♂ and ♀ Com. Ravens. Since the latter eat many foods, some being carrion, the size overlap can have little significance in terms of food consumption. Male and ♀ Roughlegs have 23% overlap, Roughlegs overlap with Ravens 36%, and their wing characteristics are very similar. Both feed heavily on microtines—as do owls, jaegers, and gulls, but hunting methods probably differ strikingly. (Also note overlap and nonoverlap of territories in Reproduction, below.)

Nest sites   Ravens and Gyrs nest early and get the sites best sheltered by overhangs; the later-nesting Peregrine uses a wider range of generally more-exposed sites; the Roughleg an even wider range, overlapping all the others, also very exposed ledges and slopes.

Migration   Occurs almost anywhere away from extensive forest and densely settled areas. It crosses wide inland and marine waters (as in the Aleutian area, Canadian arctic, etc.). It perches off the ground or on it, if there is a wide view of surroundings.

Winter   Prairies, semidesert, open fields, marshland, bogs, dunes, and some garbage dumps (to obtain rats). Usually solitary, on hillocks, sagebrush, poles, and in trees—preferably isolated ones. Near abundant food it may roost communally at night with other raptors. Hovering, although energy-consuming, is an adaptation to open terrain and has its rewards—prey is easier to locate from a relatively stationary position even in absence of a perch. They seem to hover more frequently on arrival at winter quarters than in midwinter.

Much has been written about winter habitat partitioning by our large buteos. It is generally assumed that an adult or young bird of a species is more or less dominant in its own hunting territory but that there is a hierarchy of species and competition for space. For example, some year-round resident Redtails must reckon seasonally with others that are transient or winter resident as well as with wintering Roughlegs. Redtails are regarded as the more aggressive, but it is more of a woodland bird, while the Roughleg favors areas where trees are few or absent. Their winter diets are essentially similar. The Roughleg has the advantage in cold weather out in the open because of the insulating quality of its feathering and its ability to hunt by hovering. Redtails generally perch higher and are dominant in territorial disputes (G. Schnell 1968, Marion and Ryder 1975), but high perching is not necessarily proof of dominance. Roughlegs are very inept at perching high on small limbs and twigs, since gusts of wind upset them; hence they are better off lower within a tree or on a pole or the ground.

Near Syracuse, N.Y., in Dec., at a place termed Roughleg Meadow, Spofford (1958a) noted raptor succession as follows: At first, many Roughlegs in sight—some hunting and others perched. By 1630 hrs., most had retired to night perches off the meadow, and 3 N. Harriers appeared. At 1647 hrs., 7 and soon 10 harriers appeared; these hunted until about 1700 hrs., and several were still seen when the 1st Short-eared Owls got up to go hunting. By 1715 hrs. the last harrier had settled into the meadow for the night, and the *snerk* calls of at least a dozen owls could be heard from all sides. By 1745 hrs. it was quite dark, the owls could no longer be seen, and the *snerk* chorus had about ceased.

Diagrams by Bock and Lepthien (1976) show highest winter densities of Roughlegs

161

in areas away from (mostly n. of) Redtail abundance. Additionally, there is some occupation of terrain vacated by Ferruginous Hawks. Thus the Roughleg in winter occupies habitat vacated more or less by other buteos.   DAVID P. MINDELL

DISTRIBUTION   (See map.) Data here are almost entirely for the New World portion of the circumboreal range.

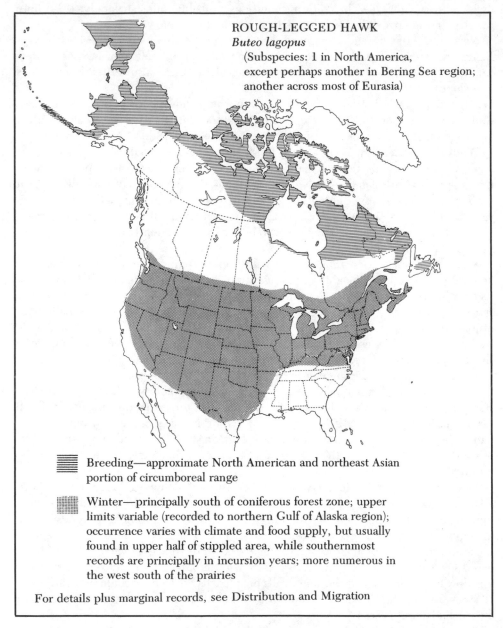

ROUGH-LEGGED HAWK
Buteo lagopus
   (Subspecies: 1 in North America,
   except perhaps another in Bering Sea region;
   another across most of Eurasia)

≡ Breeding—approximate North American and northeast Asian portion of circumboreal range

▦ Winter—principally south of coniferous forest zone; upper limits variable (recorded to northern Gulf of Alaska region); occurrence varies with climate and food supply, but usually found in upper half of stippled area, while southernmost records are principally in incursion years; more numerous in the west south of the prairies

For details plus marginal records, see Distribution and Migration

Breeds Approximately in area mapped. Has a tendency to nest in clusters—that is, less scattered than might seem likely. Appears to be a more common nester along coasts and on marine is., but this may be a function of nest site availability plus adequate food.

Nests far n. on Canadian is.—Prince Patrick, Melville, Bathurst, and Bylot; upper limits thus are far into the higharctic. Yet apparently habitable areas are frequently vacant. Nests along the Alaska Pen., also on adjacent is., and w. in the Aleutians as far as Ananiuliak I.—breeding range coincides with original distribution of native rodents (O. Murie 1959). Occurs occasionally and seasonally farther w. In the Commanders, Stejneger thought it might become established as a breeder because mice had been introduced, but it is only a winter–spring straggler; the introduced house mouse (*Mus musculus*) occurs in villages there; the red mouse (*Clethrionomys rutilus*), accidentally introduced in the mid-1800s, occurs only on Bering I., where it is abundant (Johansen 1961).

Bechard and Houston (1984) pointed out that, except near Churchill, Man., there is no proven breeding s. of lat. 60°N in w. Canada and the coterminous U.S. Southern limits of breeding do not coincide with upper limits of forest, however; this hawk nests in Nfld. (most southerly), in nw. portions of NWT, Canada, and in some forested parts of Alaska. It has rarely been found breeding in high mt. ranges of Alaska or Yukon Terr., unlike the Gyrfalcon; it appears to reach an altitudinal limit there at 2,500–3,000 ft., similar to the Peregrine Falcon.

Summer nonbreeding There are many late occurrences far s. of breeding range into s. Canada and coterminous U.S., mostly for late May–early June, when tundra birds are incubating. Perhaps many are yearlings, which do not attempt breeding until a year later, such as a June bird in s. Idaho (White et al. 1983). In Wyo. in May 1974, a pair was said to have refurbished a Ferruginous Hawk nest (1974 *Am. Birds* **28** 930).

Migration May occur almost anywhere within overall range but generally in open places. Although possibly reluctant at times, it is obviously not averse to crossing wide waters—unusual for a buteo.

Winter In the E. the birds occur principally from C. Cod, Mass., to the Chesapeake Bay region and thence w. to the s. part of the Great Lakes region and down to the lat. of n. Ky. Beyond, nearly to the Pacific coast, they are centered from just above the Canadian boundary down through 2 tiers of U.S. states or shift more s. to an area including Kans. and extreme n. Tex. w. throughout most of Nev. and n. to include se. Wash. By far the greatest number occur w. of the Mississippi.

Upper limits of winter occurrence are not well documented, G. Sutton (1932) stated that it occurs all year n. of Hudson Bay on Southampton I., but there seem to be no other reports from beyond the forest, and G. Sutton and Parmelee (1956) mentioned only breeding on Southampton. It has wintered in the Copper R. Delta, Alaska, which is far down within the forest zone. As to high density, upper and lower limits apparently shift depending on mildness or severity of season. Recorded s. limits include all s. U.S.-Mexican border states, a few across the border of Sonora (S. Russell and Lamm 1978), the U.S. Gulf of Mexico coast, and sightings in Fla. (primarily in the L. Okeechobee area plus 1 at Key West).

Straggler BERMUDA One shot in winter (Reid 1884).

ICELAND   A very dark ♀ of the N. Am. race (based on meas.) was taken Apr. 29, 1980 (for photo of this museum specimen, see 1985 *Bliki* no. 4, 60).

Recorded as **fossil** from the Pleistocene of Calif., Nev., N.Mex., and S.D.; and from **prehistoric sites** in Calif. (2), Utah (5), S.D. (several), Iowa, Ill., and the Brooks Range in n. Alaska—from Brodkorb (1964) with additions.

NOTES   There seems to be no indication of any significant change in breeding distribution in historic time. Northward beyond the Canadian mainland, known range has increased in recent decades, probably from an increase in observers.

Old reports of N. Am. birds occurring in Europe are misidentifications (Alexander and Fitter 1955).

For a fairly detailed map of Palearctic breeding distribution, see C. Harrison (1982). The Roughleg has straggled to the Faeroes and to extreme n. Africa. It is not recorded from Greenland.   RALPH S. PALMER

MIGRATION   In N. Am. Most Roughlegs live in open country, crossing the boreal forest twice annually between summer and winter quarters. Areas of greatest winter abundance apparently shift in latitude in different years, perhaps depending on time and extent of snowfall, which may affect availability of prey, or for some other reason related to a greatly fluctuating food supply. Even so, established winterers probably tend to return annually to the same place.

Most of the topography of n. Ungava has low relief (lack of preferred nesting places) except around parts of its perimeter, yet apparently more birds occur ne. than directly to the s. on e. winter range. Suitable winter habitat—marshland, extensive open areas, desirable garbage dumps—is scarce, and it would appear that movement from the breeding range of at least some Roughlegs is more or less diagonal sw. Birds banded e. of long. 80° W have been found as far w. as e. Man. and e. Kans. Movement is more vertical over the prairies. A bird banded on Victoria I. was recovered in s. Idaho (Parmelee et al. 1967). Alaskan birds must trend somewhat se. in order to travel in interior Canada and U.S. Birds banded in Alaska w. of long. 140° W have been found as far e. as e. Colo.

The birds of at least s. Baffin and nw. and w. Ungava almost surely migrate down the e. side of Hudson Bay to James Bay; on the w. side of the latter, Roughlegs have been seen (J. A. Hagar) coming in from over the water. Flight appears to be diagonal toward the n. shore of L. Superior (which, in its w. half, trends sw.) and many of the birds cross water rather than circumnavigate it. For example, after reaching the n. shore of the lake, many follow the shoreline sw. briefly and then head out over the water. Numbers seen at the w. end of the lake (near Duluth, Minn.), for example, are trivial compared with those of the Redtail—only 700+ of the former counted in fall of 1982. Thousands of raptors have been seen coming off the cent. s. side of L. Superior near Manitou I. off the tip of the Keweenaw Pen. (Sheldon 1965). Roughleg migration over L. Erie continued as late as Dec. 6 in 1964 (Kleiman 1966). Roughlegs are often active through the middle hours of the day (over land and water) and when the sky is overcast. They are much less dependent on thermals than out other buteo hawks; where "kettles" of Broadwings spiral upward and then glide, the Roughleg usually flies steadily onward—even sometimes in rain. Some fly high over water, but many have been seen from shipboard.

164

Roughlegs travel more or less spaced out, occasionally with up to 10 in sight at once. Hundreds may pass in a day. A few are early travelers both in fall and spring, and migration is protracted and on a broad front. The birds go farther s. from Tex. to Ariz. than elsewhere. First-winter birds are recognizable from older ones, and there is evidence both from observation and collection that younger Roughlegs tend to travel farther, and ♂ ♂ farther than ♀ ♀. Based on specimens collected between Dec. 10 and Feb. 14, K. Russell (1981) found that the mean lat. for 42 ♂ was 39°42′ N and for 64 ♀, was 42°33′ N, about 3° farther n. for ♀ ♀.

Fall On Oct. 13, at a slope near Indian House L. in interior Ungava, 28 birds soared, dived, and "played tag" in 2s and 3s. At least 36 were present the next morning, but by 1750 hrs. only 6 could be located. A weather change was imminent on the 14th, and most of the hawks departed that day (Clement, in W. E. C. Todd 1963).

Some Roughlegs apparently vacate n. breeding range early, especially in poor lemming years. A few arrive on winter range even before the end of Aug., yet most evidently do not leave breeding range until around mid-Sept.–Oct. Numbers of migrants increase through Sept., and main passage in s. Canada and n. coterminous U.S. occurs in Oct. (peak numbers, usually in last ⅓ of the month, do not necessarily coincide between various lookouts). Over 1,000 were seen Oct. 18, 1959, at Marathon, Ont. (1960 *Aud. Field Notes* **14** 31). Numbers diminish through Nov., but in some years some still travel even as late as the 2d ¼ of Dec. Bent (1937) gave a long list of fall dates, and later reporting has not changed the picture appreciably. Most records for s. winter range are from some time in Nov.–Feb.

Winter Although the birds are territorial, where food is plentiful they occur in local concentrations and sometimes have small communal roosts. A recognizable individual in Calif. used the same telephone pole for a perch for several months (Wilkinson and Debban 1980). There are various indications that individuals and groups—presumably the same birds—remain long in an area unless forced out by weather. For example, see Belknap (1960) for N.Y. In the Sacramento Valley, Calif., 10 were flying in a group on Feb. 26 (Wilkinson and Debban). Evidence from Sweden that Roughlegs reuse their winter territories includes a wing-tagged individual that defended the same area in 4 consecutive winters (Sylvén 1978).

Spring Some movement at s. limits of wintering and even as far n. as upper N.Y. occurs in Feb., and there is much movement in coterminous U.S. and s. Canada during Mar.–early Apr. A majority of the birds have departed from s. Canada by the end of Apr., but migration continues, diminishing, past mid-May. Many Roughlegs are funneled to the cent. s. side of L. Superior at the Keweenaw Pen.; from there, they apparently cross over, the shortest overwater distance being nw. to Isle Royale. It is possible that water is more of a barrier to migration in spring than in fall. A total of 253 were counted passing Whitefish Point, Mich., on the se. shore of L. Superior in 1 hr. on Apr. 23, 1979. Some more e. birds are funneled along the s. shore of L. Ontario, yielding relatively high counts at Derby Hill e. of Rochester, N.Y.—but perhaps they cross the lake to the e. As in fall, the birds usually travel spaced apart, yet quite often within sight of each other, and many may pass some locations in a few hrs. Migration n. across the boreal forest is heavy in late Apr. to well into May, continuing even later well out on the tundra where the spring thaw is yet to arrive. The idea (Townsend, in Bent 1937) that the birds follow the retreating snow, when runways of *Microtus* are

165

revealed, is not entirely correct regarding either the habits of voles or the reasonable constancy of migration regardless of whether the season is early or late. For example, in a recent year in sw. Yukon Terr., the 1st migrants were seen on Apr. 5 when the ground was covered by more than 0.5 m. of snow.

Here are some records of interest, for treeline and far beyond, from e. to w. Fort Chimo in n. Ungava—arrive about the last week in May (Turner, in Bent 1937) (Turner was there Aug. 6, 1882–Sept. 4, 1884). Northern Ont. at Winisk on Hudson Bay—30 seen June 1, 1981 (1981 *Am. Birds* 35 934). Also on Hudson Bay, at Churchill, Man.—100+ passing on June 7, 1936; migration had evidently been going on for some time, since 6 clutches were found in nests the following week. It was estimated that 1,000 passed June 7–17; they always seemed to be watching for lemmings, made slow headway along a narrow coastal strip, and crossed the Churchill R. (Farley, in Bent 1937). These birds were circumnavigating sw. Hudson Bay and bound for somewhere nw. Bathurst Inlet, NWT—migration May 24–28, birds flying singly (McEwen 1957). Nw. Keewatin at Perry R.—arrived May 22 (Aleksiuk 1964). Southeastern Victoria I.—they return before the thaw when the land is mostly snow covered; a single on May 10, 1962; pairs visit nesting places as early as May 24 (Parmelee et al. 1967). Banks I.— arrived May 24, 1952, and May 15, 1953 (Manning et al. 1956). In arctic Alaska on the lower (n.) Colville R.—the birds were already resident by June 4 (Kessel et al. 1953), so migration was earlier.

Flight years   Need much more investigation. There was an "immense" flight in the latter part of Oct. 1895 in the vicinity of Toronto, Ont., the birds decreasing in number until Dec. 5 (Fleming, in Bent 1937). This was followed by a lesser flight there in 1896 (Fleming 1907). Peak winters in the Toronto region listed by Spiers (1939), and stated to coincide with Snowy Owl peaks, were: 1917–1918, 1926–1927, 1930–1931, 1934– 1935, and 1937–1938. In cent. Ill. in the span 1905–1954, in Christmas counts, there were pronounced peaks in 1910, 1914–1919 inclusive (annually and collectively, much the highest), 1921, 1925 (high, as in 1910), 1929, 1946, and 1948 (Graber and Golden 1960). There is no reason to assume that any highs in Mont., for example, would correspond with any in Ill. or Pa. The above information aligns consistently neither with dates for Snowy Owl incursions—see listing of these for 54 years in Speirs (1939) or for 113 years in Palmer (1949)—nor with Goshawk or Great Horned Owl incursions.

Migration count data are affected by many variables, such as weather, height of migrants, and changes in travel routes. Correlations with actual population fluctuations have not been directly demonstrated. Migrant counts for 1935–1975 at Hawk Mt., Pa., where this is the rarest hawk, range from 0 to 36, with highs in 1939, 1949, 1961, 1964, and 1974 (Nagy, in Chancellor 1977).

At the w. end of L. Superior (Hawk Ridge, Minn.) in fall (Oct.–Nov.), migrant Roughlegs seen in 100 hrs. observation were 105–267 annually (av. 185) during 1978– 1982 inclusive (M. and D. Evans). Spring migrants (Apr.–May) near the opposite end of this lake (Whitefish Point, Mich.) ranged 134–645 annually (av. 451) (J. Kleiman and L. Baumgartner). Fall count fluctuations during 1978–1981 at the w. end of L. Erie (Holiday Beach, Ont.) correlate fairly well (correl. coeff. 85) with those from Hawk Ridge. Fluctuations in spring counts 1979–1982 at the e. end of L. Ontario and at Grimsby, Ont., near the w. end, are closely correlated (correl. coeff. 95). Spring count fluctuations do not correspond well between Whitefish Point and Derby Hill (correl. coeff. 5)—the most widely separated of the 3 spring count sites. Count fluctuations could be expected to be similar at Grimsby and Derby Hill, other factors notwithstanding, since they are relatively close and along the same general route of travel; Whitefish Point, however, is farther away, along a different general flight path, and probably contains migrants from a different wintering, and possibly breeding, region. Fluctuations at fall count sites do not correspond with those from spring sites (data from files of Hawk Migr. Assoc. N. Am.).   DAVID P. MINDELL

BANDING STATUS   In N. Am., 1955–Aug. 1979, the number banded was 1,524, with 41 (2.8%) returns (Keran 1981). To Aug. 1981 the number banded was 1,894, with 118 recoveries (Clapp et al. 1982). Main places of banding: Alaska, Wis., Minn., Que., and Dist. of Mackenzie. In addition to Wis. and Minn., smaller numbers have been banded widely on winter range, with increase in winter of 1973–1974 reflecting an incursion.   DAVID P. MINDELL

REPRODUCTION   North Am. plus Fennoscandian data. Age when **first breeds** not reported—perhaps 1 year for some and 2 for others, although there is only speculation on whereabouts of any yearling prebreeders.

Pair formation and displays   North Am. evidence of long duration of pair bond consists of various observations of birds perching and roosting in 2s in winter and some n. migration in 2s in spring. Turner (in Bent 1937) believed that the birds were mated before arrival at Ft. Chimo and immediately reoccupied or built a nest.

HIGH-CIRCLING, 1st reported in N. Am. by Henniger and Jones (1909), is seen occasionally in late winter and spring during spells of warm weather. Townsend (in Bent 1937) saw it in Mass. in Apr.–May—2 birds, "probably a pair," circling together and then heading "in direct flight" ne. With wings and tail fully spread, they rise, sometimes to a great height, swinging by one another closely at times, at least 1 giving the typical 2-syllabled call. This has also been seen rarely within the breeding range. Any pair formation occurring there must happen quickly, if the known brief spans between arrival and onset of nesting activity of breeders is any criterion.

The SKY-DANCE, described from Norway by Hagen (1952a), is of typical *Buteo* pattern. Suddenly the bird nearly closes its wings and hurtles abruptly downward, then checks its descent, climbs rather steeply, stalls with the body near-vertical, then tips forward and again hurtles downward. Calling, although not reported, probably occurs.

Captives in the prelaying period: the ♂ performed head-bobbing actions and flew back and forth frequently in the pen. Occasionally he perched, leaned toward the ♀ with half-opened wings, and offered a twig. Either foot or beak was used in offering nest material, but the ♀ did not respond. Both birds repeatedly attempted to leap straight upward—presumably in thwarted aerial display in their confined quarters (Bird and Laguë 1976).

Nest site   Described many times (see Habitat above); typically in a recess high on a cliff. Where there are several possible locations, the chosen one tends to be highest, providing the widest possible view and easiest aerial access. Overhead shelter is not a

167

requisite. In the Perry R. region, 30% were on colder, windswept, n.-facing sides of outcrops, evidently for better protection from predators, which could ascend gentler s.-facing slopes (Sealy 1966). On se. Victoria I., snow cover remaining past June 5 precludes early nesting. Roughlegs also nest there on scree, large erratics, and even flat ground; the poorer sites are occupied during lemming peaks, when cliff sites are at a premium (Parmelee et al. 1967). In the Anderson R. region, nw. Mackenzie Dist., of no less than 70 nests, 55 were in crotches of trees not far from their tops, 20–30 ft. from the ground; the others were near edges of steep cliffs, in faces of deep ravines, and in declivitous riverbanks (MacFarlane 1891).

In forested portions of Alaska lying within the Roughleg's breeding range that have been surveyed, tree nesting is reported rarely. Although further surveys may find more, single instances have been found on the Kuskokwim R., s. of Bethel, and on the Chandler R. (F. Williamson 1957, White and Cade 1975). Along many rivers having both cliffs and apparently suitable trees available, Roughlegs seem largely tied to the former. On the Labrador Pen., W. E. C. Todd (1963) found Roughlegs nesting exclusively on cliffs even where trees were available. On the South R. in w. Alaska a nest slid off a cliff ledge, and the adults were seen feeding 2 nestlings standing atop a jumble of sticks on the ground.

Olendorff (1980) listed 2 foreign references to providing man-made nest bases. In w. interior Alaska, 2 nests were on superstructures of old gold dredges (D. N. Weir).

Nest building In the Palearctic literature it is stated that the ♂ fetches material and the ♀ builds. In an abnormal situation (captivity) in N. Am., only the ♂ "was seen active in nest building" (Bird and Laguë 1976).

Nest Sticks, where available, are used; on the barrens, twigs, bones, any transportable debris. For example, on Banks I., 6 nests, including an active one, were built of fossil coniferous wood, hardly or not at all petrified, from deposits at the site (Hills 1970). The lining is of grasses, sedges, small twigs, and, as the season progresses, molted feathers and down and lemming fur. The structure varies with the site. That is, it tends to be circular on an open surface but compressed when against the wall of a niche and with more materials toward the front. Some new nests are small and scraggly, but typically nests are bulky for the size of the birds even before refurbishing in subsequent seasons. Diameter is to at least 30 in., height to 15 in., and there is a considerable bowl of about 10-in. diam. The top is usually trodden flat before the young depart; if the nest is recessed on a slope rather than a vertical or overhanging cliff, often a long train of material greater in volume than the nest itself trails down.

Nests are repaired and reused, or several may be fairly close together with only 1 active—which indicates **alternative sites** constructed within a territory over a period of years. In sw. Alaska, 1 or more inactive nests occurred within 100 m. or 25 (66%) of 38 active ones; there were 18 unused nests 1 km. or more distant from the latter (Mindell and Dotson, in Ladd and Schempf 1982).

Roughlegs do not appear to alternate between cliff and tree nests. In the treeless Perry R. region, Hanson et al. (1956) found a nest that consisted of over 10 layers of willow twigs, representing about as many annual nestings. Favored sites are apparently traditional, long used, probably by successive pairs, over a lengthy span of years.

On se. Victoria I., in years of lemming scarcity, some Roughlegs repair and defend

nests but do not breed successfully; the sites are abandoned by July or earlier, as are the breeding grounds (Parmelee et al. 1967).

Along rivers in w. Alaska, spacing of nests is not regular, as it tends to be with the Golden Eagle and Gyrfalcon (Weir, in Ladd and Schempf). Where numerous sites appeared to be available in sw. Alaska, again, spacing was not regular: nests were in clusters—smaller in number than those of the Redtail (Mindell and Dotson, in Ladd and Schempf). In arctic Alaska groups of 6–10 pairs of very dark birds clustered, as mentioned under Description, above.

Nesting/hunting territory Undoubtedly varies in size, probably down to 5–6 sq. km. or less when prey density is high. That is, spacing is related to occupation of traditional sites plus rodent numbers. Without going into details, perhaps the most striking recorded case is from the Seward Pen., Alaska: pairs increased from 35 in 1968 to 82 in 1970; in 1972 the number plummeted to 10 nesting pairs, and only 2 young

169

attained flight (Swartz et al., in Murphy et al. 1973). In the forests and bogs of n. Finland in 1963–1966 there was an occupied nest per 30–50 sq. km. area; the hunting area during the hatching period was 5–7 sq. km., increasing to 10 sq. km. during the nestling period (Pasanen 1972). In forested sw. Alaska, 7 of 14 distances between adjacent Roughleg and Redtail nests were less than 3 km. (1.9 mi.), and 2 were 0.8 km. (½ mi.) apart; it is likely that territories overlapped. Confrontation seemed to be avoided (Mindell and Dotson).

Although aggressive, nesting Roughlegs are less so than Peregrine Falcons and are sometimes forced by them to change their nesting location. One Colville R. Peregrine nest, apparently usurped from Roughlegs, contained 2 Peregrine and 2 Roughleg eggs (C. White, J. Enderson). On the lower Colville, Roughlegs were never seen to attack Peregrines, although a pair harrassed a Golden Eagle until it alighted on the ground (Kessel et al. 1953). In numerous instances, Roughlegs and Peregrines have nested successfully within 60 m. of each other. On the other hand, there was "terrific aggression" when they nested only 10 yds. apart on a cliff (White and Cade 1971). Neither of our eagles generally is tolerated anywhere near a Roughleg nest, yet on the Alaska Pen. Gianini (1917) reported seeing Roughleg and Bald Eagle nests "in close proximity to each other," but "evidently" there was "mutual respect." In Sweden, Roughlegs shared a cliff with Gyrfalcons (Lindberg 1981a). Territorial Gyrs killed 2 adult ♂ Roughlegs in Alaska (Cade 1960). Gyrs sometimes occupy a Roughleg site, probably assuming ownership early before the hawks return to it. Defense against human intruders varies from lax to vigorous, with physical contact not uncommon.

Copulation These are the only N. Am. data. A captive pair was seen to copulate 19 times in the 14 days before the 1st egg was laid. It occurred at all times of day and lasted 8–10 sec.; see Voice, above, for calling by both sexes. There were 15 copulations during the laying span (about 8 days). The clutch of 5 was removed, and within 1 hr. the pair copulated again. There were 14 copulations during postlaying, more perfunctorily than earlier, with calling not as loud (Bird and Laguë 1976).

Laying interval In the wild, possibly 1 egg per day, but some days are more likely skipped. Intervals in the 5-egg clutch laid in captivity were 2, 2, 2, and 3 days (Bird and Laguë).

One **egg** each from 20 clutches from localities across Canada from Alta. to the Ungava Pen. size length 56.22 ± 2.02 mm., breadth 44.56 ± 1.53, and radii of curvature of ends 19.16 ± 0.90 and 14.13 ± 1.10; **shape** varies from elliptical to subelliptical, many being roundish, elongation 1.26 ± 0.049, bicone −0.058, and asymmetry +0.142 (F. W. Preston). Another series: 50 measure length 42.5–62 mm. and breadth 38–48.5, av. 56.6 × 44.9 (Bent 1937). They have been confused with those of Swainson's Hawk; see Bechard and Houston (1984) for details and comparative meas., or compare with Swainson's Hawk species account in this volume.

Ground **color** very palish green or blue, soon bleaching to white. Markings vary endlessly in amount, shape, and size. Often the eggs are blotched or spotted with dark to pale browns; some are marked more or less violet, deep to pale, overlaid or intermixed with dark browns. Some are streaked. Blotching and streaking are often concentrated as a "wreath" around the larger end. A few are finely dotted with browns and are more or less violet. Some have few markings, but none are plain. (Modified from Bendire 1892.) Based on material from the Askinuk Mts., Alaska, Brandt (1943) stated

170

that the markings are of 2 general colors—red and lavender. The 1st prevailing—"brick red, hazel, cinnamon brown, and mummy brown." "Grayish lavender" is less frequent, often absent, but some eggs are "beautifully capped and blotched" with it. Usually 1 egg in a clutch is heavily marked, another meagerly, the remainder in "even gradations" in between—as though the bird ran "short of paint" as laying progressed. The shell is smooth, without gloss, and finely pitted. A fresh egg weighs about 2 oz. (56–60 gm.).

Clutch size   In n. Alaska on the lower Colville R., 17 clutches were of 2–5 eggs (mean 3.23) (Kessel et al. 1953). On se. Victoria I., 4–6 eggs; whether smaller clutches occur commonly is uncertain (Parmelee et al. 1967). On the Anderson R. in nw. Mackenzie Dist., 3–5, never more, in "no less" than 70 clutches (MacFarlane 1891). In the Perry R. region in nw. Keewatin, in 1963 three sets of 4–6 (mean 5) (Aleksiuk 1964) and in 1965 there were 17 of 2–5 (mean 3.3) (Sealy 1966). Clutches of 6 have been reported both in the Nearctic and Palearctic, but only in the latter has 7 been reported (and larger clutches are claimed for years of rodent abundance).

Dates for presumably viable eggs   "Labrador"—19 records May 2–June 23, with 10 of these June 4–10; and Alaska and "arctic" Canada—32 records May 18–July 13, with 16 of these May 30–June 20 (Bent 1937). Earliest dates for full clutches would presumably be for more s. portions of the Ungava breeding range, Nfld., forested Alaska, and perhaps also in nw. Mackenzie Dist. and n. Yukon. Clutches are laid in some years, at least, beginning in the last week in May in higharctic Canada—s. Baffin, Victoria I., and elsewhere—before the thaw. In the forest zone (Kuskokwim R.) in sw. Alaska, av. hatching dates in 4 years ranged June 10–21 (Mindell 1983b), which would indicate clutches by about the end of the 1st week in May.

Incubation   As far as is known, by the ♀, but the ♂ may possibly sit on the eggs briefly. On the Chuckchee Pen., Siberia, a pair was collected on July 16; the ♂ had a faint incubation patch, the ♀ a large one (Portenko 1972, trans. 1981). Occasional pronounced differences in development and age of nestlings, especially in large broods, indicates different hatching dates and incubation before completion of the clutch. In a captive pair, "serious" incubation evidently began with the 3d egg (of 5), the ♂ was on the nest once briefly, and (in an incubator) 4 eggs hatched July 5–7 and the 5th did not hatch (Bird and Laguë).

Incubation period   "About 31 days" (Parmelee et al. 1967) or, in confinement and with artificial incubation (Bird and Laguë), somewhat longer.

Greenery   At least during incubation and rearing, 1 or both parents "decorate" the nest with twigs of willow, birch, or, in its time and place, other obtainable vegetation.

The ♂ **roosts** on a high spot nearby, keeping a lookout when not away hunting, and usually birds are quiet in the middle hours of the night. In the 24-hr. daylight of n. Finland, the Roughleg appears to be a "clearly pronounced diurnal bird" (Pasanen and Sulkava 1971).

The ♂ fetches a lemming, vole, or other prey, calling as he nears the nest; the ♀ gets off, calling, joins him, and accepts the food in a midair pass. He may also deliver food to the nest.

Hatching success   Evidently high; in the Perry R. region 17 nests contained 56 eggs, and 48 (85.7%) hatched (Sealy 1966).

Rearing period   In n. Finland wild young grow rapidly for about 20–22 days then slower—graph of wt. increase in Pasanen and Sulkava (1971). These are from observations of a captive-reared brood in Montreal (Bird and Laguë): The nestlings could lift their heads when about 6 hrs. old and were fed. At 3 weeks the Juv. feathers began to appear, and the young fed themselves on bits of food supplied them. At 4 weeks they supported themselves on their feet, and 3 days later the oldest one left the artificial nest; mates followed on later dates. At 5 weeks they tore up 3-day-old domestic fowl, and a few days after that, the young hawks were transferred to a larger cage and given low branches on which to climb. Each then was eating 3–4 chicks or a whole rat daily.

Siblicide   There seems to be no evidence; there is mention of 2 dead Roughlegs in Roughleg nests by White and Cade (1971), and cannibalism was reported in Norway.

In n. Finland a brood of 2 young swallowed small prey whole at 10–15 days but did not dismember prey until 25–27 days (Pasanen and Sulkava).

The Finnish brood: number of prey delivered to it av. 4.9/day and had an estimated total wt. of 330 gm. The total number of prey would be around 200 for the observed 41-day period of nest life, a total wt. of 13.5 kg. After the early period of rapid growth, wt. becomes variable and decreases may occur. One nestling ingested an estimated 150 gm./day (3,300 in 22 days), the other 120 (2,400 in 20 days). In the latter part of the period the daily av. was 180 and 150 gm. for the 2 young in the wild. On this basis, the food ingested in the nestling period would weigh about 12 kg., and, allowing for an additional 18% for waste, the total wt. of whole prey would be 14–14.5 kg.—slightly more than the figure of 13.5 kg. derived from direct observation, using estimated mean wts. of prey.

If one adds food consumed by the parents and assumes both that the daily amount is $\frac{1}{7}$ their wt. and that the ♂ weighed 760 and the ♀ 1,020 gm., then they require 22 kg. of food for the entire breeding period of 86 days. This plus food for the young totals about 35 kg.

The above are, of course, approximations. In better vole years they might take as many as 500 (12/day). The number would also alter if birds of various sizes were taken.

A captive nestling at ages 7–37 days showed a wt. increase of 807 gm. from an intake of 5,160 gm. of food—an "efficiency" of 15.6% (Pasanen and Sulkava).

In the 24-hr. summer light of n. Finland, the 1st prey was usually fetched between 0500 and 0600 hrs. and the last between 1800 and 1900 hrs with few exceptions. The ♂ usually settled at his roost between 2000 and 2200 hrs. and started hunting at 0400–0500 hrs. Hunting was most intense between 0400 and 1000 hrs., and total hunting time was 15–18 hrs. daily. (From Pasanen and Sulkava.)

In N. Am. in good rodent years one may frequently find, especially when the young hawks are small, at least a half-dozen uneaten prey stockpiled on the nest. In n. Ungava in 1980 lemmings were extremely scarce, although their winter nests, runways, and accumulations of droppings were plentiful. No lemmings were caught at traps set in their runways and tunnel entrances, yet apparently Roughlegs were catching enough—judging from nest contents—to maintain their broods (R. Palmer).

Increased brood size and nesting success have been found to accompany increases in breeding pairs in Dovre, Norway (Hagen 1969), and, to a lesser extent, on the Kuskokwim R. in Alaska (Mindell 1983b). For 4 years' data from the Colville R., number of breeding pairs and av. clutch size were not well correlated.

172

The Roughleg does well when and where lemmings or voles are plentiful; a high percentage of young survive to flight age. Conversely, if a breeding area lacks prey, many of the birds disappear; one might assume that they go where conditions are better, but documentation of any sort is scarce. For example, the birds come n. presumably in good condition, and some may start the nesting cycle but discontinue it early and vanish. There is no evidence as to where they go or whether any undertake to breed elsewhere. Any suggestion that they instead remain and lay smaller clutches when food is in short supply is questionable.

Age at first flight On se. Victoria I. a 31-day-old ♂ had remiges and rectrices sheathed at the base and much visible down remained. The young were "at best weak fliers" at 31–32 days; some flew strongly at 36 days, but most remained in the nest 40 or more days (Parmelee et al. 1967). In Norway, ♂♂ fly at 34–36 days and ♀♀ at 40–45 (Hagen 1952a). In n. Finland a ♂ flew at 36 days and his ♀ broodmate at 40.5; and a captive-reared ♂ at 37 days (Pasanen and Sulkava 1971). According to F. Beebe (1974), the period of **dependence** extends to and blends with migration. Some may be independent a month or less after they first fly.

Nesting success Along 183 mi. of the Colville in n. Alaska in 1971, when ptarmigan and microtines were few, 74 pairs of Roughlegs produced an estimated 107 young (96 actually observed in 70 nests) (White and Cade 1971). Norway: 152 eggs in 43 nests; 124 (82%) hatched and 76 young (50%) were reared to flight age (Hagen 1952a). N. Finland: mean clutch size in 13 successful nests was 3.4 eggs, and 26 young (mean brood size 2.0) were reared (Pasanen 1972). A reasonable generality is that hatchability is high and about ½ the eggs laid produce young reared to flight age.

Single brood A 2d clutch is probably laid if the 1st is lost early; this might explain some known late nestings.   DAVID P. MINDELL

SURVIVAL   In N. Am., in 48 selected recoveries of dead birds, av. life span was 20.7 months, and the oldest individual lived 18 years, 1 month (Keran 1981).

DAVID P. MINDELL

HABITS   In N. Am. unless otherwise stated.

Unwariness Having little contact with man in the arctic, the Roughleg is altogether too confiding when it arrives on winter range. Brewster (1925) wrote that the Conn. R. valley was formerly a principal migration route through Mass. but that the birds were either slain or driven away by about 1880. They were easily approached and shot by a gunner in a horse-propelled vehicle but were not approachable by a person afoot. It is true today that anyone in an automobile can drive to within easy gun range. Furthermore, while they are feeding on traffic-killed hares and rabbits they in turn are killed by traffic. On 240 km. of highway in Utah, 19 freshly killed Roughlegs and 8 Great Horned Owls were found in 1 week—and probably others were missed (White, in Hickey 1969). The Roughleg is docile in captivity.

Hunting methods The Roughleg is crepuscular to a considerable extent, hunting **from a perch** or beating over the terrain "in the fading twilight" (A. K. Fisher 1893), and it is active when the sky is heavily overcast, whether or not the wind is blowing. Perch-and-wait stance is very erect. The following is modified from Townsend (in Bent

1937), based primarily on field experience in winter–spring in Mass.: The hawk flies slowly, alternately flapping and sailing, **quartering the ground** like a harrier. It is attracted to water—inland and coastal—and frequently flies close to the surface. It also **hovers,** flapping, or hangs suspended, motionless, in an updraft above the crest of a hill or a cliff. While thus essentially stationary, it turns its head from side to side, watching (and probably listening), lowers its tarsi preparatory to pouncing on prey, or may draw them up again. Or it partially closes its wings and plummets. Ipswich, Mass., is an area of sand dunes and salt marshes where there were windmills in Townsend's day, and the hawks frequently perched on these—high perches being few and mostly man-made.

Usual hunting altitude is about 15–40 m., and, since this hawk has proven ability to catch shrews and deer mice as well as to locate lemmings in the n. when they are scarce, it must have remarkable ability to hear and locate the slightest rustle. Possibly it can begin its stoop, or even complete it, without visual contact with its prey. It can dismember prey and feed while in flight.

At the Toronto airport it foraged in areas of high and low vole (*Microtus*) numbers (J. A. Baker and Brooks 1981), but in s. Sweden it was said (Sylvén 1978) to avoid poorer habitats. In Nova Scotia a Roughleg speedily killed and swallowed, intact and head first, 4 voles; then it alighted on a fence post and watched intently, but otherwise ignored, a brown rat that wandered close by (Tufts 1962).

Fishing   In Wis. a Roughleg ate from an abundance of dead alewives. Then it flew over the water, plunged somewhat Osprey-like, and caught a live fish. This happened twice. Later that day it also waded after dead and dying fish (Mueller et al. 1966). On Feb. 12, 1978, there was much snow on the ground but the Detriot R. was kept open in places by rapid current. Three Roughlegs perched in a clump of trees, and every few min. 1 would fly over the river and disappear behind an is. One returned carrying a fish 15–25 cm. long. Another observer (T. W. Carpenter 1979) saw a Roughleg eating fish near the river. Catching frogs is apparently a fairly common occurrence. Near Tacoma, Wash., a Roughleg, wet when shot, had just eaten a "field mouse" [*Microtus*]; probably the vole had been caught while swimming (Kitchin 1918).

Winter territories   To which Roughlegs may return, in Mich. were stated by the Craigheads (1956) to be larger than those of other buteos—exceeded in size only by those of the N. Harrier. One had a maximum observed diam. of 2.7 mi. and another 1.5. In a large study area, in the winter of 1941–1942, an av. of 30 hunted in fall and an av. of 13 wintered, but none wintered in 1948. The change coincided with a decline in vole numbers. Territories were smaller in spring. Although Roughlegs and Redtails have nearly identical winter diets, their territories tend to be nearly exclusive—both in raptor species and individuals. Yet there is some degree of overlap, the 2 hawks sharing an area but using it at different times.

Communal roosting   Roughlegs are social to a degree in winter as well as summer (compare with the N. Harrier). In some places on winter range they congregate at night and disperse unknown distances to their individual hunting areas by day, and individuals use the roost regularly for short periods only. They may perch close together or be spaced well apart. Roosts are associated with high rodent numbers. In Ill. there were several roosts, and up to 15 birds used a site in a single night. Five of 6 roosts were in tall conifers. The birds tended to roost earlier in relation to sunset as the year progressed, and in morning there was rapid exit before sunrise (G. Schnell 1969). Other roosts have been found in pine and cedar windbreaks, a clump of cottonwoods, a stand of 5 apple trees, and on the ground.

Some raptor interrelationships Mostly in winter (see Reproduction, above, for spring–summer). In Sept. in Man., although not actually seen to make the strike, a Roughleg had a Sharpshin as prey and tried unsuccessfully to carry it off on approach of observers. The dying Sharpshin was examined and left where found; examination 1½ hrs. later revealed that the Roughleg had torn feathers off its back (Collins and Bird 1979). In Ill. in early Jan. a Roughleg attacked a N. Harrier that was carrying a small mammal; the prey was dropped and the Roughleg retrieved it (R. P. Kirby 1959). In Feb. a Roughleg robbed carrion (a dead crow) from a Redtail; in turn, it was robbed by another Roughleg (Hogan 1983). On the Colville R. in n. Alaska, 2 dead Roughlegs found in Roughleg nests were tabulated as "prey" by White and Cade (1971). In Norway, Hagen (1952a) reported "cannibalism" at a nest, as well as 3 Short-eared Owls in Roughleg nests and 3 Roughlegs in Eagle Owl nests. In N. Am. in winter the Roughleg is less sedentary than the Redtail, more in open country, tends to perch lower, and does not move away because of snow and cold weather (G. Schnell 1968). The Roughleg hovers in a stiff breeze or wind, the Redtail seldom if ever.

Population fluctuations The Roughleg is well known for fluctuations in regional numbers in both the breeding and wintering seasons and for heavy use of fluctuating small mammal prey. This does not imply, however, that it is cyclic—which denotes predictable periodicity, or regularities in amplitude of change. Statistical analyses of apparently regular cycles of wildlife numbers generally refute periodicity (Cole 1954, M. Campbell and Walker 1977). Unfortunately, no continuous long-term data on Roughleg breeding abundance are available. The Colville R. in Alaska with 10 years' data over a 16-year span is the best documented area we are aware of, and strict cycling of breeding abundance is not suggested. The lack of a short-term (4-year) cycle is also demonstrated by 5 years of relatively consistent abundance data from the Kuskokwim R. in Alaska and by annual densities of 5, 5, 4, and 6 breeding pairs during 1963–1966, respectively, on a study site in Finland (Pasanen and Sulkava 1971). In a recent reanalysis of microtine population fluctuations, Garsd and Howard (1981) found that most data show random fluctuations rather than approximate 4-year cycles. They suggested that, although no clear mathematical cycle describes the data, microtines are regulated by complex intrinsic and ecotone system variables. Randomness in vole fluctuations alone could account for lack of periodicity in Roughleg fluctuations; however, Roughlegs are not restricted to small mammal prey. The hawks in different areas have available and use different amounts of avian prey in different years—note the Finnish work mentioned under Food, below. This tends to reduce any one-to-one correspondence between vole and Roughleg fluctuations. On the Colville R. in 1971, breeding Roughlegs were relatively abundant despite low microtine populations (White and Cade 1971). Pasanen and Sulkava (1971) found Roughleg nesting density in an area of Finland to be independent of small mammal stocks with good nesting results even in a poor vole year. In Norway, Hagen (1969) found the more well-known pattern of highs (9 pairs) and lows (none) of breeding Roughlegs to correspond with highs and lows of vole numbers.

The data available on breeding abundances illustrates different degrees of fluctua-

175

tion. Annual percent change from the av. number of breeding pairs has varied from +92 to −77 (N = 5) on the Seward Pen., +70 to −49 on the Sagavanirktok R. (N = 4), +39 to −60 on the Colville R. (N = 11), and +30 to −27 on the Kuskokwim (N = 5). Of these 4 Alaskan areas, 3 are beyond treeline, while the Kuskokwim is in mixed boreal forest and tundra. The Kuskokwim area fluctuated least. Annual percent change from the av. was also relatively low, ranging from +20 to −20, in a Finnish study area located in mixed forest and tundra (Pasanen and Sulkava 1971). The Kuskokwim and Finnish taiga zones generally experience less prolonged severe winter and spring weather than the arctic regions. The observed breeding population fluctuations in the last 2 areas mentioned are similar to those reported for more stable raptor species as summarized in I. Newton (1979). Breeders in mixed boreal and tundra habitats may have access both to prey that fluctuates less, due to milder weather, and to greater variety of prey species than arctic breeders, possibly contributing to their relative stability. Drastic declines may be the result of concurrent lows in multiple prey species or of extremely harsh weather, which negatively affects all prey. The latter scenario was suggested by major declines and lowest populations for Roughlegs as well as Gyrfalcons, Com. Ravens, and Golden Eagles on the Seward Pen. in 1971.

Roughleg breeding fluctuations are regionally independent of each other in at least some, and possibly most, instances. This is to be expected, since small mammal prey fluctuations are not uniform through vast geographic regions and occur, rather, in a changing mosaic of abundances with each area fluctuating in a random or pseudo-periodic fashion, as described by Garsd and Howard (1981). The largest known area measurement of uniform lemming abundance is 300,000 ha. (1,200 sq. mi.) near Barrow, Alaska (Pitelka 1957 and in Britton 1973), although this fluctuated annually. Near Baker Lake, NWT, lemmings fluctuated in a relatively uniform fashion over 100,000 ha. (Krebs 1964). In addition to the local nature of small mammal prey fluctuations, differential availability and use of alternative prey species would contribute to independence of Roughleg populations. Synchronous lows or highs in prey or extensive weather degradation, however, could result in synchronous Roughleg fluctuations.

Annual changes in winter density are not well documented, although regional summaries in appropriate issues of *Am. Birds* provide anecdotal evidence, and a summary for part of Ill. (Graber and Golden 1960) has been done—see flight years under Distribution, above. Regionally independent breeding fluctuations could be expected to lead to the same for winter populations. The tendency of wintering Roughlegs to concentrate in areas of prey abundance also contributes to annually fluctuating winter densities.

The phenomenon of population fluctuation in Roughlegs is not patently simple, but a summary characterization can be offered. Fluctuations are likely pseudoperiodic or random rather than cyclic. Roughleg fluctuations are related to small mammal fluctuations but not bound to them in all situations. Degree of autonomy is related to the availability and use of alternative prey. In breeders, the higharctic birds and those in areas of most severe weather extremes seem to fluctuate most; those in taiga zones appear to be comparatively stable.

Flight years   A lemming/vole crash in the n. generally occurs in the colder part of

176

the year when the hawks are absent. So they return to a very lean summer before migrating s. again. They vacate the n. every winter anyway, but the Snowy Owl leaves (has "flight years") when it cannot sustain itself there. Thus flight years of the 2 birds are not brought about in the same way and do not necessarily coincide.

Biocides Three Roughleg eggs from the Colville R., Alaska, av. 7.07 ppm. p,p'-DDE oven dry wt. (Lincer et al. 1970). Brain tissue from 3 Roughlegs av. 0.67 ppm. Of those tissues represented by equal sample sizes of 3 (egg, brain, fat, muscle), fat had the highest DDE level at 13.3 ppm. In the same study, Peregrine Falcon tissues av. much higher. In a comparison of pesticide levels in prey (shrews for the Roughleg, waterfowl for the Peregrine), the Roughleg's fare contained ¹⁄₁₀ to ¹⁄₂₀ the DDE of the Peregrine's migratory prey. It must be remembered, however, that Roughlegs take some migrant prey and Peregrines some resident. Dieldrin has been reported in the liver of Roughlegs by Prestt et al. (1968). Brain tissue of a dead bird in Oreg. contained heptachlor (Henny et al. 1984a).

Mean eggshell thickness index for Alaskan Roughleg eggs before 1947 was 2.15. Average thickness index decreased by 3.3% for eggs collected in 1967–1969 (Cade et al. 1971).   DAVID P. MINDELL

FOOD   In N. Am. with some reference to elsewhere. Small mammals principally—lemmings, voles, others occasionally; birds in varying numbers; some frogs, fishes, a lizard, and insects; carrion.

Older summaries, based on digestive tract contents, were for birds taken primarily on winter range: A. K. Fisher, Henshaw, and McAtee, cited by A. Springer (1975), who added summer data from the Seward Pen., Alaska. May (1935) summarized 16 sources, dividing the food into major categories only. Sherrod (1978) briefly summarized 8 papers for the period 1893–1975. Percentage figures given below are as stated by authors and may not all be calculated the same way.

SUMMER   Lemmings (*Dicrostonyx, Lemmus*), voles (*Microtus, Clethrionomys*) where present. Lemmings often constitute 80–85% or more of prey. Occasionally arctic ground squirrels (*Spermophilus parryi*)—probably young ones usually—and a few young tundra hares (*Lepus othus* [= *L. timidus*]).

Townsend (in Bent 1937) stated that the Roughleg "seldom or never" takes birds, which reflects earlier reports; subsequent authors seem to have made a special effort to refute this. Leffler (1971) summarized reports of birds taken in summer. Although small mammals tend to predominate even when birds seem to be available in quantity, recent studies in Alaska show considerable avian prey—9%, 11%, and 18% in the Colville R. drainage (White and Cade 1971), 17% and 30% on the Seward Pen. (Springer 1975), and 30% inland from Norton Sd. toward Bethel (Mindell and Dotson, in Ladd and Schempf 1982). Eleven (of 12) ptarmigan (*Lagopus*) on the Seward Pen. were full-grown (Springer)—probably the upper size limit of healthy birds that can be captured. Most are small: grouse chicks (*Lagopus*, rarely *Dendragapus*), a few shorebirds (Golden Plover, Red-necked Phalarope, young Whimbrels), and other small birds—including wagtails, Tree Sparrows, Lapland Longspurs, Snow Buntings, and various unidentified remains.

In n. Finland, identifiable bird remains were found in minute numbers, since the

177

majority of avian prey reportedly were plucked; microtine rodents were swallowed whole, and their bones were found in abundance (Pasanen and Sulkava 1971). In N. Am. a captive devoured, nearly whole, both mice and small birds, and bones, fur, and feathers were present in its disgorged pellets (Smith, in Bent 1937); this does not support an idea that they always pluck their avian prey, but prey typically is beheaded. Young birds' bones are not much ossified, and they may be clothed in down and partly-grown feathers. In small mammals, the teeth are especially persistent and are identifiable to species. The Long-tailed Jaeger and the Roughleg are 2 birds that appear to be too small-mouthed to swallow a full-grown varying lemming (*Dicrostonyx*) intact, yet they accomplish this regularly.

Birds may be regarded as alternative, or "buffer," species when small mammals are scarce, but numerous variables must be reckoned with. For example, perhaps some Roughlegs develop a preference for or a special expertise in catching birds; in forest, where ground cover provides refuge for small mammals, birds may be more in evidence and may require less energy to obtain. Again n. Finland: in 1964 and 1965 the food was 80–90% small mammals and the remainder birds; in 1966 the proportion of birds was about 70% when small mammals were down in numbers—yet Roughlegs had normal clutch size and nesting success was the highest. Prey taken that year was primarily shorebirds, also many young thrushes (*Turdus iliacus*), a few young grouse, and so on.

Carrion in summer   T. G. Smith (1975) specifically mentioned seal and caribou.

WINTER   Roughlegs are in country where there are more, and largely different, prey species from on their breeding range, and their diet reflects this diversity. Even so, voles (principally *Microtus*) sometimes constitute 80–90% of known diet. Other mammals reported include several weasels (*Mustela*), a few ground squirrels (*Spermophilus*), brown rats (*Rattus*), house mice (*Mus*), and assorted others. In Okla., after several passes, 1 succeeded in catching a small bat (*Myotis velifer*) in flight (Twente 1954).

Reported consumption of some species raises interesting questions. For example, long ago in Mont., prairie dogs (*Cynomys*) were labeled a "favorite food," and another author stated that this hawk feeds largely on "gophers" (a vernacular for *Spermophilus*—that is, not pocket gophers, *Thomomys*). These are hibernators, but they are above ground in spring before many Roughlegs depart.

Shrews have been mentioned by all of the following, listed chronologically: A. K. Fisher (1893), J. Munro (1929a), Errington and Breckenridge (1936), Cope (1949), Craighead and Craighead (1956), and G. Schnell (1967b). Most were big short-tailed (*Blarina*) and little short-tailed (*Cryptotis*) shrews; a few were long-tailed (*Sorex* spp.). One of 5 "marsh shrews" that a hawk ingested was obviously swallowed alive; it caused the death of its captor (V. Jackson 1941). Roughlegs get deer mice (*Peromyscus*) and pine voles (*Microtus pinetorum*), which typically are not open-country inhabitants.

Not many small birds are identified, although unidentified remains are fairly common. Poultry and pheasants are taken as carrion, perhaps as live young sometimes (Errington and Breckenridge). Birds as large as a loon and large ducks (listed as "food") were obviously not captured by the Roughleg; a small grebe and small ducks might have been cripples or carrion. The Roughleg has eaten the breasts of dead Mallards

(Racey 1922). A Roughleg killed a Snowy Egret in Fla. but departed without eating it (Sprunt, Jr., 1940).

Reptiles A lizard (Fisher).

Amphibians Various Am. authors, beginning with Thomas Nuttall in 1832, have mentioned frogs. The food in 58 Ont. stomachs was 2.9% frogs (L. Snyder 1932). In n. Finland a captive young ♂ Roughleg was fed 17 frogs over a period of time, yet no remains were found in its pellets.

Fishes See Habits, above, for fishing methods.

Insects Mostly grasshoppers, also some crickets and others. One stomach contained 70 insects, but none in 48 others (Fisher). Mormon crickets (*Anabrus*) in Utah (La Rivers 1941).

Carrion in winter Traffic-killed and hunter-killed small game: rabbits, hares, ducks, pheasants, and so on; traffic-killed domestic fowls and even such small birds as Horned Larks and Lapland Longspurs. A dead Herring Gull. Skinned carcasses of muskrats. Fishes and other dead animals cast up by the sea (Maynard, in Fisher). Dead and dying freshwater fishes. Evidently more of a carrion feeder than its more powerful relative, the Redtail. The Roughleg is adept at driving Prairie Falcons from or robbing them of their kills.　　　　　　　　　　　　　　　　　　　　　　　RALPH S. PALMER

Def. Basic

Juv.

GOLDEN EAGLE

Aquila chrysaetos

Very large and variably brownish. Rear of crown and nape with lanceolate erectile feathers having "golden" ends; legs feathered to toes. In Juv. Plumage the tail is white with black terminal band, and in the wings, the inner primaries and outer secondaries are white basally (in the primaries the white "window" may or may not show on both surfaces of the spread wing); the white usually diminishes in area or vanishes in 1 or 2 succeeding feather generations; most individuals become essentially unicolor. Within the genus *Aquila*, the Golden, judging from available evidence, is notably dark in the Juv. stage. In all flying ages and in at least parts of N. Am. and Europe some Goldens have small white "epaulettes" (see below). In its circumboreal range, goegraphical size variation is evidently slight and individual variation considerable.

Sexes similar; the iris varies from pale yellowish to reddish brown in the ♂ and is usually warm brownish in the ♀; the ♀ is larger; there is overlap in size and wt. of the sexes; in some meas. (as BEAK from cere), rather little. In N. Am., sexes combined: length 30–40 in. (76–102 cm.), wingspread 60–80 in. (152–204 cm.) (reportedly 227 cm. in a 5-month-old Swiss bird [Stemmler 1955]), wt. (with any crop contents?) ♂ 6½–9½ lb. (2.9–4.3 kg.) and ♀ 8–13 lb. (3.6–5.8 kg.). Birds in their 1st year of life are as heavy as older ones; their tail feathers are longer and more pointed (less squarish) terminally; their primaries vary to as long as those of definitive-feathered birds but av. slightly shorter.

180

Five to 8 subspecies have been listed, with various names and depending on author; there is 1 in our area (its distribution includes ne. Asia).

DESCRIPTION *A. chrysaetos canadensis.*

▶♂ ♀ *Def. Basic Plumage, in breeders acquired from early* SPRING *into* FALL *and retained a year;* some body feathering is usually retained from 1 preceding generation and portions of wing sometimes from 2 preceding generations. Basic IV appears to be the earliest definitive; perhaps some attain this condition earlier, but others never acquire all of the typical definitive pattern—some "characteristics of immaturity" recur for some years or even throughout life.

Beak blackish blue distally, paling proximally, the cere and edges of gape yellow (evidently with seasonal variation in vividness); **iris** varies from yellowish to a reddish brown in the ♂ and is usually a warm brownish in the ♀; **head** feathers on occiput and nape in fresh feathering (late summer–fall) are coppery reddish but fade to pale yellowish or straw color by late winter; these lanceolate feathers form a distinctive nuchal cape, narrow on rear of head (where a large white area is concealed), broader toward lower neck, and erectile (as in threat display). **Upperparts** overall lighter than Juv. and tend to appear somewhat variegated because older, faded feathers are intermingled and some feathers are white basally; the new ones have a purplish sheen; scapulars rather dark, contrasting with the pale (usually retained, worn) innermost secondaries and smaller upper wing coverts. **Underparts** darker than dorsum, more uniformly dusky brownish; abdomen thickly covered with long, blackish, loose-webbed plumes; under tail coverts full and thick (are extended out over feet as a muff in cold weather), their reddish brown tips scarcely concealing their white or pale grayish plumaceous bases. **Legs** feathered, the long, loose-webbed tibial plumes forming pronounced "flags" reaching the base of the toes; inner sides of legs and all of tarsi lighter brown to buffy (occasionally white or bleaching to white), the tarsi evenly covered with a dense feltwork of small feathers. Toes more or less yellowish (feet of breeding captives become light orange by Feb.—Kish 1970), talons black. **Tail** variable, often quite evenly dark distally, or most of it a grayed brownish with fairly distinct to obscure darker transverse barring; some retain more or less white ("immature characteristic") basally—as known from captives and at least 1 known-age wild individual in N. Am. Variation in N. Am. includes individuals with almost uniformly darkish tails (rare) to others with variable number (3 or more) darkish bands, the intervening more or less grayish areas marbled or irregularly marked dark—especially on lateral feathers—and often some white basally.

Wing Outer primaries blackish, those retained from previous years worn and bleached; inner primaries and the secondaries have more or less obscure barring, mottling, or marbling, especially proximally, the faded ones being retained from preceding generations; upper coverts generally lighter than back and tendency for smaller ones to be retained 2 years (each greater covert is molted with its corresponding flight feather); wing lining quite uniformly dark brownish or blackish brown, but leading edge of wing varies from fairly dark to pale yellowish brown or lighter—may appear white in head-on view of flying bird.

Molting Has been described as irregular, meaning presumably that sequence and/or time of renewal of individual feathers is variable or that molting continues intermittently all year. There is excellent contrary evidence. Molting is protracted; some feathers of 1 or 2 past generations are retained; there are several "molt centers" in the wing (which, added to retention of old feathers, is confusing); and acquisition of new feathers may not cease entirely in fall since a few feathers may get knocked out later and their replacements may grow. The upshot is that, on examining museum specimens, molting appears chaotic—that of the wing "irregular" (stepwise molting; 2 or 3 years for complete renewal). Molting of the primaries begins with the innermost, proceeds outwardly, and ceases after a few feathers are renewed; the next year, molting renews where it ceased and again continues outwardly. While molting thus progresses in annual increments, the sequence also starts over again at innermost primary. In the secondaries there are 3 centers at which molting begins annually; the sequence of renewal is outward in the distal 2 and both outward and inward in the proximal 1, with succeeding waves as in the primaries.

W. R. Spofford's unpublished data on a healthy captive through 6 years reveal that order and time of renewal of individual feathers is on a regular schedule. The head–neck start molting early and rapidly, then slow down. Body molt is prolonged, both of contour feathers and underlying down. In the tail the central pair drops 1st, then the outer pair; there is some variation in sequence of those in between. Servheen (1976) noted that the right-hand deck feather dropped 1st in 4 molting periods. Also see Jollie (1947) for various details of molting in captivity.

Variants Some individuals have "epaulettes," which show in flight as a small white patch on each "shoulder" at base of leading edge of wing. In Europe this was termed the *barthelemyi* variant (references in Jollie, also see Besson 1969). They were observed on an "adult" trapped in Tenn., another in Ga., and on both parents and the 3 successive offspring over a 6-year period in n. New Eng. (Spofford). Such a bird was seen in Oct. 1959 at Hawk Mt., Pa. According to Jollie, in w. N. Am., single white feathers on hindneck or "shoulder" region are "quite common." Cameron (1905, plate 6) showed a Juv. in Mont. with small white epaulettes; a breeding ♀ and a ♂ (Cameron 1908a) also both had them. In Utah in 1952–1970, 5 Juv. birds had epaulettes that varied from small (3–4 feathers) to large (to 20 feathers) (C. M. White). An "adult" at a nest in N. Mex. had them. White in or near the scapular area, in differing amounts, occurs in several *Aquila* species, most notably in the Imperial Eagle (*A. heliaca*).

A mounted bird from Cripple Creek, Colo., appeared all black; the feathers were "rather chestnut-brown" with black tips on occiput and nape, and there was a concealed chestnut patch on the breast (Aiken 1928).

AT HATCHING Beak grayish with darker tip, egg tooth prominent and white, cere whitish yellowing basally, feet pale grayish, talons nearer white. Down-A (prepennae) is short, pale grayish with slightly darker tips, somewhat darker on nape, back, and upper surface of wings; it is rather dark around the eye and is white at the ear. It is sparsest ventrally, in the umbilical region and on rear of tarsus from "heel" to toes. Among this down are short tufts (B). At 18 days or earlier a long woolly white down-C appears and completely conceals down-A; it bears on its tips the short down-B. It continues to grow until age about 30 days, forming a dense and nearly waterproof covering. Earlier, at about 24 days, the dark primaries begin to push out through

182

down-C, appearing at 1st as black spots. Overall, the longest Juv. feathers appear 1st and grow fastest. The contour feathers appear, remnants of down-A breaking from their tips, and the feathers in turn cover up the woolly down-C, which remains beneath them long after flight age. This is based on E. L. Sumner (1933), which is derived from Witherby (1920) and condensed in Witherby et al. (1939); it does not jibe with statements that there is a single "natal down" in the Accipitridae. Furthermore, the A and B of Witherby and Sumner are commonly combined as A and their C is labeled B—a reduction to A and B. The latter is included in annual molting.

For chronology of development of nestlings (appearance, wt., behavior), see E. L. Sumner (1929a, 1929b, 1933, 1934); for useful photographs through age 9 weeks, Hoechlin (1976); and for many behavioral details, text and photographs in D. Ellis (1979). Below, under Reproduction, some "landmarks" are given for estimating approximate age of nestlings.

▶ ♂ ♀ Juv. Plumage (entire feathering), acquired during nest life; begins to appear through the down by age about 24 days, covers the nestling at about 8 weeks, and is fully grown by 15–16 weeks. It is retained through WINTER, and then most of it is replaced during prolonged Prebasic I molting, which begins at age about 11 months; stated otherwise, the young eagle has only the Juv. feather generation from age approximately 15 to 44 weeks—parts of 2 calendar years.

Beak mostly dark; iris lightens to a clear, warm brown by 11 weeks or sooner. **Head** crown blackish; rear of crown and nape muted to fairly vivid reddish brown (which fades); nape feathers comparatively short (to 4.5 cm.) and narrow (1 cm. where widest) and not much white basally except on part of occiput; remainder of head very dark. **Upperparts** blackish brown or sooty with purplish sheen (late summer–fall) fading (winter–spring) to browner and paler; scapulars (they taper distally) blackish, contrasting with lighter browns of proximal upper surface of wing; upper tail coverts dark, the feathers with extensive white bases that give a patchy appearance. **Underparts** sooty, various feathers often with very tips pale; under tail coverts lighter, to pale yellowish brown or even whitish distally, only partly concealing the long downy basal portions; the "flags" (long flank feathers) dark, usually with light tips; inner sides of legs very pale; tarsi pale tawny to white, the feathers sometimes with dark shaft streaks, and feet white. **Tail** feathers, on av., appreciably longer than in all later Plumages, somewhat narrower, more or less wedge shaped (not squarish) terminally; proximally they are white (in some flecked dark) and with black terminal band, which varies with individual from more than ½ to (usually) less than ½ tail length (some individuals in w. N. Am. have almost no dark band), and the very tips of the feathers are pale and soon wear off. **Wing** primaries blackish, except more than ½ inner ones have white basal portions and white also extends across the inner portions of a few secondaries (especially the outer); the secondaries otherwise are dark, occasionally with some dark barring inwardly that extends onto inner primaries. Primaries av. slightly shorter than in later Plumages. Upper coverts variably brownish, fading to yellowish brown and becoming much frayed by late winter. Wing lining blackish brown.

NOTE   An outer or 11th primary is vestigial (Sumner 1933); this abortive primary in the fully grown Juv. Plumage is longer than its under covert, while in "adult plumage" it is shorter (there is no upper covert) (W. deW. Miller 1924).

Molting   From Juv. to Basic I the primaries may drop from inner to outer (descending mode), but commonly, beyond the 4th, 1 to all are retained. The secondaries begin molting at 3 centers; molting may begin with the outermost feather, separately at #5 (counting from outer toward inner—the "diastaxic center"—illus. for this species by Wray 1887), proceeding inward; and a 3d center at #17, proceeding thence outward (only?). Some smaller upper wing coverts and the wing lining are commonly retained. The tail starts with the deck feathers (central pair), follows very soon with the outer pair, and ends with those in between (sequence varies); sometimes molting proceeds quite regularly from central to outer pair. A tail feather requires 75 days to grow; in 2 captive birds a central Juv. feather was pulled in Oct. and each was succeeded by a feather with pattern intermediate toward Basic I (Jollie 1947). Retained Juv. rectrices are typically longer than the full-grown adjoining Basic I feathers.

▶♂ ♀ Basic I Plumage; most feathering is acquired from SPRING into LATE SUMMER of calendar year following hatching year (molting is described above) and retained approximately a year. Some worn and faded Juv. body and flight feathers are retained.

The new feathering is lighter overall than fresh Juv. feathering; the lanceolate feathers on rear of crown and **nape** are longer (6–7 cm.), twice as wide at widest part (2–3 cm.), and basally white. Light feather tips are largely or entirely absent from **underparts,** flags, and legs; the tarsi are darker; the pale webbing of under tail coverts is browner, yet the fluffy light basal portions are scarcely obscured. The new **tail** feathers are shorter, squarish terminally, and the white or whitish area is reduced by presence of a narrow, dark band separated from the wide, terminal, blackish band by a grayish zone variably marked or flecked darkish (usually more on outer feathers). The full extent of variation at this age is unknown, but typically considerable white is present basally in the tail. In the **wing** the new inner primaries have less white basally with correspondingly more darkish barring and marbling (no white may show in dorsal view of spread wing); white in the secondaries is largely or entirely concealed.

▶♂ ♀ Basic II Plumage, acquired from SPRING into LATE SUMMER or later of 2d calendar year after hatching year and retained nearly a year.

Some birds presumed to be in Basic II are the youngest that really look "adult." Probably variable in appearance and not recognizable as B-II unless retained and recognizable B-I and Juv. feathers are also present. It may be typical for birds in this Plumage to have 2 narrow dark tail bars proximal from the wide terminal one, the intervening areas more or less obscured by darkish markings. Any white basal area in the tail is usually (but not invariably) small and may have darkish markings. At some predefinitive stage the nape feathers become more attenuated distally and their zones of coloring become more clearly delimited.

▶♂ ♀ Basic III Plumage, acquired from SPRING into LATE SUMMER or later of 3d calendar year after hatching year, and retained a year. Some feathers from 1 or 2 preceding generations (notably in wing) are usually retained.

Largely as definitive (described at beginning of this section); no single character appears to be diagnostic of the B-III tail. (Any retained feathers of the 2 preceding generations would not include the Juv.) One would expect more tail bars in this generation and fewer individuals showing exposed white basally in the tail.

▶♂ ♀ Basic IV Plumage—definitive (described earlier), repeated (or with minor variation) annually thereafter.

184

The nape feathers by this stage, if not earlier, are comparatively long and attenuated, their lateral outlines distinctly concave. The tail has multiple barring (3–4 or
more), often not very distinct; in some there is much mottling; a few are almost evenly
dark. Some retain some white in the tail basally throughout life, as known in captives in
Britain (Lilford 1903) and Europe (Jollie 1947)—hence, this is not always an indication
of "immaturity." One nestling banded in Utah was found electrocuted about 6½ years
later; it had 40–50% of the tail area white—that is, the bird's feathering appeared to be
that of a 3-year-old at most (P. Benson).

NOTES   In the wild and in captivity, prebreeders and nonbreeders begin molting
slightly earlier, and possibly finish sooner, than breeding individuals.

The terminology used above, with Jollie's (1947) equivalent in parentheses, is: Juv.
(juv.), B-I (immature), B-II (subadult), B-III (first adult), B-IV and later, definitive
(adult). As in the present account, Forsman's (1980) data from Finland carries the birds
into their 5th calendar year.

Color phases   None; a melanistic individual was mentioned earlier.

Measurements   By Bortolotti (1984a): birds from widespread N. Am. localities
with the mean in parentheses: "adults" BEAK from cere 23 ♂ 36.9–43.5 (40.55) mm.,
and 27 ♀ 41.7–47.5 (44.21); WING across chord 23 ♂ 569–619 (595) mm., and 27 ♀
601–674 (640.4); TAIL 23 ♂ 267–310 (286.5) mm., and 24 ♀ 290–330 (307.2); REAR
TALON across chord 23 ♂ 45.9–52.9 (49.35) mm., and 26 ♀ 49.8–63.4 (55.67); and TAIL
22 ♂ 267–310 (286.5) mm., and 24 ♀ 290–330 (307.2).

"Immatures" [probably all Juv.] BEAK from cere 26 ♂ 36.2–42.6 (39.36) mm., and 31
♀ 39.9–50 (43.34); WING across chord 26 ♂ 559–636 (585.9) mm., and 31 ♀ 601–665
(632.2); TAIL 23 ♂ 269–341 (297.7) mm., and 30 ♀ 285–375 (322); and REAR TALON
across chord 24 ♂ 44.9–51.3 (47.75) mm., and 30 ♀ 49.7–58.2 (54.01).

Note that there is little overlap in BEAK and in REAR TALON and that the WING is
variable but av. somewhat shorter in Juv. birds. In general, and irrespective of age, a
bird with BEAK under 42 mm. is almost always a ♂, the ♀ generally being larger. TAIL
varies to appreciably longer in Juv. in both sexes (disparity between Juv. and definitive, sex for sex, is much less than in the Bald Eagle). It is of interest that, in nominate
chrysaetos, Forsman's (1980) WING meas. for 22 ♂ (565–610 mm.) and 18 ♀ (623–665)
show no overlap.

For a smaller N. Am. series, see Friedmann (1950); there are some meas. of BEAK
and WING chord in N. Snyder and Wiley (1976).

Weight   For curves of growth of eaglets in Calif., see E. L. Sumner (1929a, 1929b),
and for a ♂ and ♀ in Mont., D. Ellis (1979). Nestlings weigh about 100 gm. at hatching;
in 60 days wt. has increased to about 3.5 kg. (♂) or 4 kg. (♀), and then it levels off.

As for older birds, there are no useful published series, and none of the scattered
records specifically states whether it is minus crop contents. If the spans given at the
beginning of this account are converted to metric, they are: ♂ 2,950–4,300 gm. and ♀
3,630–5,900. The heaviest ♂ noted by Imler (1937) weighed 9.53 lb. (4,327 gm.). A
winter "adult" ♀ in Oreg. weighed 4,825 gm. (Henny et al. 1984a). A ♀ from the
Brooks Range, Alaska, weighed 13 lb. (5,900 gm.) (Irving 1960). Also from the Brooks
Range (Anaktuvuk Pass), in Apr. 1949: 3 ♀ 3,650, 4,150, 4,600 gm., and a ♂ 3,400 (R.
Rausch). A Juv. ♀ taken alive in Tenn. weighed 14 lb. (Spofford 1946), but it had eaten
heavily beforehand.

Hybrids None; the listing of Suchetet (1897) is based on 2 names for the same species. Captive Goldens have fostered Redtails several times. A laying captive ♀ had domestic fowl eggs substituted for her own; she hatched 3 and tended her foster offspring but seems to have reverted to type when she slew 1—a cockerel (1896 *Ibis* 261, reprinted in Prestwich 1955).

Geographical variation In the species, slight. Wing length is said to increase clinally in Eurasia going e. from the Yenisei and in the mts. of cent. Asia; it decreases going s. in Europe, and it is comparatively small in N. Am. Korean and Japanese birds are evidently smallest. These statements are derived from Vaurie (1965), whose sample sizes were minimal; considerable individual variation in size and coloring tend to limit their usefulness. The few Juv. Goldens examined in nests in the ne. U.S. had less white in wing and tail than those in the West (Spofford 1964).

Affinities The genus *Aquila*, to which the latest reviser (Amadon 1982a) assigned 10 current species, is evidently of ancient origin. Just what was ancestral to the present *A. chrysaetos* is guesswork. Currently the species has an enormous distribution around the world. It may be of interest that in w. N. Am. during the Pleistocene there were 3 species of a related genus (*Spizaetus*) of large eagles—a genus currently widespread elsewhere (13 living species). There were various *Aquila*; the Cuban fossil material includes 1 larger than any living eagle (Arredondo, in Olson 1976). Also of Pleistocene age, 590 of 960 Golden Eagles discovered in the La Brea pits in Calif., were found in the 7 most recent (youngest) pits (H. Howard 1962); any significance is unclear. The Golden obviously occurred s. of the Pleistocene ice and most likely also n. in Beringia, whence perhaps migratory birds later spread across boreal N. Am. RALPH S. PALMER

SUBSPECIES The number listed has varied—formerly sometimes up to 8, more recently (Vaurie 1965, others) no more than 5—still based on inadequate material. It is not inconceivable that the number of forms recognized may be reduced ultimately to as few as 3, with more emphasis on individual variation in these large birds: 1 most of Eurasia, 2 Korea/Japan, and 3 ne. Asia plus N. Am. For now, with approximate breeding ranges:

In our area *canadensis* (Linnaeus)—descr. and meas. given above; moderate in size, rather dark; breeds in ne. Asia from the Indigirka drainage e. and s. to Yakutsk, and in N. Am. from tundra to Mexican highlands and Baja Calif.

Elsewhere More or less from w. to e.: *chrysaetos* (Linnaeus)—pale, moderate-sized; Britain, France, Fennoscandia and across n. Eurasia to the Indigirka drainage; *homeyeri* Severtzov—small, dark; Portugal, Spain, w. Mediterranean area including nw. Africa; *daphanea* Menzbir—large, dark; s. Caspian region and Iran e. to include the n. ⅗ of China; *japonica* Severtzov—rather dark, smallest, very few in number; Korea and Japan. See various Palearctic literature for meas. and other details. RALPH S. PALMER

FIELD IDENTIFICATION In N. Am. One of our largest diurnal raptors—length 30–40 in.; usually solitary or in pairs, occasionally small groups; a tendency to gather at times where food is abundant; a few occur at Bald Eagle roosts. The birds are dark or bleached toward yellowish brown with pale nape. The youngest cohort (Juv.) is darkest

186

overall, the tail white with conspicuous subterminal black band (very tips of feathers white and inconspicuous or wear off), a white "window" basally in inner primaries (visible as a patch from below, smaller from above) and white basally in some adjoining secondaries (partially visible from below). There are intermediate (older) stages toward the dark-tailed definitive, but some individuals show more or less white later—even all of their lives.

In e. N. Am., Goldens with white "epaulettes" (see variants, above) have been suspected of being escaped falconers' Imperial Eagles (*A. heliaca*).

The wings are long, rather pointed, held angled very slightly upward, the 6 outer primaries (5 notched) extending as long, well-separated, upturned "fingers." The Golden soars easily and evenly with an occasional rippling stroke of the wings. Flight is graceful and adroit, especially in display and in pursuit of quarry; usually, however, this eagle is seen flying fairly low, "contouring" hills and ridges, or just above the trees in semiwooded country, or perched on dead snags in forested country, utility poles in w. N. Am., or crags, even on the ground in treeless places.

The head, in relation to tail area, is small in a flying Golden and large in a Bald Eagle. An occasional young Bald is mostly dark with a white tail that is more or less dark distally (as Juv. Golden), but it is large headed and broader winged, and any white in undersurface of wing is in the lining—not the flight feathers—and widest proximally. Young Sea Eagles might be confused with older cohorts of the Golden, but they have large heads, heavy beaks, squarish wings, and comparatively ponderous flight, similar to the Bald Eagle.

Buteos are smaller, with broader wings, the "fingers" less extensive (usually only 4 notched), and the head blunt (not relatively small and tapering), while the eagle's wingbeat is slower, deeper, and more deliberate. At long distance a very dark Rough-legged Hawk might be mistaken for a Golden. The Juv. and ♀ Roughleg have a tail pattern similar to the Juv. Golden. A flying Osprey has a pronounced bend at the "wrist," and its white underparts show at long distance. The Turkey Vulture's upward-angled wings and teetering flight distinguish it even at long distance.

Attempts to assign ages in the field to individuals beyond the Juv. stage and prior to typical full definitive are not easy. There are, however, some reasonably definable stages, identifiable by a kind of reverse-order thinking. Examples:

1 During the bird's 2d summer, when the 1st molting (Prebasic I) is underway, and from then into fall, the inner primaries have been renewed, thereby reducing the white area of inner primaries; in the secondaries the outermost ones (showing most white) are also renewed, reducing or sometimes eliminating visible white along the wing. The tail will show a mixture—retained Juv. (only a distal, dark bar) and Basic I (shorter feathers with an additional preterminal, narrow bar).

2 By the following summer, there is usually little (even no) white in the wings; there is still white in the tail, mostly laterally, since the central feathers have molted twice (showing 2 narrow, irregular, dark bars plus the distal, wide bar). As molting continues there is a stage in which at least most individuals show only a spot of white (visible from above) in each side of tail.

In Sweden, from knowledge of differences in details of outline and pattern, Tjernberg (1977) was able to distinguish 159 individuals, including 45 "adults."

RALPH S. PALMER

VOICE   N. Am. data. Common descriptive words are yelping, yapping, and scream-ing. Dawson (1923) regarded its so-called scream as "rather pathetic"—quite inade-quate if intended to intimidate. Audubon likened its voice to the barking of a dog, which is passably acceptable; Turner's (1886) "prolonged shrill whistle" may be in error. The data here are from the ne. U.S. (Spofford, notes), from a captive-reared ♀ in Wis. imprinted on a person (Frances Hamerstrom 1969), and from w. Mont. (D. Ellis 1979). When *weeeo* of 1 source is reinterpreted as *Skonk* by another (Ellis), there are obviously problems of phonetic transcription and interpretation. The calls are given here as described.

Adults   Utter a series of slow, measured yelps given by 1 or both of a pair when in view of or close to each other—a pronounced 2-syllabled *Kee-Yelp* or *Che-owp* or *Ki-ah* in series, rather similar to but less piercing than the food call of the eaglet; or a 1-syllabled *Kleek;* or, much softer, a mellow *Culp* (presumably by ♂ only), in series. Quiet clucking notes occasionally at the nest or when feeding. A shrill, chittering scream *Ki-Ki-Ki-Ki-* (indefinite length) when fighting or when trapped or otherwise restrained. Adults are usually quiet both at and away from the nest, even when an eaglet is yelping loudly, but occasionally the parents yelp in concert (duet?). In 9 days of nearly continuous observation a concert was heard 3 times. Two yearling captives "sang" in concert in early spring on moonlit nights *Culp-culp-culp* (long continued) (Spofford). A captive yelped before each rain (Vennor 1876).

Some specific episodes   A ♂ came in late afternoon carrying prey, and ♂ and ♀ exchanged vociferous yelping calls, the ♀ giving the loud *Kee-Yelp* in series, the ♂ responding more quietly *Ka Kaa Kaa Ka Ka Kulp* KULP KULP. Calling continued nearly 2 hrs. (till dark), the lone eaglet often adding his shrill version.

In another year at a different site: a distant yelping was heard, and 2 eagles flew in, 1 with prey, plunging out of the sky toward the cliff with sharp *Yelps* and more mellow *Culps* until almost the final moment, when they dived over a beaver meadow and shot up onto the nest cliff.

The 3 concerts mentioned above are described in Spofford's notes as "real blistering serenades" that require the presence of 2 birds. Lone birds awaiting a mate give single yelps at intervals. The longest yelping heard was from a flight-age nestling. In late afternoon, a ♂ brought in prey. The eaglet yelped plaintively on seeing the approach-ing parent and then made excited, fast yelps as the parent alighted. The eaglet immedi-ately mantled over the prey and began continuous yelping (2/sec. to 1+/sec.), and the ♂ walked around the nest for 5 min. before hopping onto a side limb, seeming to ignore the eaglet, which acted protective of its food and yelped steadily. Spofford calculated over 5,000 yelps, and the eaglet, still calling, had eaten nothing when he (unseen by either eagle or eaglet) withdrew. In nearly 2 hrs. the eaglet had yet to begin eating. The ♂ eagle was silent.

A long, rasping scream *Kee—aa-augh* was heard from a captive and once from an adult flying past a nest containing an eaglet of late preflight age. A 7-week-old eaglet approached for banding in the nest leaped at the observer, clapping his face with its wings and giving a loud hiss (Spofford).

A captive, on sighting 2 distant soaring eagles or hawks, called *Kielk Kielk Kielk* (very sharp, explosive); 10 min. later it responded to Spofford's imitation with the same, diminishing and becoming a chitter.

A captive-reared ♀ in her 4th year: beginning in Feb. a "curious, melodious song" reminiscent of but more musical than the call of a Wild Turkey. Long bouts of "singing" on moonlit nights; also daytime singing on hearing or seeing a person. Before laying her 1st egg, chicklike cheeps and soft dry grunts. April 2 (right after laying 2d egg), long continuous singing. Later, on beginning to feed a foster young Red-tailed Hawk, her "usual greeting call" and a new sound—a soft *boop*. Still later, when feeding foster Redtail young, continuous "clucky" sounds (Hamerstrom). The turkeylike call was reported from another captive by Brewster (1925).

Most of the calls described by D. Ellis (1979) appear to be different renderings of those described here; see also description of copulation (below).

Eaglets A clearly audible peeping before hatching, feeble at hatching, but developing into loud *Kee-yelp* (in series), piercing and insistent, of the month-old hungry eaglet; eventually it can be heard 1 mi. or more. A faint, chittered *K-k-k-k-k-k-* (indefinite length) of small nestling when brooded or handled. In times of great excitement, the food call of the 6-week-old eaglet may be chittered *Ki-ki-ki-ki-ki-ki-Yelp* (this uttered repeatedly). At a nest a ♀ heeded the peeping from within the egg, became restless, flew off, and returned with food (a live young crow that was brooded overnight until the eaglet hatched). The peeping was clear but not loud at age 1 week, louder and heard clearly by an observer on the talus slope below at 2 weeks, and much louder at 4 weeks, when it could be compared with yelps of adults. As the nestling approached flight age the adults were usually away from the nest, even at night, and were almost never heard even though the eaglet still called at irregular intervals. This food call served to locate the eaglet while grounded (for a week or more after leaving the nest at age 11 weeks) and for weeks thereafter when perched in thick forest or on rocky hillsides. In 1 of its early flights the eaglet landed in water on the far side of a lake and made its way ashore into dense spruce cover; its loud yelping brought the ♀, who within 1 hr. caught and delivered it a Black Duck (Spofford).

See also D. Ellis (1979) for another account of development of voice of the young.

In Yosemite Valley, Calif., 2 flying young, accompanied by their parents, yelped continually for attention (Michael 1925).   RALPH S. PALMER

HABITAT In N. Am. In general, the birds need solitude—open areas in any season for hunting and, in **nesting** season, the same but not distant from shelves on cliffs, their equivalent, or large trees. The Golden occurs in appropriate season(s) from tundra and alpine country through forested areas to sw. deserts—including Death Valley and Salton Sea (whence absent in warmest season). Many nest in niches in cliffs, escarpments, and bluffs, some in steep dirt banks along boreal rivers, but not restricted to these. Commonly on escarpments of the e. foothills of the Rockies; in Utah about 5% in trees, especially firs (J. R. Murphy); in the rolling coastal ranges of Calif. perhaps exclusively in trees. Generally at low elevations, occasionally up to about 8,000 ft. Often distant from water.

In forested e. N. Am., what might broadly be termed the n. Appalachian eagles have probably been bog hunters from at least the post-Pleistocene era, using burned areas of forest as a back-up. At present: open bogs, marshy terrain bordering watercourses, the shores of lakes and ponds, along dirt roads, in openings created by forest fires and lumbering operations, and upland fields. Bog and marsh birds, especially young Am.

189

Bitterns, are prominent on the menu. More s., in the wilder ridge country, formerly nested not far from "grassy balds" and man-made clearings. At least in the recent past, some nested near sheep pastures, where carrion, occasional small lambs and kids, and various small mammals were obtainable.

In migration Widespread—even high over cities—but mostly follow escarpments and ridges to use updrafts. Golden Eagles seem to avoid directly crossing large bodies of water, but some may pass high over large lakes.

In winter Mostly in more or less open country—in the W. in the former range of the bison and pronghorn (and the still-present jackrabbits and cottontails). This land is now largely in crops or used for grazing stock—cattle, sheep, and to some extent goats—and the eagles tend to congregate to some extent near livestock, especially sheep, and near unfrozen water. In parts of Tex. and N.Mex., for example, there is relative seasonal crowding of raptors; the winter range is loaded with inexperienced young Golden Eagles. There are numerous Golden (and usually many more Bald) Eagles on national wildlife refuges, where crippled and dead waterfowl and pheasants are a mainstay.

Golden-Bald Eagle contacts The 2 species appear to be sensitive to each others' territories and tend to avoid trespassing.

In the Alaskan interior the Golden usually nests higher up and feeds largely on ground squirrels (*Spermophilus*) taken in open alpine areas, but it also hunts on and nests close to low terrain—muskeg, forest openings, and burned areas. The Bald typically nests down in the "true" forest, generally near water, and hunts and scavenges near there. In 1971, some 50 mi. n. of Paxon, there was an "explosion" of snowshoe hare (*Lepus americanus*) numbers. A pair of Goldens nested there in alpine terrain (prime ground squirrel habitat) and raised 3 young—feeding them on hares caught in the valley far below along with a few of the also abundant tree squirrels (*Tamiasciurus*) (Spofford).

In cent Sask., the Golden usually nests on cliffs and hunts over land; the far more numerous Bald nests almost exclusively in trees and eats mainly fish. Two pair nested 1.3 mi. apart, the next smallest distance being 3.0 mi. (D. W. A. Whitfield et al. 1969).

In n. Alta. in Jan. 1907, there was a surfeit of snowshow hares. The number of eagles present "would hardly be believed unless actually witnessed"—the Golden outnumbering the Bald. Every little muskeg had 1 or 2 eagles, sometimes 4 or 5. The next year there were neither hares nor eagles (Henderson 1920).

Bald Eagles are present by the 100s in winter in cent. Utah, where they cannot avoid trespassing on territories of the resident Goldens. The strongest and most frequent interactions are seen in late Feb.–early Mar., after the Goldens have started nesting and before the Balds have departed for nesting areas to the n. (J. R. Murphy). The Golden has been known to "escort" the Bald from its nesting territory. Yet a few (young only?) associate with Bald Eagles at communal winter roosts (C. Edwards 1969).

In winter in Tex. an aircraft roused a young Bald Eagle, which flew over and joined a Golden on the limb of a low pine; they sat side by side in apparent harmony (Spofford 1964).

There are reports of the Golden and Bald feeding together on the same carrion in winter (Murphy 1973). Evidence seems to indicate that younger birds of the 2 species associate in such circumstances without discord but that older ones may tend to keep apart. At carcasses, Goldens of any age are dominant over Balds of any age.

RALPH S. PALMER

DISTRIBUTION   Panboreal, occurring widely on major landmasses and some adjacent is.; the following pertains to *A. chrysaetos canadensis* **in our area** and the generalized map (which see) is not appreciably different from Oberholser's (1906) of 80 years ago.

Breeding   Inadequate food plus weather (brevity of mild season) limit n. nesting distribution. Breeds in nw. and n. Alaska to about lat. 69° 30′ N, n. Yukon, nw. Dist. of Mackenzie, and s. Keewatin; e. of Hudson Bay on the Ungava Pen. there are enormous gaps and 3 known tundra sites: near Sugluk, Wakeham Bay, and Finger L. (Leaf R. area inland sw. from Ungava Bay) with perhaps 3 or more sites s. in Que. and at least 1 in Labrador. Possibly now breeds on Bonaventure I., Que. Breeders are concentrated w. in N. Am.; highest densities are in far w. Canada and w. coterminous U.S. Sparse nester to the e. (formerly s. into Tenn. and N.C.) and s. in Mexico (limits: n. Baja Calif., Durango, Guanajuato, and Nuevo León).

Summer   In coterminous U.S. and away from known breeding areas occasionally occurs (mostly young with banded tails) s. to the Mexican border and e. into Ga.

Winter   Withdraws from some n. areas and higher elevations where this season is long. **Northern** limits are somewhere in Alaska and across forested Canada, e. possibly to the n. shore of the Gulf of St. Lawrence. The birds become seasonally more numerous and widespread largely in more s. range of resident breeders—the vast majority in far w. Canada and 17 U.S. states w. of the 100th meridian. Northerly within the latter area, high seasonal density includes resident and locally migratory breeders and their older progeny plus an influx of birds of various ages—number and composition probably varying with mildness or severity of season (highest known densities in Mont., Wyo., and Colo.). **Southerly,** on both sides of the Mexican border, winterers are largely Juv. birds, which migrate farthest, and their seasonal occurrence includes areas where resident birds are few or absent. Mexico: Sonora and especially Coahuila (but also occurs farther s. as breeder—see above). Fla.—occasional.

Changes in distribution   In the mid-1880s, Lucien Turner found this bird in the Aleutians at least as far w. as Atka, but in recent decades there have been very few Aleutian records. (The Bald Eagle apparently fares well at some Aleutian breeding sites that are inaccessible to introduced foxes.)

No longer breeds in some areas, notably in parts of e. U.S.; most recent active nest in se. U.S. presumably in Giles Co., Va., in 1952. (Summation of recorded and unrecorded active and inactive e. sites is omitted here intentionally.) There are various changes. For example, there was an influx of Goldens in N.D. after creation of Upper and Lower Souris Migratory Wildlife Refuges; the eagles stay all winter (Henry 1939). For very widespread occurrence e. of the Mississippi in the U.S., see discussion, maps, and list of regular wintering localities in Millsap and Vana (1984).

Peripheral records   ALASKA visitor to Aleutians and St. Lawrence I. ARCTIC CANADA s. Victoria I. ATLANTIC AREA almost no recorded occurrence in Nfld., and rela-

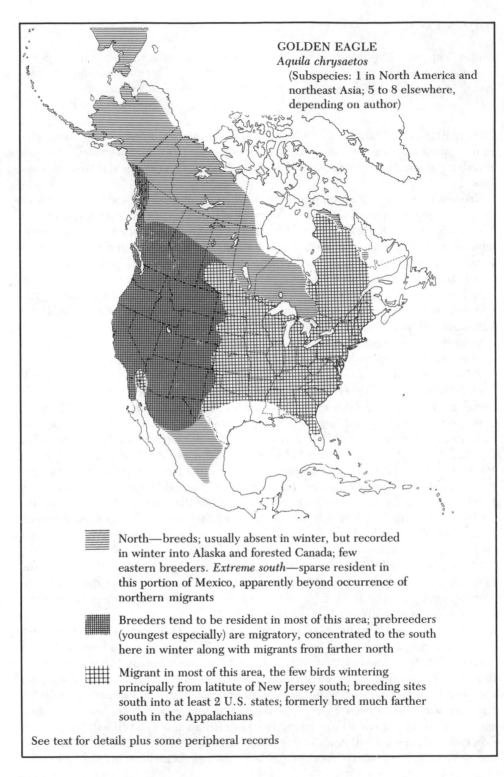

GOLDEN EAGLE
Aquila chrysaetos
(Subspecies: 1 in North America and
northeast Asia; 5 to 8 elsewhere,
depending on author)

North—breeds; usually absent in winter, but recorded
in winter into Alaska and forested Canada; few
eastern breeders. *Extreme south*—sparse resident in
this portion of Mexico, apparently beyond occurrence of
northern migrants

Breeders tend to be resident in most of this area; prebreeders
(youngest especially) are migratory, concentrated to the south
here in winter along with migrants from farther north

Migrant in most of this area, the few birds wintering
principally from latitude of New Jersey south; breeding sites
south into at least 2 U.S. states; formerly bred much farther
south in the Appalachians

See text for details plus some peripheral records

192

tively few nesting sites known in the Maritimes. FLA. recorded down onto the Keys. MEXICO Sonora, Sinaloa, Hidalgo. HAWAII Kauai—seen at various times from May 18, 1967 (escapee? released captive? natural occurrence?) into May 1984. It was in predefinitive feathering when 1st seen; with passage of time it became increasingly antagonistic toward helicopters and finally dove at 1 and was killed—at probable age of 21 years (1984 *Am. Birds* **38** 967 and earlier).

The world list of places where this species has been reported from the Pleistocene and from prehistoric sites (Brodkorb 1964) is lengthy; limiting coverage to the New World and adding data supplied subsequently by the same author yields the following: **fossil** from the Pleistocene of Oreg., Calif. (6 localities), Nev., N.Mex. (3), Tex. (2), and Mexico (Nuevo León 3); and from **prehistoric sites** in Alaska, Calif., Idaho, Utah (5), Ariz. (5), N.Mex., N.D., S.D. (many), and Ill. (See under affinities, above, for some Pleistocene contemporaries of this species.)

Many bones of the Golden Eagle were well illus. in H. Howard (1929), the skull in D. Ellis (1979).   RALPH S. PALMER

MIGRATION   In N. Am. Subarctic and at least some boreal birds of all ages travel seasonally, the youngest cohort "leapfrogging" over less migratory or resident birds to the s. There seems to be an intermediate zone n. of and perhaps astride the U.S.-Canadian boundary whence breeders and older young wander or migrate short distances, especially in severe winters and/or when food is scarce. In and near the intermountain w. (of the U.S.), the great majority of breeders and older prebreeders are locally resident—their numbers augmented seasonally by an influx of winterers and resulting in the highest known seasonal density in N. Am. in some areas. First-fall birds there disperse in almost any direction, some occasionally going some distance, but they evidently return to the vicinity of their hatching. In sw. Idaho, where "adults" have been observed in the vicinity of nesting territories throughout the year, recoveries of banded birds plus observations of marked young indicate that they evidently occur in numbers throughout the study area but that individuals do not remain at a specific location for any length of time (Beecham and Kochert 1975); but see Steenhof et al. (1984) for many recent data. In cent. Utah, 120 nestlings banded over a 16-year period (1967–1982) yielded 10 recoveries; 8 were within 50 mi. of the banding site (age of recovered birds ranged from 6 months to 7 years). The most distant recovery was a 2 year old at Temecula, Calif.—approximately 700 mi. from the banding location (J. R. Murphy). In Calif., 7 recoveries from 33 banded young indicated no extensive movement (Carnie 1954), and a much larger sample now reaffirms this (P. H. Bloom).

It is possible that the above pattern for the species may not always align with latitude, since Aleutian birds (when formerly present) were possibly resident. In the arid sw., after breeding the birds are virtually absent from hot deserts; they are said (Phillips 1947) to go higher up, even to the tops of peaks. It thus appears that breeders everywhere prefer to maintain their nesting-hunting domain or to go the shortest distance necessary to survive prolonged cold or heat, that older prebreeders may be less tied to specific locations, and birds of the youngest cohort are variably migratory.

Spring   Passage appears to be rather inconspicuous or at least not often observed except at certain localities. Older birds in Mexico and s. coterminous U.S. leave winter quarters in late Feb. or (mainly) Mar., some yearlings not until late Apr., May, or rarely June. Thus considerable numbers of winterers (subarctic-boreal birds?) still remain in N.Mex. in Mar., after egg laying is well under way in Colo. and Wyo. (Boeker and Ray 1971). High counts at some w. localities are weeks after peak Bald Eagle passage. Not far from Colorado Springs, Colo., at least 23 sleet-covered Goldens were grounded on a day in Mar., 1926, and 5 were run down and captured (Aiken 1928). At a locality in Park Co., Mont., Mar. 30, 1982. 21 Golden and 70 Bald Eagles were on the wing and others were on the ground (1982 *Am. Birds* **36** 875). Passage in the Bear R. region of Utah is in Mar. (O. Scott 1956). Many migrant Goldens are back on high-latitude territories in late Mar. or early Apr.; at Anaktuvuk Pass in the Brooks Range, Alaska, they pass in Mar.–May (Irving 1960), mostly before ground squirrels are out of hibernation.

In e. N. Am., spring passage, depending on locality, extends early Feb.–May, with occasional young birds later. Near se. L. Ontario at Derby Hill, they pass Mar. 10–May 5, peaking Mar. 25–Apr. 25 (G. Smith and Muir 1978).

Summer Altitudinal shift was mentioned above. An occasional (healthy?) bird lingers or remains through the season on s. winter range.

Fall Larger numbers, better recorded, often pass after marked deterioration of weather to the n. They leave the Brooks Range, Alaska, by early Sept.—food supply decreases since ground squirrels are hibernating (Irving 1960)—and the Alaska Range soon afterward (parents accompanied by still-dependent young). Aside from a few early travelers, throughout much of the U.S. w. they begin appearing in late Sept., and many pass in Oct. (Most raptor migration is earlier in the w. than the e., although this eagle is comparatively late; it probably travels higher in the w. because of higher cloud base—some thermals extend up to 10,000 ft.) Sizable flights occur along the Bighorn Mts. and the Laramie Range, moving s. into Colo., beyond into w. Tex. and N.Mex. (relatively snowless sheep country), and some into Mexico. Forty were counted in 1 hr. on Nov. 1, 1959, passing w. of Casper, Wyo. (O. Scott 1960); 35 on muskrat houses in a 200-acre marsh at Malta, Mont., Nov. 3 and 5, 1955 (1956 *Aud. Field Notes* **10** 33). A 6-year study in N.Mex.: the birds began to arrive in Oct., were at peak numbers in Dec.–Feb., began to leave in Mar., and were gone by mid-Apr.; a high percentage of "immature" birds passed beyond to the s. in Nov. and to the n. in Mar. (Boeker and Ray 1971). The numbers censused in sw. Tex. and e. N.Mex. 1964–1968 (Boeker and Bolen 1972) were fairly constant and low. In Okla., there was a "mass migration" of 50 eagles (Golden and Bald) on Dec. 10, 1953 (Van den Akker 1954).

It would seem that migrant birds of the youngest cohort are scattered where they can find adequate food and few older eagles are there to compete with them.

A "immature" bird banded at Ft. Smith, NWT, Sept. 23, 1965, was recovered in Mont. on Oct. 25, having traveled about 1,000 mi. in a month (Kuyt 1967). A nestling banded n. of Fairbanks, Alaska, in July was trapped in B.C. in Nov. (W. R. Spofford). Of 10 recoveries from 92 young banded in Canada, 9 were in coterminous U.S., and 4 of these were more than 1,200 mi. from banding site (Boeker 1974).

In e. N. Am., knowledge is relatively extensive in proportion to the small number of Golden Eagles. The Appalachian route is well known; the birds traverse the ridges down to the s. highlands. A few decades ago, when they were more numerous, they passed through w. Pa. from Sept. 15 to Nov. 22 (mainly in Oct.), and "immatures" av. 50% of a 5-year total (Broun 1939). October plus the 1st ⅓ of Nov. is the best time for eagle watching there, but the total time of passage may be summarized thus: end of Aug. (rare), more often beginning after Sept. 10, and most birds pass from early Oct. to late Nov. (peak about Nov. 5–10). They usually pass in early afternoon, seldom before noon, moving with other migrant raptors on days when nw. winds provide lift over the ridges; they soar high on calm days and sail close to the slopes when there is a strong wind. Sometimes they hunt the slopes in quartering flight or play with a wind-blown leaf. They begin to perch long before dusk and may be relatively inactive until toward the following midday. Easterly ridges include Mt. Tom in Mass., the Shawangunks and Hudson Highlands in e. N.Y., Kittatinny Mt. in N.J., and the Blue Ridge through Pa. and Va.

One nestling banded near Wakeham Bay in Hudson Strait on July 26, 1967, was trapped and released at Hawk Mt. in w. Pa. on Oct. 23 of the same year (D. Berger). One banded as a nestling in Maine in July was "found dead" in Nov. of the same year, 60 mi. s. of Hawk Mt. (W. R. Spofford). An emaciated Juv., captured at Montezuma Refuge in upstate N.Y. in Nov. 1970(?), was fed and gained wt. from 7½ to 10 lbs. and was released at Shining Rock wilderness in w. N.C. Thirteen months later it attacked and killed a captive Wood Duck in s. N.J., was recaptured and released at Brigantine Refuge (N.J.), and was there shot (injured) by a duck hunter and taken to Patuxent Research Refuge (Spofford).

Ganier (1931) thought it probable that a few birds from w. N. Am. migrate into the se. U.S., but the small numbers do not support this.

A few Goldens pass around or between the Great Lakes at Duluth, Minn., along L. Michigan, and along the n. shores of Lakes Ontario and Erie. An occasional bird passes along the ne. Atlantic seaboard.

Speed of flight is usually of the order of 28–40 mph. (ground speed), but this bird can fly rapidly for some distance. Abroad, Darling (1934) claimed to have timed 1 with a stopwatch, the bird covering several mi. at 120 mph.!—a speed credited to the Peregrine Falcon. The late Leslie Brown claimed to have seen 1 stoop faster than a Peregrine.

Winter   Some birds remain in Alaska in the warmer perimeter of the Gulf of Alaska and nearby. Counts of Goldens at winter Bald Eagle roosts in the arid w. interior of the U.S. vary within brief spans of time, probably in response to changes in weather. A remarkable concentration of eagles in n. Alta. in Jan. (see Habitat, above) would indicate that migrants may go no farther than necessary to find plentiful food.

RALPH S. PALMER

BANDING STATUS   In N. Am. From the banding of 834 individuals in the Rocky Mt. states, 1955–1970, Boeker (1974) reported 41 recoveries (5%). The number banded in N. Am. from 1955 to Aug. 1979 was 2,866, with 120 (4.2%) returns (Keran 1981). The total number banded to Aug. 1981 was 3,666, with 282 (7.7%) recoveries (Clapp et al. 1982).

This bird has been banded in small numbers over a vast area, but principal banding has been in the n. U.S. Rocky Mt. states and in Sask. Banding data have been used in limited quantity in numerous papers, also quite extensively in the migration study by Steenhof et al. (1984). Apparently there are only 5 recoveries of birds banded as nestlings in e. N. Am.—mapped by Millsap and Vana (1984).

In addition to bands, wing markers are now used extensively in some areas (Kochert et al. 1983, Steenhof et al. 1984). RALPH S. PALMER

REPRODUCTION North Am. data unless otherwise indicated. Age when **first breeds** undoubtedly varies with individual, depending on circumstances—from some time before attaining definitive feathering to any time afterward. There are few relevant data as yet, but it appears certain that both sexes are capable of fertile mating before the usual age of attaining "adult" (definitive) feathering.

Prebreeders return to the vicinity of their rearing—that is, they are near established breeders and, at least in places where nesting density is high or saturated, must include individuals already past potential breeding age; marked birds first appeared on territories in their 4th to 7th years (Steenhof et al. 1984). Since preferred (traditional) nesting territories are occupied much longer than the av. lifespan of breeders, obviously there is a turnover of occupants. If 1 of a pair is lost (at least within the long breeding cycle), the survivor (either sex) remates very soon with an unattached bird. The number of vacancies (opportunities for replacement) is related to the survival rate of breeders. If their av. lifespan is long, then available potential mates will include birds that have been excluded longer from breeding; if survival av. shorter, choices among replacements will have a somewhat younger av. age. This schematic outline is modified considerably by indications that a surviving established breeder remates with whatever unmated bird of the opposite sex is conveniently available—regardless of its age. The birds probably have "known" each other for some time. Mated nesting pairs with 1 of them (as yet no records of both) in some predefinitive stage of feathering have been reported here and abroad. The following examples will suffice:

In an 11-year study in sw. Idaho, 17 (5%) of 340 territorial pairs included a "sub-adult" (2 ♀, 4 ♂, 11 sex unknown), occurrence of these pairs did not coincide with periods of food abundance, and 3 mixed pairs failed to lay eggs (Steenhof et al. 1983). The ♀♀ of 2 breeding pairs in Scotland had white wing patches and conspicuous white in base of tail; both laid fertile eggs, and 1 reared 2 young (Payne and Watson 1983). In Alaska, Spofford observed and photographed a ♀ at a nest with 2 eaglets; she was in an early stage of 1st molting (Prebasic I)—that is, she was a yearling and could have been a foster mother.

Thus it is evident that more or less participation in the nesting cycle is a normal attribute of birds of various early ages, but the age at which either sex becomes capable of fertile mating remains speculative. It is of interest that participation in the breeding cycle by individuals having "immature" characteristics of feathering is more frequent than is the retention of such characteristics past the usual age of attaining definitive feathering.

Evidently there are other arrangements. Paired birds excluded from traditional or ideal nesting sites may persist in occupying and attempting to breed in less satisfactory places. Some ground nests may be in this category. Further, from his Calif. experience, J. B. Dixon (1937) had doubts that **pair-bond** form was invariably life-long. He claimed to have observed an unmated ♀ that built a nest, laid an infertile clutch, and persisted until successful in acquiring a mate. Dixon also believed that he had witnessed several instances in which 1 of a pair banished its mate and supplanted it with a younger bird. The banished bird would stay nearby and was harassed by 1 of the ruling pair though tolerated by the other. When yearlings insisted on returning to an area from which Dixon stated they had been driven perviously, invariably the larger bird (♀) of the resident pair did the "chastising" and the smaller one (♂) did not fight—in some instances he joined the "chastised" bird and even perched beside it but later departed with the bird that had been doing the punishing.

There seems to be no indication that prebreeders anywhere form stable pairs, but young birds occasionally hunt together, and some individuals likely become attached to areas with which they are familiar. Although this species has striking displays that relate in large measure to territoriality and perhaps synchronization of reproductive cycles, formation of a pair bond (by birds of similar or different ages) can occur rapidly. There is one indication (Dennis 1983), from Scotland, of probable **trio-bond.** The various circumstances suggested here would seem to create considerable opportunity to enter the breeding population, even where nesting density is high, yet any assumption that all individuals eventually breed may be questionable. In sw. Idaho, along with younger prebreeders, there are nonterritorial "adult floaters"—3 trapped in 1977 (Snake R. Birds Prey *Spec. Res. Rept.* 1979).

Displays Quite buteolike. Except for High-circling, any relation to pair formation or maintenance seems tenuous. Sky-dance is most often described, and it intergrades with an abrupt form: tumbling.

HIGH-CIRCLING Especially in winter, small gatherings, sometimes of both predefinitive-feathered and older birds, ride upward in a thermal "bubble" (cone) and soar in circles. As with a soaring buteo, occasionally there are several rapid wingbeats. Sometimes 1 dives at another in mock attack. The "attacked" bird may flip over and present its talons upward to the "attacker." Mated pairs do this, quite commonly in the span when the nest is being readied for use; the ♂ dives and sideslips downward, the ♀ flips over as he approaches. In Tenn. on Jan. 3, as many as 4 Goldens were circling in "playful flight," diving at each other (Ganier 1953); on that date, 7 were present, but only 2 were "fully adult." Near Brevard, N.C., Mar. 14, 1956, 2 eagles that were riding a thermal high went into a long glide with wings folded and alighted on the ground. Then both quickly caught a thermal and rode very high, like 2 aircraft in tight formation. The ♂, slightly above and behind, descended until he seemed to alight on the ♀'s back, where he remained briefly; they separated, repeated this twice, and then sailed out of sight (M. Edwards).

Near winter Bald Eagle roosts, when soaring conditions are favorable, both Balds and Goldens may be seen circling high overhead.

SKY-DANCE The bird (or birds) fly an up-and-down undulating course, making oscillations of greater amplitude when higher above the ground. The Sky-dance may be directed toward another bird in the distance to discourage territorial invasion, it may appear spontaneously, or toward a mate, and it may be a mutual "dance" between mates, but its typical function is to maintain territory. It is seen in Idaho even after the young are on the wing (Kochert 1973); it has been seen Oct.–June in n. Colo., whence

Harmata (1982) provided the best account. It occurs all year. The following gives some indication of variation:

In Calif., a flying bird called in the distance. A 2d bird left its nesting ledge and High-circled. Before the latter got as high as the former, it hurtled downward with closed wings (tumbled), checked its flight when close to the ground, and began a series of acrobatics; it rolled, "stood" on its head or tail, and sideslipped with extended wings. In between these activities it performed flights reminiscent of a skater cutting figures on ice. It terminated when aligned with its nest and made 3 perfect loops in the air, culminating right at the nest ledge. Meanwhile its mate was High-circling. The "resting" eagle flew upward from the ledge. The distant bird flew down and performed the same routine as had the other. Such flights always ended with 3 loops (Sky-dance) terminating at the nest ledge. The whole may have lasted 1 hour. Finally, mates were together on the ledge and departed together for a hunting area. This may have occurred more often but was observed only 1 day in a season (Lofberg 1935).

Also in Calif., Hanna (1930) mentioned High-circling by both birds, then "flight antics" over the nest, such as swooping and loop-the-loop. In J. B. Dixon's (1937) description, the ♂, from his home area, went up some 2,000 ft. and dived in loops in the direction of a distant eagle. At a Calif. location in Jan., Emelie Curtis saw 2 pairs in joint diving display. In s. Ariz. in Mar. 1973, there was a pair on Silver Peak (reared 1 young) and another pair on Portal Peak (breeding?). The latter were 1st seen to dive; the former appeared at about 1,500 ft. and also dived, with sharp yelping (possibly both pairs called). For about 2 min. all 4 eagles looped and dived, then each pair withdrew toward its nesting place (Spofford). In Ill. in late Dec. a lone "immature" was about 100 ft. overhead; suddenly it darted upward, turned over, and swept downward, somewhat in the manner of a flycatcher, repeating this a number of times (Bellrose 1936).

In Colo., a ♂ climbed to about 2,000 ft. and was joined by his presumed mate, High-circling. One bird, above and upwind, half-folded its wings and made a swooping approach toward its mate, which turned over and presented its talons. This was repeated. In another instance the presumed ♀ spiraled upward over the aerie to at least 1,500 ft. in circles at least 1 mi. in diam. and then began to Sky-dance (Olendorff 1975).

Utah, Apr. 23: a nest had 2 small eaglets, the presumed ♀ was brooding, and the presumed ♂ circled up beneath a passing Ferruginous Hawk. A few min. later the ♂ made 2 great dives, rocketing upward with closed wings. A 3d "adult" appeared, and the ♂ at once made 2 display dives toward the interloper. After more dives the interaction became a tail chase. After they were a mi. away, both High-circled (Spofford).

North of L. Umbagog, N.H., a ♀ flew out from a mountainside and began making dives and close circles. Then the presumed ♂ appeared, carrying prey. There was then evidently a food pass (♂ to ♀), and an eagle came to the nest carrying an Am. Bittern (Spofford). In Alaska a ♂ came to the nest with prey and, right after he left, began a series of undulating drops; the whereabouts of the ♀ (she was not at the nest) was unknown (Spofford).

Near Roswell, N.Mex., in Mar., while photographing wintering eagles from a small aircraft, a pilot overtook an "adult" that appeared almost under the right wing tip. The

198

bird folded its wings and dived out of sight, very quickly reappeared right at the wing tip, again plunged with closed wings, and soon was up again eye-to-eye. This apparent Sky-dance was repeated until the pilot, who had been flying at almost stalling speed, had to dive to gain momentum in order to remain aloft (Spofford). Some pilots claim that eagles wheel and come at them, but to impugn attack may be questionable. A bird in Hawaii (see Distribution, above) attacked helicopters. Abroad, this eagle has been stated to attack aircraft on occasion—perhaps when a displaying pair is approached (Bruderer 1976).

TUMBLING May be described as an exaggerated, to near-vertical, downward portion of a Sky-dance oscillation. Suddenly the bird drops like a rock, similar to the display of the Com. Raven. It is spectacular. In Mont. in Feb., when a pair was renovating a nest, the ♀ tumbled, and tumbling is common to both sexes later. In Mar. a perched ♂ took flight and soared skyward, suddenly closed his wings, and dropped head foremost "like a spent rocket," then spread his wings to check his descent. Then he shot upward, tumbled again, and rested at his perch before resuming this aerial display (Cameron 1908a).

Talon grasping and cartwheeling are not separate displays but are among the possible consequences of territorial disputes. Such interactions are apparently most likely to occur when a single bird enters the domain of a breeding pair; an owner dives at the interloper, who flips over with feet extended upward, and the 2 catch or lock talons and tumble or rotate (cartwheel) toward earth until they disengage. There are variants. In Utah on Apr. 23, 2 eagles were in a fast chase; 1 changed direction, and they met beak-to-beak about 200 ft. above ground; they grasped talons and gyrated earthward, then separated and continued pursuit. When at a distance, they High-circled with no evidence of conflict (Spofford). In Okla. in Sept., 2 eagles dived at a 3d, who sought refuge on the ground; later the 2 flying birds "came to grips" and whirled earthward "in a series of breathtaking evolutions," halting their descent just before they would have crashed (G. Sutton 1934).

Two dead eagles were found in Scotland with talons still locked; apparently they had fought to the death over territory (L. Brown and Amadon 1968 1).

Lifelong monogamy May be the rule, but evidence of exceptions was given above. A lost mate is soon replaced—in 5 cases in ne. Wyo. "within a few days" (R. L. Phillips et al. 1984). If both birds disappear, others may occupy the territory as early as the same season (Kalmbach et al. 1964).

Territoriality A major factor in regulating nesting density. In a saturated population, pairs tend to be spaced evenly enough so that, if the whereabouts of some are known, the location of others can be predicted. Further, data from Britain, Europe, and N. Am. indicate that territories frequently support more—to many times as much—food than is needed (although there may be borderline cases in e. N. Am.). Boundaries are definite, occasionally with overlap in hunting areas (usually those not visible from the aerie), and they (Dixon) may vary in dimension with changing ownership. The birds use diverse methods to hunt diverse prey (and locate carrion) in diverse habitat in a defended area, which enhances hunting success. Since pairs have preferred hunting places, other parts of the overall territory may be regarded as seldom or unused controlled space.

J. B. Dixon (1937) diagramed 28 contiguous areas (27 occupied) in San Diego Co., Calif., of 19–59 sq. mi. (av. 36), of varying configuration, smaller where there were many changes in elevation and larger on flatter terrain. In Mont. in 1964 an av. of 66.3 sq. mi. for each of 19 pairs (McGahan 1968), and 54.8 for 23 pairs in the same area in 1967 (H. Reynolds 1969). In the densely occupied Snake R. canyon in sw. Idaho in 1975–1977, for radio-tagged birds the av. was 22 sq. mi. (Snake R. Birds Prey *Spec. Res. Rept.* 1979). The figure was 38 sq. mi. in cent. Utah in 1968 (Camenzind, in Murphy et al. 1969), and, like Dixon, Camenzind indicated that nests tended to be near a margin of the defended area. Dixon also noted that adjoining pairs prefer to nest where they can keep an eye on each other, which must be a factor in the spacing of active aeries. (Sometimes when pairs nest close an intervening ridge blocks the view.) As a rule, breeders do not hunt close to their aerie, but if the ♂ is lax in providing food, the ♀ may do so occasionally in his absence. Undefended areas are used by single (unmated) birds.

In the saturated population of the cent. Alps in 1980–1981, breeding density of 51 pairs varied 75–191 sq. km. in 5,565 sq. km. Four pairs studied in summer obtained all necessities in 22–48 sq. km. each. They were permanent residents. In winter, 8 pairs studied used much smaller portions of home range and generally flew only when the sun reached favorable slopes (most flying was in middle hrs. of day); their diet when marmots were hibernating included carrion (Haller 1982).

A measure of density is distance between active aeries. Mont.—minimum of 1.2 mi. and max. 10.5 (McGahan 1968). Utah—2 were only 0.7 mi. apart and max. was 16.1 mi. (Camenzind, in Murphy et al. 1969); and 34 active nests in e. Great Basin, 1.12–10.3 km. (av. 3.71 ± 1.1) (D. Smith and Murphy 1982). Snake R. area of sw. Idaho—56 active aeries 0.5–10.0 mi. (av. 2.7) apart (Kochert 1972), and a much longer study there gave an av. of 3.8 km. (2 mi.), the closest 0.97 km. (⅗ mi.) (Snake R. Birds Prey *Spec. Res. Rept.* 1979).

Intruding singles are attacked by occupying breeders; such encounters are presumably the most frequent cause of conflict. Again the cent. Alps: territorial challenges by singles affect breeders to the extent of reducing their nesting success to 0.4–0.6 young reared/year; in earlier years when the birds were persecuted and fewer, success was often above 1 eaglet raised/nest/year. (Haller 1982).

Nest site Ideally this should be located where an eagle burdened with prey can arrive without hindrance on a favorable wind or updraft and where there is shelter from excessive heat or cold. As for exposure, analysis of 166 cliff nests showed: Alaska—directional preference to the se. (avoidance of cold), Utah—equal preference to nw. (avoidance of heat), Mont.—to the s. (lat. plus elevation), and Tex.—no significant orientation in small sample size (Mosher and White 1976). Exposure to excessive heat or sunlight may be reduced by nesting earlier or at higher elevation.

In Sweden, mostly in coniferous forest, analysis of 158 tree and 61 cliff nests: 50+% of the former were exposed to the sw., the remainder scattered in other quadrants; the majority (62%) of cliff nests also faced s. to w. Furthermore, although cliff sites would seem to have advantages (more durable; more difficult for predators, including man, to reach), on 43 territories having both options, 28% used cliffs only, 35% trees only, and 37% both. (From Tjernberg 1983a, which see for many details and comparisons.)

In Calif., Dixon thought that the ♀ decided on the location of the future nest and that she also "for no apparent reason" would switch from 1 to another. Often the nest is visible from a distance, but whether it has any signal function is moot. At some boreal cliff nests, splashes of defecation nourish a conspicuous growth of orange lichen (as with the Gyrfalcon and Rough-legged Hawk). Near tree limit in extreme nw. Canada, and in absence of cliffs, 10 nests were on steep earth banks, and 2 were in "tall spruce pines" where the soil was too sandy to form banks (MacFarlane 1891). In the cent. Brooks Range 40 mi. from timber, a scanty nest on a slope (J. M. Campbell 1960). In McKinley [Denali] Park, Alaska, 23 all on cliffs (A. Murie 1944); over Alaska generally (65 examined), 2 in trees, 2 on brink of dirt banks, and remainder on rock base— boulder to large cliff (C. M. White). In Mont., 93 (occupied and unoccupied)—62% on cliffs, 29% in Douglas fir, 7% in other trees, and 2 on the ground (McGahan 1968). In Wyo., Colo., and N.Mex., 79 (occupied and unoccupied)—87% on cliffs, 11% in trees, 1 on ground (Wellein and Ray, in McGahan). Thirty-one in cent. Utah—27 on cliffs, 2 on man-made structures, and 2 (1 probably an abandoned Ferruginous Hawk nest) on the ground (Camenzind, in Murphy et al. 1969). Lack or scarcity of acceptable sites undoubtedly affects nesting distribution in parts of N. Am. In the cent. Alps, most nests were on cliffs down just within the forest zone, and the birds foraged higher up on alpine areas (Haller 1982).

Ground nests are probably built more often than they are used. In Millard Co., Utah, in 1970, 2 eaglets were on the ground, and as the sun changed position they had to follow the shadow of a post to get what little shade existed (Madsen 1970). Tree nesters in Calif. prefer oaks and eucalyptus (Dixon); in forested e. N. Am., cliffs primarily, but also large white pines. Almost everywhere Great Horned Owls, which are early nesters, occasionally preempt eagle nests; much less often the Red-tailed Hawk, Com. Raven, and Peregrine Falcon preempt nests, but the last may also use a nest for a feeding platform.

In Wyo. in 1980 a nest containing young was moved to another site, continued to be tended, and the young attained flight; the next year the adults nested at another man-made site some 2.5 km. from their original site (Postvit and Grier 1982). There is a growing literature (see Fala et al. 1985) on human manipulation of artificial sites.

Nest building The birds select from what is available close by, but finer material for a lining may be fetched from some distance. Typically the bulk of the nest is large dry sticks broken off trees or picked from the ground. Sometimes much construction of a new nest occurs rapidly, within perhaps 4–5 days. A bird fetching a stick flies in the accipiter manner, close to the ground if terrain is open, unobtrusively and silent, and when almost beneath the site swings abruptly upward and drops onto the rim. Departure is similar; the bird drops over the rim nearly to the ground and flies away. Both sexes fetch material, but evidently the ♀ works it into place. Texas data: building was from Jan. onward, 4–6 weeks, leisurely, rarely more than ½ hr./day but sometimes for a ½ day; from later observations—they work quite actively from daybreak to about 1100 hrs. and then are absent until near dark, when they return to roost on the cliff for the night (R. Strandtman, notes). In Okla. a nest was built in Dec.; the pair was not seen again until after Feb. 4 (1956 *Aud. Field Notes* **10** 392). In San Diego Co., Calif., construction began with the first heavy fall rains and continued through winter; nests often were built and not used the first year as the birds left, going to an older, previously used, nest to lay (J. B. Dixon 1937). Usually the nest was worked on after the morning hunt was over. Large material is usually transported by foot but may be transferred to the beak; smaller material is carried in the beak. A bird on a half-dead juniper tree walked out on a dead branch, broke off a stick with its beak, and carried the stick in its beak to the nest (Willard 1916a). At a N.Y. site in Mar., the ♀ made trips about every ½-hr. At another N.Y. site the pair circled high overhead; the larger dropped in a stoop into maple-beech treetops, seized a long thin branch, and took it to the nest on a nearby cliff. The ♂ soon appeared, empty footed; the ♀ spent many min. working the stick endwise into the nest, then pulled it out and again slid it in carefully, holding it sideways in her beak; sticks were worked in carefully, not just dropped (Spofford).

The lining is typically of much finer material; M. S. Ray (in Bent 1937) stated that it varied from 1 site to another. Examples: coarse roots in a nest on a barren mountain side; eucalyptus leaves in an oak-wooded canyon; elsewhere, 1 with gray-green oak moss; and in humid coastal Calif., rabbit fur, mosses, eagle down (probably accumulated during incubation and later). In San Diego Co., Calif., previous year's leaves of Spanish dagger, which, after several weeks, the bird shreds to form a soft mat (J. B. Dixon 1937). In semiarid valleys of w. Utah, sprigs of "Mormon tea" (an evergreen shrub *Ephedra*) for lining and, later (see below), "decoration" or greenery (J. R. Murphy). Olendorff (1975) mentioned yucca roots and dead yucca spears, an occasional green yucca plant, and dry grass. In ne. woodlands, small branches of white pine (some with needles) and undoubtedly other material. In Colo.: cow bones, deer antlers, barbed wire, burlap bags, rags, newspapers, stockings, and other rubbish

(Olendorff). In S.D., a cowboy hat (but no sign of cowboy, horse, or boots) (Moriarty 1966).

Nest size   Very variable, probably about a meter across at first. It has been incorrectly stated to be greater in trees than on cliffs. A tree nest may increase to some 2.5 m. (8 ft.) in diam. and be as tall or taller; volume of cliff nests varies with what the site will hold and amount added over the years. Reused nests may have little new material added, but some double in size in a season.

Alternative or supernumerary nests   Very common. Individual birds (or pairs) seem to vary in nest construction or usage, so that there is no obvious pattern. A pair may have several cliff nests, or several tree nests, sometimes 1 or more of each. In the Snake R. area of sw. Idaho the number varied 1–12 (av. 6) per pair, and some ♀ ♀ lay in a nest the year it is constructed (Beecham and Kochert 1975). As noted in Calif., the birds watch each other, and the "worst insult" is for a pair to steal sticks from another's nest; even if they rob an old unused nest, it provokes conflict (J. B. Dixon 1937). Both sexes join in battle. In Mont., McGahan (1968) stated that the birds generally use the same nest in consecutive years but that they may repair supernumerary ones and tend them regularly until the clutch is laid. Over half the pairs had supernumerary nests—1 pair had 8, with 2 of these only 0.3 mi. apart; 11 pairs had an "extra" nest each, others had 2 or 3. Rarely, two nests may almost touch; usually they are spread up to several mi, apart or even more. In nw. Wash., 1 pair apparently bred in alternate years; another nested in alternative nests in successive years; a 3d used the same nest 4 consecutive years (Bruce et al. 1982). Perhaps successful nesting predisposes a pair to return to the site and failure may induce it to use an alternative one.

Long use of sites   Certain sites are virtual magnets and have a succession of owners. In n. New Eng. an eagle, or eagle's nest, mountain is known from about 1689, and another, not far distant, from 1879 (and both were probably long used before first reported). One was mentioned in print in 1736, the other in 1838, the 1st again in 1936—at 100-year intervals. At the earliest-reported site an eaglet was raised in 1986. In ne. Man. at Hell Gate Gorge on the Nelson R., there was 1 cliff nest in 1819 and 2 in 1900 (Preble 1902). In Oreg., near the Malheur Refuge, a site known to have been active in 1870 was in use in 1970 (E. Hemphill). Various Utah sites, presently productive, are known at least back to the 1930s and with indications that some had long previous use (J. R. Murphy). There are other long N. Am. records, undoubtedly exceeded by records from abroad.

Nests at some cliff sites must be more durable than those in trees. Of 3 on a cliff in n. New Eng., 1 (with good overhead shelter) existed unused for over 30 years and was then reoccupied (after an alternative tree-site had been used?); a 2d has fallen out twice; a 3d, on a sloping ledge, usually slides out after 3–4 years.

Copulation   On open terrain like soil or ledge or at the aerie, repeatedly, from some time before laying and decreasing in frequency during early incubation but reported even when young are 2 weeks old. The ♀ calls loudly before, during, and for a few sec. afterward; the ♂ is silent. The ♀ crouches with lowered head, and the ♂ rests his tarsi with "fists" closed ("balled") for an av. of 11 sec. See D. Ellis (1979) for illus. and further details. Mates may perch together briefly afterward. At a Mont. aerie the total span of occurrence extended from the beginning of Mar. until about May 10—55 days after clutch completion—and frequency was several times/day early and again late during this period (Ellis and Powers 1982).

Nonviable or infertile eggs   Common. A pair laid a clutch each year for 3 years, incubated each for approximately 6 weeks, and none hatched (Sandermann 1956). In an area in sw. Idaho in 1970, 22% of all eggs laid were infertile (Kochert 1972). A pair in N.Y. reared an eaglet in 1957, then refurbished and sat on their alternative nests the following 8 years without ever hatching—if indeed they laid (Spofford). (See also productivity.)

Breeding in captivity   In Europe since 1922 or earlier (in Engelman 1928); in the U.S. a pair bred successfully in the Topeka, Kans., zoo in 1971 (Kewata 1973) and for 5 years thereafter. In 1972 Frances Hamerstrom and J. Grier were successful in artificially inseminating a Golden Eagle (C. Snow 1973b).

Egg dates   In the Brooks Range, Alaska, eggs by late Apr. (J. M. Campbell 1960). (Many young in Alaska attain flight in early Aug.) In "arctic America," May 27–June 29 (5 records, probably not all fresh eggs); Calif. to Tex., Feb. 9–May 18 for clutches taken (272 records with 136 in the span Feb. 26–Mar. 24) (Bent 1937). In Tex., eggs Nov. 6 through winter to June 20 (viable?), and young ready to fly as early as Mar. 1 (Oberholser and Kincaid 1974)—hence nesting while winterers are present. An early Calif. date is 2 eggs the 1st week in Jan. (L. and M. Walker 1939). Slevin (1929) took 18 clutches in Calif. in Mar., but Willett (1912) had stated earlier that, if eggs were fresh after Mar. 12 they were a replacement set. Central Utah: dates vary from year to year as well as within a given year—1st eggs Feb. 25–Mar. 6 (Camenzind, in Murphy et al. 1969). In cent. Utah there is some variation in dates with elevation—nests at lower altitudes have eggs 1st—but there are exceptions; a pair in 1 of the Wasatch canyons at about 5,800 ft. consistently has eggs by Feb. 20, a full 10 days to 2 weeks before adjacent valley pairs, which are a full 1,000 ft. below (J. R. Murphy). In ne. U.S. in March and Apr. (young just hatched May 29 and June 5).

Laying interval   In captives in N. Am., 3 eggs in 4 or fewer days (Kish 1970). In 3 instances in the wild in Scotland the interval was 96–120 hr., according to Nethersole-Thompson, who witnessed an egg being laid (Gordon 1955).

Clutch size   From table in McGahan (1968), in N. Am.: 89 clutches (of 1 egg), 367 (2), and 44 (3). For comparison: in 82 Scottish aeries 15 (1), 59 (2), and 8 (3) (Gordon 1927). In Oreg. in a year of jackrabbit abundance, 5 (3) and 2 (2), but in all other years of the study combined only three 3-egg clutches (Griffee 1941 and letter 1961). In Calif., a ♀ regularly laid 3-egg clutches (Slevin 1929); this is also true for some individuals elsewhere. For example, in Scotland, 3 eggs each year for 9 years, and 3 young raised in each of 8 years (Gordon 1955)—a phenomenal success. In Calif., a 4-egg clutch (Ray 1928) seems authentic, even though the nest held only 2 the previous year. In Scotland the 4th egg was a runt (Gordon 1927). Again Calif.—5 eggs in a nest included 1 stained and addled (DeGroot 1928), but the other 4 may have comprised the clutch.

Replacement clutches   May go unrecognized unless the birds are watched through the season; they may switch aeries before the ♀ again lays. Central Utah: clutch of 2 abandoned about Mar. 17, and 6 days later new "decorations" at the alternative nest 0.7 mi. away; on Apr. 11, 2 eggs were reported at the later site, and estimated interval before relaying was 24 days. Another clutch was abandoned on Apr. 11, and 25 days later, 2 eggs were in an alternative nest and presumably laid by the same ♀. These data are from Camenzind (in Murphy et al. 1969), who reported that 3 pairs used different nests the same year. J. B. Dixon (1937) stated that the interval between clutches was 28 days, that the 2d set was usually in another nest, and that he had known of a 3d, even 4th, set laid in a season under favorable conditions. Willett (1912) did not go that far, stating that he had been informed that a bird would lay a 3d set. (Many Calif. aeries were visited often by collectors.) Seton Gordon (1955) mentioned only 2 replacement clutches in Scotland, which seems odd in view of the number of aeries raided by collectors.

Eggs Nineteen clutches in Calif. and 1 Utah: **size** length av. 74.38 ± 3.40mm., breadth 57.30 ± 1.63, radii of curvature of ends 23.55 ± 1.63 and 16.23 ± 1.84 (F. W. Preston). Bent's (1937) av. for 59 N. Am. eggs was 74.5×58 mm. One measuring 89×66.6 mm. (C. Sharp 1904) may be the largest on record. Based on eggs "laid over a twenty-year period by 2 pairs of eagles," eggs decrease in size and their shells become thicker as the birds age (Dixon). **Shape** usually oval but rather variable. The shell is more or less granular, without gloss, **color** slightly off-white (toward creamy or buff), and eggs vary from nearly unmarked to heavily marked with blotches and/or dots of various warm to cool browns—well distributed on some, but concentrated toward 1 end on others. A ♀ tends to lay similarly marked eggs from year to year; her eggs can be recognized (Dixon). Hanna (1930) stated that the wt. of 31 eggs varied $113.87–176.5$ gm., av. 141.4 (just under 5 oz), stage(s) of incubation not stated.

Incubation behavior Sitting on the nest, at least by the ♀, may begin days before the 1st egg is laid (D. Ellis 1979). Incubation thus begins with the 1st egg and is mostly by the ♀. Her mate hunts in the morning, evidently feeds himself, and delivers food for her around 0700 hrs.; she leaves the nest and feeds at a nearby plucking site. The ♂ departs or roosts not far away. Around noon he returns, often coming in high, occasionally calling, and drops onto the nest. The ♀ leaves immediately—you might think that the same bird that had alighted left (Dixon). The off-duty ♀ now rests or perhaps hunts occasionally. At evening or sooner there is another changeover and the ♂ leaves. In captivity, only the ♀ incubated at night, and she became aggressive during incubation (Kish 1970). In the wild the ♂ generally has a roost not far away, say 150 m., preferably overlooking the aerie; occasionally an alternative nest gets used more or less as a roost, rarely as a feeding platform.

Some ♀♀ sit extremely tight and cannot be scared off by noise; they only get off when very closely approached (Slevin 1929). Occasionally 1 can be touched on the nest (Camenzind, in Murphy et al. 1969). Most often, the adults are gone before a person comes near. Being curious as to which sex was on the eggs at night, J. B. Dixon (1937) visited a nest and at first thought that the bird was dead—her head lay forward on the nest and her wings drooped. Later he saw birds in this posture during the day, apparently sound asleep. As is well known and revealed in various photographs, the incubating eagle lies very low, its back approximately a horizontal line—quite unlike the higher humped position when brooding nestlings.

As a reaction to humans, the incubating bird flattens down on the nest—a response not given to passing cattle, deer, coyotes, and other animals. A very high percentage of nesting failure is human induced, and eagle watchers, even at a distance and using a telescope, may keep the parent(s) away. An easy mistake to make, or avoid.

Greenery As with other raptors, fresh greenery is delivered to the nest during the reproductive cycle and at other times. Typical greenery is small branches or sprigs, usually pine where available but also deciduous or something else. Examples: soap-weed (Cameron 1905), elderberry (Sumner 1929a), "Mormon tea" (mentioned above), and birch twigs. Greenery concealed 1 clutch (Slevin 1929). One ♀ was seen to make 6 trips in rapid succession for pine or birch. She got 1 large branch by hanging on it, upside down, and flapping until it broke off. Then she carried it to a lookout perch, carefully tore off a small terminal twig, dropped the big piece, and delivered the small piece to the nest (Spofford). Getting such greenery may be a "killing" action (breaking off a branch) with delivery of the substitute or symbolic prey (branch) to the nest. It may advertise ownership or reinforce attachment to territory. Some birds fetch green-ery in any season; some do it to all nests in their territory, including those not in use for rearing a brood; see Wimberger (1984).

Incubation period Forty-three to 45 days, much longer than the 28–35 often quoted from Bent (1937). An egg (incubation already started?), kept under con-secutively 3 domestic hens, hatched on the 41st day (Abbot 1924). Period 43 days according to Dixon (L. and M. Walker 1939). In Nebr., an egg hatched in 45 days (G. Mitchell 1968). In captivity, at least 40–43 days (in Kewata 1973). In Scotland the 2d egg of a clutch hatched in 43–44 days (Nethersole-Thompson 1951).

Hatching Requires more than 1 day; the voice of the eaglet from within the shell stimulates the ♂ (or ♀) to fetch food. The hatching interval was 2 days in 12 clutches in Idaho (T. Edwards and Collopy 1983).

In Maine in 1960 an adult was seen delivering prey in late afternoon. The next morning, June 5, the eagle was brooding with wings out, and a partly grown Am. Crow came out from beneath her and went back underneath again; the eagle's egg was hatching. On inspecting the nest a week later, there was an eaglet—and a few black feathers (Spofford).

Nestling period Now there is a marked change in behavior of the parents. The ♀ sits high when brooding; the ♂ may brood occasionally (whereas he sat on the eggs rarely), and his killing rate increases greatly. The nestlings are seldom left untended during approximately the 1st half of their nest life, and in their 1st week or longer, generally a supply of food in great excess of immediate need accumulates in the nest. Birds are usually plucked before delivery, mammals are decapitated and their fur is more or less removed, generally at a plucking place not far from the aerie. From there the ♂ delivers them or the ♀ comes to get them. One eaglet was surrounded by 11 cottontails and a jackrabbit (L. and M. Walker); at a nest with 2 eaglets there were 22 fresh ground squirrels (Work and Wool. 1947). The aerie serves as a food cache, which is especially useful if prolonged inclement weather interferes with hunting.

During the 1st month or so the ♀ may stand all day in the hot sun, shading the eaglets; blackflies may gather on her face, and she rubs them off against her wing. As the sun drops low, she may leave quickly, circle up 1,000 ft. or more and sweep across the near sky for ½-hr. (Spofford). In sw. Idaho, late in nestling life (7th to 9th weeks), ♀ ♀ contributed 43% of prey biomass (Collopy 1984).

Weight of nestlings Increase follows a sigmoid curve, from about 100–140 gm. (3½–4¾ oz.) at hatching to about 3,800 (♂) or 4,000 (♀) gm. at around 60 days, then levels off; the most rapid gain is approximately in 4th through 7th weeks. In sw. Idaho, eaglets in multiple-nestling broods received more food from adults than those in single-nestling broods (Collopy 1984); quantity delivered was evidently tailored to brood size. The physical development of the young is described here briefly (from E. L. Sumner's papers) as an aid in estimating approximate age of preflight young:

JUST HATCHED Mostly covered with pale short down; eyes not fully open; legs and feet pale flesh color; nestling unable to distinguish objects and chirps incessantly; wt. about 100 gm. ONE WEEK Can sit up and stretch neck forward; chirps for food, follows observer's finger and accepts small bits of meat; the later (white) longer down is just beginning to grow; wts. 232 and 257 gm. TWO WEEKS Chirps continuously when handled; 1 persisted in crawling away; the white down now well developed; sheathed beginnings of primary quills just beginning to show; talons darkening; wts. 585 and 1,023 gm. THREE WEEKS Young rear up "in feeble menace" but soon settle down or may chirp and retreat to far side of nest; longest primary about ¼ in; talons blackish; egg tooth vanishes at 22–25 days; wts. 1,662 and 1,273 gm. FOUR WEEKS Smaller nestling waddles and hisses, beak open, wings raised, but larger nestling quiet; legs and feet seem enormous; longest primaries 2 in. (½ in. out of sheath); wts. 1,880 and 2,669 gm. FIVE WEEKS Smaller bird aggressive, advancing with open beak, feebly striking with upraised wings, utters hissing gasp; primaries to 5 in. (2 in. out of sheath); tail about 2½ in. (1 in. unsheathed); wts. 2,270 and 2,870 gm. SIX WEEKS Smaller bird more hostile, hissing, buffeting with wings, its voice still high pitched; larger bird docile, squeals with earlier high-pitched voice but usually makes deeper note; primaries to 7 in. (4 in. out of sheath); wts. 2,607 and 3,582 gm. SEVEN WEEKS Smaller eaglet uses talons occasionally, larger one is docile; when put on ground, both use wings and legs when retreating into grass; if placed on a limb, are too weak to sustain themselves; primaries to 9 in. (5½ in. out of sheath), tail 6 (3 unsheathed); at around 50 days the contour feathers of head–neck become visible, being about the last to appear—only 15–20 days before eaglet attains flight; wts. 2,802 and 3,852 gm.; nest now quite trodden and flattened, indicating much activity. EIGHT WEEKS Smaller bird stands most of time; larger shows hostility (or defense) and, for the 1st time, utters a rasping croak; wingspread 53 and 62 in.; primaries to 10 and 11 in. (7 in. unsheathed); tails 6 and 7 in.; wts. 2,442 and 3,402 gm. (a decrease, perhaps indicating much exercise). NINE WEEKS Much as before, but both are stronger; wts. 2,982 and 4,062 gm. TENTH WEEK Nest empty.

From E. L. Sumner (1934): Fear was evident at about 3 weeks, but even when much older there seemed to be no hostility, only escape; preening and exercising (much wing flapping) began at about the 5th week and occupied an increasing amount of time thereafter. From about 40 days onward the parent ♀ slept away from the nest, but returned to feed the young even when they could feed themselves. Curiosity of nestlings was evident at 5 weeks, and at 49 days one toyed with a pocket knife. "Mantling" over prey occurred by age 8 weeks. E. L. Sumner (1933) stated that wt. increase per gram of food consumed increased during nest life; working with 3 *Buteo* species, Olendorff (1974b) stated that highest efficiency of wt. gain occurred during the 1st week and decreased throughout the growth period. For many additional data on nestling Golden Eagles, see especially D. Ellis (1979), both text and illus.

After feeding the eaglet(s), both ♂ and ♀ may make several visits to the nest fetching greenery. At first the ♂ feeds both nestlings and mate, but after the young are well feathered, the parents may come to the nest only briefly during daylight. Then the ♀ does some hunting on her own, lightening the burden on the ♂; she may begin earlier if the ♂ is a poor provider. In 1 instance in n. New Eng., when a lone eaglet was under a month old, 1 parent landed on the nest with prey, and seconds later the other delivered prey; 1 brought a small hare, the other a small woodchuck, and both sexes had almost surely made a kill (Spofford).

The ♂, at least, will sometimes return after delivering a carcass and carry it away to a plucking place for his own consumption. In n. New Eng. in May an adult came to a nest and removed a carcass to the top of a dead snag and there fed for 10 min. or more. In July the ♂ came in and removed an almost intact Am. Bittern, which it carried to open rocks about 100 yds. away, and fed; at that spot after he left were the remains of 3 Bitterns and other prey.

The nestlings back to the rim of the nest, elevate their hind ends, and squirt semiliquid fecal matter outward, producing an area of "whitewash" below. The parents keep the nest cavity clean during incubation (carry debris away) but not after hatching (Camenzind, in Murphy et al. 1969); the ♀ removes fecal matter and debris from the nest (D. Ellis 1979). In Maine in late July a 2-month-old nestling dug a large recess in the side of the nest to escape the hot sun; it spent much of the day out of sight, appearing on top only occasionally to yelp briefly (Spofford).

Brood reduction So-called siblicide is widely known in this species, being reported in N. Am., for example, by E. L. Sumner (1934), Beecham and Kochert (1975), D. Ellis (1979), and T. Edwards and Collopy (1983). In the past it has been supposed that, when the young get inadequate food and are hungry, a stronger eaglet may attack a weaker one, eventually causing its death. This generally occurs when the young are under 3 weeks of age. The dead nestling may be treated by its sibling(s) as food (as though it were prey), be trodden into the nest, or disappear (carried away?). Percentage of surviving young may be greatly reduced in the past supposedly to fit the amount of food the parents can provide. The parents make no attempt to distribute food equally among the brood, nor do they interfere when 1 nestling acts aggressively toward another; see T. Edwards and Collopy (1983) for additional information.

This apparently instinctive predatory reaction by nestlings is far more prevalent in the Golden Eagle (when older, an aggressive hunter of agile prey) than in the Bald (a fisher and scavenger, primarily). In the Black Eagle (*A. verreauxi*), closely related to the Golden, the regular killing of the weaker eaglet is quite unrelated to hunger, being part of inbred behavior; when the larger is already gorged, it may immediately attack the smaller (Gargett 1978). During periods of jackrabbit scarcity in N. Am., when parent eagles must turn to other food, there seems to be little evidence of increased siblicide (see also below for reproductive fluctuations).

Age at first flight Usually about 65 days. Camenzind (in Murphy et al. 1969) gave the spread as 59–70 days, the shortest being for an eaglet that was alone in the nest for its final 7 weeks with plentiful food. In some instances, young are frightened from the nest early and cannot get back by themselves; in others, the young may have flown but return to feed and/or roost. If the young are flushed prematurely and rotate with spread wings or somersault to the ground, they walk uphill and hide; the parents respond to their food call and tend them wherever they are (Hickman 1971).

Does a parent assist flying young?   In Calif., on word of a reliable informant, Loye Miller (1918) reported the following: The mother "roughly handled" the eaglet and "allowed" it to drop 90 ft.; she would then swoop under it, the eaglet would alight on her back, and she would fly upward; this was repeated. On July 11, 1937, at Lower Ausable Lake, N.Y., for more than 30 min. an adult allowed the young to alight on her(?) back and assisted it in flying high in the air, then dumping it off; the eaglet would fly, calling continuously as it came down lower and lower, and the older bird would fly under it and repeat the process. At times they were directly above 4 observers, as reported by 1 of them (Chester L. Reagan) to W. R. Spofford. A similar episode was observed by Eva Sherman in the 1970s at King and Bartlett L., Maine. It also was observed in Utah in 1914, as reported in the autobiography of Wilbert Snow (1974: 200). The statistical likelihood that the persons seeing these episodes had knowledge of each others' observations is nil. An adult eagle is presumably unable to transport anything as heavy as its own young—certainly not far—but a flapping eaglet boosted from below by a parent is possibly another matter.

Reproductive fluctuations   There is little doubt that clutches av. larger when food is plentiful, although a few ♀ ♀ appear to be quite consistent in laying large clutches. Major foods such as jackrabbits, ground squirrels, cottontails, and snowshoe hares all fluctuate (not synchronously) from very scarce to extremely abundant. A positive correlation between jackrabbit numbers and overall breeding success has been reported, for example, in sw. Idaho (Beecham and Kochert 1975), cent. Utah (Murphy 1974), and se. Colo. (1974 *Am. Birds* **28** 930).

In N. Am., fluctuations are as great as in the Ferruginous or Rough-legged Hawks. The generalized pattern in low food years is to 1 return to nesting site but not attempt to rebuild, refurbish, or add greenery; 2 add greenery throughout the nesting season but lay no eggs; 3 lay eggs, then desert them; or 4 lay smaller numbers of eggs than "normal," some of which hatch and may be raised. The following example from 1985, an extremely low-food year, will suffice, although most of the w. U.S. then suffered a low rabbit year. The Powder R. Basin, Wyo., contained 127 occupied territories of which 62 contained eggs and 47 reared young to flight age (A. Beske); Black Butte, Wyo., contained 22 territories of which 17 were occupied, 4 contained eggs, and 2 reared young (S. Platt); Utah contained 195 known territories (530 nests checked within them) of which 23 contained eggs and 14 produced young (66% of nests had 1 eaglet) (K. Keller); in e. Idaho, 9 of 44 occupied territories contained young, while in a smaller, more intensely studied area, 26 territories were occupied and 2 produced young (K. Steenhof, M. Kochert). In the latter area the occupancy rate of territories still was near "normal."

In n. Sweden, whether the birds produce clutches is probably determined by prey numbers before the laying season (Tjernberg 1983b). In Utah in 1969, six of 14 pairs had 3-egg clutches; of these, 5 each produced 3 young to flight age (Arnell 1971). This approaches a Scottish record mentioned above under clutch size. (For tabulation of many relevant U.S. data for 1966–1981, inclusive, see M. Jenkins and Joseph 1984.)

This example of a breeding cycle study is from the Snake R. area of sw. Idaho, 1970–1978, inclusive; it relates to 365 breeding attempts: Average clutch size was 1.98, and there were no 3-egg clutches 1973–1976. Hatchability, when clutch size and number hatched was known, was 69%. Losses: 15 infertile eggs, 3 with dead embryos during normal incubation, 37 eaglets died when nests were abandoned, 2 were lost due to human disturbance, and 27 died of unknown causes. The mean number of young hatched per "breeding attempt" was 1.40; in nests that hatched any young the mean was 1.77 for all years combined. Nestling survivorship (to flight age) in 111 nestings av. 71%. In 105 cases of nestling losses, of 50 where cause was known, 21 died from heat stress, 15 from trichomoniasis, 8 from human disturbance (including shooting), 2 from falls out of the nest, and 4 from fratricide. Of 234 eggs monitored, 110 (47%) produced young to flight age. An av. of 1.03 "per attempt" and 1.62 "per successful attempt" attained flight (Snake R. Birds Prey *Spec. Res. Rept.* 1979).

Many other data could be given. In brief, in 10 studies in w. U.S. lasting 1–15 (av. 5.4) years and rounding off figures, the number of young attaining flight per successful nest was 1.3–1.7 (av. about 1.5). It is, of course, lower when failed attempts are included. Human disturbance causes many failures. There are many variables; it was stated (Boeker and Ray 1971), for example, that some pairs apparently nest only in alternate years. In 1971–1978 in the Snake R. area, mentioned at length above, nonbreeding pairs comprised 0–44% of the total number of pairs occupying territories. In Haller's (1982) study of a saturated population of 51 pairs in the cent. Alps, breeding success was low by any standard in the presence of nonbreeding intruders (territory defense resulted in nesting failure). Such failures were a density-dependent result of overpopulation; nesting success was not limited by food supply. Prebreeders were thus a factor in bringing population dynamics into equilibrium. At an earlier time there, when birds were fewer (population not saturated), breeding success was higher.

There is little useful available information for e. N. Am.; among observed fall migrants in recent decades, the ratio of individuals identified as "young" (may include more than 1 age class) to those termed "adult" is uncomfortably low.

Duration of family bond Parents often watch and guard their flying young. The latter at first may be "branchers," staying nearby and returning to the nest to be fed; alternative nests are occasionally used by them as feeding platforms and/or for roosting. On Aug. 4 in Alaska, 2 young recently out of the nest were on a grassy slope some 300 ft in elevation above their nest. One had a sort of well-used ground "nest" for several days. Food (hares, ptarmigan) was delivered there. The young would sprawl out after eating at their chosen places. Both could fly well (Spofford).

The young, at least of resident birds, may be fed for up to several months after they can fly, during which time they improve their flying ability and gain some proficiency at hunting. At first they make frequent, short flights from perch to perch. Soon they become interested in their own prey and still-hunt from stationary perches (soaring is for more experienced birds). They make frequent changes of perches when unsuccessful.

Many families in which the parents are essentially resident are presumably disrupted by the young migrating or dispersing in their first autumn, but in other instances (as from n. Alaska) families at least begin migration together. At Hawk Mt., Pa., what appear to be migrant family groups have been seen. The existence not only of birds associating in pairs but also what appear to be family groups on winter range in Tex. argues strongly that some families continue to remain intact. If the unit has persisted this long, it perhaps continues until the onset of the next breeding cycle (the

2 age categories not necessarily migrating together), when the yearlings are banished from the territory.

The following anecdotes (from Spofford) indicate long parental bond, attachment between individuals, and so forth:

Near Apache, Ariz., Nov. 14, 1972. At about 1000 hrs. a Golden circled low over the highway, rose higher when attacked by 2 Com. Ravens, then dropped back toward a spot near the road and circled very low, flapping constantly and fast, crisscrossing the highway. It had the white "epaulettes" of the known ♂ of the local pair. On driving to the spot, an alive, apparently paralyzed, eagle was seen next to the road. It was removed but died within a few hrs., apparently of internal injuries. It was a young ♀ (white on each side of the tail). In the road at the site was a partially eaten carcass; presumably the eagle had been hit by a vehicle when the eagle attempted to leave the carcass. The ♂ was attending her when discovered. The following afternoon the ♂ was seen there again, apparently searching for the ♀.

November 16 at 1105 hrs., s. of Apache (3 mi. from the above occurrence)—2 eagles circled at about 1,500 ft. One was a Juv., the other almost surely the above-mentioned ♂. Soon there was a loud yelping and the adult plunged vertically, directly in front of the auto. He seized a small cottontail carcass, carried it off in 1 foot, and settled in grass some 100 yds. to the w. There was renewed yelping as the young bird plunged down, ungainly, in an amateurish stoop with feet widely separated, checked its flight 20 ft. up, and then dived where the ♂ had taken the carcass. Almost at once the ♂ sprang up and flew out of sight. Evidently this was a transfer of prey to a young bird aged about 8 months.

RALPH S. PALMER

SURVIVAL In N. Am. From 130 records of banded birds recovered dead, av. length of life was 19.6 months, which the oldest lived 11 years, 1 month (Keran 1981). In Idaho, 52 of 56 banded birds were found dead ranging from 4 months to 4 years old within 108 mi. of where they were banded (Kochert 1973). The greatest losses among flying birds are during the Juv. stage and are attributable to their inexperience (Ellis et al. 1969, references therein). Many more young than adults get killed, and many more ♀♀ than ♂♂, as discussed by Bortolotti (1984b). Common causes of losses, particularly of young birds, include starvation, impact injuries, shooting, electrocution, ingesting poisons, predation, disease, and (much more, formerly) getting caught in steel traps set for furbearers and other such animals.

Causes of some nestling losses have been mentioned earlier. Although siblicide in this species has been discussed frequently, actual reported losses are few.

A bird kept in captivity since a nestling laid no eggs 1973–1976, inclusive, then in 1977 laid 4, none in 1978, 2 in 1979, and 3 in 1980—the last in her 28th year (D. Bird and Tinker 1982). A number of captives have survived at least into their 4th decade, one to 48 years.

Scotland: It was calculated that 75% of Golden Eagles that attained flight were dead before they reached sexual maturity; further, if a pair is reproducing at a rate of less than 1 eaglet/yr., then it takes them 10 years to produce 2 birds to replace themselves (L. Brown and Watson 1964). This has been considered applicable in N. Am. (Spofford 1971) and in Norway (Hagen 1976).

Central Alps: Haller's study (cited above) showed that the population improved markedly with protection and that high productivity was followed by low productivity as the population approached saturation. As discussed above, density and survival are interrelated.   RALPH S. PALMER

HABITS   The Golden is a "far nobler" bird than the Bald (Bent 1937), but its vast distribution diminishes its potential as a regional symbol.

Hunting behavior   Common prey includes small to medium-sized mammals that are active in the subdued light of morning and evening. The eagles take flight early, sweeping the slopes. This is the best time to observe them. Their flight is labored; there is no "lift" in the air, and their wings may be damp from condensation. Quite obviously they can not transport heavy prey. If a bird does not make a kill in early morning, its chances are often slim until the active period toward evening. Thus in general the eagle hunts when the sun is fairly low—unless it is hungry or pressed to support a mate and brood. It can fast for days; then it gorges and can fast again. A bird that has fed is likely to perch quietly or soar for a few hrs. As the sun gets higher and thermals develop, the birds may circle very high, at times in a kind of social affair. They may also seek water to drink and bathe and are social at watering places. (Adapted from Spofford 1964.)

For perching an eagle needs an elevated spot on an escarpment, dead snag, utility pole (preferably on higher ground), rockpile, haystack, or even a muskrat house. From there it heads for the nearest updraft and then rises to an altitude that gives it a commanding view as it heads for its hunting grounds. On its own territory a Golden Eagle knows the terrain and air movement above it—the whereabouts of updrafts that will support it through calm air or a downdraft to the next updraft. Seldom does an eagle kill in a downdraft area, apparently aware that it cannot load its digestive tract and still get into the nearest updraft. On occasion after a bird has eaten its fill it is unable to become airborne. A Juv. with full crop in a downdraft area in Utah in Nov. was captured by hand (Camenzind, in Murphy et al. 1969).

Attack   Usually upwind. A bird may drop nearly vertically a short distance or even from soaring; as it nears its prey it extends its wings partly to follow the quarry, drops its legs, and then binds firmly with a foot. Then it may also grasp with the other foot. It may spread its wings and tail—"mantle" over its food—especially if another predator is in sight. When transporting a ground squirrel, young marmot, or other prey, the eagle conserves energy by not taking the most direct course to its destination but instead remaining in updrafts, where the going is easier.

Goldens search from high or low flight, or any perch, rarely even from the ground; from head movements, at times a perched bird appears to be listening. The following examples are indicative of diversity of hunting methods:

Soaring   The eagle floats high above a prairie dog "town" on motionless wings in wide sweeps and circles so as not to alarm its prey; the "dogs" become very alert if the bird passes right overhead. The eagle descends to 75–100 yds. If a particular prey singled out still remains above ground, the eagle suddenly folds its wings and plunges headfirst. The "dogs" scramble to their holes. When the eagle is about 3 yds. above ground, it checks its flight, follows the quarry, and grasps it with a foot. (From Cameron 1908a.) (See perch-hunting, below, for pursuit of jackrabbits.)

In the cent. Alps, aerial hunting was more successful than perch-hunting (Haller 1982), but the latter can often be seen and is more readily followed.

Aerial attack   Stooping, chasing, and so on is used in pursuit of birds.

Contouring the terrain   May be rapid or slow, even with frequent changes in direction. When hunting ground squirrels, for example, the bird flies low, keeping out of sight except when it clears the top of a rise. A squirrel away from its burrow and surprised at close range is the quarry. Such hunting is done on a percentage basis, since location of prey and whether away from a safe haven are not evident before attack is initiated. Success rate must depend considerably on abundance of prey; there are many misses. A good example of contouring, from J. B. Dixon (1937), is the following: A ♀ eagle would leave her nest and fly conspicuously until at a distance, then drop down and contour the terrain to a place where Am. Coots (*Fulica*) fed ashore near a fence. The eagle would get between the water (escape route) and the coots and would then rise over the fence and quickly seize a bird.

Perch-hunting   Or still-hunting, the usual method of inexperienced young birds whose coordination and skills are not yet perfected; it is also a method of older birds where perches are convenient for the purpose. This is the waiting game, from an elevated lookout. The prey is seen as it moves into the open and the attack is then launched; success rate is comparatively high.

Cottontails are relatively small in size, often use burrows or rockpiles for escape, stay fairly close by, and cannot escape quickly. They can be spotted for quick attack from a utility pole. Perch-hunting requires little expenditure of energy to obtain this rather small quarry. Jackrabbits are much larger. They are wide ranging and depend on fleetness to avoid predation. Hunting from the air (it allows wide visibility), although energy consuming, is more or less compensated by capturing quarry of this size. In brief, the best way for the eagle to hunt cottontails is from poles and to hunt jackrabbits is from the air. See discussion in Benson (1982). This could result in some individual eagles becoming specialists on a particular prey and presumably perfecting techniques for getting it.

Flushing   In Ariz., a pair swooped down and drove a jackrabbit to cover under a mesquite bush. Then 1 alighted on the ground and began to walk toward the rabbit, which dashed from shelter and was seized by the other eagle, which had been hovering close overhead (Willard 1916b). In Calif., a pair was hunting and 1 missed a ground squirrel that ran into a heavy bush. The eagle grasped the bush and flapped its wings while "screaming." The other bird waited in case the quarry flushed, but the quarry was an experienced squirrel and remained out of sight (J. B. Dixon 1937). These episodes also qualify as cooperative hunting, discussed below; see also winter hunting in the West as described under Bald Eagle.

From a ground perch   A ♀ missed a ground squirrel, so she waddled to the top of a squirrel mound and appeared to fall asleep—she was very still but turned her head. Soon the squirrel surfaced, and when it was foraging away from its burrow, the eagle took wing and caught it easily (Dixon).

Versus rattlesnakes   According to Cameron (1905), the bird feints several times to make the snake uncoil (tire it) and then seizes it behind the head with a foot and grips it farther back with the other. Then the snake is carried to a feeding place, its head is removed and devoured, and the remainder is carried to the aerie.

213

Cooperative hunting Reported rather frequently by both mates (tandem hunting) and more birds. In sw. Idaho (Collopy 1983), in that portion of the reproductive cycle in which the ♀ is fully occupied at the nest, there are few opportunities for tandem hunting; it occurs later. The ♂ flies in front, apparently directing the hunt—he can locate prey and attack 1st—and the ♀ attacks when he is unsuccessful. Yet the method is less rewarding than solo hunting.

The writer has seen no report of obvious cooperation by only Juv. birds, but individuals other than "adult" are sometimes involved. Cooperation has its advantages, especially if prey is large. In Sask. in winter in pursuit of a fox, an "immature" bird stooped from behind, an "adult" from above; the fox was knocked down several times and weakened; on the 4th stoop, both birds grasped it and soon killed it (D. R. M. Hatch 1968). Note combined effort in killing, as reported above in Calif. by Carnie (1954). A fox can use its tail to foil a solo eagle (J. S. Dixon 1938, Seton Gordon 1955). Hatch mentioned 3 eagles cooperatively hunting a fox; C. J. O. Harrison (1968) mentioned 4. There are a number of reports of Goldens cooperating to hunt large quarry, such as deer when disadvantaged by snow (and perhaps in poor physical condition), where a lone bird would likely have little chance of succeeding. For example, in a severe winter in Mont. when the eagles were famished, 3 cooperated in killing a pronghorn (*Antilocapra*) (Cameron 1908a). The Golden has been reported to cooperate in hunting Wild Turkeys in Tex. (J. Thomas et al. 1964).

In winter in Mont. a solo bird would kill a Barrow's Goldeneye (*Bucephala islandica*) and its "mate" would come immediately to share the food (W. Sharp 1951); this might be termed cooperative feeding.

Hunger panic (of Hagen 1952a) may be explained as hungry birds attacking or feeding on prey with apparent disregard of their own safety. Most such birds are young and inexperienced. In n. Ill. in Dec., 2 eagles were feeding on the remains of a hog; they swooped at a person who approached them; 1 fell dead when shot, the other renewed its attack until disabled—so stated E. W. Nelson (1887). In Mont., 1 attacked a dog and was killed with a stick (Cameron 1907). At Goffstown, N.H., Oct. 22, 1961, an eagle tried to carry off a beagle and was shot by the dog's owner; a photograph shows a small eagle (♂?) in 1st-fall feathering. (See also mistakes, below.) In Maine in Aug. 1879, an "adult" eagle seized a domestic goose. A child attacked the eagle with a club and the bird faced her, still grasping its prey. The child's parents came and "quickly dispatched" the eagle (Brewster 1925). Near Bennington, Vt., on Oct. 26, 1934, an eagle was captured alive while intent on eating a goose; it was a young bird and made no resistance to capture (Thomas Foster).

In Norway an extremely lean bird killed a cat and was about to eat it when a man approached; it left its prey and attacked the man and later in captivity was aggressive toward humans and other animals (Willgohs 1961).

Perhaps unprovoked attacks on humans by "young" birds (Gullion 1957) fit in the present category. In Brit. Columbia a Golden Eagle seized a 9-year-old child by 1 arm; a neighbor attacked the eagle, partially disabling it, and the child's mother decapitated the bird with an ax (Forbush 1927).

Fanciful stuff is omitted here, except for an instance in which an attack was manufactured. A weakened captive bird was tossed (for the benefit of a photographer) by 1 boy at the head of another: "Eagle Attacks Boy," *Life*, Mar. 8, 1948 (or see Arnold 1948).

214

Mistakes Young birds, especially, attack prey they cannot kill. In Mar. in sw. Alta., an "immature" eagle landed on the back of a steer and hung on for some 300 m., then repeated this on another steer (Dekker 1985). Some sightings of large mammals such as deer or bighorns being harassed evidently fall in this category; some appear to be a less serious exercise. Encounters with porcupines (*Erethizon*) in N. Am. can be hazardous. In Minn., an emaciated bird with underparts full of quills was killed with a club (Lano 1922). In N.Y., a young ♀, shot when killing a cat, was emaciated; there were many quills in its feet and legs (D. Stoner 1939a). In Vt., a bird with wings, breast, and feet full of quills died of starvation (Bennington *Evening Banner* Jan. 6, 1960). Other examples could be cited. Yet at Minerva, N.Y., in Nov. 1962, Goldens were said by an expert observer (Greenleaf Chase) to be feeding on porcupines. In Europe, the little hedgehog (*Erinaceus*), whose spines are firmly planted in its skin, is fairly common prey.

In Colo., a Golden alighted at the water's edge and waded toward a Pintail decoy (Sperry 1957). In Tex. 2 Pintail decoys were attacked and showed talon damage (Alford and Bolen 1972).

Amount of food eaten Three captive eagles maintained at relatively constant wt. and fed once a day (Fevold and Craighead 1958) consumed the equivalent of 5.7% of wt. (the larger ♀) and 6.6% and 5.5% (2 smaller ♂). It varied inversely with wt. of bird and environmental temperature. An increase in nutrition appeared necessary during molting—the additional food being needed to grow feathers. This study also discussed exercise v. food intake.

From estimates of predation and consumption, McGahan (1967) concocted a formula that indicated an amount of just over 1 lb. of prey/day (includes wastage), which might convert into 40–50 prey indivdiuals/100 days. In captivity the figure would be lower. Another approach is Olendorff's (1973) calculations of biomass in the area he studied. The rodent biomass was between 62 and 95 times the raptor biomass. In 152 days in 1972, eagles (combined with eaglets) consumed about 6% of the nonraptor avian biomass plus rodent biomass. The figure for the previous year was 3.8%. (Certain prey items, including rabbits, were omitted because their numbers in the area were not known.) For calculations of amount of food needed/day at existence level, see Lasiewski and Dawson (1967).

Generally speaking, through nest life an eaglet might av. ½ lb./day and an adult year-round 8–12 oz. of digestible food—the larger amount in cooler months. Parts of the prey, such as fur, feathers, and feet, are wastage; any such parts ingested are not assimilated (ejected as castings). A wild bird may gorge itself and then fast for several days.

It was estimated that the food of a pair of wild eagles in Scotland amounted to 174 kg. of live prey plus carrion per year, 163 of it ingested and the rest waste. A preflight eaglet required about 54 kg. (39 ingested) and flying prebreeders about 43 kg./year (42 ingested). It was further calculated that the food required from a territory to maintain a stable population was 271 kg./year (includes 54 for a nestling) of carrion plus live prey. These figures are "undoubtedly open to argument" but probably not far from actuality (L. Brown and Watson 1964, L. Brown 1969).

Raptor interrelationships In general, if more than 1 raptor species is in a small area, there is hostility (although not necessarily attack) if 1 or the other is territorial, but away from territory and in nonbreeding season they can get along—spaced apart—provided the weaker does not unduly harass the stronger or the stronger is not hungry. Anyone with much field experience could add to the following observations; see Habitat, above, for Golden Eagle-Bald Eagle contacts.

In Brit. Columbia a Goshawk's remains were lodged in an eagle aerie (Preble, in Bent 1937). The Golden may occasionally take over a Gyrfalcon site, but the only record of Gyr remains in an eagle's nest is Hagen's (1952a) for Norway. Gyrs become very excited and noisy if a Golden comes anywhere near their eggs or young. In Alaska, when Rough-legged Hawks harassed a Golden, it took refuge on the ground (Kessel et al. 1953). Goldens will not tolerate Ferruginous Hawks or Roughlegs in their territory (Olendorff 1975), and the reverse probably also holds. A presumed Ferruginous nest was the site of a Golden Eagle nest (see Reproduction, above). Red-tailed Hawks are aggressive and drive any eagle from their territory (R. Hardy 1945), but when food is scarce the Golden will kill breeding Redtails and Great Horned Owls; J. B. Dixon (1937) saw eagle pairs do this. Great Horned Owls, which are early nesters, occasionally appropriate a Golden Eagle aerie; whether this results in conflict is unreported, but the number of these owls killed by the eagle is cause for suspicion. For example, in at least 3 incidents in Utah, Great Horned Owls were killed adjacent to Golden Eagle nests but not used as food; possibly this was territorial defense (J. R. Murphy). In N.D., a shot and wounded Great Horned Owl landed in an open field; a pair of Goldens swooped down, and 1 of them made off with the still-struggling owl (Henry 1939). In Kans., remains of a Redtail were found in the crop of a Golden Eagle (Gloyd 1925). In Pa. in fall a migrating Golden killed a migrating Red-shouldered Hawk that harassed it (Broun 1947). In Mass. in Nov., a Golden struck an Osprey as it was leaving the water, held it under, and then dragged the carcass ashore; other food was probably scarce (LaFontaine and Fowler 1976).

Nesting Peregrines harass Goldens, at times for obvious reasons. An eagle landed on a Peregrine aerie and broke the eggs (R. Bond 1946), and in Calif. an eagle pair forced Peregrines to abandon a cliff (J. B. Dixon 1937). Three fledgling Peregrines were released at a natural site in Sequoia Natl. Park, Calif.; 2 were captured and eaten by eagles and the 3d was recaptured by biologists to prevent a similar fate (Wildl. Mgt. Inst.). Prairie Falcons harass Goldens but may nest as close as 200 ft. from an eagle aerie with only "limited conflict" (Olendorff 1975). Goldens were chased by Calif. Condors, evidently in defense of their young.

These may be categorized as **kleptoparasitism.** In Alaska, 3 Magpies acting cooperatively robbed a Golden Eagle of a ground squirrel (J. S. Dixon 1938). Feeding Goldens are harassed by ravens, occasionally by crows, seeking food. In Utah in winter, Goldens may feed at Bald Eagle kills. In Colo., 2 coyotes followed a flying eagle, perhaps hoping to steal a kill or to capture a rabbit if 1 flushed (Engel and Vaughan 1966). Migrants in sw. Alta. attempted to rob ground squirrels from each other; some thus lost their prey, but others ate seemingly unperturbed (Dekker 1985). One Redtail was robbed in the air, another on the ground (Dekker).

What might be termed **mixtures of raptors** is of interest; here are 2 of many observations: In Mar. in N.Mex. an "adult" Golden with full crop was flushed from a dead jackrabbit in early morning. The rabbit was cold and had Great Horned Owl feathers entangled in its toes; apparently it had been killed by the owl in the night. Presumably the owl fed, and at dawn the eagle flushed it from its prey and fed on cold rabbit. A ♂ N. Harrier was on the ground some 20 ft. away, waiting its turn (Spofford 1964). In Cedar Valley, Utah, along 12 mi. of road on Dec. 21, on poles were 18 Roughlegs, 5 Golden Eagles, 2 Com. Ravens, 3 N. Harriers, and a Prairie Falcon (D. Ellis et al. 1969).

The following, although not a mixing of species, is notable. In Idaho in winter, where jackrabbits were abundant, many Goldens roosted at night on power-line structures. Half of them roosted singly, the others 2, 3, or more per structure. In Feb., they roosted so close together that no space was seen between them, which suggests that they shared warmth (T. and E. Craig 1984).

Play In June in S.D., a flying young bird repeatedly carried a stick about 1 × 8 in. in size, dropped it, then plunged to grasp it again (R. Pittman). The same has been observed abroad—for example, on the Isle of Mull (Coomber 1977). Possibly these are an extension of nestling behavior—pouncing on a stick to "capture" it? A captive ♀ was fond of playing with a smooth, round stone almost as big as a grapefruit and much given to uttering a mellow *heu* 5 to 7–8 times in rapid succession (Brewster 1925). An observer told Ganier (1940) that he had seen Goldens in Tenn. chase colts and calves downhill, perhaps in a spirit of playfulness—as a falcon will stoop at a vulture. In Tenn. on Dec. 6, 1952, there were 4 Goldens and 8 Balds (latter all "young") at a waterfowl refuge; 1 Bald "repeatedly engaged in playful flight" with a Golden (Spofford). On Jan. 3 in Tenn., 7 Goldens were in sight (only 2 "fully adult"); as many as 4 were flying in circles in playful flight, diving at each other (Ganier 1953).

Bathing In w. Mont., nestlings performed a wing-flop-rump-dip action, probably associated with bathing; this was usually seen during rain showers (D. Ellis 1979).

A preflight nestling aged 64 days was placed in a shallow pan of water. It cried, moved about uneasily, did not drink, and then crouched beside the pan and made bathing movements; 3 min. later it entered the pan and took a "real bath," which it did thereafter nearly every day, although it did not drink for a month (E. L. Sumner 1934). On San Francisco Mt., Ariz., a pair came every morning to bathe and drink in a pool of clear meltwater above timberline at 11,000 ft. (F. M. Bailey 1927). Also in Ariz., in the Chiracahua Mts., 12 were seen bathing in the spray of a waterfall and in the pool beneath it, at 8,000 ft. (Morrow, in Brandt 1951). In w. Tex. they congregate in numbers of up to 10 at stock-watering places and other locations (Spofford 1964).

Weight that a Golden Eagle can transport This has been a subject of guesswork and frequent exaggeration. Cameron (1905) mentioned carrying lambs. Later Cameron (1907) stated that a bird could carry a 7-lb. jackrabbit. Still later he (1908a) discussed the subject at length. He was informed that a ♀ flying into the wind lifted a lamb, "probably weighing between 10 and 12 pounds, for some distance" before she was compelled to drop it. He had seen an adult jackrabbit transported only once (when young jacks are plentiful, most of those taken are not fully grown). It seems likely that an adult ♀ eagle with empty crop might transport a 7-lb. jack at least a short distance, but larger prey is dismantled and only a portion is carried any distance.

In 1937, C. C. Sperry tested the wt. lifting capacity of a wild eagle caught in Tex.; it could not rise from the ground with 5¼ lb. of attached wt. (Arnold 1954).

217

Sometimes cited are experiments, of dubious design, with Caesar, a captive, trained, ♀ Golden in good physical shape. With a 1-lb. wt. attached to each foot, and tossing the bird off a 15-ft.-high platform, flight was "normal, effortless, playful." Doubling the load produced a noticeable strain, but the bird made 64 and 58 yds. with a 20-min. pause in between. Doubling it again (4 lbs. tied to each foot), the bird, when tossed, used every effort to keep from crashing—and failed (L. and M. Walker 1940). Huey's (1962) conclusion is amusing, or perhaps instructive; he compared Caesar with a ♀ House Finch (*Carpodacus mexicanus*), calculating that the former carried about 21% of its wt. as a load, the latter 23%.

In Scotland, L. Brown and Watson (1964) estimated that loads of about 2 lb. were carried to the aerie. A pair nesting in Ireland supposedly carried hares over the water from Scotland (C. Deane 1962).

Adverse effects on the Golden Eagle Practically all relate directly or indirectly to humans. This has been emphasized by various authorities. It makes little difference how many protective laws, refuges, and so forth we create if we are unwilling to leave the birds some relatively undisturbed space for nesting and hunting. Aside from eagle catching by native peoples (it must have had local impact), the pressure on eagles, especially the degradation or total loss of habitat, began fairly early in e. N. Am. but became serious in the West only within the present century. A catalog of human activities that are deleterious to eagles would be prohibitively long. Human disturbance was responsible for 85% of nesting failures along the Front Range of the Rockies in Wyo., Colo., and N.Mex. (Boeker and Ray 1971). If disturbed, Goldens will abandon their territories, sometimes moving to higher elevations to nest (Murphy 1974). Much else of relevance could be cited.

Bounties Paid in Brit. Columbia from 1910 to 1924, probably with some young Bald Eagles mistakenly included as Goldens; the $3 fee of 1910 was eventually reduced to $1; even so, 7,095 eagles were bountied in 1922 alone. After 1924, wardens could still take Golden Eagles (again, young Balds probably included), and 902 were killed 1948–1952, inclusive (Imler and Kalmbach 1955).

Shooting apparently eliminated the resident birds in w. Tex. (Heugly, in C. Snow 1973b), and it was the most frequent cause of mortality in Utah (C. Edwards 1969). Many statements of this sort can be made. Young birds, perched conspicuously (as on utility poles) or in preflight stage when standing on the nest, are tempting targets and continue to be shot.

Shoot-offs Occurred from the 1930s to past the 1960s, into the period when legal protection existed. Aside from the gruesome statistics and excluding much of the biased and/or questionable material extant, the following at least gives a hint of some possible attributes of the Golden Eagle. The data are from Spofford (1964) except as otherwise indicated.

Eagles were shot from aircraft in Tehama Co., Calif., as early as fall–spring of 1935–1936, when over 200 were killed by "sportsmen" (Dale 1936). One pilot shot 160, including 13 in a day.

In 1937 ten were shot from a light aircraft e. of the Pecos, Tex. But the real shooting began in the fall of 1940 when a rancher lost 19 yearling sheep weighing some 75 lbs. each—not likely to eagles! Ranchers formed the Big Bend Eagle Club (there were also

218

at least 7 smaller clubs) to engage in eagle "control." A hunter for the Big Bend group reportedly killed 28 in a day, 1,008 in a year (fall–spring), av. 850/year (*Life*, June 13, 1949). This was reported also by Buechner (1950, or see Spofford 1964); for 1941–1942 to 1946–1947, inclusive, the number taken varied from 667 in 1942–1943 to 1,008 the next winter (6-yr. av. 803).

The largest number shot in a day by 1 individual was 38, mostly over the Eagle Mts.—a record that stood for some years. Then 2 other individuals each claimed to have killed 40 in a day. One man was reported to have shot 512 eagles in 2,800 hr. of flying time in 8 years; another was reported to have killed 149 in Jan. 1961.

Although all reports are not to be taken literally, it is "now clear" that for over 20 years at least 1,000 and perhaps 2,000 Golden Eagles were killed from aircraft each fall–spring in far-w. Tex. and se. N. Mex. (Spofford, in Hickey 1969). *Incident at Eagle Ranch* (Schueler 1980), a sobering coverage of man v. eagle in this period, seems almost unreal in retrospect.

An eagle may circle upward in a thermal and outfly an aircraft, but more often the pilot can outfly it and shoot it down. If 1 is shot at, it often drops quickly toward or onto the ground; then to approach close enough to shoot from a plane is too dangerous. (When harassed by helicopters; eagles land and crouch—D. Ellis 1975.) One person told Spofford that if an eagle survives a few aerial pursuits, it learns to get close to the ground or to alight and shield itself behind some obstruction. This person also stated that many eagles go down with a broken wing and may fly again after being grounded for a few weeks. The eagle's mate often will "arrive at once and will attend it, bringing food until it can take care of itself again." Spofford examined a dead eagle taken in a trap; its right wing had broken and healed. Another person who shot 100s of eagles from the air stated that when an eagle is hit another often joins it and spreads its wings over the fallen bird. He claimed to have seen this many times. In many cases the 2d eagle will bring food to the grounded one.

A few days before lambing time a rancher would contact a hunter, and several days' shoot-off would follow until, apparently, virtually all eagles were eliminated from a large area. Then others would drift in from surrounding areas. Two or 3 weeks later there would be a 2d shoot-off. Such slaughter accomplished no more than a temporary reduction—the shooting being an "incredibly wasteful destruction" of a generally admired bird.

Northwest of Roswell, N. Mex., much of the country is "level plain or low rolling hills, stony and with very scant vegetation," lacking natural perching sites. Small man-made monuments are favorite perches, hence favorable places for successful eagle trapping. On the s. Edwards Plateau, eagles were taken by placing traps on a sheep or deer carcass or even a deer hide pegged to the ground. In 1962–1963, a time when shooting from aircraft was prohibited, perhaps several hundred were trapped or shot from the ground.

An estimated 800 eagles (5 were Bald) were killed from the air in Wyo. and Colo. "since last September," according to an Aug. 4, 1971, news release. It was noted that the price paid for killing an eagle was $25 and that a great many were found in a mass grave on federal grazing land. In the winter–spring of 1970–1971 in Wyo. and Colo., nearly 1,200 eagle deaths were documented: 30+ by poisoning, the 800+ just mentioned as killed from the air, and 300+ from electrocution or shooting along power lines (Olendorff et al. 1981).

Eagles have died from eating rodents killed by eating poisoned grain (Kalmbach et al. 1964). Carrion has been poisoned in coyote control operations. In Scotland carrion was, by wt., ¼ of summer and over ⅓ of winter diet (L. Brown and Watson 1964).

Legislation On Apr. 1, 1963, Part 11, Title 50 of the Code of Federal Regulations was revised to give the Golden Eagle essentially the same legal protection accorded the Bald Eagle 23 years earlier. Governors of states could still request permission to take Golden Eagles for any period deemed necessary to protect livestock. Golden Eagles could not be taken from aircraft or by poison. On Feb. 8, 1972, the president of the U.S. issued an executive order banning the use of poisons on federal lands and by federal agencies. Other restrictions, not always long-lasting, have also been mandated.

Eagle and livestock interrelations It is important to determine whether eagle food was taken alive (predation) or was carrion. This has been dealt with by R. Packard et al. (1969), R. Wiley and Bolen (1971), Alford and Bolen (1972), and Bolen (1975); see especially the photographs in Wiley and Bolen. Talon punctures with subcutaneous hemorrhages are "a priori indications of eagle predation," indicating damage done while the victim was alive. Yet some stockmen maintain that such wounds are often absent from eagle-killed lambs and that the eagle kills by impact—the feet closed in a "fist"—or in some other way alien to the known method of killing by a crushing grip (binding firmly to the quarry, as falconers say), the talons piercing and penetrating deeply. Killing is by laceration and suffocation. An absence of hemmorhaging around the wound indicates that the animal was dead when lacerated. Also, if there is no soil or debris in the hoof cleft or any evidence of hoof wear, it is almost certain that the lamb (or kid) was stillborn and any damage to it was scavenging.

Wiley and Bolen described these situations: **1** "pure" predation—healthy animal taken by an eagle; **2** carrion feeding—lamb or kid dead from other causes; **3** "enhanced" already ill from disease or some other cause; and **4** predation by an eagle, then the carcass used by 1 or more other species, then by the eagle again. The 3d situation—culling—is very important and may be the most difficult to detect. Eagles that take lambs and goats mostly are young birds, under a year old.

Signs to note: removal of eyes and tongue is usually the work of ravens or vultures; bones picked clean but unbroken, also skin cut or partly removed, is done by a bird; chewed and crushed bones indicate a mammal.

An oversimplification, sometimes applied broadly toward predation on the w. range, is as follows: Grassland deteriorates when grazed too heavily. Perennial vegetation is supplanted by seed-producing annuals (shrubs and weeds). Rodents and lagomorphs multiply, which encourages an increased predator population. Then, rather than recognize or deal with the underlying cause (land abuse), ranchers blame predators unduly for livestock losses. In some cases this may be relevant, yet elsewhere there may be so many variables and the situation may be so different that each case deserves independent appraisal. As for the Golden Eagle specifically, in large areas it is only a minor predator—although the most conspicuous one. Locally and in season, but not in many documented cases, it has been a serious predator of lambs and kids. Some individuals undoubtedly become habituated to prey so easily obtained

220

during a brief portion of the year when it is vulnerable. Their efficiency probably improves with experience. Livetrapping and releasing these offending individuals elsewhere is costly.

Pressures for eagle control come from sheep and goat ranchers; some, however, regard damage as rather negligible—a reasonable trade-off for removal by eagles of rabbits and rodents that compete for forage. Sheep, for example, are introduced aliens, selectively bred, and usually ranched as a monoculture, or sole crop. On ranchland one must also reckon with predators other than eagles, the availability of "natural" prey, the time and circumstances of lambing, whether carrion (as stillborn lambs or coyote prey) is left exposed, the effects of bad storms and hot weather, screwworms, disease, and so on. Although it has far more to do with coyotes than eagles, an especially thought-provoking case study of predation in Mont. is that of O'Gara et al. (1983). From an earlier, and simpler, day, here are 2 contrasting situations, from Kalmbach et al. (1964):

North of Ft. Collins, Colo.—foothills, buttes, prairie, brushy slopes. There was an estimated 1 pair of eagles/township. The sheep were usually herded in flocks of about 600; lambing occurred from late Mar. to mid-May, usually in sheds where ewes and lambs were kept 10 days. Sheep were closely supervised; grazing pressure was moderate to heavy. None of the sheepmen had ever seen eagles preying on sheep, but they did observe them quickly finding dead ones and eating them.

Texas w. of the Pecos—scattered mt. ranges, rolling hills and flat valleys, scrub in lowlands, also semiarid grassland, and some brush on steeper slopes. Peak of lambing in mid-Mar., out on pasture. Grazing was heavy to severe. From an examination of carcasses, it was learned that some lambs had been killed by eagles, but the ranchers agreed that eagles seldom attacked lambs more than 7–10 days old.

In the se. U.S. there are reliable records of Golden Eagles preying on lambs and kids and eating sheep as carrion. An old report (A. K. Fisher 1893) of their being destructive to sheep in S.C. claimed that a person killed over 40 eagles one spring, "principally by using strychnine." Obviously the eagles were feeding on dead animals (poisoned carcasses).

Electrocution Has been a serious problem in some parts of the w., although now rectified in places. (It has occurred in the e. and might be a greater problem if there were more eagles.) An eagle making final flaps when alighting on the crossarm or other component of an energized transmission line may touch 2 live wires or 1 and a ground-wire, be electrocuted, and cause an expensive power outage. Sometimes this happens when a bird spreads its wings to dry after a rain. Ancillary actions such as defecating on the strings of insulators also cause electricity to spark over. The problem has existed at least from the 1920s, is most serious in winter, and is most acute in treeless areas. Common victims are young eagles, perched above good ground cover such as sagebrush inhabited by cottontails. It is beneficial to add perches above the wires, but the generally most desirable solution is to separate the wires so far (5 ft., or 152 cm., minimum) that they cannot be bridged (shorted out) by a bird as large as an eagle. For the many problems there is a variety of equipment design—see Olendorff et al. (1981) for text, diagrams, and an annotated list of relevant literature.

Where natural perches are common the eagles make little use of power lines. But

221

where they are few or lacking, the birds use the poles or other structures—the highest available perches—for increased visibility and easy takeoff. They tend to use poles and towers more on hills and ridges for the added advantage of more favorable air currents (Boeker 1972).

In 6 w. states, 82.5% of 416 eagle carcasses were found near power lines. Fifty-one were fresh enough to determine the cause of death. Of these, 80.6% died of electrocution in winter, and only 5.8% of these were "adult." In cottontail habitat, 36% of poles had eagle carcasses under them. No carcasses had gunshot wounds. These figures are from P. C. Benson (1982), who discussed measures for lowering eagle electrocution— routing lines around preferred prey habitat, locating poles in topographically low areas, and insulating pole conductors.

Organochlorine pesticides and related matters Have been studied considerably. A good example is Kochert's (1972) work on mercury in sw. Idaho. The eagle's food chain is short, jackrabbits being the main prey. Since they (and other herbivores) accumulate low pesticide levels, the same holds for the eagles. Further, since the Idaho birds are resident, they are less exposed to higher levels of contamination. Heptachlor was implicated in the deaths of 8 birds in Oreg. One fell from the sky, hit the ground, and began convulsing; another, found alive, had no coordination; the remaining 6 were found dead (Henny et al. 1984a).

Indians and eagles in N. Am. A vast subject. The Golden is deeply embedded in numerous cultures—beliefs, aesthetics, a wide spectrum of rituals, numerous taboos, totems, heraldry, and various utilitarian functions. Veneration of the eagle, a belief in the sacred character of the birds or even their feathers, was widespread. The Thunderbird—creator of the world, messenger of the gods, the Great Spirit himself (C. Snow 1973b). Bones of eagles (and other predatory birds) are not rare in prehistoric sites; see final paragraph under Distribution of various species in this volume.

Pit trapping, with its attendant rituals, was used to obtain both of our eagles, but principally the Golden, from the Great Plains w. and s. The remains of many ancient pits still exist, mostly on bluffs and escarpments, from the upper Missouri drainage w. The catcher hid within; there was a hole in the covering overhead, and beside it lay bait such as a dead jackrabbit. When an eagle grasped the bait, the hunter reached through the hole, seized the bird by the legs, and then drew it inside, where, in close confinement and darkness, it was helpless (J. Jensen 1923). In the sw. (as among the Pueblos) and to the n., not only were eaglets taken from nests but flying birds were also captured in built-up stone enclosures. Bait was placed inside and young Goldens would enter but could not escape; older, experienced birds were too wary.

An enormous variety of ceremony and human behavior associated was with eagle catching. Among the Mandan, being a catcher and the singing of certain songs was hereditary. Among the Hidatsa, the 1st eagle captured was tethered near the pit as a decoy; others taken were strangled, transported away, and plucked. (We now know that the decoy will attract other young eagles but that older ones will see that the restrained bird is in trouble and will avoid the site—Harmata, in Gerrard and Ingram 1985.) Among the Arapaho it was said (Kroeber 1902) that 50 or 100 eagles might be caught in 4 days. Different tribes kept various birds of prey captive, usually in order to pluck their tails when fully grown; the birds then might be released. The recorded

222

keeping of eagles by the Hopi (and Zuni) dates from the time of Fray Marcus, advance agent of the Coronado Expedition of 1540–1542 (Winship 1896). A Zuni eagle cage was illus. in the narrative of Maj. John Wesley Powell (1895) of Colorado R. fame. Those interested in pursuing this general subject further might begin with G. Wilson (1928), but see also below.

A particular ceremony that required a large diurnal predatory bird and was loaded with symbolism, formerly existed quite widely from Calif. s. in w. N. Am. and (continuously?) through Cent. Am. and far down the S. Am. Andes. Within at least part of its past range, the Calif. Condor was the principal bird (eagles were secondary). In part of Cent. Am. in former times, the Harpy Eagle was evidently the chosen bird. Correspondingly, in much of its w. range and especially within what is presently the coterminous U.S., the Golden Eagle was—and is—the prime bird. (In turn, when eagles are unobtainable, a large buteo may be substituted.)

The Hopi ceremony is best known and most fully recorded. Much of the information here is from an informant who spent 10 years on a reservation and attended 2 eagle hunts. The Hopis take the birds under permit, on the basis that they are used for religious purposes (Pub. Law 95–341, Aug. 11, 1978). Different hunting areas belong to different clans, which try to maintain the breeding population by never taking more than ½ the nestlings—young that will be feathered by the time of Niman (Home-going) dance in late July. Not all hunts are successful. Furthermore, any single eaglets are not taken. At least formerly (Fewkes 1900), when the birds were taken to the pueblo, in due course 1 was always released with a prayer stick attached to a leg so that it could return to its comrades carrying the hunter's prayers.

The preflight eaglet is carried to the village. After some days in captivity it is anointed with watery whitish clay and given a name. Then it is tethered on the roof. It belongs to whomever brought it in and is fed fresh rodents or rabbits by many members of the clan. It is talked to and given gifts brought by kachinas on dance days. Since its sex is unknown, children give miniature bows and arrows (boys) and plaques and dolls (girls) that are tied to its perches. The morning after Home-going dance, the bird is given a present and sent home—smothered (sacrificed). If the young bird is not sufficiently feathered—that is, its quills hard basally—the dance is postponed with much apology and expressions of great appreciation for the eagle's gift of its feathers. (Most aspects of the ceremony have variants; note Fewkes (1900).)

Most of the feathers are then removed, small downy ones being distributed to all present and worn in the hair until lost. The eaglet's body is prepared for burial as a child's would be—a small cradleboard of reeds is provided and used in the Hopi manner. Then it is wrapped and taken with its toys either to a place where young children are buried or to an eagle cemetery. Food is placed nearby, and a stick is stuck into the burial mound so that the eagle can climb out and go home on the 4th day. The bird's feathers, used in numerous rituals, symbolize its ongoing presence. To get rid of evil, for example, many small ones are tied to a bush; they wear away in the wind and are supplanted by something spiritually good. See also Fewkes (1900, or in Hodge 1907), J. Jensen (1923), O'Kane (1953), Waters (1963), S. and J. Page (1982)—text and illus.—and J. and S. Page (1982) for abbreviated coverage. There is an interesting autobiographical account by a Hopi, Don Talayesava (b. 1890), edited by Leo Simmons (1942). The importance of the Golden Eagle to the Pueblo Indians is well conveyed by H. Tyler (1979).

The most spectacular use of eagle feathers was in the so-called war bonnets of the Plains tribes, which have become almost a cliché of the American Indian. Their frequency in anthropological collections would indicate the capture of a considerable number of Golden Eagles; furthermore, the manufacture of these and other gear for a commercial market has been remarkably persistent. A full headdress extended down in a long train and was decorated with tail feathers arranged evenly from longest at the top to shortest at the bottom. A minimum of 60—that is, all the tail feathers from at least 5 eagles—was required. Eagle feathers were attached to shields and spears and were a component of fans and other items. Feathers and other eagle parts were included in ceremonial bundles, certain feathers were used in fletching arrows, and talons were used in necklaces. There seems to have been some sort of hierarchy of feather uses that may have included children to some extent but perhaps not women; one searches in vain for women wearing feathers in published collections of early photographs. For interesting prehistoric evidence of feather usage, see Ubelaker and

Wedel (1975). Some of the finest awls from prehistoric sites appear to be splints of eagle bone, presumably useful in making better-grade garments.

The "black eagle" (dark Juv. Golden) was most highly prized. Its tail feathers, strikingly white with black distal portion, are somewhat longer than those of older birds (which also have a more complicated pattern). Yet for many tribes the taking of eagles is now much out of fashion, and the lands of some are sanctuaries. Indians who currently need feathers, and only for their own use, can probably get them from salvage material stored by the U.S. Dept. of Interior. For manufacture of finely crafted items for sale, white turkey feathers with dyed ends make an excellent substitute for tail feathers of the Juv. Golden Eagle and without dye supplant the tail feathers of the Def. Basic Plumage of the Bald Eagle. These are used and/or sold already. The shaft of an eagle feather has a V-shaped groove on the underside, a turkey feather a U-shaped one (R. Laybourne); use of the latter should help dry up the market for eagle feathers.

In Colo. in Mar., 1928, Indians captured Golden Eagles to transport to Okla., where they were kept in confinement and plucked for the manufacture of war bonnets (Aiken 1928). An unpublished 1931 thesis included a mention of 36 Golden and Bald Eagles taken by Indians for their feathers. Into at least the 1930s, boys' magazines advertised Golden Eagle feathers for sale. In Zacatecas, Mexico, in 1954, the Golden was regarded as a serious predator on calves; many were shot and a large collection of talons appeared to be all from this species (J. D. Webster 1958). Much else could be mentioned.

For a formerly very widespread eagle dance, see under Bald Eagle in volume 4. Lest the Inuit be omitted here, it may be noted that the only information at hand is a limited amount of myth and folklore; Inuit cultural involvement was insignificant as compared with Indian tribes. The Inuit had, of course, less exposure to eagles.

Reference to Old World **symbolism, mythology,** and **folklore** was made earlier in volume 4, under attributes of the Bald Eagle, in some measure because of transference of concepts relating to the Golden Eagle to the New World. Eagles got into Christianity early (*Ezekiel* 1) as a symbol of the resurrection; this probably derived from ancient myth—the bird flew to the sun, then plunged into the sea to renew its youth. Eagles had a place in medieval manuscripts before A.D. 700, often as a symbol of St. John the Evangelist, their image therein generally indicating lack of firsthand knowledge of the subject (Yapp 1981). The eagle-transporting-child theme is ancient. Jupiter took the form of an eagle and carried off the youngster Ganymede, who became his cup bearer. Corregio painted this subject in the early 1500s (Kunsthist. Mus., Vienna): Ganymede, far heavier than his Golden Eagle captor, is positively serene and unruffled while holding onto the airborne bird! The same theme is indigenous to some N. Am. native peoples; since it has also been introduced from abroad, one might say that we in N. Am. are doubly infected and do not discriminate as to species when applying this idea to an eagle. William Holmes McGuffey, professor of moral philosophy, utilized it for his purposes (see under Bald Eagle species account). The theme is alive and well.

Place names Those incorporating "Eagle" are numerous. When applied to is. and bodies of water in N. Am., the usual association is with the Bald, but, inland especially, those applied to elevations and related topography are often Golden-derived. The frequency of the latter in the e. of this continent may be unrealized. An unusual example: Eagle Nest Pond, N.Y. (near a onetime Golden aerie).

The culinary eagle   Samuel Hearne, at the end of his account of his 1770–1772 journey from Hudson Bay to the mouth of the Coppermine R., described common brown fishing eagles (actually the Golden). He wrote that before the young can fly, their nests were filled with so much food that the Indians could obtain a "most excellent meal of fish, flesh and fowl from their larder." The Indians believed that arrows fletched with eagle quills were superior. Eagle flesh was eaten by most Indians, but it is known to be "always black, hard and fishy," and even eaglets, though their flesh is "delicate white," are so rank as to render them very unpleasant to some persons. except in times of necessity (J. B. Tyrrell 1934). Hearne seems to have scrambled 2 eagle species, the n. bird being the Golden.

Habituation   Individual Golden Eagles and pairs vary greatly in the ability to cope with human disturbance. Much has been written or implied about the readiness with which this bird will desert its aerie and abandon its territory. Some nesters, for example, are so sensitive that even watching them at a distance through a telescope is enough to keep them away; others, especially if not directly and suddenly intruded on or if human activity is repetitious, differ remarkably. Around civilization they become "very tame in some instances and usually wind up being shot by some passing hunter" (J. B. Dixon 1937). In Utah, several pairs continue to nest in historically used aeries that are now close (min. about 300 yds.) to freeways and other major highways. In 1 canyon there is an active nest on a cliff not 50 ft. above a main railroad line, and an engineer could actually see downies in the nest from his locomotive cab. This pair has habituated to trains passing beneath them day and night, with accompanying noise, diesel exhaust fumes, and so forth (J. R. Murphy).

In Tex. an experienced eagle shooter told Spofford (1964) that eagle behavior changed after the ban on eagle shooting went into effect in 1962. In the shooting years, eagles fled or dropped to the ground and hid if possible on the approach of an aircraft. But in 1964 they seemed indifferent. Often it was difficult to get them to fly long enough to be photographed.

Olendorff (1975) observed a nest from a stationary vehicle 200 yds. away. The sitter watched him, her evident attention diminishing as the season advanced. If he was out of his truck and in plain view, he was a source of alarm. In Maine some decades ago, a ♀ became more trustful as each week passed, finally just flying to a nearby perch when the investigator approached in routine fashion on his periodic visits; yet in N.H. an eagle never accommodated to college students hiking nearby (Spofford).

Again J. B. Dixon (1937) in Calif.: 1 pair of eagles would follow a man plowing, and when the horses flushed a ground squirrel, the ♀ would pounce on it. Then she would stand a few ft. from the plowman and eat. When he stopped his team and snapped his whip playfully, she would move only a few ft. farther away.

Most wild-caught Goldens readily become tame. On the other hand, Vennor (1876) wrote of a captive that took a great dislike to a disagreeable caretaker; it would attack whenever possible and even recognized this man after years of separation. (For another hostile bird, see hunger panic, above.) Quite different are reports of several captives (all ♀ ?) that seemed to adjust to captivity, after a while even "talking" regularly to their captors; examples: Hamerstrom (1970), Collier (1982). Evidently because of the habituation factor, if a captive is to be freed, then the sooner this is done the better its chances of survival.

Hunting with Golden Eagles   An ancient practice. In parts of Asia they are transported on horseback on a wooden perch affixed to the pommel of a saddle since they are too heavy to manage more than briefly on the fist. They are still used, generally at least 2 at a time (cooperative hunting), to handicap or capture quarry as large as small antelopes and wolves. In Britain in former times they were reserved for royalty—flown only by kings. Treatises on falconry have much information on the Golden. For an excellent, brief introduction to living with eagles, some history, and how hunting with eagles is practiced in cent. Asia, see *Beyond the Caspian* by Douglas Carruthers (1949). *Hints on the Management of Hawks* by Harting (1898, 1981) is also first-rate.

Ability to cope   In considerable measure this is a factor in the following matters: Any buffer zone created that curtails or prohibits human activity to protect nesters should surely be a minimum of 1 mi. (1.6 km.) in diam., more or less centered on the aerie. Suggested size varies (Suter and Joness 1981), but obviously a zone that small would not protect both nesting and hunting areas. As indicated above, some nesters appear more tolerant of human presence and activity than others, but this can be misleading; the birds may seem to accept such intrusion, only to abandon the area once their brood has departed. Providing artificial nest bases or platforms to enhance nesting opportunity is feasible in some circumstances (Olendorff 1980). Eaglets need shade to prevent heat prostration or death; they also need shelter from the wind. Such sites may also be occupied by other raptors. Some recent experiments have demonstrated that a platform with nest and eaglets may be moved some distance without abandonment of the young or that eaglets may be shifted via a series of platforms to a safer location.

Numbers in N. Am.   The Golden is a "sensitive species" in relation to land-use changes; its relative number among diurnal raptors in Canada is low and stable (Fyfe, in Chancellor 1977). It is doing well in part but not all of its U.S. range—notably the very few nesters in e. N. Am. Golden Eagle numbers on this continent have been greatly underestimated (less than 10,000—Spofford 1964) to overestimated (around 100,000—Braun 1975). An acceptable current figure would be about 70,000.

From a census of winterers in Wyo., Wrakestraw (1972) calculated over 11,000 birds in that state. More recent studies of Wyo. breeders indicate clearly that Wyo. nesting habitat is saturated (R. L. Phillips et al. 1984). This implies different population dynamics than where Goldens are fewer (note references to Haller's study in the cent. Alps, above).

A carefully prepared estimate of the number of Golden Eagles in winter in 16 states in the w. U.S. yielded a figure of 63,242; to these add a "few hundred (or thousand)" in Canada, Mexico, and elsewhere (Olendorff et al. 1981). It was further calculated that about 65% (41,000) were "adults," a potential of 20,500 breeding pairs in the 16-state area. States having over 5,000 in winter were: Mont., 13,138; Wyo., 10,072; N. Mex., 8,789; Colo, 7,081; Utah, 5,993; and Calif., 5,046. For Tex., where a shoot-off in the winter of 1943–1944 purportedly resulted in the death of 1,008 eagles, the wintering figure was only 1,591—less than a 6th as many as were in adjacent N. Mex. Oregon and

Wash., parts of which are Bald Eagle domain, had fewer than 400 each. Nesting density is high in the intermountain stages; the birds are essentially resident, with an added increment of winterers. More to the e., as from N.D. to e. Tex., the number of resident and migrant birds is greatly diminished.

Eastern N. Am. In any season nowadays, far from ideal Golden Eagle country; yet there have been few nesting birds throughout recorded history. The count of fall migrants at Hawk Mt., Pa., 1934–1975, inclusive, varied annually from 31 to 80 birds with a slight downward trend through the period (Nagy, in Chancellor 1977); most probably came from n. of the St. Lawrence R. In the 1st 5 of these years, ½ the birds were "immature" (Broun 1939), but these later declined (Cottam 1962), indicating poor (or poorer) production of eaglets. Since some time in the 1970s the ratio of "immatures" has improved somewhat. The former poorer production, and reduced numbers of migrants generally, parallels the decline in breeding success of the Bald Eagle and Osprey together with the virtual disappearance of the Peregrine Falcon from the Appalachian region. The explanation seems to be that during the breeding season e. Goldens hunt to a great extent over the most open available habitat—bogs, swamps, marshy margins of lakes and streams—preying on Am. Bitterns, young Great Blue Herons, and the like, which are top predators in the aquatic food chain. What might be termed the "Bittern ecosystem" has evidently suffered adversely from biocides, acid deposition, or a combination of these. In any event, the food chain is strikingly different from that on w. rangeland—the home of jackrabbits, prairie dogs, and ground squirrels. It would appear that any modest improvement in reproductive success is probably among Canadian nesters, which are transients when counted.

Many reports of the fate of e. birds within the U.S.—mostly young in 1st fall–winter—are at hand. Although many deaths are undoubtedly unreported, the majority of those that are resulted from shooting. Even today, some hunters seem to regard Goldens as irresistable targets. Several have been killed while trying to capture domestic fowl, cats, and dogs; others have been found starving; a few have had obvious injuries; 2 were electrocuted. Included here are the following from Va.: records of 36 shot (J. J. Murray 1952), and of 3, badly decomposed, found hanging in a tree in July 1953 (C. O. Handley). Any notion of augmenting the local stock (Nelson, in Hickey 1969) should not be encouraged in view of the poor chances of survival to breeding age.

An appraisal After many studies of eagle biology in general and of predation in particular, we have an adequate base from which to arrive at sensible judgments. Yet the facts will need to be explained or interpreted in the future to those whose foremost image is of the bird's purported destructiveness to domestic stock and/or "beneficial" wildlife. The attention that this bird attracts by its very conspicuousness is generally out of proportion to its importance in range management. The conflict over whether human or bird has the dominant claim to portions of the environment will cost the eagle some ground. In this ongoing interaction, anthropomorphism comes easily because the bird often seems "intelligent." It can change and adapt, which assures that it is here to stay.

References The literature on the Golden Eagle in N. Am. is short on books, as compared with Europe, and long on journal coverage. Informative books include Frances Hamerstrom's (1970) account of a captive ♀ and Olendorff's popular treatment of this species in its w. environment. The *Aquila* bibliography by LeFranc and Clark (1983), which appeared after the present account had been drafted, is a time-saver for those seeking sources. The number of reports and journal articles on the Golden Eagle is large and is growing at an increasing rate. Over 700 sources were consulted and 242 were cited in preparing the present account. RALPH S. PALMER

FOOD   In N. Am. In terms of total biomass, principally rodents, hares, and rabbits. In more detail: wild mammals, mainly of squirrel to hare and marmot size (but occasionally much larger); small young of smaller domestic mammals to a very limited and local extent; carrion frequently (dead lambs and kids, road-killed jackrabbits and cottontails, etc.); wild birds and occasional poultry; a few cold-blooded vertebrates (mostly snakes).

   Summaries   In chronological order: Oberholser (1906), May (1935), Arnold (1954), Schorger (1954 MS), Kalmbach et al. (1964), Olendorff (1976), and Sherrod (1978), who summarized 10 reports and previous summaries. In sw. Idaho, in a comparison of direct observations of prey delivery with estimates of food habits from analyses of castings and prey remains, there was no difference in estimated species composition—percentage or volume (Collopy 1983).

   Various data are from contents of digestive tracts, others from prey remains found in and near nests, and a few are observed deliveries. Notable biases in the study of prey remains include 1 the seasonal nature of prey; 2 carrion may not be recognized as such; 3 heavier items (including carrion) are not transported to the nest; 4 prey is occasionally fetched and then removed and eaten elsewhere; and 5 small prey may be consumed and leave no trace. Winter studies are particularly hard to make because much prey is eaten on the spot and one must see it happen. Olendorff's 1976 summary of 7,094 prey items tabulated: mammals 83.9%, birds 14.7%, reptiles 1.0%, and fishes 0.4%.

   Mammals   Where ground squirrels (*Spermophilus*) are available, the Golden often preys almost exclusively on them. Elsewhere Goldens prefer prairie dogs (*Cynomys*), a food source now vastly diminished. Marmots (*Marmota*) are taken in high country. These 3 genera are hibernators, only available seasonally. Golden Eagles take hares (*Lepus:* jackrabbits and snowshoe hares) and rabbits (*Sylvilagus:* cottontails) year-round; they are a mainstay on much of winter range. In spring–summer, young jacks are frequent quarry. Eagles tend to concentrate (at least in winter–spring) where many jackrabbits and/or cottontails are killed by road traffic and in turn may be killed by vehicles.

   Goldens have been reported to prey on full-grown deer (*Odocoileus*), but doubt remains that deer can be killed (as by eagles hunting cooperatively) unless already injured or otherwise handicapped. A "good-sized" blacktail was reportedly killed in Mont. (C. Morrison 1889); a 4-point whitetail in Ariz. foundered in deep snow, was attacked, succumbed, and was dragged downhill where 3 eagles fed on it (Willard 1916a). Deer fawns are taken with some frequency in certain places (Longhurst et al. 1952, Riney 1951). In sw. Yukon, the capture of several Dall's sheep lambs was observed; there was a scarcity of usual prey (Nette et al. 1984). The evidence for taking pronghorns (*Antilocapra*), especially small fawns, is solid (for Tex., see Buechner

229

1950), but evidence from eagle digestive tracts—of this as well as other species—could pertain to carrion. Grown pronghorns are more likely to become victims in severe winters; see, for example, Bruns (1970). Five Goldens fed on a ♀ pronghorn killed by 1 or more of them (Lehti 1947). Two cooperated in killing an elk (*Cervus*) calf (O. Murie 1951). There is insignificant predation on young caribou, bighorns, and mountain goats (many authors); young eagles sometimes harass them, possibly a form of play.

The subject of livestock v. the Golden Eagle was dealt with above. So far as adequately reported, eagle predation is mainly on very young sheep in exposed situations and locally in place and time; except in unusual circumstances, too few are taken to justify eagle persecution to maintain or enhance livestock production. Much that is consumed is stillborn young and other carrion. The taking of very young goats may be fairly regular in some places but has been little reported—hardly more than the reported taking (and attempted taking) of cats and dogs. Piglets have been preyed on at widespread localities; see J. S. Campbell (1934), J. B. Dixon (1937), and others.

This eagle has attacked both young and full-grown red foxes (*Vulpes*) successfully, and on the North Slope in Alaska it hunts near arctic fox (*Alopex*) dens, getting some pups (Garrott and Eberhardt 1982). It preys on both adult and young coyotes (*Canis latrans*) (H. Ford and Alcorn 1964); trapped and debilitated coyotes are partially eaten (Cameron 1908a). Relations with the coyote, however, seem to be at somewhat of a stand off. The Golden has kept them from an elk carcass (Flook and Thomas 1962), but in other observations coyotes have persevered and been successful (Bowen 1980), and coyotes have trailed a flying eagle, as noted above.

Since the eagles appear to be opportunists and generalists within limits, though some are certainly specialists when possible, a list of known mammalian prey additional to species already mentioned would be long. It ranges from opossums to shunks, muskrats, tree squirrels, wood rats, and assorted others, in size down to voles (*Microtus*) and deer mice (*Peromyscus*).

Carrion Eaten commonly, especially in winter. In mammals, see above. In an experiment conducted in Tex., C. C. Sperry determined that the carcass of a jackrabbit or lamb dead 2 or more days was preferred over live lambs in the immediate area (Kalmbach et al. 1964). In the days of millions of bison there must have been far more carrion of various sorts than is now available.

Birds The largest recorded as taken are Whooping Crane (Windigstad et al. 1981), Trumpeter Swan (Eklund 1946), Wild Turkey (young?), and Great Blue Heron (young only?). Eklund stated that in B.C. the eagle strikes the flying Trumpeter occasionally but never recovers the fallen bird. Avian quarry varies in size down to (rarely) larks and sparrows. Among the numerically more evident are open-country gamebirds—ptarmigan, grouse, pheasant, Gray Partridge, and Chukar—and magpies. Many gamebirds are taken before fully grown. In Wyo. the Sage Grouse was said to be vulnerable (J. Scott 1942), but under other circumstances in Utah recently there was no eagle predation. There seem to be few records of gulls as food. Except for the Great Horned Owl, known captures of raptorial birds are few (and usually at least the owl is killed in territorial squabbles—not to eat). (Compare with n. Sweden; 6 species of diurnal raptors and 7 of owls found in food remains—Tjernberg 1981.) Ravens are plentiful in much eagle country and are seldom taken; except for inexperienced young, perhaps

230

they are difficult to capture. Crows are more agricultural than woodland birds, which may explain their near absence.

Reptiles Includes a number of snake species (rattlers rarely), evidently many individuals of some species (Bent 1937; McGahan 1968; Olendorff 1976; Voelker, in Sherrod 1978). Gopher snakes and bullsnakes are notably conspicuous.

A horned lizard (*Phrynosoma*).

An occasional tortoise (Bent 1937); a box turtle (McGahan 1968). There is no evidence of carrying tortoises aloft and dropping them, as reported from Bulgaria by W. Fischer (1980 and earlier papers).

Amphibians One record—a frog (see below).

Fishes Suckers and perch (Carnie 1954). Three references to fishes in eagle diet in sw. Idaho (in Collopy 1983). A few Goldens consort with Bald Eagles and feed on dead or spent salmon, as at McDonald Creek in Glacier Natl. Park in late fall.

Insects Stated to eat Mormon crickets (La Rivers 1941). Migrants ate grasshoppers (Kuyt 1967).

NOTES There are scattered observations for the ne. U.S. These items have been noted: **1** terrestrial and aquatic—Common Loon (partly grown), Am. Bittern (many; mostly young in July), Great Blue Heron (mainly Aug., young), Black Duck, red fox (young), mink, muskrat, woodchuck, snowshoe hare, cottontail, domestic goose, and a leopard frog delivered alive to the aerie; **2** from top of forest canopy and above—Red-tailed and Broad-winged Hawks, Barred Owl, Com. Raven (2, probably inexperienced young); and **3** from a nest—Am. Crow (preflight) (W. R. Spofford).

Here is an example of a comprehensive study in the W. In the Snake R. area of sw. Idaho, 1971–1978, inclusive, Black-tailed jackrabbits were most important in frequency and biomass (volume)—nearly 60% of the latter. Next came cottontails (their numbers were relatively constant, but jackrabbits fluctuated) and the introduced Ring-necked Pheasant (important in diet only at aeries adjacent to agriculture). Total biomass: mammals 81.9%, birds (more than 30 species) 16.1%, reptiles 0.7%, and fishes 0.9% (Snake R. Birds Prey *Spec. Res. Rept.* 1979; see also Collopy 1983). RALPH S. PALMER

231

Family FALCONIDAE
Crested Caracara
Falcons

CRESTED CARACARA

Polyborus plancus

Common Caracara; Mexican Eagle—the national emblem; Carancho—in many S. Am. countries. A fairly large, stout-beaked, crested, rather long-necked, trim-bodied, long-legged (ambulatorial), diurnal raptor. Caracara ancestral stock (from which falcons are also derived) evolved toward more or less vulturine habits. The compressed deep beak is decidedly hooked and without "tooth" in upper mandible; nostrils narrow, elongated, diagonally situated in upper anterior portion of cere; forepart of face naked except for some bristles. Wing distally wide, primaries nearly twice as long as secondaries; counting from outer, the 1st is shorter than the 6th, with #3 and #4 longest; inner webs of outer 4 (and adjoining one to lesser extent) incised or narrowed. Tail longish, nearly square ended. Talons rather long but not strongly curved.

Coloring and pattern vary to some extent geographically, with these features constant in presently extant birds in definitive feathering: dark cap with elongated, pointed feathers at upper nape, remainder of feathered head and upper throat light, much of body and wings dark with at least part of breast and anterior back white barred black, lower abdomen and all tail coverts light (to white) and plain or barred, spread wing shows large, light area in outer primaries (but was obscure in a recently extinct subspecies), tail light with a dozen or more narrow, dark crossbars plus a wide, dark, terminal band. Juvenal birds tend toward browner coloring and heavy longitudinal streaking (venter especially). Basic I is nearer definitive than Juv.

Sexes similar in appearance and nearly so in size (♀ somewhat larger). Within this widespread species, larger birds measure: length of ♂ to 22 in. (56 cm.) and ♀ to at least 24 in. (61 cm.); wt. of ♂ to 30 oz. (850 gm.) and ♀ to 36 oz. (1,025 gm.).

235

There are 4 or 5 subspecies altogether, with 2 limited to is.; in our area there is 1 preponderantly mainland and 1 (extinct) is. subspecies.

DESCRIPTION   *P. p. audubonii.* One Plumage/cycle with Basic II earliest definitive (Bent 1938, Friedmann 1950); molting in Fla. begins in SPRING and ends in FALL (about Apr.–Oct.). Molting of primaries begins with #4 counting from inner (V. and E. Stresemann 1960).

▶ ♂ ♀ Def. Basic Plumage (entire feathering). **Beak** variably palish blue; bare skin (extends back to eye and onto chin) generally described as a red (ruby? magenta?), but within a few sec. can alter from pale yellow to salmon pink to vivid red (Vuilleumier 1970)—that is, not a hormonal (gradual) change. The black **cap** extends to nape, where the feathers are elongated, pointed, and erectile. Feathers of neck down onto **breast** and sometimes on **back** white or somewhat buffy with variable amount of black crossbarring that merges ventrally to solid blackish abdomen and thighs. Both upper and under **tail coverts** (and posterior abdomen) white, plain or with some dark barring. Legs and **feet** yellowish, talons black. **Tail** basally white with 11–14 narrow, dark bars (progressively wider and darker distally), then a very dark terminal band about 2 in. (5 cm.) or more wide. **Wings** mostly dark above and below, except for white portion in more than basal ½ of outer primaries, which is slightly interrupted with some broken darkish barring.

AT HATCHING   Beak whitish, face pale, iris brownish. The downy covering is light buffy or white with most of head a deep reddish brown, a spot of lighter brown on each scapular region, thigh, and rump. Photographs of small downies: Bent (1938, plate 24), H. Schroder (1947), and 1971 *Am. Birds* **25** 728. The pattern may persist, but nothing is reported on succession of natal downs.

▶ ♂ ♀ Juv. Plumage (entire feathering) begins to emerge through the downy covering by the time the nestling is 10 in. long (Bent). **Beak** whitish or tinged bluish, cere and **facial skin** gray to pinkish, depending on amount of flushing with blood. The **cap** is muted brownish, with abbreviated forerunner of crest at rear, **iris** dark brownish, darkish feathers of foreneck and **breast** have prominent light shaft streaks, many dark feathers of dorsum are tipped or terminally margined very pale. Legs and **feet** pale (may be gray or faintly bluish or yellowish). **Wing** has "adult" pattern but is browner. Photographs: A. Cruickshank (1947), H. Schroder (1947).

Molting   Bent (1938) stated that the Juv. feathering is retained about a year; that is, in Fla., Prebasic I molting usually begins between Jan. and Apr. New spotted feathers appear on breast, then molting encompasses rest of body, then wings and tail. According to Bent, this produces the following:

▶ ♂ ♀ Basic I Plumage (entire feathering) worn about 1 year. Pattern as definitive; **breast** feathers pale pinkish buff, edged with muted brownish, and with very dark shaft streaks, and some have wedge-shaped transverse dark spots; **upper back** and **abdomen** solidly dark; light areas tinged buff (are not white as in succeeding Basics) and dark areas dark brownish (not blackish). For a much fuller description, see "immature" in Friedmann (1950). (In *P. p. cheriway* in the Netherlands Leeward Is., according to Voous (1957), "subadults" have blackish crossbarring on light buffish ground on center of abdomen, lower breast, and median upper wing coverts.)

236

Color phases   None; an "albinistic" specimen from S. Am. was listed by Gylden-stolpe (1951).

Measurements   Birds from Fla., Tex., Ariz., and Mexico: 10 ♂ BEAK from cere 30–36.5 mm., av. 33.5, WING across chord 370–418, av. 393, TAIL 228.6–254, av. 240.5; and 10 ♀ BEAK from cere 30–36 mm., av. 33, WINGS across chord 373.5–408, av. 391, TAIL 223.5–254, av. 242 (Friedmann 1950, repeated in E. R. Blake 1977). Note that sexual size dimorphism is rather slight in this carrion-eating raptor.

"Adult" ♂ ♂: 13 from Fla. BEAK from cere 31–36 mm., WING across chord 380–410, TAIL 200–225; and 15 from nw. Mexico and Ariz. BEAK from cere 30–32, WING across chord 320–387, and TAIL 197–210 (van Rossem 1939).

[The species: 66 specimens, both sexes included and the Guadalupe I. birds omitted, flattened WING meas. 356–451 mm., av. 394.6 (Vuilleumier 1970).]

Weight   Panama birds (2 subspecies occur or intergrade there), with standard error of mean: 14 ♂ 834 ± 35.5 gm. and 10 ♀ 953 ± 20 (Hartman 1961). This indicates appreciable sexual dimorphism or perhaps some bias in the samples.

Hybrids   None.

Geographical variation   In the species. Birds of Cuba and Fla. resemble those of Tex. to the Isthmus of Panama. Off the Mexican Pacific coast, the Guadalupe I. birds, from isolation and/or rapid evolution, came to differ from adjoining mainland birds in being preponderantly brown with more broken pattern and without black ventrally. Farther s., the Tres Marias birds are somewhat smaller and are not invariably paler than mainland birds; ♂ ♂, at least, also have narrower terminal tail band. The birds of n. S. Am. have dark areas black (not almost black) and other minor differences; s. from the Amazon (and in the Falklands) the birds have notably fine dark barring on breast, the same extensively down the back, and are the largest birds of the species.

Affinities   The Crested Caracara seems less falconlike and more vulturine than the other extant species. It is assumed to be in direct line of descent from *P. prelutosus* (Howard), which, on Pleistocene fossil evidence, was also very widely distributed geographically.   RALPH S. PALMER

SUBSPECIES   As is often the case, birds once described as separate species are now united. Thus the Guadalupe I. birds were treated as a species until, most recently, by L. Brown and Amadon (1968 2). The s. S. Am. birds were also regarded as specifically distinct. The birds included here as a species are all unique among caracaras in having a compressed, large beak with elongated, obliquely placed nostrils and other characters. Within this assemblage, combining birds formerly treated as subspecies has gone the limit. Recently birds from s. U.S. to the Amazon were united under a single name; here divided at Panama. Listing is from n. to s.

In our area   *audubonii* Cassin—descr. and meas. given above. Mainland from s. U.S. down into Panama, also Cuba and Isla de la Juventud [Isle of Pines]. Lumped with subspecies *cheriway*, listed below, by Stresemann and Amadon (in Mayr and Cottrell 1979).

lutosus Ridgway—extinct; in definitive feathering a rather finely broken pattern overall, mostly of browns; no black ventrally. Light area of tail with diffuse brown bars and mottling; an area distally in wing is only noticeably lighter (not mostly white and

237

strikingly evident). Size approximately as preceding. Guadalupe I. off Baja Calif., Mexico. See Friedmann (1950) for meas. Monochrome illus.: Greenway (1958); color illus.: L. Brown and Amadon (1968 **2** plate 132).

Elsewhere *pallidus* Nelson—slightly smaller than adjoining mainland birds; av. paler, but variable (not a diagnostic feature); ♂ ♂ in definitive feathering have narrower dark terminal tail band than mainland birds, also shorter wing and tail (same may hold for ♀ ♀, but not enough material to establish this); some "adults" match mainland birds in coloring, and a greater proportion of "immature" birds cannot be distinguished (P. R. Grant 1965). Occurs on several of the Tres Marias Is. near the cent. w. (Nayarit) Mexican coast. For meas., see Friedmann (1950).

cheriway (Jacquin)—in definitive feathering, dark areas black (not blackish gray); otherwise quite like *audubonii* (with which it is combined by Stresemann and Amadon, in Mayr and Cottrell 1979). A "well marked" subspecies (Vuilleumier 1970). Panama well into S. Am., w. to n. Peru and e. to the Amazon Delta. Island occurrence includes Pacheca (Gulf of Panama), Trinidad, Blanquilla and Margarita, and Netherlands Leeward Is.: Aruba, Curaçao, and Bonaire. For meas., see E. R. Blake (1977); for a few meas. from Aruba, and so forth, see also Voous (1957).

plancus (Miller)—larger than any of the preceding; finely barred down the back; ventral barring fine and extensive. Apparently intergrades with preceding in lower Amazon drainage. Large range on the S. Am. mainland s., continuing across the Strait of Magellan on Isla Grande and Isla de los Estados [Staten I.]—nearest occurrence to the Falklands, which it also inhabits. For meas., see especially E. R. Blake (1977).

RALPH S. PALMER

FIELD IDENTIFICATION **In our area**—but useful much more widely. A hard bird to confuse with any other. About 2 ft. long with 4-ft. wingspread, largely terrestrial, usually conspicuous, alone, in small numbers, and in groups (as when feeding on carrion with vultures). Sexes similar. When perched, a somewhat elongated bird with erect stance; usually where commanding a wide view. Heavy beak, black cap with erectile crest at rear, remainder of head and neck pale, legs quite heavy and long. Runs swiftly at times. Often silent, but may advertise its presence by cackling or grating call that carries well.

In flight, compared with other raptors, body slender and both neck and tail relatively long; a dark bird with conspicuous large white area in outermost portion of wing; light tail with broad blackish terminal band, heavy beak, and light foreparts with black cap. White of wing and tail are visible at long range. A few rapid wingbeats and then a long glide, graceful and fairly swift, rising and falling, often with quite abrupt changes in direction. A noisy rustling of wings heard during flapping flight at close range. May circle high overhead on thermals, its trim body with wings amidships distinguishing it from hawks. Kilham (1979) could distinguish the sexes of a nesting pair in Costa Rica—the ♂ was smaller and had less barring on his white breast.

Juvenal birds are decidedly brownish where older ones are blackish and buffy or tan where older ones are whitish or creamy; Juvs. have gray or pinkish facial skin where older ones are vivid yellow to reddish orange; Juvs. have grayish feet and legs, while older birds' feet are vivid yellow.

RALPH S. PALMER

238

VOICE   Of the species. *Caracara* is of Indian origin, imitative of the voice of the bird—a "barbarous" word, from some S. Am. dialect (Coues 1882); of Brazilian origin (Barbour 1923). Nobody seems to have indicated whether voices of the sexes may differ. The following reports, from widely scattered locales, indicate a limited vocabulary.

"Adults"   FLA.   Rattle-call-with-head-toss (J. Layne). TEX.   The calls in Oberholser and Kincaid (1974) are as in Barbour (1923), from Cuba, and Friedmann and Smith (1950), from Venezuela—both given below. MEXICO   In Sonora, *cre-a-ak cro-ak crea-ak* with head tossed back, the display and call repeated within 1 min. (Tinkham 1948). Guadalupe I.—"curious gabbling noise" when squabbling (in Ridgway 1876). CUBA   Tame bird, when frightened or irritated, a "high-pitched shriek," and, from high perch in morning and before sundown, a "high cackling cry" with head tossed backward (Gundlach, in Barbour 1923). COSTA RICA   Piglike bass rattle that may be delivered with backward toss of head from lofty perch or the ground; another call rustles like a dry palm frond; also a 1-syllabled, heavy *ĕ-ĕ-ĕ-ĕ-ĕ* (Slud 1964). Paired birds in rainy season "greeted each other" with "vibrating heron-like bass croaks," or "ripples that altered with either a light or heavy chatter"; "resonant bass rattle" (Slud 1980). Nesting pair: single *wuck* or *g-wuck* notes when 1 caracara was approaching the other, carrying prey or debris when its partner was on the nest (Kilham 1979). PANAMA   Rattling, clattering, almost mechanical in its sound (A. Wetmore 1965). VENEZUELA   A "pebbly *eh-eh-eh-eh*" sounding somewhat like "a person clearing his throat" (Friedmann and Smith 1950); also described similary from elsewhere. FALKLANDS   Usually a loud harsh *cruk*, singly or "repeated quickly in higher pitch"; perched bird may utter it 5 or more times, rapidly, followed by loud purring call while head tossed back on "shoulders," followed by more *cruk* calls as head returned to normal position (R. W. Woods 1975).

Young   Downies—no information. COSTA RICA   Young bird on wing uttered an "insistent hoarse peeping" (begging?), quite unlike the "subdued asthmatic scream" uttered once to several times by other young birds (Slud 1980). RALPH S. PALMER

HABITAT   Of the species. Generally regarded as a subtropical and tropical bird of open and semiopen lowlands, preferably arid, but occurs to considerable elevation in Andean foothills and to cool climate of extreme s. S. Am. and the Falklands.

In our area   FLA.   Now primarily the Kissimmee Prairie region (grassy terrain with scattered clumps of trees and shallow ponds); also other open dry and wet areas; improved pasture lands; even relatively wooded areas with more limited stretches of open grassland (Layne, in Kale 1978). TEX.   Prairies; grazed and cultivated areas with clumps of oaks; mesquite areas of Rio Grande coastal plain; to some extent where open country extends between wooded mountains.

Elsewhere   MEXICO AND CENT. AM.   Grasslands, cultivated areas, semidesert, scrub of various sorts, coastal lowlands, beaches. In Sonora, Mexico (van Rossem 1945), and elsewhere, for the same reason as the Black Vulture, most likely to be found in vicinity of human habitations—commonly at slaughterhouses, anywhere that offal is discarded. In the Tres Marias Is., where iguanas are a principal food, occurs in many unexpected places; frequently seen in tops of trees in unbroken forest (E. W. Nelson 1899) and hunts on the forest floor. SE. BRAZIL   Usually on beaches, in 2s and 3s (M.

Mitchell 1957). FALKLANDS and some other far s. habitat includes tussock grass and is windy. RALPH S. PALMER

DISTRIBUTION (See map.) On morphological grounds, is. stocks are derived from the nearest mainland birds, although this does not seem obvious for the now-extinct Guadalupe I. birds.

In our area FLA. At present, principally in the prairie region n. and w. of L. Okeechobee, with occasional occurrence in recent years n. into Alachua, Duval, and Nassau cos. and s. into Dade and Monroe cos. (lower Fla. Keys). It is evident that there were more birds in larger area in Audubon's day, with decrease when mapped by A. H. Howell (1932) and further decrease when mapped by Layne (in Kale 1978). A 1984 estimate: 150 breeding pairs and 100–200 prebreeders (Layne).

These data are listed geographically from w. to e.:

CALIF. Straggler to cent.-w. area: Monterey, 1916; 3 at Pilot Knob, 1928 (Bent 1938).

ARIZ. Probably never common; tame and confiding, easily destroyed (A. R. Phillips 1968). A few may have bred in extreme cent.-s. Ariz. on the Papago Indian Reservation, where Levy (1961) found 2 or 3 breeding pairs in 1960—apparently the 1st such recorded for the state since 1889. Millsap (1984) listed a "vagrant" in s. Ariz. in each of these years: 1971, 1972, 1974, 1976, 1977, and 1981.

N.MEX. May occur periodically in Rio Grande valley; also reported in sw. part of the state. Specimens: Ft. Thorn, 1876; Mesquite, 1914. One nesting record: Rio Grande valley at Bellen, s. of Albuquerque, 1953 (J. S. Ligon 1961).

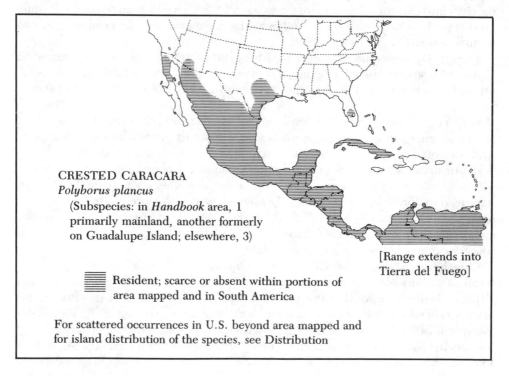

CRESTED CARACARA
Polyborus plancus
(Subspecies: in *Handbook* area, 1
primarily mainland, another formerly
on Guadalupe Island; elsewhere, 3)

[Range extends into Tierra del Fuego]

Resident; scarce or absent within portions of area mapped and in South America

For scattered occurrences in U.S. beyond area mapped and for island distribution of the species, see Distribution

TEX. Sizable range with year-round occurrence; records were mapped by Ober-holser and Kincaid (1974); there is occasional later mention in issues of *Am. Birds*. There appears to have been a considerable, and continuing, decrease generally. On the Welder Refuge, breeding pairs declined from 35 in the 1950s to 1 or 2 in the mid-1970s (Porter and White, in Chancellor 1977).

OKLA. Kaufman Co.—nest with 2 young, July 1980 (1980 *Am. Birds* 34 909).

LA. Although regarded by some early authors as fairly common, the only record that Bent (1938) found was an 1854 specimen from Calcasieu Pass. Lowery (1955) was vague: "decidedly rare," noted only in cent.-s. and sw. areas; unrecorded for more than ½ the months of the year; unconfirmed reports of nesting. In his 1974 revision Lowery listed it as a decidedly rare permanent resident—1 or 2 pairs in Cameron Parish, whence the majority of sightings.

MISS. Hillside Natl. Wildl. Refuge—1 seen Mar. 13–14, 1981 (Woodson and McClellan 1981); 2 other recent records (J. A. Jackson).

Stragglers Northward in N. Am., or perhaps all of the following were escapees: WASH. At or near Westport, ♂ shot June 1936. WYO. Yellowstone Natl. Park, seen Sept. 8–12, 1984. IDAHO Near Montpelier, seen May 30, 1984. S.C. About 10 mi. from Charleston, seen May 1, 1943. N.C. Pineycreek, seen Feb. 19, 1933. PA. Pittsburgh Zoo escapee survived in area through winter of 1955–1956. N.Y. Western end of Long I., "immature" seen Sept. 28–Oct. 5, 1946. ONT. Near Port Arthur (n. shore of L. Superior), found dead July 18, 1892.

Elsewhere A derivation of the Fla. stock inhabits Cuba and Isla de la Juventud [Isle of Pines]. Accidental in Jamaica.

MEXICO Apparently rare in n. Baja Calif. Elsewhere across the n. interior, obser-vations of A. R. Phillips indicate that by the 1970s one could travel long distances in summer without seeing this bird—that is, an obvious decline. PACIFIC IS. Extinct on Guadalupe (off cent. Baja Calif.), occurs on Santa Margarita and probably San Ignacio (s. Baja Calif.), and the Tres Marias (off coast of Nayarit). [Socorro I. (far at sea sw. from the Tres Marias)—listed as occurring by Friedmann (1950: 508), an error probably based on some early source.]

CENT. AND S. AM. Part of the Cent. and all of the S. Am. mainland is included on E. R. Blake's (1977) map, but the bird is absent from large areas. Island distribution off the Venezuelan coast includes Aruba, Curaçao, and Bonaire (Netherlands Leeward Is.), Margarita and Blanquilla (only indigenous bird of prey there), and Trinidad, but evidently not recorded from Tobago. Far s., at the Falklands, not reported by Darwin in 1833–1834 (the negative is hard to prove); currently widespread, presumably rely-ing on refuse from sheep farming; only locally common (R.W. Woods 1975). (Another caracara, the Johnny Rook *Polyborus australis*, also occurs there and Darwin reported it plentiful.) Southernmost range: part of Tierra del Fuego.

The species is recorded as **fossil** from the Pleistocene of Peru, Ecuador, Brazil, and Argentina, and from a **prehistoric site** each in Tex. and Fla. (Brodkorb 1964, with additions). The fossil record is interesting. The presumed precursor (*P. prelutosus*) of our present caracara was widely distributed in Pleistocene time. At least 1 caracara (*P. creightoni* Brodkorb), named from the Bahamas, occurred in the W. Indies. Also, a "problematical" form is recorded from Puerto Rico (Pregill and Olson 1981).

RALPH S. PALMER

MIGRATION The species—quite sedentary, with some dispersal of young birds. Pairs appear to occupy the same large territory, which includes nest sites, all year. The young wander after leaving the family group; prebreeders occasionally form aggregations (J. Layne). In Tex. long ago, Merrill (1878) thought that there were more birds in winter than summer, from an influx of young birds.   RALPH S. PALMER

BANDING STATUS Such Fla. banding as has been done has not resulted in any published information. Very few have been banded in Tex. and almost none in Ariz.
                                                                         RALPH S. PALMER

REPRODUCTION Much remains unknown; the data from our area are bolstered with other information.

Age when **first breeds** unknown; a "subadult" (sex?) collected in Curaçao had "active gonads" (Voous 1957). A "subadult" ♀ taken in Argentina had enlarged gonads (C. M. White).

Display In Costa Rica an adult with a large lizard was joined almost immediately by another bird. The owner lifted the carcass in its beak at each hesitant approach of the other bird and withdrew a few steps. Later they stood "obliquely opposite one another," and both performed the RATTLE-CALL-WITH-HEAD-TOSS, uttering a bass croak as each bird's head moved backward until the crown rested on the upper back. The 1st bird continued to guard the prey if the 2d came near, but the lizard came apart so that each could feed on a portion. Each bird's crop protruded like a yellow golf ball (Slud 1980). In Sonora, Mexico: While the head rested on the back, throat feathers were fluffed out, and the bird uttered a peculiar grating call 3 times. This was repeated within a min. The other adult, possibly ♀, stood still. The 1st then seemed to search for food, and then they ambled off (Tinkham 1948). Such actions presumably relate to **pair formation**. Mates preening each other (Kilham 1979) may relate to bond maintenance.

In Costa Rica a pair already nesting was never heard to call, except for a 1-syllabled greeting, or to have any display flight (Kilham). Yet a bird may call in alarm, as when driving another Caracara from the vicinity of the nest. In Fla., pairs associate year-round and occupy a more or less exclusive home range (Layne, in Kale 1978); it is about 5 mi. in diam., and the birds often make extended flights of 1 mi. or more (Layne).

Nest site In the U.S. on the plains it is in low bushes, but along forested river bottoms it may be 40–50 ft. from the ground (A. K. Fisher 1893). Typically it is in the crown of a solitary tree or a high tree in a grove, commanding a wide view. In Fla., of some 40–50 nests seen, all were in cabbage palms except 3 in oaks and 1 in a pine (Nicholson 1928a). A nest in a large, solitary pine was illus. in Bent (1938, plate 23). In Tex., in live oaks, huisache, cabbage palm, even hackberry; 1, 8 ft. (2.4 m.) from the ground, in crotch of a Spanish dagger yucca; 1 on branches of a sapling under larger trees (Bent). In desert regions, sometimes on branches of giant cactus. Reportedly nests on cliffs (Bent), but no definite records from our area. In Ecuador, usually high in trees, also early reports (cited in Marchant 1960) of nesting on the ground and under overhanging stones. In palms (*Copernica tectorum*) in ne. Venezuela (Mader 1981). On Curaçao, occasionally on the highest installations of an oil refinery (van der Werf, in Voous 1957). In the Falklands on cliffy places. Everywhere, requisites are command of a wide view plus an elevated perch not far away for the mate's guard site.

Nest Among the Falconidae, only caracaras build nests. The Crested Caracara usually builds its own, which is often refurbished and reused, but may occasionally occupy and refurbish a hawk nest. Thus the nests become layered in structure and very bulky. Although the last annual additions may be of finer material, there is no real lining.

In Tex., birds came each Jan., 1955–1959, to a nest in a live oak (Dillon 1961). Of 35 Tex. nests examined, ⅔ were reoccupied annually, but whether by former owners was unknown (Schultze 1904). Also Tex., 30 (of 35) nests examined by Brandt were composed entirely of broomweed; 2 others contained fine briers as well; 3 others contained corn husks, small sticks, broomweed, mesquite sticks, and so on. Nests were bulky, with deep cavities, and usually showed successive layers (Bent 1938). Other Tex. nests have contained trash, dry dung, and pieces of mammal hide. In Costa Rica, in addition to bringing sticks, only bones and tendons were delivered on 7 visits (Kilham 1979). A Tex. nest in a solitary huisache in a wet meadow contained some 50 nests of the Great-tailed Grackle, with 7 of these crowded underneath the Caracara's (Brandt, in Bent). Fla.—nest of "green tough bushes, broken off by the birds," also briers, in a heap and trampled until sometimes "quite a decent hollow" is formed; sometimes some **greenery**—a few green leaves or pieces of grapevine—are added (Nicholson 1928a).

There are no data on duration of construction or refurbishing other than that work evidently begins promptly on occupation or reoccupation of the site.

One **egg** each from 20 clutches (Tex. 14, Fla. 6) **size** length 59.15 ± 2.78 mm., breadth 46.65 ± 1.38, radii of curvature of ends 20.59 ± 1.09 and 12.17 ± 1.52; **shape** usually short subelliptical, elongation 1.26 ± 0.050, bicone -0.120, and asymmetry $+0.226$ (F. W. Preston). Fifty-seven eggs av. 59.4×46.5 mm. (Bent) and they varied considerably in size. The shell is smooth; **color** is in 2 layers, the inner varying from very pale to (usually) a medium brownish, more or less (sometimes almost completely) covered with fine markings to blotches and patches of darker browns—somewhat resembling the eggs of the Peregrine Falcon and Merlin. Rarely, an egg is nearly plain.

Clutch size Two or 3 eggs, more often 2, rarely 4 (Bent). At some 35 Tex. nests, ⅔ had clutches of 3, the remainder 2 (Brandt, in Bent).

Egg dates For presumably viable eggs: Fla.—30 records Dec. 28–Apr. 7 (15 of these Jan. 30–Feb. 28); Tex.—80 records Jan. 30–June 4 (40 of these Mar. 15–Apr. 18); Mexico—10 records Mar. 2–Aug. 10 (5 of these Mar. 6–May 10) (Bent 1938); see also below.

Incubation Bent stated that it is by both sexes. Most likely it is at least preponderantly by the ♀, with the ♂ overseeing from an elevated perch.

Incubation period Thirty-two days (Glazier, in I. Newton 1979), probably determined in captivity; "about 30 days" (Layne, in Kale 1978) in Fla. Both of these are longer than stated in Bent.

Nestling period In the dry season (late Jan.) in Costa Rica, when 2 nestlings were nearing flight age, the adults brought food at a rate of slightly more than once an hr. It was torn apart and presented bit by bit, most being freshly killed—that is, little carrion. A decapitated cotton rat was delivered in the feet. Since both parents were at the nest after 1 fetched food, possibly both fed there, along with the young (Richmond 1976). In 26 hrs. of observation at that nest, items delivered included: 3 jacanas and an unidentified bird, a peccary lower jaw and a cotton rat, 8 lizards (3 genera), a large frog,

2 small fishes, a tarantula or large insect, and 3 pieces of unidentified carrion (Richmond). At another Costa Rican nest, of 13 items delivered, 11 definitely and 2 probably were birds, all partially plucked or dismembered; 2 presumably were teal (taken alive or found dead?); the pair also fed on carrion (Kilham 1979).

The nestling period is 42+ days (Glasier, in I. Newton 1979); young **attain flight** "at about 8 weeks of age" (Layne, in Kale 1978).

Family groups In Tex., stayed in the vicinity of the nest for some time, hence nesting success was easy to determine—2 young each year 1955–1959 except 1 in 1958. Families could be seen until late June or July when they departed, and none were seen thereafter until nesters returned the following Jan. (Dillon 1961).

Is the Caracara double-brooded? Or does it have a discontinuous or prolonged breeding season? The evidence is not clear. A Fla. nest contained a nestling estimated at about age 5 weeks on Dec. 27 (indicating laying in Oct.); on the following Apr. 7 the nest contained another set of eggs, but whether by the same parents was unknown (J. Howell, in Bent, 1938; H. Schroder 1947). Sonora, Mexico—nesting is in late summer, but also in spring (L. Short 1974). Baja Calif., Mexico—nest with 2 young a few hrs. old on July 26 (Brewster 1902) would seem to be out of phase with the expected breeding season. Costa Rica—flying young were still receiving parental care when a pair was seen copulating (Slud 1980). Northeastern Venezuela—pair copulating the last week of Apr., and young apparently just out of the nest the last week of Sept. (Friedmann and Smith 1950).   RALPH S. PALMER

SURVIVAL   No data from the wild; a captive lived 30 years.   RALPH S. PALMER

HABITS   The species. The following excerpts from information at hand clearly reveal the Caracara to be a versatile opportunist.

Aerial hunting The bird may fly at moderate height, searching for live prey to pursue or for carrion; in low harrierlike flight it likely flushes some prey at very close range and so takes it by surprise. Many aerial hunts, once begun, continue as long and persistent chases, successful and otherwise. In Tex. it quarters over highways at daybreak, earlier than the vultures, to feed on animals killed by traffic during the night (Glazener 1964); it does the same in Fla., where it may, in turn, be hit by speeding traffic (Layne, in Kale 1978). It seeks road carrion in Mexico (G. Sutton and Burleigh 1940), in Venezuela (Friedmann and Smith 1950), in Argentina (C. M. White), and undoubtedly elsewhere. In Bolivia it followed moving trains to seize bits of meat that the trainmen held out on sticks (Eisentraut 1935).

Flapping rate In Fla. in summer, 3.3 wingbeats/sec. (C. H. Blake).

Bird catching In Nuevo León, Mexico, neither A. M. Sada nor A. R. Phillips has ever seen a Caracara catch or even pursue a bird; further, Phillips cannot recall ever seeing small birds appear agitated by the Caracara's presence. Others have had similar experience, which has given rise to the notion that perhaps only injured birds are taken. In Tex., the abundant Scissor-tailed Flycatcher pestered the Caracaras—even riding on their backs for a mi., leaving behind a wake of pulled feathers (Brandt, in Bent 1938). In ne. Venezuela, a Caracara used its feet to capture an injured Fork-tailed Flycatcher and its beak to kill it (Friedmann and Smith 1955). In Cuba long ago,

Gundlach reported a White Ibis overcome and killed (Barbour 1923). In Argentina, several pursued and killed an egret (Hudson 1920). On the Argentine pampas it has captured the S. Lapwing (*Vanellus chilensis*) (Hudson 1920, Myers 1978). In Fla., preying on Cattle Egrets appears to be a regular occurrence, especially in winter and early spring (dry season), when the Caracaras have high energy demands for nesting (Layne et al. 1977). (See also cooperative hunting, below.) In the Netherlands Leeward Is. it is said to catch domestic fowl by nonchalantly crossing a farmyard and taking its prey by surprise (Voous 1957).

It eats any available eggs, or occasional nestlings, that it finds. In Argentina in mid-Oct., at a nest of the Chimango Caracara (*Polyborus chimango*), Crested Caracaras made a large hole in each of the 4 eggs and ate the contents. At intervals they erected their crests and half-spread their wings—apparently a posture of menace—and the flying pair of Chimangos kept their distance (Azetegui 1975).

Pirating food It robs various raptors (and the Caracaras rob each other—Merrill 1878, later authors) and pelicans, and D. Evans (1982) added gulls. A few examples will suffice: In Fla., a Bald Eagle carrying what appeared to be a marsh rabbit was pursued by a Caracara, 2 vultures, and many crows; the outcome was not observed (in Bent 1938). Similar interactions of several raptors, including Caracaras, were recently reported in Fla. (Paulson 1985). Crows forced a N. Harrier to drop its prey, which was seized by the leading crow, only to be lost to a Caracara (Savary, in Bent). In Tex., it robbed a harrier without an intervenor (K. Hamilton 1981). In ne. Venezuela, 1 forced a White-tailed Hawk to drop a large lizard (Friedmann and Smith 1950). In Tex., Caracaras drove Turkey Vultures into flight from carrion. In each of 4 instances the Caracara pursued until the vulture disgorged, some of the food being seized in midair; in 3 instances the Caracara also alighted to feed on the fallen food (Glazener 1964). On an is. in Laguna Madre, Tex., the Caracaras ignored outward-bound Brown Pelicans, but homecoming laden ones were harassed over land; the Caracaras attacked with shrill screams, and the pelicans disgorged their food (Goss, in Bendire 1892).

Possible cooperative hunting In Tex., the Crested Caracara was commonly seen in couples to hunt prairie dogs (Lloyd 1887). In Sonora, Mexico, a Caracara remained hidden while another danced before a young lamb, purportedly (Lloyd, in Bendire 1892) trying to entice it away from its mother; the lamb began to follow, but the ewe called it back. In 3 of 4 aerial hunts for birds in ne. Mexico, a Caracara would initiate pursuit and would then be joined by another. In 1 case, members of the duo alternated in making passes at a Brown Jay. The other 3 hunts, for Cattle Egrets, failed, but there was other evidence of predation on them (Whitacre et al. 1982).

Terrestrial hunting About midway down the Baja Calif. Pen. in Apr., a dozen or more Caracaras followed closely behind a tractor; they seemed to be seeking insects, mice, and probably lizards. They leapfrogged over one another, hopped aside when the tractor turned to go in the opposite direction, and continued to follow. They seemed to play as they worked back and forth, chasing each other, engaging in mock battles, being agile both afoot and just above the ground (Wiggins 1969). They have also followed vehicles in S. Am.

In Sonora, Mexico, in Mar., 1 pulled a small log aside and started scratching for insects like a hen (Tinkham 1948). The now-extinct Guadalupe birds scratched similarly (in Ridgway 1876). In Honduras one scratched among semi-dried cow dung (G. C. Taylor 1860). In Guatemala there was an "invasion" of grasshoppers, and 12 Caracaras fed on them in much the same manner as turkeys (Griscom 1932). In ne. Venezuela in Dec., some 75 assembled on a golf course to eat beetle larvae that had reached plague proportions (Friedmann and Smith 1955). On the Tres Marias Is. off w. Mexico they were often encountered in thick woods, walking about in search of snakes and lizards (Grayson 1872). Probably many small rodents, such as cotton rats (*Sigmodon*) in Tex., are stalked afoot; they are eaten there in quantity (A. K. Fisher 1893).

In Fla., Sprunt, Jr. (1946), saw a yellow-bellied turtle completing the process of laying and burying its eggs on the bank of a drainage canal. Returning 20 min. later he saw a Caracara digging out and eating the eggs, which the bird perhaps watched the turtle lay and cover. In Panama, turtles lay in holes they dig in slopes above a marsh; Caracaras seek the nests, scrape them open with their feet, and eat the contents of the eggs; the emptied shells are a common sight (A. Wetmore 1965).

Fishing By wading in shallow water. They were repeatedly seen fishing in Sonora, Mexico (Lloyd, in Bendire 1892). There are several other reports, as Barbour (1923) for Cuba, and fish have been seen being delivered to the nest.

Transporting items In Fla. a bird made 8 trips to the nest always carrying food in the beak; at the nest, a small turtle was held with the feet and dismembered with the beak (Grimes, in Bent). In ne. Venezuela, 2 Caracaras were eating a dead iguana; when approached, 1 grasped the large lizard with its feet and flew 50 yds., which is unusual, since they commonly carry objects in their beaks (Friedmann and Smith 1955). Heavier nesting material (and prey) is carried in the feet and small items in the beak.

Versus livestock The raising of sheep or goats (or cattle) in large numbers is usually a monoculture, or sole crop in an area. With sheep, this provides dying and dead ones and seasonally a percentage of unhealthy and stillborn lambs—an artificial food supply that favors the birds but has resulted in many decades of relentless persecution. Such has been the situation in sheep-farming areas on the mainland from the s. U.S. to the remotest parts of S. Am. and on various is., including the Falklands. The believable allegations include attacking ewes in labor (R. Peterson 1961, A. W. Johnson 1965, others) and pecking out the eyes of young lambs; on Guadalupe, pecking out the eyes of a burro caught between rocks. Most explicit was Johnson, writing of s. S. Am. He stated that the birds gather around and wait for opportunities to separate newly born lambs from their mothers. Attacking from the ground, 1st they peck out the eyes, then kill with the beak. They also eat the placenta. In winter they attack weakened sheep, pecking out eyes and tongue. Hence—as elsewhere—a price on the Caracara's head. (See also d'Orbigny 1835.) An Argentine rancher claimed to have set fire to 100s of its nests (Peterson).

On Guadalupe they were said to feed on live kids as well as skinned goat carcasses (and other foods).

In the Falklands, in addition to feeding at livestock carcasses, it is said to attack a newly fallen sheep; this gives a sheep a stimulus to stay on its feet, thus resulting in its survival where shepherds are scarce (R. W. Woods 1975).

In s. Baja Calif., 120–150 were seen daily in midafternoon at a slaughterhouse where pigs were butchered. Turkey Vultures also came then and in the morning (the Black

Vulture does not occur there). When the Caracaras were not feeding, each of the many tall cacti thereabouts was apt to have a Caracara perched on top (A. R. Phillips).

In ne. Venezuela, both the Caracara and vultures come to foul carrion, the former apparently to feed more on the associated insect larvae (Friedmann and Smith 1950). A similar supposition is reiterated by Glazener (1964) from observations in Tex.

Sunning The Caracara may perch for hours in an exposed place, with ruffled feathering and half-spread wings (A. K. Fisher 1893). In Fla., Layne has never seen this posture; at most, they open their beaks, compress the feathering, and allow their wings to droop slightly at the "shoulders." In ne. Venezuela the Caracara has a habit reminiscent of anting by Passerine birds. It sits on its haunches in the dust, tail outspread and flat in support of its body, and head erect; locally, it was said to be "refreshing itself" (Friedmann and Smith 1950).

Mutual preening Mentioned under Reproduction, above. In Tex. it has preened with a Black Vulture (NG and Jesperson 1984).

Wariness By and large, where persecuted, Caracaras tend to keep their distance. In other situations they come to cultivated areas, even farmyards, and they fly, scolding, directly toward a collector and are shot. In Fla., they often perch along roadsides close to moving traffic. Some will remain if a vehicle stops nearby, even allowing a person to approach close on foot (Juv. birds are more likely to do this); others take wing (J. Layne).

Captivity There was a Caracara from Aruba in the Schönbrunn Zoo, Vienna, as early as 1784 (Jacquin, cited in Voous 1957).

In Cuba long ago, Gundlach kept 1 as a free-living pet for 15 years (Barbour 1923).

A man named Drent captured 4 birds on Guadalupe I. and transported them to Calif. He stated that they were easily domesticated, did not allow strangers near them, were fed raw meat, and would come to him when called (C. G. Abbott 1933).

In the Dresden zoo, 2 were hatched and reared in 1927, 2 nestlings were lost in 1928, and the next year 2 were hatched and reared (Flower, in Prestwich 1955). Presently, there are about 3 score in the world's zoos.

W. J. Hoxie of Ga. had a pair that became very tame. After Hoxie had been absent for several years, the ♂ escaped, and Hoxie was then able to call it down from a tall tree and return it to confinement. Some years later, when the bird was about 12 years old, it made a fuss when Hoxie visited it, and so he pacified it by scratching its head through the bars of its cage (Bent 1938).

In the spring of 1955 a Caracara escaped from Highland Park Zoo in Pittsburgh, Pa. It wandered for a while, then wintered in the Oakland district, roosting with pigeons among the ornamental architecture on buildings. Although there was some traffic-killed food (cottontails, squirrels, pigeons, probably rats), it was seen feeding on pigeons more often than could be accounted for from the number of available dead ones. It survived a fairly cold winter, began wandering in spring, and vanished (K. C. Parkes).

Folklore In fulfillment of an ancient omen, in A.D. 1325 the Tenocha tribe of Aztecs began to build the city of Tenochtitlán on a rise of land within the lake where Mexico City presently stands. The omen was an eagle perched on a cactus devouring a snake—the Mexican Eagle, or Caracara, the national emblem of Mexico today. (The

adapted from von Hagen (1957)

"most sumptuous city ever raised by indigenous man in the Americas" (von Hagen 1957) was destroyed by Cortez in 1521.)

The notion prevails in Ecuador and Peru that the Caracara, mated with domestic fowl, produces fierce fighting cocks (Marchant 1960).

Status and history   In our mainland area, the Caracara's range is somewhat diminished and its numbers have declined. Although protected by law, it is a fine, large, conspicuous, frequently unwary, and tempting target. A dead one, most unfortunately, can no longer participate in the sanitation roles of scavenging or prey on rodents and harmful insects. In Fla., the major threat to it is habitat loss.

On Guadalupe, off the Baja Calif. mainland, the local Caracaras were 1st made known to science in 1876 from specimens taken the previous year and became extinct just about ¼ century later. All that remains is about 40 specimens, at least 1 skeleton, and a couple of eggs of questionable provenance. Aside from those taken by collectors, they were shot and poisoned by goat farmers (W. Bryant 1887)—one of the "few cases of a bird population having been purposefully extirpated by man" (Greenway 1958). For the brief, unhappy recorded history of these is. birds, see especially W. Bryant (1887), C. G. Abbott (1933), and Greenway (1958).   RALPH S. PALMER

FOOD   Of the species. Sherrod (1978) summarized 8 sources, not including many scattered items of interest. Seldom is it possible to ascertain from a digestive tract whether a bird captured an item or found it already dead. Audubon's captives "fed indifferently on dead and living animals"—rats, cats, various fowls. Various information given above is relevant here. Below is a condensation from references at hand, listing not every recorded item and few of the sources.

Carrion   If available, usually comprises some portion of the diet. It is insignificant or entirely lacking in various times and places. Offal at slaughterhouses, burial pits, and wherever discarded. Sheep, goats, and pigs that have died or are incapacitated, especially the very young. Skinned carcasses. The kills of other predators. Injured and dead traffic victims of all sorts. Some specualtion that, at foul carrion, the birds may be more interested in the attendant insects and larvae.

Mammals   The larger species, especially, both as carrion and alive: skunks, jackrabbits, cottontails (widely), prairie dogs, ground squirrels, tree (fox) squirrel (carrion?), rats (partly carrion), cotton rats, and numerous "mice."

Birds   Taken alive include: White Ibis, an egret, Cattle Egrets, S. Lapwings, grown and young domestic fowl, Rock Dove, and various birds approximately from large jay down to bunting size. Blue-winged Teal and Pectoral Sandpiper, both perhaps as carrion. Dead petrels (Guadalupe I., formerly), dead penguin (Falklands). Bird eggs and nestlings—perhaps more often than realized.

Reptiles   Young alligators (alive, dead), lizards alive or dead and in size up to include *Cnemidophorus* and *Iguana,* various snakes (most captured are rather small), and numerous live turtles (from a few in. long to only recently hatched). Turtle eggs where available.

Amphibians   Bullfrog (Audubon), other frogs.

Fishes   Small ones—live, stranded, dead, and (Fla.) occasionally some discarded by fishermen.

Invertebrates   Beetles, grasshoppers, crickets, assorted larvae, ticks on mammals (2 or 3 authors), "hard-shelled worms" (Audubon), crabs, crayfish, any edible material exposed by falling tide or stranded—as shellfish and (Falklands) an octopus.

Vegetable   In Suriname, along with Black Vultures, 2 Caracaras came and fed on the drying flesh of coconuts (Haverschmidt 1947).   RALPH S. PALMER

KESTREL; EURASIAN KESTREL

Falco tinnunculus

A small true falcon with "toothed" upper mandible; length about 12–14 in. (31–36 cm.); rather long tailed—4¾–6 in. (12–15 cm.); wingspread to over 26 in. (66 cm.); usual wt. about 6–9 oz. (170–250 gm.). The 2 outermost primaries are deeply notched (emarginated) on the inner side; counting from the outermost, #1 and #4 are about equal in length and decidedly shorter than #2 (longest) and #3 (nearly as long as #2). Feathering soft and lax; coloration of the sexes conspicuously different after the Juv. stage (especially different head coloring and tail pattern); ♀ av. slightly larger than ♂.

▶ ♂ Def. Basic Plumage **head** slaty with narrow black malar stripe ("mustache" mark) and whitish chin–throat; **dorsum** some variant of reddish brown with scattered longitudinal black markings; **venter** buffy or pale tan with elongated to more or less transverse dark markings; **tail** slaty or bluish with wide black subterminal band and white tip. ♀ Def. Basic **head** mostly muted browns with hint of a "mustache"; **dorsum** reddish brown with heavy transverse dark barring; **venter** brownish buff with much dark longitudinal marking; **tail** palish tawny-chestnut to rather grayish with numerous narrow blackish bars, a wide subterminal bar, and white tip. ♂ ♀ Juv. more or less like ♀ Def. Basic, but tail barring heavier. ♂ ♀ Basic I and II are said (Witherby et al. 1939) to be intermediate stages toward Def. Basic.

This little falcon might possibly be confused with the ♂ Merlin, but much more likely with the Am. Kestrel (which see). Some 11 subspecies are recognized (wide-

250

spread in Eurasia and Africa, including on various is.); 2 recorded in our area. In Transcaucasia, USSR, where both Kestrel and Lesser Kestrel (*F. naumanni*) are colonial, mixed colonies occur, and hybrids from Osmolovskaya are in the Zool. Mus., Moscow Univ. (Dementiev and Gladkov 1951, trans. 1966). A captive produced ♂ *tinnunculus* × ♀ *naumanni* is reported.   RALPH S. PALMER

DISTRIBUTION   Much of Eurasia, Africa, and various is. This falcon is migratory (n. birds) to resident (in warmer climates). The following records and reports must be considered with due regard for a likelihood of more or less assisted passage (transport aboard ship, etc.) and the possibility of escapees; no evaluation is made here of various alleged sightings.

Atlantic, in our area   GREENLAND   C. Farewell (Winge 1898), questioned by Bent (1938) but accepted by Salomonsen (1951).

MASS.   Nantasket Beach in town of Hull, ♀ shot Sept. 29, 1887 (correct details in Forbush 1927); it is a Juv.-feathered *F. t. tinnunculus* Linnaeus (Pinchon and Vaurie 1961). Possibly a natural occurrence. (This falcon has occasionally been imported.) There is no indication of oil or grease on the preserved skin.

N.J.   Ne. of C. May Pt., Juv. ♀ livetrapped, photographed, banded, and released Sept. 23, 1972; petroleum-based grease on underparts suggests assisted passage (1973 *Am. Birds* **27** 37, W. S. Clark 1974). This species reportedly seen at C. May on Oct. 9, 14, and 15, 1979 (1980 *Am. Birds* **34** 145, C. Sutton 1980).

Atlantic, outside our area   The following are of some interest. In the e. Atlantic this little falcon occurs over water and makes some crossings there; fairly frequent instances of resting or traveling aboard ship are to be expected,

LESSER ANTILLES   W. coast of Martinique at Le Carbet, an "adult" ♀ in exhausted condition and extremely emaciated was taken by hand on Dec. 9, 1959; it soon died and was preserved (Pinchon and Vaurie 1961). ICELAND   Most common "accidental" falconiform species—some 30 records, 11 being specimens (Oct. 21, 1903, and thereafter) (A. Petersen). FAEROES   Rare vagrant (Salomonsen, in A. S. Jensen et al. 1934). SPITZBERGEN AREA   1 came aboard a vessel e. of Bear I., Aug. 7, 1924; saved as a specimen (Løvenskiold 1963). AZORES   At least 4 records.

Pacific-Bering   ALASKA   Outermost Aleutians. Shemya—*F. t. interstinctus* McClelland, "immature" ♀ Sept. 5 and 9 (when collected), 1978; and a "similarly-plumaged" individual seen Oct. 2–6, 1978 (Gibson 1981). Attu—♂ seen May 4 and 7, 1981 (1981 *Am. Birds* **35** 853) and this species also in summer of 1984.

CANADA   Cariboo region of B. C.—♂ taken at Alkali L., Dec. 10, 1946 (R. W. Campbell 1985).

DETAILS LACKING   ♀ boarded a ship bound from Japan to Humboldt Bay, Calif. The specimen was turned over to Humboldt State Univ. about 1978 and was seen in 1979 by C. M. White, who suggested it might be *F. t. interstictus* on basis of dark coloration.   RALPH S. PALMER

OTHER TOPICS   This small falcon is best known for hovering, in the manner of the Am. Kestrel, when seeking prey. Thus it is conspicuous and not particularly shy, in open and even in suburban terrain. Like its Am. counterpart, it is seen at airports.

Usual clutch size is 4-5 eggs, laid on a sheltered shelf on a cliff, in old nests of large birds, on ledges of buildings, etc. Incubation is mostly by the ♀, period 28 days; the nestling period is up to 32 days; the young become independent some 4 weeks thereafter. A common and available raptor, it has been much studied in Europe, Britain, and elsewhere. The 1954 monograph on it by Piechocki was in its 6th rev. ed. in 1982.

RALPH S. PALMER

AMERICAN KESTREL

Falco sparverius

Formerly called Sparrow Hawk, but it is a falcon (and 2 *Accipiter* species are called Sparrow-Hawk, *nisus* in the Old World and *bicolor* in lower Cent. and S. Am.).

Our smallest, and rather trim, falcon. The usual "toothed" falcon beak; wings long, pointed, the 2 outer primaries with inner webs emarginated, and, counting from the outer, the 2d and 3d primaries nearly equal in length and longest, the outermost much shorter; tail about ⅔ as long as wing and rounded; tarsus feathered in front for approximately upper ⅓; feathering overall soft but compact. The sexes from Juv. stage onward are conspicuously different, the ♀ remaining essentially as Juv. throughout life. Two black bars down side of head, varying in the species from wide and conspicuous (as usually in our area) to much reduced, and a black spot or patch on side of nape. Rich coloration includes some slaty on head, also wings of ♂ (and some are darker outside our area), dorsum variably reddish-rusty (to darker), and tail same, variously barred dark (to black) depending on sex and geographical area. It is commonly stated that there are 2 color phases—light and dark (reddish)—but they are bridged by intermediates, the extremes being most dissimilar in Cuba.

In temperate N. Am.: ♂ length about 8¾–10½ in. (21.5–26.5 cm.), wingspread 20–22 in. (51–56 cm.); and ♀ length about 9–12 in. (23–30.5 cm.), wingspread 22½–24 in. (57–61 cm.). The ♂ weighs 3–5 oz., av. 3⅗ (80–143 gm., av. 103) and ♀ 3–5⅘ oz., av. 4⅕ (86–165, av. 120 gm.). The birds are considerably smaller in the Gulf states. The larger and smaller birds of our area combined include approximately the total size range of all the birds elsewhere.

Currently recognized are 3 subspecies in our area including Baja, Calif., and 14 elsewhere; combined breeding range extends from Alaska and Canada to Tierra del Fuego.

DESCRIPTION   *F. s. sparverius* of most of *Handbook* area. As far as is known, differs from our other native falcons in that **1** the sexes differ markedly from the Juv. stage onward, and **2** the Juv. feathering (other than most flight feathers and a few body feathers) is molted in fall of year of hatching (into Basic I). Then, beginning in 2d calendar year of life, there is a renewal of all feathering annually—1 Plumage/cycle. Plumages are described here first, beginning with Basic II, then molting at end.

▶ ♂ Basic II and later Plumages (all feathering) acquired in SUMMER–FALL and retained a year.

Beak bluish tipped black; cere and eyelids yellow (or toward orange), **iris** dark brownish. **Head** upper sides and top slaty bluish with rufous crown patch (varies from large to small, occasionally lacking); sides of face and throat white or very pale, anterior of side with black stripe ("mustache" mark) down it, rear of white area bordered with parallel black stripe, and behind that (toward rear side of neck in an area usually buffy-tan or matching dorsum) a black spot. These last, as viewed from the rear, resemble a pair of ocelli, or "false eyes." There is individual variation in size of head markings, especially the "mustache." **Upperparts** some variant of rufous, the anterior dorsum rarely with any markings, the larger scapulars and interscapular region with many to few (rarely no) black bars or spots. **Underparts** vary from nearly white toward reddish buff (usually much lighter than back), becoming paler posteriorly, with black streaks and spots rarely on breast and most numerous and largest on flanks. Legs and **feet** yellow, talons black. **Tail** variably rufous dorsally (as back), much paler ventrally, with black subterminal band (usually wide) and white or grayed brownish tip; other tail markings exceptionally variable, but outer feather usually, and outer web of next often, white with black patches; often there are black spots or black-spotted white areas along margins of remaining feathers. **Wing** upper coverts and parts of secondaries slaty-blue, usually with black spots; primaries black with white patches on inner and sometimes outer webs; all flight feathers of wing tipped with white or pale grayish when new; axillars and wing lining white, barred or spotted black.

▶ ♀ Basic II and later Plumages (all feathering) acquired in SUMMER–FALL and retained a year.

Beak, eye, and **head** much as ♂, with similar individual variation. **Upperparts** and **tail** some variant of rufous, barred black (this reduced on rump, upper tail coverts, and outer **tail** feathers), tail tip white or toward buff. **Underparts** basal color less vivid than in ♂, streaked (usually quite evenly and heavily) with some shade of brownish except plain posteriorly. Legs and **feet** as ♂ or paler. **Wing** upper coverts as back; primaries and secondaries blackish with light rufous spots on inner web, and all are tipped whitish or pale rufous in unworn condition; axillars and wing lining white, heavily barred or spotted rufous.

AT HATCHING   The pink skin is covered with short, silvery-white down. The

254

"tooth" in the beak is already evident; the nestling's eyes are open, and it can grasp with its feet. The later, longer down is also white. Last remnants of the 1st down usually wear off the tips of the Juv. feathers around age 30 days.

▶ ♂ ♀ Juv. Plumage (entire feathering) acquired during nestling period, then (at least as known in ♂ ♂) almost all of head–body and some inner secondaries molted in 1st FALL and remainder beginning in following SUMMER (Parkes 1955). Iowa data: age 7 days—Juv. pinfeathers show; 16 days—feathers out of sheaths enough so that sexes distinguishable; 26–29 days—initial flight (See also Reproduction, below.)

The sexes differ greatly, approximating older birds of corresponding sex, but note these predefinitive characteristics: ♂ **1** streaking and spotting on upper breast; **2** dark barring on anterior dorsum; **3** tips of tail feathers, especially central pair, usually pinkish buff; and **4** brownish crown-patch feathers have well-marked gray centers; then **1**, **2**, and **4** disappear in 1st-fall molting and **3** is obscured by wear—1st-winter birds may be distinguishable by relatively greater tail-wear. The ♀ is not always separable with certainty from subsequent Basics, but the following criteria seem to be typical of most individuals: **1** crown with heavy shaft streaks, the reddish brown and blue-gray areas poorly defined and blended; **2** subterminal black band of tail typically no wider than those anterior to it (except perhaps on central pair of feathers); **3** ventral streaks tend to be broader (but much individual variation) and less sharply defined.

▶ ♂ ♀ Basic I Plumage (almost all of head–body and usually inner feathers of wing) acquired (at least in ♂ ♂) mainly in SEPT.–OCT. of 1st calendar year of life. Sex for sex, as later Basics, except worn with retained Juv. flight feathers. The new feathering, rich in coloring like later Basics, is retained until SUMMER–FALL of 2d calendar year of life, when all feathering is replaced during Prebasic II molting.

Molting This is our only native raptor that molts out of much Juv. feathering in fall of hatching year (although a similar schedule is evident in other small *Falco* and at least 1 kite). Many Kestrels first breed as yearlings (2d calendar year of life), by then evidently being on the usual raptor schedule of beginning molting concurrently with breeding. Also, numerous Kestrels are double brooded at some time in life, but whether this may affect progress of molting is unknown.

Allowing for variance among authors, it appears that wild breeding ♀ ♀ begin molting about at onset of incubating the 1st (or only) clutch of the season, captives some time afterwards, and ♂ ♂ from perhaps a week to over 2 weeks later than their mates.

In captives, Willoughby (1966) noted that molting of flight feathers of wing extended throughout the period of body molting, there were no substantial differences in molting between the sexes, and none between "old and young" birds (included a ♀ that began at age 8½ months). Although there was some individual variation, the same author reported molting sequence as follows (slant line indicates 2 feathers dropped within a day): primaries (counting from inner to outer) #4, 5, 6, 7, 2, 8, 9, 10/1; secondaries #5, 6, 7, 8, 4, 9, 3/10, 1, 2; and tail feathers (center outward) # 1, 2, 3, 6, 4, 5. Wings and tail molt concurrently.

In Calif., 2 wild ♀ ♀ "completedly omitted" molting flight feathers; in others the largest number missing at the same time was 8 (6 wing, 2 tail) in a ♀ with young just out of the nest. She caught prey as readily as her mate (Balgooyen 1976). Kestrels can fly reasonably well without any tail feathers (D. Bird).

NOTES A **gynandromorph**, in feathering part ♂ and part ♀, was taken in N.D. in Apr.; the bird was of ♀ size and was sexed as ♀; the feathering was exceedingly worn, and the bird evidently was not breeding (Brodkorb 1935). Another, with ovary undeveloped and feathering essentially ♂, was taken in Ont. in late Sept. (L. Snyder 1960).

As known for some other raptors, ventral tarsal scale pattern is unique for each individual, even among siblings and parent v. offspring (D. Bird).

At least 3 authors have speculated on possible function of the dark ocelli on sides of the nape; see Balgooyen (1975).

Albinism Not rare. Among 1,952 museum specimens, 1 was "partly albinistic" and 1 entirely white (Roest 1957). A captive ♂ had "normal coloring" until molting "prior to its 8th year," when it became totally white and the new feathering "wore rapidly" (J. Parker 1985). Dark-eyed birds with mostly white feathering have been seen.

So-called **color phases** are bridged by intermediates—that is, better called a tendency to dichromatism. Individuals vary from pale to rufescent (or dark) in N. Am., especially ♂♂. In the species, this variation reaches maximum development in the resident Cuban subspecies, where strikingly different birds are seen in both Juv. and Basic feathering: light—underparts largely whitish, all dark markings much reduced; and dark—underparts deep rufous, back of ♂ sometimes dark slaty like wing coverts. Extremes and intermediates can be present in the same brood. Field count: 28 light, 5 intermediate, and 12 rufescent (D. Davis 1941); museum specimens sorted as 2 categories—38 light and 16 rufescent; and, from Isla de la Juventud [Isle of Pines], 7 light and 1 rufescent (Vaurie 1957).

Measurements *F. s. sparverius* (WING is the usual and probably most useful mensural criterion of subspecies). Breeding season birds (May–July) WING flattened, w. N. Am. 54 ♂ 181–200 mm., av. 187.8, and 44 ♀ 188–206, av. 196.4; and e. U.S. and Canada 22 ♂ av. 186.3 (R. Bond 1943). Also e. U.S. and Canada 12 ♀ 181–203, av. 193.2 (K. Parkes). As far as is known, birds in Juv. feathering are not measurably different from older ones.

Weight A 130-gm. ♀ weighed 179 gm. after gorging on food; hence, except for birds with empty alimentary tract, recorded wts. have little comparative value (R. Bond 1943). The body fat of ♂♂ decreases from Apr. to early Sept., increasing sharply in late Sept.; in ♀♀ it decreased from Apr., to late July, increasing steadily during Sept. (Gessaman 1979b). For responses to food deprivation, see Shapiro and Weathers (1981).

Age classes combined, of birds from B.C. into Mexico 88 ♂ 80–143 gm., mean. 102.5, and 72 ♀ 86–164.8, mean 119 (Roest 1957).

In Calif., live wts. around the year 69 ♂ 111 ± 9.3 gm. and 111 ♀ 120 ± 9.2 (Bloom 1973).

Hybrids In the wild, none known. After cross-fostering with the Eurasian Kestrel and being visually isolated in winter, captives were offered a mate choice. There was no distinct pattern of mating with either their own or the other species (D. Bird).

Variation in the species Individual size variation is considerable. The larger ♀♀ are more variable in size than ♂♂, with great overlap of the sexes. Judging from published meas., the ♂ becomes smaller in relation to ♀ size going s., or at least in S. Am.

256

IN OUR AREA   In coloring, birds of any age in new feathering are essentially alike across N. Am. but become bleached or "sunburnt" (Dwight 1905) in desert areas. Average size decreases from n. to s.; the largest birds occur in interior w. Canada, the smallest (more richly colored, largely resident) birds from s. Ga. through Fla. and w. into La. Size variation westerly was discussed by R. Bond (1943) and easterly by James (1970). In coterminous U.S. and s. Canada, there is an increase in av. clutch size with increase in lat. (Henny 1972).

CENT. AM.   Rather small, dark rufous dorsally, crown patch usually reduced or absent. CUBA AND NEARBY   Slightly larger than the small Fla. birds, greatest disparity between extremes of light and dark individuals. HISPANIOLA   About as temperate N. Am. in size, but paler and with reduced dark markings. OTHER CARIBBEAN IS.   Relatively small, heavily marked. S. AM.   In Guianas and vicinity rather small and pale, wing longer and underparts more richly colored farther w.; from sw. Ecuador to n. Chile, larger, ♂ pale with well-spotted underparts, ♀ vivid rufous dorsally and with considerable white on forehead; in Brazil rather small, variable in pattern and color; farther s., size about as in temperate N. Am., pattern and color variable, both sexes usually with pale collar, dorsum quite highly colored and marked, ♀ often with ends of secondaries and most of inner vanes of primaries white. Juan Fernandez Is. (Pacific Ocean off cent. Chile), ♂♂ variable, much like birds from adjacent mainland, ♀♀ darker and more heavily marked ventrally.

Affinities   This is hypothetical: Ancient falcon stock in S. Am. invaded warmer parts of the Old World, there proliferating into various gray and brown kestrel species. Much more recently, kestrel stock from Eurasia reinvaded the New World, here evolving into our present Kestrel, which spread throughout the Americas and differentiated into 17 subspecies. The Kestrel is unique in that the sexes differ in Juv. Plumage. Its nearest Old World relative may be the Lesser Kestrel (*F. naumanni*).

RALPH S. PALMER

SUBSPECIES   **In our area** presently reduced to 3.

sparverius Linnaeus—descr. and meas. given above; largest breeding range of any subspecies; n. birds are migratory, some wintering in ranges of other subspecies listed below.

paulus (Howe and King)—s. Ga. through Fla. (except lower Fla. Keys) and w. into La.; mostly resident, but some seasonal movement indicated, for example, by occurrence on Fla. Keys where not known to breed. Smaller than *sparverius* (Fla. birds are small extreme of a cline in WING-length, Ga. birds somewhat larger) with relatively larger beak; markings reduced, especially ventrally, where ♂♂ usually almost immaculate. E. G. Holt and Sutton (1926) stated that soft parts are more vividly colored in *paulus* and that field identification is possible due to smaller build, rapid flight, shriller voice. Nearly extirpated from most of its range not long ago, but now considerably recovered. WING flattened of Fla. birds in definitive feathering 15 ♂ 166–180 mm., av. 173.2, and 10 ♀ 175–188, av. 181.9 (meas. by K. Parkes). For clinal variation, see James (1970).

peninsularis Mearns—s. Baja Calif. e. and s. into Sinaloa, Mexico.

Elsewhere   The number of subspecies recognized has changed from 12 (Hellmayr and Conover 1949) to 14 of recent authors, as E. R. Blake (1977), and Amadon (in Mayr and Cottrell 1979), which see for various details. They are listed here going s., with main distribution. None is highly migratory. *tropicalis* (Griscom)—extreme s. Mexico, Guatemala, and n. Honduras; *nicaraguensis* T. Howell—lowland pine savanna in Honduras and Nicaragua; *sparveroides* Vigors—Cuba and Isla de la Juventud [Isle of Pines]; *dominicensis* Gmelin—Hispaniola, including Ile a Vache and Tortue and Gonave Is.; *caribaearum* Gmelin—Puerto Rico, Virgin Is. to Grenada in Lesser Antilles; *brevipennis* (Berlepsch)—Aruba, Curaçao, and doubtfully Bonaire (Netherlands W. Indies); *isabellinus* Swainson—the Guianas, Trinidad (resident?), most of Venezuela and part of adjacent Brazil; *ochraceus* (Cory)—mts. of e. Colombia and nw. Venezuela; *caucae* (Chapman)—w. Colombia in mts. bordering Cauca Valley; *aequatorialis* Mearns—Ecuador n. of Chanchan Valley; *peruvianus* (Cory)—sw. Ecuador, Peru, and extreme n. Chile; *caerae* Cory—tableland of Brazil w. to Bolivian boundary; *fernandensis* (Chapman)—off cent. Chile on Juan Fernandez Is. (Mas Afeura, Mas a Tierra), said to occur also on the Desventuradas (San Ambrosio, San Felix); *cinnamominus* Swainson—w. and s. S. Am. to Tierra del Fuego (partly migratory). RALPH S. PALMER

FIELD IDENTIFICATION **In our area** (but applies to a large extent elsewhere). This is our most numerous falcon, also the smallest (larger than a robin, usually about 9–11 in. long), and the only one (also including small hawks) with reddish tail. It is most similar, especially the ♀, to the Eurasian Kestrel, which is larger, very rare in our area, and discussed earlier in this volume. It might be confused with the Merlin but is separable by the contrasting black-and-white facial markings and reddish back and tail; these differences may not be evident if an Am. Kestrel is soiled or is viewed when strongly backlit. The sexes differ—see Description, above. Note that, with minor modification, the "adult" pattern is present in each sex in all flying ages.

Hovering, which is commonly seen, is conspicuous and diagnostic. The Kestrel usually hovers about 50–100 ft. from the ground and rarely for more than 1 min. If nothing is spotted by the bird, it shifts elsewhere and hovers again. It spends much time perched upright on poles, wires, and buildings; it frequently, especially soon after alighting, pumps its tail and occasionally bobs its head.

Flight speed is slower than the Merlin's (R. Bond 1943) and less purposeful, even though (E. Poole 1938) the Kestrel has less wing area per gm. of wt. W. Stone (1937) described its flight as 7–12 strokes, a short glide, then another set of strokes.

According to Bloom (1973), "young" kestrels cannot be distinguished from "adults" by feathering, contrary to some authors. Yet Juv. ♂♂ are usually heavily streaked ventrally, while older birds have plain anterior underparts. In ♀♀, separation is probably impossible. It must be remembered that young birds lose the Juv. head–body feathering in fall of year of hatching, hence appear to be "adult" even before their 1st winter; see Description, above.

Possibly an experienced observer may be able to identify the smaller birds of s. Ga. and Fla. around into La. to subspecies; see Subspecies, above.

A tendency everywhere for individuals (of both sexes) to vary from lighter through intermediates to darker ones reaches maximum expression in Cuba. The difference there is striking. In light birds, all of the venter is white, the back rusty, and wing coverts slaty; dark ones resemble the Am. Robin, having reddish-rusty venter and dark upperparts.

In Puerto Rico and part of the Lesser Antilles, according to Voous (1955), this species does not hover.

The Am. Kestrel is not compared here with other small raptors of Cent. and S. Am. DAVID M. BIRD

VOICE F. s. sparverius. Limited repertoire, basically of 3 vocalizations and combinations thereof: the klee or killy, the whine, and the chitter.

Individuals vary in tonal quality, pitch, and frequency of notes uttered in series. Generally, voices of ♀♀ are lower pitched and harsher than those of ♂♂, and, according to Willoughby and Cade (1964), larger birds have lower-pitched voices than smaller ones regardless of sex. (This trend is said to be accentuated in the small F. s. paulus, of Fla. and thereabouts.) One most often hears the klee or killy (depends on author) from an excited or stressed bird, such as during aggressive encounters with their own or other species, in aerial displays, or in foiled attempts at catching prey. It generally consists of a rapid series of 3–6 notes and carries quite far.

The whine, which may last as long as 1–2 min., has been divided into simple whine and treble whine (Willoughby and Cade), the latter characterized by higher intensity. The simple whine usually, but not always, has a rising intonation, whereas the treble whine does not. The latter may be broken into 3 distinct segments with a stop before each. Transitions between the 2 extremes reflect intensity of expression. The simple whine is uttered by both sexes during food-passes ("courtship feeding") and copulation, whereas the treble whine is seldom used by the ♂. The latter is used by both the breeding ♀ and flying young begging for food.

The chitter is pulsed at about 20/sec. and is the most frequently used call by both sexes in ♂–♀ interactions. Varying in loudness, duration, and state of arousal, the chitter is associated with "friendly approach" and bodily contact (Willoughby and Cade) during the breeding season. Balgooyen (1976) encountered chitter calls from territorial individuals, indicating some element of aggression or fear due to high stress. He also noted that several whines may be followed instantly by chitters.

A whine-chitter may be given by either sex during food transfers. Mueller (1971) associated it in captives only with ♀♀ and extremely hungry Kestrels, but Balgooyen's field observations do not concur.

Mueller also described a klee-chitter call from hungry captive Kestrels after food was removed from them.

S. C. Bishop (1925) described the call of a ♀ during and after copulation as a low pee-'p pee-'p pee-'p while fluttering her wings.

Nestlings by age 2 weeks can produce whine, chitter, and klee. DAVID M. BIRD

HABITAT In our area The Kestrel inhabits open terrain from sea level up to about 13,000 ft. (3,960 m.), including plains, deserts, fields, meadows, and unforested portions of mountainsides, where there exists both adequate prey supply and perching sites. The latter include telephone and hydro poles and lines, fence posts, rock outcrops, tree stumps, small shrubs, trees wholly or partially dead, and a large assortment of man-made structures. The Kestrel occurs commonly in suburban and urban environments. Widespread deforestation and land development have facilitated a conti-

259

nentwide population increase of this remarkably adaptive species, and it would probably be easier to describe where it does not occur.

Open habitats with high perches are likely to attract Kestrels. For example, 7.6-m. poles were more acceptable than 1.8-m. ones on Venezuelan savanna. In an experimental study on Mich. grassland and where the difference was less (1.5 v. 2 m.), the Kestrels showed no preferences (K. Harrison 1977).

These data pertain to various parts of the range in various seasons, going s.: In s. Yukon Terr., the Kestrel is the most common diurnal raptor of woodlands and burned areas. In Idaho, shuns thick woods but is attracted to slashings resulting from logging operations. In n. Wis. in forested country, found only in open farmland, extensive marshes, large bogs, and beaver meadows. In Mont., prefers cottonwood forest over shrubland, sagebrush, and pine-juniper woodland; breeds at forest margins and in groves, ranging out over adjoining prairie, cropland, and badlands. In Colo., a roadside survey (Bauer 1982) revealed that winterers preferred to perch on hydro wires and poles and that most birds preferred cropland and pasture habitats.

At Sagebrush Creek, Calif., Kestrels breed (but do not winter) in burned forests and along edges between sagebrush and forest habitats. Unoccupied and apparently unsuitable habitat includes extensive meadows, sagebrush flats, dense pine forest, brushy fields, and talus slopes. Regrowth of burned areas excludes the Kestrels for some 20–40 years. (From Balgooyen 1976.) Dead eucalyptus trees are favorite perches of Kestrels migrating through s. Calif. Off the coast on San Clemente I. this bird is occasionally seen hovering over brushy mesas and cactus-covered hillsides.

R. Morris (1895) provided an early account of successful **urban nesting,** on a 6-storey building in downtown Springield, Mass. It has bred in towns and villages for a long time. Kestrels appear regularly on bird censuses in all seasons in towns and in urban areas of various sizes. Generally it is difficult to study this falcon in large cities due to inaccessibility of nest sites. Some pairs have territories in urban cemeteries.

Breeding habitat   Highly dependent on availability of nesting cavities. Thus, in Adams Co., Miss., they nested almost colonially or socially in an area of many old stumps with holes. Nesting in boxes provided for them dates back at least to 1909. Frances Hamerstrom et al. (1973) caused a dramatic increase in Kestrels in an area in Wis. by erecting nestboxes. Nestboxes have been used successfully to concentrate Kestrels for research and to increase numbers along transmission lines (Stahlecker 1979) and on reclaimed surface mines (T. Wilmer). (See Reproduction, below, for design of a suitable nestbox.)

Koplin (1973) showed **differential habitat use** by Kestrels wintering in n. Calif. A prevalence of ♂♂ was discovered in orchards and small pastures and fields surrounded by trees, whereas ♀♀ were more numerous in expansive pastures and fields devoid of or with few trees. Mills (1976), who did a study in Tex. that supported Koplin's findings, provided a good review of the subject. It was suggested that the more dominant ♀♀ force the more adaptable ♂♂ into less suitable habitats, thereby lessening competition for food. Layne (1980) noted a preponderance of ♂♂ in his winter roadside counts in s.-cent. Fla., 1968–1976, but noted that the sex ratio favored ♀♀ in other parts of Fla. (See also Tabb 1977.) Females are more out in the open, hence get more small mammals, while ♂♂ get more insects. For Ky. data and discussion of earlier reports, see Sferra (1984). In Ga., Stinson et al. (1981) found ♂ Kestrels more abundant where vegetation was over 1 m. high, hwereas ♀ ♀ preferred it lower; this was thought to reflect sexual preferences for the different prey found in each type of habitat.

These are a few examples from **outside our area.** In the Bahamas, the Kestrel is commonly seen on golf courses and in wooded areas. In Jamaica, it prefers cultivated areas, coconut and citrus groves, wooded pastures, woodland-savanna, scrub wood-land, and suburban areas. In Hispaniola, it occurs among palms of the lowlands and lower hills, among open pine woods at higher elevations, and in suburban gardens but is absent from tropical rain forest. In Trinidad, it is (was?) a rare resident of marshes and mangrove swamps. In e. Guatemala, resident birds (subsp. *tropicalis*) breed in scrubby pine and pine-oak woodland, while wintering nominate *sparverius* is found abundantly in lowlands. In Honduras, it breeds in highland pine and in lowland pine-savanna. In mainland Venezuela, it is abundant at edges of deciduous forest and on savannas, especially where telephone poles and lines provide perches. In Tierra del Fuego, it frequents open scrub country and forested areas.   DAVID M. BIRD

DISTRIBUTION   (See map.) Total breeding range of the species in the w. hemisphere has been mapped variously, based on differing amounts of information and uncertainty (especially s. of Mexico) of extent of areas where it is presumably absent.

In our area and nearby   Breeds from w. wooded Alaska across to include Nfld. and s., but not very far from the Fla. mainland down the Fla. Keys. From Tex. w. it breeds s. beyond the Mexican border, rarely into Nuevo León to the e. and far down in the interior and w., including the length of Baja Calif.

Although the Kestrel probably occurs almost anywhere within overall limits of range in some season, it is presumably absent as a breeder from certain habitats—for example, sw., s. coastal, and se. Alaska and adjacent B.C. (but is at least a fall migrant in part of this area); alpine and extensive forest areas in Canada and w. coterminous U.S.; some desert areas; and extensive grasslands remote from tree-lined watercourses and their banks. Yet in much of the arid sw. it is the most common desert falcon; it is resident.

Distributional changes in our area   Occurrence in Nfld. was regarded as hypothetical as recently as 1951; less than 2 decades later, L. Tuck (1968) stated that this was the most plentiful and widely distributed falcon. Approximately within the zone of transition from migratory to resident status across N. Am., a tendency to remain farther n., in urban areas especially, in winter appears to be fairly recent. The small Kestrels of the se. U.S., now recovering from a drastic decline in numbers, are also tending to breed in what were formerly considered unusual places; this may be a consequence of loss of natural habitat.

Marginal records northward   ALASKA on Unalaska I., in the Aleutians; Barrow; near mouth of Colville R. close to Beaufort Sea; CANADA in s. Victoria and nearby Jenny Lind I. in Dist. of Franklin; Chimo on the Labrador Peninsula (♂ and ♀ 1983).

Pacific oceanic   MEXICO on Guadalupe I. off Baja Calif. (resident); HAWAII on Oahu in 1970 (natural occurrence? assisted passage?).

Western Atlantic/Caribbean   Migrants and winterers from N. Am. occur in Ber-

261

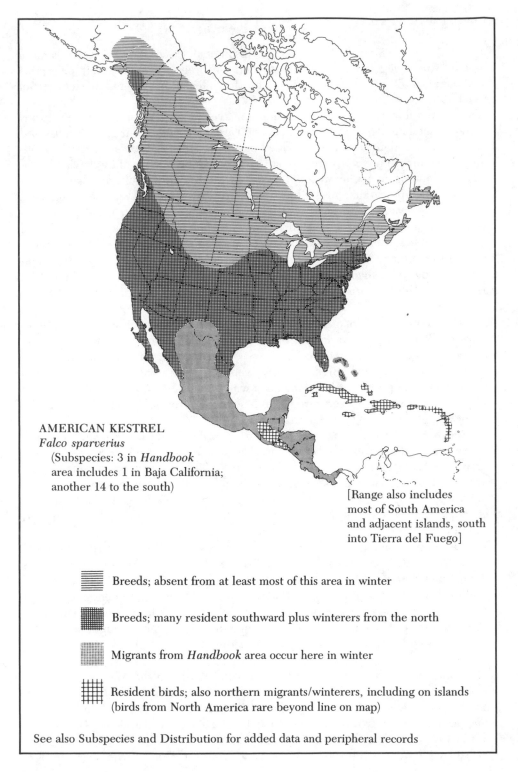

AMERICAN KESTREL
Falco sparverius
(Subspecies: 3 in *Handbook*
area includes 1 in Baja California;
another 14 to the south)

[Range also includes
most of South America
and adjacent islands, south
into Tierra del Fuego]

≡ Breeds; absent from at least most of this area in winter

▓ Breeds; many resident southward plus winterers from the north

▒ Migrants from *Handbook* area occur here in winter

▦ Resident birds; also northern migrants/winterers, including on islands
(birds from North America rare beyond line on map)

See also Subspecies and Distribution for added data and peripheral records muda (winter, not regularly), the Bahamas (where another subspecies is resident), and Cuba (common). Limits of seasonal occurrence of birds from N. Am. in the Caribbean are speculative.

Changes in Caribbean distribution   There has been a remarkable change in the Bahamian region and beyond since about the 1940s (J. Bond, 1978, 1980). The Hispaniolan *F. s. dominicensis* has reached Jamaica and is now a common resident; the Cuban *F. s. sparveroides* has invaded the Bahamas, spreading n. to Long I. and San Salvador (nesting on both); it also is reported from Haiti and Jamaica. Bond noted that *F. s. sparverius* wintering in the Bahamas is usually much shyer there than *F. s. sparveroides*.

Eastern Atlantic/Britain/Europe   Although various falcons are noted for traveling aboard ship (assisted passage), the following Am. Kestrel records have been treated as presumed natural occurrences: DENMARK in 1901; AZORES in 1968; SCOTLAND (Fair Isle) and ENGLAND (Cornwall), both in 1976.

A ♂ shot near Tallinn, Estonia, in June 1963, was suspected by Mank (1965) to have been brought to Europe and escaped. A ♀ shot on Malta in 1967 presumably came off a ship (Bourne 1969 *Ibis* **111** 134). Captives were for sale in June 1972 in a market in Barcelona, Spain, and not identifiable (from photographs) to subspecies—reported by A. Coles (1982) with appended suggestion that perhaps they had been imported from Mexico. The Am. Kestrel bred in captivity in Freiberg, Germany, beginning in 1961 (Koehler 1968).

F. s. paulus of the se. U.S. is generally regarded as resident. Yet it has been recorded away from wooded breeding range in Tex., once in the state of Veracruz, Mexico, and may occur in winter well down the Fla. Keys. This could be movement of young in their 1st fall–winter.

Cent. and S. Am.   *F. s. sparverius* of our area reaches at least Panama but is apparently unrecorded beyond there. The species is not reported from Tobago, is apparently a rare resident in Trinidad, and occurs on Margarita I. Far to the s., there are few Falklands records, but it may breed ne. there (Cawkell and Hamilton 1961). It is resident on some oceanic is. off Chile.

The question arises as to whether extensive deforestation in Cent. and S. Am. may have resulted in changes in breeding distribution (assuming nesting sites are available).

Based on Brodkorb (1964) and later records, the species is recorded as **fossil** in the Pleistocene of Calif. (6 sites), Nev., S.D. (3), N.Mex. (3), Tenn., Tex. (2), Fla. (5), Bahamas (New Providence), also Mexico (Nuevo León) and Brazil; and from **prehistoric sites** in Oreg., Idaho, Utah, Ariz. (6), S.D. (3), Ark., Ill., Pa., and in Puerto Rico (2) and Peru.   RALPH S. PALMER

MIGRATION   *F. s. sparverius*. This attempt to present a pattern is subject to revision when there is further analysis of banding data.

Based on Henny's (1972) use of recovery data, there is a change from migratory birds n. through a zone in which the proportion of migrants decreases and residents increase, to all resident s. This zone extends from about lat. 44°N down to about 36°. Thus the area of transition overlaps a comparable one for the Red-tailed Hawk. Northern Kestrels migrate through areas occupied by residents and short-distance migrants, some going very long distances. Example: a Kestrel banded in Alta. was killed in s. Mexico. Southern migrant Kestrels of breeding age apparently travel relatively short distances, their young in 1st fall evidently going farther. (In general, judging from Lincer and Sherburne 1974, Kestrels in their 1st fall migrate farther than older ones.) Apparently most birds of breeding age in Pa. and Md. are resident, while their young are recovered most often in S.C. and Ga. New Eng. birds partially bypass them, being recovered in S.C. and beyond. Migrants from the s. Canadian prairies e. to the Great Lakes region winter in some numbers in Ark., La., and Tex. Migrant Kestrels have winter territories.

Many birds banded in fall migration in N.J. and a scattering of others (presumably including birds banded as nestlings) from places to distances as far as Ont. and N.S. have been recovered in peninsular Fla., while others banded on winter range in Fla. have been recovered up to points equally far distant n. (Layne 1982). Minimum speed of 4 individuals was 80–120 km./day. Since numerous Kestrels go beyond Fla. to Caribbean wintering localities, they travel more than the 2,700 km. straight-line distance from N.S. to s. Fla.

In Fla. (Layne), there is some indication that migrant ♀ ♀ tend to winter farther s. than ♂ ♂; in Ohio (Mills 1975) ♀ ♀ also greatly outnumbered ♂ ♂.

In Calif., birds hatched at higher elevations begin moving s. in mid-Aug. They winter in agricultural and coastal areas, and some go well down into w. Mexico. Even so, Kestrels can be found throughout Calif. in winter to at least 7,000 ft. in optimum habitat. Most hatched below 3,500 ft. do not migrate, except from arid and desert regions where seasons are harsh. (Data from P. Bloom.)

Kestrels make water crossings and feed en route on the wing (or aboard ship sometimes) on small birds. They have been seen from and on shipboard on the Great Lakes (J. Perkins 1964), and they fly from the (Fla.?) mainland to Caribbean is., as previously noted. At least 4 birds, as reported by 3 observers, have been seen in the Gulf of Mexico (1 headed n. from Yucatan), but their main route is around it—even though Van Tyne and Trantman (1945) reported migrants leaving the n. shore of Yucatan in early Apr. They feed while migrating over land as well as water.

Migration over relatively flat country is spread out; elsewhere Kestrels are concentrated along ridges, near coast, and, to some extent, at margins of inland waters, which many traverse.

Spring   Passage may generally be graphed as fairly flat in numbers (high peaks are unusual), mainly extending for a month or more; late travelers are perhaps young birds that have yet to establish breeding territories. Males often reach their destinations a short time before ♀ ♀.

Migration must begin in Feb. in n. S. Am. and in Cent. Am. and is mainly in Mar. in n. Mexico. In Calif., most birds have begun leaving wintering areas by mid-Feb. (P. Bloom); some s. birds there already have clutches in the last ⅓ of Mar.; and transients pass until some time in Apr. Winterers begin leaving Fla. in Feb., and almost all have left by Apr. In s. states from the Rockies e., there is much movement at least from early Mar. into Apr., and in n. states mainly mid-Mar. to mid-Apr. On the s. Canadian prairies, most movement is in the last 3 weeks of Apr., but it continues to about mid-

May. Since lookouts near the Great Lakes have not reported spring concentrations of migrants, evidently the birds approach these waters on a broad front and usually cross over rather than circumnavigate them.

Summer In n. U.S. and adjacent Canada, flying young and postbreeders disperse beginning in July to places where food is plentiful, sometimes occurring together in numbers. Apparently they may go in any compass direction; a few recoveries suggest that some young go n. before their fall migration. This is also the time when some birds move to above timberline.

Fall In Sept. there is much movement of migrants in Canada and n. U.S.; it dwindles rapidly around mid-Oct. At Bend, Oreg., the local birds drift s. in Sept., movements depending on available food and weather, but are gone by midmonth; then, during mid-Oct., transients from farther n. cross the region (Roest 1957). At Point Diablo near San Francisco, Binford (1979) reported 276 Kestrels in 6 autumns, 1972–1977, approximately 3.3% of all raptors seen. They appeared there as early as Aug. 11–20 and as late as Nov. 11–20, and the median date was 3 days later than at Hawk Mt., Pa. Easterly, there are large numbers of migrant Kestrels in the latitude of N.J. about the 3d week in Sept., and most have passed by Oct. 10. Yet there are late dates in the cent. states, supposedly of migrants, into Nov. and even early Dec. Arrival in Fla. begins in Sept. and lasts at least well into Oct. The birds arrive in s. Cent. Am. down to Panama beginning in mid-Oct.

Unusual fall concentrations A large flight of 1,000s of Kestrels was witnessed near Albuquerque, N.Mex., along the Rio Grande on Sept. 13, 1914, by J. E. Law (1915). The birds moved in a continuous stream, and 100 or more could be seen at a time, often perched. None were seen 2 days later some 200 mi. to the s. At C. May Pt., N.J., on Oct. 16, 1970, Choate (1972) recorded an unprecedented 25,000; it was rainy, with strong nw. winds. Roughly 18,000 were observed between 0900 and 1200 hrs. Generally, at most hawk lookouts, a strong nw. wind provides good flights.

Winter Kestrels increasingly tend to winter in n. urban areas that have a year-round food supply and warm roosting places (Mills 1975, D. Bird). In other n. places, a cold spell in winter causes the birds to be absent temporarily. Also, there are various places where winterers plus residents add up to a relatively dense population, as in Oreg. (Roest 1957), Fla. (Tabb 1977), and Ohio (Mills 1975).

Homing In Pasadena, Calif., Kestrels returned after being trapped and released 20–40 mi. away; 1, deported 70 mi., returned in a subsequent winter (H. and J. Michener 1938). In Ohio in winter, 2 (of 4) ♀♀ returned to their trapping site after being released 1.6–4.8 km. away, and a ♂ brought into the area from 24 km. n. was seen near its point of release over 1 month later (Mills). Few band recoveries are obtained miles away and not at sites at which birds were banded as nestlings. Once Kestrels have established a breeding territory, however, they have a strong tendency to return each year, not necessarily to the identical nesting site.

There is much evidence of homing to winter territories by migrants—Mills (1975), Tabb (1977), Bolen and Derden (1980), and Layne (1980). Layne suggested that fewer Kestrels reach Fla. in seasons when the weather to the n. is comparatively mild.

F. s. paulus is commonly referred to as resident, which would imply that none are migratory. One would expect, at minimum, dispersal of young. This little Kestrel

265

occurs on the Fla. Keys in winter in places where it apparently does not breed. In a part of Miss. where it breeds there are no winter records, and *F. s. sparverius* then is common (Burleigh 1944). A ♂ was taken Oct. 19 n. of Jalapa, Veracruz, Mexico (Lowery and Dalquest 1951), a considerable distance from the hitherto known range of this subspecies.   DAVID M. BIRD

BANDING STATUS   Among diurnal raptors in our area, the Kestrel is exceeded only by the Sharp-shinned Hawk in total number banded. To Aug. 1981, the number of Kestrels banded was 65,670, with 1,832 (2.8%) recoveries (Clapp et al. 1982).

Main places of banding: N.J., Ont., Calif., Wis., Ohio, Pa., Mass., N.Y., Md., Colo., Minn., Fla., and Alta. A considerable number have been banded even in Mexico and a scattering at other s. places.

Various banding data have been published, most extensively as follows: survival rates (Henny 1972); e. migration (Lincer and Sherburne (1974); s. Calif.—movements (P. Bloom 1983 MS); Tex.—fidelity to wintering areas (Bolen and Derden 1980); and Fla.—winter recoveries (Tabb 1977) and migration and survival (Layne 1982).

                                                                DAVID M. BIRD

REPRODUCTION   The Kestrel is a remarkably flexible bird, as evidenced by its willingness to breed under all kinds of constraints in the wild and, especially, in captivity. It has frequently been used for research into toxicity and general biology; hence many data on reproduction originate from laboratory studies, some being included here to augment data on wild birds. Birds in our area (mainly *F. s. sparverius*) are dealt with principally, with incidental mention of birds elsewhere.

Age when first breeds   Both sexes are capable of breeding as yearlings, and Henny's (1972) data suggest that about 82% do so. It may depend to some extent on whether a bird can secure a territory and mate. Hand-reared yearling ♂♂ demonstrated poor fertility but, when older, surpassed natural-raised ♂♂ in the laboratory (D. Bird and Laguë 1982b).

Arrival   Males arrive on territory a few days ahead of ♀♀, according to most authors, this perhaps applying to previously established breeders. In Oreg., Roest (1957) observed ♀♀ arriving only a day or 2 after ♂♂. In Alta., ♂♂ almost invariably arrived 1st, ♀♀ about a week later (W. and J. Salt 1976). In e.-cent. Ill., of 9 pairs, ♂♂ arrived 1st 5 times, a ♀ once, and 3 times they arrived together; the breeding population increased from Jan. 11 to mid-Apr. (Enderson 1960). At Sagehen Creek near L. Tahoe in Calif., where there is annual snow cover, the sexes arrived more or less together (Balgooyen 1976).

Breeding cycle preliminaries   Generally begin immediately unless delayed by adverse weather. Balgooyen, for example, emphasized late snow cover as an important limiting factor. Low temperatures do not halt displays. In Ohio, Skaggs (1974) described aerial competition between ♂♂ over a ♀ as early as Jan. 31, with clutch laid by Mar. 19 during freezing temperatures. Several captive pairs at Montreal, Que., stimulated by artificial photoperiod, laid during temperatures as low as −14°C (D. Bird et al. 1980). In urban areas, such as Montreal, ♀♀ have been seen going in and out of cavities during a warm spell at the end of Feb. (R. Galbraith). After arrival, Kestrels are occasionally seen in groups of both sexes of 4 or 5. While ♂♂ are busy establishing (or reestablishing) territories, there may be promiscuity in the 1st 1–2 weeks, principally among ♀♀ and ♂♂ on adjacent territories; see Balgooyen (1976) for discussion. It is doubtful that such activity generates any fertilization because (D. Bird and Buckland 1966) the maximum length of time for storage of viable sperm within ♀♀ is 12 days and the 1st egg is generally not laid until 2 weeks later.

Displays Comparing Merlin and Kestrel, Feldsine and Oliphant (1985) stated that displays of the former are decidedly more complex. For the Kestrel, Flutter-glide and Dive-display were described by Willoughby and Cade (1964), these being falcon versions of HIGH-CIRCLING and SKY-DANCE, respectively. The Flutter-glide is much like Flutter-flying of the Merlin and is performed mainly by the ♀ Kestrel, being more common by the ♂ in the Merlin. The Kestrel's Dive-display is similar to Undulating-flight of Peregrine and Gyrfalcon (R. W. Nelson 1977). The Merlin's behavioral repertoire and display intensity seem, subjectively, to be more similar to the large falcons than to the Kestrel.

Willoughby and Cade described 5 behavioral categories: aerial display, whining and chittering, "courtship" feeding, copulation, and nest-site inspection. In Flutter-glide the ♀ flies slowly and buoyantly with quick, shallow wingbeats, the wings spread fully but arched below the horizontal axis of the body. Although done thus by the begging ♀, the ♂ also does it sometimes during aerial food-transfer and in copulation. Dive-display consists of a series of climbs and dives, with powerful wingbeats, and 3–5 *klee* notes uttered near the peak of each ascent. Vertical depth of dives is around 30–60 ft. The diving ♂ usually achieves great speed, dropping at about a 50° angle, then climbing steeply. It is most frequent early in the display period, and its principal function is to advertise territory—to exclude another bird. The ♂ may dive 2–6 times, sometimes directly over the ♀. There are variants. In one described by Balgooyen, the ♂ ascended in a spiral course between dives and was silent. Cade (1955a) thought that aerial displays occur after the nest site is established, and Balgooyen stated that they may precede and even influence site selection. Spofford's (1943) description of Dive-display in fall, and where Kestrels are double brooded, favors the latter. Vocalizations are important throughout the entire breeding cycle.

Experimentally widowed ♀♀ perform aerial displays, presumably to attract a replacement mate (R. Bowman, D. Bird).

To supplement and extend the above, the following behavioral components seen among captives (Mueller 1971) are outlined here briefly: *Curtsy*—bird raises feathers of back and may present its dorsum toward an adversary, indicating hostility. *Bow*—bird nearly horizontal, head–body feathers raised, tail usually spread, and making *klee* call; observed only in response to presence of humans. *Confrontation*—by 2 birds 10–15 cm. apart, very erect, and body feathering compressed; birds may cease or may Curtsy or (rarely) fight. *Fighting*—birds grapple with their feet and fence with their beaks; the birds are not injured by this; the subordinate one may utter *klee* call. *Tail-spreading*—in general, a fear response; *Tail-pumping*—in various situations, feathering compressed, suggests conflict or indecision, as before launching an attack on prey. *Mantling*—hungry bird with food in talons spreads its wings; well developed in the nestling period, presumably to hide food from siblings (or, in older birds, from any potential robber).

Food pass Or transfer of prey is usually aerial and from ♂ to ♀. It apparently strengthens the pair bond, and it provides nourishment for ♀ and brood. Normally it is beak-to-beak, but a very aggressive or hungry ♀ may snatch the prey with a foot. According to Balgooyen, this type of feeding the ♀ lasts some 9–11 weeks, starting some 4–5 weeks before laying and ending 1–2 weeks after hatching. Since its primary function is to produce a brood, he called it "production feeding." (Either parent may offer food to flying young.)

In captives, the 1st sign of a tendency to engage in this activity is the ♀'s willingness to wait and watch the ♂ as he eats; within a few days she begins whining and chittering, sometimes following the ♂ and gently trying to remove food from him if he is unwilling to offer it. In an unusual instance in the wild, Bird and Spiegel (1975) observed the ♀ providing the ♂ with a vole; he then gave it back to her and she ate it. The 1st indication of a captive ♂'s tendency to food pass is his utterance of simple whines on sighting food. Soon he is whine-chittering when picking it up and chittering as he flies toward the ♀ and offers it. Throughout, both may head-bob, erect their feathers, flutter wings, and chitter. There are many variants in the wild and in captivity—see Balgooyen (1976) and Willoughby and Cade (1964).

Olendorff (1968) observed **reciprocal preening** by captives—occasional pecks by 1 bird at the head or neck, sometimes at the beak, of the other. In a variant, the perched ♂ tail-bobbed and squatted slightly while reaching out to peck the ♀'s beak several times; then he squatted lower, rolled subtly from side to side (perhaps 10° each way), wings partly spread, as if bowing before her. This suggests some elements of Dive-display.

Copulation   Often described. Either sex may initiate it, and attempts early in the season are often clumsy and, as noted above, most likely do not result in fertilization. Sometimes a captive ♀ tries to stimulate the ♂ by wedging herself beneath him. Typically, she leans forward, her dorsal areas aligning as a platform, and the ♂ alights from behind, resting on underside of his tarsi and with feet clenched ("balled"). As he lowers his tail, the ♀ wags hers in the opposite direction and elevates her rear. The ♂, balancing with his wings, leans back and makes cloacal contact by pushing, sometimes repeatedly. Both birds may chitter; the ♀ invariably whines before, during, or after contact.

According to Balgooyen, ♂♂ cannot copulate as frequently as ♀♀, the refractory period being about 2 min. One ♀ copulated twice in 20 sec. with 2 ♂♂. Frequency of copulatory behavior reported by various authors includes 3 times in 15 min., 5 in 25 min., 5 in 10.5 min., 14 in 36 min., 6 in 27 min., and 10 times/hr. A single attempt generally lasts 2–18 sec. Such behavior may continue 6–7 weeks; frequently increases as egg laying approaches and then decreases. It has been observed well into incubation. Balgooyen estimated a total of 690(!) copulatory acts to fertilize a 5-egg clutch, but D. Bird et al. (in Chancellor 1977) indicated that twice weekly insemination is enough to insure a fertile clutch. In view of duration of fertility in ♀♀ (D. Bird and Buckland 1976), this would seem unnecessarily high, and, as Balgooyen suggested, not all acts involve passing of sperm. Semen production by captive ♂♂ extended for 103 days, Mar. 19–June 21, according to D. Bird and Laguë (1977), which see for other details.

Nest-site inspection   Both sexes actively inspect cavities (♀♀ visit only familiar ones—Balgooyen) for possible egg deposition. The ♂ leads the search with the ♀

following him (Balgooyen). The chittering ♂ may employ various displays, with or without food, to stimulate her. Or he may enter the cavity, remain there for a few sec. or even min., chittering all the time. The ♀ then may duplicate his action, and copulation may ensue after she emerges. Sometimes the ♂ may sit peering out of the cavity, chittering periodically. The ♀ apparently makes the final selection. See Balgooyen (1976) and Olendorff (1968) for details.

Pair formation As previously noted, Kestrels are sometimes seen in small groups after arrival in breeding areas. In s. Calif., pairs are formed 12–14 weeks before laying (Cade 1955a), and farther n. at Sagehen Creek (Balgooyen 1976) the period is only 6–7 weeks. Debate exists as to whether pair formation is based on sexual attraction or on site selection; at Sagehen, however, the brightly colored ♂ attracts the ♀ to his area. Balgooyen claimed that if a member of the pair does not return, the remaining bird will leave the territory. However, the presence of numerous yearling prebreeders and some older nonbreeders would allow for a very rapid replacement of a lost mate of either sex (and both have been reported). There is much agreement that mate selection is by the ♀ (Roest 1957). Willoughby and Cade (1964) demonstrated experimentally with captives the unimportance of body size in the pair bond, and the experiments by D. Bird and Goldblatt, in Cooper and Greenwood (1980), with *F. sparverius* and the larger *F. tinnunculus* in the laboratory showed that cross-fostered individuals of the smaller species readily selected the larger as mates. Porter and Wiemeyer (1970) and D. Bird (1982) randomly paired birds in the laboratory with no regard for body size, and there were no ill effects on reproductive performance. Further, it may be noted that the strikingly different so-called color morphs (and intermediates) in the Cuban race *sparveroides* pose no barrier to interbreeding. Additional mate-selection studies in 1983 (J. Duncan and D. Bird) revealed that ♀ Kestrels in 27 choice tests chose their brothers 8 times, chose nonsiblings 11 times, and made no choice on 8 occasions. A father-daughter pairing in the wild is known (R. Bowman and D. Bird).

Banding results from Que., Ont., Conn., and Calif. indicate that young Kestrels surviving to breeding age rarely return to the vicinity where they were reared. This promotes random mating.

Sustained monogamy Monogamy through successive breeding seasons seems to prevail in Kestrels. There is little certain evidence that the bond is continuous around the year as long as both mates survive, and winter habitat segregation of the sexes, at least in some circumstances, would seem to preclude it. Yet some Kestrels reportedly remain paired through winter—**lifelong pair bond** (Cade 1955a, Czech 1968). The following situations are atypical: In Pa., 2 ♀ (a ♂ present) fought over a territory (Saenger 1984). Late in the breeding season in W.Va., a pair reared a brood; 2 additional Kestrels, which also defended the site, were possibly Juv. birds (Wilmers 1983). There was a **trio bond** in N.Y.—2 ♂ alternately delivered prey to a ♀ at a nest containing 5 young (Wegner 1976).

Territory size In some areas Kestrel pairs seem very tolerant of others nesting in proximity; thus, in the Utah study by D. Smith et al. (1972), 5 nests were located within 61 m. of at least 1 other nest, and 2 were only 12.2 m apart. The av. was 4.5 pairs/sq. mi. in 1969 and 3.2 in 1970, but only 0.65 outside the study area. In Ill., 0.29 (Enderson 1960), in Mich. 0.44 (the Craigheads 1956), and the 4-year mean in Pa. was

3.25/½-sq. mi. (Heintzelman 1964). In the last-mentioned, 7 nests were in ½-sq. mi. in 1961. In Ont., Speirs (1977) estimated 10 pairs/100 acres in an East Whitby forest plot but found only 1 pair/100 acres in urban Pickering and 6 pair/100 acres in urban Whitby. Diameters of "home ranges" of breeding pairs include 0.66 km. in Jamaica (Cruz 1976), 0.82 in Utah, 2.42 in Mich. and Wyo., and 2.3 in Ill. Such large variation may be a function of food and nest-site availability. Smaller home ranges in the Utah study indicate high densities; pairs bordered by adjacent territories had smaller home ranges than did solitary pairs (D. Smith et al. 1972). Available nesting sites do affect breeding density; erection of nest boxes can concentrate the birds and also can extend them into otherwise unusable habitat.

Intra- and interspecific territorial defense   Kestrels tend to return to their previous territories but not necessarily the former nesting site. In some instances the same site is used for several successive years. Switching sites can be a result of investigator disturbance. The Calif. Kestrels at Sagehen Creek (Balgooyen 1976) defended not just the nest site but the total territory against other Kestrels. Females engage in little defense, but ♂ ♂ are very active, chasing ♂ ♂ from their territories. In the Utah study (D. Smith et al.), no Kestrel/Kestrel encounters were observed despite overlapping defended areas. Kestrels are quite capable of driving off Red-tailed Hawks, Goshawks, Cooper's Hawks, and Barn Owls and occasionally strike human intruders. Urban-nesting Kestrels in Oklahoma City showed no interest in curious humans (G. Sutton and Tyler 1979), but both members of a pair in Springfield, Mass., readily attacked people (R. Morris 1895). Cade (1955a) noted that urban Kestrels were "tamer." Attitudes of captive breeding pairs toward laboratory investigators vary greatly, and defensive behavior is usually triggered by the presence of eggs in the nest box (D. Bird). Kestrels are evidently unsuccessful in driving off predatory raccoons. It is common to observe passerine birds (Am. Robins, kingbirds, grackles, etc.) harassing and mobbing nesting pairs (Sherman 1913), yet passerines nesting near nesting Kestrels were not molested by the falcons (Morris 1899).

Balgooyen contended that Kestrels are clearly dominant competitors for nest cavities at Sagehen Creek, evicting or out-competing several woodpecker species, European Starlings, N. Flickers, bluebirds, chipmunks, and small squirrels. Kestrels do not always win contests with starlings, and F. Craighead and Mindell (1981) expressed concern that increasing numbers of starlings in w. Wyo. may affect Kestrel numbers and nesting success in the future, especially in late spring seasons.

Kestrels have been found in cavities containing Wood Duck eggs. In B.C., they used 24 of 137 new boxes put up for Barrow's Goldeneyes (Savard 1982). In one instance (F. A. Sumner 1933) the Kestrels actually reared a Screech Owl with their own brood.

Nest sites   The common denominator at virtually all sites is a hole or cavity. Among its advantages is protection from larger raptors (Kestrels have shared trees with Red-tails and Long-eared Owls). See Balgooyen for events leading to acquisition of a hole in burned and sagebrush habitats of Sagehen Creek, Calif. Roest (1957) gave what might be termed a very conservative list of sites, in decreasing order of importance: flicker holes, natural cavities, woodpecker holes, cavities in buildings, magpie nests, and holes in cliffs and eroded stream banks. Use of excavations, as old kingfisher and other

270

holes in eroded stream banks and holes or recesses in cliffs is more frequent away from trees. Gallup (1927) described a flicker and Kestrel trading sites over 2 years. Of 41 sites in Utah (D. Smith et al.), 19 were in flicker holes, 2 in magpie nests, 7 in natural cavities, 11 in buildings, and 2 in cliff niches. Kestrels have nested in drainpipes, chimneys, hollowed-out fence posts, and many other places. On the is. of Dominica, tree cavities are scarce; sometimes (J. Bond 1941) the Kestrel takes over a stick nest at the base of a frond of a tall coconut palm. In Cuba, Kestrels nest in the tops of dead royal palms (the interior of the trunk rots). In Jamaica, 85% nest in woodpecker holes (Cruz 1976). In Venezuela, Kestrels have used hollowed-out termite nests (Friedmann and Smith 1950).

In Colo., the Kestrel "not infrequently" takes possession of a deserted magpie nest and makes a few "crude repairs" (Rockwell 1909). The bird toys with or occasionally "rearranges" the nesting substrate or adjacent material. Richards (1970) regarded this as relict nest building; at least as likely (as in other falcons), it is done out of boredom, curiosity, or perhaps (as in greenery brought by *Buteo* and other species) to advertise occupancy of a site.

Dunlavy (1935) thought that Kestrels nest in high trees and seek refuge in low ones, but they will use a site anywhere from less than 1 m. from the ground to as high as a suitable cavity exists. The majority of Roest's nests were 3.1–9.1 m. up, and height of 43 others (Balgooyen) was 2.1–24.3 m. (mean of 7.8). The highest reported nest is probably one 108.6 m. up on a 22-storey building in Ottawa (Iola Price).

Orientation of nest opening　Balgooyen concluded that e.-facing holes were preferred and were advantageous in inclement weather. Of 54 boxes occupied in Lessen Co., Calif., 19 faced s., 17 n., 11 w., and 7 e., and w.-facing boxes had a high failure rate (Bloom and Hawks 1983). The most recent Calif. study (Raphael 1985) indicated that, regardless of availability, selection is e.-facing—that is, nonrandom—more often than otherwise.

Size of entrance　Based on experimentation with hole sizes, Balgooyen believed that Kestrels select those, especially tight-fitting ones, commensurate with their body size. They may overdo it. S. and J. Schmutz (1975) removed flea-ridden nestlings from a cavity so narrow that some were on top of others, and F. A. Merriam (1896) reported use of a hole so small that the brooding bird had to wriggle in and out. The interior cavity must have at least adequate diam. for the bird to incubate, and it varies in depth (to about 1 m. reported).

Nest boxes　Various designs have been put up for Kestrels since at least very early in this century, and 1,000s currently exist. Reports of Kestrels appropriating boxes from doves and pigeons and of accepting man-made boxes in both rural and urban areas, led Frances Hamerstrom et al. (1973) to demonstrate that the number of available sites limits breeding density. In the 20 years before boxes were erected on a Wis. study area, only 3 nests produced Kestrels, while in 5 years young were reared successfully from boxes 51 times. Those placed on buildings were preferred. Bloom and Hawks (1983) reported similar findings in Lassen Co., Calif.; their Kestrels preferred boxes without obstruction at entrances and open to moderate, but never dense, canopy coverage.

These are sketchy details of what might be described as a standard nest box, easily

271

produced in quantity. Most of it is cut from a 1 in. × 10 in. × 6 ft. smooth board. Sides are about 14¾ in. high at the back and slope 1 in. to the front. The bottom of the 3-in. entrance hole in the front is up 9–10 in.; there is a small shelf inside, below the hole, and its surface is roughened to facilitate exit of the young. One side is designed to be opened periodically (for cleaning), the bottom has small holes (for drainage), and the box is put up at least fairly well out in the open, say 10 ft. or higher, on a 2-piece pole joined for pivoting to lower the box for inspection or cleaning. See also Bloom and Hawks (1983). In Idaho, Craig and Trost (1979) found no significant differences in productivity when comparing natural cavities with nest boxes.

Willoughby and Cade showed that, in the laboratory, absence of a nest hole neither delayed nor interfered with displays. A pet Kestrel once amused Taverner (1921) with its extreme interest in a cigar box with a hole in its side. Presence of a nest box is enough to stimulate laying in unpaired naturally raised ♀ ♀ in the McGill colony (D. Bird and Buckland 1976). Some even lay eggs on the floor of colonial cages containing several ♀ ♀. Finally, Kestrels raised on open ledges always preferred nest boxes for nesting when given a choice, indicating an innate preference for nest holes (L. Shutt, D. Bird).

Laying The eggs are deposited on the existing substrate in the cavity—rotting wood or whatever. Grass sod, wood shavings, peat moss, pine needles, and sawdust have been used in nest boxes. Eggs laid on bare board may suffer breakage.

Laying dates In Ont., laying begins in early Apr., young are in the nest as early as May 14, and eggs are as late as June 23. In Idaho, Craig and Trost (1979) calculated incubation to have begun in mid-May in 1975 and 12 days earlier in 1976. In w. Wyo., laying was 31 days later in 1975 than in 1947; heavy prolonged snowfall and reduced prey availability were possible causes of the 1975 delay (F. Craighead and Mindell 1981). In Pa., egg dates ranged from Apr. 15, 1961, to (renesting?) July 4, 1959 (Heintzelman and Nagy 1968). In Ohio, a ♀ was laying as early as Mar. 19 (Skaggs 1974, 1976). The earliest clutch in e.-cent. Ill. was completed about Apr. 22 and the last by Apr. 29 (Enderson 1960). The latest date for laying near Laurel, Md., was July 16 for a renesting pair. In Calif. at Sagehen Creek, Kestrels began laying in late May or early June, av. June 6 (Balgooyen), and in Lassen Co. median date over 4 years was May 22 (Bloom and Hawks 1983). For dates for presumably viable eggs taken in various stages of incubation, see Bent (1938); the localities are spread from New Eng. to the prairie provinces and s. to Fla. and Baja Calif., Mexico. There are numerous Mar. dates for warmer parts of the U.S. and s. In Venezuela, nesting has been observed Jan.–Apr., and Chilean birds are said to have 1st broods in Oct. (Two broods/season is discussed later.)

In the captive colony in Md., birds from Fla. always laid later than local birds (both exposed to natural daylength), without overlap, 1966–1968; there was a tendency, however, both for laying dates to come closer together as well as for laying to be progressively earlier each year (Porter and Wiemeyer 1972). Willoughby and Cade (1964) showed the importance of photoperiod (increased daylength) and presence of a nest hole in triggering laying in captives. D. Bird et al. (1980) also altered lighting to induce laying during freezing midwinter temperatures. Such work raises questions as to genetic v. environmental control. In the related *F. tinnunculus* of Eurasia, food availability apparently restricts laying date (Dijkstra et al. 1982).

Egg size   In our area, 169 eggs av. 35 × 29 mm., extremes being 39 × 32, 31 × 28, and 33 × 26 (Bent 1938). One egg each from 20 clutches (15 were from Pa.) **length** 35.13 ± 1.14 mm., **breadth** 28.42 ± 0.63; **shape** typically short elliptical but varies, radii of curvature of ends 12.50 ± 0.40 and 9.49 ± 0.65, elongation 1.24 ± 0.033, bicone −0.055, and asymmetry +0.131 (F. W. Preston). One egg each from 20 Calif. clutches av. very similar (Preston); see also Balgooyen (1976) for 58 eggs from Calif.

One egg each from 23 Fla. clutches: **length** 34.01 ± 1.28 mm. and **breadth** 27.96 ± 1.05 (Preston), and Bent gave av. of 45 as 34 × 28 mm. That is, the eggs of the small *F. s. paulus* of Fla. av. about 1 mm. less than the other eggs just listed in both length and breadth.

Of 887 captive-laid eggs, meas. were: **length** 29.7–38.0 mm., mean 33.8, and **breadth** 24.2–30.2, mean 28.2; length decreases significantly before end of the laying season (D. Bird and Laguë 1982a). Porter and Wiemeyer (1972) measured 1st eggs of the clutch of captive 3- and 4-year-olds and 1st and 2d generation progeny. They were much the same in size. There was no change with age and no direct correlation between size of ♀ and her eggs.

Egg color   Ground color varies from white through cream to a yellowish or light reddish-brown, overlaid with blotches, spots, and mottling (sometimes only at 1 end) with various shades that are more or less violet-magneta, grays, and, particularly, browns. Occasionally they are unmarked. J. P. Norris (1888b) described the usual range of variation in appearance and gave meas. of 23 Calif. sets. Giles (1924) recorded a white egg in a clutch of 4, and D. Bird has seen several in white eggs in otherwise normal clutches of captives at McGill. Generally, eggs are not glossy. Balgooyen (1976) noted that coloration fades and surface **texture** goes from rough and dull to smooth and shiny during incubation. Camouflaged egg patterns suggest that ancestral Kestrels may have nested in open sites.

The ♀ has been known to incubate Wood Duck eggs, and eggs of captive Kestrels can be switched from nest to nest; this suggests inability of the bird to recognize its own eggs.

Egg weight   In Calif., 53 weighed 10.0–18.0 gm., av. 13.8 gm. (Balgooyen 1976), and Hanna's (1924) data on 36 are almost the same. In the captive colony at McGill, 803 fresh eggs weighed 9.81–18.65 gm., mean 14.65, and declined significantly by late in the laying season. Neither ♀ body wt. nor age affects egg wt.

Laying interval   Ordinarily an egg is laid every other day, not infrequently 1 day apart, and occasionally 3 days apart. The interval av. 2.4 days in captives; birds forced (by egg removal) to lay an excessive number of eggs become more irregular (Porter and Wiemeyer 1972). At least in captivity, eggs are laid at any time during day or night, and the ♀ typically appears lethargic, almost ill (D. Bird).

Clutch size   Ordinarily 4–6 eggs. Summarizing unpublished data from 7 regions (1 in s. prairie Canadian provinces, 6 in coterminous U.S.), number of eggs varied 2–6 inclusive, and mean figures included 4.81 ± 0.68 (largest clutches) in Canada and 4.00 ± 0.71 (smallest) in Fla. (Henny 1972). That is, clutch size decreases going s. Many published regional data could be cited, also clutches of 7 (rarely) and 1 of 8 (discounted as probably by 2 ♀). The mean for 160 captive-laid clutches at McGill was 474 ± 0.06 (D. Bird and Laguë 1982a). Up to 5 years of age, mean clutch size increased by 0.20 egg/year. There is general agreement that clutch size decreases through the season.

Adding and removing eggs (Porter 1975) did not establish whether this species is a determinate or indeterminate layer. Yearlings laid repeat clutches less often than older birds.

Incubation patches Both sexes develop bare oval areas (approximately 3–4 × 2–3 cm.) on each side of the breast. Willoughby and Cade (1964) gave data on patches on 2 Kestrel pairs. The 2 ♀ developed them at the same time, whether or not a nest hole was present; only ♂ ♂ paired with egg-laying ♀ ♀ developed them.

Incubation Typically begins at laying of 3d or 4th egg, the 1st 2 or 3 eggs often being cold to the touch. Some incomplete clutches with as many as 4 eggs are still cold, despite the ♀ sitting on them. Porter and Wiemeyer (1972) observed that incubation commenced after 2 eggs were laid in a 4-egg clutch and after 4 or 5 in a 6-egg clutch. Females attending eggs are more prone to leave the nest upon disturbance before the onset of full incubatory behavior. The latter is associated with a lack of both copulatory behavior and vocalizing; nests are difficult to locate during this period. In nest relief the Flutter-gliding ♂, with or without food, whines and chitters to draw the ♀ from the nest. Then she proceeds to eat food either from a transfer or delivered from a cache. The ♂ dictates the timing, but if the ♀ wishes to evict him afterwards, a particular behavioral pattern is necessary. Details in Balgooyen (1976). The extent to which the ♂ incubates varies with individual. Sherman (1913) noted that the ♂ incubated only once during the entire period, but Roest (1957) observed a ♂ to incubate regularly at night. Males incubated about 4 hrs./day, usually for a spell each morning and evening (Balgooyen). Wilmers (1983) reported that the ♂ incubated at night in pairs in W.Va. and Pa. Generally, however, the ♀ does the larger share. Olendorff's (1968) captive pair never allowed the eggs to be uncovered for more than 3 min., yet Kestrel eggs must be quite hardy as incubation advances. The majority of eggs laid by pairs experimentally induced to lay in midwinter hatched even after the incubator was shut down twice for several hrs. because of power failure (D. Bird et al. 1980). Weekly egg weight-loss was approximately 0.43 gm. and the overall mean weight-loss in 458 instances for the 28-day period was 1.70 ± 0.04 gm. (D.Bird and Laguë 1982c). For details of conditions for incubating Kestrel eggs at 37.5°C and 50–60% relative humidity, see D. Bird (1982) and Snelling (1972). Embryonic development was described and illus. by D. Bird et al. (1984).

Incubation period Usually 28–29 days, sometimes longer in the wild. For 15 Idaho eggs the mean period was 29.6 days, ranging 26–32 (D. Smith et al. 1972). It was 29–30 days in 3 clutches in Iowa (Sherman 1913), 30–31 days in Oreg. (Roest 1957), 30 in 8 clutches in Pa. (Heintzelman and Nagy 1968), and 29–31 days in Calif. (Balgooyen 1976). Captive birds av. 27 days in 19 instances (Porter and Wiemeyer 1972).

Fertility Data indicate that fertility of all eggs in a clutch is not assured. Of 168 eggs in Calf., 3 (1.8%) were infertile (Balgooyen). Sherman (1913) removed an infertile egg from her study nest; Stahlecker and Griese (1977) removed 2 from a clutch of 5 laid in mid-Apr. and found 4 infertile eggs in a clutch of 5 on Aug. 8. D. Bird and Laguë (1982c) reported about 75% fertility in 268 eggs laid by captive pairs randomly paired for breeding—that is, some incompatibility existed. Fertility declined significantly through the breeding season, best explained by corresponding decrease in semen production (D. Bird and Laguë 1977). Semen production usually peaked daily in very early P.M., and it declined considerably around June 21. D. Bird and Buckland (1976)

274

reported a mean duration of ♀ fertility of 8.1 days, ranging 4 to 12. Onset of fertility is, at most, a day, allowing another for egg production.

Hatching   A clutch of 5 eggs hatches in 2, sometimes 3, days. Each egg takes about 48–52 hrs. from the pipping stage. Females have been observed helping young out of the shell, and the empty shell is either trampled into the nest or eaten by the ♀ (D. Bird).

Hatching success   Heintzelman and Nagy (1968) felt that a 78% hatching success for Pa. Kestrels was rather high; excluding losses to predation, infertility, chilling, and wind, Balgooyen reported virtually 100% success. The following reports include such factors: In Utah, 69 of 103 eggs (67%) hatched (D. Smith et al. 1972). In Idaho, success was just over 80%, varying slightly between 1975 and 1976 (Craig and Trost 1979). In Lassen Co., Calif., 79% of 157 eggs hatched during 4 years (Bloom and Hawks 1983). The number of eggs hatched per clutch in 6 instances in w. Wyo. was 3.9 in 1947 and 1.5 in 1975, the latter season being cold and late (F. Craighead and Mindell 1981). Adverse weather also occurred in 1982, when 454 of 999 eggs in nest boxes in Ont., Pa., Minn., and Va. failed to hatch (Roger Jones). D. Bird and Laguë (1982c) showed a significant annual variation in hatching success and also found that eggs laid later in the season hatched poorly. Kestrel eggs artificially incubated from day 1 also demonstrated poor hatching success (D. Bird).

Replacement clutch   Kestrels will readily lay a 2d clutch on loss of the 1st, sometimes in the same nest or, if available, in an **alternative site** in the same territory (M. Morrison and Walton 1980). This has been known since as early as 1878. Ten pairs were forced to relay by clutch removal in s. Que. (Bowman and Bird MS), and 5 of 8 renesting pairs raised young. The renesting interval was 8–15 days, av. 11.6. Clutch size decreased by an av. of ⅕ egg. All 5-egg clutches were replaced by others the same size, and two 6-egg clutches were replaced by 5-egg ones. Egg traits, fertility, hatchability, nestling quality, and survival to flight age did not differ between 1st and replacement clutches. First clutch progeny did attain flight earlier than their successors, however. In Porter and Wiemeyer's study (1972), replacement clutches had fewer and longer eggs with thicker shells. No differences were found in egg wt., fertility, and so on. The renesting interval is shorter if the 1st clutch is taken sooner, and it is shorter in older, experienced layers. In the wild, a zealous collector took 4 clutches from a single pair, and captives do as well or better. Up to 26 eggs have been removed as laid by a single ♀ (Porter 1975, D. Bird).

Nestlings   The nestling dries off within 1 hr. of hatching and is covered with sparse white down on pink skin. The legs are yellowish pink, and the cere, beak, and talons are whitish pink. There is less down on the abdominal region, which protrudes to form a tripod arrangement with the 2 legs for sitting erect. The egg tooth (may be as long as 2 mm.) is prominent, and the typical falcon "tooth" on the beak is present; dark bluish black eyes are open for short periods, especially during whining or gaping for food; the feet can grasp slightly; the head can be raised shakily; and the beak is capable of nibbling at a finger. The newborn nestling is not totally helpless. At Sagehen Creek, Calif., young just hatched weighed 10–12 gm. (Balgooyen). The overall mean fresh wt. of 241 young hatched from eggs laid in captivity was 10.1 ± 0.06 gm., equal to about 69% of fresh egg wt. (D. Bird and Laguë 1982b).

By age 3 days a peeping sound is replaced by an immature *klee,* and the young can crawl nimbly. When not begging to be fed, they doze. The oil gland appears as a small knob about 1.6 mm. long (E. L. Sumner 1929b).

Age 1 week—skin is more bluish on wings, shoulders, back and crown; talons are darkening; dark brown irises with a deep bluish pupil are visible in wide-open eyes, and the nictitating membrane is functional. Wing quills are just developing. Occasionally a fear response—the young flattening itself on the nest substrate—and a defense attitude—the bird rolling on its back and presenting its talons—are seen. The young are able to follow movement of objects in front of them. The abdominal down has worn off and body temperature is 38.3°C.

Age 11 days—the egg tooth may be gone by 10 days but is sometimes retained as long as 14 days. The young are very lively and scream in excited tones. Beak and talons are gray, and the oil gland is about 3 mm. long.

Between ages 2 and 3 weeks—feathers appear over the entire body, thickest on wings, tail, back, breast, and crown. Primary tips emerge enough to distinguish the ♂'s blue-gray wings from the ♀'s rufous ones. Tail quills are about 2–3 cm. long. See Balgooyen (1976) for growth of tail and for wt. of hand-reared nestlings. Feather lengths may be a more reliable measure of age because of low variation; the outer tail feather is the last to reach full length.

Age 16 days—the young spend most of their time on their feet and emit a begging call during feeding and a *klee* call when excited. Several authors have noted a more aggressive temperament—the ♂ ♂ are quite meek—at this stage. The oil gland of 18-day-old nestlings is about 11 mm. long.

Age 20 days—nestlings are well feathered, have tail feathers 6–6.5 cm. long, and spend much time preening.

Nestling weight During their 1st few days, the young eat about 2–4 gm. of food daily, but by 7–10 days they require about 25 gm. See Sherman (1913) for daily wt. of 2 ♂ and 2 ♀ to flight age. E. L. Sumner (1929b) and Balgooyen (1976) also provided data on wt. increase and feather growth. At 16–17 days the young weigh the same as adults. This initial peak is followed by a decrease just before attaining flight. The drop is due to voluntary decrease in food intake, not to the parents starving them to induce departure. For comparison of growth of several body components in parent-raised v. hand-reared Kestrels, see D. Bird and Clark (1983).

Nestling sexual size dimorphism Evident (♀ ♀ larger than ♂ ♂) by about day 6 of nestling life. Males, however, tend to grow faster than ♀ ♀ in some parameters. From D. Bird and Laguë (1982b): hand-reared young grew slower but tended to "catch up" in body wt.; their physical dimensions remained permanently smaller, however, and the heavier ♀ ♀ tended to be larger than ♂ ♂ in certain physical dimensions.

Parental care After the young hatch, the ♂'s absences from the nest area are frequent, whereas the ♀'s are few and brief. Balgooyen did not see any brooding of young by ♂ ♂. By 8–10 days posthatching, diurnal brooding terminates, but the ♀ returns at night to the cavity. Generally, the ♂ is the sole provider of food for the 1st 7–10 days; then both parents bring it. The ♀ is the more frequent provider overall, accounting for roughly 70% of feeding visits (D. Smith et al. 1972, Balgooyen). Occasionally the ♂ transfers food to the ♀ to feed the nestlings, but once she begins to hunt, such transfers no longer occur.

Available data on feeding activity were provided by a camera unit at the nest entrance (Balgooyen) and by a one-way glass window in the back of a nest on a building (D. Smith et al.). In the latter case, food was brought shortly after 1st light, periodically throughout the day, and shortly after sunset (before darkness). Two feeding peaks occurred, 1 between 0900 and 1200 hrs., the other between 1600 and 1700 hrs. Balgooyen noted bunching of feedings, particularly by ♂ ♂. D. Smith et al. provided data on prey numbers and pattern of feeding relative to time of day. Between 2.5 and 3 items were brought hourly, roughly 40 items daily for a total biomass of 165 gm./day for 5 young. Balgooyen computed that the ♂ needs to supply about 153 gm. daily for a family of 4 young plus his mate and himself. Judging from the ♂'s hunting success, 100 daily feedings necessitate the ♀'s help. Sherman (1913) determined an av. length of 2 hrs., 20 min., between feedings of 4 young, while intervals observed by D. Smith et al. ranged from 1 min. to 1 hr., 44 min. Grouped feedings—1 adult feeding several items in an uninterrupted bout—were common in Balgooyen's birds. Contrary to Roest (1957), both sexes do feed the young, the ♀ more often. Occasionally both parents feed the young together.

The nestlings will respond vocally to the calls of adults and N. Flickers and Killdeers. Usually, when a parent arrives, the largest nestling rushes up 1st, the others standing ready. No fighting takes place, save for some brief, gentle tugs-of war. Once satiated, a youngster moves out of the way of hungry siblings. Items of insect size, carried in the parent's beak, are stuffed head-first into the nestling's throat. Larger prey, carried in the talons, is dismembered into bite-size portions. Early on, the ♀ gives only flesh to the young. According to Balgooyen, parents deliver whole, unprepared prey to nestlings beginning at 7–14 days, but Sherman (1913) did not note this until about 19 days. The parents usually leave immediately after delivery. Generally, the young Kestrels back up, raise their tail, and defecate on the walls of the cavity.

Siblicide Neither proved nor disproved, there being no pertinent observations of preflight brood behavior of this hole nester. For example, Young and Blomme (1975) listed 2 apparent instances of cannibalism; these could have been nestlings "which had died of other causes before being eaten by their nest-mates."

For parasites and maladies of nestlings, see Balgooyen (1976).

Age at first flight Occasionally a preflight bird perches in the nest hole; typically, members of a brood leave over a period of several days. Sherman, for example, noted that 4 young departed at the rate of 1/day in this order: ♂ – ♀ – ♂ – ♀. Departure is usually at age 29–31 days. The period was 28–30 days in Lassen Co., Calif. (Bloom and Hawks 1983), and was between 27 and 30 days in Sherman's birds. Older young usually leave 1st. Captives first fly at 26–28 days (D. Bird). In captivity, the 1st nestling hatched in 29 nests flew at an av. age of 28.4 days (Porter and Wiemeyer 1972). First-flight behavior in urban Kestrels was described as more of a crash landing (Black 1979), such that those young unable to fly needed human rescue to survive. Only 1 or 2 managed to fly to an open field across the street. (The young may also reach relatively distant perches.) In Calif., Balgooyen observed young birds and parent ♀ ♀ reentering the cavity at night for up to 12 nights.

Breeding success Has been reported in various ways, preferably being the number of young that fly from successful nests. The figure is high, ranging about 88–

100% in wild birds. In 168 captive-reared young it was 95% (D. Bird and Laguë 1982c). Henny (1972) reported a 7% decrease since 1959 in the number of young banded per successful nest in the ne. U.S., but it was not statistically significant.

Postnesting dependency   Food is still provided for the young up to 12 days after nest departure. At first, short flights are made by flutter-gliding, and the young stay fairly close to one another. Hyperactive young make mock attacks on small inanimate objects, make exaggerated head-bobs and tail-pumping, emit whining noises, and watch alertly for the parents. Soon they frequently fly to the parent for food. Prey items are recognized during nest life, yet when Sherman put live sparrows in a nest, they were not molested. D. Bird observed a Kestrel attempting to catch a butterfly within minutes after leaving the nest. See Balgooyen for similar evidence, also information on parental defense. The young often perch close and imitate one another, frequently travel in pairs, and 6–14 days out of the nest they perch and fly with unrelated Juvs. in groups of 2 or 3; such lack of aggression in the nest area may facilitate Juv. band-formation (D. Lett et al. MS).

Sex ratio   Heintzelman and Nagy (1968) reported a 1 : 1 ratio among nestlings over 8 years; D. Smith et al. (1972) combined 3 years' data for a ratio of 62 ♀ : 38 ♂, similar to Roest's (1957) findings; using only complete clutches, Balgooyen recorded a 92 ♂ : 100 ♀ ratio in Calif.; Bloom and Hawks, in Calif. over 4 years, reported 47 ♀ and 52 ♂; Porter and Wiemeyer (1972) also found a 1 : 1 ratio in complete clutches of 8 captive pairs and a 1 : 1 : 1 tertiary ratio in 19 pairs. Fall, winter, and spring records of Kestrels indicate that ♂ ♂ are more frequently recorded than ♀ ♀; Roest reported that 65% of all returns of banded birds were ♂ ♂. D. Smith et al. noted equal numbers of the sexes in spring and fall in Utah. Beginning with Willoughby and Cade (1964), several authors have reported winterers in an area to be of 1 sex—habitat segregation of the sexes. Balgooyen averaged out all reports to an approximate 1 : 1 sex ratio in the wild.

Duration of family bond   According to Cade (1955a), young in Calif. stay with parents as a family unit for periods ranging from 2 weeks to a month or more. During that span the young receive some food from parents. In late summer, those young that have not strayed are driven off by the parents. Cade observed social hunting groups— several broods banding together to as many as 20 individuals—occupying, but not defending, an area of some 200–300 acres. By mid-July and at various places, all young are generally independent (Roest 1957). In Idaho, D. Smith et al. observed that group hunting by families on nesting territory persisted up to 3 weeks after the young could fly but saw no large bands of Juvs. At Sagehen Creek, Calif. (Balgooyen), family flocks persisted until late Sept. Late in the season, adults occasionally would wander outside territory, pursued by whining youngsters. The Juvs. leave before the adults, and Balgooyen suggested that the oldest leave 1st. The adults depart separately. Surrounding (and even marginal) areas are occupied by dispersing young Kestrels, which are tolerated by territorial ♂ ♂ and ♀ ♀.

Two broods/season   Reported from Fla. (Stahlecker and Griese 1977) to Ont. (Tozer and Richards 1974) and from the Atlantic (n. Va.) to the Pacific (San Francisco Bay region). In captive pairs the "renesting interval" was 11–16 days in 22 pairs, about the same as the span between pairing and laying (Porter and Wiemeyer 1972). For data on many 1st plus 2d broods in cent. Mo., see Toland (1985b). A ♂, while still feeding flying young, also was feeding a ♀ who was laying a new clutch (W. Spofford).

278

In Chile and adjacent parts of Peru, Bolivia, and Argentina, the 1st brood is raised in Oct., the 2d in Dec. or Jan. (A. W. Johnson 1965). Although it has been stated that the Kestrel lays eggs year-round on St. John, Virgin Is., the evidence is better for a season extending from late Feb. into June (Robertson 1962).   DAVID R. BIRD

SURVIVAL   R. Bond's (1943) report of 75% mortality in fall of hatching year was questioned by Parkes (1955), who pointed out that loss of most Juv. feathering that season accounted for apparent disappearance of young birds. Roest (1957), using data on 150 kestrels of known age when banded, arrived at mortality rates of 70–43%, av. 57%. Henny (1972) calculated mortality rates for 1925–1945 and 1946–1965. "Adult" rates did not differ, but 1st-year mortality apparently had decreased since 1945. Recovery of shot birds declined (decrease in shooting pressure), particularly of the more vulnerable birds in their 1st calendar year. He detected no change in overall mortality rates.

Of birds recovered dead, 1,017 records revealed an annual av. survival of 12.6 months, the oldest bird being aged 9 years, 10 months (Keran 1981). The oldest reported by Clapp et al. (1982) was aged 11 years and 2 months. Captives at the McGill Univ. colony live an av. of 5 years and 2 months, the oldest being a 14-year-old ♂, and both sexes still are breeding at 10 years of age (D. Bird).

Of 185 banding returns where cause of death was known, 45 (possibly more) were shot and 40 were trapped and/or captured (Roest 1957). Of 139 deaths recorded by rehabilitators at Univ. of Minn., 122 were man-caused. Of 1,017 deaths recorded at the Bird Banding Laboratory, known man-caused ones included 158 killed by traffic and 186 by other means; 29 were killed by predators (Keran 1981). A few Kestrels have diseases or abnormalities, including missing toes and talons and a condition called bumblefoot (D. Rogers and Dauber 1977). Kestrels lose their lives in other ways. Examples: going down chimneys, drowning in watering tanks and pools, and collisions with wires and windows; at least formerly, many caused expensive electric power failures via "insulator flashovers" (Michener 1928)—that is, they were electrocuted. The Kestrel has been trapped in fresh tar on a newly resurfaced road when pursuing prey already immobilized there.

There were several hundred dead Kestrels close to Key West, Fla., just after passage of a cold front (Layne 1980). In cent. Ohio, Mills (1975) observed a rapid decrease of winterers after the 1st cold spell but did not witness actual mortality. Kestrels in spring at boreal limits of occurrence, where the temperature can drop suddenly, have been found dead. In the captive colony at McGill, the most mortality occurs with onset of the 1st cold spell in autumn; as many as a dozen died in 1 night (D. Bird). Urban habitat is a mixed blessing, especially because of the hazards to young out of the nest before well able to fly; they spend much time on the ground, and some are victims of dogs, cats, and automobiles, some starve, and some are "rescued" by humans. Orphaned young are the most frequent raptor patients at rehabilitation centers.   DAVID M. BIRD

HABITS   Mainly of *F. s. sparverius*.
The sexes differ less in size than do Peregrines and take the same kinds of prey in about the same proportions (Cade 1960), although some differences are now reported.

A bird may develop a propensity for a particular prey species, to the frequent exclusion of others. Basically, the Kestrel kills only when hungry (Mueller 1973b), yet it may store a considerable surplus of food (see below).

Flapping, hovering, and soaring are common daily activities. Flapping rate is about 2.8 wingbeats/sec. in still air or (C. Blake 1948) 4.6/sec. against a moderate wind. A speed of 20 mph is easily maintained (Roest 1957). Migrants at Hawk Mt., Pa., had speeds of 22–36 mph with flapping flight in nw. winds that varied 4–25 mph (Broun and Goodwin 1943). The Kestrel dives swiftly, but not as spectacularly as the larger falcons. It has evolved efficient flight patterns to reduce caloric demand (Balgooyen 1976). Low wing loading (ratio of total wt. to wing area) of about 0.3 gm./sq. cm. facilitates hovering; this costs more but also yields more per unit of time than perch-hunting (Rudolph 1982).

L. Miller (1954) noted a fairly strict schedule of a wintering ♀ Kestrel that roosted in his house eaves. In 26 instances, arrival time before sunset was 4–21 min., av. 12.7, and 2 morning departure times were 17 and 15 min. before sunrise. The weather varied. Kestrels hunt more or less irregularly and continuously throughout the day (R. Bond 1936), and Balgooyen's Kestrels in Calif. exhibited no peaks of activity. They rarely began by 0700 hrs., preferring to catch insects that became active around 0900 hrs. In semidesert, however, Kestrels hunted in morning and evening (Bartholomew and Cade 1957). Female Kestrels wintering on agricultural lands in nw. Calif. spent 6.6% of an 11-hr. photoperiod in flight activities and the remaining time perched (Koplin et al. 1980). Eighty percent of the latter was spent searching for prey.

Of 151 wintering Kestrels sighted in an automobile survey in e. Tex., 92% were on utility lines (Bildstein and Grubb 1980), and Craig's (1978) auto survey in se. Idaho revealed that most Kestrels perched either on the tops or the wires of power poles rather than on the cross arms; 15% were on fence posts. Pet Kestrels commonly choose the highest available perch. To sleep, the bird stands on 1 foot and tucks its head under the scapulars; to doze, it pulls the head low on the neck and closes its eyes.

Kestrels in Humboldt Co., Calif., fed on rodents and shrews in absence of insect prey (Collopy 1973). According to Hart (1972), in Wis., Kestrels compensated for vole scarcity by taking more birds and insects, thus indicating flexibility and lack of dependence on fluctuating rodent numbers. After the young are on the wing, entire families move to timberline basins in Calif. to eat grasshoppers, which are plentiful in late summer and fall.

Grass fires attract many Kestrels, which hunt along the edge (usually the windward side) for insects, rodents, and small reptiles. They dash close to the flames, sometimes alighting on stubs or fallen branches in thick smoke (Schorger 1917), or hover, performing shallow stoops (Smallwood et al. 1982).

Kestrels seek prey essentially in similar microhabitats using the same methods, according to Balgooyen (1976). The birds he studied in the Sierra Nevada of Calif. mostly still-hunted (97%) in areas of low open vegetation. In heavier cover they waited longer to locate prey. Stinson et al. (1981) recorded longer flight times by ♀♀ over low vegetation with no high perches than over intermediate or high vegetation. In a series of prey-capture experiments in the laboratory, Sparrowe (1972) demonstrated that the length of time suitable prey is exposed to the Kestrel controls whether an attack is initiated, carried through, and/or successful. This in turn is controlled by cover density and contrast of prey with background.

Hover-hunting Particularly in areas lacking prominent perches, Kestrels hover over 1 spot, apparently only when there is some wind to minimize energy costs (Balgooyen). They hover more as wind speed increases (Rudolph 1982). Usually the tail is spread fully and angled below the body, the head in motion scans the ground below, and the wing tips winnow in a small amplitude of about 10–15 cm. Posture varies somewhat with wind speed. Sometimes the wings are essentially motionless, kitelike. Most hovering is at altitudes of 12–25 m., and duration seldom exceeds 1 min.

When prey is sighted, the bird may partly fold its wings and drop lower down or even repeat this several times before attempting a strike. If no prey is spotted, the Kestrel may wheel away in a semicircular glide for perhaps 100 yds., then turn again into the wind, stretch the head up, ascend a few ft. before becoming relatively stationary, and finally restore the head to a downward-looking position. Judging from the literature, at least most Kestrels in the tropics also hover. Roest (1957) noted that hovering Kestrels dive headfirst at mammals and feetfirst at insects but take both in the feet. Mills (1976) watched a concentration of 11 Kestrels, mostly ♀♀, hovering to capture insects from a freshly plowed field; some, however, hunted from the ground.

Soaring The Kestrel spreads its wings to full extent (they appear less pointed than usual) and spreads its tail (but less so than in hovering), which aids in controlling direction. The bird moves mostly in circles and figure eights.

Still- or perch-and-wait hunting The Kestrel perches on an elevated site and awaits the appearance or movement of prey. If success rate is unsatisfactory, the bird goes elsewhere. Perch height apparently bears no relationship to strike distance, the av. distance being around 34 m. and maximum 275 m. (Balgooyen). Actual attack is often preceded by much head-bobbing and tail-pumping. The Kestrel watches the flight of a grasshopper. As soon as the insect alights, the bird flies close to the spot, checks its flight, and usually flushes the insect. Then it usually makes the kill on the wing. If the grasshopper does not flush, the Kestrel alights and walks about, attempting to flush it, searching usually for less than 10 sec. (Balgooyen 1976). Tadpoles and water beetles in ditches are captured by still-hunting from overhead perches, and lizards are picked deftly off tree trunks and rocks. Costa Rican Kestrels still-hunt over pastures and lawns but hover primarily over longer grasses (R. Jenkins 1970).

Coursing At times low over the ground in the Merlin manner, is not a common hunting method (except perhaps at times in migration), but is used in pursuit of flying prey (including insects). In Tierra del Fuego, Humphrey et al. (1970) considered that *F. sparverius* hovered less than does *F. tinnunculus* in Europe; instead, it resorted to skimming the ground in rapid, dashing flight. When migrants in N. Am. are traveling thus, they seem also to be on the lookout for potential prey.

Insect catching (See also perch-hunting, above.) Most of the older reports of taking flying insects were summarized by Rudolph (1983). In perch-hunting, the Kestrel flies out, makes a capture, and then returns to feed on it. Even tiny prey is taken in a foot. In a variant of flight-hunting, the Kestrel soars and flaps upward and away from its perch, then stalls or dives abruptly to its target, reportedly taking it in the beak. It may eat the insect during flight, return with it to a perch, or feed it to a young Kestrel. In another variant (Locke 1961), a ♀, on sighting a dragonfly, would dart from a perch, tilt her body, and attempt to strike down the insect with a wing. Then she would drop to the ground, seize the prey, and return to a log to eat it. Wings and head were discarded. Occasionally she made several passes at a dragonfly without capturing it. In n. Sask., Nero (1963) found dragonfly wings in a Kestral nest site even before eggs were laid.

Aerial bird-hunting Small birds utter alarm calls on approach of a Kestrel, so they recognize it as a danger even though it seldom kills them. Apparently they are taken more often when they are moving about conspicuously, as during spring migration when other Kestrel food is less accessible. Size of kills has ranged from Calif. Quail and Mourning Dove down to 2 records of hummingbirds, and ♂ Kestrels are thought to be partial to avian prey. See summary by Mills (1976); also note birds as listed under Food, below.

Nest robbing To a summary of earlier reports, Richards (1967) added that a Kestrel searched several trees, aparently in a "rather systematic manner," that Kestrels have been seen inspecting House Sparrow nests while the adult sparrows fluttered help-lessly nearby, and that 1 Kestrel was seen to tear the roof off such a nest. Whenever it finds a brood of nestlings, the Kestrel keeps returning until it has removed all of them.

Robbing burrows and nests of swallows has been reported most often. In cent. N.Y., Kestrels were seen 40 times perched on or near the edge of Bank Swallow colonies. A Kestrel flew to a swallow burrow 25 times, taking 9 nestlings. The swallow colonies were within Kestrel territories, and usually this raptor appeared when the young swallows were approximately 14–16 days old, at which age they move close to the burrow entrance to facilitate rapid feeding from their parents. It is of interest that flying Kestrels disturbed the parent swallows (whose alarm calls may function to warn their broods) and that the swallows quieted down when a Kestrel alighted anywhere within a colony. For details, see Freer (1973) and especially Windsor and Emlen (1975). The Kestrel has taken nestling phoebes (R. Cowles 1928); it also took a young bluebird and extended its foot into the nestbox attempting to get another (Drinkwater 1953). To extract a Cliff Swallow from a nest, a Kestrel hung upside down by 1 foot and reached in with the other (Bonnot 1921). In se. Brazil, Kestrels tried to raid the nests of Gray-breasted Martins (*Progne chalybea*) (M. Mitchell 1957).

Bat catching About 7 genera are known prey in N. Am., and apparently the Kestrel seldom misses in a capture attempt. It may snatch a bat off the bark of a tree (D. Stoner 1939b) or catch it in flight. At a cave, J. K. Baker (1962) observed a Kestrel entering an outgoing bat flight several times, catching 1 each time, but only killing and eating the last 1 taken. The Kestrel also attacked the incoming flight, with unknown results. Usually the Kestrel perches near the cavern entrance, awaiting the bats. Eanes (1924) reported 2 Kestrels killing as many as 20 bats in an evening without eating any. In this instance the tactic was to fly above a building and descend rapidly, striking bats as they flew away from the walls. If they missed, they ascended and again at-tacked. Level of illumination was not reported. When it was less than 1 foot-candle at 0458 hrs., however, Twente (1954) saw successful capture of a *Myotis*. Several dives may be made before the quarry is caught in a foot. One knocked a bat to the ground, then retrieved it. Bats are frequently caught from behind in straighaway flight. Most of the earlier accounts of captures were listed in S. Garber's (1977) summary, and see also Holroyd and Beaubien (1983). Taking bats in the dim light of dusk or dawn seems to be at variance with Fox et al. (1976), who reported that Kestrel visual acuity declined sharply in poorer light. In contrast, Pierce's (1937) pet Kestrel had no difficulty in gaining a perch upon escaping at night or finding food in a darkened box. In any event, it appears that bats are easy to catch, even in diminished light.

Ground foraging   Whether the Kestrel pounces from the air or engages in terrestrial pursuit is a thin line, but at least most of the following relate to opportunity to move afoot. A Kestrel ran about on a lawn like a Killdeer, occasionally flapping to gain speed, and another foraging bird jumped along in an alfalfa field (Marshall 1957). A Kestrel had some method of getting many cecropia moth cocoons (R. Miller 1905) and corn borer larvae (Petrovic and Mills 1972). It has taken small chickens (Steidl 1928), young Killdeer (Meyerriecks 1957), Least Terns (Fisk 1972), and Mallard ducklings (Follen 1976). For obvious reasons, frogs, lizards, and small mammals are attacked from flight.

Kestrels have not only taken birds immobilized in banders' mist nets but can also be a nuisance where other traps are on the ground. They reach into, or even enter, them to kill and eat the occupants.

At the beginning of Apr. in Toronto, a ♀ Kestrel joined feral pigeons that were being fed bread. At first she came only when the pigeons were feeding. On the 1st day she held the bread in her feet, dismantled it with her beak, and may not have swallowed any. Later she still wasted much of it. The next day she carried it to her perch, in beak or feet, definitely ate some, and lost her apparent dependence on foraging by pigeons. By the 3d day, she no longer pounced on the bread (as on a grasshopper) but ran about like an Am. Robin, carrying bread in her beak to a perch. On the 4th day she used this method to capture rained-out earthworms. The next day was cold, so she returned to a diet of bread (Warburton 1952).

Earthworms are taken during walking forays after rainfall in suburban areas (Cade 1982), and in the Puget Sd. area the Kestrel feeds primarily on earthworms in normal winter weather (F. Beebe 1974).

Carrion   Fresh or decayed flesh is eaten rarely.

Caching   The killing and concealment of surplus prey is known in both wild Kestrels (Eanes 1928) and captives (Nunn et al. 1976). It is done by both sexes and in any season; for example, see Balgooyen (1976) for roles of the sexes in the breeding season. Usually the Kestrel transfers prey from a foot to the beak and pushes or wedges it into the chosen site. Tordoff (1955) watched 2 birds hover over a cache site briefly, suggesting that they memorized its location for retrieval. Lizards, snakes, frogs, birds, and rodents (but not insects) are cached but not necessarily decapitated beforehand. Several sites may be close together, as in a tree. Stendell and Waian (1968) watched a ♀ (or pair?) cache 17 items at a site over a 40-day period, and in Balgooyen's study, ♀♀ maintained more sites than ♂♂. According to Bildstein (1982a), cache sites serve to hide, as well as store, prey, and Kestrels often conceal food if about to be disturbed. They also become excited if a site is approached by a potential thief. Nunn et al. (1976) observed a ♀ kill and cache up to 20 provided mice in succession before eating any. Such abundance of easily gotten prey may trigger caching. In Collopy's (1977) study,

283

Kestrels apparently continued to hunt immediately after storing prey. In 90 observed instances in 2 years, 51% were of storage, 36% were retrievals, and 13% were attempts to retrieve. Occasionally prey is retrieved and then stored again.

Toland's (1984) study was done year-round in Mo.; he listed much of the literature and reappraised some of it. He observed 30 Kestrels cache 116 times (95% rodents, 5% birds) and retrieve 77.5%. The prey was hidden in grass clumps (often, by both sexes), hollow railroad ties, tree roots, bushes, fence posts, building gutters, tree limbs and holes (very often, by ♂ ♂), and tops of power poles. Height of sites varied 0–20 m. In spring–summer, 93% of cached items were uneaten and in fall–winter 42%. Only 32 prey were decapitated—a low figure compared with some other studies. Prey was not placed in any preferential position, and sometimes the site had apparently been selected beforehand. When a number of mice were released at about the same time, a Kestrel killed them while in flight and stored all in the same site. Seven prey were cached together in a 5-min. period. Extra food was stored for a few hrs. to several days and thus would be a reserve to draw on during unfavorable hunting weather or to meet the needs of a growing brood.

Visual acuity Remarkable (see Pierce 1937), but not 2.6 times that of humans (Hirsch 1982), as had been reported. Actually, it is about the same. Stereoscopic depth perception has been demonstrated (R. Fox et al. 1976). Kestrels head-bob to separate planes and to improve distance judgment: Grinnell's (1921) principle of rapid peering. The body may move on a swaying branch or during hovering, yet the head may remain relatively stationary to maintain a "fix" on potential prey.

Prey recognition and selection Balgooyen (1976) felt that Kestrels recognize potential prey before they are old enough to fly; they were reluctant to accept unusual offerings (such as lean beef) but readily accepted "normal" prey. Further, parents deliver or drop prey to their flying young, which have had no previous experience with it, and they accept it readily. (Do they associate acceptable food with parent?) Live sparrows placed with nestlings elicited either a fear response or none at all (Sherman 1913). From laboratory experiments, Mueller (1977) concluded that predatory responses by Kestrels were largely innate and that experience plays a minor role in the development of recognizing, capturing, and killing mice. In the 1970s and early 1980s various studies were published of attempts to elucidate the importance of specific search images, movement, oddity, novelty, conspicuousness, familiarity, conditioning, hunger, and so on. Authors do not necessarily agree, but time may tell. Meanwhile, it appears that an active mouse, of "usual" color and pattern, is living dangerously if it is near a Kestrel.

In wild birds in s. Calif., the sexes showed no preference as to prey size in winter; in the breeding season, ♂ ♂ usually chose smaller prey than ♀ ♀. Larger prey were preferred by hungry birds, as were "normal"-colored rather than white mice (Bryan 1984). Elsewhere in Calif. in the breeding season, the sexes took similar-sized prey (Balgooyen). A Kestrel caught a spadefoot toad, shook its head repeatedly while attempting to eat it, and discarded it (Mills 1977). A tame bird repeatedly rejected parts of frogs (Ingles 1940). From the evidence in Mills (1976), it would appear that ♂ ♂ are more apt to take birds. Kestrels seem to have good memory; a captive-bred released ♂

284

returned a year later to steal a day-old chick (it had been raised on chicks) through the wire of a captive Kestrel's cage (D. Bird).

Prey capture The quarry is usually taken with a foot (or the feet?) and killed with the beak; when ground-foraging for insects, some prey is seized in the beak. Regarding a pet Kestrel, Pierce (1937) found it "almost unbelievable how tiny an insect he could hold in his talons." Balgooyen believed that the notching of the maxillary tomium aids in efficient penetration of a prey skull and neck and that the "tooth" reinforces the beak's tip.

The bird may dive at prey with wings partly closed or flutter downward, checking and controlling its descent. Attack and strike vary in angle; see Goslow (1971) for velocities and for angles of pelvic limb joints. A flashlike sideways movement was used in capturing a hummingbird in the air (Mayr 1966). Lamore (1963) watched 1 capture a lizard with its feet, then strike it twice with the beak. Nunn et al. (1976) described a tame Kestrel using its talons to grasp a young rat by the neck; then it bit the eyes, cranium, and nasal bones to kill it. In the wild, with mouse-sized prey, the Kestrel may kill either at the capture site, while it is aerially transported, or after arrival at a nearby perch. For ways in which hand-reared "naive" Kestrels manage prey, see Mueller (1973b).

Kestrels generally ingest smaller insects whole but may initially tear off the head and devour it, sometimes with entrails attached. The legs, wings, and occasionally overly large rear portions of larger insects are discarded, but the entrails are eaten. Avian kills are often found with heads or eyes missing, skulls torn open exposing the brain, and/or breast partly eaten along with contents of upper abdomen. Pierce's pet bird swallowed whole, then later regurgitated, a small lizard. R. Bond (1936) observed that, like other falcons, Kestrels lift their heads every 3d or 4th mouthful to look about. Small prey is sometimes transferred to the beak and consumed during flight over land, perhaps more often over water.

Capture success Varies with prey density and type, cover, origin of attack (as perch v. hovering), and so on. Collopy observed a success rate of 51%. Of 233 captures, 85.4% were invertebrates, the remainder vertebrates. A quarter of dives on vertebrates were successful, also 64% of 309 dives on invertebrates. Fifty-two percent of 403 dives from a perch were successful against only 22% from hovering. In the Sierra Nevada of Calif. (Balgooyen), 70% of 813 attempts succeeded; ♀♀ and ♂♂ differed little. Success rate went from 40% in early spring to 90% in late summer. As prey densities increased, Kestrels became more efficient, especially with emergence of grasshoppers. Kestrels in Mich. made 17 captures in 47 attempts from perches and 1 from hovering (Sparrowe 1972). G. Page and Whitacre (1975) watched 3 captures from 15 attempts on small shorebirds on the ground. In vegetation of intermediate height, ♂♂ were successful in 4 of 6 attempts, and ♀♀ caught 18 prey in 36 attempts (Stinson et al. 1981). Success rate in Costa Rica was 39% of 246 attempts (R. Jenkins 1970).

Maximum weight transported Balgooyen observed ♂ Kestrels carrying maximum loads of 89 and 57 gm. and ♀♀ 80, 51, and 45 gm., but not without difficulty. Maillard (1928) watched a Kestrel (sex?) attempt unsuccessfully to carry off a road-killed Calif. Quail (ca. 200 gm.) and Lamore (1956) witnessed a ♂ carrying an adult Am. Robin (ca.

74–85 gm.) under labored flight. Marshall (1957) described a ♂ unable to get fully airborne with a full-sized Juv. Am. Robin, but its mate flew away more easily with it. On 2 occasions, Southern (1974) saw adult ♀ Kestrels carrying full-grown rats, but less than 0.3 m. above the ground, indicating some ability to transport prey approaching twice their own wt. Occasionally the Kestrel kills prey heavier than itself.

Food consumption   Crop capacity is about 12 gm., and Kestrels eat a maximum of 8–12 gm. per meal (Collopy 1977). For data on food for raising a family, see Reproduction, above. Off and on in the span Dec. 25–Mar. 25, L. and A. Wing (1939) measured food consumption of a wild ♂ held in captivity. At temperatures of 1.9–21°C, it ate 24 gm. daily (about 21% of its body wt.). Their data agree well with the 42 cal./gm. body wt./day computed by Barrett and Mackey (1975). Daily food intake of wild Kestrels was about 40 gm. for fall–winter and 27 for spring–summer (the Craigheads 1956). A 114-gm. ♂ had ingested 71 corn borer larvae comprising 95% of stomach contents.

Pellet formation   Kestrel pellets are more or less an elongated elliptical shape but may taper to somewhat of a point at either or both ends; there is, of course, variation depending on what was eaten. Of 142 pellets collected from Chilean Kestrels (Yanez et al. 1980), mean and standard error: length 24.7 ± 0.51 mm. and diam. 11.3 ± 0.33; dry wt. 0.48 ± 0.01 gm. Regurgitation, or egestion, by captives in Calif. was discussed by Balgooyen (1971), who gave volumes of 222 pellets as 1.59 ± 1.18 cubic cm. The mean time of ejection was 21 hrs., 33 min., after eating any of several types of meals, and wt. differed with type of food. The usual rate was a pellet a day, but consumption of unusually large amounts of indigestible material resulted in multiple ejections. Seeds and fruits have germinated from regurgitated Kestrel pellets, suggesting a mechanism for long-range plant dispersal—"endornithocory" (Balgooyen and Moe 1973). The Kestrel sheds its stomach lining (McAtee 1917).

Use of water   Pierce (1937) knew of captives that bathed regularly, yet his pet bird avoided water for its 1st 6 months before it began to drink small amounts and wanted to bathe. There are records of Kestrels drowning in livestock watering tanks and troughs; in se. Idaho (Craig and Powers 1976), this may be a significant mortality factor. Captives can be maintained without access to water and apparently breed normally (D. Bird). They may exist on water content of prey items and water manufactured within the body (Cade and Greenwald 1966); a ♀ studied produced very concentrated urine in comparison with some other raptorial birds and also had high ionic concentrations in blood plasma. Compared with 6 other raptors (M. Hughes 1970), the Kestrel had, relative to body wt., the heaviest kidneys.

Metabolism   Breathing rate varies 35.4–54/min. (K. Daniels and Duke 1980). Roest (1957) reported a body temperature of 38.3°C (at ambient temp. 20°C) for nestlings, but more reliable 40.5°C of Bartholomew and Cade (1957). High ambient temperatures increase it by 2–4° only. This, combined with apparent independence of surface water and with diurnal hunting patterns, enables the Kestrel to dwell in deserts. Mean body temperature of 11 captives measured at night at 27°C was 39.3 ± 0.4°C and declined by 0.2–0.4° daily during fasting (Shapiro and Weathers 1981). For many additional data on metabolism of wild and captive birds, see especially Gessaman (1979a, 1980), Gessaman and Findell (1979), Hayes and Gessaman (1980), and Koplin

286

et al. (1980). Balgooyen (1976) provided an argument for sexual size dimorphism based on energy expenditure.

Play   Documented in pet Kestrels (see Pierce 1937) and probably occurs also in the wild. Whether attacks on unlikely targets, as egrets, are attributable to playfulness, hunger, lack of experience, or some other motivation is conjectural.

Grooming   Captives generally have 2 daily grooming peaks, in early morning and midafternoon, with special attention paid to the alulae and primaries. Beak wiping is associated exclusively with feeding. Lefebvre and Joly (1982) categorized grooming bouts into long and short, discussing in detail organization rules and timing.

Wintering behavior   See Habitat, above, for differential use of habitat by the sexes at this season. This may reduce intersexual competition for food (Koplin 1973), while winter territoriality serves to maintain adequate hunting ground. Costa Rican Kestrels are solitary, apparently territorial, and, once holding a food-rich territory, become quite sedentary (R. Jenkins 1970). Cade (1955a) experimentally demonstrated territorial behavior in Kestrels wintering in Calif. Live or stuffed "intruders" elicited indifferent to very violent behavior from both sexes. Males were less inclined to attack intruding ♀ ♀ (see also Mills 1975). Physical contact usually involves a pair grappling to the ground. Mills noted 5 cases of ♂ and ♀ sharing territory. In Calif. (Cade 1955a), pairs with permanent pair bonds began to defend winter territory in late Aug. against migrants. Apparently the presence of a roost is an important aspect of territoriality; many of Mills's birds entered old buildings at dusk. Bildstein (1978) also noted that wintering Kestrels in Ohio preferred to occupy areas within 75 m. of active farm sites, which other raptors avoided.

The av. diam. of winter territories in Ohio was 1.4 km., the largest 2.4 km. (Mills 1975). Smaller than 2.4 km. were reported for Ill. (Enderson 1960), but were 3.5 km. in Mich. (the Craigheads 1956). A Costa Rican ♂ took up winter residence in an area 400 m. in diam.

Densities varied 11–18 birds per 100 km. of roadway in s. Tex. and 9–16 in s. Ariz. (Mills 1976). Occasional large concentrations of Kestrels, such as 10 ♀ and 1 ♂ in a 90-acre freshly plowed field, were found in Ariz., where several chases were observed. On Oct. 5, Mills saw 15 ♂ and 7 ♀ in an area less than 1.6 km. in diam. Birds were perched in 2s or 3s, often of the same sex, and no aggressive interactions were seen. Overall densities in cent. Ohio (Mills 1975) were 17–27 per 52 sq. km., compared to 4–10 per 111 sq. km. in Ill. (Enderson 1960) and 5 per 96 sq. km. in Mich. (the Craigheads 1956). In road surveys, Koplin (1973) found 34 ± 11 per 161 km. in Calif. coastal and Coast Range habitats and 115 + 25 per 161 km. in Central Valley habitat. In se. Idaho, Craig (1978) encountered 0.59 Kestrels per km. of roadway. In se. Fla., Layne's (1980) study area contained 0.48 birds per sq. km., ranging 0.25–0.71. Other specifics included a trend of fewer Kestrels wintering there.

Some interspecific relations   Migrating Kestrels harassed buteos and eagles at Hawk Mt., Pa. (Broun 1939). Wintering Kestrels have chased Red-tailed and Sharp-shinned Hawks and a Merlin (Mills 1975) and have struck a Cattle Egret (R. Roberts and Kale 1978). Wintering Kestrels may be clumped with spatial separation from shrikes (Bildstein and Grubb 1980). A shrike perched only 5 yds. from a ♂ Kestrel and stole a mouse from it (Hill 1945). Kestrels may rob one another (Marshall 1957, Fetterolf 1979).

Kestrels have few known enemies but have been found in diets of the Goshawk, Redtail, Sharpshin, Cooper's Hawk, Peregrine, and Barn Owl. A crow killed and ate a ♀ (M. Walker 1974). Kestrels seem to particularly dislike and harass Redtails but avoid accipiters (yet successfully defend their nest and young from them). They also defend their nest sites against other cavity nesters. In the breeding season, chasing other raptors consumes about ⅘ defense time. A Kestrel may attack a raptor and then briefly redirect the attack against some nonraptor. Generally they are on the offensive, but they have been defensive against hummingbirds, swallows, Am. Robins, blackbirds, and Chimney Swifts. An Am. Robin knocked a young Kestrel from its perch. Mobbing by Bank Swallows was ineffective against flying Kestrels, and the swallows quieted down when the predator alighted near their burrows (Windsor and Emlen 1975).

Ethnology Kestrel remains have frequently been found in the ruins of abandoned Indian dwellings, which suggest that they were kept as pets and/or killed for various purposes (A. Miller 1932). They are often found in the sacred bundles of the Plains tribes, thus being associated with human burials (Gilmore 1932), and they were pets among the Paiutes (A. Johnson 1936).

Biocides Known to have caused Kestrel deaths, yet (Henny 1977b) chemical contaminants did not result in a drastic decline in numbers. Northerly Kestrels accumulated DDE where they wintered (Lincer and Sherburne 1974). From study of wild and captive Kestrels, much has been reported on effects of organochlorines, other chemicals, metals, oil, and radionuclide concentrations—all this not summarized here. Diseases and parasites are also omitted, and the published sources are scattered.

Kestrel numbers Based on an assumed density of a pair per 100 sq. km. n. of lat. 45°N and a pair per 5 sq. km. elsewhere, Cade (1982) estimated 1,000,000 pairs in N. Am. and suggested that Cent. and S. Am. numbers were equally large—and possibly increasing due to such human activity as deforestation. Henny (1972) calculated that, on av., breeding ♀♀ must produce 2.88 young to flight age annually to maintain a stable population. A figure of 3.92 indicated stability before 1959, but a subsequent decrease plus reported declines in migrants seen suggested a slight drop in numbers.

In the period 1934–1975 there was a long-term increase in migrants seen at Hawk Mt., Pa. (Nagy, in Chancellor 1977). Winter counts 1946–1979 in Wash. indicated a high in the mid-1940s, decline 1951–1961, and a rather steady increase from the mid-1960s onward (D. Smith and Knight 1981).

As laboratory animal The advantages of the Kestrel for research were discussed by Porter and Wiemeyer (1970), D. Bird and Rehder (1981), and D. Bird (1982). Information is already available on captive maintenance, breeding techniques, hand-rearing, artificial insemination, semen preservation, assay teachniques, and a host of other topics. Kestrels are maintained in captivity by the 100s.   DAVID M. BIRD

FOOD   *F. s. sparverius*.   Largely insects (especially grasshoppers and allies), small mammals (especially voles and cotton rats), birds (mainly small, also preflight young), small reptiles, a few amphibians, and a few miscellaneous items. Some foods and methods of capture were mentioned in previous pages. The Kestrel takes at least several times as many insects as vertebrates.

Of 703 stomachs examined in the U.S. Biol. Survey, the main categories and the number of stomachs in which they were found were: Orthoptera (grasshoppers, etc.) 491, beetles 207, mammals (especially voles) 192, spiders 153, caterpillars 150, lizards 41, birds 38, moths and butterflies 22, and snakes 21 (McAtee 1935). These data, which had accumulated over many years, include the material in A. K. Fisher (1893). For some recent papers, the reader interested in details should consult Sherrod (1978).

One's first impression is that the Kestrel is very flexible, using whatever hunting method is appropriate to take whatever is of manageable size and is readily available. Yet, from reading one study, one might assume that food is principally grasshoppers, in another it is voles, and in yet another, birds. To a great extent, this is due to individual Kestrels developing a proclivity to take particular prey; they develop specific search images and concentrate on a single species or group—grasshoppers, dragonflies, or birds—as long as such remains available, while ignoring other acceptable quarry (R. Bond 1936, later authors). Also, when brood rearing, they tend to concentrate on vertebrates, which yield much nourishment per item captured.

Mammals Usually open-country species, including rodents of at least 12 genera. Small (young) ground squirrels (*Spermophilus*), wood rats (*Neotoma*), pocket gophers (*Geomys*), red squirrel, chipmunks, Least Weasel (*Mustela*), and such mouse-sized species as voles (*Microtus*) northerly and cotton rats (*Sigmodon*) southerly, house mice (*Mus*), and so on. Bats of about 7 genera. Largest mammal reported is "rabbit" (carrion?) and smallest is shrew (*Sorex*).

Birds Of numerous species, from Mourning Dove (*Zenaida*) and quail (*Callipepla*) size to many species of approximately meadowlark (*Sturnella*) to swallow size, and even smaller—to wrens, bushtits, and (twice reported) hummingbirds. Least Sandpepers at Bolinas Lagoon, Calif. Many House Sparrows (*Passer*) are taken in rural to urban areas. Horned Larks on the high plains. A breeding pair in n. Ont. took many Brown-headed Cowbirds (*Molothrus*). Chicks of domestic fowl and Ring-necked Pheasant; Mallard ducklings; preflight young of various other precocial birds; nestlings of various small altricial birds removed from nests, bird houses, or (Bank Swallows) burrow entrances. Some avian prey was tabulated by Mills (1976).

Reptiles Include various genera of small lizards, some being labeled skink, swift, anole, race-runner, chameleon, and so on. At least seasonally, lizards appear to be a mainstay in some warmer areas. Small snakes of 3 or more genera. A horned "toad" (*Phrynosoma*) occasionally.

Amphibians Frogs of several species, tadpoles, toads.

Insects The long list is headed by large and conspicuous ones, such as grasshoppers, dragonflies, crickets, and June beetles. Many others, especially beetles, some down to surprisingly small size, such as weevils.

Miscellaneous Crayfishes, centipedes, scorpions, spiders, earthworms, and a snail. Bread (see Habits, above).

Carrion California Quail and Screech Owl. A noose trap for catching Kestrels was baited with thawed carcasses of mice, voles, and House Sparrow (Wegner 1981).

F. s. paulus   Of 25 stomachs from Fla., 24 contained insects and none birds (A. Howell 1932). **Mammals**   Cotton rat (*Sigmodon*) and deer mouse (*Peromyscus*). **Birds**   Yellow-rumped Warbler and E. Phoebe (F. C. Baker 1980). **Insects**   Mainly grasshoppers and other Orthoptera, katydids, field crickets, cave crickets, dragonflies, long-horned beetles, carrion beetles, and lepidopterous larvae. **Miscellaneous**   lizards, tree frog (*Hyla*), and spiders.

Extralimital   A study in "Mexico" (Sherrod 1978) is interesting because of the number of sizable birds taken: Killdeer, 6 White-winged Doves, 28 Mourning Doves, 6 Common Ground-Doves, a Red-billed Pigeon, various cuckoos and woodpeckers, and 10 Great-tailed Grackles; also smaller birds and insects.

Recent Kestrel studies in S. Am. are not summarized here, but many small rodents and large insects are taken on the mainland. The resident birds of the Netherlands Leeward Is. were seen repeatedly catching small and medium-sized lizards from the ground—16 of 18 stomachs contained them (also other foods) (Voous 1955).

DAVID M. BIRD

♂ Basic

♂ Basic

♀ Basic

♀ Basic
drawn from life

P.P.P.

MERLIN

Falco columbarius

Pigeon Hawk, so-called formerly in N. Am. Small, stocky falcon with compact feathering; in configuration more or less a diminutive Gyrfalcon. Usually some dark on anterior cheek, but not a prominent "mustache"; area from eye to cere nearly bare. Lower forehead light or white, this extending narrowly over eye. Dark dorsally from head to most of tail, except more or less interrupted by mixed white and tan or darker across nape (nuchal patch). Tail slightly rounded. Wing—counting from outer primary, the 3d (longest) is slightly longer than the 2d, and 1st (outer) shorter than 4th. There is some narrowing distally of webs of outer primaries, most pronouncedly the inner webs of outer 2 feathers.

In definitive feathering the sexes differ greatly; the ♀ throughout life essentially repeats the Juv. pattern and coloring but with grayish or bluish rump. The ♂ differs in coloring and pattern. Sexes and all flying ages: underparts light with little to much dark streaking (or widened barring). Definitive ♂ varies geographically from a very deep to a palish slaty bluish dorsally and tail (dorsal view) from black interrupted with white bars to (part of Pacific NW area) same with faintly indicated or lacking lighter bars (and somewhat similar in some extralimital populations). Definitive ♀ toward a muted brownish dorsally and feathers without obvious light ends; dark ventral streaking sharply defined; tail with variable number (often 4–6) blackish bars, in some populations much wider than the conspicuous to faint intervening light ones. Juvenal ♂ ♀— dark feathers of dorsum with tan margins; ventral streaking slightly diffuse; tail variable: in N. Am. with transverse dark and light bars to same with white reduced to nearly absent, in much of Eurasia mostly with alternating blackish brown and light (buffy to tan) bars, varying in width.

291

In the species the ♀ av. larger, the sexes overlapping slightly in meas. (? none in BEAK) and in wt. In N. Am., sexes combined: length about 10–13 in. (25.4–33 cm.), wingspread 22–26 in. (56–67 cm.). Weight of ♂ about 5.3–7.6 oz. (150–215 gm.), ♀ 6.6–9 oz. (187–255 gm.). That is, on av., the ♂ is about ⅘ as large as the ♀ and weighs about ¾ as much.

A circumboreal falcon with 9 subspecies usually recognized; in our area 3; 3 others (1 Pacific, 2 Atlantic) have occurred on islands as stragglers.

DESCRIPTION *F. c. columbarius.* One Plumage/cycle with Basic I earliest definitive; age and sex differences are diagnosed briefly above (see also Subspecies, below); fairly prolonged spring–fall molting. Abbreviated descriptions follow; see Freidmann (1950) for further details.

▶ ♂ Def. Basic Plumage (entire feathering) ALL YEAR, renewed by molting described beyond. Considerable individual variation, but essentially as follows: **Beak** bluish with dark tip, cere yellow, **iris** very dark brown. **Head** with very dark cap; lower forehead white, this extending narrowly back over eye; chin and throat white or tinged tan, often with some dark shaft streaks. **Upperparts** individually variable from a slaty bluish toward a darker slaty, interrupted by a nuchal patch—that is, a light area (white, tan, and black intermixed) across nape and extending laterally downward. Most of **underparts** vary from whitish to same tinged tan or even rusty (especially flanks), and many feathers have wide dark shaft streaks, which, on sides and abdomen, may widen several times on an individual feather and, on the feathers collectively, may combine into more or less barring. **Tail** (dorsally) colored as lower back or darker (to black) with about 4 exposed white bands; the subterminal band is widest and black, the very tip white. Underside of tail appears paler. Legs and **feet** yellow, talons black. **Wing** most upper coverts like back; flight feathers, especially outer secondaries and the primaries, are crossed on inner webs with white bars or spots that align but are otherwise very dark; lining mixed whitish and tawny, the feathers with dark shaft streaks and some darkish barring (very broken pattern).

▶ ♀ Def. Basic Plumage (entire feathering) ALL YEAR. **Beak,** cere, and **iris** about as ♂. **Head** pattern approximately as ♂, but considerable pinkish laterally; chin–throat white with tan cast. **Upperparts** a dark drab, in some with hint of slaty (especially lower back and rump), the feathers without lighter margins. Most of **underparts** vary (with individual) from whitish to a pinkish tan or even rusty (especially flanks) with dark streaking, which varies in width and amount. Legs and feet about as ♂. **Tail** (dorsally) a dark neutral color, the pale, narrow cross barring usually a buffy tan or paler, on middle pair of feathers a medium grayish. **Wing** pattern much as ♂, but bars or spots on flight feathers generally larger and variably buffy tan or even toward orange.

AT HATCHING The down is rather short, toward buffy or with hint of brownish dorsally, grading to white ventrally; intermixed are some very short tufts of white down. A later down is longer, coarser, and replaces the short tufts (as in Peregrine, which see); it is grayish brown dorsally and white (gray basally) on underparts.

▶ ♂ ♀ Juv. Plumage (entire feathering) worn from time of nest leaving into following spring, then a period of molting so that entire Basic I is not acquired until late summer or fall of year after hatching.

Largely as ♀ Def. Basic. Main differences: **upperparts** browner, dull, no hint of bluish or slaty, many feathers have ends or margins more or less toward buffy-tan or tawny (it may wear off); nuchal band wider and more toward pinkish buff; **underparts** vary with individual from buffy toward palish cinnamon-buff, the dark streaking not as sharply defined; the light **tail** bands gray or buffy (♂) or buffy and less well defined (♀); in the **wing** the pale markings on flight feathers pale to vivid tawny-buff, and no barring on anterior web (at least in some).

For Basic I, see Molting, below.

According to Temple (1972a), there is a subtle but constant difference between ♀ Basic and ♂ ♀ Juv.—rump and upper tail coverts of ♀ Basic are slaty brown (= toward grayish or bluish), contrasting with dark brown of back; in Juv. birds the back, rump, and upper tail coverts are same shade of brown. The difference may be obscured by extreme bleaching.

Molting   Most statements on Prebasic I (out of Juv.) are apparently derived from Witherby (1920) or as stated by him in the 1921 portion of the *Practical Handbook* 2 for *F. c. aesalon:* body begins molting into Basic I in Feb., Mar., and Apr., but wings and tail "do not appear" to be molting before July, with entire Prebasic I molting completed about Nov. of 2d calendar year of life—that is, there is molting of head–body (into Basic I) in 1st winter, then molting of all feathering annually thereafter. Gradual molting (as in Peregrine) would minimize any flight handicap of missing feathers in an extremely agile falcon.

This is known for breeders in N. Am.: considerable molting occurs concurrent with the reproductive cycle, beginning some time in May or soon after. There is early molting of some primaries, starting at #4 (counting from inner) and going both ways, and in the secondaries at #1 (outermost) going inward, at #5 going both ways, and at innermost going outward. The tail starts with the central pair ("deck feathers") and continues outward, and from outer pair inward, the next to outer pair usually last. Adult birds molting both body and flight feathers are frequent in Aug.

Color phases   Swarth's (1935) suggestion that the "Black" Merlin (*F. c. suckleyi*) may be a dark phase is apparently not valid.

Measurements   "Adults": Easterly 28 ♂ BEAK from cere 11–13 mm., av. 12.5, WING across chord 182–200, av. 188.9, TAIL 114–128, av. 121; and 32 ♀ BEAK from cere 13.5–15 mm., av. 14.2, WING across chord 192–215, av. 207.8, and TAIL 120–140, av. 133.6.

Westerly (formerly "*bendirei*"): 25 ♂ BEAK from cere 11.5–13 mm., av. 12.2, WING across chord 177–198, av. 190.9, TAIL 118–130, av. 124.5; and 16 ♀ BEAK from cere 14–15 mm., av. 14.4, WING across chord 207–215, av. 210, and TAIL 135–146, av. 140.7. All of the above are from Friedmann (1950), which see for geographical origin of specimens measured.

"Adults" 38 ♂ WING across chord 189.2 ± 4.6 mm., TAIL 115.5 ± 2.9; and 33 ♀ WING across chord 211.7 ± 3.9 mm., and TAIL 127.6 ± 4; "immature" (= Juv.) 33 ♂ WING across chord 190.5 ± 5.1 mm., TAIL 117.1 ± 3.1; and 40 ♀ WING across chord 211.5 ± 4.3 mm. and TAIL 130.2 ± 3.8 (Temple 1972a).

In fall at C. May Pt., N.J.: WING across chord "adult" 40 ♂ 190.4 ± 4.2 mm. and 73 ♀ 211.7 ± 3.8; Juv. 546 ♂ 190.2 ± 5 and 759 ♀ 210.4 ± 4.3.

In spring at Sandy Hook, N.J.: WING across chord "adult" 22 ♂ 190.1 ± 3.4 mm. and 39 ♀ 211.9 ± 44; Juv. 3 ♂ 188 ± 2.4 and 39 ♀ 210.5 ± 3.8. Cape May and Sandy Hook data from W. Clark (1985).

From the above and from other series from elsewhere in N. Am. (see Subspecies, below), it is evident that the sexes can be distinguished by BEAK from cere— ♂ 13 mm. or less (often about 12) and ♀ over 13 mm. (usually about 14). Regarding ages, on av., the Juv. has slightly longer WING and TAIL than birds in definitive feathering. For sexing nestlings by meas., see Reproduction, below.

Weight (No allowance made for contents of digestive tracts.) In fall at C. May Pt., N.J.: "adults" 40 ♂ 158.6 ± 11.6 gm. and 72 ♀ 217.7 ± 14.3; and Juv. 506 ♂ 152.7 ± 10.7 and 27 ♀ 211.3 ± 15.6. In spring at Sandy Hook, N.J.: "adults" 22 ♂ 169 ± 13.7 gm. and 39 ♀ 243.6 ± 21.6; and Juv. 3 ♂ 155.9 ± 10.2 and 40 ♀ 234.4 ± 13.4 (W. Clark 1985).

In N.J. in fall, "adults" were significantly heavier than "immatures" (Juv.). In spring, Merlins were considerably heavier than in fall. They can be sexed (♀ ♀ larger) by a plot of wt. v. WING across chord, even though there is slight overlap in either between the sexes (W. Clark 1985).

Hybrids Presumed natural ones × ♀ *Falco tinnunculus* have been reported (Ackermann, also Suchetet, cited in Annie Gray (1958).

Geographical variation In N. Am.; the effects of Pleistocene events were postulated by Temple (1972b); his treament is here abbreviated as follows: 1 The Merlin crossed from ne. Asia to Alaska and spread across boreal N. Am., then continentwide glacial ice forced the birds s., w. and e of the prairies. 2 As the ice waned, a 2d invasion entered N. Am. via the same route and reached its s. limit on the prairies—between w. and e. birds of the previous invasion. 3 Then another glacial event isolated (a) w., (b) prairie, and (c) e. birds to the s. 4 With waning of the last glaciation, w. and e. birds shifted n. and joined in continuous boreal distribution, while the prairie birds (from 2d invasion) remained essentially in place. Thus there is currently a fairly homogeneous continentwide boreal population and a pale prairie population. Details of the scheme also allow for long occupation of extreme w. Canada, where the birds are very dark. This would account for color saturation, which is not clinal. Regarding size, there is little variation except that open-country (prairie-parkland) birds have appreciably longer wings and tails—as diagrammed by Temple.

For Eurasia, Vaurie (1965) probably oversimplified matters by stating that variation is clinal—the birds becoming paler and larger going from w. to e., with cline in coloration reversed in Anadyrland and coastal Pacific regions, and so on. A reconstruction of past history of the Merlin in Eurasia might be helpful.   RALPH S. PALMER

SUBSPECIES   Concise treatment. The 1st 3 are N. Am. breeders; stragglers to our area include 1 in extreme n. Pacific and evidently 2 via the n. Atlantic. Winter ranges of subspecies in N. Am. and to the s. evidently overlap greatly.

In our area As breeders. *columbarius* Linnaeus—"Northern" Merlin; descr. and meas. given above; av. moderately dark (lighter than the next listed below and darker than the 2d). Boreal forest and peripheral tundra. Primarily a long-distance migrant. In transcontinental breeding range, perhaps a percentage of individuals can be differentiated geographically—dorsum av. paler (w.); the several proximal dark tail bands of the ♂ usually narrower than the intervening light ones (w.) or usually the opposite (e.). Swarth (1935), Rand (1946), and others were unable to recognize w. *"bendirei"* as separable. Vast winter range from within Canada s. into n. S. Am. Reported from Greenland in error and from Scotland possibly naturally or via assisted passage.

suckleyi Ridgway— "Black" Merlin. Melanin-saturated birds. Breeds in extreme w. Canada (sw. B.C. n.) into se. Alaska. Heavily marked ventrally; light barring of tail reduced or even obscure. Evidently more or less resident, but some dispersal or migration (recorded nearly to the Mexican border and e. as far as Wis.)

"Adults" 7 ♂ BEAK from cere 11.5–12.5 mm., av. 12.1, WING across chord 186–197, av. 188.7, and TAIL 115–122, av. 119.2; and 14 ♀ BEAK from cere 13–15 mm., av. 14.2, WING across chord 207–215, av. 211.6, and TAIL 127–140, av. 131.1 (Friedmann 1950).

Mean and standard error: "adults" 13 ♂ WING across chord 189.9 ± 2.4 mm., TAIL 117.4 ± 1.9, and 18 ♀ WING across chord 210.4 ± 4.5, TAIL 129 ± 3.4; Juv. 26 ♂ WING across chord 189.9 ± 3.6, TAIL 117.3 ± 3.1, and 42 ♀ WING across chord 210.1 ± 5.1, TAIL 130.5 ± 2.7 (Temple 1972a).

richardsonii Ridgway—"Prairie" Merlin. Much paler overall than other N. Am. Merlins (quite like *F. c. pallidus* of Asian steppes); whitish nape (no brownish); ♂ has narrow dark tail bands, proximal bands 5–10 mm. wide, most distal band 15–25 mm.; ♂ ♀ underparts very pale, streaking toward medium brownish. Partly resident and partly migrant. Recorded e. to s. Ont., Mo., Ill., and Iowa; s. into nw. Mexico; may have occurred w. beyond the Rockies—F. Beebe (1974) listed several very pale birds taken in B.C.; Browning (1974) stated that all Oreg. records are doubtful.

"Adults" 12 ♂ BEAK from cere 12–13.5 mm., av. 12.5, WING across chord 195–203, av. 197.7, and TAIL 117–132, av. 124; and 10 ♀ BEAK from cere 13.5–15 mm., av. 14.1, WING across chord 210–228, av. 220.2, and TAIL 126–149, av. 137.4 (Friedmann 1950).

Mean and standard error: "adults" 29 ♂ WING across chord 197.6 ± 3.3 mm., TAIL 120.5 ± 2.5, and 22 ♀ WING across chord 217.2 ± 4.4, TAIL 132.1 ± 3.7; Juv. 31 ♂ WING across chord 198.1 ± 3.1, TAIL 121.7 ± 3.1, and 27 ♀ WING across chord 218.8 ± 4.7, TAIL 134.1 ± 3.2 (Temple 1972a).

Elsewhere　More n. subspecies, going from w. to e., are listed 1st. Some are evidently highly migratory, others to a lesser degree. There is reasonable agreement on 6 subspecies, although combining the 1st 2 has been suggested. Stragglers to our area are mentioned under 3 names.

subaesalon Brehm—moderately dark dorsally; tail of ♂ almost entirely dark above, the proximal area with a few narrow blackish markings. Iceland. Some remain all year, but others cross wide waters to n. Britain (principally) and W. Europe (a few). Taken in e. Greenland (Angmagssalik, July 3, 1914), but other Greeland records may pertain either to this or to *F. c. aesalon*. Faeroese birds are said to be few in number, resident, and nearer in size to Icelandic than to Scandinavian ones. Many birds from n. and w. in Britain fall within the size range of Icelandic birds, based on examination of 300 specimens (Butterfield 1954); also note meas. of WING flattened in Picozzi (1983).

aesalon Tunstall—essentially as preceding in appearance; size av. smaller, but great overlap. Faeroes (but see *F. c. subaesalon*), Britain, and e. to the Yenesei drainage. Has straggled widely, including n. to Novaya Zemlya and aboard ship near Spitzbergen.

There are over a ½-dozen Merlin records, from 1867 onward, for Greenland—Angmagssalik (e.), C. Farewell (s.), and Godthab Dist. (sw.)—at least some of which may fit better here than being assigned to Icelandic origin.

insignis (Clark)—paler birds; e. from range of preceding to the Kolyma drainage. Doubtfully recorded from the Commander Is. (see *F. c. pacificus*).

pacificus (Stegmann)—still paler than the preceding; ne. Asia, including Sakhalin I. The ♀ taken June 10, 1913, on Bering in the Commander Is. is a specimen in poor condition that cannot be assigned to subspecies but, on geographical grounds, likely belongs here (Vaurie 1965).

These occur farther south:

pallidus (Sushkin)—palest of all Old World Merlins. Asian steppes from e. of the Urals nearly to the Altai.

lymani Bangs—av. largest of all Merlins; mountainous cent. Asia approximately from Kazakhstan e. to L. Baikal. RALPH S. PALMER

FIELD IDENTIFICATION **In our area** In flight, at 1st glance might be mistaken for a member of the pigeon family, especially the Mourning Dove—hence the vernacular Pigeon Hawk. The wings usually move in a swift, short arc from horizontal downward, and tips seem to flip back at termination of stroke. Flight habit plus small size (about as Mourning Dove or Golden Plover) are diagnostic. Much wt. in proportion to wing area (high wing loading). Very agile. Fast, vigorous, steady flier. Rather blocky body profile, different from the comparatively slender and longer-tailed Am. Kestrel (a hoverer). No red in dorsum or tail; no prominent facial markings. Both sexes and all ages appear quite dark overall (paler on the prairies)—nothing very distinctive except contrasting tail pattern consisting of alternating white or very light bars separating the several blackish ones (light ones obscure or absent in Pacific coastal Canada). Underparts streaked dark on light (in far w. Canadian birds the streaks broadened to blotches and barring). Sometimes a hint of white along trailing edge of secondaries.

Sometimes confused with the Sharp-shinned Hawk when this bird is flying fast and strong (not its slower flap-and-glide), but this accipiter has rounded wings and relatively long tail. When perched, the Sharpshin's longer tail is diagnostic.

Except at times when migrating or displaying, the Merlin often flies low, only 2–3 m. from the ground, with occasional glides. Sometimes it mounts to considerable heights over its territory or when riding thermals during migrations. Usually seen as a migrant, with numbers occurring only at a few places, or as a breeder or year-round resident in urban areas of the s. Canadian prairies. Perches in trees, on rocks, even on the ground, in erect manner of the large falcons. Takeoff is fast and can be nearly vertical; may fly low and then shoot upward to alight gracefully in a tree or on a cliff. Does not bob its tail, which the Am. Kestrel does frequently. Occasionally an Am. Kestrel becomes so soiled and abraded in winter that it could be mistaken for a Merlin.

In definitive feathering the ♂ Merlin is slaty backed, hence easily distinguished from the brownish-backed ♀ and young in Juv. Plumage, which ordinarily are inseparable afield.

Might be confused with Juv. Mississippi Kite or Juv. Aplomado Falcon, both treated elsewhere in this volume. Also compare with the N. Hobby and the Eurasian Kestrel, stragglers to our area that are treated briefly in this volume. From our s. border beyond into n. S. Am., the Merlin might, at a glance, be confused with some other small falcons, such as the largely dark-bodied Bat Falcon and the Aplomado.

NOTE In European field guides the ♂ Merlin's tail in dorsal view is described and illus. as dark except at very tip—that is, not with prominent contrasting bands as in most of N. Am. and part of Asia. RALPH S. PALMER

VOICE Somewhat like our larger falcons, but faster and higher pitched. Probably has all calls of Peregrine and Prairie Falcons. They are shrill, chattering, or clipped, or even trailing or lisping, all being higher pitched in the ♂. The *Tic* call is a staccato version of *Eechip* of the larger falcons, omitting the initial segment. The begging whine of the ♀ and the copulation chutter are almost as in the larger falcons, and the *Ki-ki-kee* is the equivalent of *Kac-cao-cac* of the larger species. (Largely from Feldsine and Oliphant 1985.)

Although calls and variants and their variant names are scattered in the literature, treatment here mostly is a condensation from the listing of 4 vocalizations of "adults" by Feldsine and Oliphant.

1 *Ki-ki-kee*—by ♂ and ♀, most common call; polyvalent—used in various displays and in territorial or other aggressive encounters. Very distinct from Am. Kestrel (Oliphant); a variant is "almost precisely" like Am. Kestrel (Brewster 1925). 2 *Tic*—by ♂ and ♀, repeated in indefinite series; used in almost all display interactions. 3 Copulation chutter—brief, by ♂ (usually), going up the scale; indicates desire to copulate; and by ♀ (occasionally) when ♂ returns with prey and gives no vocal signal. Also used by nonresident ♂♂ and ♀♀ when approaching a resident ♀. 4 Food-begging whine—by ♀; monotonous; like #1 but very slow; used to urge ♂ to feed her or to urge him to go hunting. Occasionally uttered by ♀ during and after copulation. A whining in alarm on approach of a flying predator (L. deK. Lawrence 1949).

From pipped egg, quick peeps, about 2/sec., in short series; much resembles call given a few days posthatching when out from under brooding parent.

Nestlings Peeping—when becoming cold. Chirp—possibly an alarm call of newly hatched young (and perhaps also uttered from pipped egg). Begging—soft, rapid, pulsating, rasping; louder in older nestlings; presumably evolves into #4 listed above. RALPH S. PALMER

HABITAT In our area As a breeder, primarily associated with trees (strong preference for conifers), laying in tree nests of other birds and in cavities (natural ones and Pileated Woodpecker nesting holes). The falcon equivalent of the Long-eared Owl (Houston and Schmidt 1981). In some areas also on cliffs or the ground.

Boreal forest birds breed primarily where woodland is discontinuous or patchy, such as areas of birch or willow and conifers; adjacent to watercourses; near man-made clearings; where forest fires have created openings; or at edge of treeline. On rolling plains and prairies: in fragments of forest, or in parkland, groves, tree-lined watercourses, and mature planted shelterbelts. Before Caucasian settlement, probably the major prairie breeding habitat was along river systems. Then settlers controlled prairie fires and planted shelterbelts—that is, much breeding habitat now is man-altered or man-created (Oliphant and Thompson 1976). (See below for nesting habitat change in Britain.)

The other obligate factor is open country close by for foraging.

Cliff aeries may be on loose rubble or on stick nests built there by other birds (such as ravens). Ground sites tend to have a fairly wide view; some are known to be sheltered under low woody growth. There is no information as to whether birds near timberline have aeries on cliffs or lower down within forest. Several at treeline in Alaska were on the ground.

Urban nesting In Yorkshire and Lancashire, England, Merlins nested in "industrial districts," away from gamekeepers who tended grouse moors (Jourdain, in Bent 1938). In N. Am. there was an aerie, evidently a crow's nest, in Ottawa in May–June 1936 (H. Lewis and Smith 1939). A pair occupied a crow's nest in Vickers Park, Ft. William, Ont., in Apr.–May 1941 (Allin 1941). Just when Merlins 1st bred in definably urban habitat on the prairies seems to be moot; see historical data in Houston and Schmidt (1981). For example, they cite records of aeries "from Calgary," along the Bow R., in 1894 and 1895. Early in the 1960s, Merlins began breeding in Saskatoon, Sask., shortly after there had been an influx of crows and magpies, whose nests the falcons use (Oliphant 1974). Around that time they began breeding in residential areas of Edmonton, Alta. Six birds were released in Regina (where there were no nesters) in 1978, and the current breeding population there presumably derives from them. Merlins have continued to do well in urban habitat, House Sparrows and Bohemian Waxwings being important foods, and they have expanded rapidly into small towns to the s. in Man., Sask., and Alta. Their increase from 1 to 16 pairs in Saskatoon, 1971–1982 inclusive, was described by Oliphant and Haug (1985).

In other seasons in our area Mainly edges and open habitats, as grasslands, bogs, fresh and saltwater marshes, shorelines, dunes, and alpine areas; also arid areas, including deserts. Preferably where small flocking birds are present.

South of our area (Migrants in boreal winter and austral summer)—a mixture of shelter and open country; semiarid areas. In ne. Venezuela, most often "deciduous seasonal forest edge" (Friedmann and Smith 1950).

Elsewhere A ground and cliff nester in Iceland, the Faeroes, the Orkneys, and elsewhere that woody growth is stunted or absent. In part of Britain, where tree planting (afforestation projects) have created suitable environment, many Merlins now breed within these stands and others out on the ground. In n. England, where they used conifer forest, it was estimated that 94% of prey was taken in open country, which composed less than 20% of the surrounding area (J. Watson 1979).

Commensal relationship In Norway and Sweden, Fieldfares (*Turdus pilaris*) nest near Merlin aeries in birch forests. Hooded Crows also nest there, and Merlins occupy some of the structures they build, both species beginning their breeding cycle earlier than the Fieldfares. The latter tend to nest within 40 m. of a Merlin aerie, and the falcon drives away such nest robbers as ravens, crows, and magpies. In breeding season Merlins do not forage near their aeries (yet they do in Saskatoon, Sask.)—that is, they do not take Fieldfares, although they do later on. The 1st of several papers on this subject was by Hagen (1947); recently Wiklund (1979) reported that Merlins were more successful breeders when in Fieldfare colonies. RALPH S. PALMER

DISTRIBUTION   A circumboreal falcon; more or less (some populations extensively) migratory. Makes long water crossings. The map for our area (which see) is
probably reasonably accurate as to current breeding distribution (based, in part, on
Oliphant 1985), although subject to modification in deatils; especially along s. limits.
The following supplements the map.

Boreal warm season   From the Pacific coast going clockwise, these data relate to
the periphery. B.C. apparently absent from the Queen Charlotte Is. ALASKA breeds
on Kodiak I.; rare on the Alaska Pen. w. of Katmai; very rare in inner Aleutians; rare n.
beyond height of land in the Brooks Range and nw. COMMANDER Is. one (? straggler
from Asia). NW CANADA breeds nearly to Beaufort Sea, this (where forest extends far
n.) being the most n. breeding occurrence on this continent; for summer occurrence
over a wide area of the barrens w. of Hudson Bay, see summary in Harper (1953).
UNGAVA PEN. (tree sites and ground aeries known)—inland, evidently breeds sparingly as far n. as there are fragments of forest (Indian House Lake, Chimo) and, on the
Labrador coast, n. to Makkovik, possibly beyond to C. Chidley (summer specimens
taken). NFLD. most common diurnal raptor (nesting on ground, in trees, and on cliffs).
SOUTHERN BORDER of breeding range across N. Am. may have changed considerably
(examples: formerly bred in Iowa; now appears to be scouting new territory in w. N.
Am.).

Migrations   May occur almost anywhere, lingering if small flocking birds are plentiful. Concentrated only along and near coasts, along Appalachian ridges, and, evidently, e. foothills of the Rockies.

WATER-CROSSINGS   Within the continent the Merlin crosses such waters as the
Great Lakes. Occurrences in the w. N. Atlantic—off our e. coast—have included
many "coastal" and 25 "offshore" (87 ± 56 mi. from land) records; 9 sightings in a line
from N.S. to C. Cod or farther s. (Kerlinger et al. 1983). The Merlin crosses Cabot
Strait, the Gulf of Maine (includes is. hopping in numbers), has occurred off Fla. in the
Dry Tortugas (spring records only?), and occurs around the perimeter and in the
Caribbean and beyond to S. Am. (Freidmann 1950 listed many is.). There seems to be
only indirect evidence of crossing the Gulf of Mexico, such as occurrence to the s. at
Cozumel I. and the Swan Is.

E. N. ATLANTIC   Merlins regularly cross the North Sea; they also traverse the
Atlantic between Iceland and Britain/Europe. This would allow for some vagrants over
a very large area. Example: 2 came aboard ship 300 mi. s. of Iceland, Sept. 23, 1956
(McLean and Williamson 1958). There are additional records in Mees (1977).

Boreal winter   ALASKA recorded on Amchitka; rare in the interior; probably regular in small numbers (resident?) approximately from Anchorage to the sw. B.C.
apparently resident on much of the Pacific slope, although some depart. MAN., SASK.,
and ALTA. formerly sporadic, now regular, approximately in s. ½; expansion in winter
range has coincided with urban breeding, the falcons feeding on Bohemian Waxwings,
which in turn feed on fruits of planted ornamentals; city birds are resident but rural
Merlins are migratory. ONT. s. edge; QUE. sw.; N.B. occasional; N.S. occasional;
NFLD. recorded (not rare?).

Boreal winter/austral summer   MEXICO especially in coastal lowlands and apparently scarce or absent from extensive inland areas away from any water. CARIBBEAN
scattered is. records, perhaps mostly "winterers," perhaps some bound to or from S.

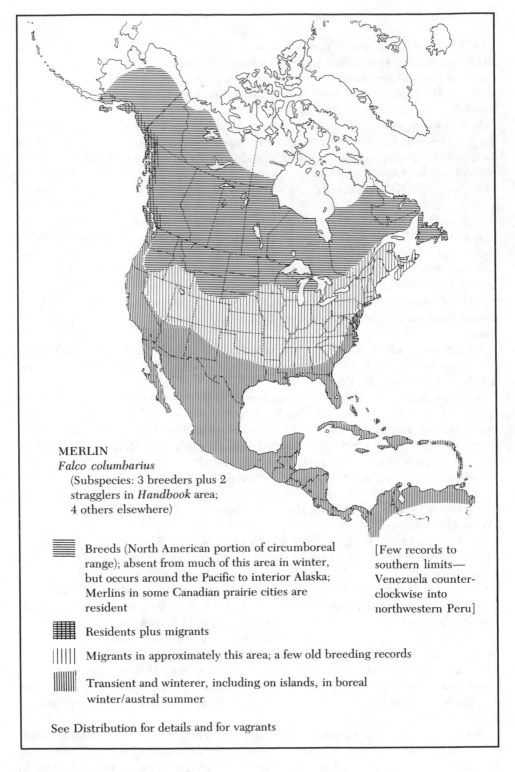

MERLIN
Falco columbarius
   (Subspecies: 3 breeders plus 2
   stragglers in *Handbook* area;
   4 others elsewhere)

| | Breeds (North American portion of circumboreal range); absent from much of this area in winter, but occurs around the Pacific to interior Alaska; Merlins in some Canadian prairie cities are resident |

[Few records to southern limits— Venezuela counter-clockwise into northwestern Peru]

	Residents plus migrants
	Migrants in approximately this area; a few old breeding records
	Transient and winterer, including on islands, in boreal winter/austral summer

See Distribution for details and for vagrants

Am. CENT. AM. scattered; unrecorded from sizable areas. S. AM. according to A. Wetmore (1965), "comparatively few" reach the Isthmus of Panama and n. S. Am. SOUTHERN LIMITS mainland Venezuela, n. and w. Colombia, and nw. Peru. Atlantic is. off the S. Am. mainland ("winterers" and transients not distinguished): Netherlands Leeward Is., La Tortuga, Margarita, Trinidad, and Tobago.

Vagrants The question may be asked as to how far away N. Am. Merlins may have occurred. The 1957 AOU *Check-list* listed *F. c. columbarius* as "accidental" in Scotland (S. Uist in Outer Hebrides, 1920) and at Kangeq, Godthab Dist., w. Greenland. The 1st is from Alexander and Fitter (1955) and was reported most recently by Cramp and Simmons (1980). Assuming it was correctly identified to subspecies, was this an assisted passage? The Kangeq record dates from Oldenow, was doubted as to subspecies by Salomonsen (1951), and was omitted from Salomonsen (1967).

Assisted passage These are examples (and see above): In the Spitzbergen area, a Merlin (listed as *F. c. aesalon*) was shot from the rigging of a whaler, May 1, 1910 (Løvenskiold 1963). A large ♀, believed to have been Icelandic (*F. c. subaesalon*), was caught aboard ship not far from Bahia, Brazil, in early Nov. 1963 (Baars-Klinenberg and Wattel 1964).

In our area the Merlin is recorded as **fossil** from the Pleistocene of Calif. (2 localities) and from **prehistoric sites** in Calif., Idaho (2), and S.D. (3); for both categories, the extralimital list now is much larger than it was in Brodkorb (1964). RALPH S. PALMER

MIGRATION As observed at C. May Pt., N.J., the birds probably use powered flight before sunrise; later, thermals form, and Merlins take advantage of them until the thermals weaken in late afternoon; then the birds drop to low levels and begin hunting flight. Unlike some raptors, they migrate on overcast, drizzly days. They also fly late in the day, long after other raptors have ceased migrating. (From W. Clark 1985.) Their usual speed probably av. around 40–50 kph. In overwater flights they have been observed flying low, just above the waves. The following appear to be valid generalizations:

1 Most boreal birds of all ages migrate, and their winter plus austral summer range extends from n. temperate into distant subtropical areas. 2 On more s. breeding range, where food is available and weather conditions permit, birds tend to be resident or to migrate short distances. Evidence from banding at urban centers on the s. Canadian prairies suggests that urban birds are not migratory. In Saskatoon, Sask., 1st-fall birds appear to scatter more than older ones. 3 Occurrence of subspecies overlaps away from breeding range in the nonbreeding season. 4 Migrants are scattered, as are the small flocking birds that they prefer as prey; there is some concentration along and near coasts, along some ridges and foothills, and at various water crossings. 5 In spring (in N.J.) ♂♂ precede ♀♀, and combined span of passage in numbers is only about 15 days (♂♂ arrive on territory ahead of ♀♀). In fall (in N.J.), the peak for ♀♀ is some 2 weeks earlier than for ♂♂, and numbers are high for over a month (W. Clark 1985). These statements do not separate birds by age class (92% of fall birds captured by banders are Juv.). 6 Most migrant winterers are on the mainland, and apparently not many go as far as S. Am.; some occur on is. around the Caribbean and off the Venezuelan coast. 7 The above statements may need some revision when there are more banding data.

In terms of currently recognized subspecies: **1** boreal birds include some traveling farthest s.; **2** the prairie birds, especially the young, that scatter s. rarely reach Mexico (there is a correlation of increasing breeding density with much increase in winterers); and **3** the dark birds of extreme w. Canada and adjacent Alaska appear to be more or less resident, but there is some seasonal scattering—individuals recorded into U.S. states bordering Mexico and e. into Wis.

The following is an indication of seasonal movements:

Spring In ne. Venezuela, migrants in Apr. "followed the great flocks of Dickcissels (*Spiza americana*)" (Friedmann and Smith 1950). Sightings at Half Moon Cay, Brit. Honduras, spanned Apr. 7–May 6 (S. Russell 1964). North of the city of Veracruz, Mexico, maximum daily count was 4 on Apr. 6, the last was seen on the 20th, and Thiollay (1979) suspected that Merlins had passed earlier than his observation period. Migrant Merlins begin arriving in Saskatoon, Sask., by Feb. (L. Oliphant), these presumably not having traveled far. At C. May Pt., N.J., they do not appear in numbers until after Apr. 20, and most have passed by May 5 (W. Clark 1985). They arrive in interior Alaska occasionally as early as late Mar. but principally in the last ½ of Apr. (K. Laing 1985).

These are banding data (W. Clark 1985) for the e. "Northern" Merlins: From Wis. bandings there have been Latin Am. recoveries in the Dom. Republic (1), Colombia (2), and Ecuador (1). A bird from Ont. was recorded in Honduras and one from NWT in Costa Rica. Of birds banded at C. May, recoveries include Ga. (1), Fla. (2), and Greater Antilles (8). It is not clear whether there exists or is substantial Caribbean is.-to-is. passage between N. and S. Am.

A Merlin banded in fall at C. May was recovered to the n. in Conn. the same season (W. Clark).

Fall The combined overlapping spans of 1st-fall birds (earlier) and older ones (later) make for a protracted migration. From upper to lower limits of breeding, young birds beginning in late Aug., and some of them migrate with Sharp-shinned Hawks, notably in Alaska (C. M. White, T. Cade). In Wood Buffalo Park, for example, Soper (1942) many times noted a marked movement of Merlins late in Aug. In the lat. of cent. Calif. across to the Chesapeake Bay, there is much movement by the 2d week in Sept., diminishing rapidly in the latter ½ of Oct. In s. U.S., principally Oct. to mid-Nov. There are few data beyond to the s. In sw. Ecuador, Marchant (1958) stated that migration is "very noticeable" in Oct.–Nov.

"Prairie" Merlins banded at Edmonton, Alta., spread out to the s.; places of recovery extend from extreme s. Calif. e. to s. N.D. and s.-cent. Kans., and s. to sw. Tex.; 9 (of 14) recoveries were of birds in their 1st year (A. R. Smith 1981). A prairie bird was collected in mid-Nov. in Coahuila, Mexico (Ely 1962).

"Northern" Merlins from w. breeding range apparently migrate principally via the e. foothills of the Rockies and farther e. They tend to follow Lapland Longspur flocks that move down the Alcan Highway in Alaska, Yukon, and n. B.C. These are apparently from areas n. of the Alcan. In former times, when they were separated as "*bendirei*," birds so identified were recorded e. into Wis., La., Fla. (including Dry Tortugas), S.C., the Bahamas, and possibly some other places (Friedmann 1950). This would indicate some diagonal movement across the continent (as in some Broad-winged Hawks, Swainson's Hawks, etc.). Also, when Merlins were divided, specimens from S. Am., including adjacent is., were listed mostly as e. ones; w. ones were listed for Panama (several) and n. Colombia (see E. R. Blake 1977). This is further indication that boreal e. and w. Merlins do not have disjunct ranges during the boreal winter.   RALPH S. PALMER

BANDING STATUS   To Aug. 1981, total number banded was 5,417, with 131 recoveries (2.4%) (Clapp et al. 1982). At Edmonton, Alta., 1975–1980, 76 nestlings and 2 adults were banded, with 13 recoveries, mostly within 20 km. of their birthplace (A. R. Smith 1981). A banding sample of 1,550 of the species in N. Am. had 29 recoveries (1.8%), 23 of them ♀ ♀ (W. Clark 1985). For a similar number from w. Canada, the rate was 1.97% (Fyfe and Banasch 1981).

   Main places of banding: C. May Pt. and Sandy Hook, N.J., and urban centers on the s. Canadian prairies, notably Saskatoon, Sask. These are ongoing studies. A few have been banded in Wis., Va., and elsewhere.   RALPH S. PALMER

REPRODUCTION   Older data forms a background for more extensive recent studies—the latter largely of prairie birds. In our area, this little falcon is principally a tree nester, such sites being easier to find than, for example, ground sites, which are used exclusively in Iceland and to a great extent in Britain and parts of Europe. North Am. data are given unless otherwise indicated.

   Age when first breeds   Usually 2 years, but individuals of both sexes breed when younger. A yearling ♀ mated to a definitive-feathered ♂ laid 4 fertile eggs (Bent 1938). There were yearling ♂ ♂ at 3 (of 20) breeding sites in Nfld., and broods were raised at these nests (Temple 1972a). In Sask., there were 4 yearling ♂ ♂ at 4 successful nests (Oliphant and Thompson 1976).

   Territory   (Includes hunting areas.) The ♂ may arrive up to a month before the ♀. In Alta., although most marked ♂ ♂ returned to their previous territories, only 2 (of 8) ♀ ♀ returned (Hodson 1975). (In Wales, however, the same ♀ returned to the same valley for 8 consecutive years   J. Roberts and Green 1983.) On the Minn.-Ont. border at Gunflint L., in suitable forest habitat, aeries were at least 2 mi. apart and near water (the Craigheads 1940). A tendency to nest near water has also been noted elsewhere. In Mont., home ranges of 3 telemetered ♂ ♂ were 12.6, 23.1, and 28.1 sq. km. and elongated in shape (from nature of habitat); maximum distances that the ♂ ♂ traveled from aeries approximately 8–9 km. (Becker and Sieg 1985). There was little overlap near aeries, but it was substantial in hunting areas. Two urban pairs in Saskatoon, Sask., nested only 1.8 km. apart; densest was 5 aeries within 1.3 sq. km. with high prey availability evidently the most important contributing factor (Oliphant and Haug 1985). A lack of perch sites can limit use of some areas, such as agricultural land.

   Since this falcon regularly uses the nest of some nest-building species for its aerie, and since such nests in disrepair are not very long-lived, it is evident that fidelity of the falcon is more to a general location than to a specific site. In Britain and elsewhere it is known that the same or successive Merlins use the same location more or less continuously. In Yorkshire, even though both mates were shot year after year, there was renewed occupation of specific locations (Rowan 1921–1922). In Northumberland, locations have been used over periods of 70 or more years (I. Newton et al. 1978). In Britain there are places haunted by generations of Merlins and, at least in the past, well known to generations of egg collectors. Territories are traditional. There is some characteristic, or combination of characteristics, as yet unknown to humans, that constitute a powerful attraction to successive generations of Merlins. Burning vegetation may disrupt the pattern until there is new growth; a single patch of heather was reoccupied 19 successive years (Rowan).

In territorial defense in Denali Park, Alaska, Merlins chased the Golden Eagle, N. Harrier, Com. Raven, Gyrfalcon, Black-billed Magpie, and Willow Ptarmigan (K. Laing 1985). If the aerie is climbed, both sexes are aggressive, but not reported to strike.

Displays The named components here are from Feldsine and Oliphant (1985) with some terminology altered slightly (example: "Prominent perching" becomes High-perching). Some listed components certainly should be combined as a single named display. As for homologies, an example is Power-diving, which is equivalent to the Sky-dance of buteos, eagles, and others. The ♂ Nest-display (such as on a magpie nest) obviously is homologous with the Ledge-display of the Peregrine. Displays, as far as is known, are more complex than in the Am. Kestrel, but there are similarities. As usual, functions are assigned subjectively; some actions are obviously polyvalent. Feldsine and Oliphant included diagrams. Their study was based on an expanding population of well-fed urban Merlins; this may account for little described interaction with other flying raptors and relatively little between Merlins.

1 POWER-FLYING by ♂; strong flapping flight with deep wingbeats, accompanied by rolls that show dorsal and ventral aspects of feathering. Boundary defense. **2 POWER-DIVING** by ♂; apparently an intense variation of #1 with different angle of flight; may be terminated with U-shaped climb, #1, or #3. Territorial defense and advertisement. **3 ROCKING-GLIDE** by ♂ ♀ (♂ more often); less intense variation of #1; no flapping; bird comes out of #2 and sets wings to glide. *Tic-tic* call by ♂ to attract a mate or uttered on return to established territory; by ♀ against an intruding ♀. Often terminated by #6. **4 FLUTTER-FLYING** by ♂ (only?); rapid shallow wingbeats. Mild territorial advertisement or display to perched mate. Male may call in flight, and ♀ often answers. **5 HIGH-CIRCLING** by ♂ ♀; 1 or more (to 4) birds observed, height to several hundred m.; may circle on set wings (soar); resident and nonresident birds. Probably mild territorial display (by residents) or a means (by others) of surveying another territory from advantageous position. **6 SLOW-LANDING** by ♂ commonly; terminal component of other displays. Done while coming to a perch; alights stiff legged, with head bowed. May precede or follow copulation. Silent or with calling. **7 BEGGING** by ♀; generally from a perch, with monotonous whines or wails. There are various ♂ responses, including motivating him to go hunting. **8 FOOD-TRANSFER** by ♂ to ♀ ("courtship feeding" of authors), in 3 forms: air-to-air, air-to-perch, and perched. In aerial transfer, the birds approach nearly breast-to-breast in stalling climb. The ♂ has the food in his beak. The ♀ seizes it with a foot. Transfers begin rather late during displays and increase in frequency until egg laying. After the young are on the wing, both parents may deliver to them via transfer. **9 SUPPLANTING** bird drives another (generally ♂) from its perch. Occurs in various contexts; aggression; when between

304

mates, may express ♀ dominance and encouragement of mate to hunt. **10** TAIL-CHASING ♀ chases ♂; seldom seen; very aggressive; in confinement, ♀ may capture and kill ♂. **11** HIGH-PERCHING usually by ♂; at prominent point near nest; territorial advertisement or merely loafing; some vocalizing. **12** PRECOPULATORY DISPLAY of ♂; may call frequently, may bow and fan his tail; may stand tall, stare intently at ♀, and utter copulation chutter. There are variants. **13** SOLICITATION by ♀, to copulate; she bows deeply and fans her tail; there is various calling. **14** NEST-DISPLAY of ♂; both sexes enter potential sites, with *Tic* call; ♂ settles on nest, arches back, droops and trembles wings, and fans his tail. Silent. The ♂ at edge of aerie. As observed in British captives and called Site-Selection-Display by Ruttledge (1985): the ♂ held wings high, then partly lowered them and walked about in stilted manner before starting to bow toward ♀ while he was horizontal with tail cocked up and usually spread. Soft *Tic* call. There were mutual bowing displays on the site.

Pair bond Fairly well along in the display period; a pair bond is indicated by the ♂ feeding the ♀ (#8 above); typically, he is her only source of food from incubation until well along in the rearing period. There are data from Saskatoon of mates repairing early in the season (L. Oliphant). Also, resident pairs display on territory after the breeding season. Outside N. Am. it is known (Newton 1979) that, if either mate is lost, the other remates the same season; also, **polygamy** (with separate nests close together in an area normally occupied by a single pair) is reported.

Copulation Occurs repeatedly, displays described above; see also K. Laing (1985).

Aerie On a cliff or the ground the ♀ may crouch or even make a "scrape" at several places before settling on her choice, but tree nesters must, for lack of multiple sites close together, be restricted in this activity. The aerie is an unoccupied nest of crow, magpie, Com. Raven, Steller's Jay, hawk, tree squirrel, and probably others. Hollow magpie nests provide a stick roof overhead, which deters crow predation (F. Beebe 1974), but L. Oliphant found them using the top even though the nests had apparently suitable cavities. Nests in conifers are favored. In se. Mont., 48 aeries were Black-billed Magpie nests in ponderosa pines on sideslopes of buttes (Becker and Sieg 1985). Randall (in Bent 1938) reported a structure used in 2 successive years by Merlins, then by Swainson's Hawk. Natural holes in tree trunks and nesting cavities of Pileated Woodpeckers are used, but seeking records of these is not highly rewarding.

Cliff sites may be on friable rock or on an old stick nest built there, for example, by Com. Ravens. Some clutches were laid on shaley cliffs in the Anderson R. region of nw. Canada (MacFarlane 1891); a few have been reported elsewhere, such as in Ungava by Hantzsch (1928–1929). Ground sites are probably used to some extent across boreal N. Am., as known in Alaska, Ungava, and (regularly) Nfld. Some Nfld. sites were under overhanging brush or stunted trees (Bent 1938), as were some in Alaska (D. Wier, C. White).

Greenery Or "decoration," delivered to the site during the breeding cycle (or longer) by many raptors; the Merlin gathers greenery only very close to or at the site. In Rowan's Yorkshire study, the incubating bird at the ground site would break off heather or add bits of bracken to the site if the material was close at hand. In Northumberland, ground sites were scraped out, and small pieces of stiff vegetation, within reach, were often placed in the hollow, "occasionally forming a substantial lining."

This occurred from before laying into incubation. Sitting birds also nibbled at thick heather stems. (From I. Newton et al. 1978.) A captive ♀ pecked at debris (bones, pebbles, feathers), drawing these toward her and sometimes constructing an elevated rim on one side of her scrape (J. A. Campbell and Nelson 1975); similar rims have been found at cliff sites. For further data on such activity by captives, see Ruttledge (1985).

Clutch size   Usually 4–6 eggs (2–7 recorded). The av. for all N. Am. populations was 4.8 (Temple 1970) or, for pre-1950 through 1969, av. 4.35 (G. Fox 1971). In Denali Park, Alaska, 4 clutches of 5 (K. Laing 1985). In se. Mont., total of 48 clutches over 4 years—4.3 ± 0.8 and not significantly different in any 1 year (Becker and Sieg 1985). [There were annual changes in Finland (Wiklund 1977).] Becker and Sieg also tabulated other studies of "Prairie" Merlins, a combined total of 205 clutches, the different samples varying in means from 3.4 to 4.6 (the highest being for 156 clutches in Alta. and Sask.).

Laying interval   Said to be 2 days but probably varies.

One **egg** each from 20 clutches of boreal birds from Nfld. to Man. **size** length 40.02 ± 1.75 mm., breadth 31.68 ± 1.16, and radii of curvature of ends 13.39 ± 0.80 and 10.70 ± 0.60; **shape** short elliptical, elongation 1.26 ± 0.054, bicone −0.043, and asymmetry +0.106 (F. W. Preston). For comparison, 55 eggs in Bent (1938) av. 40.2 × 31.3 mm.

Prairie birds—one **egg** each from 20 clutches (Mont. 2, Sask. 12, Alta. 6) **size** length 40.92 ± 1.43 mm., breadth 31.75 ± 0.68, radii of curvature of ends 13.39 ± 0.61 and 10.32 ± 0.55; **shape** as above, elongation 1.28 ± 0.046, bicone −0.044, and asymmetry +0.123 (Preston). For comparison (Bent), 48 eggs av. 39.8 × 31.2 mm.

There are no available data on *F. c. suckleyi*.

One egg each from 16 Icelandic (*F. c. subeasalon*) clutches av. 39.33 ± 2.20 × 31.60 ± 2.225; and 1 each from 20 "European" (*F. c. aesalon*) clutches av. 39.78 ± 1.72 × 31.34 ± 0.90 (Preston). Both av. slightly shorter than N. Am. eggs.

The shell is smooth, with little or no gloss. The eggs resemble those of the Peregrine, except for smaller size, and are said to av. slightly darker, which is doubtful. **Color** variably rusty brownish, overlaid in more or less even pattern with variably small, irregularly-shaped deep brownish or chestnut markings.

Replacement clutch   In prairie birds, according to Randall (in Bent 1938), if the 1st clutch is taken, the birds often occupy another site not far away and lay a 3-egg clutch.

Clutch dates   Laying is generally completed in se. Mont. by May 20, but in Sask. this is the peak date (in Becker and Sieg 1985). In Denali Park, Alaska, clutches completed by 3d week in May (K. Laing 1985). Bent (1938) gave few data for presumably viable clutches: "Arctic Am."—8 records May 25–June 29; Alta. and Man.—19 records May 7–June 6 (10 of these May 18–June 4); Ont. to Nfld.—14 records May 18–June 27 (7 May 24–June 9); and "Labrador"—8 records May 15–June 30.

Caching food   If the ♂ fetches unwanted prey and lingers, the ♀ drives him away (Temple 1972a). This may account for his depositing some quarry in trees or on the ground during the breeding cycle (both sexes also cache and retrieve food in other seasons—see Habits, below). There are variants. The ♂ may cache it. He may deliver it to the ♀, at or away from the aerie, and she may cache what is left after a feeding bout. Apparently it is always cached within the defended territory, merely being

306

stored some place like the fork of a tree or under loose bark. It is not concealed, at least not covered, and it may fall to the ground.

Incubation Usually begins on completion of the clutch (with synchronous hatching), occasionally earlier. In Nfld., the ♂ was at the aerie about ⅓ of the times birds were flushed (Temple 1972a), but only 15% of the time in Alaska (K. Laing 1985). A ground aerie in Yorkshire was watched through the night, and the ♂ incubated (Rowan 1921–1922). Both sexes, but primarily the ♀, incubate.

Incubation period In captive British birds, between 31 and 32 days, nearer the latter (Ruttledge 1985), which is more accurate than the usually stated 28–32 days. As noted in captivity and in the wild in N. Am., the eggshells are removed or eaten (J. A. Campbell and Nelson 1975, K. Laing 1985). For a wild Merlin with part of an eggshell in its beak, see 1977 *Brit. Birds* **70** (9): photo #105. In Denali Park a dead nestling was found on a stump used as a plucking perch (Laing).

Nestling period The ♂ supplies food for young and mate. Typically, she flies out to get it in an aerial food pass. Occasionally he delivers directly to the aerie (sometimes a beak-to-beak food pass), and she feeds the brood. If prey is delivered intact, the ♀ plucks and dismantles it at the aerie; if it is delivered beheaded and partly plucked, sometimes the ♂ has already consumed part of it.

The ♀ broods the young only during the 1st week, and even then she is absent for progressively longer periods (K. Laing 1985). Females do not make important contributions to food getting (at Saskatoon, one does not see her hunting until after the young fly—Oliphant); contrarily, L. deK. Lawrence (1949) stated that when the nestlings are at least 10 days old and just beginning to feed themselves, the ♀ hunts for herself and brood; Temple (1972a) also found evidence that ♀ ♀ hunt. The ♂ may deliver food and may even feed the young occasionally in the ♀'s absence. There is little aggression among siblings, although they may snatch food from one another when hungry. Details of home life at a ground aerie in Yorkshire, England, were charmingly recounted in the final installment of Rowan's (1921–1922) serial paper, to which the reader is referred.

Growth and development Oliphant and Tessaro (1985) described 2 pairs of hand-raised prairie Merlins, here condensed. NEWBORN eyes open by 3d day. SMALL DOWNY 4–8 days, enter period of rapid growth, 2d down develops; 9–11 days, sheathed contour feathers appear, can sit erect. LARGE DOWNY 12–14 days, primaries break sheaths, 1st casting; 15–17 days, secondaries break sheaths, can stand upright; 18–21 days, flight feathers developing rapidly, leveling off of food consumption and wt. gain. BRANCHER 22–28 days, maximum wt. attained, down visible only on head by 28 days, short jumping flights. "FLEDGLING" 29–34 days, become capable of sustained flight; 35–40, develop flying abilities, show interest in prey, 1st bath; 45–50, kill flying insects, 1st bird kill (by ♀ at day 42), some down still on head, completion of feather growth; 50–60, become INDEPENDENT, disperse. The authors also included graphs of wt. gain and food consumption. It is of interest that, on the diet supplied, Merlins were capable of flight at 32 days (♂) and 34 (♀)—6 days longer in both sexes than in wild birds in Britain (Orkney), discussed next.

Picozzi (1983b) studied the development of 17 nestlings of *F. c. aesalon* in the wild in Orkney. Weight increase of growing young soon clumped along 2 curves; the assumed ♀ ♀ (9) attained maxima in excess of 235 gm.; the assumed ♂ ♂ (8) grew at a slower rate, and none exceeded 210 gm. In both sexes wt. leveled off when they were about 20 days old and in 3 birds decreased thereafter. Females developed heavier tarsi and feet. Beak and rear talon were still growing when the birds last were measured (they attained flight at 26–28 days). In the various linear meas. taken, later records showed almost no overlap between the groups. For example, BEAK from cere in the assumed ♂♂ measured 11.4 ± 0.32 mm. and in the assumed ♀♀ 12.7 ± 0.37. One could sex nestlings with some confidence by about age 13 days using wt. in relation to WING flattened and/or length of outer (10th) primary.

To return to Oliphant and Tessaro's study of urban prairie birds, they calculated prey requirements for a pair with 4 young reared to age 55 days (120-day total breeding period) in terms of birds of House Sparrow size (each would contribute about 25 gm. of useful food). The figures arrived at were 78 prey/young and 210/adult—total of 732 sparrows. On a somewhat different basis, including 1 less nestling, L. deK. Lawrence (1949) calculated it at 450 birds.

In 43 nests in se. Mont., the young attained flight capability in 26–33 (mean 29) days (Becker and Sieg 1985); this combines the sexes, but ♂♂ ordinarily fly 2 days earlier than ♀♀.

Family bond In Denali Park, young did not fly often in the 1st week out of the aerie; they then became more active; they called frequently, often in unison; they chased each other and mobbed adults returning to the breeding area with prey. They chased other raptors—Am. Kestrels, Juv. N. Harriers, a Golden Eagle, a Sharpshin, also 2 Black-billed Magpies. All this appeared to be playful. Kestrels and Sharpshins sometimes turned and chased the Merlins. Kestrels and Merlins sometimes perched together in the same tree. (From K. Laing 1985, see also Cade 1982.) In se. Mont., young remained in vicinity of aeries for 7–19 (mean 13) days "after fledging" (Becker and Sieg 1985). Presumably they were independent thereafter and could support themselves.

Breeding success Boreal birds: In Nfld. in 20 nests in 1969 there were 3 young/successful nest (Temple 1972a); in Denali Park, 4 clutches of 5 and 15 eggs hatched; 1 nestling died, but all others attained flight (K. Laing 1985).

Prairie birds: Becker and Sieg (1985) summarized 8 studies for 1964–1981 in a table. In 7 studies, av. clutch size varied 3.4–4.6 eggs and brood size 1.9–4.0; in 4 studies, av. number of young attaining flight varied 2.8–4.0 in successful nests. Egg losses were perhaps due largely to predation, and nestling losses to predation and inclement weather. Another study, of urban birds at Saskatoon: 82 breeding pairs (1971–1982) produced an estimated 302 young; av. number of young in 68 successful nests was 4.2 ± 0.03, and the av. for all 82 nesting attempts was 3.7 ± 0.07 (Oliphant and Haug 1985). There was a 26% increase in breeding population per year.

Although there are various technical papers on biocide-related **eggshell thinning** in prairie birds especially, they are not cited here because apparently there was little, if any, negative effect on Merlins or their reproduction.   RALPH S. PALMER

SURVIVAL Since there is evidently no local segregation by age of migrants, and since 92% of Merlins captured for banding in fall at C. May Pt., N.J., are Juv., perhaps 1st-year losses are of the order of 60–70%. This would allow some increase in birds traveling along the Atlantic coast, which Oliphant (1985) and others stated has occurred over the past 10–15 years. The mortality rate must be lower for resident urban Merlins than in the species generally. Average life span unknown. The oldest bird listed by Clapp et al. (1982) was aged 7 years, 10 months.   RALPH S. PALMER

HABITS   In N. Am. unless otherwise specified. The Merlin is very active and full of energy and purposefulness. Its small size and swiftness enables it to capture fast-flying small birds. Although often solitary, 2 are sometimes seen outside the breeding season; in fall in Saskatoon, Sask., some of the resident pairs display and maintain territory (L. Oliphant). In winter it is not unusual to find several in a fairly small area, and they may roost communally. Communal roosting has been noted abroad by various observers (cited in van Duin et al. 1984), even associating with Sparrowhawks (*Accipiter nisus*) and N. Harriers, the Merlins arriving latest in evening.

Hunting from a perch   The most productive hunting method. In winter in Mont., in pursuit of a Bohemian Waxwing (*Bombycilla garrulus*) separated from a flock, the quarry tried to fly to cover and the Merlin attempted to stay below it and force it up into the open. One, however, spiraled upward and outflew the Merlin (Servheen 1985). Birds capable of fast sustained flight (waxwings, blackbirds) maintain flock unity and ring upward, regularly outflying the Merlin. If not struck to the ground in an instant, the House Sparrow (and our native sparrows) dodge and may escape into cover.

Searching flights   The Merlin often courses about 2 m. above ground or cover, keeping out of sight until coming on its quarry suddenly and swiftly. With flocking sandpipers, for example, it appears that experienced individuals capable of flock synchrony are in the center, while inexperienced, young ones are at risk on the periphery (Boyce 1985, D. P. Whitfield 1985). A hungry Merlin can usually make a capture and move on, barely slowing. If it misses, the Merlin shoots by, losing some momentum before it can change course.

The above indicates that evasion techniques vary with prey species and age; other examples are given below.

A Merlin hunted for voles (*Microtus*) in Saskatoon in winter (Warkentin 1985). On set wings, the falcon glided slowly to a point above the vole, then plunged downward with extended feet. When it tried to hunt from ground-level perches, it failed. In Wis. in Apr., there were crippled and dead Purple Martins (*Progne subis*) on a road; a Merlin took those that exhibited some movement rather than the dead road-kills and evidently cached them (Haug 1985).

Prey is carried to a perch or plucking site, and the ♂, at least, usually eats the head in any season. The carcass is plucked, dismantled, and often mostly eaten.

It has been stated that the Merlin does not **stoop** from a height in the Peregrine manner, yet a number of observers (H. Laing 1938, others) down to the present have seen it happen.

In the experience of falconers, the Merlin will "wait on" overhead for only short periods of time (unlike the Peregrine) for quarry to be flushed beneath it; instead, it is cast from the fist immediately when prey is flushed from the ground.

In the heyday of **falconry** abroad, the Merlin was a ladies' bird and was trained to hunt Skylarks. This is a combination of perch-hunting and ringing flight. The lark is flushed from the ground; the Merlin is cast from a gloved hand, and, if there is no ground cover for escape, the lark flies steeply upward. The Merlin, with its heavier ratio of wt. to wing area, gains altitude less rapidly. Thus it becomes a contest in stamina. The Merlin spirals upward; it may get above the lark and seize it in a short stoop. If the lark outflies its pursuer, the latter spreads wings and tail and glides back to earth. The entire flight may extend at least several hundred m. upward and a km. horizontally. Often a 2d Merlin was cast off at the quarry. In 1883 a British falconer "of some experience," using 3 Merlins (2 were ♀♀) killed "(on very first-rate ground on Salisbury Plain) no less than 136 larks" (Lascelles 1892). Larks are less easily taken after about Sept. 1, when they have finished molting and are in full feather.

On the Minn.-Ont. border in summer a ♀ Merlin was seen to "glide lazily" above a lake, then drift toward a burned tract. Tree Swallows (*Tachycineta bicolor*) suddenly appeared and darted at her as she "spiraled lazily up and up." When so high that the swallows looked like tiny insects, the falcon suddenly dived earthward with the swallows in pursuit. With increasing speed she pulled away from the swallows and, when almost to the ground, suddenly turned and shot upward. The swallows did likewise, but now they were pursued. From increased downward momentum, the hawk pitched up faster than the light swallows ahead of her—and she "deftly snagged a swallow as it seemed to hang motionless" in the air (the Craigheads 1940).

In Ont., a Merlin dived into a flock of "blackbirds" and "came out the other side with one in each fist" (McIlwraith 1886).

Catching dragonflies   Near an aerie, the ♀ swooped down from the tops of jack pines and took dragonflies on the wing (Breckenridge and Errington 1938). A ♀ caught and ate one on the wing (the Craigheads 1940). In Calif., according to R. Bond (1951), the flying Merlin spotted its flying prey from overhead; then it dived with great speed and seized the quarry in a foot. Once it was seen to perch and eat a dragonfly, discarding the wings. The Merlin occasionally eats during flight (Bent 1938), reaching downward with its beak to prey held forward in a foot; aside from insects, however, it usually carries its prey to a perch.

A Merlin may fly headlong into brush to flush quarry (Shelley, in Bent 1938) in the accipiter manner.

Large Prey like a Rock Dove may be killed by strangulation, the Merlin not having the Peregrine's strength to break its neck (Lascelles 1892).

Castings or pellets av. about 25 × 12 mm. and taper at 1 end (W. Johnson and Coble 1967).

Cooperative hunting   By 2s, has been seen a few times in N. Am., most recently on 2 occasions in Saskatoon by L. Oliphant. It is better known and more often reported in Britain and Europe; the account by Bengtson (1975) is quite detailed. Such hunting evidently occurs in any season—sometimes a smaller (♂?) and larger (♀?) together. Falconers have commonly flown 2 or 3 trained Merlins at quarry.

Using a beater   The Merlin follows the N. Harrier, seeking prey flushed by the larger bird. Van Tyne and Mayfield (1952) repeatedly saw Merlins following harriers in the Bahamas. Such behavior has been reported a number of times in Britain and Europe, most recently 8 instances in Ireland by Dickson (1984). It follows hunting

310

dogs in Sask. and on one occasion killed several passerines that were flushed (L. Oliphant). An unusual variant occurred in Sonora, Mexico, in Feb.; 6 Merlins were observed through the windows of a train, making kills of small birds flushed by the moving locomotive (Kenyon 1942).

Play As noted above (see Reproduction), Merlins newly on the wing chase various birds, in part perhaps hoping to be fed. They not only chase such potential prey as large flying objects but also strike at inanimate objects borne on the wind—thistle down, feathers, and so forth. Older Merlins seem to have abundant energy and great confidence in their own safety: they harry and torment Peregrines, Gyrs, N. Ravens, and Am. Crows with persistence, to the considerable discomfort of their victims. On the Maine-N.H. border in Sept., Brewster (1925) saw 3 Merlins chasing one another, "like so many swallows playfully inclined." Presumably when not hungry, Merlins spend much time "half-heartedly" chasing after birds; this complicates the matter of determining what is "for real" and what is "for fun" in calculating success rates.

Raptor interactions Not treated further here other than to note that it is fairly common for migrant Peregrines to rob migrant Merlins. Definitely a reverse situation occurred near Albany, N.Y., in Mar.—a Merlin struck and killed a Red-tailed Hawk (Klem et al. 1985).

Food caching And retrieval (see also Reproduction, above) occurs in various seasons, is done by both sexes, and is now well known here and abroad. In breeding season at Saskatoon, Sask., when the ♂ did almost all hunting, he offered prey to the ♀, and if she refused it, he cached it. Carrying the prey, often decapitated and partly plucked, he would fly to a perch close to the aerie, uttering a variant of the normal aggressive *Ke-ke-ke-ke-keee*. If the ♀ did not appear, the ♂ uttered a series of single *chip* notes. After several min. he would fly to a nearby tree and cache the food. Birds already partly eaten were also cached. A ♀ cached the uneaten remains of a bird in a spruce close by, and later the same day, when the ♂ failed to provide food, she retrieved it. In s. Alta., food was cached both in trees and on the ground. Retrieval was usually in afternoon or evening, the food being transferred to the ♀ or, once, eaten by the ♂. The ♀ "did not appear to remember" the cache site and so searched for it (Oliphant and Thompson 1976). Generally speaking, Merlins usually cache food well within 50 m. of the aerie in breeding season. Sometimes a cache is in the vicinity of a plucking site (K. Laing 1985). They seldom repeat caching at the same site in summer, perhaps to avoid piracy by magpies and crows, but in winter they tend more to reuse a site (Warkentin and Oliphant 1985).

At Sheridan, Wyo., a ♀ killed a House Sparrow, flew to a squirrel nest, and partly plucked the prey before caching it there. Then she captured another one and cached it at the same nest. She carried prey in a foot but transferred it to the beak when being cached (Pitcher et al. 1979). In winter in Saskatoon, 3 radio-tagged Merlins each used a site consistently for caching and for retrieval after cold nights (Warkentin and Oliphant).

Prey consumption In the breeding season, discussed under Reproduction, above. It would seem that Merlins could deplete their food supply if they hunted only close to the aerie. In another season in Calif., wt. of food/day was calculated at 20.5–128.6 (mean 71) gm. (G. Page and Whitacre 1975). Newfoundland data (Temple 1972a) suggested that the smaller ♂ prey on smaller quarry than the larger ♀—as current theory would have it.

Captivity Treatises on falconry and the experience of recent handlers are in agreement that the Merlin readily becomes tame and, in the hands of a qualified person, is quickly trained. E. "Lewis" (1938), an Englishman, put it well when he stated that the Merlin is a "grand resolute flyer and a most delightful bird." He noted that trained Merlins rise into the sky "till I needed a glass to follow them" and that, at aeries, they "dash to and fro in short shallow stoops, as they do to the lure when trained." Several people in N. Am. have raised Merlins in captivity, the 1st young having been reared in 1974 (Cade et al. 1977).

Numbers There have been various studies of diminished reproductive success, supposedly related to chemical contaminants, in Canada, Britain, and Europe; they are roughly similar, although differing somewhat in timing. Yet it is now believed that the picture in N. Am. was nowhere near as bad as was painted. In the 1980s, prairie Merlins (supposedly the most adversely affected) were increasing and may be the most numerous population. The boreal birds have a vast range but, except in a few places (as Nfld.?), appear to be thinly spread. The dark *F. c. suckleyi* of part of the Pacific fringe of breeding range remains the least known—only 14 nestings "potentially attributable" to it have been reported (Oliphant 1985) since 1950. Easterly autumn flights of Merlins in N. Am. were improving by the mid-1970s (Arbib 1976), and in Wash. state an analysis of Christmas counts from the early 1960s onward showed a gradual increase in numbers (D. Smith and Knight 1981).

Literature For a useful list of Merlin papers, see D. Evans (1982).

RALPH S. PALMER

FOOD Around the world the Merlin is a bird eater, hence seems to be independent of rodent fluctuations, yet in Norway (Hagen 1952a) breeding success is better in good than in bad vole (*Microtus*) years. It eats large insects, and perhaps dragonflies are a mainstay for short periods when available in quantity. Other foods (vertebrate and invertebrate) comprise a short list of species but are few in quantity.

North Am. data Summarized several times in the past. Earliest is A. K. Fisher (1893). May (1935) summarized 8 sources and added original information. A 1954 MS by A. W. Schorger was based on some 60 "principal references," and Sherrod (1978) added some later ones. Various recent papers were included in Warkentin (1985), and there is an up-to-date list of domestic and foreign literature by Becker (1985).

Based on available information: **1** medium-sized to small birds are primary prey; **2** many of these are (a) open-country flocking species—Horned Larks, longspurs, Water Pipets, Rosy Finches, Snow Buntings, small sandpipers, and (b) others that flock seasonally—waxwings, Com. Starlings, swallows, various Icteridae (such as Rusty and Red-winged Blackbirds), and Am. Robins; **3** away from prairies, alpine areas, and barrens, and more often in breeding season, many small woodland birds; also **4** young birds recently out of the nest (and growing evidence that young still in the nest are taken regularly); and **5** dragonflies are important, by no means exclusively in the breeding season. Ancillary data follow.

312

Birds The Merlin will attack birds that are impossibly large for it to capture; see, for example, Bent (1938). Those it can manage are mostly from about flicker and jay size down to include various sparrows and wood warblers. About 70 species are recorded. The largest actually captured include a Willow Ptarmigan (it also takes young), purportedly (Audubon) Green-winged (Common) Teal, and others have added young ducks and chicks of domestic fowl, Rock Dove, Passenger Pigeon, Mourning Dove, Am. Woodcock, and Black-bellied Plover. In Labrador, 1 "foraged" among Eskimo Curlews (Coues 1861). Smallest include Brown Creeper, Ruby-crowned Kinglet, Blue-gray Gnatcatcher, and (Lowery 1938) Ruby-throated Hummingbird. Some rather notable reports include Leach's Storm-Petrel brought aboard ship in the Gulf of St. Lawrence and eaten there (Murdoch 1877). Chimney and Vaux's Swifts, both fast fliers, are known prey. Merlins occasionally specialize, hunting a single species more or less exclusively. Said to be particularly fond of Black-bellied Plovers in w. Canada (Taverner 1926). In Pa., it entered boxes repeatedly to get at and prey on domestic pigeons (Warren 1890). At an aerie in Butte Co., Idaho, there were remains of 18 Mourning Doves (Craig and Renn 1977). The Merlin is a successful shrike hunter.

Young birds are frequent prey in the nesting season. In our area, evidently the 1st indication of nest robbing was L. deK. Lawrence's (1949) suspicion that it took nestling E. Kingbirds. It has robbed kingbird nests in the Saskatoon area (L. Oliphant). Such robbing may occur primarily when the ♂ Merlin is under pressure to supply food for both his mate and the growing brood; the evidence might vanish, being completely digested (nothing in castings). As for flying young as food, a good example (K. Laing 1985) is of many taken July 10–Aug. 6 in Denali Park.

Availability factor Obvious when comparing urban Merlins in Saskatoon with those of the prairies (Oliphant and McTaggart 1977, Hodson 1978). Nearly all hunting in breeding season was by the ♂, and birds were the only recorded prey. The city Merlins captured: House Sparrows 69%, Horned Lark plus Bohemian Waxwing plus Am. Robin 14%, and 15 additional species 17%. On the other hand, analysis of 2,070 prey items on shortgrass prairies yielded: Horned Lark 50%, Chestnut-collared Longspur 37%, and miscellaneous 13%. The Merlin is closely associated with large winter flocks of Bohemian Waxwings. In se. Mont. in winter, birds were 91% of prey and 93% of biomass; the majority of prey species were typical of grasslands or prairie (Becker 1985).

Dragonflies Listed in at least 8 primary sources. They are taken by breeding adults, are prey of young Merlins just learning to hunt (5 references in D. Evans 1982), and are also taken at least by fall migrants. For example, breeding season food at 7 nests (Ont. 4, Minn. 3) was chiefly dragonflies, in part also swallows (the Craigheads 1940). Food in 41 stomachs from C. May, N.J., included 115 dragonflies and 34 birds (Pearson 1933). In files of the U.S. Biol. Survey were "389 records of dragonflies in 727 stomachs," many of the Merlins having been taken on Fishers I., N.Y. (McAtee 1933). Earlier, A. and H. Ferguson (1922) had reported that 298 "stomachs" sent to the Biol. Survey from Fishers I. contained 4 mammals, 318 birds, and 967 "insects."

Mammals Few species, usually few individuals: voles, deer mice, house mouse, ground squirrels (*Spermophilus*), shrews. Inexperienced Merlins may find mammals easier to catch than birds (Warkentin 1985). Bats at least occasionally--*Lasiurus borealis* and *Myotis* recorded—1 of latter seen captured in daytime (yet a Merlin took a Horned Lark in the beam of auto headlights—Gerow 1943).

Insects Other than dragonflies: grasshoppers, crickets, cicadas, butterflies, moths, caterpillars, June beetles and allies, wood borers (Cerambycidae) and water bugs (Belostomatidae).

Miscellaneous Garter snakes, horned "toads" (*Phrynosoma*), toads, crayfishes, scorpions, spiders.

There is some indication that (omitting dragonflies) invertebrates are taken more often in arid and semiarid areas. There are no reports of carrion, but the Merlin has taken crippled birds.

Outside our area To the s. there is little information; hunts in semidesert, dry country, and over wetlands. Old World data are not included here.

RALPH S. PALMER

314

APLOMADO FALCON

Falco femoralis

Colorful, long-tailed, long-legged, bird-hunting falcon of desert grasslands, high-elevation scrubland, and Neotropical savannas. About the size of Cooper's Hawk, slightly smaller than the Prairie Falcon; ♀ larger than ♂ with slight overlap in linear meas., none in wt.; the sexes combined: length 12–15¾ in. (30–40 cm.), wingspread to 31½ in. (80–90 cm.), wt. of n. birds 8¾–17⅗ oz. (250–500 gm.). Bold striped facial pattern, slaty dorsum, pale upper breast, dark "cummerbund," cinnamon lower abdomen, white-banded tail. Color pattern suggests that of Bat Falcon (*F. rufigularis*) or Orange-breasted Falcon (*F. deiroleucus*).

Three subspecies, 1 (very rare) in our area.

DESCRIPTION   *F. f. septentrionalis*. Basic 1 Plumage is earliest definitive; sexes similar, except ♂ tends to be immaculate on breast and with bolder white barring on "cummerbund." Feathering has sharply defined areas of color. No data on molting. See Friedmann (1950) for details that supplement the following terse treatment.
▶ ♂ ♀ Def. Basic Plumage (entire feathering) ALL YEAR. **Beak** black grading to bluish gray basally; cere, gape, and eye ring yellow to orange-yellow; **iris** dark brown (usually appears black). **Head** crown and nape blackish or dark slaty; a white or buffy stripe extends from eye to back of nape, bordered ventrally by a broad blackish stripe on upper side of face with forward extension downward (malar stripe). **Upperparts** slaty gray, fading toward brownish. Lower sides of face, chin, and **breast** white to pale cinnamon (breast plain or with scattered dark streaks). A well-defined dark brown to black area (the "cummerbund") extends from axillars across lower breast and upper abdomen, in most individuals in N. Am. becoming quite narrow midventrally; lower abdomen to tail cinnamon. Legs and **feet** vivid yellow, talons black. **Tail** dark with 8 narrow white transverse bars and very tip white. On the dark **wings** the secondaries are

315

tipped white, forming a trailing edge; wing lining blackish with evenly scattered small whitish bars.

At hatching The down is white; a later down is dark gray. Cere bluish, legs and feet greenish yellow.

▶ ♂ ♀ Juv. Plumage (entire feathering) becomes evident at age 3–4 weeks. Pattern essentially as Basic, but lighter areas are deep buffy or cinnamon—and fade. **Beak** dark, cere and eye ring blue-green at nest leaving, gradually changing to pale yellow; **upperparts** slaty or brownish gray, appearing slightly brownish because the feathers are margined buffy or cinnamon and fade; upper breast has broad dark longitudinal streaks, sometimes nearly obscuring the ground color; legs and **feet** pale yellow.

Color phases in the species Were termed (Friedmann 1950) white and cinnamon. In e. Mexico, birds in Basic feathering have breasts varying from nearly white to deep cinnamon or grayish. There appears to be a spectrum of individual and perhaps some sexual variation, with Friedmann's designations applying to the extremes—that is, not disjunct phases.

Measurements From Hector (1981) except BEAK from E. R. Blake (1977). Six ♂ BEAK from cere (of 8) 16–18 mm., av. 17, WING flattened 251–262, av. 258, TAIL 146–185, av. 162, and TARSUS 39–51, av. 44; and 5 ♀ BEAK from cere (of 7) 17–20 mm., av. 19, WING flattened 255–296, av. 279, TAIL 168–200, av. 185, and TARSUS 42–49, av. 45.

Weight From e. Mexico: 7 ♂ 208–305 gm., av. 260, and 6 ♀ 310–500, av. 407 (Hector 1981).

Hybrids None.

Geographical variation See Subspecies, below.

Affinities Stegmann (1933), N. C. Fox (1977), and Cade (1982) regard the Aplomado Falcon as most closely related to the Orange-breasted and Bat Falcons and the New Zealand Falcon (*F. novaeseelandiae*), but this needs confirmation.

DEAN P. HECTOR

SUBSPECIES See also E. R. Blake (1977) in addition to the following data.

In our area *septentrionalis* Todd—descr. and meas. given above. Ground color of upper breast highly variable in Basic; amount of streaking there highly variable in Juv. and Basic, but in general, the Juv. more heavily streaked. "Cummerbund" often very narrow midventrally, even interrupted. Very rare in U.S. (formerly nested regularly in Tex., N.Mex., and Ariz.), thence s. to Nicaragua.

Elsewhere *femoralis* (Temminck)—smaller and paler than either the preceding or following. "Cummerbund" nearly always complete. There is geographical variation within this subspecies. Eighteen ♂ WING flattened 223–250 mm., av. 235, TAIL 146–185, av. 162, TARSUS 39–51. av. 44; and 8 ♀ WING flattened 254–274 mm., av. 263, TAIL 168–200, av. 185, and TARSUS 42–49, av. 45 (D. P. Hector). Costa Rica to Tierra del Fuego; lowlands; see Distribution, below.

pichinchae (Chapman)—darker than either of the above; upper breast often very buffy; tawny abdominal area deeply colored, "cummerbund" usually narrows abruptly from "armpits," becoming nearly (often completely) divided on venter; larger than the preceding. Seven ♂ WING flattened 256–280 mm., av. 268, TAIL 158–193, av. 181,

TARSUS 42–50, av. 46; and 8 ♂ WING flattened 275–318 mm., av. 292, TAIL 185–200, AV. 200, AND TARSUS 41–53, av. 48 (D. P. Hector). Mainly the Andes; see also Distribution, below.   DEAN P. HECTOR

FIELD IDENTIFICATION   This falcon is so striking that identification of **perched adults** should be easy. Key field marks: 1 white eyebrow stripe (this in itself would be distinctive, except many Prairie Falcons have at least a suggestion of the same pattern, as do some Merlins), 2 long barred tail, 3 dark "cummerbund," 4 long accipiterlike tarsi, and 5 white trailing edge on the wings. In frontal view, typical individuals in Basic Plumage are tricolored: whitish upper breast, dark abdominal band, and rufous lower abdomen and under tail coverts. The pale upper breast is visible at a great distance. In some, the upper breast varies to deep cinnamon or grayish. **In flight,** identification is more difficult; directly overhead, however, barring and length of tail are both good field marks. To some degree, Aplomados in flight look like smallish Peregrines; both are dark falcons with grayish dorsums and blackish barred underparts. Both have pale upper breasts. The Aplomado, however, has longer tail, narrower wings, a shallower wingbeat, and much dark in the axillars (the Prairie Falcon is not the only bird of prey of our area with dark "armpits"). Flight profile at a distance is similar to that of the Am. Kestrel, but the Aplomado is larger.

Aplomados in Juv. feathering are less readily identified. The Basic pattern is less apparent, yet facial pattern, tail, and general proportions should be diagnostic.

Unfortunately, like most easy-to-identify raptors, it is still possible to confuse the Aplomado with Am. Kestrels, Mississippi Kites, Bat Falcons, Caracaras, and other species. Mistakes usually occur when identification is rushed, perhaps by self-imposed pressures to observe rare species. In flight, Juv. Mississippi Kites are especially similar to Juv. Aplomados—both have streaked breasts, white-tipped secondaries, long tails, and long pointed wings, which are rather narrow close to the body.

DEAN P. HECTOR

VOICE   Most frequently heard at nest sites is the typical falcon *kek-kek-kek-kek* (indefinite length) uttered on appearance of other Aplomados or predators. Similar to analogous call of Prairie Falcon and Peregrine, but faster-paced and higher-pitched.

Aplomados utter a sharp *chip* when they see prey. When 2 falcons hunt together and only 1 has sighted a vulnerable quarry, this call seems to attract attention of the other to the same potential food. Thus the *chip* may assist Aplomados in coordinating cooperative pursuit. It is also uttered by the ♂ when he returns with prey to the nesting area, when he perches briefly at a prospective nest site during the display period, and immediately before copulation. It may be the counterpart of the Peregrine's *ee-chip*, but with 1st syllable faint or lacking.

A plaintive wailing is given by the ♀ at the nest site when the ♂ has been gone some time. It increases in loudness and duration when, finally, she sees the ♂ returning with food.

A high-pitched chittering is uttered both by nestlings and young recently out of the nest before a feeding or when some time has passed since they have last eaten.

DEAN P. HECTOR

HABITAT   In our area, was desert grassland and coastal prairie with scattered mesquites and yuccas (Merrill 1878, Bendire 1887, J. S. Ligon 1961). Elsewhere, tropical habitats include various savanna associations dominated by palms, oaks, or pines (T. Howell 1972, Hector 1981, Mader 1981). In the altiplano of Argentina, Ecuador, Peru, and Chile in nearly treeless associations (D. Ellis, R. Glinski, C. M. White).

Occasionally, Aplomados hunt over marshes and along beaches, also in vicinity of riparian woodlands that cross more open terrain (Henshaw 1875, Willard 1910, Cherrie 1916, Hector 1981). A. Miller (1946) found it in desert thornscrub in Colombia.

DEAN P. HECTOR

DISTRIBUTION   (See map for our area.) The subspecies *septentrionalis* occurred formerly from se. Ariz., s.-cent. N.Mex., and w. and s. Tex. (but now very rare in U.S.) s. through Guatemala and along the Pacific slope perhaps as far s. as Nicaragua (T. Howell 1972, E. R. Blake 1977). Most U.S. nesting records were from near Brownsville, Tex. Also nested near Ft. Huachuca, Ariz. (Bendire 1887); in the Animas and Rio Mimbres Valleys and Jornada del Muerto in N.Mex. (F. M. Bailey 1928, J. S. Ligon 1961); and near Midland-Odessa in w. Tex. (Strecker 1930). Highest densities now occur in tropical lowlands of Mexico.

F. f. femoralis occurs from Costa Rica through remainder of Cent. Am. In S. Am. it occurs e. of the Andes s. to cent. Tierra del Fuego; it is found on the savanna-grasslands of Venezuela, Suriname, Trinidad (rare), Brazil, Paraguay, Uruguay, Argentina, e. and w. Ecuador, Peruvian lowlands, and s. Chile (T. Howell 1972, E. R. Blake 1977). Accidental in Falklands.

F. f. pichinchae is the Andean bird—Cauca Valley of Colombia s. to part of Tierra

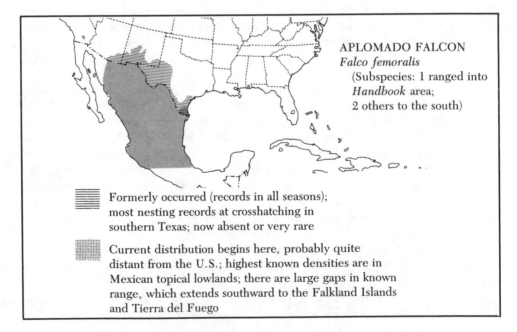

APLOMADO FALCON
Falco femoralis
(Subspecies: 1 ranged into
Handbook area;
2 others to the south)

Formerly occurred (records in all seasons); most nesting records at crosshatching in southern Texas; now absent or very rare

Current distribution begins here, probably quite distant from the U.S.; highest known densities are in Mexican topical lowlands; there are large gaps in known range, which extends southward to the Falkland Islands and Tierra del Fuego

318

del Fuego; higher elevation in nw. Argentina (E. R. Blake 1977). Down to near sea level on Chilean coast (A. W. Johnson 1965).

The species is recorded as **fossil** from the Pleistocene of Ecuador and Peru (P. Brodkorb).   DEAN P. HECTOR

MIGRATION   Little information. It has been suggested that birds withdraw from n. and s. extremities of range when winter approaches. Hector observed Aplomados in spring moving n. (along with Mourning Doves and Peregrines) on the Gulf coast of Mexico. Somewhat puzzling, however, is the fact that most Aplomado Falcons collected in the U.S. were taken in winter; a set of eggs was collected in Jan. in Tex. It seems unlikely that winter conditions, which are rather mild in the n. portions of the species' range, would encourage any widespread s. movement. DEAN P. HECTOR

BANDING STATUS   Twelve nestlings of the n. race were banded by Hector, with no returns.   DEAN P. HECTOR

REPRODUCTION   Little information; the emphasis here is on the n. race, with added data from elsewhere.

In e. Mexico, Aplomados HIGH-CIRCLE together and occasionally dive in tandem to a common perch. Males fly to prospective nest platforms and give the *chip* vocalization, perhaps to attract the attention of the ♀. Adults hunt and feed together during this period and at other times of the year when not breeding, which would indicate a long-maintained **pair bond.**

Breeding site   In most cases the pair selects an old stick nest in which to lay the clutch. Within the U.S.: nests of the Chihuahuan (White-necked) Raven, Swainson's Hawk, and Caracara were used (Merrill 1878, Bendire 1887, Strecker 1930). In e. Mexico, nests of Roadside Hawk, Brown Jay, Caracara, Black-shouldered Kite, Lesser Black Hawk, and Gray Hawk (Hector 1981, Meitzen's ool. records). Five stick platforms used by this falcon in e. Mexico had a top diam. of 28–100 cm. (Hector 1981).

Several aeries in the state of Veracruz appeared to have been freshly constructed and may have been taken by force from the original owners. There is no evidence that this falcon ever constructs its own aerie. A few Mexican sites were in the crowns of large arboreal bromeliads; the falcons seemed to have worked out a depression there which served as a nest bowl.

At least 1 clutch is recorded as having been taken from a stick platform on a cliff (F. B. Armstrong); in treeless areas possibly such sites are used, or eggs may even be laid on the ground.

Laying season   For the n. subspecies, Jan.–June (most eggs laid in Apr.). Elsewhere: Trinidad—begins laying in Apr. (Herklots 1961); Venezuela—found breeding in mid-Jan. (Mader 1981); and Chile—eggs have been taken in Sept.–Oct. (A. W. Johnson 1965).

Clutch size   Typically 2–3 eggs; the mean for 45 e. Mexican and s. Tex. clutches was 2.58 (Hector 1981). Four is apparently the maximum number. There is good evidence that the purported clutches of 4, collected in s. Tex. by F. B. Armstrong, are actually composites—that is, eggs from different sites were combined to make up sets that are not true clutches (Hector 1981).

One **egg** each from 20 "clutches" (Tex. 17, Ariz. 3) **size** length 44.82 ± 0.87 mm., breadth 34.74 ± 0.87, radii of curvature of ends 14.38 ± 0.72 and 11.26 ± 0.78; **shape** short elliptical, elongation 1.28 ± 0.034, bicone −0.047, and asymmetry +0.116 (F. W. Preston). Twenty-eight eggs from e. Mexico av. 43.75 × 35.06 (L. Kiff). Ground **color** whitish to buffy, nearly obscured by cinnamon spots and blotches.

Incubation By both sexes, the ♀ sitting for most of the daylight hrs. and at night, in most pairs. In the tropics, both adults may spend an hr. or more away from the eggs. The bird on the clutch may even leave to assist its mate in securing prey. Sometimes the ♀ is relieved by the ♂ only long enough for her to preen and stretch; at other times she may spend over an hr. hawking insects nearby.

Incubation period Thirty-one to 32 days—single record from state of Veracruz (Hector).

Nestlings Small young are brooded throughout the day for most of their 1st week, then only at night in 2d and 3d weeks. Either the ♂ carries prey directly to the ♀ at the nest or else she receives it from him in an aerial transfer or at a perch. She almost always feeds the young; on the rare occasions when the ♂ takes food directly to the young, the ♀ soon arrives and takes over for him. Throughout their development, nestlings feed quietly, accepting food from their mother with minimal conflict. The ♀ feeds even older nestlings and flying young with small bits of food that she tears from prey animals. Unlike many raptors, there is little jostling among the young for favorable positions near the ♀ during feedings. Especially after the young can fly, the ♂ will assist the ♀ in feedings. In these, the ♀ may divide prey between herself and her mate; thus the ♂ can feed a nestling while the ♀ feeds the other(s).

Age at first flight At 4–5 weeks posthatching the young fly to nearby trees. For 2–3 days they may return to the "nest" to roost at night. Gradually they wander farther afield but may return to the original nesting area for at least a month. Siblings remain together for some time after becoming independent and hunt together.

An Aplomado nestling was hatched in captivity in 1982 at the Chihuahuan Desert Research Inst., Alpine, Tex. (1982 *Am. Birds* **36** 993) and elsewhere they have also been raised from eggs.   DEAN P. HECTOR

SURVIVAL No information.

HABITS Although not gregarious, Aplomados are social to the extent that mated pairs hunt together and can be found together throughout the year. They hunt cooperatively when chasing avian prey (Cherrie 1916, J. S. Ligon 1961, Hector 1981, Mader 1981). Pairs often hunt even after sundown (J. S. Ligon 1961, Hector 1981). The ♂ tends to range more widely from the breeding site in his attempts to locate food. When he finds suitable prey within sight of the ♀, he attempts to force it from cover and begins uttering his *chip* call. The ♀ then flies to the location and either helps drive out the prey or else joins in pursuit as it takes wing. At other times both birds may spot prey from the same perch, then dash off together in pursuit. The Aplomado is extremely swift in level flight, being capable of outflying such species as Mourning Doves, Rock Doves, and Killdeer. In addition, it is agile afoot and often runs down ground-oriented prey, such as Bobwhites.

Insects are almost always captured by Aplomados hunting singly, usually in brief slow-flapping, hovering, or gliding flight. Often several insects are captured, dismembered, and eaten during a single flight. Larger insects are taken to a plucking perch to be dismembered and eaten. Large moths are pursued more like avian prey—in rapid chase.

Plucking perches Usually avian prey is killed quickly by bites to the neck and head. The falcon may then decapitate the bird and remove some or most of the remiges and rectrices before carrying the quarry to a perch where the remaining feathers and other inedible parts are removed. Typically, such perches are more or less horizontal large limbs within the crown of a tree. Others have included logs, fence posts, and upper larger branches of tall, sparsely branched trees.

Cache sites Uneaten prey is cached in arboreal bromeliads, crooks of branches, on bare ground, in clumps of grass, or in small shrubs. At a Veracruz site at least 3 cached prey were retrieved and fed to the young without an intervening successful hunt. Cache sites, with or without stored prey, are often defended aggressively by the falcons from other predators.

Kleptoparasitism Aplomados occasionally take prey from other falcons. A ♂ pursued a smaller falcon (Am. Kestrel?) that was carrying prey; after a brief climbing chase, the smaller bird dropped its burden, which was caught by the Aplomado and taken to a small tree and eaten.

Disadvantaged prey Locusts are forced to flee from advancing range fires. A. Brooks (1933) witnessed this falcon foraging for locusts in s. Tex. Hector has observed them at fires in Campeche, Mexico. In Venezuela they chased ground doves flushed by an approaching motorcycle (Mader 1981).

History The following, almost entirely pertaining to our area, is based on published sources and data from egg collectors.

The 1st specimen record of this falcon in the U.S. dates from 1852 (Heermann 1854). It was common in at least part of the range mapped in the present volume; 98 years after it was 1st recorded, there had been a minimum of 55 museum skins and 125 clutches of eggs taken in the U.S. Peak numbers of eggs were taken 1890–1910, mostly in the vicinity of Brownsville, Tex. The species was also taken at Ft. Huachuca, Ariz.; the Animas and Rio Mimbres valleys and the Jornada del Muerto, N.Mex.; and Midland-Odessa and Alpine, Tex. J. S. Ligon (1961) found Aplomados nesting on the Jornada del Muerto in 1910–1920, and R. D. Camp found birds on the Palo Alto Prairie near Brownsville in the 1920s (F. M. Bailey 1928, Hector 1981). The most recent documented nesting attempt occurred in 1952 near Deming, N.Mex. (J. S. Ligon 1961). Only scattered sightings in the U.S. are known since that year.

Habitat alteration Encroachment of woody vegetation (principally mesquite *Prosopis* sp.) on the desert grasslands and coastal prairies of the sw. U.S. have drastically altered many former nesting areas of the Aplomado Falcon, especially on the Tex. coast n. of Brownsville and in N.Mex. on the Jornada del Muerto. Conversion of grassland to farmland on the Tex. coast, along the Rio Grande Valley in s. Tex., and in the Animas valley of N. Mex. further depleted available habitat. Even so, much open grassland survives within the former U.S. range of the species. Furthermore, efforts to eradicate brush in s. Tex. are rapidly creating additional open prairie. Yet the Aplomado remains a rarity n. of Mexico. Possibly pesticide use has blocked or at least slowed recovery of the species in the U.S. In tropical Am., deforestation is undoubtedly creating additional Aplomado habitat.

Biocides A diet heavily biased toward avian prey has exposed this falcon in e. Mexico (and presumably elsewhere) to contamination by DDT. Kiff et al. (1978) found a sample of Aplomado eggs from within the DDT era (1956–1967) from the Gulf of Mexico coast to have shells 25.4% thinner than pre-DDT eggs from the same area. A more recent sample (1977) av. 24% thinner. DEAN P. HECTOR

FOOD Principally birds, but this falcon is also highly insectivorous. Other recorded foods: small mammals, reptiles, and fishes. The quantitative dietary study of the n. subspecies in e. Mexico (Hector 1981), as later published (Hector 1985), includes extant information for the species. In Hector's study, birds contributed an estimated 97% of prey biomass. The most commonly taken birds were White-winged Doves, Great-tailed Grackles, Groove-billed Anis, and Yellow-billed Cuckoos.

Birds A list of all known avian prey would require naming over 50 species plus some generalizations such as plovers, sandpipers, and hummingbirds. Largest recorded prey is the Chachalaca (*Ortalis vetula*); most are dove- to robin-sized; smallest, listed from Venezuela by Friedmann and Smith (1950, 1955), are hummingbirds. Many kinds of birds taken tend to be in the open at least part of the time, using exposed perches, foraging on the ground, or making flights to feeding or watering areas.

Other vertebrates These are recorded for the species: bats (Ligon 1961, ffrench 1973, Hector 1981, 1985, Mader 1981); mice and other rodents (Bendire 1887, A. Wetmore 1965); small reptiles (Bendire 1887); lizards (Wetmore); and small fishes (Cherrie 1916). The stomach of an Argentine specimen contained a grasshopper, a passerine, and a lizard (C. M. White).

Insects In Hector's study, most frequently captured and eaten were moths, beetles, and locusts. Locusts (Bendire 1887, A. Brooks 1933, Haverschmidt 1968); beetles (Cherrie 1916, Haverschmidt 1968, M. Mitchell 1968); cricket (in F. M. Bailey 1928); and butterflies, wasps, and bees (Haverschmidt 1968). DEAN P. HECTOR

NORTHERN HOBBY

Falco subbuteo

A small falcon; shape as Merlin, but size somewhat larger—length 12–14 in. (30–36 cm.), the ♀ larger within this span. Much of **head** very dark, patterned as in Peregrine; the dark lateral downward markings of the "hood" project into white of cheeks and down to include chin–throat. **Upperparts** very dark, the feathers light bordered in Juv. stage. **Underparts** with heavy longitudinal black markings on white (Juv.) or variably buffy (Basic), the latter altering to rich rusty posteriorly.

Hobbies have been divided into several species; the present 1 consists of 2 subspecies as currently treated, with *F. s. subbuteo* Linnaeus evidently the subspecies included here.

In or near our area Scattered sightings (1 bird photographed), mostly in the region of the outermost Aleutians; allowance must be made for possible assisted passage aboard Japanese fishing vessels. All sightings in chronological order: Cordova, Alaska, Sept. 19, 1977 (Roberson 1980); near Merritt, B.C., May 22, 1982 (1982 *Am. Birds* **36** 876); 200 mi. nne. of Attu I., July 1982 (1983 *Am. Birds* **37** 1017); "observed at Attu," May 20, 1983 (1983 *Am. Birds* **37** 902); 98 mi. ssw. of Aggatu I. aboard a Japanese fishing vessel, June 19, 1983 (1983 *Am. Birds* **37** 1017); and 95 mi. n. of Attu, also aboard a Japanese salmon catcher, **photographed,** June 25, 1983 (1983 *Am. Birds* **37** 1017–1018); Aug. 15, 1984, St. George I., Pribilofs (1985 *Am. Birds* **39** 91).

This is a Temperate Zone falcon of the Eurasian mainland and is. Although it breeds in part of Kamchatka, it is apparently not recorded from the Commander Is., which are not distant and lie between there and the Near Is. (outermost Aleutians). This migratory falcon is not averse to making certain water crossings.   RALPH S. PALMER

PEREGRINE

Falco peregrinus

Peregrine Falcon; formerly, in N. Am., Duck Hawk. "The typical falcon is by common consent allowed to be that cosmopolitan species to which unfortunately the English epithet 'Peregrine' (i.e., strange or wandering) has been attached" (A. Newton and Gadow 1896). Big-footed Falcon is appropriate worldwide.

About the size of a large crow, the Peregrine is a true falcon—upper mandible "toothed," lower with a notch, and circular nostril with a central bony tubercle. It has 2 **color phases** in S. Am. In N. Am., the Peregrine is distinguished from other falcons as follows: inner toe (minus talon), when laid alongside middle toe, does not quite extend to next to outermost joint of the latter (it extends to or past it in both Gyrfalcon and Prairie Falcon); next to outer primary longest or else the 2 outer about equal, in the folded wing extending beyond the outer secondaries for more than ½ the length of the wing; inner web of outermost primary emarginated, and outer web of adjoining primary slightly narrowed; very little of upper forepart of tarsus feathered; tail less than ½ as long as wing. The feathering is compact; the black malar stripe ("mustache mark"), which may extend to include the side of the head, is very conspicuous (more so in Basic than Juv.); the elongated flank feathers ("flags") vary from whitish to creamy to variously brownish (but not chestnut) and are usually barred blackish.

▶ ♂ ♀ Basic Plumage. The dark feathering of the head is essentially black and at least the chin white; upperparts some variant of slaty (bluish to blackish); underparts vary

324

from whitish to buffy to salmon or almost tawny-rufous, with variable amount of (to much) horizontal dark markings; dorsal surface of tail usually quite similar, with blackish crossbars, its undersurface typically paler—darkish bars (distal one widest) separated by buffy to tan.

▶ ♂ ♀ Juv. Plumage. Much of head and malar stripe very dark; dorsum some variant of sepia, the feathers light-margined (which may wear off); chin typically plain, but rear of cheek (usually) and all of underparts vary from whitish toward tawny with heavy blackish longitudinal streaking down to lower abdomen; tail dorsally quite similar to back except crossed with 5–6 visible rows of light patches (align as bars or large spots) varying with individual from pale (contrastingly conspicuous) to obscure, and on undersurface dusky barring with intervening (often much narrower) buffy to tawny areas, the pattern often so muted as to be quite inconspicuous.

Sexes essentially similar. Based on WING meas., ♀ ♀ av. about ⅐ larger than ♂ ♂, and, sex for sex, Juv. birds measure slightly larger than those in Basic. In N. Am.: ♂ length about 15–18 in. (38–46 cm.), wingspread to about 39 in. (99 cm.), and middle tail feather 5–6¼ in. (12.7–15.9 cm.); ♀ length 18–21 in. (46–55 cm.), wingspread to 44 in. (112 cm.), and middle tail feather 6¼–7¼ in. (15.9–18.4 cm.). In Basic feathering, wt. of ♂ about 1⅛–1¾ lb. (500–800 gm.) and ♀ 1½–2⅝ (750–1,200 gm.). The sexes have essentially no overlap in meas. and little in wt.

There are about 19 subspecies worldwide, of which 3 breed in our area. Evidently another straggles to Hawaii.

DESCRIPTION   *F. p. anatum.* One Plumage per cycle with prolonged molting in warmer part of the year. Basic I is earliest definitive.

▶ ♂ Basic Plumage (entire feathering). **Beak** muted bluish grading to black tip and yellowish basally; cere, eye ring, and some confluent orbital area yellow or toward orange; **iris** very dark. **Head** upper portions and part of sides blackish (darker than back), sometimes with narrow (2–3 mm.) off-white band across lower forehead; black on sides of face may be extensive, including malar and auricular area, but, if less, the white of auricular area is not closer than 11–16 mm. (av. 13) from the eye. **Upperparts** variably dark bluish gray, toward slaty, the rump paler; somewhat obscure darker bars on back become more evident on rump and upper tail coverts. **Underparts** chin throat, and upper breast usually plain and near white; the remainder, which varies from a rich tawny-buff toward grayish, has blackish markings varying from narrow shaft streaks on center of breast to transverse bars, chevrons, and/or spots lower down; barring heaviest on flanks and thighs; under tail coverts pale with transverse spots or narrow blackish barring. Legs and **feet** as cere. **Tail** dorsally light bluish gray or darker, the feathers tipped whitish and crossed with up to 12 blackish bars, which are progressively wider distally; ventral surface paler and pattern less evident.

Wing   Upper surface in general as back; greater coverts have more or less evident darker barring, other coverts narrowly tipped pale; primaries blackish distally, very narrowly tipped whitish (may wear off); remainder of inner webs light with about 10–14 very dark bars on longer feathers and fewer on shorter ones; secondaries barred throughout, but fewer bars; underwing coverts whitish or toward buff, narrowly barred black, hence wing lining appears light.

▶ ♀ Basic Plumage, on av., differs from ♂ thus: soft-part coloring appears muted (yellowish); whitish buff of nape feathers basally may extend outward on them so as to be visible more often; underparts more buffy and more heavily marked black, these markings extending up onto breast or even crop area; sides, flanks, and thighs with grayed cast and more and wider barring.

Although Basic I may be somewhat darker than later Basics in both sexes, there is no evidence that Peregrines thereafter become progressively lighter with age.

AT HATCHING   Beak palish gray, iris black, feet grayish. The most useful data are on *F. p. peregrinus*, in Witherby (1924, slightly revised 1939). Most sources list raptors as having only 2 "natal downs," i.e. combining Witherby's A and B as down-A, with his C thus becoming down-B. According to Witherby:

The down is sparse at first = A (prepennae) and whitish or slightly toward buffy. Also present is B: very short tufts of white in among A. Later the nestling becomes covered with coarse, long down-C, which is a grayed buff dorsally and toward creamy ventrally. C succeeds B (latter is pushed out on its tips) and also grows in places where there was no previous down. C, when fully grown, nearly conceals A. About the time that C begins to grow, the Juv. feathers push out A, which is attached to their tips and later breaks off. Down-C is molted when the Juv. feathers are nearly grown, late in nest life.

According to T. Cade (letter), the above is essentially or entirely correct for the Peregrine and other falcons. He noted that **1** he had difficulty in confirming the existence of B but that it can be seen on ventral tracts; **2** most of C grows from follicles that contain no down at hatching; **3** C is shed profusely at about the time of 1st flight; and **4** the definitive body down presumably grows from the same follicles that produced down-C (preplumulae).

Downs to Juv.   Lumping Witherby's A and B as A, the 2d, grayish, down emerges by day 7 (except belly still retains A) and by the day 9 is fully emerged. Juvenal tail feather sheaths can be seen on the day 13 and are 2 mm. longer by day 14–15; by day 20 the primaries are clearly visible and facial feathers are appearing; by day 30 the nestling is largely feathered, but wisps of down remain on head, flanks, thighs, and rump; by day 40 the bird is in full Juv. feathering with no obvious down except perhaps on forecrown.

▶ ♂ ♀ Juv. Plumage (entire feathering) develops as stated above; the ♂ develops faster than the ♀ until about the start of the 2d week; flight is attained in 5th–6th week (♂ ♂ several days earlier than ♀ ♀). Females tend to be somewhat darker overall than ♂ ♂. This feathering is retained through WINTER into SPRING (Mar.–May), when Prebasic I molting commences (see below).

Beak as Basic; cere and orbital skin may be bluish, greenish, or a more muted yellow than in Basic. **Iris** very dark brown. **Head** crown and nape variably dark brownish (chestnut); some have more or less of the following: buffy-rufous streaking on head, buffy forehead band, pale streak through eye, and pale basal portions of feathers on rear sides of cheek and nape may extend out so as to be visible. Malar stripe usually narrower than in Basic; usually less dark separating pale auricular area from eye; auriculum may be somewhat streaked; rarely, the dark malar is interrupted by a lighter horizontal brownish streak. **Upperparts** variably darkish brown, the feathers often with rufous or buffy margins and sometimes an ashy overwash. **Underparts** heavily streaked brownish on rufous-buffy background, the streaks on abdomen, sides, and

326

flanks broadening to chevrons, even bars, especially on flanks and under tail coverts. Legs and **feet** variably bluish to yellowish, talons black. **Tail** dorsally as back or darker, the central pair of feathers unmarked or may have 5–6 transverse spots on each web in place of bars and, on the others, barring tends to be discontinuous across each feather; ventral surface paler. **Wing** dorsal coverts as back but may lack light edgings; primaries dark brownish where black in Basic; undercoverts have wide dark barring, the intervening pale areas appearing as spots.

Subsequent Plumages are definitive.

Molting   North Am. temperate-arctic birds. Timing in breeders varies depending on dating of the breeding cycle, earlier below lat. 55°N and in the nw. Pacific coastal area and later and perhaps more protracted to the n. The ♀ generally starts molting during egg laying or soon after, and molting has been documented at the aerie in Alaska-Yukon during the breeding cycle in time-lapse photography by Enderson et al. (1972). Males normally begin considerably after ♀ ♀. Molting may slow down or cease for a time during brood rearing.

Flight feathers of the wing molt in the *Falco* mode; that is, primaries and secondaries start molting within each series and it proceeds in both directions (centrifugally). The primaries, counting from inner to outer, molt in this sequence: #4 5 3 6 7 2 8 1 9 10; the secondaries, counting from outer to inner: #5 7 4 8 3 9 2 10 11/1; and the tail, from middle pair of feathers outward: #1 2 3 6 4 5. Primaries occasionally vary, either #4 or #5 1st, for example. In the tail, sequence between middle and outer is somewhat variable. Although the tail starts molting after the primaries begin, usually it is completed before them, especially in n. birds. Head–body begin (anteriorly) soon after the primaries start, and rate of progress varies.

Prebasic I molting (Juv. to Basic I Plumage) is more variable in timing than subsequent Prebasics, and some Juv. feathering is frequently retained. (This is especially true of captives.) Birds in their 2d calendar year of life: an arctic ♂, still in Ecuador on Apr. 8, had acquired only ¼ of its Basic feathering; a bird in Utah on Aug. 26 had acquired ½ of Basic I; and 1 in n. Alaska had not yet begun molting on May 1. In general, n. (migratory) birds show more variation in timing, progress, and interruption in molting than s. ones.

Females (at least in higher lats.) may have a pause in molting beginning when they start to hunt food for the nestlings, and some birds of both sexes have interrupted molting (wing, tail, body) during migration, while others do not. Southbound migrants in Basic in 1st week of Oct. frequently have rectrices #4 and/or #5 partly grown. For some data on variation in molting of fall birds on the Tex. coast, see W. G. Hunt et al. (1975).

Molting ordinarily requires about 5 months but varies from 4½ to at least 6 depending on source of the birds. Some migrants from the N. Am. arctic into S. Am. still have primary #10 incoming in Jan.—9 months after molting began.

NOTE   Identification of individuals is possible by the unique toe-scale pattern of each bird (Stauber 1984).

Color phases   The breeding Peregrines of S. Am., in all feathered ages, have a pallid phase that is conspicuously different from the "normal"; intermediates are not known (see *F. p. cassini*, below).

Measurements *F. p. anatum* varies clinally—e. continental (formerly) were larger, w. and Canadian and Alaskan taiga smaller. After severe reduction or even extermination over much of the range, reintroductions are of birds from various areas—that is, of different stock—and their meas. may differ from those of the original stock, which are given here.

WING flattened is longer than WING across chord (of Friedmann 1950, present author), differences averaging, in Basic feathering, ♂ 5 mm. and ♀ 7.5, in Juv. ♂ 6 mm. and ♀ 8.7.

Basic feathering: ♂ 11 from e. N. Am. BEAK from cere 17–21 mm., av. 20, and 40 from w. N. Am. and taiga 18–22, av. 19.8; WING 12 from e. N. Am. 308–322, av. 318, 16 from w. N. Am. 291–318, av. 306, and 6 taiga 310–322, av. 313; TAIL 13 from e. N. Am. 131–155, av. 147, and 35 from w. N. Am. 130–155, av. 142; ♀ BEAK from cere 28 from e. N. Am. 22–27 mm., av. 24, 45 from w. N. Am. and taiga 18–22, av. 19.8; WING 27 from e. N. Am. 340–372, av. 357.6, and 43 from w. N. Am. 333–363, av. 349.8; TAIL 28 from e. N. Am. 165–185, av. 179.2, and 43 from w. N. Am. 160–187, av. 170.2. Note that meas. of BEAK shows no overlap of the sexes.

Sex for sex, Juv. birds meas. larger than Basic, except difference in beak—too slight to record here: ♂ WING 10 from e. N. Am. 304–330 mm., av. 316.5, 44 from w. N. Am. 293–324, av. 310.2, and 13 from taiga 314–335, av. 323; TAIL 10 from e. N. Am. 148–165, av. 159.2, and 46 from w. N. Am. 137–162, av. 152.5; ♀ WING 17 from e. N. Am. 342–375 mm., av. 360, and 48 from w. N. Am. 339–367, av. 352; and TAIL 15 from e. N. Am. 170–193, av. 183, and 49 from w. N. Am. 161–191, av. 177.

Weight Poorly documented. Most data are from trapped migrants from unknown localities. Some omit season or condition of bird. Falconers frequently give "trained weight," not necessarily applicable here. Female wt. is perhaps 50–100 gm. heavier just before laying a 40–50-gm. egg. Males in Basic feathering av. 6–8% more than Juv. and ♀ 7–9%. The birds formerly in e. N. Am. weighed (Basic feathering): ♂ 600–800 gm., av. 718, and ♀ 900–1,300, av. 1,184. In w. N. Am.: ♂ 588–690 gm., av. 678, and ♀ 870–1,201, av. 1,038. Peregrines weigh more in winter and early in the breeding season, when they have more subcutaneous fat.

Hybrids A ♂ Peregrine and ♀ Prairie Falcon, both released from captivity, bred in the wild (see Prairie Falcon species account). More recently (1986, in Utah), released birds of these species successfully crossed in the wild (C. White).

A "presumed natural" cross with the Lanner (*F. biarmicus*) (Suchetet 1897, cited in Gray 1958) dates from decades prior to known attempts at artificial insemination. A ♂ Peregrine × ♀ Saker (*F. cherrug*) natural cross, in captivity, listed in I. Newton (1979), was based on Cade et al. (1977).

Many *Falco* hybrids (including some reciprocal crosses and back crosses) have been produced by artificial insemination. There is great variation in feathering of offspring, hence a "norm" cannot be described. Proportions and structure of feet, legs, and wings can be like either parent or intermediate. Examples: ♂ *peregrinus* × ♀ *sparverius*— an offspring was similar to a large Moluccan Kestrel (*moluccensis*), although coloring was more like Juv. *columbarius* and feet were of Merlin or Peregrine structure; *peregrinus* × *mexicanus* (including reciprocal)—often offspring look like the latter but are darker, like Juv. *peregrinus; peregrinus* × "white" to darkest *rusticolus; peregrinus* × *columbarius*.

328

There have been various crosses produced in U.K., Germany, and elsewhere, sometimes imported into N. Am. and probably sometimes lost to the wild. Current breeding attempts are aimed, in part, at developing a stock having characteristics that will satisfy falconers and is adapted to climates abroad.

Fostering   In the wild, a Prairie Falcon was given Peregrine eggs, which it incubated until they were removed; another, provided with 3 captive-produced Peregrine nestlings, successfully reared them. Wild Peregrines have been provided with substitute or additional eggs or (more often) young of their own kind and have usually reared young to flight age. Experimental fostering and cross-fostering of eggs among several *Falco* species in captivity have been done repeatedly and successfully; see Fyfe et al. (in Temple 1978).

The Eurasian Kestrel (*F. tinnunculus*) sometimes lays its clutch in a disused N. Raven nest. The Peregrine is twice known to have then taken over the site. In an observed instance in Scotland, the eggs hatched and the Peregrines successfully reared the brood (Ratcliffe 1963).

Geographical variation in the species   Generally follows Gloger's rule: pale in high lats. and arid regions, where browns and reds prevail (reduction in melanin)—such as tundra birds and in n. Africa. Peregrines are dark, heavily pigmented and marked in humid climates—as in nw. Pacific N. Am. and part of Asia into s. China. As for size, based on averages of published meas. of WING, N. Am./Greenland birds are large and S. Am. ones slightly smaller; Eurasian temperate/arctic birds are somewhat larger than in N. Am.; African/sw. Asian (arid country) birds are smallest, with Australian birds slightly larger; and oceanic is. birds (based on very small series) are intermediate. Peregrines might separate better via multivariate analysis than on this single character.

WING length relative to wt. or length of TAIL is longer and more attenuated in arctic migrants than in residents to the s. The TAIL is relatively longest in nw. Pacific N. Am. and shortest in the Middle East, part of s. Asia, and Australia. Island populations contain few individuals and are presumably less variable than those of continents, where there is greater opportunity for gene flow. Any named race of Peregrine occupying a large geographical area (continental or on archipelagoes) shows some sort of clinal—in addition to individual—variation within its range. In *F. p. anatum*, for example, e. birds av. darker, less reddish brown than w., and n. ones are lighter and with reduced ventral markings (grade into *F. p. tundrius*).

Affinities   Cade (1960) suggested that the main evolutionary trend in *Falco* (size differences) was a result of exploitation of different food niches as these became available during the Tertiary era.

Within the genus, Peregrines constitute a subgenus, based on "hardness" of feathering and some other morphological traits (see Friedmann 1950). The "limits" of the species *peregrinus* have been placed variously, certain Old World desert and arid-country birds being included or omitted depending on author. They are included here. The Teita Falcon (*F. fasciinucha*) of cent.-e. and s.-cent. Africa appears to be a close relative. The Orange-breasted Falcon (*F. deiroleucus*) of s. Mexico to Peru bears considerable resemblance but is now regarded as not even closely related. The derivation of species may possibly be clarified by biochemical and genetic studies. The fossil record—so far—has not been helpful.   CLAYTON M. WHITE

SUBSPECIES   Many trinomials have been applied to Peregrines, but gradually they have been synonymized under some 22 names or fewer—19 here, including Old world desert birds. Even so, because of similarity and individual variation, many specimens cannot be labeled satisfactorily. This is particularly true where names are applied to portions of a gradient (cline) in characteristics. Elsewhere in this volume, recognition of subspecies is denied the Bald Eagle, its variation apparently being gradual and in a single character (size) over much area with no obvious subdivision anywhere; in the Peregrine, some changes at least are abrupt and there is a tendency toward recognizable geographical populations. Additionally, there are groups of more-alike Peregrines, such as arctic-subarctic birds, those of Old World arid lands, and so on. Since Peregrines return to their natal area to breed, local groups persist in minor distinctive characteristics. For convenience here, N. Am. breeding birds are treated 1st in some detail, then those of S. Am. (also in some detail), and the remainder are listed with their distribution. There are comparative N. Am. data by C. M. White (1968a, 1968b, and in Ladd and Schempf 1982).

In our area   *anatum* Bonaparte—detailed descr. and meas. are given above. Large, fairly richly colored darkish Peregrines (but neither as large nor as dark as *pealei*). Much black on side of head (typically little or no white in auricular area). Except on the perimeter of the Gulf of Alaska plus the Aleutians and Commanders (occupied by *pealei*), has very large N. Am. breeding range extending approximately from treeline s. into Mexico. To the n. it intergrades more or less clinally with *tundrius;* to the nw., it is not known to intergrade with *pealei* because of geographical and ecological barriers. Northerly *anatum* are (or were) migratory. Numerous specimens are extant (including many mounted birds), but adequately documented museum material is scarce. This subspecies became extinct or nearly so over much of its range during the 1940s to 1970s, the biocide era, and reintroduced birds of other stock may not be comparable. There is a large literature on the original population extending well into the 1960s; notable are R. and K. Herbert (1965) on biology and Hickey (1969) on early coverage of decline in numbers.

pealei Ridgway—largest Peregrine, with most extensive dark markings. Coloring varies from less dark in Wash., B.C., and se. Alaska, to darker in the Aleutians, and darkest in the Commander Is. This is a relatively sedentary humid-climate bird of archipelagoes and other is., and a few breed on nw. coastal headlands. It has occurred in winter down the coasts of Wash. and Oreg., several times into Calif., and once into Baja Calif., Mexico. That it breeds in the n. Kuril Is. seems doubtful; 2 dark specimens were taken farther s., in Japan (Hokkaido). No intergradation with other N. Am. subspecies is known. The following is condensed; for some further details, see Friedmann (1950).

▶♂ ♀ Basic differs from *anatum* as follows: Cere and orbital area pale yellowish. **Head,** neck, and back darker (to slaty blackish), often with powdery grayish bloom; trailing edge of malar stripe sometimes poorly delineated from lighter whitish to grayish auricular area due to spotting and marks on latter; birds from se. part of range frequently have a light forehead band greater than 5–10 mm. wide, especially ♀ ♀. **Upperparts** dorsal barring more obscured because of darker background; rump more bluish than back, the broad dark barring more evident. **Underparts** throat and crop often white (no shaft streaks or spotting) in ♂♂ of B.C. and se. Alaska, thus differing from Aleutian birds; upper breast with many large spots and teardrop-shaped markings, becoming more barred on lower belly and boldly barred on flanks and thighs; frequently an olive cast to an otherwise light grayish to pale yellowish overwash— Aleutian birds being noticeably grayed and se. birds more yellowish; ♀♀ av. more spotted and marked on breast and especially lower belly, the thighs and flanks sometimes with bars wider than intervening light areas. Legs and **feet** muted yellow. **Tail** as *anatum* except bars more often obscured by darkness of ground color and some Aleutian ♀♀ show no evident bars on central tail feathers.

▶♂ ♀ Juv. Variable; feather edging yellowish to olive-yellow, often buffy. In B.C., coloring varies from palish-headed muted brownish to buffy birds with black malar patch interrupted (as in *tundrius*) by a lighter transverse line below eye, to deep chocolate brown, nearly black, as in the Aleutians. **Head** frequently with palish streaks extending back from forehead; feathers of rear sides of head and the nape basally off-white to yellowish buff, this sometimes extending outward so as to be visible; **upperparts** very dark with varibly lighter feather edgings, muted yellowish or buffy (not rufous). **Underparts** more or less as *anatum* but more muted and with more buffy to a yellowed olive cast. Legs and **feet** vary from a bluish gray or greenish to pale yellowish by some time in 1st year of life. **Tail** essentially as *anatum* except central feathers more frequently unicolor or with spots on each side of rachis (no definite bar). **Wing** essentially as *anatum*, but darker.

The birds of the Aleutians and especially the Commanders are definitely recognizably darker than, for example, those of B.C.

Measurements From White (1968a); these do not indicate slight differences between Aleutian and other birds; "adults" 15 ♂ BEAK from cere 17–22 mm., av. 18.8, WING chord 309–328, av. 318.6, TAIL 143–162, av. 151; and 15 ♀ BEAK from cere 23–27 mm., av. 24, WING chord 347–375, av. 363, and TAIL 172–189, av. 179.6.

Juvenal birds—BEAK av. slightly smaller than the above; WING chord 13 ♂ 314–335 mm., av. 323.5, TAIL 157–172, av. 162; and 27 ♀ WING chord 352–383 mm., av. 368, and TAIL 175–201, av. 189.

Weight "Adults" ♂ 638–1,058 gm., av. 867, with Juv. less; and ♀ 1,201–1,590, av. 1,390, with Juv. 1,150–1,251.

Major papers include F. Beebe (1960, 1974), Blood (1968), C. M. White (1975), R. W. Nelson and Myres (1976), and R. W. Nelson (1977).

tundrius White—palest N. Am. Peregrine, much nearer to *calidus* of boreal Eurasia than to *anatum;* in size, similar to latter in w. N. Am. Size and color vary clinally from smallest and palest in Alaska to largest and darkest in Greenland. Intergrades s. on continental breeding range with taiga *anatum* (where and if extant). Highly migratory, most of them going well s. in S. Am. and remaining there through the austral summer.

▶♂ ♀ Basic. The ♀ is generally darker than the ♂, with heavier ventral barring and, in new feathering in fall, tends to have more rufous and buff.

Beak, cere, and eye as *anatum*. **Head,** although sometimes lacking a whitish forehead band, typically has one, to an excess of 10 mm. wide (especially ♂), but av. 3–6 mm. (less in Greenland birds); black malar stripe generally narrow and uniform in width, seldom wedge shaped as in some other N. Am. individuals; white of auricular

331

area extends up to about 8–10 mm. from the eye, usually not as close in Greenland birds (and much more distant, if at all, in *anatum*). **Upperparts** toward bluish gray—that is, paler than *anatum*, more or less barred darker. **Underparts,** especially in worn condition, almost white with less buff or toward tawny-pinkish of other N. Am. subspecies, but may be quite buffy in new fall feathering. Chin to upper breast usually plain except in Greenland birds, which usually have spotted upper breast. Flanks and thighs toward palish gray with dark barring generally lighter and less defined than in *anatum*. **Legs** and **feet** yellow, even toward orange in ♂ (as *anatum*). **Tail** variable, often somewhat as *anatum* but paler. **Wing** as *anatum* but mostly paler.

In fall migrants in cent. Alta., 1969–1978, about ⅓ of the birds in Basic showed a buffy or brownish cast to the tail dorsally; some Juv. birds also had "red" tails—color varied from dark reddish brown to strikingly pale buffy-orange (Dekker 1979).

▶♂ ♀ Juv. Variable; approaching *anatum* in Greenland birds. **Head** generally with pale stripe over eye; streaking variable; that is, head appears light when feathers have wide light edges and dark when they are narrow. In many, the palish head color is confluent with the basally light feathers on rear sides of neck and nape (a feature also of some w. *anatum*); malar stripe varies from a narrow streak to as broad as in *anatum* or *pealei* of B.C., often interrupted by a transverse pale line below the eye (but less often in Greenland birds). In 28 ♂ and 28 ♀ the narrowest width of dark between eye and upper end of pale auricular area av. 3 mm. in ♂ and 6 in ♀, and width of auricular patch av. 16 in both. **Underparts** paler than in *anatum*, the streaking on flanks and thighs usually linear to lanceolate, seldom broad and barlike as in some *anatum*. **Legs** and **feet** vary from pale bluish to greenish to palish yellow when older. **Tail** usually more conspicuously barred with a wine-buff color than in most *anatum*, but some, especially ♀♀, lack barring; also note "red" tails mentioned above under Basic.

Measurements From White (1968a); these do not indicate difference between w. and e. parts of breeding range. Basic feathering: 66 ♂ BEAK from cere 17–21 mm., av. 18.7, WING chord 292–330, av. 308.3, and TAIL 130–154, av. 140.2; and 64 ♀ BEAK from cere 21–25 mm., av. 22, WING chord 333–368, av. 352, and TAIL 153–180, av. 168.6.

Juvenal 30 ♂ BEAK from cere 17–19 (1 at 22) mm., av. 18.3, WING chord 295–321, av. 311, and TAIL 143–162, av. 152.4; and 32 ♀ BEAK from cere 19–24 mm., av. 21, WING chord 333–367, av. 350.6 and TAIL 167–189, av. 177.

Additional meas. of migrant *tundrius* in fall: ♀♀ in Basic and ♂♂ and ♀♀ in Juv., in N.J. and Tex. (Henny and Clark 1982) are about as the above. As would be expected, however, based on WING chord, the somewhat larger size of Greenland birds is reflected in meas. made in fall down the Atlantic coast in N.J. (Meas. of WING of live migrants are somewhat larger than those of dry museum skins.)

Weight No data on ♂♂ in Basic; Basic 21 ♀ 825–1,185 gm., av. 961; Juv. 5 ♂ 477–662, av. 570, and 8 ♀ 844–925, av. 897 (White 1968a).

Live-trapped birds at C. May Pt., N.J., presumably are at least mostly Greenland birds that have made overwater crossings and then do not linger; fall migrants at Padre I., Tex. (a few reach Padre via C. May), forage there and gain wt. during a stay of variable length. Cape May Pt., Basic feathering: 2 ♀ 834 and 889 gm.; Juv.: 41 ♂ 496–782 (578 ± 53) gm., and 63 ♀ 580–1,042 (831 ± 83). Padre I., Basic: 16 ♀ 925–1,175

(1,056 ± 71) gm.; Juv.: 14 ♂ 560–695 (610 ± 43) gm., and 57 ♀ 720–1,200 (946 ± 111) (Henny and Clark).

Relevant literature includes Calef and Heard (1979) for Keewatin, W. G. Hunt et al. (1975) for Tex., and J. T. Harris (1979) and Burnham and Mattox (1984) for Greenland.

South America *cassini* Sharpe—breeds from equatorial Ecuador s. along the Pacific side of S. Am. to the s. tip, also from n.-cent. Argentina southward, plus Tierra del Fuego and the Falklands. In n. part of breeding range found mainly in sierras, along rivers, and on the coast.

Color phases At least to the s. Vasina (1975) stated that it is migratory. (Migrant *tundrius* from the arctic-subarctic occurs in at least a large portion of the range of *cassini* during the austral summer.) The S. Am. Peregrine is of N. Am. derivation, with some slight resemblance to Australian birds. It varies more or less clinally—"normal" phase birds paler in Chile than in Argentina and darkest in the Falklands.

▶"**Normal**" **phase,** without going into details: ♂ ♀ Basic—essentially as *anatum*, much darker than *tundrius*. ♂ ♀ Juv.—also much like *anatum*, the malar stripe usually broader, even side of head mostly black and nearly confluent with nape.

▶**Pallid phase** (formerly *Falco "kreyenborgi"*): ♂ ♀ Basic—quite variable. Pale beak and talons in all flying ages. Rather like *tundrius* but **pale headed,** the forehead white, crown and nape palish tan streaked dark in variable amount, malar stripe typically narrow, large auricular area whitish or pale tan and this extending up to eye, bluish **dorsum** has much narrow blackish barring, **underparts** white to tan with fine darkish markings, **tail** palish tan barred black. ♂ ♀ Juv.—**head** overall light; forehead very pale, crown and nape pale (whitish to tan) with some dark streaking, side of head to nape mostly white to pale tan with narrow malar stripe and often a dark streak extending from eye backward and downward; **dorsal** feathers muted brownish with tan markings and edging (overall, appear warm brownish) but vary with individual to slaty with white markings and edging; **underparts** white with variable amount of fine darkish streaking, this in some broadening at least to teardrop shape on sides and flanks; **tail** white, usually tinged tan, with black bars. Color photographs: Ellis and Garat (1983).

The pallid morph is not known throughout the range of *cassini* and is most plentiful to the s. in Argentina and Chile (arid country). Breeding pairs of "normal" × "normal," "normal" × pallid, and pallid × pallid are known (and sometimes their preflight young), and although there is considerable individual variation (more so in pallid birds), the morphs are not known to be bridged by intermediates.

For much biology of S. Am. Peregrines, see Vasina and Straneck (1984) and Schoonmaker et al. (1985); for the pallid phase and the literature on it, see McNutt (1984).

Eurasia/Africa *peregrinus* Tunstall—Britain, temperate and boreal Europe into e. USSR (intergrades with *calidus*). In the past often divided into various subspecies on the basis of slight regional differences. Northerly birds migratory. Greenland birds are not of this race (Jourdain 1933, later authors) but are American. Captives have been imported into N. Am.; see, for example, J. Cooper (1971). The relevant literature, popular and technical, is vast, plus major emphasis in many treatises on falconry. W. Fischer's (1968) monograph has gone through various printings and revisions; Ratcliffe (1980) is primarily a British monograph.

calidus Latham—cooler and temperate boreal USSR, intergrading to the w. with *peregrinus* and to the e. presumably with *japonensis*. Pale birds. Highly migratory, as is also the next one listed.

japonensis Gmelin—reportedly darker than the preceding but evidently has considerable geographical variation. Northeastern Asia s., including is. on the landward perimeter of Okhotsk Sea (Sakhalin, etc.) and at least the s. Kurils, Japan (Hokkaido, Honshu), and s. Korea. Migrant in the Commanders (where *pealei* breeds). Long-distance migrant (equivalent of New World *tundrius*) to s. Asia and even s. Africa.

A ♂ reported as a Siberian *calidus* (Hanna (1940), taken near C. Prince of Wales, Alaska, in 1939 and listed as *harterti* (synonym of *japonensis*) in the 1957 AOU *Check-list*, is identical with certain *tundrius* individuals from widespread localities (White 1968b). Individuals may cross between ne. Asia and Alaska, but proof must await recovery of banded birds.

Hawaiian sightings, also a specimen reported by Clapp and Woodward (1968), are evidently of *japonensis*.

Biology: Egorov (1959).

brookei Sharpe—Iberian Pen., is. in the Mediterranean, and across s. Europe and beyond to the Caspian. For many data, see especially W. Fischer (1982).

The next 2 following are regarded here as Peregrines but have been considered (combined) a separate species by some authors (Vaurie 1961a, Cade 1982); treatment as in L. Brown and Amadon (1968 2) seems preferable.

pelegrinoides Temminck—Barbary Falcon. Notably pale desert birds, in a general way resembling our Prairie Falcon. Canary Is., perimeter of nw. Africa and, to some extent, far inland; and in e. Africa approximately from the Nile drainage e. plus s. end of the Arabian Pen. Literature: Vaurie (1961a) and Cade (1982).

babylonicus Sclater—Red-naped Shaheen. Palest (desert-adapted) of Old World Peregrines, even paler than the preceding; part of Asia from e. Iran into China (including Mongolia).

peregrinator Sundevall—Black Shaheen. Pakistan, India, Ceylon, e. to s. coast of China (apparently no Peregrines breed to the s. in se. Asia). Reference: Ali and Ripley (1978).

minor Bonaparte—part of s. Africa and at least also a belt across the widest part of the continent s. of the Sahara. Apparently scarce. Reference: McLachlan and Liversidge (1959).

Australia Two races have been listed, those to the n. slightly smaller and darker than those to the sw. This is based in part on a belief that they are more or less geographically isolated; it may be that current known distribution and variation preclude recognition of a separate sw. population (R. Weatherly).

macropus Swainson—Australia except part of the interior, the sw., and Tasmania. References: Condon and Amadon (1954), J. and L. Cupper (1981), Pruett-Jones et al. (1981), and Czechura (1984).

submelanogenys Mathews—sw. portion of Australia. Doubtfully recognizable.

Islands and archipelagoes *madens* Ripley and Watson—C. Verdes. Very small population. References: Ripley and Watson (1963), de Naurois (1969).

radama Hartlaub—e. part of Madagascar and the Comoro Is.; little known. Reference: C. W. Benson (1960).

furuitii Moryama—only known breeding place is a 6-mi.-long is. in the Volcano group, s. of Honshu, Japan. Specimen taken on Torishima, Izu Is. Condensed account: W. King (1979).

ernesti Sharpe—Sumatra, Borneo, Celebes, e. into New Guinea and n. to the s. Philippines. Reference: Mayr (1941).

nesiotes Mayr—n. of New Zealand in the New Hebrides, Loyalty Is., Fiji, and New Caledonia. Reference: Clunie (1972).   CLAYTON M. WHITE

FIELD IDENTIFICATION   The species—**in our area**   Above medium size for a falcon (about as an Am. Crow, Prairie Falcon, or Cooper's Hawk); usual length 17–21 in.; sexes essentially alike except ♀ larger.

In flight, thickset or solid, appearing heavier forward, wings quite long and tapering, tail comparatively short for size of bird (it is slightly rounded when furled). At a distance, before details of pattern can be made out, the powerful fluid wingbeats through a rather narrow arc are evident. In combination of smoothness of flight, speed, acceleration, and maneuverability, this is the ultimate of perfection among our native raptors. Unhurried flight is direct and purposeful, interspersed with short glides. Not a soaring bird ordinarily, but rises on updrafts and in thermals, wings extended and tail so fully spread that its lateral edges nearly touch the trailing edge of the wings. Migrating Peregrines soar and glide under suitable conditions. (See Reproduction and Habits, both below, for other flight actions.)

Basic feathering   A Peregrine is obviously "hooded" blackish, this extending down laterally in the black malar stripe ("mustache" mark) or this expanded to include much of side of head; dorsum blue-gray to slaty to a blackish brown; venter varies from whitish to buffy to salmon or toward tawny with little to much mostly transverse blackish marking—individual and geographic variation—except throat unmarked white; the tail dorsally is not as dark as the back, is sometimes brownish, with a series of dark crossbars, and is overall paler ventrally; wing lining mixed light and darkish, the underside of the patterned flight feathers somewhat lighter basally.

Juvenal Plumage   Upper areas of head mostly dark, extending down as "mustache"; dorsum variably dark, from brownish to nearly neutral; venter light and moderately to very heavily streaked (not barred) dark (heaviest on is. in B.C. and counterclockwise through the Aleutians and beyond); tail sometimes toward reddish brown dorsally (tundra birds); wing lining less evenly patterned than in Basic.

As noted in fall migrants in Tex., Basic and Juv. are readily separable afield on the difference in ventral markings (barred Basic v. streaked Juv.) and dorsal coloration ("blue" Basic v. dark brownish Juv.) (W. G. Hunt et al. 1975).

When perched, the Peregrine is an erect, solid bird, stout at the "shoulders," facial pattern recognizable at considerable distance.

Confusing species   Prairie Falcons (both sexes) tend toward browns overall and have proportionately longer tail; they are not as dark nor as contrastingly patterned as Peregrines. Head capped (not hooded) dark with narrow "mustache," dorsum various browns, venter varies with individual from whitish toward tan with fairly large (but usually rather few) dark markings. A most important field character is the usually largely blackish wing lining.

Large ♀ Peregrines overlap in size with small ♂ Gyrfalcons (the largest species of falcon). The latter tends to be much more evenly colored overall, not obviously "hooded," with hardly a hint of "mustache" in Basic (but is like the Peregrine in Juv.), and individuals vary in general coloring from almost entirely white through grays to slaty or darker. The Gyr's wings are wider at junction with the body and are comparatively rounded distally. Peregrines and Gyrs are easily confused at a distance.

The Merlin, on the other hand, is much smaller—about Mourning Dove size—with dorsum dark bluish (♂) or brownish (♀), no "mustache," and much longitudinal streaking on the buffy to brownish venter.

NOTES Although one may be tempted to guess the sex of a Peregrine based on judgment as to its size, this is risky unless mates (♀ av. ⅓ larger) are within view together. The smaller ♂ has faster wingbeats than the larger ♀, a rather subtle difference.

Our native falcons are now protected species. Various falcons (some not native) have been maintained by falconers and at breeding facilities in N. Am. and crosses and back crosses have been produced by artificial means (some hybrids were listed earlier). Some escapees, if not obviously such from wearing jesses and bells, could create insoluble problems of field identification.

In S. Am., migrant Peregrines from boreal N. Am. may be confused with the locally reared austral birds in "normal" phase; briefly, the latter tend to have lighter heads and variable (av. paler) upperparts. In part of its s. range the latter also have an even lighter, distinctive, pallid phase (see *cassini* under Subspecies, above).

RALPH S. PALMER

VOICE Generally silent when solitary, but noisy at times at the aerie, and some vocalizing can occur whenever and wherever vestiges of the family or the sibling bond exist. At least most calls are used in various contexts (are polyvalent) and in various intensities, which has resulted in much variation among describers. They relate to advertising, display, copulation, feeding, and territorial and other defense, and all are modifications of a few main types. The ♂'s voice is higher pitched than the ♀'s. There are many N. Am. data on voice by Hagar (in Bent 1938), R. and K. Herbert (1965), Wrege and Cade (1977), Cade et al. (1977), and R. W. Nelson (1977). Most of the following is condensed and modified from Nelson and in no special sequence.

Adults *Cacking* harsh, rasping, staccato (♂ ♀), variously spaced; may continue at length if a person or other intruder remains near the aerie; the most commonly described call; as a rapid-fire scream it signals attack; after the young are flying, a parent may utter it in self-defense to drive them away. *Waik* (♂, or pair) especially when perched high (advertising); ♀ signaling readiness to copulate. *Eeechip* (♂ ♀) in various mutual displays, including Ledge-display; ♀ soliciting, also during copulation; ♂ ♀ with head feathers raised (threat) or when in horizontal stance (threat); also in pursuit, fighting, and so on. *Chuckles* (♂ ♀) when making a scrape. *Treble-whine* ("wailing") ♀ begging for food; ♂ or ♀ mantling over (defending) food; either sex when threatened with attack. *Eep-eep-eep* (♂ especially) in aggressive chase. *Upchip* (♀) signals readiness to copulate. *Chitter* (♀) as preceding; also when threatened with attack. *Chup-chup* (♀) not ready to copulate. *Chutter* (♂) mounting and copulating. *Eee* and *nyaah* (♂ ♀) when threatened with attack.

336

Young There is a *cheeping* sound within the egg before it hatches; modified and rapidly repeated, it evolves into the treble-whine. Sherrod (1983) stated that the following develop more or less during preflight and are afterward used by young of both sexes: *Treble-whine* "begging" (food solicitation). *Playful scream* much as preceding, but in playful context. *Cacking* rapidly repeated, when disturbed or threatened. *Chitter-scream* high-pitched chitter in extreme alarm. RALPH S. PALMER

HABITAT Emphasis on N. Am. The number of bird species worldwide that regularly fly in unobstructed airspace exposed to the Peregrine's attack is not large; the number of a size suitable for consistent use is smaller still (F. Beebe 1974). Peregrines also occur locally where special conditions make available to them a broad spectrum of prey species not ordinarily taken (Beebe). Stated otherwise, unavailability of suitable prey restricts the Peregrine's occurrence. This is an open-country raptor in all seasons, and it fares better in moderate climates than at extremes. According to M. Nelson (in Hickey 1969), in the mt. states of w. U.S. it is doomed to breeding failure at elevations below 6,000 ft. if exposed to direct rays of the sun; it is a late breeder and is far more sensitive to heat and cold and direct sunlight than either the Prairie Falcon or Gyrfalcon.

The is.-resident Peregrines around the perimeter of the nw. Pacific are especially adapted to cool, humid conditions. They have a powdery bloom consisting of particles of down that perhaps adheres by secretions from the oil gland. It functions as waterproofing, and these birds do not become soaked by winter rains. They specialize in capturing seabirds (as do those of Baja Calif. and elsewhere). They occupy a special niche.

In some tundra areas, the only diurnal raptor that exceeds the Peregrine in numbers in summer is the Rough-legged Hawk. On the other hand, within the Peregrine's breeding range, there are miles of seemingly suitable unoccupied cliffs, such as in the foothills of the Rockies. Again, in Nfld. one searches in vain for the Peregrine (few cliffs even have Roughlegs).

There is much yet to be learned about the nature of conditions and amount of flying time the Peregrine spends crossing various waters. Our most marine falcon, it feeds at sea, taking prey from the air (usually); it even travels over water to some extent after dark.

Breeding Peregrines prefer sites at least fairly close to water—niches in cliffs, steep banks, rock islets, and so on; not at high elevations. A few mammals may affect local breeding distribution. In N. Am. the scavenging raccoon (*Procyon lotor*) and ringtail (*Bassariscus*) are able to reach some aeries. In the Baltic region, where Peregrines lay on bog hummocks, the predaceous mink (*Mustela vison*), which has escaped to the wild in Europe, is not reported to be a predator or else has not reached these areas. The scavenging raccoon dog (*Nyctereutes*) has spread into the Baltic area recently. Although some tundra Peregrine sites are on the ground, only those on safe rocky elevations are free from fox predation, especially in years of fox abundance. Some sites are robbed of eggs by ground squirrels (*Spermophilus*).

In Greenland, this falcon prefers inland places, away from the cooler and less sheltered coast. Elsewhere, some breed on an assortment of man-made equivalents to

337

natural sites (see Reproduction, below). Tree sites are used on various continents, but enough of such usage to extend breeding distribution is limited essentially to part of Australia. Tree nesters hunt over the forest canopy, waterways, and clearings.

Migrations   North Am. tundra birds are long-distance migrants, and more s. ones are less migratory or resident. Traveling Peregrines may occur anywhere (such as in cities, seeking pigeons), but most prefer open country or water—prairies, lake and river margins, marine shorelines, beaches, dunes, and the sea. There is an important staging-area for migrants on the Atlantic edge of the U.S., from N.J. into S.C., and another on barrier is. of the Tex. gulf coast. The relatively level terrain of both is an ecological counterpart of tundra. The birds hunt and the young gain wt. before continuing the long journey that many of them will take—to open landscape far s. in S. Am.

Winter   Those traveling to distant "winter" (austral summer) range were just mentioned. In much of temperate N. Am., ♂ ♂ at least seem to be territorial much of the year, going if necessary in colder months only far enough to find a food supply. Prebreeders scatter more widely.

Versus the Gyr   Based on Alaskan studies, Cade (1960) stated that the Peregrine is "numerically more successful" than the Gyr because it adapts to changing climatic conditions, is less exacting in choice of aeries, has no difficulty in obtaining plenty of food through summer, and escapes the arctic winter by migrating. Although breeding ranges of Peregrine and Gyr overlap some 15° lat. in N. Am., the cold-adapted Gyr is a true arctic bird; the 2 species have insignificant overlap of winter range. Some aeries are used by either species in turn (or by the N. Raven). The earlier-breeding Gyr needs a site that is snow free early. In the zone of overlap of occurrence, the Gyr breeds at higher elevations. The Gyr is more of a ground-hugger and takes more mammals; the more aerial Peregrine takes more birds. Nearby water seems to be more important to Peregrines than to Gyrs.

Versus the Prairie Falcon   The Peregrine's breeding range has the entire breeding range of the Prairie Falcon within it. The latter is a true desert bird; it can tolerate more heat, drier conditions (is less tied to water), and tends to use sheltered sites (such as cliff holes) for aeries. The Peregrine prefers higher sites, more in the open, where the young are sensitive to heat and sunlight. Even so, the 2 falcons are more or less compatible and may have sites along the same cliff or switch ownership in different years. At higher elevations, the Prairie Falcon exceeds the Peregrine in flight capability (a matter of wing loading). The Prairie Falcon is a ground-hugger, perhaps even more than the Gyr, and feeds considerably on mammals; the Peregrine, true to form, usually hunts higher, for birds. Generally speaking, the Peregrine, although not plentiful, can breed successfully under desert conditions if near a marsh, lake, or river.

Versus man   There seems to be reasonable understanding that breeding Peregrines are intolerant of human disturbance. The rule can be bent—Peregrines have bred above busy city streets (rarely for more than a few seasons) and at natural sites from which some human activity was visible. As for habituation, original conditions are long past in Britain, and Peregrines now leave the vicinity of the aerie when man intrudes; in N. Am. they have not yet reached this stage and may attack the intruder (compare with the Goshawk).   RALPH S. PALMER

338

DISTRIBUTION (See maps.) Although there are some absences, the breeding range of the Peregrine may be described as nearly worldwide (except polar regions), on continents and many is. It is recorded far at sea, on is. where it does not breed, and n. beyond breeding range. The following pertains principally to our area.

During Pleistocene glaciations, it is probable that there were breeding Peregrines (as well as Gyrfalcons) in arctic refugia (in both Old World and New), the Peregrine being migratory. Subsequent occupation of terrain exposed by waning of the ice age allowed n. and s. birds to meet and blend, thereby permitting a continuous breeding range. Resident insular birds of the nw. coastal perimeter occupy areas unaffected by late glaciations, and this extended period of continuous occupancy is reflected in unique development. In Greenland Peregrines may have shifted s. from primarily Gyr country as the climate warmed, or perhaps Peregrines extended their range from Canada to s. Greenland relatively late. These are hypotheses, but they seem to align with the Peregrine's recent evolution and migratory behavior. (The Canada Goose has a comparable leapfrog pattern, but none migrate as far as tundra Peregrines.)

Peregrine and Gyr now have lat. overlap in breeding distribution in N. Am. but tend to ecological separateness locally. The Peregrine's total lat. breeding distribution in N. Am. is about 22°–72°N. It is resident in the Commanders and the Aleutians, where the Gyr (at least presently) is not known to breed. On the other hand, the Gyr is plentiful in Iceland, where the Peregrine is not known to breed. The 2 falcons sort out somewhat in Greenland: only the Gyr to the n., both to the s. (Peregrine seasonally absent). Breeders are thinly scattered in interior n. Mexico. The Peregrine has reached Tasmania but not New Zealand.

GREENLAND Breeds from C. Farewell n. up the w. side to Quanak Dist., although sparingly n. of Nûgssuaq; much more common in interior and fjord country than on the coast; straggler n. to Thule Dist. On the e. side has bred at least in Angmagssalik Dist. and straggled n. to Scoresby Sd. Dist. (See comment under Migration, below, for possible former wintering.)

Winter Eastern U.S., based on Christmas count analyses. From 1940 to 1975, Peregrines were widespread but showed a steady decline in numbers; details in Bonney (1979). In 1976–1977 through 1982–1983, in N.C., S.C., Ga., and Fla., numbers improved slightly the last 2 winters, with most winterers seen in Fla. (1983 *Am. Birds* 37 387).

Summer Some N. Am. individuals (prebreeders or nonbreeders) occur both n. and s. of breeding range, as well as within it.

Peripheral records Recorded (Ross 1974) in the Canadian Higharctic on AXEL HEIBERG I., above the lat. of the Thule Dist. of Greenland. [Beyond the Siberian mainland, the Peregrine was reportedly seen long ago on BENNETT I., n. of the New Siberian Archipelago (Uspenskii 1963), which is nearly as far n. as Axel Heiberg.] BERMUDA rare (Bradlee et al. 1931), later listed as regular in fall and spring (Bermuda Aud. Soc. 1959). GULF OF MEXICO is almost surely crossed by Peregrines. WEST INDIES-CARIBBEAN area sparse migrant (so far as known), and some remain in winter; fewer records to the e.

On the Pacific side, in BERING SEA a fall record for St. Lawrence I. (A. M. Bailey 1956). Far to the s. in the HAWAIIAN GROUP recorded from Hawaii, Oahu (5 records),

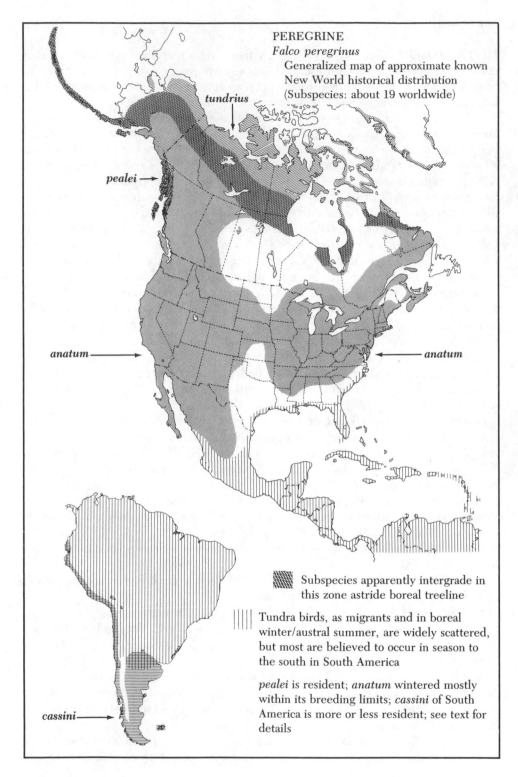

PEREGRINE
Falco peregrinus
Generalized map of approximate known
New World historical distribution
(Subspecies: about 19 worldwide)

tundrius

pealei

anatum — ← → — *anatum*

cassini →

▨ Subspecies apparently intergrade in
this zone astride boreal treeline

‖‖ Tundra birds, as migrants and in boreal
winter/austral summer, are widely scattered,
but most are believed to occur in season to
the south in South America

pealei is resident; *anatum* wintered mostly
within its breeding limits; *cassini* of South
America is more or less resident; see text for
details

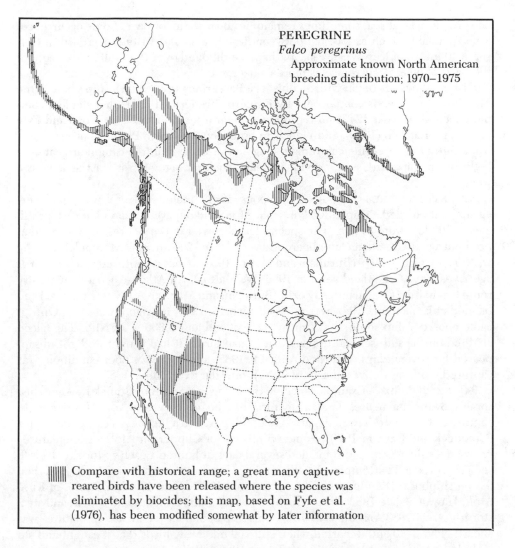

PEREGRINE
Falco peregrinus
Approximate known North American
breeding distribution; 1970–1975

Compare with historical range; a great many captive-
reared birds have been released where the species was
eliminated by biocides; this map, based on Fyfe et al.
(1976), has been modified somewhat by later information

Lisianski, Midway, Kure, and French Frigate Shoals. All were probably from ne. Asia, including (Clapp and Woodward 1968) a specimen.

SOUTH AMERICA   Our tundra birds occur in S. Am. in the austral summer (see Migration, below), and a few linger long after others have departed n. The Peregrines breeding in S. Am. number perhaps only a few hundred pairs. Their breeding range extends from Tierra del Fuego and the Falklands n. on the mainland into s. Argentina or beyond, s. Chile, and breeding is scattered n. in the narrow Pacific drainage to a known site less than 10 km. s. of the equator.

At sea   The Peregrine and Osprey are the raptors most likely to be found remote from land. This ties in with their hunting over water—rivers, lakes, seas—even when breeding. G. Tuck (1970) wrote of numerous instances of Peregrines in all principal

341

oceans, often far at sea, sometimes remaining aboard ship for days. Some occurrences are explainable, such as passage between Scandinavia and Britain or a bird in Oct. some 40 mi. w. of Key West, Fla., perhaps southbound over the Gulf of Mexico, but the basis of other occurrences is more conjectural.

Historical records begin with an illus. of a Peregrine perched on a ship's bow in the MS copy of the treatise on falconry by Emperor Frederick II of Hohenstaufen, completed about the year 1247 and reproduced 7 centuries later in C. A. Wood and Fyfe (1943) and Ratcliffe (1980). Individuals in both Juv. and Basic Plumage occur at sea. Apparently the Peregrine can remain long on the wing; seabirds caught are eaten in flight or on shipboard, and individuals may "book passage" for at least as long as a week.

ATLANTIC RECORDS   Reported by Voous (1961), included 1 of a presumed Peregrine that boarded a ship 1,300 km. from Africa and departed 2 days later when still over 1,100 km. from S. Am. The species has occurred in the Azores. A ♂ banded at preflight age in Greenland later boarded a vessel some 200 mi. e. of Montauk Pt., Long I., N.Y., on Oct. 3, 1979 (Burnham and Mattox 1984); it was recaptured as a breeder at age 7 years at a Greenland aerie in 1986 (W. Mattox). An Atlantic oceanic migratory route to and from Greenland may exist (Burnham and Mattox). A Juv. bird, reared and banded at Edmonton, Alta., was released June 13, 1985, in Algonquin Park, Ont.; it came aboard a ship some 1,000 mi. w. of Scotland and 1,000 e. of Nfld. The falcon alighted on the ship several times to eat "small birds" it had caught in flight, disappeared for several days, returned Aug. 14, 1985, apparently in poor condition, was captured, and was delivered ashore in N.J. on Aug. 21 (Connor 1985).

PACIFIC RECORDS   Examples include the following: South of Umnak I., Aleutians, some 418 km. from nearest land, a "mature" bird boarded a vessel Apr. 24, was seen to capture 5 storm-petrels, and departed as the ship passed a Japanese vessel 2 days later (Craddock and Carlson 1970). Some 65 mi. ne. of Clipperton Atoll an "immature" boarded a ship in Oct. and remained several days; it hunted Leach's Storm-Petrels (8 seen captured in 11 attempts), usually removed head and wings during flight, and then fed on shipboard (W. Rogers and Leatherwood 1981). Four hundred mi. e. of Kure Atoll, Hawaii, in late 1982 a bird remained aboard a ship for a day and caught and ate 2 storm-petrels (1983 *Am. Birds* **37** 152). On a ship bound for Japan, an "immature" was aboard Nov. 3–10 and departed when still 700 mi. away; birds that it caught and ate included a tern and at least 2 Bonin Petrels (Byers 1957).

NOTES   Erroneously reported breeding on St. George, Pribilofs (1957 AOU *Checklist*). Supposed records of Am. birds in Britain, based on sightings of dark individuals, have been widely accepted on both sides of the Atlantic. A possibility of migrant birds from Greenland would seem more logical, but there are almost no Peregrine records in between for Iceland and very few for the Faroes. Ratcliffe (1980) would disallow British reports of Am. birds unless based on recovery of banded individuals.

In N. Am. reported as **fossil** from the Pleistocene of Calif. (2 sites), N.Mex., Idaho, and Fla. (3); and from 3 **prehistoric sites** in Utah and 1 each in the Brooks Range of Alaska and in Calif., Ark., Ill., Ohio, and Pa. In S. Am. from the Pleistocene of Ecuador and Peru. These are from Brodkrob (1964), with additions. Old World records are mostly from Europe and Britain; in the latter, historical records appear from the 8th century onward, thus overlapping 9th and 10th century archaeological finds in Shetland; details in Ratcliffe (1980).   RALPH S. PALMER

MIGRATION   In the Americas. In the New (and Old) World the Peregrine has a leapfrog pattern; high-lat. (tundra) birds bypass those farther s. and go farthest—a few evidently to Fla. and vicinity, some to Caribbean localities, perhaps a few to Cent. Am., but mostly to s. S. Am. Some that bred in more temperate lats. were (before regional extirpation) intermediate to short-distance travelers, although most established breeders (at least at lower elevations) were essentially resident. Some were forced to leave their territories in colder months to seek food elsewhere; in s. N. Am. breeding range there was (and is) some scattering during the heat of summer.

Temperate birds in 1st fall tended to travel farther than established breeders (and return to natal areas subsequently), but apparently few of any age from within the s. Canadian mainland and coterminous U.S. went beyond the N. Am. s. breeding limits of the species. Whether captive-reared birds of *tundrius* or mixed parentage, when stocked where breeding *anatum* was extirpated, are genetically programmed for long distance migration is moot.

The n. Pacific Peregrines of the Queen Charlottes and counterclockwise to include the Aleutians and Commanders are an exception to the above, being resident. Currently, unknown numbers of Peregrines also migrate in both spring and fall along the nw. Pacific perimeter.

It has been stated that some birds are locally migratory or resident in s. Greenland. There are late seasonal records, and a few possibly wintered during a climatic optimum now past, but banding evidence indicates that they are long-distance migrants.

The breeding Peregrines s. in S. Am. are said (Vasina 1975) to be migratory. Apparently there is at least some seasonal dispersal.

Peregrines migrating over land travel mostly in daytime and roost at night. They often hunt in early morning and in evening—they do not travel or rest on an empty stomach—and 100–200 mi./day may be the av. rate of progress. A southbound telemetered Juv. ♂ in early Oct. in N.C. "periodically reached altitudes of several thousand feet in thermals" (Cochran, in Harwood 1985); gliding and soaring high in thermals probably makes long passage feasible and may also explain why there are few recorded occurrences in some areas (such as Cent. Am.).

That Peregrines cross wide waters is well known, and there is growing evidence of night travel. For example, traveling between Scandinavia and Britain/Ireland would surely place them over water after dark unless they departed from land very early in the day. Occurrence at sea at distances more than a day's flight from land (see Distribution, above), is further evidence of nocturnal flight. In daylight, at least, much travel over water is low, under 100 ft. altitude, with much flapping (powered flight).

Transient young tundra birds, especially in fall, may linger for days at a staging area to hunt and fatten. This occurs on Atlantic coastal beaches (notably Assateague I., Md.-Va.) and the Gulf of Mexico barrier is. on the Tex. coast (notably S. Padre). In the C. May region of N.J., "adult" ♂ ♂ are few at staging areas, perhaps being forced away by

343

♀ ♀ (Dekker 1979); at S. Padre there are few "adult" ♂ ♂ along the outer beach (none trapped there), but a possibility exists that they are inland nearby (W. G. Hunt et al. 1975).

Fall   Within Greenland, migrants are reported to travel s. inland (away from the coast), feeding on Snow Buntings (Salomonsen 1951). That would imply that they subsequently leave Greenland well s. and that the most direct water crossing would be wide, toward the Labrador Pen. In bad weather they possibly rest on icebergs or ships or perish at sea. Very likely they then go down over the interior plateau (there is a banding recovery some 150 km. n. of Montreal), and many Peregrines occur, or at least are most often observed, farther s. near, on, and off s.-trending coasts. There is a good flight beginning in early Sept. along the inner periphery and also out over the Gulf of Maine. Peregrines occur along the beaches of Long I., N.Y., from about mid-Sept. to late Oct. To the s. in Md.-Va. at Assateague I., numbers peak approximately from the last few days of Sept. to mid-Oct., and repeated sightings and high recapture rates there (Ward and Berry 1972) demonstrate that this is a staging area. The number trapped and banded there in 1984 was 151 birds. A few from Assateague go diagonally sw. to the Tex. coast, a few are seen in winter in the se. U.S., and, via Fla., some island-hop in and around the Caribbean, some scattered birds remaining there and others presumably continuing on to S. Am. Birds banded at Assateague I. have been recovered at places extending from Greenland to Argentina.

Birds banded in Greenland have been recaptured or recovered on the n. shore of the St. Lawrence; on Long I., N.Y. (several); along the Atlantic coast (many); on the Tex. coast; in Cuba (2); Dominican Republic (2); and Ecuador (W. Mattox). To this list add Bolivia (1979 *Am. Birds* **33** 161).

Many central tundra (and formerly some more s.) birds come down mainly via the Great Lakes region and w., leaving Canada mostly in the last ⅓ of Sept. and 1st week of Oct. They move on in the Mississippi drainage and divide; some head e. toward Fla. and some go toward the Tex. coast. Beyond Tex. their route is speculative. Records of Peregrines at this season in Cent. Am. are few and scattered; the few recoveries to the n. in S. Am. seem to be concentrated on the Pacific side. Farther s., occurrences are mainly in Uruguay and Argentina (E. R. Blake 1977, map). According to White (1968b), *tundrius* occurs in winter probably to lats. 35°S in Argentina and 40°S in Chile.

In n. Alaska, family groups are still centered on the aerie until migration begins (Cade 1960). Interior Alaska and Yukon Terr. birds go s. inland (a few along the Pacific coast?), lingering at times where shorebirds or other open-country prey is plentiful, and continue on through the U.S. along the foothills of the e. side of the Rockies. In cent. Alta. the majority pass Sept. 10–Oct. 4 (Dekker 1979), and most of them cross the Canada-U.S. boundary in the last 3 weeks of Sept. They occur in numbers at the S. Padre staging area in Tex. principally in the 1st ½ of Oct. (span of about Sept. 23–Nov. 8). "Adults" arrive 1st, then peak numbers of 1st-fall ♂ ♂ are soon followed by a peak of 1st-fall ♀ ♀ (W. G. Hunt et al. 1975). "Adults" quickly pass on, but the young may linger, some up to several weeks. A total of 157 was banded there in Sept.–Oct. 1981. They continue on, their route speculative. Here again it is suggested that they travel high in thermals. A more or less Pacific route (for birds that stop at S. Padre) in S. Am. would seem to be logical. Enderson (1965) reported that "immatures" banded on the middle U.S. Atlantic coast had been recovered in fall in Ecuador (also in spring in Ecuador and Colombia and in the boreal winter in Uruguay).

An "immature" ♂ was captured n. of Green Bay, Wis., on Oct. 12, 1974, fitted with a transmitter, and released. It went s. into La., then sw. into e. Tex., and crossed into Tamaulipas, Mexico, on Oct. 25. It was radio-tracked over this distance. Combining the data with a small amount from other tagged birds, av. distance covered daily was 111 mi. (included 13 in low hunting flight) for 1,637 mi. in 4,766 min. of flight at av. speed of 21 mph. There was great variation in speed, depending on wind and availability of thermals.

The bird tracked to Mexico was perched (eating, sleeping) 58% of the time, in low hunting flight 6%, in low migratory flight 7.5%, and in circle-soaring migratory flight 28.5%. Birds hunted and ate in the morning (beginning before sunrise), then flew in uninterrupted migration (av. 5 hr. 18 min.), and then hunted (not always successfully) in the evening. They did not migrate at night. They made flapping flight at 30–300 ft. when thermals were unavailable and did not fly during extended periods of headwinds. They flapped little or not at all in thermals, and 2 birds were estimated to have exceeded 3,000 ft. altitude "on numerous occasions." Peregrines flapped between weak, widely spaced thermals but glided when thermals were plentiful. Movement essentially ceased during low overcast and rain. Nights were spent in wooded areas. There is a distinct migratory pattern that, once it is functioning, excludes all other activities (Cochran 1975).

Austral summer Migrant N. Am. tundra birds are s. in S. Am. from about the beginning of Nov. to the end of Mar. (recoveries to the n. in S. Am. extend at least from early Oct. into May). Three interesting banding recoveries: 1 nestling banded on the Thelon R.. NWT, July 29 and killed 9,000 mi. away in Argentina in the following Jan. (Kuyt 1967); 2 banded at Cedar Grove, Wis., Oct. 1 and recovered in Uruguay Dec. 8, averaging 128 mi./day over the intervening distance (Cooke 1943); and 3 a young ♂ banded at Cedar Grove Sept. 27 and shot near Montevideo, Uruguay, the following Mar. 2 (Mueller and Berger 1959). In the last instance the authors gave a straight-line distance of 5,900 mi. but suggested a probable route via the Antilles and Brazilian coast of 9,000 mi. Such records invite comparison with Arctic Terns, many of which take a much more circuitous route to cover approximately the same straight-line distance.

Boreal winter In former times, when breeding Peregrines occurred generally in s. Canada and coterminous U.S., there were few winter sightings in s. Canada (coastal is. of B.C. excepted). In the U.S. those breeders that vacated their territories for more or less time flew to nearby rivers, waterfowl refuges, and other waters. Easterly, there seems to have been movement to or toward open country of Atlantic coastal estuaries, bays, and inlets. There seems to have been no particular concentration in Fla. The species seems to have been present s. in Tex. and perhaps for some distance beyond to the s. The few birds presently (mid-1980s) occurring in winter in the se. U.S., including Fla., may be from the tundra.

On the Pacific coast of the coterminous U.S. there was (and is) little migration.

Banding evidence (P. Bloom) clearly suggests that birds from within Calif. go inland to interior Mexico; this inland pattern also may apply to birds that bred (and breed) in the s. Canadian and U.S. Rockies.

Spring Many breeders in N. Am. temperate lats. (before regional extirpation) were present and active at aeries by Feb. or early Mar. The tundra birds that pass the austral summer in S. Am. probably start n. beginning at that time and probably retrace fall routes somewhat. North of the city of Veracruz in se. coastal Mexico, Thiollay (1979) saw 48 (estimated 65) Apr. 6–May 6, 1978. A bird banded in Oct. in Tex. was recaptured in Tex. in the following June (Enderson 1965), presumably having been elsewhere in the interim. In Tex., some birds pause at S. Padre I. in Apr.–May. A telemetered "adult" ♀ flew from S. Padre to Wis. in 8 days (W. G. Hunt). A few are seen at the e. end of L. Ontario, where the usual peak is Apr. 15–May 5 (G. Smith and Muir 1978). Far to the w.. they pass through cent. Alta. May 4–23, foraging en route; from 1969 to 1978, "adults" peaked May 4–7 and "immatures" May 12–15; those seen departing were headed n., soaring and sailing high; some "adults" traveled against headwinds (Dekker 1979). Peregrines are much more plentiful there in spring than in fall (Dekker 1984). Those bound for forested interior Alaska arrive in Apr.–early May and go to the breeding cliffs immediately; mates appeared to arrive simultaneously (Cade 1960). In n. Alaska the probable peak of arrival is after mid-May, much later than in the Yukon drainage. Peregrines return to their Greenland aeries beginning in the latter ½ of May.

East-west There are a few records of lateral shift. One banded at preflight age in N.Y. in June was shot in Nebr. the following Nov.—1,200 mi. to the w. (A. and D. Smiley 1930). RALPH S. PALMER

BANDING STATUS **In N. Am.** A total of 5,439 had been banded to Aug., 1981, with 321 recoveries (Clapp et al. 1982); these figures include Greenland birds. In Greenland, banding (with Danish bands) began in 1946, and through 1958 a total of 35 had been banded, with 3 recoveries (Salomonsen 1959). An Am. project was begun in cent.-w. Greenland in 1972, and through 1985 a total of 467 Peregrines (438 nestlings, 28 adults, and 1 Juv.) had been banded, with 19 live recaptures; the most distant recovery was in Ecuador (W. Mattox).

Nestlings have been banded throughout the N. Am. breeding range. Examples: 870 under a single permit 1967–1980 in w. Canada (Fyfe and Banasch 1981); widely in Alaska (mostly *anatum*, half as many *tundrius*. 40 *pealei*) for a total of some 900, 1952–1983, inclusive; about 200 in Calif. Many have been banded at aeries in Yukon Terr., Dist. of Mackenzie, Alta., and the Queen Charlottes. Banding of migrants has been done widely. Examples in coterminous U.S.: some at Cedar Grove, Wis.; many along the midsection of the Atlantic coast (especially C. May Pt., N.J., and Assateague I., Md.-Va.); many on the gulf coast at S. Padre I., Tex. Rice and Berry (in Hickey 1969) reported the banding of 437 Peregrines at Assateague in 12 autumns (1954–1965); of the 171 banded there by Rice, there was a recovery rate of 5%.

Captive-reared and banded young birds have been released widely—over 1,000 from 1975 through 1983—some in ongoing programs.

Among papers using recovery data, notable are Enderson (1965) on N. Am. migration generally (with recoveries mapped) and Henny and Clark (1982) on fall migrant arctic birds.

Elsewhere Peregrines have been banded in Britain, Eurasia, Australia, and other areas. No British-banded individual has been recovered elsewhere (Ratcliffe 1980). Swedish- and Norwegian-ringed (banded) birds have been recovered in Great Britain. For some w. European data, see C. Mead (1973), also Ratcliffe. Victoria, Australia: 212 nestlings banded in 11 years, 69% at cliff aeries, the others in trees (Emison and Bren 1981).   RALPH S. PALMER

REPRODUCTION North Am. data augmented with various information from elsewhere. Earlier sources for our area pertain almost entirely to *F. p. anatum* before it became regionally extirpated, and information for approximately the past 2 decades pertains to *F. p. tundrius*. Data for these are combined in some instances. Various activities of captives have been reported in even more detail than for wild birds, and some reference to this is also made.

Age when first breeds Usually 2 years. Some begin breeding when older, but many never breed in captivity, and some evidently never breed in the wild. It is firmly established that an occasional yearling ♀ (mated to an older ♂) lays a clutch and may rear a brood; it is probable, but more difficult to establish, that yearling ♂ ♂ (mated to older ♀ ♀) fertilize a clutch. It is well known (A. Brooks 1927b, others) that when 1 of a pair of breeders disappears, its replacement (either sex) may be a yearling. No breeding pairs consisting of 2 yearlings have been reported. Some yearlings of either sex have incubation patches (White, in Hickey 1969). A yearling ♀ in Md. laid 2 eggs (incomplete clutch?) that were taken by a collector (Wimsatt, in Hickey 1969); in 1946 a yearling ♀ in Philadelphia laid 3 (Hickey), but evidently most mated yearling ♀ ♀ do not lay.

In s. Scotland, some live-trapped yearling ♀ ♀ did not have incubation patches. Of 6 trapped ♂ ♂ (classed as breeders from having a mate and clutch), 4 1st bred at 2 years, 1 at 3, and another at 4 or 5 (his whereabouts not continuously known). A ♂ at age 3 years was territorial, mated to a nonlaying ♀. Of 16 trapped ♀ ♀, 2 1st bred as yearlings, 13 at age 2, and 1 at age 3 (but past the yearling stage they might have bred elsewhere). Five additional yearling ♀ ♀ that were not trapped also laid eggs, and 12 other paired ones apparently did not lay. There is some indication that ♂ ♂ begin breeding at an older age than ♀ ♀ (R. Mearns and Newton 1984).

Displays Related to defense of territory, pair formation, or bond renewal and to synchronize the cycles of the sexes; they have much overlap in timing and vary in duration. Some Peregrines have been seen in 2s (paired?) as migrants and winterers, and some, high-lat. breeders at least, appear to be already paried on arrival at established sites. For the latter, time available for displays and related activities is brief since laying begins within a few days. Nowhere does the Peregrine need time for construction of an aerie, since it makes only a "scrape" in which to deposit the clutch.

This is the approximate sequence in milder climates. The ♂ is present 1st and evidently has more attachment to the breeding site than the ♀. He advertises his presence and ownership by being noisy while HIGH-CIRCLING—soaring and flapping—and HIGH-PERCHING (both to be conspicuous). The ♀'s arrival causes great excitement, and the birds engage in an elaborate repertoire of spectacular aerial performances. In time, she accepts food offered by him, and her repeated acceptance indicates that the pair bond is formed (or renewed). The ♂ then concentrates on getting the ♀ to occupy a particular site, potentially one where the clutch will be laid. Copulation begins well beforehand and continues frequently. After the ♀'s interest is concentrated on the site, the ♂'s shifts elsewhere—primarily to getting food for his mate and himself. Many facets of behavior were assigned names by R. W. Nelson, and the whole subject was included *ad libitum* in Cramp and Simmons (1980), to which the interested reader is referred. The following covers the salient points:

EARLY PHASE   There is High-circling above and near the potential breeding site, mainly by the ♂; frequently it is in a strong updraft above the face of a cliff. Both sexes (but ♀ seldom) engage in High-perching, often for long periods, the breast being conspicuous. The ♂ may utter a *waik* call. Sometimes there is swift straightaway flying (by ♂, rarely ♀, silent). The undulating or roller-coaster SKY-DANCE (Czechura 1984, diagram) consists of a series of rather steep dives and pullouts. This varies to diving by the ♂ (silent), with many changes in direction—a vertical drop, then upward flight, then another drop; he may turn on his side or even upside down. Dance and dive are territorial advertisements. The ♀ (silent) may follow or pursue the ♂. The pair may hunt cooperatively (both silent). They may defend the site cooperatively (♂, ♀, *cack* call). In slow landing the ♂ (silent) tips forward briefly, as if off-balance. Postures when perched include a vertical stance with head feathers erected (threat?), giving the head a blocky shape in frontal view. In mutual roosting (♂, ♀, *waik* call sometimes), typically the 2 can see each other. In bowing (♂, ♀, sometimes with *eechip* call), the body is tipped forward quickly; there is a horizontal posture (♂, ♀, *eechip* sometimes) that occurs in several contexts.

Aggressive territorial defense includes all manner of pursuit, attack, and strike, by either or both sexes, usually chittering. The owner may stoop or dive from above, or it may turn over and thrust the feet upward at the intruder. They may lock talons and tumble earthward. A few fatal fights, at least between ♂ ♂, are known. If a bird of either sex passes over or through a defended territory, it flies high, often slowly, which seems to inhibit attack.

LEDGE-RELATED   The ♂ (silent) passes the ♀ and flies toward or to the ledge; the ♀ (silent) may follow or pursue the ♂. In the LEDGE-DISPLAY (Wrege and Cade 1977), the ♂ (with *eechip* call) stands, walks, bows, or is horizontal, mainly near the scrape; he may stand in it, briefly or even for many min. The ♀ also displays, with the same call. In mutual Ledge-display (♂, ♀, *eechip* call) both are at the site, horizontal or bowing; variable. In scraping (♂, ♀, with *eechip* and chuckles), the bird is on its breast, kicking back with 1 foot or alternating both, and it may use its beak to roll some loose material (as detritus), which then may form a slight rim. Scraping occurs over a span of days, is done by both sexes; serves to indicate attachment or occupancy, and is the focal point of mutual activities. If several scrapes are made, evidently the ♀ selects the one for the eggs. Scrape making occurs at a particularly sensitive time, and a disturbed bird will shift elsewhere nearby if a satisfactory alternative location exists.

FOOD-RELATED   Begging by the ♀ (with *waik* or whine) occurs in various situations; it signals that the perched bird requires food, which the ♂ may not then have. A flutter-glide (♀, whine or *waik*) is slow, with quick, shallow wingbeats—aerial soliciting. In an indirect transfer of food away from the aerie (♂, ♀, *eechip* call), the ♂, silent or calling, caches food in an open spot, and the ♀ may or may not soon retrieve it. Or the ♂ (with *eechip* call), if perched, rips prey with exaggerated movements; then, in flight, he passes slowly near the ♀ or aerie, carrying it. If she approaches, he lets her take it or drops it for her to seize in midair. In another form of food-pass (♂, ♀, *eechip*, treble whine), the ♂, perched and horizontal, awaits the ♀, and there is beak-to-beak transfer; or there is a flutter-glide, and she takes it from the ♂ in flight. The ♂ may begin feeding the ♀ up to a month before laying, at least in resident birds.

COPULATION-RELATED The ♀ solicits in various ways. Often she tips forward, even for long periods, her back toward the ♂ while watching him at the same time. During mutual Ledge-display she may bend far forward (strongly motivated posture), uttering *eechip*. When less motivated, the soliciting ♀'s vocalizations include *waik*, *eechip*, *upchip*, and chatter. If the ♀ is not ready, she may be silent or utter *chup-chip* and prevent the ♂ from alighting. The ♂ has various tactics and postures to induce the ♀ to copulate; sometimes he is silent, while at other times he utters a *chutter* or low *chip* rapidly repeated. **Copulation** occurs more or less daily for up to several weeks, increasing in frequency as time of laying approaches.

Sexual nexus The pair bond is usually **lifelong monogamy** (maintained as long as both partners survive). In 1976–1982 in s. Scotland, 1 ♀ was present at an aerie for all 7 years of the study, 3 were present for at least 6 years, 2 at least 5, 4 for 4, 12 for 3, and 8 for 2 years. Two ♂ (1 aged 9 years) were present for at least 4 years, and 2 for at least 2 years. Few ♂♂ were captured. Few data on mate fidelity were obtained, although 2 pairs were known to have stayed together for at least 3 years. In general, there appears to be fidelity to both breeding site and mate at undisturbed sites. (From R. Mearns and Newton 1984.)

Trio bond Polygamy or its possible occurrence has been reported rarely in this much-studied raptor. At a tree site in Tenn. the ♀ disappeared. Then, in spring, there were 2 ♀—one small, the other a large dark yearling. The ♂ ignored the small ♀, fed the other, and no eggs were laid. The following year, 3 "adults" were present; 1 large ♀ laid and incubated, the other small ♀ settled on the eggs when the large ♀ got off and vacated when she returned. This was a successful breeding attempt (Spofford 1947a, and in Hickey 1969).

In Scotland in 1971, 2 aeries with clutches were some 3.5 km. (2 mi.) apart. The ♂ flew between the 2 sites. One produced a nestling while the other had an addled egg (Weir, in I. Newton 1976b; Ratcliffe 1980). In Ireland in 1978, 2 aeries were barely 100 m. apart; 3 young had flown from 1 when there still were 2 downies at the other; the "defending" ♂ perched at the vacated aerie (Ratcliffe). Ratcliffe also cited an old report of a ♀ shot at an aerie whose one-legged (hence identifiable) mate returned with both ♂ and ♀; all 3 occupied the site.

Replacement of lost mate In Scotland, during the breeding cycle, when either sex is killed, "a mate is speedily found by the survivor" (A. Wilson and Bonaparte 1832 3). Eleven other authors reporting this were cited in I. Newton (1979); sometimes it

349

occurs within a day. In Montreal the same ♀ was present and laid eggs annually, 1940–1952, inclusive. She had 3 different mates during that span; the fate of 1 was known—it was killed when 2 pairs fought for the breeding site (G. H. Hall 1970).

Breeding associates   At Langara I., B.C., Peregrines that live within colonies of nocturnal seabirds (burrowing species) do most of their hunting of such prey from, or over, the aerie, in such weak light as to be essentially dark (F. Beebe 1960). Peregrines have had aeries near or among night herons; they may share a ledge with cormorants, as on Bering I. (Dementiev and Gladkov 1951, trans. 1966) and at Grand Manan, N.B. (W. Wood 1871). Tundra-breeding geese nest near aeries (Kessel et al. 1953), as do other waterfowl, shorebirds, and various small birds. There is a partial list in W. Fischer (1968). Yet there is evidence from Greenland (Burnham and Mattox 1984), where prey is not plentiful, that the taking of small birds within some 400 m. of an active aerie can depress their numbers significantly.

Return of prebreeders   A return to the natal area or nearby appears to be the rule. Yearlings returning in spring to natal sites were deterred from staying by pairs already in residence (Fyfe, in I. Newton 1976b). In Mass., "extra" ♀ ♀ were occasionally fed by paired resident ♂ ♂, but Hagar (in Hickey 1969) suspected that these ♀ ♀ might have been progeny visiting the sites of their hatching the previous year—that is, continuation of family bond. In s. Scotland, 39 breeders (24 ♀ and 15 ♂) banded as nestlings were retrapped subsequently, their dispersal between birthplace and where they bred are not necessarily generally representative. Males did not disperse as far as ♀ ♀, in general; median recorded distances were ♂ 20 km. (max. 75) and ♀ 68 (max. 185). They went in any direction, and there was no indication of preference for a site similar to where they hatched. Peregrines generally make their longest movements in their 1st year of life and in any direction; and having acquired a breeding territory, they remain in that general area thereafter (R. Mearns and Newton 1984). The situation possibly differs in migrant birds.

Territory   May be defined as defended area, which is small, as distinguished from total hunting range, which is much larger. Peregrines do not patrol the borders of either—although High-circling and Sky-dance are warnings to potential intruders.

The area regularly defended may extend in radius about 100 yds. from the aerie, but the distance at which the falcons attack depends on what species is approaching—in Alaska, they attack Golden Eagles when more than 2 km. away, but Com. Ravens can approach within 100 m. and Rough-legged Hawks within 50 m. (White, in I. Newton 1979). The Peregrines that breed in s. S. Am. "vehemently" attack the Com. Caracara to a radius of 300–400 m. from the aerie (Vasina and Straneck 1984). Response of intruders varies. The Bald Eagle, if attacked from above by a single bird or pair, may turn over and extend its feet upward. The Snowy Owl does likewise (Sutton and Parmelee 1955). Most intruders retreat hastily. In territorial disputes among themselves, fighting Peregrines may grapple and even crash to the ground (R. and K. Herbert 1965). Pairs fought for the breeding site on the Sun Life building in Montreal, and a ♂ was found dead on the "nesting ledge," its breast partly eaten; it was apparently the resident ♂, which had been there some years (G. H. Hall 1970).

Although the actively defended area is small, the entire hunting range in the breeding season can be as much as 40 sq. mi. (10,000 ha.), as on some Scottish grouse moors

(Ratcliffe 1980), and food supply probably determines its size. Total hunting areas of breeding pairs of Peregrines frequently overlap.

In s. Scotland, of 7 ♀ that changed territories, 4 moved to adjacent ones, 2 moved across 2 other territories (to sites 29 and 33 km. away) and 1 across 3 (32 km.). Three moved after breeding failure (1 was a nonlaying yearling ♀). No information was obtained on ♂♂ at these sites (R. Mearns and Newton 1984). In a 10-year study of 26 aeries in France, only 1 pair used the same aerie all 10 years (Foman 1969).

Territory in winter The breeding locale is occupied in all seasons in mild climates—except when and if it is vacated temporarily. The ♂ is believed to show greater attachment to it than the ♀ (as in R. and K. Herbert 1965) and will defend it, but there is some evidence that the ♀ sometimes remains when the ♂ is absent. (Obviously, if mates are separated, they hunt in different areas.) Both sexes may roost at or near the breeding cliff, and a resident bird may sleep at the aerie, and/or use it as a plucking site, and may sometimes hunt directly from it. Yet apparently there is a tendency to hunt some distance away. Vleugel (1950) saw 2 Peregrines in a prolonged fight that was apparently a boundary dispute on Dec. 31.

Aerie It has been defined as the general location containing the breeding site or, as here, the immediate area containing the clutch—more or less the spatial equivalent of a raptorial stick nest. Among elevated sites, variation includes cliffs (and substitutes), stick nests of other birds on cliffs or in trees, and tree cavities. What might be termed intermediate sites are such places as recesses or level spots at or near the tops of eroded river banks. Nonelevated sites are on an eminence, a slope, a boulder, a dune, a bog hummock or islet, or even on the ground if there is little or no topographical relief.

Ideally the aerie commands a wide view, is near water, has plentiful prey in its vicinity, and is seldom disturbed. A sheltering overhang is common at cliff sites. There should be some debris, such as soil or rocky material, in which to make the "scrape" for the eggs; some of this debris may be pulled toward the sitter to form a rim sufficient to keep the eggs from rolling about.

The Peregrine generally lays on a fairly level spot, preferably at least 2 ft. (60 cm.) in diam.; it is advantageous to have more space for the young to move about as they grow. If a cliff aerie is small, the young become crowded, and 1 or more may fall off; such losses are probably more common than is realized (F. Beebe 1960).

It has been noted by various observers, but especially as reported by Cade (1960) in Alaska and Enderson (1965) in the U.S. Rockies, that the birds do not necessarily select an aerie that one might expect. Thus, in parts of Alaska, Peregrines frequently use a low bluff only a few hundred yds. from a high cliff; and in the foothills of the Rockies there are 100s of mi. of unoccupied but apparently suitable cliffs, while "poorer" sites are occupied regularly.

The ♂ typically has a perch not far away, from which he can view the aerie.

Hickey (1942) divided cliff sites into 3 categories from excellent to poor. Inadequate sites are visited by Peregrines and may be plucking sites. Hickey inferred that the ♀ selects a mate that has a good site, but conclusive evidence is lacking. Cliff sites are typical of the Peregrine almost everywhere, some even being small rock outcrops on is. In the N. Hemisphere they are unmodified (usually), or contain a stick nest of the Com. Raven (favored, often sheltered), Roughleg (less favored, often unsheltered), or occasionally the Golden Eagle or Redtail. A stick nest on a cliff, after use by the Peregrine, may revert to a former owner or be used by some other species. In the n., early-breeding Gyrs and Com. Ravens may get the sheltered sites, while the later-breeding Peregrine will use a wider variety, including more exposed ones. Gyr and Peregrine may occupy a particular site in different years. Active young Peregrines may dismantle the stick nest of the Com. Raven in which they are reared, as in Greenland.

Alternative sites Usually described for cliff breeders, but occur more generally. If there are several suitable sites, such as along an escarpment, individual pairs (and their successors) may change about in different years—a spread of up to several mi. They may also shift to a different cliff. One or 2 alternative sites are common; up to 7 in 16 years were reported by Ratcliffe (1962). An alternative site may serve as a plucking site. If no alternate site is available, the pair tends to stay put.

Substitutes for cliff sites Man-made ecological counterparts reportedly include church towers, castle ruins, bridges, quarries, raised platforms (some under roofs), a barrel in a marsh, and assorted buildings (mostly urban) at scattered N. Hemisphere locations plus a building close to the equator at Nairobi, Kenya; see plates 30–36 in Hickey (1969). (In a few alleged instances the birds have proven to be Eurasian Kestrels, not Peregrines.) Best known are urban sites, all evidently having been used briefly except for 1936–1952 on the Sun Life building in Montreal, which was "enhanced" by the provision of a box of sand. In N.Y., when a ♀ laid on the bare metal of a bridge, the eggs cracked from the heat (Bull 1964). Many more buildings are occupied seasonally by migrants and winterers than by breeders.

Sites can be enhanced or created, such as by shoveling recesses in cutbanks (as for the Prairie Falcon) and blasting them in cliffs. In nw. Calif., 44 of approximately 1,000 cliffs were rated (Boyce et al. 1982) for possible enhancement. Willow baskets off the ground but low in trees have been used frequently by nesting ducks, such as in Sweden. For Peregrines, the same, partly filled with forest litter, have been placed (and used) in old pines as substitutes for formerly used and badly weathered stick nests in Germany (Mebs, in Hickey 1969).

Stick nests In various parts of the world the Peregrine has appropriated stick nests (usually disused) in trees (alive or dead) of such diverse birds as members of the crow family, the Osprey, Black Stork, Roughleg, Com. Buzzard (*B. buteo*), *Haliaeetus* and *Aquila* eagles (including the Wedge-tailed Eagle in Australia). The structures are solid, rarely flimsy (as are heron nests). Stick nests in trees are perhaps best known in the Baltic region. Except for 1 or 2 records, and speculation in probability of others, in Alaska, stick nests in trees are not known Peregrine aeries in N. Am. After no record in Britain/Ireland for 100 years, a pair occupied a disused N. Raven nest; this coincided with recovery in numbers of Peregrines—that is, population pressure (Ratcliffe 1984b).

Tree cavities Clutches have been laid in these, including the hollow tops where limbs broke off. Colonel Goss (1878) discovered several in 1875–1877 in woodland near Neosho Falls, Kans. One site was a knothole in a cottonwood tree, the entrance "apparently" having a diam. of not over 5–6 in. Robert Ridgway (1895) found 3 aeries in large sycamores near Mt. Carmel, Ill., in May 1878. One, a cavity with overhang where a branch had broken off, was 89 ft. from the base of the leaning tree, which Ridgway assisted in cutting down—thus terminating not only the site but also 3 of the 4 "full-fledged young." There were a few tree-cavity nesters in lowlands lacking cliffs in Tenn. (R. Herbert and Spofford 1943, Spofford 1947b and earlier; see plates 28, 29 in Hickey 1969). Generally speaking, the Peregrine has used few such sites compared with the number (worldwide) that have used stick nests in trees. In Australia, where both hollows in eucalyptus trees and stick nests are available, it is suggested (Pruett-Jones et al. 1981) that such usage has enabled the Peregrine to colonize large inland areas that lack cliffs but are apparently otherwise suitable. (The same applied in a very limited way to the few birds, before the large trees were felled, in bottomlands within the Mississippi drainage.) The Peregrine was suspected of using tree cavities in B.C. (R. W. Campbell et al. 1977).

Terrestrial sites Widely used; although tundra birds prefer cliff sites and eroded banks of watercourses (the latter are unstable), they also lay on hills, slopes, dykes, and, where terrain is quite level, on boulders, hummocks, or the ground. Locations near fresh or salt water are much preferred. In N.D. and Mont., 2 sites were near the tops of cutbanks (Coues 1874c)—in effect, ground aeries. Slopes are known in Britain, even sites in heather; dunes in the Netherlands; ground sites from n. Fennoscandia e. across n. Eurasia; hummocks and islets in bogs in Finland and Estonia. Most of the Finnish breeding population was (is?) in bogs, and some Peregrines may alternate between a ground site and a stick nest in a tree.

Long site occupation Records exist of the use of specific breeding locations in Britain from at least the 13th century to the present. There is repeated reference to this: Ferguson-Lees (1957), I. Newton (1979), and Ratcliffe (1980). Ferguson-Lees reported the known high numbers of birds shot from the same aeries in stated numbers of years, indicating the attraction of particular vacated sites to other Peregrines. Among Dementiev's long records for Eurasian tundra birds, at least 1 dates from the 17th century and was reported in use at least into the 19th century (in Dementiev and Gladkov 1951, trans. 1966). North Am. has obviously not had records for as long as Britain, but we do have some for over a century in Alaska (see Cade 1960) and in Mass. as noted by Hagar (in Bent 1938 and in Hickey 1969). Various sites where occupancy terminated in the biocide era will undoubtedly attract Peregrines again. In the W. in the meantime, many vacated sites are used by Prairie Falcons. In n. N.Mex., for 10 consecutive years, many eroded holes along a cliff (Ponton 1983).

Spacing of aeries An abundance of food plus plentiful sites for aeries can result in a high concentration of breeding Peregrines. For Langara I., B.C., F. Beebe (1960, fig. 9) diagrammed 6 "preferred" (and other) sites along irregular shorelines within a straight-line distance of about 1¼ mi. Food and breeding sites were plentiful, and there was good productivity of young. Highest breeding densities of the subspecies *pealei* in B.C. were in areas containing colonies of small alcids (auklets), and lowest densities were in sections where alcid colonies did not occur (Beebe). Near Okanagan, B.C., in 1906, Allan Brooks saw 3 breeding pairs of Peregrines along about ½ mi. of inaccessible lakeshore cliff (Nelson, in Hickey 1969). Occupied sites at Wager Bay in ne. Keewatin were 3.2–19.3 (av. 8.0) km. apart and on se. Melville Pen. 4.8–12.9 (av. 9.2) km. apart (Calef and Heard 1979). In scattered portions of the Aleutians, resident pairs occurred on an av. of 5–8 mi. (8–12.8 km.) of shoreline (White, in Murphy et al. 1973). In cent.-w. Greenland, closest distance was 2 km. apart, and the mean distance apart of 34 producing aeries was 7.7 km. (Burnham and Mattox 1984).

353

In parts of Britain the av. was 4.8 km. (Ratcliffe 1972) or, fairly regular, at 4–5 km. (Newton and Mearns 1981). Occasionally, occupied aeries are very close—down to 100 m. apart. Breeding as close as 2–3 km. apart evidently is not especially unusual in Britain; see table on close nesting and another on breeding density in Ratcliffe (1980). Breeding densities in N. Am., as of the mid-1980s, are probably highest on some is. and tundra areas, the Yukon drainage, and in Ariz. and vicinity—all places where there has been a continuum of birds and no releases of captives. Some of these approach the av. British density.

Nonbreeding Almost all yearlings and some 2-year-olds and older are prebreeders (eventually breed), yet a considerable percentage of birds of breeding age are non-breeders. Some ♀ ♀ may never lay (R. Bond 1946). The number of paired nonlaying ♀ ♀ was estimated at about 15% in some local populations in N. Am. before the biocide era, when it rose to virtually 100%. There also are records of single birds holding territories. Cade (1960), for example, reported a cliff occupied for 3 years by a non-productive ♀ and gave other observations of apparently unmated birds on location in summer. Sometimes it appears that, when satisfactory breeding sites are occupied, unsatisfactory ones may attract Peregrines but provide inadequate stimulus for mating and/or breeding. In effect, in a fully populated area, birds may become breeders only by succeeding lost members of breeding pairs or by occupying vacated breeding sites.

Prolonged adverse weather at high lats. can undoubtedly prevent breeding, even by established pairs, but there is better evidence for reduced success in some years. In captivity, only about ½ of the pairs breed, in spite of all attempts to increase the percentage.

Egg-laying territory Begins some 5 days before the 1st egg is laid. The ♀ is silent and often stands or perches (at least in daylight) listlessly, seeming to doze, for relatively long periods. This signals her continuing readiness to copulate; she is completely dependent for food on her mate, who delivers it to her (no aerial food pass). This condition wanes gradually after she begins laying.

Laying interval Some 30–35% of ♀ ♀ have paired ovaries, 1 functional (C. White 1969). In the wild the usual span between egg depositions is about 48 hrs.; they are laid at any time, but usually in the morning. The gap may be longer, to 72 hrs., between the 3d and 4th egg. (When a clutch exceeds 4 in the wild, there seem to be no data on spacing.) In captives, the interval av. 52–62 hrs., so that time of laying shifts steadily as the clutch increases (Cade, in Ratcliffe 1980).

Clutch size In N. Am. av. larger at mid-lats. than at extremes of climate (marginal conditions). Thus there is an increase from a mean of 3 eggs in the arctic/subarctic to 4 in temperate regions. Even in n. Alaska, a clutch occasionally contains 5 eggs. West of the Rockies the trend is reversed slightly going s. into interior Mexico (av. slightly smaller clutches), but probably no decrease around the Gulf of Calif. and including Baja Calif. There are biases in samples, such as inclusion of incomplete clutches and inclusion of replacement clutches, which av. smaller—in e. U.S. from a mean of 3.72 (282 1st clutches) to 3.0 (22 2d clutches) (Condensed primarily from Hickey 1969.)

Known clutches (which are few) from yearling ♀ ♀ are of 2 or 3 eggs. In Montreal a ♀, definitely believed to be the same individual, laid 11 known clutches of 4 plus 1 of 5 in 1940–1952 and reared 2 young to flight age when she was at least 19 years old (G. H. Hall 1970). Nearly all captives that breed lay 4-egg 1st clutches and cease laying at around 19–20 years with no terminal decrease in clutch size (Cade, in Ratcliffe 1980). In captives, egg size and wt. decreased with age of bird and in replacement clutches (Burnham et al. 1984).

Bent (1938) stated that clutch size is 3 or 4, occasionally 5, and "very rarely" 6 or even 7. (Presumably the 6 and 7 were seen in egg collections.) The maximum number of nestlings found at an aerie evidently is 5. There were 6 eggs in approximately 1% of 282 clutches (Hickey 1942). In s. Wis., a Peregrine laid a clutch of 7 eggs, collected on April 21, 1933; she laid a 2d clutch at another site that contained 5 eggs 23 days later and 6 eggs when examined on June 11 (in Hickey 1969).

Britain: 12 clutches (of 2), 146 (3), 313 (4), and 8 (5), mean of 3.66 for all 479 (Ratcliffe 1980).

Replacement clutches/multiple clutching This supplements information given above. In wild birds in N.Y., a ♀ repeatedly lost clutches and laid 4 (of 4 eggs each) in a single season (R. and K. Herbert 1965). A long-established pair may repeat at the same site, at least initially, but robbed birds commonly move to an alternative site nearby, and they may shift again if another clutch is taken. The original site may be occupied by them the following year. Some ♀ ♀ that lose their clutch evidently do not lay another.

In captives, the interval before the 1st repeat clutch is initiated was said to be "invariably" 14 days (Cade and Temple, in Chancellor 1977), but others have given a slightly longer interval. By removing clutches as laid, a ♀ may lay up to 16–20 eggs. The eggs may also be taken as each is laid. As the season advances fertility and hatchability decrease; so also in the wild. Many problems are associated with getting captives to breed and with double- and triple-clutching, and so on; see especially Fyfe et al., also Cade and Fyfe, both in Temple (1978). In biocide-contaminated birds, it is said that double-clutching helps to detoxify the ♀ and increases success in hatching eggs and rearing young to flight age (Lindberg 1981b). Procedure with captive ♀ ♀ is to take early eggs (which are placed in an incubator) and to allow the ♀ to incubate some later ones.

Egg size Worldwide: ordinarily, length varies 46.9–58.9 mm. and breadth 36.3–44.9, this being the range in 300 eggs of *F. p. peregrinus*. That is, existing records for various other subspecies (including *cassini* of S. Am.) were within these limits (Schönwetter 1961). Ratcliffe (1980) reported smaller ones—a British clutch of 4 av. 32.5 × 46.5 mm. From Sonora, Mexico, M. Jenkins (1984) reported a clutch of 2 that were shorter still but wider. See Jenkins for some data on size variation with age of layer, geographical size variation in Australia, and a table of minimum and av. meas. of eggs of 5 subspecies.

F. p. anatum: one egg each from 20 clutches (Mass. to Calif.) **size** length 53.23 ± 1.74 mm., breadth 41.26 ± 1.15, and radii of curvature of ends 17.59 ± 1.13 and 12.34 ± 0.88; **shape** typically between elliptical and short elliptical, elongation 1.28 ± 0.035, bicone −0.063, and asymmetry +0.165 (F. W. Preston). Sixty-one others varied in length 48.5–57 mm., in breadth 38.5–43.5, and av. 52 × 41 (Bent 1938).

In largest Peregrines (*F. p. pealei*): 34 eggs varied in length 48.5–58 mm., breadth 39.1–43, and av. 53.3 × 41 (Bent).

In Britain/Ireland (*F. p. peregrinus*) the mean for 2,253 eggs was 51.5 × 40.8 mm. (Ratcliffe 1980).

According to Ratcliffe, eggs in replacement clutches may av. either smaller or larger than in the 1st set, and the same applies to layings by the same ♀ in successive years. Yet he also noted that in series of clutches of 6 ♀ over 6 or more years, there was a tendency for av. egg size to decrease slightly.

Egg weight   Twenty fresh British eggs had av. meas. of 51.6 × 40.9 mm. and weighed 38.5–52.6 gm., av. 45.5, a 4-egg clutch thus weighing 16% of av. ♀ wt. of 1,140 gm. (Ratcliffe 1980). Eggs lose wt. from evaporation as incubation proceeds; this, from laying to pipping, is approximately 0.18 gm./day, for a total of about 16% of initial wt. (Burnham 1983).

Egg color   Peregrine eggs are regarded as outstandingly beautiful, even among falcon eggs. The shell is fairly smooth, at first without gloss, and richly patterned, but coloring fades toward brownish and the shells acquire a gloss from the oiled feathers of the sitter. Therefore, in a fairly fresh clutch, the last egg laid may be recognized by having the most vivid coloring. Fresh eggs have the reddish brown typical of the genus *Falco*. Ground color varies from pale creamy to brownish toward reddish, this largely (even wholly) overlaid by dots, spots, blotches, and patches of various warm browns, some toward reddish—great variation. Rarely an egg is wholly darkish, overlaid with even darker markings. Sometimes the outer pigment is concentrated, such as toward or on the larger end.

Egg dates   Full 1st clutches in N. Am. vary from early Mar. (commonly in the last ½ of the month) to the s. to the last ⅓ of Mar. and Apr. in temperate climates, to late May and 1st ½ of June (rarely later) in coldest parts of range (including Greenland). In Alaska, resident Aleutian birds are laying about a month earlier than migrant birds of the mainland tundra. (In Australia, Peregrines begin laying early in the austral spring; the same also to the s. in S. Am., but probably late Dec. or early Jan. there near the equator.)

North Am. egg dates in Bent (1938) are for presumed viable clutches taken during incubation.

Using data for 1891–1932 from the Pocono Mts. of Pa., Street (1955) stated that dates for full 1st clutches varied greatly with weather, from mid-Mar. to Apr. 7. Along the lower Hudson R. in N.Y., in tardy seasons there was late laying, reduced clutch size, and poor breeding success (R. and K. Herbert 1965). In the Aleutians, laying time varied with spring weather; when it was bad, the prey (alcids) stayed offshore, which had a negative effect on breeding (White, in Murphy et al. 1973).

Egg losses   Result from infertility, death of embryos, mammalian (and avian?) predation, eggs rolling away from scrapes (quite often), and such miscellaneous causes as rockfalls and violent storms. In general, losses av. less than 1 egg/clutch.

Incubation   Mostly by the ♀. Evidently the eggs are covered, at least at night, before regular incubation begins. the ♀ is on at night during incubation (R. W. Nelson 1970). Males did not seem to incubate at night (R. and K. Herbert 1965); some ♂ ♂ were on clutches as night approached and may have incubated at night (Enderson et al. 1972). The ♂ has traces of incubation patches (Cade 1960). In captive breeders (Cade), the ♂ incubates for up to ¼ or more of daylight, but there is much individual variation, and only the ♀ is on at night. The ♂'s stints diminish as incubation progresses.

The ♂, with quarry that is fresh or is retrieved from a cache, typically flies to a perch visible from the aerie, uttering *eechip* calls, and the ♀ gets off the clutch to take the

356

food, perch, feed, defecate, and preen. Or the ♂ may fly by the aerie and the ♀ will fly out for the aerial food pass. She may perch, feed, preen, and so forth, and remain off the eggs for a considerable time. The ♂ often settled on them but departs immediately when she returns.

The ♀ shuffles to a standing position over the eggs and settles down, her toes together and limp to avoid damaging the eggs. She erects her breast feathers as she settles to bring the eggs into contact with the 2 bare incubation patches and rocks her body until all is arranged comfortably. Her back is low and horizontal, her feathering relaxed, perhaps to dissipate heat. She may doze at times or rise more or less to change position, at which time she may turn the eggs—her beak open, supposedly to reduce the risk of puncture. She may get off the clutch, walk about on the ledge, and preen. Sitters often toy with debris within reach. She watches any moving thing within sight and may react if the ♂ is nearby and shows alarm.

Some sites can be approached rather closely, but typically the ♀ gets off, much alarmed and *cakking* hoarsely, before danger is near and may remain in the vicinity, watching from the air, or disappear. Some birds get off silently. The ♂ may sight an interloper first, in which case his alarm also causes her to react. If an occupied aerie must be visited for any valid reason, the time spent there should be very brief.

Hatching   The embryo begins making cheeping sounds before the egg is pipped; this causes a behavioral response in the parent bird that probably is communicated to the mate (if not gotten directly from the egg). The shell is pipped for 3 or fewer days (50–55 hrs. in captives—Cade) before hatching. In captives, pipping to hatching generally requires about 48 hrs. The embryo breaks the shell a number of times near the pipping hole; then, in 30–45 min., it makes a complete revolution counterclockwise (as viewed from the large end of the egg) and hatches, as reported by Burnham (1983)—which see for further details. In wild Peregrines in temperate climates, the hatching span for the entire clutch is usually as long as 2 full days; this indicates that incubation (not mere sitting) begins approximately with laying of the 3d egg. It is said of arctic Peregrines that incubation begins with the 1st egg (covered to prevent chilling), which results in a hatching span approaching the laying span (longer asynchronous hatching). That all eggs hatch within a "few hours of each other on the same day" in Montreal (G. H. Hall 1970) might have been an assumption by the author, or possibly ♀♀ differ as to when they begin to incubate. The eggshells are not removed from the aerie.

Incubation period   For *F. p. anatum* in the wild was given correctly as 33–35 days by Hagar (in Bent 1938) and for the race *paelei* as 32–34, possibly 35, by R. W. Nelson (1972). The data in Burnham (1983) suggest a normal incubation per egg of approximately 33.5 days. The period was long reported in standard works as 28 or 29 days and, using these figures to back-date (calculate laying dates) introduced a 5–6 day error, which persisted in various literature until past 1960.

Food caching   Up to the present at least, is known to occur only during incubation and rearing. It has been reported in Germany (Mebs 1956), Britain (Treleaven 1977, 1980; A. Parker 1979), in B.C. at Langara I. by R. W. Nelson (1970), and in N.Y. The ♂ deposits prey at some spot not distant from the aerie, and the ♀ retrieves it; an uneaten portion may again be cached and retrieved. Presumably caching assures a supply of food during bad weather, when hunting is difficult. At least sometimes it is triggered by an abundance of available prey. In spring on the lower Hudson R. in N.Y., when Peregrines were breeding and Blue Jays were migrating across the river, the Peregrines were capturing the jays over water and were "storing them up like nuts on the ledge." They had so many that they "didn't know what to do with them" (Spofford, in Hickey 1969).

Brood size   The percentage of successful aeries (at which at least 1 young attained flight) has varied greatly in different studies. As to size of successful broods, a very general statement would be that 1 nestling/brood does not survive to flight age.

Somewhat condensed, here is the way figures are given—in this case for cent.-w. Greenland, 1972–1981, inclusive. Of 86 pairs on territories, 73 had young; av. of all 86 sites gave a mean of young in each of 2.3, but av. of only the successful sites gave a mean of 2.8. The total number of occupied sites (21 by singles, 86 by pairs) was 107, and mean production was 1.8 young/occupied site (Burnham and Mattox 1984). Using the Hickey and Anderson assumption (in Hickey 1969) of 1.16 young/year required from all breeding pairs to maintain a stable population, the Greenland birds are thriving. (Comparable figures for successful sites are 2.4 for England and 2.5 for N. Am. before the biocide era.)

Without going into numerous details (including which years), the following figures are: **1** number of occupied territories, **2** number of successful aeries (at least 1 young reared), and **3** mean or av. number of young/brood: Alaska (arctic) 25–14–2.5 (Cade 1960); Alaska (Yukon R.) 20–14–1.9 (Cade 1960); Alaska (Yukon R.) 17–12–2.3 (Cade et al. 1968); Alaska (Aleutians) 57–38–2.7 (White, in Murphy et al. 1973); B.C. (Queen Charlottes) 34 successful aeries av. 2.7 (F. Beebe 1960) and 76 av. 2.5 (Blood 1968); N.Y. 38–16–1.4 (Hickey 1942); N.Y. (lower Hudson region) 72–28–2.4 (R. and K. Herbert 1965); and Pa. 65–35–2.3 (Rice, in Hickey 1969).

At a continuously occupied site (eggs annually 1940–1952, inclusive) in Montreal: total of 50 eggs, 26 hatched, and 22 young "survived to take wing" (G. H. Hall 1970).

Calef and Heard (1979) compared 1975 productivity from arctic Alaska to w. Greenland: 65 of 199 sites were occupied and 37+ sites produced 79+ young. Not included were Wager Bay (ne. Keewatin) or the se. portion of the Melville Pen., censused in 1976 and 1977. These areas, considered undepleted by biocides, proved to be the most productive known for tundra birds: 42 of 46 known sites occupied and 28+ sites produced 79+ young. The number of young/occupied site in 1976 av. 2.08, and number of young/successful aerie av. 2.45; the comparable 1977 figures were 2.21 and 2.95. There is much other valuable information in this important study.

Of interest: in Victoria, Australia, brood size av. 2.4 for all sites hatching young (Pruett-Jones et al. 1981).

In Great Britain in 1981: at least 1,058 breeding territories (included 783 occupied by pairs and 80 by apparent singles); at least 531 pairs and probably another 81 had eggs; of these, at least 363 reared young (Ratcliffe 1984a).

Brood losses   Caused principally by bad weather, most such mortality being in the 1st 2 weeks posthatching. In such weather, hunting requires extra time or may be impossible. There is some loss to predators, such as the Golden Eagle, and to mammals if the aerie is accessible. Especially if food is in short supply and is monopolized by older and stronger nestlings, a younger, smaller nestling may weaken and die. Its demise, therefore, is not attributable to direct attacks by siblings. Dead nestlings have been found at plucking sites, undoubtedly delivered there by a parent.

Preflight period Very young nestlings huddle together, dozing and sleeping for the most part, but respond to the ♀ by cheeping. They are brooded almost continuously for some 10–14 days, by which time they are becoming better insulated by their 2d coat of down. Their eyes are closed at first, or perhaps half-open at times, for several days, and they respond to parental alarm calls by becoming silent. By the end of the 1st week they have some visual response to the parent, and an untended nestling utters a mixture of chitter and treble-whine.

In the 2d week they make various movements, such as stretching, but locomotion is still a mere shuffle. They soil the site at first, but by this age they raise their rear ends and squirt fecal matter radially from the scrape. They have good vision, better coordination, and, when hungry, call noisily and shuffle toward the parent. They continue to spend much time dozing and sleeping until past 2 weeks of age. Sometimes a nestling wanders from the scrape beginning in this week, but mostly the young still maintain bodily contact.

In the 3d week they are growing feathers and have considerable thermoregulation; the amount of time that they are brooded begins to decrease steadily. They utter the "adult" *kek-kek-kek-kek* alarm. By the end of this week, they spend little time in bodily contact and are too large to be effectively brooded. It is around this time that competition among broodmates for food may cause a younger and less responsive nestling to weaken and die.

By about 4 weeks the young begin to scatter along the breeding ledge or about the site. They are noisy on approach of a food-carrying parent, seize the prey, and attempt to dismantle it. Between feedings they rest, doze, preen a great deal, do much wing-exercising, raise their feathers ("rouse"), and walk about considerably. Now they can go to the cliff edge and, with rear ends outward, eject their fecal matter over the edge.

At 5 weeks the feathers are well grown, although wisps of down remain. Much time is spent exercising the wings. If they are in a loosely constructed stick nest, they may scatter the sticks about. It is increasingly difficult for a parent to deliver food, since the nestlings are aggressive when it is delivered.

Weights in gm. of growing captive *F. p. peregrinus:* ♂ 31/at hatching, 210/10 days, 383/15, 538/20, 630/30; and ♀ 36/at hatching, 210/10 days, 410/15, 640/20, and 915–30 (O. and M. Heinroth 1927).

For many details from time-lapse photography, see Enderson et al. (1972) for Alaska-Yukon Terr. and Hovis et al. (1985) for w. Greenland.

At first, only the ♂ parent fetches food, for both brood and mate, but the ♀ does progressively more hunting as her brooding declines. The timing and duration of this changeover period varies considerably at different aeries. According to R. Bond (1936), avian prey almost always and mammals frequently are headless when delivered to the aerie; Bond thought that the ♂ parent lived "largely, if not exclusively" on heads at this time, but there are indications that the ♂ does some hunting for himself, consuming prey away from the breeding territory. The ♂ may deliver prey to a nearby perch, and the ♀ gets it there, or she may meet him in the air and get it in an aerial food pass or drop; sometimes the ♂ delivers food directly to the young, especially if the ♀ is absent. The ♀ may get food from a cache or even return any uneaten portion there.

The young get more aggressive in seizing food from a parent as they approach flight age, and a nestling may "mantle" over food lest a broodmate attempt to seize it. For about ½ the nestling period the aerie is kept clean; that is, the ♀ removes uneaten or discarded prey remains; later, parts of prey are scattered about on the site, and evidently it is hazardous for the ♀ to attempt sanitation since her young become aggressive. She hunts more as time passes to help support a growing, hungry brood.

In Calif., telemetered distances flown from aeries in Apr.–June: ¼ of the ♀'s flights were within 1 km., 64 exceeded 1 km., 12 exceeded 3 km., and 2 were 8 km.; the ♂ had few short flights and hunted in all directions from the aerie; of 26 of his flights over 1 km., 7 were beyond 3 km. and 2 were about 7 km.; that is, foraging flights were up to 7 km. (Enderson and Kirven 1983).

At Mono Rock (a marine site), Calif., after the ♂ died, the ♀ foraged only within sight of the aerie—that is, was the sole but inadequate provider (E. Johnson 1980). There are instances in which either parent, deprived of its mate (at least in the nestling period), managed to rear at least some young.

Age at first flight   From Sherrod (1983): Departure is a result of maturation. It is time to go. For some time beforehand the young are extremely restless and noisy and may move about if they have the room. They are aggressive toward the parents as they approach flight age. If there is an updraft, the young may launch, to glide and flap, alighting even at same height as takeoff. Normal departure of known-age young; 10 ♂ 39–46 days, 12 ♀ 41–49 days, but tundra birds on reduced food supply possibly remain longer at the aerie. Much shorter spans have been given in the literature, probably for disturbed birds, and it is doubtful that they could survive if they left when 35 days old or younger. First flights av. about 100 m. (Sherrod).

It is incorrect that the parents lure the young from the aerie or starve them out. The notion of luring probably originated from seeing a parent fly by repeatedly, carrying prey, awaiting an opportunity to alight or to drop it without a potentially dangerous attack by the young. Prey dropped in vegetation is not retrieved. The ♀ may alight away from, but near, the young, deposit prey, and the noisy young rush to it. There is a stage during which preflight young are frightened by live prey yet take dead prey brought to them.

Postnestling stage   The parents "attend" their flying young (MacFarlane 1891). This subject fills 200 pages in Sherrod (1983) and only certain aspects can be included here.

Once the young are on the wing there are perch-to-perch flights, soaring, pursuit of parents or other adults, mock combat among siblings, and pursuit of inanimate objects, of insects, and of birds in due course. These are the major aerial activities, and a single flight may include several of them. Details vary; for example, a young bird may flutter-glide (solicit) while pursuing an adult. A parent is pursued on sight and hence becomes secretive and evasive. Catching a butterfly is a waste of energy (Forbush 1927) but a useful experience.

Pursuit of birds varies from mild to intense, the young at first having only a "remote interest" in them. (This equates somewhat with pursuit that is not "serious" later on.) The young Peregrines become more accomplished with practice, but prey-capture rate is very low, probably zero at first. They may pursue unsuitable prey, such as large birds, there is even a record of white-tailed deer. They are social, following or accompanying each other; 1 may pursue prey and the others will join in—an antecedent to the cooperative hunting of breeding pairs. Thus it appears that there are great advantages in a young bird having siblings.

In general, it appears that the young develop motivation and ability to kill consistently when hungry after they are on the wing about 3 weeks, but many do not become independent (are still being fed) until much later.

Many factors play a role in the initial killing behavior, such as size of prey, hunger, individual aggression, and ability. After the young bird has experience and exposure to flying prey and has reached a certain stage of motivational development, the act of killing (including lethal bites and plucking) begins. After several associations between capture of prey and satiation are made, the general pattern of pursuit terminating in capture becomes established. The young are genetically programmed to capture and kill.

Food passing varies. Transfer to the young may be made at a perch. The young may take it from the talons of a parent. In a "dead drop," the flying parent drops it and the young seizes it in midair (it may be lost if it falls to earth). Some drops are "intentional," but the parent may be pressured to drop to avoid aggressive attack by the young. In a "live drop," the adult is more or less stationary in the air or is pursued by the young. As the young (positioned for pursuit) approaches, the live prey is dropped. If the young bird fails to take it, the adult may recapture it and release it again. There is a considerable literature on a parent evidently training the young to hunt; for example, F. Beebe (1974), I. Newton (1979), and Ravel (1981).

Family hunting forays begin when the young are strong enough to chase the parents for several km. while soliciting aggressively. That is, the young are usually following before the adult makes a capture. A young Peregrine that has received prey may go into an exaggerated flutter-glide, in effect aerial "mantling" (guarding its food).

In the short arctic season, Peregrines are still in family groups until the beginning of migration, and the parents are still supplying some food. In temperate climates there is longer association in the vicinity of the aerie—up to 2 months, sometimes longer. The young are not driven away, as explained earlier. Yet after wild offspring are on the wing for 5–6 weeks, the adults eventually become aggressive—even though they still may be providing some food. They will attack if the young birds beg continually. Sherrod stated that this change occurs when there is a "recrudescence of courtship behavior" of the parents (resident birds), but the timing is hard to explain. Onset of migration may often be the time of termination of the family bond, but not always. Some families probably disperse then, but in others a parent accompanies the young (or vice versa), and in a few instances migrant young have been observed soliciting food. Sometimes the young continue together—in some arctic birds at least to Tex. It was mentioned earlier, citing Hagar, that yearling ♀♀ may return to their natal area, where the resident ♂ may feed them.

Occasionally a young migrant is playful, making mock attacks on inanimate objects (C. Floyd 1982). They still go through the motions of killing and plucking tufts of vegetation, and there are mock aerial battles.

The most difficult time for a Peregrine is when it must hunt for itself. Young birds may starve to death because of poor hunting ability (Cade 1960).

Captive breeding and releases Apparently the earliest record of egg laying in captivity is in a book by the German falconer, Renz Waller (1937); furthermore, this ♀ hatched 3 young in 1942, of which 1 was reared (see Prestwich 1955). The essential information on captive breeding is in a manual by Weaver and Cade (1985) and on releasing in the wild in a manual by Sherrod et al. (1982). RALPH S. PALMER

SURVIVAL For a "life table" by Enderson, based on recoveries of birds banded as nestlings, see Hickey (1969). Some generalizations about losses of eggs and preflight young are included under Reproduction, above.

Judging from the percentage of yearlings seen among breeders, it is clear that there is heavy mortality in the 1st year of life. It begins early. Between 12% and 36% of birds hacked in the e. reintroduction program, 1975–1980, inclusive, died or had to be returned to captivity. The number that departed normally was 205, or 76% (Sherrod 1983). The survival of hacked and of wild-reared young birds is about the same (Barclay 1980, or see Barclay's data in Sherrod 1983). At least most Peregrines do not breed until 2 years old (and some older, some never), and it seems probable that a bird that survives to the usual breeding age has an av. total life expectancy of 5–6 years—¼ potential longevity (20 years in the wild and in captivity).

Enderson estimated 1st-year mortality to be 70% and av. annual adult mortality to be 25%, and, in a selected sample of returns from banding, 50% of yearlings and 33% of older birds had been shot. There is much less shooting now (mid-1980s), but it continues.

Hickey and Anderson (in Hickey 1969) cited a paper on *B. buteo* in which it was concluded that 1.16 young are required of all pairs attempting to breed to balance the Fennoscandian population—and added that the statistic must be "fairly close" in a stable Peregrine population. That is, if the figure is smaller, the population is declining; if larger, it is increasing. This has been cited frequently when comparisons of productivity (such as counts of nestlings/aerie) are made (see above). This is easier than compiling information on birds in later life, but so many banded nestlings have flown that statistics derived from them are to be expected. There must be regional differences, for example, between resident and highly migratory birds, and temporal differences, such as between stable, declining, and increasing populations.

From banded birds, Mebs (1971) estimated av. annual adult mortality as 19% for Finnish and 28% for German birds, this was in excess of replacement (populations then declining). The figure was 32% for Sweden (Lindberg, in Chancellor 1977).

For interior s. Scotland, Newton and Mearns (1981) estimated maximum annual adult mortality as 17%. More recently, the figure was even lower—9% for breeding ♀♀, but a reduced estimate of 7% and, combining the sexes, 11% (Mearns and Newton 1984). Apparently the population was dense and stable. There was a problem of reconciling such figures with longevity. Thus, on 10% annual mortality from the 2d year onward, some 15% of birds that reached their 2d year would survive on their 20th year, and 6% on their 25th. From this it was deduced that mortality presumably increases "after a certain age" (to keep within potential longevity).

RALPH S. PALMER

HABITS   The species. Earlier we have dealt with symbols—condor and eagles—and now we come to that most popular and most propagandized of all raptors—the Peregrine—the glamour bird. No thoroughly comprehensive treatise on it exists, no doubt partly from the bird having been so idolized by falconers and others around the world that a good grasp of all aspects of its biology and of the record of recent centuries of human interrelationships with it could fill the working lifetime of a dedicated and scholarly raptorphile. Some works of recent vintage include W. Fischer's (1968 and later editions) small monograph, Hickey (1969) on Peregrine biology and biocides, and Ratcliffe (1980), who emphasized wild birds in Britain. The number of journal papers, especially from the 1940s onward, is very large. Therefore, only a few matters can be touched on here.

Being specialized for capturing aerial prey, the Peregrine is very fast and extremely agile. Its remarkable skill is especially well attested in the various episodes recounted in Forbush (1927). Although there is a somewhat stereotyped popular image of it as a hunter, the following shows that it is very adaptable and versatile.

Still or perch-and-wait hunting   Although superb fliers, wild Peregrines ititiate a major—and evidently most successful—portion of hunting from a stationary position. From a high spot, such as a prominence or a tall tree, the bird watches on all sides and above, evidently being able to track flying objects even beyond range of human vision. Many seemingly prospective targets may pass close by. Then suddenly, having made its selection, the falcon launches an attack. If the quarry is below it, it has the added advantage of a swift down-angled approach; then it may make a shallow stoop or rise higher above the quarry and stoop at tremendous speed. The quarry tries to dodge and to reach cover if possible.

If the initial strike fails, the Peregrine mounts rapidly and stoops again. It may make repeated attempts, ending in capture or in tail-chases, or the prey may gain cover. Variants are many. For example, after an initial failure, the falcon may "bind to" (grasp) the quarry on the next pass. If the quarry is nearing cover, the Peregrine may get beneath it, turn over, and seize it from below. Sometimes the quarry is forced upward; then the Peregrine gets above it and stoops to capture it. Migrant tundra Peregrines on coastal is. of Tex. manipulate their prey in yet another fashion; the falcon stoops and appears to miss a Rock Dove intentionally. It guides the quarry to the ocean and may force it into the surf; then the pursuer awaits near the water's edge as the bedraggled prey washes ashore (W. G. Hunt et al. 1975). Inland, the Peregrine pursues or forces prey out over rivers.

If the chosen target is high overhead, typically the falcon faces into the wind on takeoff, then "rings up" (spirals upward) in spectacular flight to get above the quarry. A fast bird such as a teal may try to keep above the falcon or to outdistance it in straightaway flight. Slow fliers try to keep above their pursuer (like swallows above a Merlin). This may succeed, or the quarry may become too exhausted to dodge its

363

sky-
scanning

sunning

Juv.

rousing

R. M. Mengel

364

attacker. A final resort is for the quarry to plummet earthward, closely pursued; generally this fails and a capture occurs quickly. Sometimes, however, the prey gets to the ground; if if alights in inadequate cover it may be killed.

In Alta., prey captured in air was carried to earth; it did not fall, helpless or dead. Binding to the quarry may be the common method (Dekker 1980), even with smaller prey. In most captures that Dekker observed, the prey appeared to be stunned by the strike but showed some life or even got free in the air or on the ground. In 2 instances the flying Peregrine brought the prey (small sandpiper) forward in flight, probably to bite and thus kill it.

Some hunting is done from the aerie, also much from nearby perches, where the ♂ spends time sunning and preening when not hunting or delivering prey.

The Peregrine has some memory of the spot where it downed prey and returns to claim its food (Hyde 1953).

From soaring and quartering The Peregrine circles overhead; in trained birds, this is the "waiting on" of falconers. It may stoop at a lower target or switch over to "ringing up" after higher prey. Variants are many.

In the classic stoop at larger birds, the victim is struck with such speed that, having greater inertia, the falcon rips right through and fails to hold. It is believed that the toes are more or less together and that the rear talon slashes the victim (the strike may be made with either foot, sometimes both). In high-speed photography under experimental conditions, a stoop was managed so as to provide a glancing blow, the feet were not very far forward (as they are in the Prairie Falcon), and the toes were extended, but they closed at impact (Goslow 1971). The sound of the strike carries well. Feathers fly and the prey may be dead as it falls. The Peregrine half-circles and alights. Whether or not the quarry is still alive, it is bitten near the base of the brain; this sometimes breaks the neck. A Juv. bird aged 77 days seized a pigeon and crashed with it on a building; the Peregrine's neck was broken, but the pigeon "was still firmly held in its talons" (G. H. Hall 1970). Heavy prey is generally partially plucked and fed on where it is struck down. The falcon bites and partially rotates its head, ripping flesh and notching the sternum—unlike the broken bones and sheared flesh characteristic of mammalian predation. In the breeding season it is typical for the ♂ to carry food to one or more plucking sites; usually the ♂ eats the head before delivering prey to mate or aerie.

Some quarry, even though knocked down, may be full of fight; a grounded cock pheasant may be more than a ♂ Peregrine can manage.

Contouring This is the harrier method and, among falcons, a Gyr specialty. The Peregrine cruises low or quarters the ground, keeping out of sight as much as possible behind vegetation or irregularities in terrain. On tundra, the falcon thus encounters some prey at very close quarters. Migrant tundra Peregrines also hunt in this manner on the barrier is. of Tex. using dunes as a shield (W. G. Hunt et al. 1975). Peregrines hunt in this mode in Colo., also in coastal marshes, as if imitating the harrier (Olendorff 1975). Both Gyr and Peregrine use this method at sea—the Peregrine tries to keep in shelter of the waves in pursuit of marine birds. If the quarry attempts to escape by diving, the Peregrine may wait overhead; the prey dives repeatedly and, when exhausted, is picked from the surface of the water.

Some ground-hugging flight is done in deliberate attempt to flush potential quarry from vegetation.

From straightaway flight Migrant Peregrines make search flights in morning (before migrating) and evening (after the day's travel). They also get some food opportunistically while migrating. Thus they watch other migrant raptors, for example, quite frequently stooping at Merlins to rob them.

In forested regions The Peregrine has several tactics. Best known is when quarry leaves shelter and is exposed when crossing above water (see above). A preference for such hunting conditions has often been noted, the pattern of some prey species probably making them more vulnerable. Rock Doves are favored targets, as are Mourning Doves (to some extent), Com. Flickers, Blue Jays, and Red-winged Blackbirds. When the now-extinct Passenger Pigeon was abundant, undoubtedly a great many were taken at water crossings. Another tactic is to keep concealed in or below the forest canopy and then rise suddenly when close to birds perched overhead (Cade 1960).

Aerial feeding Some small prey is eaten on the wing. Apparently such feeding is sometimes done if the falcon is timid about alighting (R. Herbert and Hickey 1941), but not necessarily so. In Alta., ♂ ♂ fed while sailing or soaring, after ♀ ♀ had attempted to rob them (Dekker 1979). Probably such prey as bats, lemmings, voles, and insects, which are unsuitable for plucking, are at least partially dismembered and then eaten during flight. In Queensland, Australia, even adult Peregrines hawk flying insects leisurely (Czechura 1984), an activity generally attributed to young newly on the wing. Some small marine birds are eaten aboard ship, but others over the sea, and surely some Peregrines habitually feed in the latter fashion. It feeds on storm-petrels far at sea (Voous 1961, Craddock and Carlson 1970). An "immature" Peregrine in Oct. in the Pacific was successful in 8 of 11 attempts to catch Leach's Storm-Petrel; usually the head and wings were removed while in the air, and the falcon then brought its quarry to the ship's rigging (W. Rogers and Leatherwood 1981). A Peregrine captured a tropicbird, rather large quarry, at sea (Casement 1973). For partial summary of aerial feeding, see Anderle (1982).

Specialists Many Peregrines favor some particular prey. In falconer's terms, a bird develops a "set"—that is, is fixated on a prey species with which it has recurring experience. If a falconer's bird does this, the pattern either cannot be altered or to do so is not worthwhile. In wild birds, specialization is often overridden temporarily by needs of feeding a hungry, growing brood; the Peregrine is then less choosy about what it captures (R. Bond 1936). In s. Que., a pair took Blue Jays until June 7 and blackbirds and swallows thereafter (Bird and Aubry 1982). Wild Peregrines in Britain may specialize on the Black-headed Gull, the Puffin in preference to other auks, or a smaller member of the crow family (Ratcliffe 1980). Preference for the N. Fulmar is a hazard because this seafowl ejects oil from its nostrils in defense of the breeding site (A. Clarke 1977). In sw. Scotland, 26% of live-trapped Peregrines were more or less oiled; it was the time of year when ♂ ♂ do most of the hunting, yet ♀ ♀ were also oiled; this can be fatal to the Peregrine (R. Mearns 1983b). The large Peregrines at Langara I., B.C., concentrate on Ancient Murrelets (R. W. Nelson 1970), which are crevice nesters and are nocturnal when ashore. On se. Victoria I. in the Canadian arctic, there were numerous remains of Sabine's Gull at an aerie (Parmelee et al. 1967). For whatever-reason, apparently the Peregrine does not specialize in some common birds; for example, it seldom kills the Am. Crow. In Wales, several pairs specialized in young rabbits (H. A. Gilbert1927).

The domestic pigeon, or Rock Dove, is so generally preferred that other quarry may be relatively safe in its presence. (In N. Am. the Mourning Dove is no adequate substitute.) Clearly, the presence of pigeons in numbers influences the falcon to occur in urban situations as a migrant, winterer, and occasional breeder. Even migrant tundra birds conform in the austral summer—in Rio de Janeiro the bold hunting of pigeons attracts widespread attention (Sick 1960).

In former times in N. Am., many Peregrines specialized in taking the then-abundant Passenger Pigeon—even to the extent of following migrant flocks (and the Merlin did likewise). G. B. Grinnell (in Ludlow 1875) graphically described a pursuit and capture. The hunted pigeon alighted on a horse's saddle within arm's length of the observer, fled when the Peregrine was above it, again sought shelter near man, again fled, and was captured.

In Alta. in spring (Dekker 1980): Some Peregrines attacked, in succession, species belonging to different "prey groups," while others pursued birds of only 1 group during up to 15 hunts before a kill was made. Some recognizable individual Peregrines hunted the same prey—specialized—3–4 consecutive days; some employed particular techniques, but others varied.

Reactions to the Peregrine The Passenger Pigeon incident above brings up the point, well known to falconers, that pursued quarry may become "tame," seeking the protection of proximity to humans. On the other hand, when the Peregrine is not hunting "seriously," many birds recognize this and either do not move or else depart without panic. (For comparison, perched buteo hawks elicit fear only when in erect, slimmed, prehunting stance, while the mere presence of an accipiter causes panic.)

Terrestrial activity According to R. Bond (1936), Peregrine and Merlin "have a specific antipathy" to taking prey on the ground and, if not too hungry, usually flush a standing or swimming bird before seizing it. There are exceptions, such as in Australia (Czechura 1984). Although better known for buteo hawks, ground hunting is fairly common to inexperienced young Peregrines, which seek large insects or other obtainable food. Large slugs eaten by a Peregrine recently of flight age, on an is. off the B.C. coast (R. Bond 1946), must have been gotten in this manner. Young Peregrines ran about in a salt marsh for 3 weeks, catching fiddler crabs (Sherrod 1983). Dekker saw 2 young ♀ ♀ walking on grass, apparently getting insects. Sizable terrestrial mammals, such as full-grown ground squirrels and partly grown hares are usually killed by a series of stoops at the head and neck; the prey is stunned or blinded or the skull fractured. R. Bond (1936) did not know of any wild falcon habitually using such tactics when smaller game was available. It has been stated that lemmings are hunted afoot, but they are quite active and many are probably snatched from the ground by flying Peregrines.

A terrestrial activity of captive falcons, and presumably wild ones, is ingesting pebbles and grit—**gastroliths** (the "rangle" of falconers)—later cast (regurgitated). N. Fox (1976) and Albuquerque (1982) discussed this habit, and Fox provided such material for his trained birds.

Mock attacks   At the Bear R. marshes in Utah the Peregrine did much hunting for food in early morning; later it pursued any flying bird "merely for the pleasure of the chase, seldom killing" (Wetmore, in Lyon 1916). This is a well-known trait. From 958 observations in Alta., mostly in spring, Dekker (1980) reported as follows: Many Peregrines hunted in a "half-hearted" way, and he believed that they were more selective than when "deadly serious." Migrant Peregrines appeared to have a "warming-up period" during which they tested prey by a single swoop and quit if the quarry dodged successfully. After several such episodes, the hunter became more "serious" or tenacious—and successful. Some passes are made to flush quarry, as mentioned earlier.

Hunting success   A Peregrine that is highly motivated to take quarry appears purposeful and has a particular wingbeat and attitude—different from ordinary cruising, less motivated chases, or obvious play. At least some prey species appear to recognize the difference.

Success rate varies greatly, mostly in the range of about 8–40% of attempts. The subject was reviewed by Roalkvam (1985); see also Dekker (1984). These are among the variables: On first attaining flight, Peregrines "attack" even inanimate objects (see Reproduction, above) but soon concentrate on more appropriate targets. Inexperienced Juv. birds are less efficient than their elders, and some probably starve. Breeding Peregrines appear to be more motivated, and more successful hunters, than in other seasons. Prey species then are not flocking (lone birds are easier to catch), and there are many inexperienced young quarry (easily taken). In any season, some prey are easier to capture than others, and some Peregrines are more expert than others. Topping the success list was a captive-reared released ♂ that hunted passerines and shorebirds from a marshland perch. One season it was successful in 95 of 102 hunts; in 44 days in the following May–June it captured quarry in 68 consecutive hunts (Cade 1982). Although trained birds flown at grouse might match this, it is the best record in the wild.

Using a beater   According the Alexander Wilson (in Wilson and Bonaparte 1832), the Peregrine, "it is said, often follows the steps of the gunner, knowing that ducks will be aroused on the way, which will afford it an almost certain chance of success." On Amchitka, in the Aleutians, it is known to "escort" a person to catch small birds that take wing (Kenyon 1961). (Compare with a Gyr following a trapper.) Occasionally the Peregrine uses the N. Harrier (which see) as a beater. In bygone days when men hunted with dogs, wild as well as trained Peregrines watched for them to flush game. If the dogs became inactive or flushed nothing, the Peregrine sometimes stopped and struck a dog to make it get going. This was formerly quite well known to falconers. In a recent instance (the bird was a Prairie Falcon—which see), it struck its trainer several times.

Cooperative hunting   A specialty of the Sea Eagle, it is well known in the Peregrine and is more efficient than solo hunting. For example, 2 trained birds may be flown at formidable quarry. In the wild, so far as reported, cooperative hunting seems to be limited to mates in the breeding season. Sometimes both parents hunt, and their newly flying young follow along to receive food. There is some evidence that the ♀ may maneuver quarry into favorable position for the ♂ to make a strike. There is an old report of a Peregrine delivering food to another caught in a trap and thought to be its mate. Arnold (1942) regarded cooperative hunting as necessary for capturing such elusive quarry as the White-throated Swift; it is common prey, hence this method of hunting it may be common.

Bat catching   W. Fischer (1968) listed occurrence in these regions: Brazil, India, Burma, Vietnam, Mesopotamia, Turkmenia, and Saudi Arabia. North Am. records begin with Stager (1941) and Sprunt, Jr. (1950), both for free-tailed bats (*Tadarida mexicana*) at Ney Cave, Tex. In Aug., several Peregrines were noisy and seemed to have "warming-up" exercises at the cave mouth. Toward evening, when the dark cloud of bats flew out, the falcons cut into the rushing mass and seldom emerged on the opposite side without prey. They also hunted during the morning return flight when the bats were less concentrated, hence less easily captured (Stager). On several occasions a Peregrine fed in flight in the manner of the Swallow-tailed Kite; the foot holding prey was brought forward, the falcon lowered its head to reach it, and the bat was torn to pieces; the discarded wings fluttered down like dark leaves (Sprunt). Peregrine aeries in the Gulf of Calif. region of Mexico contain bat remains (R. D. Porter).

Migrant tundra Peregrines capture bats in the austral summer in S. Am.—in Paramaribo, Suriname (Pierson and Donahue 1983), and in Rio de Janeiro (Sick 1961) and Porto Alegre (Albuquerque 1978) in Brazil.

Fishing   Heads and other remains of fishes have been found at Peregrine perches and aeries in N. Am. and abroad. It is possible that some fish taken were stranded— that is, carrion if dead. At Umiat, Alaska, Cade (1960) reported seeing graylings breaking the surface, and a ♂ Peregrine captured 1; the ♀ flew out, the ♂ dropped the fish, and she caught it in midair. White and Roseneau (1970) summed up the earlier known instances of fishing in N. Am., adding the report by A. C. Bagg and Eliot (1937) of a Peregrine pirating a fish from a flying Osprey. Identified fishes in N. Am. and/or Britain-Europe include pike, perch, grayling, and brown trout. The Peregrine is capable of retrieving prey dropped into the ocean (D. Fisher 1978), as one would expect. It has been reported fishing at sea (Tatum 1981). Reports of a Peregrine capturing a Eurasian amphibious rodent (*Arvicola "amphibius"*), if they were taken from water, are an approximation of fishing. There are almost no records of frogs and toads (none for N. Am.), probably taken from water. Cautionary note: Peregrines "flight-bathe," hitting the water with a splash, at a low angle, then veering upward (W. Fischer 1968, illus.); this might be mistaken for fishing.

Bathing and drinking   Frequent; one bathing method was just mentioned. Usually the bird waddles or shuffles into water up to its breast, douses its head, splash-bathes vigorously, drinks, and, when well soaked, manages to reach a perch to dry. On the Yukon and Colville in Alaska, a gently sloping gravel bar was the ideal site, and Cade (1960) stated that every aerie in the region was near one of these. Captives have a great fondness for bathing and drinking, as known for centuries.

Sherrod (1983) described bathing and drying or sunning behavior of young birds. While still in the aerie, the young make bathing movements during rain. After attaining flight, they are frequently stimulated to bathe when they see the edge of water; they alight near it and sometimes execute bathing behavior before, even sometimes without, entering it. They bathe in high grass, wet from dew, and they do not appear to

369

be averse to bathing in salt water. After a bath the bird jumps to a stone or branch, shakes its feathers ("rouses"), and flaps its wings. The most common drying position is with back to the sun with wings and tail partly spread—the usual sunning posture of the Peregrine.

Thermoregulation   Older nestlings may rest or sleep with a leg extended back and outward (R. W. Nelson 1970), and in warm weather a ♀ may incubate with foot and part of tarsus exposed. This may help to maintain a stable internal body temperature; see Mosher and White (1978) for details. Raising the feathers may function at times to "ventilate" the bird.

Daily routine   In the rearing season, the tiercel (♂) may be motivated to hunt through the day, although ordinarily much time is spent sunning and loafing. In the far n. there is a lull during the continuous daylight—no appreciable action 2100–2300 hrs. in Greenland (A. D. Fox and Stroud 1981). In s. Que. in 1980 a pair reared 2 young, and 78% of hunting by both sexes occurred 0500–1000 hrs. (Bird and Aubry 1982). At least most of the year, "serious" hunting is done in morning and again toward evening, the latter probably more often when the bird was unsuccessful early in the day. See also Mueller and Berger (1973).

Speed   For over half a century the Peregrine has been credited with a flight speed of 200 mph. According to Ratcliffe (1980), estimates vary from 100 (conservative) to 250 (extravagant). He cited (from Hantge) timed maximum speeds of 170 mph at a 30° angle of descent and 220 at 45°. Also, measurements of level flight suggest a norm not exceeding 60 mph (100 kph). Flapping rate is 4.3–4.4/sec. when hunting (Meinertzhagen 1955). The smaller ♂ flaps faster than the larger ♀. Speed is ordinarily about 40–60 kph. Ratcliffe cited Orton's calculations that a Peregrine in a vertical stoop of 5,000 ft. would reach a terminal velocity of 230–240 mph, with more normal strikes to some 100 mph slower. According to Cade (1982), citing Parrott, the calculated terminal velocity of a Laggar (*Falco jugger*) is 223 mph, and the more compact and streamlined Peregrine should do "somewhat better."

Prey size limits   Wild Peregrines have struck down and/or killed the Black-throated Loon, Common Heron (*Ardea cinerea*), Red-faced Cormorant, Pelagic Cormorant, Graylag Goose, Lesser Snow Goose, Brant, Barnacle Goose, Red-breasted Goose, Shelduck. ♂ Capercaillie, Mallard, and Great Black-backed Gull. Occasionally, therefore, the victim of an attack is too heavy for even the ♀ Peregrine to transport. It sometimes briefly carries prey that is heavier than itself. The Peregrine feeds on large kills where they fall. Inexperienced young ones, evidently when very hungry ("panic hunger") occasionally attack targets that are inappropriately large—Sherrod (1983) mentioned white-tailed deer. Sometimes there is a question as to whether it was a mock or genuine attack. As to lower size limit, small birds taken include Redpolls and Willow Warblers, while large insects are still smaller.

Prey size v. Peregrine size   A subject much debated is whether the smaller ♂ takes prey averaging smaller than does the larger ♀, but it evidently does not; see R. Mearns (1983a). Both sexes readily take birds the size of ptarmigan, grouse, and pigeons, but logistics indicate that the larger ♀ can transport larger prey farther or with less fatigue.

Abnormal prey   Whether Peregrines select for abnormal (such as sick, injured, or otherwise disadvantaged) individuals of its prey species is an ongoing subject. Dekker

370

observed that there was a higher take of individuals showing abnormal escape behavior. As R. Bond (1946) pointed out, crippled birds "seem to hold a fascination" for Peregrines; falconers bait wild Peregrines by using a tethered pigeon (appears handicapped), which even attracts Peregrines that have just gorged on food. According to Ruggiero and Cheney (1979), prey movement is the most important factor eliciting predation, while oddity (novelty, being unfamiliar) reduces the probability of attack. If, for example, the outermost individuals of a sandpiper flock are young ones low in the social hierarchy, they are the most vulnerable.

Wanton killing? Taking quarry in excess of need occasionally and in special circumstances has kept this topic alive. For example, Theodore Roosevelt, at Oyster Bay, N.Y., in Sept., saw a Peregrine fly into a flock of young Black-crowned Night Herons and "kill three without picking up any" (in A. K. Fisher 1893). One might assume that the falcon was overstimulated by multiple easy targets. F. Beebe (1960) reported the taking of unneeded prey in B.C., and Spofford (see Reproduction, above) saw the Peregrine piling up Blue Jays. Both observations were in the breeding season and could indicate that the aerie served as a cache site (as it does in some other raptors). For a few British observations, see Ratcliffe (1980).

Food consumption Migrants in Alta. (Dekker 1980) apparently killed several birds daily; Peregrines specializing in waterfowl apparently killed twice daily. Those that pursued small shorebirds foraged at least 3–4, even 5–6, times daily. Three falcons, each after eating a small bird, immediately chased prey again. Cade (1960) estimated that, on av. in Alaska, parents and their brood require 540 kg. of food—the equivalent of 100 ptarmigan or ducks or about 2,000 songbirds—in the 4-month period of May–Aug.

Captive ♂ ♂ (mean wt. 683 gm.) that the Craigheads (1956) studied had a daily food requirement av. 104 gm. (max. 147 gm.) in autumn and winter. A ♂ during summer (wt. av. 721 gm.) av. 83 gm. of food (max. 120) daily. Thus they consumed the equivalent of 11.5% (summer) and 15% (winter) of their own wt.

A ♀ (av. wt. 1 kg.) needs about 129–154 gm. of food daily (Cade, in Ratcliffe 1980). Food varies as to percentage that is digestible, and so on. Probably at least ⅕ of prey wt. is waste. Ratcliffe estimated that the smaller ♂ needed a Cuckoo (*Cuculus canorus*) or Mistle Thrush (*Turdus viscivorus*) daily, the ♀ a Jay (*Garrulus glandarius*) or Golden Plover (*Pluvialis apricaria*). These are lesser amounts than in some projections and guesses. The Peregrine can do well without feeding every day.

Newly flying young Peregrines continue for several weeks to eat consdierably more than adults, building up reserves of fat (Cade, in Ratcliffe 1980).

Food caching Apparently limited to the breeding season (see Reproduction, above), which is different from some other falcons.

Pellets Or castings, are elongated and blunt-ended and usually measure about 3.5–5 cm. long and 2.5 in diam. A pellet may contain feathers and/or fur, claws, chitin, little or no bone, extraneous matter such as vegetation from the digestive tracts of prey—and sometimes metal or plastic bird bands. A pellet is usually ejected daily, rarely in flight. There may be an accumulation of pellets at aeries, plucking sites, and below perches. Unlike owls, for example, a Peregrine seldom ingests anything whole, even if small. Large insects are dismantled. Bones of larger prey may be broken while

371

still attached to the body of the prey. Bones are usually completely digested; any bone in a pellet from a wild falcon is rare. No matter how much bone is fed to a growing captive Peregrine, none is regurgitated (R. Bond 1936).

Some raptor interactions Various encounters have various outcomes, and only a few are mentioned here, in part to expand some information given earlier (see Reproduction). Many recorded episodes relate to Peregrines defending their breeding territories; others concern piracy or whether the Peregrine kills or is killed by another raptor. The Golden Eagle is dominant, yet breeding Peregrines attack it with great vigor even when distant from the aerie; it rarely, if ever, flips over and presents its talons upward as does the Bald Eagle. The Bald is attacked; if it flies near an aerie frequently, it perhaps lowers Peregrine breeding success. Sea Eagles and Peregrines had breeding sites in the same tree in Mecklenburg, and the latter attacked, although not when the eagles were on their site (Deppe 1972). Many migrant raptors cross between Spain and Morocco via the Strait of Gibraltar; in defense of territory, the resident Peregrines attack these passage birds, the Short-toed Eagle being the one most commonly struck down (Garcia 1978).

As mentioned in other contexts, Gyr and Peregrine tend to be ecologically separated where both breed. There is some competition for aeries and food, and the larger, earlier-breeding, Gyr is dominant. A Gyr killed a Peregrine in Greenland (Meridith, in Cade 1960).

Peregrines have eaten other Peregrines (Ratcliffe 1980); possibly some victims died in territorial skirmishes and then were treated as usual quarry, but details are lacking. Migrant Peregrines, at least, rob other Peregrines; see Dekker (1980) for interesting details. Peregrine and Prairie Falcon are about at a standoff; if their aeries are fairly close, they avoid one another—usually. Peregrines quite readily kill (and eat) smaller falcons, which tend to be wary of the larger raptor.

Breeding Peregrines probably attack any approaching *Buteo*, but N. Am. observations relate principally to the Rough-legged Hawk; being less feared than the Golden Eagle, it is permitted closer approach before being attacked. A Peregrine killed a ♀ Roughleg and laid its own eggs with those of the hawk (in Ellis and Groat 1982). Roughlegs attempting, or succeeding, in robbing migrant Peregrines were described by Dekker (1980). The Red-tailed Hawk, Swainson's Hawk, N. Harrier, and crows were seen to flush migrant ♂ Peregrines, which then transported their prey long distances before feeding (Dekker). Common Buzzard (*Buteo buteo*) remains have been found in aeries, and a Peregrine was flushed from a carcass in Wales (Ratcliffe 1980). The Eurasian Sparrowhawk has been found in Peregrine aeries; also (Rudebeck, in Cade 1960), a migrant young Peregrine specialized in taking this small raptor. The Peregrine has robbed the Sharp-shinned Hawk and has occasionally killed it. It has killed the Red-shouldered Hawk.

The Great Horned Owl is a serious predator on the Peregrine, getting young ones in or near the aerie at night. The Peregrine attacks it by day, sometimes knocking it down or even killing it. The Peregrine captures and eats small owls. Four Short-eared Owls were found in an aerie in Norway (Hagen 1952a), and this is the most widely reported owl taken. It is inadvisable for British-breeding owls to nest near Peregrine aeries, since the Peregrine has taken all 5 species (Ratcliffe). It has killed the Snowy Owl (Forbush 1927).

The N. Harrier and Peregrine have a varied relationship. The Peregrine may use it as a beater (see above). The 2 species have fought over food in Calif. marshes (Cade 1960). Not all harriers yield their prey to the Peregrine (Dekker 1980). In Alaska, a Peregrine killed a harrier in a territorial fight, then used it for food only incidentally (L. Bishop 1900).

Peregrine and N. Raven have a long recorded history of conflict. Usually this is related to the possession of breeding sites; they may breed nearby but out of each other's sight. Much of the fighting (the Peregrine initiates it) is sham, some genuine, and sometimes the Peregrine suffers injury from attacking such a clever adversary. The particular vocalizing of a threatened or attacked Raven is diagnostic and memorable once heard. The Peregrine has killed the Raven and has even eaten it. The Raven may be forced to abandon its clutch. Sometimes the 2 reach accommodation, mostly by avoidance, when they share the same cliff.

After breaking off the attack on an eagle, large owl, or Raven, the Peregrine may redirect its aggression toward some other convenient avian target or even a mammal. A number of raptorial birds have this trait.

Piracy Already mentioned. Peregrines are robbed of food by larger raptors (although no report of the Goshawk) and others down to smaller buteo hawks and sometimes the N. Harrier. A young Prairie Falcon visited a Peregrine aerie, where it obtained 3 prey that had been delivered to the occupants (Ellis and Groat 1982). In Greenland the Com. Raven may rob food from a Peregrine aerie in absence of its owners, and it also searches for cached prey (Sherrod 1983). Peregrines rob various raptors, in N. Am. from at least N. Harrier down to Kestrel size, but probably the Merlin most commonly.

Mammalian Predators Mentioned above.

Versus biocides This is a brief coverage of a very large subject, here mostly minus references. Especially important are papers by Enderson, listed in the bibliography by Porter et al. (1986).

North Am. Peregrine populations seem to have been relatively stable until well into the 1940s. Then, rather suddenly, there was much reproductive failure in parts of N. Am. as well as in Britain and Europe. Egg breakage was extensive, and sometimes a parent bird ate the contents. Eggshell thinning began in Britain in 1947 (Ratcliffe 1967) and started in the U.S. (Calif., Mass.) also in that year (Hickey and Anderson 1968). For example, J. A. Hagar first observed broken eggs in aeries in Mass. in 1947 and assumed that raccoons were responsible (in Hickey 1969). Eggs of the well-known pair that bred on the Sun Life building in Montreal disappeared in 1948, 1949, and 1951; in one of these years, G. Harper Hall actually saw the ♀ eating the contents; he did not report it until later (G. H. Hall 1958, 1970). In Britain, Ratcliffe's writings contained arguments that shell thinning had to be a pesticide effect, and he concentrated his thinking on the probability that it was dieldrin. Evidently the 1st paper linking a biocide to shell thinning was Hickey-Anderson, cited above, in which DDE (a breakdown product of DDT) was shown to be associated with shell thinning in Herring Gulls. The matter was proven in controlled experiments at Patuxent, Md., showing that DDE produced this effect and PCBs did not. These are the bare bones of a team effort.

Serious decline in part of Britain began in 1956 and spread rapidly. By 1963, breeding populations were greatly reduced, in n. Europe to a small fraction of previous numbers; Peregrines were present at fewer than ½ their aeries in Britain and France. By 1964, in the coterminous U.S., neither breeders nor territorial nonbreeders could be located e. of the Mississippi, where at least 350 breeding pairs had bred ¼-century earlier. Most were also gone from mainland Canada s. of the boreal forest, and numbers were down in the w. U.S. The decline did not seem as abrupt as, for example, in Cooper's and Sharp-shinned Hawks, being masked by seasonal presence of migrant tundra birds. It was more obvious in conspicuous birds, such as the Bald Eagle and Osprey.

The nw. Peregrines on the rim of the Pacific, although contaminated to some extent, have escaped serious levels of biocides. Elsewhere, by the early 1970s, there had been a reduction in boreal forest and tundra birds, the latter acquiring most of the pesticides from food ingested during migration and in Latin America during the austral summer. A severe decline occurred in the USSR (whence little information) and apparently in Japan. Thus it became evident that DDT and its metabolites were a worldwide problem, minor in some areas but serious in highly industrialized regions. Various is. Peregrines and some others seem not to have declined noticeably, but eggshell thinning was noted even in the remotest parts of Australia. Historians take note: "Death Comes to the Peregrine Falcon," *N.Y. Times Magazine*, Aug. 9, 1970, pp. 8–9, 43–45. Publicity has been enormous. The Peregrine has received more concentrated attention than any other bird in the world (I. Newton 1976a).

Use of DDT and dieldrin were greatly restricted in the U.S. in 1972 (for brevity's sake we omit other pollutants of raptors), and, in the long view, some changes have been rapid. Going back to World War II, the Peregrine in Britain was severely persecuted (not eradicated) to protect carrier pigeons. Yet so rapid was the subsequent recovery from remnant stock that the yet later, rapid, postbiocide recovery, again from remnant stock, does not seem dramatic. A national survey in 1981 found more occupied territories in Britain than known at any previous time in the 20th century. This provides some background for what might occur in parts of N. Am.

The decline in Peregrines had ceased in parts of N. Am. around the mid-1970s, although there was a lag in some places, such as n. Alaska. In the Yukon drainage in that state, the local stock had bred up to its previous level by 1979 or 1980, but the birds were still scarce to the n. Breeding sites throughout most of N. Am. have been checked at intervals, and it is clear that, wherever there was a healthy remnant breeding stock, recovery has been rapid. For example, by the early 1980s there were as many breeders in the arid sw. U.S. as had ever been known; numbers of wild birds were increasing (augmented by releases) in the U.S. Rockies; in Calif., from 2 known pairs in 1970 there was an increase to 50 occupied territories in 1982 (but the biocide level was still high enough to impede reproduction); along the Yukon there were more Peregrines than ever known before; and they were doing well on the Labrador Pen. Any concern about tundra birds seems to have subsided. In 1980, 3 pairs (4 parents were released birds) reared the 1st-known recent wild-bred young e. of the Mississippi. In 1985, e. population growth was graphed at 40 pairs observed, 25 breeding attempts, and 16 productive pairs (*Peregrine Fund Newsletter* no. 13: 3).

Captive breeding Useful for restocking in parts of N. Am. that were depleted (although not everybody favors improving the lot of raptors), but not in Britain, where the species (never eradicated) has built up naturally. There is a breeding facility in Sweden to supply Fennoscandia. (Rearing birds for falconry is another matter.)

The above temporally overlaps restocking programs. Once the s. continental N. Am. race of the Peregrine had acquired official "endangered" status, recovery programs were the order of the day. (Congress passed the Endangered Species Act on Dec. 28, 1973.) The birds could be bred in captivity (it had occurred in Germany in the early 1940s), and Cade (1973) estimated that 30 breeding pairs (not all captives breed) could produce 200 young in a year. (None of the breeding facilities has had even 1 bird of e. U.S. stock.)

Production can be increased by so-called multiple-clutching (see Reproduction, above). In the wild (as in the Rockies), eggs and nestlings, which are readily fostered by the Peregrines, are substituted for defective ones. The other method is to breed young in captivity to about 10 days before flight age, then place them in an empty aerie (or equivalent site) to be fed by hack-site attendants, who maintain, but keep out of sight of, the growing Peregrines, which attain flight and become independent. This is a modified form of "hacking," since the birds are not "taken up" (returned to captivity) after flying—as a falconer would do. All this is spelled out by Sherrod et al. (1982). Birds have been hacked on cliffs, platforms, bridges, buildings, and in habitats from marshlands to mountains to cities, in Canada and the U.S. In the early 1980s it cost US$1,500–$3,000 to breed a Peregrine and hack it to flight age (Harwood 1982). As would be expected, most hacked birds have vanished, just as some 8 or 9 of every 10 wild-produced birds do not survive to flight age. There were only 20 captive-reared Peregrines in 1973 at the facility at Cornell University, yet enough were produced to release birds into the wild beginning in 1975. From various facilities, over 1,000 young Peregrines were released in Canada and the U.S. by the end of 1982. About then there began serious discussion, in the U.S. at least, that federal support for hacking various raptors should be terminated.

Wildlife reintroduction projects (especially of raptors) generate questions, including those about tradeoffs in values, and the Peregrine has not escaped. As an example, historically, the few urban breeding sites in N. Am. had only brief occupancy by wild birds, except one in Montreal. Even so, birds have been hacked in at least Norfolk, Philadelphia, Washington, D.C., Baltimore, Grand Rapids, Mich., Los Angeles, Salt Lake City, Montreal, Toronto, Ottawa (Hull), Albany, N.Y., and Portland, Maine. Some Canadian cities have been "saturated" with hacked birds, in hope of assuring that pairs (and recruits) would breed there—76 in Montreal and Hull in 1976–1982 (1982 Am. Birds 36 957). Although Peregrines (especially passage birds) have presumably visited all these urban areas, seeking pigeons, many places have no breeding tradition—hence a question of whether publicity attendant on such releases (however funded) warrants putting captive-produced birds there instead of in more typical settings. (The Merlin has become an urbanite, but under other circumstances.)

In time, matters may get sorted out. Captive releases are done more or less on a presumption that empty former habitat remains acceptable to the Peregrines. It is reasonable to assume that more or less of this habitat, in time, would have been repopulated naturally. Once a few birds are present, a build-up will probably be rapid (as in Britain). The initial phase may be hurried along by releasing birds where the species was extirpated and to augment other stocks that are depleted and contaminated. The Osprey, formerly in a desperate way, has done very well with less direct assistance—and much less promotion. The Bald Eagle, regionally extirpated, has had liberal direct assistance and has "recovered" rapidly—with much promotion. Meanwhile, the Peregrine—the glamour bird—is still on its way up. The bird, of course, will not be quite the same genetically as its predecessor (which may not matter), and it will have much less privacy than when there were fewer people.

Numbers Without going into details, at the beginning of the 1980s, Cade's (1982) estimate for N. Am. was 2,846–3,862 breeding pairs. This included 2,000–3,000 pairs in "boreal regions." There are accurate data for Britain and good information for at least most of Europe. Elsewhere there is little to go on, although it is thought that there are between 3,000 and 5,000 pairs in Australia. Cade came up with a world figure of between 12,000 and 18,000 breeding pairs of Peregrines (as he defined the species), with concentrations in Australia, the n. Pacific-Bering perimeter, Britain, and Spain.

Falconry Just when the Peregrine and/or its warm-climate relatives in the Old World became closely interwoven with human culture dates back several millenia. The best-known early evidence, at least on the fringe of the occidental world, is Horus—the Egyptian falcon-headed god of gods, symbol of sun and sky. Although it has been suggested that this earliest of Egyptian bird-gods was derived from the conspicuous Black Kite (*Milvus migrans*), a Peregrinelike bird was worshipped, its image, for example, being a very early ideographic hieroglyph. Recastings of ancient Egyptian falcon sculptures are admired and marketed to this day. By 1200 B.C. (hardly a firm date), large falcons were used for hunting from Japan w. to the Arab lands. By about A.D. 860 (a firmer date), falconry reached Britain and became the chief spectator sport—more accurately, passion—especially of the aristocracy, for centuries. (We omit here which social stratum was allowed to use which raptor, except to note that the Peregrine was high up, next to the Gyrfalcon.) Then it suffered a severe blight in some parts of the world from a combination of circumstances, the invention (reinvention?) of gunpowder and the development of firearms for fowling being heavy contributors. Guns, traps, and other means were turned against all raptors, generally to conserve game for shooting. Despite invention, social change, and all the side-effects of an exploding human population, falconry (and hawking) has survived (as in Japan, central Asia, Europe and its vicinity, and especially in the Arab world) and expanded (as into the New World and Australia). It is of interest that, after the Egyptians had portrayed the Peregrine with remarkable realism, in the occidental world, at least, there is a gap of at least 2,000 years before the bird was again portrayed as well.

Falconry has considerable appeal, but very few persons who are impressionable are liable to acquire the expertise and have the other necessary ingredients to succeed at it. Fundamentals include apprenticeship to an accomplished falconer and an ongoing heavy investment in time, patience, and material resources. It is an addiction. Be warned—the evidence is solid that self-immolation in this pursuit can wreck a marriage. Where permitted at all, stringent laws may apply, and, especially in settled areas, the activities of such a predator are liable to cause public relations problems. Assuming that all these matters are reckoned with satisfactorily and one has access to open country, the subject of this chapter is the ideal bird—and legally protected

376

except for certain very specific nonfalconry purposes. The Peregrine is easier to train than some other raptors and, when properly managed, adjusts quite readily to captivity. When cast off, it "waits on" overhead best of all; under most circumstances an experienced falconer can reclaim his bird by use of a lure if the quarry is missed; he knows the individual traits and effects of early conditioning of any bird that he flies. Braun (1977) stated that there were 2,800 licensed falconers (many probably were not using Peregrines) in the U.S. Later, D. Evans (1982) stated that the number of Peregrines kept for falconry was unknown, a reasonable estimate being 100–200. If one must possess (legally) a raptor, the Redtail might be a possibility (where permitted). We now have much information on nutrition and diseases of captive raptors, even some indication that escapees to the wild may manage fairly well.

The proper practice of falconry and hawking have been described innumerable times. The falcon is fitted with jesses (leather straps), permanently attached to its legs, in turn attached to a swivel-double-ring, and this to a leash used to anchor the bird to a block (perch) or elsewhere. Small, spherical, quite musical bells are fastened to the legs; by their sound a falconer may follow the flight of the bird, or locate a lost one, or ascertain whether it is restless or quiet on the block. A carefully fitted hood covering the eyes has a calming effect, and a hooded bird can be handled or carried a great distance, even among strange activities and noises.

Afield, the hooded bird is perched on the gloved fist, where it stays quietly, even when "sharp set" (hungry). The hood is removed, the leash disengaged, and the falcon is cast off and spirals upward to "wait on" until someone below, or a dog, flushes the quarry. The falcon pursues and stoops and, if it makes contact, may "bind to" the prey, or the prey may fall injured or dead to the ground or escape. If prey is taken, the Peregrine is allowed to feed on it briefly; then the trained bird is taken up on the fist, rewarded with a bit of food, and hooded. If the prey escaped, the falcon may "wait on" until prey is again forced from cover and then again pursue; or, by using a lure, the falconer may retrieve his bird. Falcons may be flown from the fist directly at game, the usual method when hunting with accipiter hawks and the Golden Eagle.

Falconry literature   Extensive, with no end in sight. Harting's bibliography (1891, reprinted 1969 with additions) listed 378 entries in 19 languages. C. A. Wood and Fyfe (1943) stated that the number could easily be tripled, including items from at least 24 languages, and proceeded to add around 670 titles. Most remarkable of the great treatises is *De Arte Venandi cum Avibus*, the original manuscripts completed nearly 750 years ago by Frederick II of Hohenstaufen and discussed under the Gyrfalcon.

Persons entirely unfamiliar with falconry and wanting an attractive and informative introduction should consult the *National Geographic* article by Fuertes (1920). For our area there is a useful primer, although hawking oriented, by Jameson and Peeters (1971, revised 1977); a good British manual is Woodford (1960). The pocket-sized book by Lascelles (1892, reprinted 1980) contains many interesting reminiscences of falconry. For sources of information on wild Peregrines, the starting point should be the bibliography by Porter et al. (1987), containing over 3,500 citations and published after the present account was completed.

Various falconry books have more or less extensive glossaries, those in French perhaps having the longest listings. In the present account it has been convenient to use (and define) a few special terms and phrases, to which may be added the following because they sometimes turn up in literary works and elsewhere. *Eyass* (eyess, etc.)—a bird taken from the aerie and so called all its life. *Falcon*—in a restricted sense, the ♀ Peregrine. *Haggard*—bird that was "adult" when trapped. *Passage bird* (passager)—one trapped while in "immature" (Juv.) feathering, usually on migration (passage). *Tercel* (tircel, tassel of Shakespeare)—the ♂, which is about ⅓ smaller than the ♀.

An extensive search has turned up **no evidence of falconry** (or hawking) in early times **in the Americas.** The subject is included here because of a section on "Falconry in America" in a famous work by Schlegel and Verster de Wulverhorst (1844–1853), the French text reprinted with accompanying English translation in 1937 and this cited as proof of Aztec falconry by E. Austin (1976). The city of Tenochtitlán was founded in A.D. 1325, and the Caracara (which see) was involved in selection of the site. Eventually it included an enormous aviary, described many times, briefly and recently by Martin del Campo (1945). Montezuma II was especially interested in raptors, kept many species captive, and, when he traveled, took along eagles and other raptors, principally to show his greatness and supremacy.

There is no indication of any Aztec falconry, although the Spaniards, awed by the number of species of captive raptors, suggested its practice to them. There is a description of robbing raptors of their nestlings, a garbled account of what appears to be the N. Harrier, and description of a method of capturing falcons by using a duck with snare or noose attached—a counterpart of the bal-chatri widely used by falconers to capture passage birds. Were raptors taken for the zoo? Or for their feathers? On Aug. 13, 1521, the beleagured city of Tenochtitlán fell to the conquering Spaniards, who demolished it (no doubt including Montezuma's bird house) building by building "in order to hurt the Aztecs more" (Cortez). The purported practice of falconry near Quito, Ecuador (cited by Schlegel and Verster de Wulverhorst), is nonsense.

In retrospect The Peregrine's relations with humans have taken peculiar twists and turns. Here is a final example—for now. A means of protecting wildlife or game in some areas has been to destroy this raptor. On the other hand, in the Arab world, a way to protect wildlife is related to the presence of this raptor (or its allies)—that is, areas restricted to falconry are, in effect, wildlife preserves. RALPH S. PALMER

FOOD The Peregrine preys principally on other **birds** and, worldwide, is recorded as having captured well over 250 species. There is no point in listing them. Emphasis here is on N. Am. The Peregrine prefers to take flying prey, out in the open. These vary in size from heavier than itself down to very small birds, but, in terms of usable food gotten for energy expended in getting it, many are from ptarmigan to sandpiper in size. The bulk of prey taken in any area usually consists of a few common open-country species—for example, pigeon, Starling, Lapwing, and Skylark in Europe, Lapland Longspur, Snow Bunting, Wheatear, and Com. Redpoll in cent.-w. Greenland, and so on. Individual Peregrines commonly have preferences as to prey species, but when under pressure to feed a growing brood a parent may be less selective. For this and for other reasons, the contents of pellets and the food remains found in the vicinity of aeries may not typify what is taken in other times and places. Schorger's 1954 MS,

378

summarizing many older N. Am. sources and largely derived from stomach analyses in all seasons and numerous places, gave a very long list of prey species.

See Habits, above, for size limits of prey, specializing in particular prey, preference for domestic pigeons, hunting at sea, getting food from the ground, ingesting gastroliths, catching bats and fishes, and so on. The following are principally additional matters.

There is a summary of 14 major compilations of food items in N. Am. by Sherrod (1978). Recent additions would include, for Alaska, Ambrose (in Ladd and Schempf 1982), listing 74 prey species and 696 individual prey identified, and Mindell (1983b) listing 562 identified prey. A useful older source for the Peregrine in general is Uttendorfer (1952).

The Rock Dove, or domestic pigeon (a feral nester in places), is a highly preferred food around the world. This has been reported for cities in N. Am. from the 1860s or earlier—pigeons attract Peregrines to cities. It favored this species even long before the Passenger Pigeon (a major prey species) was exterminated—which does not preclude the latter from having been a primary food in earlier times. (In Britain, as a "crude gross estimate," the domestic pigeon may well constitute "around 50%" of food, by wt., considering all districts and seasons—Ratcliffe 1980.) In N. Am., aside from the Passenger Pigeon, no wild pigeon (or dove) is known to be taken in any quantity. Domestic fowl and pheasants are minor prey under most circumstances.

There is not much useful evidence on seasonal change in quarry. A switch from Blue Jays to blackbirds and swallows in the breeding season was mentioned earlier. In the Aleutians, alcids (especially auklets) are less available in winter, and the resident Peregrines switch to Rock Ptarmigan and Snow Buntings (C. White 1975). Tundra breeders certainly find the selection different when they migrate to S. Am.

Small petrels, which are nocturnal when ashore, are taken at sea in various seasons; the Am. record begins with Grayson (1871), if not earlier, and continues to the present. At least 3 species were identified as food on Amchitka (C. White 1975). Seabirds are greatly preponderant in the Aleutians, Queen Charlottes, Baja Calif., and elsewhere.

Unlike some of the smaller falcons, there are few reports of the Peregrine taking preflight young birds. This is perhaps because the Peregrine does not favor secluded or stationary prey or because some evidence is destroyed by thorough digestion. It took young terns in Conn. (C. H. Merriam 1877), 4 Canada Goose goslings on the Colville R. in Alaska (C. White and Cade 1971), and downy young Brown Boobies near St. Thomas, Virgin Is. (1983 *Am. Birds* 37 916). Dense booby colonies provided prey for overwintering Peregrines.

Mammal The list of species taken worldwide is fairly extensive. W. Fischer (1968) considered this list to be incomplete: shrews, bats, rabbits and young hares, pikas, tree squirrels, chipmunks, ground squirrels, lemmings, and voles. The brown (or Norway) rat is taken on Amchitka and probably at least in the littoral zone throughout the Aleutians and in some other areas. From s. Ireland there is a suggestion of perhaps taking the hedgehog (Ussher, in Ratcliffe 1980). Porcupine quills in castings in Alaska may have been gotten secondarily (Ritchie 1982).

We have snail eaters among N. Am. raptors, but perhaps only the Peregrine is reported to have taken **slugs** (see above). **Fiddler crabs** (*Uca*) were taken on the ground for 3 weeks (Sherrod 1983).

Insects Catching dragonflies is more typical of the Merlin than the Peregrine, and taking large grasshoppers is far more typical of some buteo hawks than of young Peregrines. Young Peregrines pursue (and capture) large insects, such as beetles, butterflies, crickets, and grasshoppers. Adults seldom do this.

Carrion Feeding on carrion is not a falcon trait. According to F. Beebe (1960), evidence of a killed bird, such as a ring of feathers on a mudflat, will cause a Peregrine to investigate and feed if there are edible remains. He saw 1 fly off with a dead Am. Coot. Ratcliffe (1980) had very few records of carrion feeding. It probably occurs occasionally in winter. Ralph S. Palmer

GYRFALCON

Falco rusticolus Linnaeus

Gyr-Falcon; Gyr Falcon; Jerfalcon—the best spelling if we consider the etymology of the word (Coues 1903). Vernacularly called the Gyr. Also "partridge hawk" across boreal N. Am.

Largest and most n. falcon. Length of outside and inside toes about the same, as in the Prairie Falcon (but outer decidedly longer in the Peregrine). In the wing, counting inward from the outermost primary, the feathers are progressively shorter in this sequence: #2 (longest), #3, #1, #4, but reportedly (Dementiev 1960) some variance in Asia. (Sequence is #2, #1, #3 in the Peregrine.) This gives the Gyr a slightly rounded distal outline to the spread wing. The outermost primary is deeply incised on its inner vane, and the next one is narrowed (both are incised in the Peregrine). (Also compare with the Prairie Falcon.) The tarsus is densely feathered except at rear for nearly the upper ⅔ (or, in Asia, occasionally only ½ feathered), and only in the Gyr is there a scattering of small feathers lower down. A malar stripe ("mustache" mark) is more or less evident in many "gray" birds but not throughout the species. The feathering is less compact than the Peregrine's, being better developed for insulation—can be fluffed out by a perched bird, concealing the toes.

Individuals vary from white with some darkish markings dorsally (including on tail), to having increasingly more dark (to black) throughout at the expense of white or lighter areas, to an extreme that is very dark overall (not actually black). In Basic feathering, the markings may be more or less streaky and variably tear shaped when minimal on "white" individuals, but otherwise and when not so extensive as to coalesce, markings are mostly transverse barring. Some ♂ ♂ have fewer dark markings

381

ventrally and are lighter overall than ♀ ♀, but the opposite has been noted in at least Greenland and Iceland. The ♀ is larger and heavier, and sexes overlap somewhat. In Juv. birds the amount of dark parallels that known in Basic feathering, lightest ones having the venter plain white; then they vary from narrowly to heavily streaked dark with intervening light; and darkest individuals have coalesced coloring—little to no intervening light. Most non-"white" individuals have rather wide light margins on the dorsal feathers, but these are darker in darkest birds.

Length ♂ about 19–22½ in. (48–57 cm.), av. about 21 in. (53 cm.), wingspread 40–49 in. (101–124 cm.); ♀ length about 20½–25½ in. (52–65 cm.), av. about 22 in. (56 cm.), and wingspread 47–53 in. (120–135 cm.). Males weigh about 28¼–46 oz. (800–1,300 gm.), av. about 2½ lb. (1,140 gm.); ♀ about 40–70 oz. (1,130–1,980 gm.), av. about 3½ lb. (1,585 gm.). Other specifications have been reported; for example, ♀ to 2,600 gm. in e. Siberia (Dementiev 1960).

No subspecies recognized (see below).

DESCRIPTION   One Plumage/cycle with Basic I earliest definitive. Captives show no change with age—that is, from Basic to Basic. "White" birds are described 1st, although variably "gray" Gyrs are most likely to be encountered in most of N. Am. range.

▶ ♂ ♀ Def. Basic Plumage (entire feathering) worn from FALL to early SPRING with long period of molting in the warmer months.

"WHITE" birds. The lightest are almost entirely white, the **beak** yellowish brown, **iris** dark brown, legs and **feet** yellow. The white **dorsum** may have a variable amount of dark (brownish to blackish) markings, varying from streaking to tear shaped to pendant shaped when few and toward barring if many; if the **tail** has dark markings, they tend to be concentrated centrally when minimal. **Wing** as dorsum—that is, white to same with variable amount of dark marking, the primaries dark distally.

"GRAY" birds (includes brownish ones), except darkest ones. **Beak** tipped black, grading to bluish toward yellow cere, **iris** very dark. **Head** usually has some white adjoining cere across forehead; cap usually slaty or darker, solid or even widely streaked white; chin white; sides of head and the neck with dark markings on light (to white), some with narrow black "mustache mark" extending down from near eye. **Upperparts** variably slaty in overall appearance, the feathers with even darker barring and pale distal margins. **Underparts** tend to contrast sharply, the light or white base anteriorly streaked or barred slaty to blackish and posteriorly barred, especially heavily on sides and flanks. **Tail** white or light barred dark; whether it appears as dark as dorsum or lighter depends on relative widths of dark and light bars, the tip white; in others it is essentially unicolor in the medium to dark gray range, in some of these becoming darkest adjoining the white of very tip. Legs and **feet** yellow, talons black. **Wing** upper surface as dorsum, the primaries distally black; the wing lining has a variable amount of dark markings on white (or light) with conspicuous light/dark barring on flight feathers.

DARKEST individuals vary to almost entirely sooty brownish, or the feathers show somewhat lighter margins. If there is any light on the **head**, the "mustache" mark may instead be a patch, but individuals vary from head overall dark to nearly all white. On

382

"gray" Juv.

"gray" Basic

"white" all ages

"darkest" Juv.

R.T.P.

underparts the feathers may be entirely dark or somewhat bicolored (have somewhat lighter areas). The **tail** may be either fairly dark with even darker barring or uniformly dark, the tip palish brown.

Molting Begins in the ♀ at least by the time her brood is acquiring its 2d down, and begins somewhat later in the ♂. The following is known from captives. Wing and tail begin 1st, and the body follows soon, the entire process requiring about 5 months, but whether there is a slowing down or pause in the wild when the duties of feeding the brood are heaviest is unknown. At any rate, wing molting is rapid at first, then slower, with feather renewal occurring so that flight capability is not seriously diminished. Counting from the inner primary, molting starts with #4 and goes in both directions (is centrifugal), the feathers dropped in this sequence: #4 5 6 3 7 2 8 9 1 10. In the secondaries (counting outer to inner), the 4 outermost molt in outward sequence, the others inwardly. Tertials molt outwardly. The alula starts in the middle and molts centrifugally. Some upper coverts in the wing are sometimes retained until the next annual molting. There is early renewal of body down, probably related to brooding young in cold climates; it may be shed or plucked in hot weather, this perhaps related to thermoregulation.

In the tail, the central pair of feathers (#1, #2) drop 1st, some adjoining ones (order varies somewhat) 2d, the outermost pair (#6) 3d, and, when the new outermost feathers are about fully grown, the adjoining pair (#5) drop last. Thus the bird always has lateral tail feathers, which are important aerodynamically.

Molting into Basic I (in 2d calendar year of life) sometimes starts as early as Feb. or Mar. (only in captives?). If the birds breed that year, molting may be interrupted and not completed (Dementiev 1960).

AT HATCHING Both 1st and 2d downs are white, or the latter slightly buffy. There is little information. The 2d down is said to be considerably developed by about age 10 days.

383

▶ ♂ ♀ Juv. Plumage (entire feathering) nearly perfected when flight is attained, worn into the following year, then molted over considerable time (see above).

"White" young in n. Greenland are white overall except for some dark markings on the dorsum, tail, and dark wing tips; yet in some in which both parents may be categorized as "white," there is also some narrow darkish streaking on the venter. At least through hatching year, beak, cere, eyelids, and feet are bluish; the iris is very dark.

In "gray" birds, soft-part coloring is at first as above, but cere, eyelids, and feet become greenish or yellow later, definitely by the time of advanced Prebasic I molt. Juvenal "gray" birds differ most strikingly from Basic "gray" ones in that the venter has narrow to wide variably dark streaks (vertical), not bars (horizontal), and the dorsum has more conspicuous light feather margins. As in Basic, the tail may be either barred or almost entirely unicolor.

Darkest Juv. birds are almost uniformly dark or show some indication of wide ventral streaking (minimal amount of light), dorsal feathers with appreciably lighter edges, tail 2-toned dark (obscure barring) or plain dark. Soft parts as in lighter birds.

Color phases   Inappropriate designations. Because of variations from nearly (entirely?) white to almost or entirely dark ("black"), the Gyr has been described as having color phases, morphs (as dimorphic or trimorphic), variants, varieties, and so on. Most of these are misleading, and any attempt to categorize Gyrs is subjective. Therefore, without drawing any definable point(s) of separation, they may be regarded arbitrarily as **1** light (includes "White"), varying from essentially white to same with considerable darkish markings, and **2** dark (various "grays" and browns to very dark overall), continuing from the preceding to darkest individuals.

W. E. C. Todd and Friedmann (1947) and later Friedmann (1950) made much of plain-tailed (unicolor) v. bar-tailed "varieties" occurring in both Juv. and Basic Plumages—characteristics independent of whether an individual is light or dark. The earlier paper also mentioned "plain-tailed young" (Juv.) molting into "bar-tailed" (Basic) feathering. The 2 tail "varieties" were known to Frederick II in the 13th century (C. A. Wood and Fyfe 1943). Another example of independent variation is head coloring in very dark Gyrs; usually they are dark headed, but they vary to almost white headed.

A "white" and a "gray" bird may mate and breed (Salomonsen 1951, Dementiev 1960, Burnham and Mattox 1984). Example: on the upper Colville R., Alaska, the ♂ parent was as "white" as n. Greenland birds, the ♀ "very dark gray," and their 1967 offspring were 3 dark (heavily streaked ventrally) and 1 "white" (W. Spofford; photo: White and Cade 1971). Near Hooper Bay, Alaska, in 1963: ♂ bluish gray with some brown on head, the ♀ white with a few blackish gray dorsal bars (White and Springer 1965). A breeding pair in Anadyr: ♂ "white" and ♀ "gray" (Portenko 1939). Occasional individuals have mixed characteristics—dark birds with areas of whitish feathers—including an individual from Greenland (Dementiev 1960). There is a dearth of information on homogeneous and mixed broods and their parentage, although when both parents are "white" in the extreme they seldom (if ever?) produce other than "white" young.

In simplest form, the scenario could approximate pure "white" as homozygous recessive (although multiple alleles are probably involved), off-white to dark brown as

384

heterozygous, and "black" as homozygous dominant. True "blacks" are not known to produce anything but "black," while dark browns can have variably gray (to off-white) young. This could be the case if Alaskan and Greenland experience is representative (Clayton M. White).

Measurements "Adults" from N. Am. and Greenland (but Juv. and Basic "white" birds are indistinguishable and both undoubtedly included): 42 ♂ BEAK from cere 20–25 mm., av. 22.8, and WING across chord 340–378, av. 364.3; and 63 ♀ BEAK from cere 23–27.9 mm., av. 25.2, and WING across chord 368–423, av. 400.5 (W. E. C. Todd and Friedmann 1947). Note that BEAK in the ♂ is 25 mm. or less and the ♀ 23 mm. or more, the overlap of the sexes being only in the 23–25 mm. range. For more N. Am. and also other meas., see especially Vaurie (1961b).

Live Juv. passage birds in Greenland, WING flattened: 4 ♂ 370–386, mean 378.5 mm., and 9 ♀ 404–420, mean 414.3 (Mattox 1970).

There is enough variation in meas. of WING of "gray" and "white" Greenland birds to negate any difference suggested by Schiøler or Salomonsen (Mattox 1969).

Weight Given earlier in rather general terms. A captive Juv. ♂ in Jan., not fed for 24 hrs., weighed 39.7 oz. (1,123 gm.), which increased to 49 oz. (1,391 gm.) after gorging on a bird (R. Widmeier). A ♀ from the Brooks Range, Alaska, trained and flown daily, weighed 44 oz. (1,245 gm.) in Aug. and Sept. with crop empty; in early Oct. she weighed 59½ oz. (1,680 gm.) with crop full (H. Webster).

Live-trapped passage Juv. birds in w. Greenland, with no allowance made for contents of digestive tracts: 4 ♂ 1,021–1,219 gm., mean 1,112.7; and 10 ♀ 1,262–1,687 gm., mean 1,470 (Mattox 1970).

Hybrids None reported in the wild. In captivity, by artificial insemination, ♂ parentage listed 1st: Gyr × Peregrine; Peregrine × Gyr (Cade et al. 1977); Gyr × Prairie Falcon; Gyr × Merlin; Gyr × ¾ Prairie + ¼ Red-footed Falcon; Gyr × Red-naped Shaheen; Peregrine × "Silver" Gyr; Peregrine × "Black" (chocolate colored with brown feather edges) Gyr (1980 N. Am. Falconers' Assoc. *Journ.* **18/19** 74–83).

Geographical variation Slight regional size differences do not warrant nomenclatural recognition (Cade 1960, Vaurie 1961b). As to light v. dark Gyrs in and near our area, evidently stocks were separated by Pleistocene ice and are now joined on formerly glaciated areas. This was resulted much more in overlap and mixing than in regional differentiation. Additionally, shifting and vagrancy are a consequence in specializing in food that is both annually migratory and very scarce periodically.

Going clockwise around the world, variably "gray" birds are vastly preponderant in much of present N. Am. range, while "white" ones not only occur beyond at high lats. but are also scattered far s. The Labrador Pen. has "white" Gyrs, "gray" Gyrs, and perhaps the majority of darkest individuals—yet some are scattered far to the w. Gyrs are "white" in higharctic Ellesmere I. and n. Greenland (Pleistocene refugia), but, going s. in Greenland (lowarctic and subarctic), the majority are gray, and some are a match for dark Labrador birds. Thus the entire spectrum (see plates in Schiøler 1931 or Krabbe 1934) occurs in Greenland. Selection for darkest, in moist habitat, may be postglacial and with some individuals subsequently scattering.

Icelandic breeders are "gray" with more or less streaked venter, possibly the most homogeneous regional stock ("white" Gyrs are winter visitors). Reportedly, only "grays" breed in Scandinavia and e. to include the Kanin Pen.; beginning approximately at the Pechora Basin, there are some "white" and "semiwhite" birds (about 5%); beyond, from the Lena to Kamchatka and Anadyrland, "whites" increase to about 50%. So said Dementiev (1960). It seems as likely that "white" birds are vagrant w. to Europe as that they reach there only by going that far e. from n. Greenland.

Affinities and origin   The Gyr is believed to be derived from the same steppe or open-country stock in Eurasia as the Saker (*F. cherrug*), some Gyrs being hard to distinguish from some Sakers. Regarding the Gyr's evolutionary past, there is a useful working hypothesis by Johansen (1956) that may prevail even if modified or expanded. The gist is as follows:

The stock from which the present Gyr is derived occupied part of Eurasia. During a long interglacial (Mindel-Riss), when extensive steppes connected cent. Asia with n. Siberia, many species (large falcons included) expanded their distribution n. Then, with slow development of a succeeding cold period, the Gyr became adapted to arctic conditions, and during the last interglacial, it spread in high lats. w. to Scandinavia and e. into N. Am., Greenland, and Iceland. During the last glaciation it differentiated somewhat (Johansen said into subspecies) in various unglaciated areas. In N. Am., the "originally dimorphic" ne. Siberian ancestral stock developed "white" in n. refugia (such as Ellsemere/n. Greenland) and "gray" s. of the icecap. In its general area of origin in e. Asia, the Gyr has remained fairly unchanged; today there are about as many more or less "white" as "gray" ones. Dark birds (an extreme within the "gray" category) evolved in response to humid conditions on the Labrador Pen.

NOTE   Western Alaska adjacent to Siberia seems to have the greatest variation of any local region. One 90-km. stretch of river had 7 pairs, with "adults" and young ranging from "white" through grays and light chocolate brown to "black" (Clayton M. White).   RALPH S. PALMER

FIELD IDENTIFICATION   **In our area**   Largest falcon (wingspread to at least 4 ft.), but size is deceptive, and some ♀ Peregrines are larger than some ♂ Gyrs. If surprised while feeding on prey on the ground, the Gyr can vanish from sight almost instantly, keeping low and getting the nearest rise or other hindrance between itself and the observer.

Basic feathering   Varies with individual from essentially white through various grays (appear quite bluish or toward slaty in flight) to a chocolate brownish overall. None is really black. In the gray range, dorsum and barred venter appear about equally dark—not dark dorsum and light venter as in Peregrine and Prairie Falcon. The Gyr's wing is somewhat rounded distally, not pointed as in the others, and relatively wider near the body. Wing action is decidedly heavier and slower, with motion appearing to be concentrated distally. Almost all of the underwing usually has a fairly even broken dark/light pattern in both "gray" Gyrs and Peregrines, but only a variable amount of the lining is very dark, contrasting with the remainder of the underwing, in the Prairie Falcon. The head may be mostly dark in darker "gray" Gyrs (and the Peregrine), but it varies to almost all white even in darkest Gyrs. A "white" Gyr might be confused momentarily with an albino Red-tailed Hawk, and darkest ones with dark Rough-legged Hawks or possibly dark Redtails, but differences in proportions and flight

386

characteristics are great. Hardly to be confused with the bluish-slaty Goshawk, which has very rounded wings.

Juvenal feathering Again, individuals vary from essentially white through grays to very dark. Any ventral pattern is vertical streaking, not horizontal barring, dark on white or very light; the latter varies from buffy to rich tan in Peregrines; the Prairie Falcon appears whitish ventrally, usually with much narrower darkish streaking. Darkest young Gyrs are nearest to dark young Peregrines (subsp. *pealei*) in appearance, but the latter usually have more obvious ventral streaking. Both are rather long tailed, so can be confused when perched at a distance; also, a perched dark Roughleg appears fairly long tailed, and the white basally in the tail may not be visible.

Sexing When mates are seen at an aerie, the ♀ Gyr is the larger (a difference also evident in older nestlings), and she has a lower-pitched voice. A smaller bird may have somewhat faster wingbeat.

Aging Most likely to be seen s. in winter are "gray" Gyrs in Juv. Plumage; they have the streaked venter, which distinguishes them from older birds, which have a barred venter.

Hybrids (Captive produced) listed earlier; the possible occurrence of an escapee must be kept in mind. RALPH S. PALMER

VOICE Noisy at times in the breeding season, and *chupping* once heard from birds in flight display in winter. Voice closely resembles that of large desert falcons (Wrege and Cade 1977). Persons experienced with the Gyr recognize calls and variants and have a conception of their functions or meanings. The ♂'s voice is higher pitched than the ♀'s. Principal sources of information from N. Am. are J. B. Platt (1977) for birds in the wild and Wrege and Cade (1977) for captives; both sources contain details not given here. Main categories of vocalizing are as follows:

Cakking is guttural, harsh, hoarse, uttered by both sexes, in threat (including against humans), by ♂ when High-circling with mate, and so forth. *Wailing* indicates anxiety, by both sexes; most commonly heard from ♀ when ♂ approaches with food, also if he lingers afterward. Used by solitary ♂ to attract mate. Also in some displays. Variable, as a buzzing or whining; a recognizable variant uttered by a captive ♀ during copulation. *Chupping* may be a single syllable or repeated; contact call by both sexes and used during aerial and perched displays; differs in speed, volume, and otherwise. Used by parent to announce arrival with food to nestlings. *Chattering* and *chittering*, repeated, speeded-up version of the preceding; variants used by both sexes in particular situations; variant by ♂ during copulation.

Other calls have been reported, including a somewhat liquid trilling, function unknown.

Begging nestlings have a *mewing* call that evidently evolves into *wailing*. They are capable of rudimentary *cakking*, and flying young are said also to utter a pleasant sound that is not understood (contact call?). RALPH S. PALMER

HABITAT **In our area** **Breeding** necessities are a suitable aerie and plentiful available food. Suitable sites are at cliffs inland and in mountainous areas, river bluffs, and rocky elevations and other coastal and marine sites. Ideal is a recess in a cliff having a sheltering overhang, as chosen by the Com. Raven, whose stick nests it frequently appropriates. It also occupies old stick nests of the Rough-legged Hawk on cliffs and, in some areas, in trees. Yet the Gyr is not an obligate parasite on nest builders because it also uses sites that have only a bare substrate of earth or rocky materials. As to food, it is a ptarmigan specialist, but again the tie is not obligate, since it takes various other prey. It prefers to hunt in the open, close to ground or over water.

Winterers   A few evidently remain at fairly high lats. through at least most of the season, but little is known other than that aeries are used as plucking perches and sleeping places for a much longer span than the breeding cycle. Most are presumably concentrated in lowarctic and subarctic areas, in more or less open country. The few that go still farther s. also are generally found in open situations. RALPH S. PALMER

DISTRIBUTION   (See map.) Circumboreal breeder, from the higharctic down to and regionally well within treeline; in N. Am., overlaps s. about 15° of lat. with the Peregrine. In other seasons, and mainly birds in their 1st winter, occurs s. to well below the boreal forest belt.

In our area and nearby   The Gyr **breeds** (or has bred) as follows: Formerly on Bering (Commander Is.). Breeds widely in mainland Alaska and recorded on St. Lawrence, Nunivak, and Kodiak is., but apparently absent (except as transient or vagrant) in the Aleutians. In Canada in much of Yukon Terr. and probably extreme n. B.C., thence, e. approximately from within treeline n. across Canada to the outer coast of the Labrador Pen. Island distribution extends at least from the Belchers in Hudson Bay and Akpatok in Ungava Bay n. into the higharctic to include n. Ellesmere, but some is. probably have no suitable breeding sites, and the Gyr is scarce on some others. Breeds throughout the seasonally snow-free perimeter of Greenland, except extreme nw.

Winter   Northern limits are not definitely known, but breeders (in addition to Juv. birds and some older prebreeders) in high lats. and other areas seasonally or periodically lacking adequate huntable prey (especially ptarmigan, which are migratory) must move elsewhere. Some Gyrs probably remain at fairly high lats., at least near open water (polynyas) and seafowl. The Gyr occurs all year in at least s. parts of the Canadian Arctic Archipelago.

Migrants   Gyrs that cross the international boundary into the coterminous U.S. are rather few in most years, mostly Juv. birds and some other prebreeders. Many are "gray" (including dark birds, as from the Labrador Pen.), and some are "white" (may include individuals from the higharctic). Extremes of s. occurrence are approximately from n. Calif. to Kans. and Okla. and to Pa. and Del.

Elsewhere   Going e., the Gyr **breeds** and is essentially resident in Iceland (there are no Peregrines) and on the Eurasian mainland from interior s. Norway n. and then e. across the continent to include the Chuckchee Pen. and probably Kamchatka (where breeding not proven). It has reportedly bred on the s. is. of Novaya Zemlya, and it breeds on Wrangel I. As **migrants** in the Atlantic area, n. Greenland ("white") birds reach Iceland at least. The Gyr has reached the Faeroes infrequently, Oct.–Mar., and occasionally Britain. There are at least 2 records for Svalbard (Spitzbergen). "White" birds have reached Finland, Svalbard, and s. Europe—as likely to be strag-

388

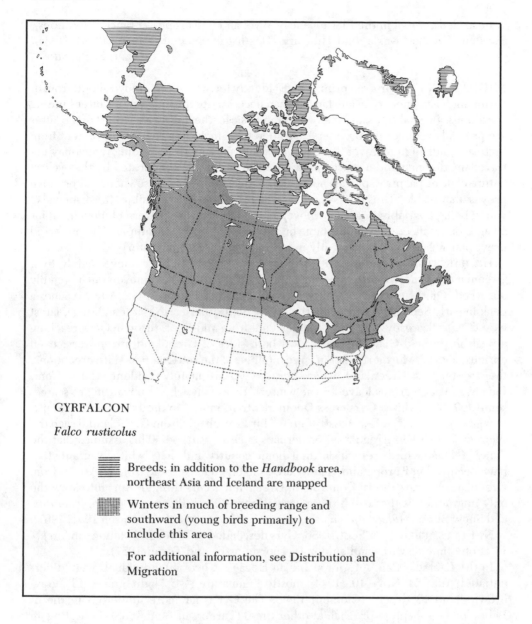

GYRFALCON

Falco rusticolus

Breeds; in addition to the *Handbook* area, northeast Asia and Iceland are mapped

Winters in much of breeding range and southward (young birds primarily) to include this area

For additional information, see Distribution and Migration

glers w. from e. Asia as e. from Greenland. On the Pacific side, the Gyr reaches the Commander Is. and n. Japan. **Winter** occurrence parallels that in N. Am.; that is, breeders tend to remain n. of s. limits of breeding, but younger birds travel, with southernmost recorded limits very exceptionally to Portugal, n. Italy, L. Baikal, and somewhere in Japan.

Introduced unsuccessfully from n. Greenland into the German Alps, probably in 1938, by agents of Hermann Göring.

389

Recorded as **fossil** in the Pleistocene of Wyo. and in Europe—France (5 localities), Sweden, Czechoslovakia, and Hungary. This list is updated from Brodkorb (1964).

RALPH S. PALMER

MIGRATION **In our area** primarily. Evidently territorial Gyrs move about, from or within high lats., not going any farther than necessary to find adequate winter hunting conditions. Juvenal birds and many fewer in Basic feathering (at least most of the latter are probably younger prebreeders) are migratory, including regular movement from high lats., although many of those from warmer parts of the breeding range may not travel any distance under most conditions. The picture is complicated by the cyclical nature of principal prey species, necessitating that the birds go elsewhere if alternative prey is unavailable. Thus the Gyr tends to be resident where possible, the dispersal of young being a variably migratory movement, and the entire pattern of movement for all ages being affected by an unstable or seasonally absent food supply. The preferred prey, ptarmigan, fluctuates greatly in numbers and is also migratory.

HIGHARCTIC N. GREENLAND Juvenal and some other birds move mainly to s. Greenland for the winter; since they travel near coasts, their movement is readily observed. On the e. coast n. of Scoresby Sd., passage beings in late Aug., reaches a peak in early Sept., and is over by the end of Sept. (there are 2 later sightings, latest Nov. 27). At Scoresby Sd., movement extends from mid-Sept. through Oct., reaching a peak in the mid-Oct. Migrants down both sides of Greenland are unwary, even curious, and were formerly shot in large numbers at the settlements. With exceptions, they winter in s. Greenland, where "gray" Gyrs are mainly resident, as also Com. Ravens (but Peregrines leave for the winter). Especially when ptarmigan are scarce, some 200–300 "white" Gyrs cross Denmark Strait, mostly in the 1st 3 weeks of Sept., to winter in Iceland. A few, mostly "gray," birds, probably from Greenland, reach the Faeroes and Britain irregularly, or perhaps even w. Europe. (This assumes that the "gray" Icelandic birds remain in their home country and that "white" vagrants that have occurred in Europe and vicinity are as likely to have come from e. Asia as from Greenland.) Spring return from s. to n. Greenland occurs through Apr. into May; the only migrant birds that reach there earlier are the Rock Ptarmigan (*Lagopus mutus*) and Snow Bunting (*Plectrophenax nivalis*). (Based mainly on Salomonsen 1951, 1967.)

N. ELLESMERE I. In Sept. 1956, Gyrs descended on a weather station "in force," 11 at one time on wires and antennas (Thorsteinsson and Tozier 1957).

In the Labrador Pen. interior at Indian House L., over 40 individuals were differentiated Aug. 24–Nov. 10, 1944, mostly "immature"—5 "light gray," 13 "gray-brown," and 13 "black" (Clement 1949). The Gyr is far more numerous in the n. Labrador Pen. Sept.–Apr. than at other times (Turner, in Bent 1938), indicating an influx from the n.

ALASKA Regular fall movements in the Kotzebue Sd. and Cold Bay areas and at Kodiak I., with migration mainly coastal and believed to extend s. as far as the outer coast of Vancouver I. (Cade 1960). Spring data are lacking. In the outer Aleutians at Amchitka, the Gyr apparently occurs sporadically in fall to spring (Kenyon 1961).

N. COTERMINOUS U.S. Gyrs occasionally appear around mid-Oct., but most reported sightings are in Dec., and Gyrs are usually seen last around mid-Mar.

390

Possibly homing   A Gyr, whether the same one is unknown, was at a locality in se. Pa. for 5 consecutive winters (1983 *Am. Birds* **37** 285).

Flight years   Irruptions, as noted to the s., are presumably triggered by a cyclic low in ptarmigan numbers over a wide area. The following list of winters in which notable numbers of Gyrs reached s. Canada and the coterminous U.S. undoubtedly could be expanded: 1905–1906 (in Bent 1938), several in Pa. in fall of 1934 (Bent), 1938–1939, 1944–1945, and 1981–1982. (Compare with flight years listed for the Roughleg.) In the last winter listed, Gyrs occurred from Calif. to Pa., with 19 Idaho records and 3 birds together in Pa. (1982 *Am. Birds* **36** 263, 278). RALPH S. PALMER

BANDING STATUS   Banding has been done on a limited scale principally in Yukon Terr., Alaska, Dist. of Mackenzie, Dist. of Franklin, Keewatin, and Que. Very few migrants and winterers have been banded—from Pa. to Wash. Some banded captives have been released. In Greenland, banding (with Danish bands) began in 1946, and 51 passage birds (most, if not all, Juv.) had been banded by 1965; of these, 5 were recovered later, all in Greenland (Mattox 1970). In 1967 a total of 10 ♀ and 4 ♂ Juv. birds were banded in autumn at Disko; 2 ♀ were recovered to the s. later. In 1972–1981, a total of 15 nestlings and 8 autumn passage birds were banded, with no recoveries (Burnham and Mattox 1984).   RALPH S. PALMER

REPRODUCTION   North Am. and Greenland data primarily. Probably **first breeds** at age 2 years (in 3d calendar year of life) or older, and some captives do not reproduce until much older. It has been stated (Dementiev 1960, others) that both sexes are capable of breeding (and eggs laid) when yearlings. Reports of Gyrs breeding while still retaining (as yearlings) some Juv. feathering need confirmation.

The breeding cycle in Alaska is longer by some 2–3 weeks than in Peregrines, and timing varies more from year to year in response to climatic variables (Cade 1960).

Territory   Established breeders in interior Alaska, nw. Canada, and presumably widely elsewhere have a strong tendency to maintain territories around the year unless a food shortage forces them to move; surely there would be more evidence of continuous occupation if aeries were more accessible for winter study. Sometimes only the ♂ remains; if he is absent temporarily, he is evidently back on station early. In Yukon Terr., solitary ♂ ♂ also held cliffs throughout the breeding season, but lone ♀ ♀ did not (J. B. Platt 1977).

There may be more continuous territory occupation through successive breeding seasons near some seabird colonies (stable seasonal food supply), but where the main prey base (such as ptarmigan) fluctuates from abundance to near-absence, aeries tend to be vacant in years of scarcity. It is possible that Gyrs nesting among some colonial birds do not take nearby prey but hunt other quarry at a distance and so might have nonbreeding years (Dementiev 1960), but the evidence is against this. Along the Colville R. in arctic Alaska, distance between aeries varied 3.2–38 km., av. 17.4 (10.8 mi.) apart (Cade 1960), and hunted area of pairs varied about 208–1,040 sq. km. In sw. Greenland, distance between inland sites was 10.4 km. for occupied sites, and av. 12.3 for those that were successful; the minimum distance between coastal sites was about 15 km. (Burnham and Mattox 1984). Greatest reported density in Iceland is 7 occupied aeries in 440 sq. km., or a pair/63 sq. km. (Wayre and Jolly 1958). Most remarkable use was 10 pairs in some 10 sq. mi. in n. Sweden in a peak lemming year (Hagen 1952b). In Yukon, the defended portion was longer than wide. In interior Alaska a Gyr may travel some 12–15 km. from the aerie when hunting (White and Cade 1971); the ♂ goes farther than the ♀, as judged by her briefer absences (at least at first). Pairs at some seabird colonies are known to have a stable food supply at hand.

Both sexes defend the aerie, but the ♀ is the chief aggressor. The N. Raven and Roughleg, if they approach (perhaps to visit a site they had occupied formerly), are sometimes killed (White and Cade, others), and the Golden Eagle can be forced to abandon its aerie after persistent attacks by territorial Gyrs (J. B. Platt 1977). In instances of accommodation, such as of Raven or Roughleg and Gyr, the species usually occupy sites some distance apart and preferably out of each others' view. Close nesting is exceptional, and quarreling is frequent. On the Seward Pen., Alaska, aerial battles initiated by the Gyrs were seen (Roseneau 1972). Yet in many situations the Raven is clever enough to avoid or escape its assailant. (The "partnership" in which the Raven supplies stick nests that later become Gyr aeries has resulted in much literature on their interrelationship.) Peregrines and jaegers may harass a Gyr, and the former can outmaneuver it. On the Colville R., Gyr and Peregrine may nest as close as 35 m. (White and Cade 1971), but in sw. Greenland, where prey is limited and these raptors have much dietary overlap, they do not share the same cliff because of competition for food (Burnham and Mattox 1984). A Gyr killed a Peregrine in Greenland (Cade 1960). The Gyr's severest and most persistent attacks are against the Golden Eagle, which, in some instances, may be trying to visit an old aerie of its own that is now possessed by Gyrs. It is alleged that the eagle preys on Gyr nestlings, which is logical but lacking in solid evidence. A dead Gyr was found in a Golden Eagle aerie in Norway (Hagen 1952a). The Gyr attacks various mammals, such as fox and wolverine, even though they cannot reach its aerie. When humans approach, the ♂ Gyr seldom stays nearby but circles high overhead and drifts away; some ♀♀ are also shy, but others, with much *cakking*, may circle for a while before leaving or may even make passes at the intruder. In Iceland, for example, a ♀ dived repeatedly at Cereley (1955).

Most aeries in Yukon, being sheltered, are winter loafing sites and/or night roosts. A site on Ellesmere I. consisted almost entirely of arctic hare bones piled 2 ft. high (MacDonald 1976), and one in sw. Greenland consisted of a "layer of excrement over 2 m. thick" (Burnham and Mattox 1984). Since breeding Gyrs keep the aerie clean of food remains and do not defecate there, these sites were obviously occupied outside the breeding season. Stated otherwise, if a wintering Gyr is located, its continued presence is more or less predictable.

Pair bond Evidently lifelong, uninterrupted in some instances and temporarily more or less interrupted by seasonal absence of 1 or both birds in others. There were 3 Gyrs at a wintering locality in Pa.; a "white" and a "gray" one flew close together (1982 *Am. Birds* **36** 278, photo) apparently in "passing-and-leading" display. This was either pair-formation behavior or, more likely, was related to bond maintenance while remote from breeding range. In Alaska ♂ defended a breeding cliff on dates to Apr. 22, and no ♀ was seen, yet 12 days later a ♀ was incubating 3 eggs (Bente 1981); possibly the ♀ had been present unseen, but more likely there was a prior-existing bond and she proceeded to lay in minimal time after arrival.

Mate replacement In ne. Greenland a ♀ was shot at an aerie on May 19, and on July 14 another Gyr flew from the site—hence, evidently the ♂ had another mate (Manniche 1910).

The aerie Requisites are a safe site with easy aerial access plus adequate prey within the ♂'s commuting distance. The ideal aerie is an existing N. Raven nest of sticks or trash in a cliff niche, protected by an overhang, oriented in any compass direction, and where snow either does not accumulate or disappears early. Many breeding Gyrs, therefore, are potentially dependent on Ravens. Roughleg aeries, preferably the less exposed ones, and occasionally a Golden Eagle's, are taken over, with occupancy sometimes switching back and forth in different years. Many Gyr sites have no structure (as in falcons generally), being a recess in a cliff or eroded dirt bank or even out in the open, without shelter. The eggs are laid in a spot scraped in whatever substrate exists. If Gyrs occupy a Peregrine site before the latter returns, in a later year they may not use it and it may revert to the Peregrine. Gyrs in Alaska occupied a gold dredge, an abandoned pile-driver, and a sluice box, taking over stick nests built under overhangs on these man-made substitutes for cliffs (White and Roseneau 1970).

Stick nests become dislodged (Cade 1960). In sw. Greenland, Gyrs depend on Ravens for stick nests at some 65% of inland aeries, but other cliff sites are more regularly occupied. The young Gyrs usually dismantle the Raven's nest; therefore, before the site can be reoccupied by Ravens, they must rebuild or else build elsewhere on the cliff (Burnham and Mattox 1984). So it is widely held in s. Greenland that the Gyr is not found without its Com. Raven "partner" (in Chapman 1899).

Most tree sites in N. Am. are probably Roughleg aeries, which have good access, while Raven nests are often quite concealed. In the Anderson R. region in nw. Canada, an aerie was on a ledge, another was in the side of a deep ravine, and 18 were in the tallest trees, "generally in pines" (MacFarlane 1891). Perhaps all tundra sites beyond were already occupied (Cade 1960). There are very few other reports of tree aeries in N. Am.; see, for example, Kuyt (1962). Gyrs in Eurasia use some stick nests in trees, including in larches, and presumably built by Roughlegs; in some Asian localities in forest-tundra they utilize tree nests of crows.

Alternative sites Common, a total of at least up to 3 along the face of a cliff, apart or close (Dementiev 1960). Potential alternative tree sites are, of course, those of Roughlegs.

Nonbreeding Territories near or at a stable food base may tend to have breeding Gyrs annually. This appears to be so at some seabird colonies in N. Am. and Greenland and is known at some Icelandic locations (there are N. Ravens but no Peregrines or Roughlegs) but not where the Gyr is dependent on fluctuating numbers of prey. When the Alaskan landscape is under snow, ptarmigan are the almost exclusive prey, and their periodic scarcity caused periodic reduced breeding success or failure in the Gyr. Six consecutive breeding years at a site there was considered exceptional (White and Roseneau 1970). In e. Murmansk in the USSR, an aerie has been known since the 17th century (Dementiev 1951), although probably not occupied continuously.

Statements that Gyrs occupy cliffs only in alternate years seem to carry the erroneous connotation that Gyrs are unable to breed annually. The presence of prebreeders might lend support to this misleading impression.

Associates   Some Greenland Gyrs breed among nesting Barnacle Geese. Also, there seems to be some habituation to Gyrs at some seabird colonies. In Alaska, scattered pairs of waterbirds nest near active Gyr aeries (White and Springer 1965), and ground squirrels are often common nearby (Cade 1960). Yet a ♀ Gyr took live prey experimentally released nearby (see below).

Displays   There is little point in listing all designations that have been applied to components of Gyr displays. The following is based primarily on Wrege and Cade (1977) for captives and J. B. Platt (1976c, 1977) and Bente (1981) for birds in the wild.

Many of the Gyr's aerial actions are modifications of HIGH-CIRCLING, while the "undulatory roll" of Platt, the sudden steep plunging and then swinging upward, and some others, are variants of the SKY-DANCE. Within this framework, plus some displays when perched, there are numerous variations depending on time of year, soaring conditions, number of individuals present, physiological state of participants, and so on.

Beginning early (sometimes before a ♀ is present), the ♂ makes himself conspicuous by High-perching, a variant of High-circling. In the latter the ♂ soars above the breeding site, probably often aided by an updraft at cliff sites, and there also is mutual soaring in circles and other configurations. This is done silently, as far as is reported. Platt described a gradual descent with wings partly closed, "mutual-floating," the ♀ *cakking*. Soaring and some other display activity almost certainly occurs on territory during warm spells in winter and if mates are present. It definitely occurs from onset of territorial advertising until well into the rearing period, and Bente stated that flying young also do it.

In "aerie fly-by" the ♂ advertises the site to a ♀. In his "roll-display" his body partially rotates, showing it off to advantage; he dives steeply and shoots upward again. Usually he makes 1 or 2 of these sudden dives. In "passing-and-leading" display the birds (mated) are close together. In "mutual floating" the ♂, *cakking*, is 3 m. or less above the ♀, and with tail spread, legs lowered, and wings partly closed, the pair gradually loses altitude. Variants and combinations are numerous. For example, the ♂ may take the lead (as in "passing-and-leading") and partially rotate his body. In "aerie fly-by" the ♂'s flight path criscrosses over the aerie, but there are all sorts of variants; the ♂, *wailing*, often carries prey, which stimulates the ♀'s involvement. He may deliver it to the aerie, as if inducing her to alight there, then fly off with it. Presumably the ♀ then gets it via an aerial food pass. (It is suggested here that, if prey were so scarce that the ♂ could not get any to display with, the breeding cycle would be disrupted—as in the Snowy Owl when it cannot find lemmings.)

At the aerie, again, numerous behavioral components have been labeled, but LEDGE-DISPLAY in its various forms includes at least most of them. It begins by visiting, by either sex or both together. Both may be in horizontal posture, head lowered, *chupping* rapidly. Either may squat and rock the body, "scraping," with head up. Other components may be interwoven, such as ♂ fetching food to the ♀, mutual stroking with the beak, and so on. The ♂ delivers food to the ♀ (aerial food pass, for example, or he may use it to entice her to the aerie) usually begins at least 10 days before laying, and the ♀ is dependent on him for all her food once she begins to accept it. Thus the pair bond is established (if new) or reaffirmed. After a food pass the ♂ may immediately perform an undulatory flight display before departing (Platt). Procedure varies. The ♂ may begin to *wail*, to announce his approach to the aerie, while still a long way off. The ♀ flies toward him, beating her wings in a distinctive shallow arc, and the prey is transferred. Usually he has fed beforehand, as evidenced by his distended crop. Very infrequently he proceeds to the aerie with food. Once she has possession, she may face him in horizontal posture, which causes his immediate departure. (Generally speaking, when the birds are perched, a vertical position indicates submissiveness, a horizontal one antagonism.) She may feed at the aerie or carry food to a nearby plucking place; she may cache any uneaten portion at no great distance and unconcealed; the ♂ does not disturb it, and she may retrieve it later.

Greenery? Before copulation, the ♂ sometimes "symbolically" fetches a small twig (Dementiev 1960); one wonders if this was a captive bird delivering a prey substitute. Turner (in Bent 1938) found twigs of larch and spruce on the rim of an aerie in what is now n. Que. One cannot exclude the possibility that they had been brought earlier by a Roughleg.

Copulation In the wild, it is attempted at least a month before the 1st egg is laid (and even earlier in captives), it is more frequent in the 10 days before laying, and it is known to continue at least until the 3d egg is laid. It takes place wherever the ♀ happens to be, at any time (or times) of day. The ♀ may solicit it; that is, either sex may initiate it. Preliminaries range from almost none to very complex. The ♂ is erect and silent, his neck arched (curved-neck posture, which elicits ♀ response); the ♀ is horizontal, whining. The ♂ mounts, and both sexes are calling (♂ chattering or chittering); afterwards the ♀ usually flies to a perch. Captives outdoors in Alaska: the 1st attempt occurred 40 days before laying; there were other attempts, then "successful" 13 days before laying. Intensity of this behavior seemed to depend on ambient temperature, peaked 3–5 days before laying, and they copulated before laying each of the 1st 3 eggs in a 4-egg clutch (Seifert, in Ladd and Schempf 1982).

Prelaying behavior Begins some 5 days before the 1st egg is laid. The ♀ may lie down and "doze" for some time at her usual perches; her flight becomes labored or is even avoided (she awaits the ♂ rather than going to him); she may visit the aerie, "scrape" the depression for the eggs, or lie quietly (J. B. Platt 1977). A captive ♀ outdoors in Alaska was in "incubation posture" for up to 2 hrs./day for a week before laying (Seifert, in Ladd and Schempf).

Laying interval It av. 56 hrs. in a 4-egg clutch (Seifert).

Egg dates On the Colville R. in arctic Alaska, by back dating: laying began the last week in Apr. (3 aeries), 1st week in May (4), and 2d week (3) (Cade 1960). (Dates should have been earlier if he calculated using 29 rather than 35 days' incubation.) A captive ♀ outdoors in Alaska began a clutch of 4 on Apr. 10 (Seifert). In n. Yukon, based on 3 years' data, laying requires 8 days and occurs Apr. 5–30 (Platt 1976c). In ne. Greenland a ♀ was flushed from an aerie on Apr. 20 (Manniche 1910). Bent (1938) gave these dates for presumably viable clutches: Greenland, May 6–June 13 (5 records); arctic Am., May 9–June 12 (6); and "Labrador" (now n. Que.), May 22–28 (3). There is not much lat. difference in timing except in Greenland. Gyrs lay very early in captivity at lower lat. (Cade et al. 1977).

Clutch size Usually 3–4 eggs (1 more in the arctic than the Peregrine). Goodnews

Bay, Alaska: 11 clutches of 2–7, av. 3.8 (Cade 1960). Greenland: most frequently 3 (Salomonsen 1951). In extreme n. Norway: even 7–9 in 1906 when food abundant (Dementiev 1951).

Replacement clutch Two records in Yukon; the interval from loss of initial clutch to relaying was 14 days; details in J. B. Platt (1977).

Egg size There are 2 series in Bent (1938), as follows: in 90 eggs length varied 53.5–64.4 and breadth 41.4–50.8, av. 58.7 × 45.7 mm.; in 55 eggs length was 56–63 and breadth 42–48, av. 59.4 × 43.5 mm. **Shape** usually between short elliptical and elliptical. Basal **color** creamy white or this suffused with some variant of pale reddish cinnamon. It is overlaid (usually quite evenly) with spots and blotches of various reddish browns, but eggs vary from unmarked (rarely) or nearly so to nearly uniform brownish. The shell is granular, without gloss. Bendire (1892) stated that they more nearly resemble those of the Prairie Falcon than the Peregrine (latter usually much darker). A fresh Gyr egg weighs about 70 gm.

Incubation The ♀ sits from laying of the 1st egg, but not tightly (actual incubation) until later—probably from laying of the 3d egg. At some aeries she can be approached very closely before getting off. She does most of the incubating, although the ♂ (who has 3 incubation patches) may sit for as much as ⅓ of daylight (J. B. Platt 1977). Observations were made at an Alaskan aerie over a span of 28 days during incubation (Bente 1981). After rising and standing or rousing, the ♀ would reposition herself on the clutch while pumping her head once or twice. The interval between these settling movements decreased as hatching approached, then became even shorter. The ♂'s role was minimal in this instance. Usually he fetched prey, and, after transferring it to the ♀, she was off the eggs for a few min. at most—the time she spent eating at a perch governed the length of the ♂'s stay. Once he arrived without food, the ♀ departed, and he sat on the clutch. Two days before hatching, the pair soared together over the aerie for about 10 min. On occasion, she got off the eggs to pursue intruders seen from the aerie—Golden Eagles, Long-tailed Jaegers, and red foxes. Her incubation shifts av. over 4 hrs. (but Platt reported much longer ones). They gradually shortened, and in the final 5 days, the ♂ sat on the eggs more than he had in the preceding 30 days. This carried over into considerable brooding during hatching, an interest that continued until the nestlings were about 5 days old.

Incubation period Per egg, 35 (34–36) days (J. B. Platt 1977), which is longer than previously reported. In Seifert's 4-egg clutch in Alaska, the 1st egg hatched in an incubator in 33.8 days and the other 2 that hatched (outdoors) required 3–5 days longer. Ordinarily the hatching span for the clutch is about 36–48 hrs.; that is, they do not hatch synchronously but in much shorter time than the laying span.

Nestling period At first the ♂ is sole provider for mate and brood, the ♀ being in nearly constant attendance at the aerie for 10 days or longer; he delivers food several times a day throughout the long daylight hours. The ♀ shelters the nestlings from cold and later, if there is direct sunlight on the aerie, from excessive heat. Any brooding by the ♂ is brief. Around 10 days, the 2d nestling down of the young is evident (it is long and dense), and nestlings have at least considerable thermoregulatory capability. Ordinarily the ♂ does not feed the brood, instead delivering food (in beak or talons) to the ♀ or the aerie edge, and she feeds the young. If he does start to feed them, she displaces him quickly and he departs. Most food is delivered between about 1100 and 1800 hrs., as was also noted in a time-lapse photographic study by M. A. Jenkins (1974, 1978). In the Holsteinborg Dist., Greenland, the young were fed at intervals around the clock, with a minimum after midnight. Feedings peaked at 1500–1600 hrs. and were lower around 1600 hrs.—probably related to activity periods of the Gyrs and their prey species (Jenkins, in Ladd and Schempf 1982). The ♂ brought food to a talus slope, and the ♀ flew to it; he never was seen to bring food directly to the young (Jenkins). Maximum number of feedings/day was 6 (Jenkins) or 7 (Bente).

The ♀ plucked and sometimes partly dismantled prey away from the aerie before delivering it but was not observed to eat it, while any plucking by the ♂ occurred at the aerie. In captives, when the young slowed or ceased eating, the ♀ uttered her *chip* call to induce them to resume (Wrege and Cade 1977); if they did not respond, she ate it herself. Studies in the wild vary; in one, the ♂ gave food in pieces to the ♀, and she passed them to the nestlings. Uneaten food remains are carried away (Jenkins).

Typically the ♂ announces his approach by wailing, and the ♀ flies to meet him, which precludes his landing at the aerie. He may alight at a perch and await her there. She wails and then chatters, and the ♂ replies with *chip* notes. In an aerial exchange she flies close below him and turns over partly to take the quarry either from his talons or when he drops it. If they are perched, she may take it from his talons or there is a beak-to-beak transfer. Afterwards, she perches and either eats it or readies it for feeding the brood. The ♂ flies overhead briefly and then departs, presumably to hunt again. After the ♀ is hunting, either sex, on departing, may circle overhead before moving away. At first she hunted within 3 km. of the aerie (telemetry data), then at greater distances; prey transfers between ♂ and ♀ are known to occur up to 1½ km. away (Bente), perhaps also farther. The young have growing appetites, and hunting by both parents must be especially important if prey is scarce. When domestic chickens were released near an aerie, much of this "supplemental prey" was taken by the ♀, the ♂ showing no interest and the ♀ taking only live fowl; she also took "natural" prey close by; details in Bente (1981). On Ellesmere, when portions of arctic hare were placed nearby, both parents delivered them to the young (Muir 1974), as though they had retrieved cached food.

Gyr/ptarmigan timing   Most raptors have nestlings to feed during the time when prey species' numbers are augmented by a summer increment of easily captured inexperienced young. For Gyrs in arctic Alaska the timing is different. Preflight Gyrs are fed on mature ptarmigan that have survived the winter; then the young Gyrs attain flight about the time ptarmigan young begin hatching. It is advantageous for the young Gyrs to have terrestrial and weak-flying quarry; additionally, they develop a "set" on ptarmigan at an early age. This interrelationship has been noted in Norway (Hagen 1952b), Iceland (Wayre and Jolly 1958), and n. Alaska (Cade 1960).

In parts of Alaska and Canada (unlike Iceland, for example), the parent Gyrs have more choice of prey species. For example, at first mainly ptarmigan. When the ground becomes bare in places but not yet thawed, the winter surface-nests of microtine rodents are exposed, and these mammals are very vulnerable as they scurry about. When they are not plentiful they may still attract Short-eared Owls and jaegers, which, in turn, are taken by the Gyrs. Arctic ground squirrels soon emerge, and they are about as heavy prey as a Gyr can transport any distance. Soon after, young ground squirrels are out of burrows; before they have much survival experience, they are driven from the home burrow. These various mammalian quarry, like ptarmigan, fluctuate violently in numbers.

Caching food   A common Gyr activity, at least in the breeding season. It is known from before laying until at least well into the nestling period in captivity and in the wild. The quarry may be left out of sight of the aerie, not hidden but placed in a rocky or vegetated spot such as on a slope and usually within 400 m. of the aerie. Both sexes cache prey. The ♀ may cache it before or after she has fed on it. In Bente's study, maximum caching activity occurred after the young were 4 weeks old, and it was last seen the day before the 1st young attained flight. The ♀ may retrieve cached prey, the ♂ occasionally. Once the ♂ returned from hunting "empty-handed," retrieved a cached prey, and delivered it to the ♀ (Bente). If retrieved prey is not fully eaten, it may be cached again. Thus multiple recachings are possible. On Ellesmere I., a Gyr delivered portions of an arctic hare, which was presumably too heavy to be delivered intact to the aerie (MacDonald 1976); this is at least the equivalent of having cached it. In w.-cent. Greenland a cached Oldsquaw (*Clangula hyemalis*) was not retrieved (M. A. Jenkins 1978).

Age at first flight   On Baffin I., at least 46 and at most 49 days (Wynne-Edwards 1952)—presumably correct in that instance, although more variation is probable.

Dependency   The flying young are fed by their parents for a month or more while getting their early hunting experience; Cade (1960) estimated dependency as longer, at least 5–6 weeks. From laying to independent existence of young is about 105–110 days (Cade). The latter figure would seem to be minimal.

Breeding success   Thirty-five nests in arctic Alaska contained 133 eggs, and 82 young were reared; details in Cade (1960). Reproduction there is regulated by ptarmigan density (Cade): 3 young/aerie when ptarmigan are plentiful, 2.2 when they are decreasing, 1.3 when much reduced; in the worst of 5 years, no Gyrs bred on that part of the Colville R. Along 183 mi. of it in 1971 (White and Cade 1971), when ptarmigan and microtine and raptor numbers were low, 12 pairs of Gyrs produced 18 young to flight age. In an area in n. Yukon in 1974–1979, inclusive, 59–80% territories were occupied, av. 69.4%; 38.2–73.3% produced young, av. 56.7%; the number of young/successful attempt (and adding 1973) was 2.7–3.4, av. 3.1; and the "estimated total productivity of young" was 116–206, av. 173 (Mossop and Hayes, in Ladd and Schempf 1982).

In the Disko Bay region of Greenland in 1974, when hare and ptarmigan numbers were very low, Gyrs were seen at some aeries, and freshly molted feathers found at some others, but no young were found at the 14 sites examined. Nor were any active sites found near seabird colonies (Burnham and Mattox 1984).

The Gyr has bred in captivity, and its young, in turn, have bred.

RALPH S. PALMER

SURVIVAL   In Alaska, starvation can begin early, affecting nestlings. The av. number surviving to flight age over the years is about the same, roughly 100 young "per 100 paired adults per year" with very great year-to-year variation—a deviation of 100–200% from the mean (Cade 1960). (Also note breeding success, above.)

According to F. Beebe (1974), about ⅓ of all Gyrs brought into mid-lat. conditions perish in their 1st year, from aspergillin fungus or foot infections, but some have excellent health for an av. of 8 or 10 years, and some survive up to 30 years.

In Iceland, 32 birds found dead (2 were visitors from Greenland) were examined. Twelve had been shot, and 10 died from various other injuries; in 13, lesions caused by *Capillaria contorta,* which affects the alimentary tract, were so pronounced that this disease was considered the cause of death. It had affected both sexes in their 1st year as well as older birds (Clausen and Gudmundsson 1981), and it affects nestlings. Various slight physical impairments of some fall passage Juv. birds in Greenland were described by Mattox (1969), who concluded that the percentage of Gyrs surviving their 1st year "must be rather low."   RALPH S. PALMER

HABITS   The Gyr is the largest and most powerful extant falcon. It hunts near the ground and is an arctic derivative of the same stock as the Prairie Falcon and other large desert and grassland species. From above and behind, it strikes a killing or disabling blow, flies past, and on the return pass at lower speed it grips the victim in its talons and bites the neck at the base of the skull. Its tactic is one of surprise at very close range, and if its first strike fails, it continues pursuit with great persistence. It is less maneuverable than the Peregrine at high speed, but Cade (1960) stated that it is far superior in both speed and strength. It saves energy by using air currents, such as updrafts at cliff aeries, and (Jenkins, in Ladd and Schempf 1982) it obtains aerodynamic advantages from flying close to the ground. The usual hunting pattern varies. Thus the quarry may be hit in the air (over land or water), and the Gyr will bind to it and carry it to a plucking site; if prey is hit on the ground, it is sometimes fed on there, but it is frequently transported to an elevated spot, killed by the usual neck bite (if not previously), more or less plucked, and more or less eaten. During the breeding season, at least, the head is removed (the ♂ often eats it) in addition to more or less feathering (or fur), before transportation near or to the breeding site; therefore, the roughage that is ejected there as pellets generally does not contain heads.

Where a Gyr has fed, such as on ptarmigan, feathers are scattered about; the long bones are pulled from the joints, the "shoulders" (coracoids) may be broken and partly eaten, and the "keel" of the sternum is bitten and broken (Dementiev and Gortchakovskaya 1965, Bengtson 1971). Such are the indications that the kill was made by a Gyr.

Only rarely is a raptor reported carrying a prey in each foot at the same time. In Greenland, Holbøll (1842–1843) saw a Gyr carrying 2 young Black-legged Kittiwakes (*Rissa tridactyla*) and, another time, 2 Purple Sandpipers (*Calidris maritima*).

Perch-hunting and contouring   May be employed separately or be combined. The Gyr temporarily uses an elevated perch, such as a rock, knoll, or low tree; it then crosses an intervening open area (such as a valley or swamp), then hunts, usually within 2 m. of the ground, up and over the next ridge where plant growth is low or sparse. In this fashion it comes suddenly on its quarry, accelerates and rises slightly if necessary, then strikes downward. There are, of course, all manner of variants. For example, it may use a succession of high perches, scanning the landscape from each in turn, between hunting flights. Like the Prairie Falcon and Golden Eagle, more prey is commonly taken from the ground (ground squirrels, some ptarmigan, lemmings, etc.)

than in the air. For further details, see especially White and Weeden (1966) for Alaska and Bengtson (1971) for Iceland.

In the Commander Is., the Gyr successfully uses a variant of contouring to capture Harlequin Ducks (*Histrionicus*) during storms. The ducks fly close to the water; the Gyr, shielded more or less by breaking waves, comes on its quarry suddenly and seizes it before it can drop into the sea (Marakov 1966).

Because of the contouring habit, Gyrs were trained by falconers to hunt hares, and presumably wild Gyrs take the arctic hare in similar fashion. Gyrs are also said to hunt tree squirrels (Dementiev 1960), but no method is described.

Soaring and quartering On leaving a perch or the aerie (or when a trained bird is cast from the fist), the Gyr does not ascend in spirals but typically takes a more or less straight upward-angled course—thus differing from the Peregrine. It goes up several hundred ft., sometimes even out of sight, then may circle or soar and drift away. From evidence at hand, wild Gyrs have been seen to stoop from a soar rather rarely, yet some trained birds are said to "take a high pitch" as Peregrines do.

It is well known that Gyrs in their 1st autumn, being inexperienced and not yet fully coordinated, are awkward hunters, largely dependent on easily gotten quarry such as lemmings. Mattox (1969) thought that Juv. "white" Gyrs in Greenland were at a disadvantage while the ground is bare but had an advantage over darker birds after snowfall.

Using a beater such as a large mammal Undoubtedly more common than real-ized. In winter in Alaska, a pair fed on ptarmigan, killed the few Mallards at an unfrozen groundwater spring, and often followed a trapper to take ptarmigan that he flushed when tending his trapline (Bente 1981). In B.C., one seized a Mallard that a hunter had just dropped (McIlwraith, in A. K. Fisher 1893), perhaps having awaited this opportunity. The Gyr is widely claimed to be curious toward persons, on the Alaskan Arctic Slope (J. W. Bee 1958) often hovering 30 ft. overhead. In all probability, the Gyr is expecting prey to be flushed.

Prey size Trained Gyrs were flown at such outsized quarry as storks, cranes, herons, kites, and buzzards (*Buteo*), and, since wild Gyrs attack eagles with fury, F. Beebe (1974) suggested that this animosity is transferred to these other eagle-sized birds, which are attacked with more fierceness than necessary. Known avian prey in the wild ranges from a small goose and various ducks down to such small species as longspurs and redpolls. Mammals range from the arctic hare (although adults are too heavy to transport except piecemeal) down to voles (*Microtus*). Even shrews in Kam-chatka (Dementiev 1960). Although it has been stated that the Gyr can transport up to 1,800 gm. (Kokhanov 1970, Pulliainen 1975), this equals the wt. of a heavy ♀ Gyr and is more than twice that of a large ptarmigan, so this wt. certainly could not be moved very far. An instance of a Gyr striking a swan in Iceland may have been "panic hunger"—a futile attack by an inexperienced young bird.

Food consumption About 250 gm. of meat per day plus, at intervals, unplucked birds, are needed (Dementiev 1960), which is roughly the equivalent of the difference in wt. of a hungry and a gorged bird (see earlier in this account). If ptarmigan are the sole prey, parents and brood need some 200 to support them May–Aug. (Cade 1960). The Gyr probably does not hunt every day; it may also feed on the same quarry (or carrion) repeatedly. Whether it caches food in other than the breeding season remains unknown. It can fast for a week.

Pellet size   Varies depending on what is ingested; shape is approximately oval. In Norway, length 42–101 mm. and breadth 17–34, av. 61 × 23 mm. (Hagen 1952b); in Murman, length varied 30–70 mm., and breadth was about 30 mm. (Dementiev and Gortschakovskaya 1945). They are larger than the Peregrine's. They may be mistaken for the castings of large gulls or N. Ravens ("Lewis" 1938).

Bathing/drinking   Gyrs bathe, as do Peregrines, and in winter take snow baths (Waller 1939, Cade 1960). In sw. Greenland a ♀ glided to a lakeshore, hopped out on a rock before stepping into the water, and drank before bathing—as captives do (Jenkins, in Ladd and Schempf 1982).

Curiosity and unwariness   Particularly of Juv. birds in fall, often reported (and see using a beater, above). There are reports of various numbers Gyrs, mostly young birds, perched at the same time on radio antennas and other wires at n. weather stations in Canada, Greenland, and elsewhere. In Greenland, 100s were formerly shot wantonly in such circumstances; fortunately some Gyrs were salvaged for the great collection of Gyrs in the University Museum in Copenhagen. In interior Ungava in fall, they were "extremely curious," often perching on antennas (Clement 1949). In winter in Siberia, the Gyr frequently stays near towns, where it preys on pigeons and crows (Johansen 1957).

Play   An unconfined hand-reared young bird, judged from size to be a ♀, made repeated mock attacks on inanimate objects such as low bushes, clumps of grass, clods of dirt, conspicuous stumps, and so on. When she broke a branch from a bush, she carried it away while making high-pitched screams. She would strike a clump of grass with both feet, tussle with it, go through the motions of breaking the neck or biting the head, and then mantle over it in the usual falcon fashion. In aerial confrontation with a smaller (presumed ♂) Gyr, neither struck nor seemed to want to strike the other. Both were very vocal, and the larger drove the smaller bird away. For mock attacks on other birds, including raptors, and further details, see Cade (1953).

Adaptations for survival   In the Moscow Zoo a Gyr often remained for long periods of time in prostrate position, breast and belly in the snow, even to temperatures of −40°C under open sky (Dementiev 1960).

The following is from F. Beebe (1974), an experienced falconer: The hind toe of the Gyr can be rotated inwardly so that it points forward, parallel with the others. This enables the bird to lie on its breast with its feet flat underneath it. When it is sleeping in this posture is it completely relaxed, the wings hang loosely, the head rolls forward and partly to one side, resting on the ground (snow?). The bird appears to be dead and can often be touched before it will rouse. Beebe inferred that the reversible toe and profound sleep in prone posture may be adaptations for periods of quiescence with moderately slowed metabolic rate, probably under snow during blizzards "when activity is impossible and exposure probably fatal." The existence of a parallel adaptation in another raptor is indicated by the sequential photographs (Trimm 1985) of a Snowy Owl facing a blizzard and flattening facedown in the snow. (For an interesting study of the sleep of a ♀ Gyr at an aerie, see Jenkins, in Ladd and Schempf (1982).

Some history   At least since the heyday of falconry in Europe and Britain, the

Peregrine, being the "glamour bird" in the Western world, has tended to eclipse the Gyr as the raptor of highest esteem from centuries earlier—and still today in some parts of the world. In March 1276, Kublai Khan headed s. from Peking accompanied by 10,000 mounted falconers with 500 Gyrfalcons and Peregrines, Sakers, Goshawks, and others. They had eagles to hunt hares, wild goats, roe deer, and other quarry. At the time of the 1st hunt witnessed and described by Marco Polo, Kublai Khan was a gout-ridden man of 60; rather than wear himself out on horseback, he traveled primarily in a "beautiful wooden room" supported by 4 elephants. Noblemen who rode alongside him called out when they saw cranes overhead. Then the roof covering would be removed immediately so that the khan, reclining on a couch, could watch the cranes and the Gyrs loosed to strike them down. Attached to their feet, hunting birds had small silver markers that bore the names of the owners and persons in charge. A retrieved lost hunting bird was taken to an appointed official, who flew his ensign conspicuously and who kept lost property until claimed. Of the many accounts published of Marco Polo's travels, the source here is "The Khan Goes Hunting," in R. P. Lister (1976).

More remarkable in the annals of the Gyr are the 13th-century writings of Emperor Frederick II of Hohenstaufen, *De Arte Venandi cum Avibus* (*The Art of Falconry*), concluded (but never completed) by A.D. 1248. A scholar, scientist, traveler, soldier, and founder of the University of Naples (1224), Frederick was interested in everything concerning falconry. He treated it as science, and today it is shattering to think that something is new and then find that it has been a matter of record of 700 years. Although variously published in the past, the reader is referred to the definitive, annotated, illustrated English translation, based on MSS at the University of Bologna and the Vatican, by Casey Wood and Margery Fyfe (1943, reissued 1961, reprinted 1969). The book concludes with an annotated bibliography of ancient, medieval, and modern falconry (a reappraisal and extension of Harting 1891) and a glossary of falconers' terms.

A surprising amount of the long history of the Gyr in different parts of the world, but especially Czarist Russia, makes up text and illus. of a monograph by G. P. Dementiev (1951). It was updated in a 1960 German version, which, in turn, was rendered into English for limited distribution.

Without going into a host of details or examples, it should be explained that the "white" Gyr, by some standards the most beautiful of all hunting birds, long had great monetary values—literally, a king's ransom. An expedition to e. Greenland to get such birds was dangerous and very costly, yet it was a part of the annual trade of n. Europe all through medieval history. Gyrs had an important role in European and Asian diplomacy, as gifts of exchange, "which not infrequently contributed to the successful conclusion of negotiations or even the forming of alliances" (Dementiev, trans.). So much for the past. The Gyr, not necessarily "white," remains in favor and the demand for it, especially by persons of wealth in the Middle East, has had international repercussions.

Patron Saint   Although St. Hubert is usually mentioned, Dementiev (1960) added St. Bavon, a falconer who lived in Flanders.

Numbers   The following is partly from Cade (1960), who discussed the subject for the entire panboreal range of the Gyr. Assuming a possible breeding range of 15–17 million sq. km. (5.7–6.5 million sq. mi.) of arctic and subarctic lands and an av. density of a pair of Gyrs/1,000 sq. km., there are some 15,000–17,000 pairs or, reducing this by half, 7,000–9,000 pairs.

The numbers of breeders on the arctic slope of Alaska must fluctuate around 100 pairs, or about 1 pair/1,300 sq. km. (500 sq. mi.). On the Seward Pen., Alaska, on a 44,000 sq. km. (17,000 sq. mi.) study area, in 1968–1972 there was an av. of 48 breeding pairs the 1st 3 years, 13 in 1971 (a poor year), and 36 in 1972 (Swartz et al. 1973, or see Cade 1982). The best areas contained a pair/69 sq. mi., and for the entire peninsula, the av. density in good years was estimated at 70 breeding pairs (1 pair/917 sq. km., or 353 sq. mi.) (Roseneau 1972). For all of Alaska, 300 breeding pairs is a minimum estimate and more likely fluctuates around 500 (Cade 1982).

Most of the world's higharctic land is in Canada and Greenland. Gyr numbers are evidently low except in ne. Greenland; in the Canadian sector large areas may lack acceptable sites for aeries.

In Greenland, the ice-free area is about 341,700 sq. km., with indication of Gyr density of 1 breeding pair/1,000 sq. km. or less, being higher in good food years. Evidently some local concentrations exist. Cade (1960) calculated the number of breeding pairs as not less than 500 and possibly as high as 1,000, while Mattox (1970) calculated "about 855 pairs."

Most of the wide coastal area of Yukon Terr., Canada, has been searched systematically for Gyr aeries, with a minimum number of 95, or 1 pair/180 sq. km. (71 sq. mi.). When all has been searched (it probably has already), the figure is not expected to rise much above 100, or 1 pair/175 sq. km. (65 sq. mi.) (Mossop and Hayes, in Ladd and Schempf 1982).

For Iceland, where the Gyr is the national bird, possibly 300–400 pairs breed in a good year, or 1 pair/about 150–300 sq. km. of usable terrain (Cade 1982). This is an upward revision of earlier estimates of around 200 pairs.

Little is known about Gyr numbers in Eurasia. Presently, therefore, in good years the best habitat on the Seward Pen. of Alaska, Yukon Terr. in Canada, and parts of Iceland, have the highest known densities of breeding Gyrfalcons—except a very local situation once in n. Sweden (see Reproduction, above).

The Gyr has lost some breeding stations to human encroachment. There are indications that, over a period perhaps of centuries, 100–200 mostly young birds were shipped out of Iceland annually for falconry. Yet there is no evidence that this had any depressing effect on the number of breeders (Cade 1968). Although that absolves falconers, it does not include the taking of eggs and young and the shooting that slowed down but did not cease when the bird received legal protection beginning in 1940. Currently, in good food years, the number of breeding Gyrs in Iceland must be at about the saturation level.

It is concluded (Cade 1982) that there is no evidence for or against long-term change in the number of Gyrfalcons; furthermore, perhaps they have increased somewhat in part of nw. N. Am. in recent decades.

Pollutants From material collected in 1970 and 1971 on the Seward Pen., Alaska, it was found that the Gyrs contained low levels of industrial pollutants. Apparently this contamination was acquired from eating migratory birds, which, in turn, had ingested them when away from Alaska; there was no significant thinning of eggshells (W. Walker 1977). This holds for N. Am. and Greenland, where the population appears to be stable (Burnham and Mattox 1984).

Controlled harvest One means of trying to curtail the illegal taking of Gyrs (such as for breeding stock and, ultimately, for sale principally to the Arab world) is a governmentally controlled harvest on a sustained yield basis. Fundamental work on this has been done in NWT, Canada. Some captive breeding projects are already putting falcons on the world market (principally in the Middle East), and the assumption is that uncontrolled taking of wild stock will decline as these projects succeed. (From Mossop and Hayes, in Ladd and Schempf 1982.) Yet climatically better-adjusted birds (hybrids?) having some Gyr characteristics would be preferable.

Captivity As F. Beebe (1974) pointed out, the Gyr has monetary value and is a status symbol. (It also has legal protection.) Among raptorial birds, it is the most responsive to human attention. Whether taken from the nest or captured afterwards, it forms an "almost doglike attachment" to its trainer. It is so fearless and responsive that a proper falconer can have a wild-caught bird flying at quarry within a week.

RALPH S. PALMER

FOOD Principally N. Am. and Greenland data. Wild birds and mammals; occasionally domestic fowl; some carrion. The close tie to ptarmigan (*Lagopus*) species is so evident and frequently discussed that this tends to overshadow the fact that the Gyr is a generalist from necessity when its usual prey is scarce. Most of its principal prey, except seabirds, fluctuates violently in numbers (and some more or less synchronously). Thus the total number of species taken in an area can be impressive, for example: Kola Pen., USSR—although birds made up 93% by wt. (about 68% *Lagopus*), some 50 species of mammals plus birds plus other animals were recorded (Kistschinskii 1958); Seward Pen., Alaska—remains identifiable in castings included at least 6 mammal and 33 bird species (Roseneau 1972); see also long discussion in Cade (1960).

Most reports are of food in the breeding season (and some prey may be carried away or cached, hence not included); rather little is known for most regions in other seasons.

South of usual winter range In s. Canada and n. U.S. has attacked turkeys and preyed on domestic fowl, Sharp-tailed Grouse, Black Duck, and rats (A. K. Fisher 1893, A. W. Schorger MS). Has also taken, and seems to prefer, Rock Doves.

The following is given to indicate known foods in usual range and mostly from N. Am.:

BERING I. (Commander group) In 4 digestive tracts in winter, "field mice" (the introduced *Clethrionomys rutilus*) and a gull (Stejneger 1885). (The Rock Ptarmigan [*Lagopus mutus*] breeds there.)

AMCHITKA I. (Aleutians) Rats (*Rattus*) in digestive tracts (Kenyon 1961).

ST. GEORGE I. (Pribilofs) In digestive tracts, Rosy Finches (*Leucosticte*) and Snow Buntings (*Plectrophenax*). (In season, there are millions of seabirds.)

SEWARD PEN., ALASKA From castings in summer, preponderant among mammals were ground squirrels (*Spermophilus parryii*), red-backed voles (*Clethrionomys*) and varying lemmings (*Dicrostonyx*). Many bird species, in size from a Brant (*Branta bernicla*) down to a Redpoll (*Carduelis*), including waterfowl, ptarmigan, shorebirds, seabirds, Short-eared Owl (*Asio flammeus*), and various songbirds. The list included 876 Willow and Rock Ptarmigan (*Lagopus lagopus* and *L. mutus*), 155 Long-tailed Jaegers (*Stercorarius longicaudus*), 30 Golden Plovers (*Pluvialis*), and 12 Short-eared Owls (Roseneau 1972).

ALASKAN ARCTIC SLOPE   Voles, lemmings, ground squirrels, many species of birds, but ptarmigan by far the most frequent in pellets (Cade 1960, White and Cade 1971).

ALASKA   Near Hooper Bay, at an aerie in summer, anatids, gulls, various shorebirds, Savannah Sparrow (*Passerculus sandwichensis*), and Redpoll (White and Springer 1965).

LOWARCTIC AND SUBARCTIC CANADA   Depending on local availability, a variety of prey species at a few scattered aeries, but ptarmigan frequently. On the s. side of Hudson Strait at Digges Sd., there are huge Murre (*Uria lomvia*) colonies, and this species is perhaps the exclusive food in season (Gaston et al. 1985).

HIGHARCTIC CIRCUMBOREAL   A pair in interior Ellesmere was raising a brood entirely on Snow Buntings (Parmelee and MacDonald 1960). Major higharctic papers were listed by Muir and Bird (1984), and these authors observed an aerie in w.-cent. Ellesmere in 1973. Few bird and mammal species were available; by wt, the bulk of prey was young and older arctic hares (*Lepus timidus*); many varying lemmings were taken. They pointed out that seabird colonies are few and scattered in the higharctic, that ptarmigan numbers have not been reported to exceed comparatively low population levels there, and that the hare was a more dependable food source. (There are substantial numbers of ptarmigan some years, but, as far as the Gyr is concerned, when they are scarce they might as well be nonexistant.)

N. AND E. GREENLAND   Varying lemmings, when common, may be the sole food in autumn (Salomonsen 1951); in summer, a large number of stomachs of Juv. Gyrs contained lemmings and a single ptarmigan; inexperienced young Gyrs seldom capture prey more difficult to take than lemmings (C. and E. Bird 1941). (Varying lemmings occur there, but not in w. Greenland.) The fluctuating numbers of arctic hare probably provide the bulk of the food in the breeding season (or longer) in various years.

SW. GREENLAND   Jenkins (in Ladd and Schempf 1982) listed food in the breeding season as young arctic hares and flightless young Lapland Longspurs (*Calcarius lapponicus*); at an inland location when ptarmigan were scarce, at an aerie where 4 young Gyrs were raised, prey remains were almost totally the feathers of small birds; passerines were present in the vicinity in above-av. density (Burnham and Mattox 1984). Various Greenland Gyr aeries are at or close to seabird colonies.

ICELAND   Rock Ptarmigan are the mainstay inland (see, for example, Suetens and Groenendal 1976), but the list of prey depends on locality and season. The unfinished study by the late Finnur Gudmundsson was done on the 800-ha. is. of Hrisey in Eyafjord. There are no terrestrial predators, and the Gyr is the only avian one. Its staple diet is Rock Ptarmigan, and Gyr numbers fluctuate with the ptarmigan—in years of ptarmigan scarcity, many Gyrs do not breed (Gudmundsson 1970, Wynne-Edwards 1981).

CONTINENTAL EUROPE and ASIA   Omitted here, although very important work on ptarmigan/Gyr biology has been done in Norway.

Raptors as food   Aside from striking or killing other raptors in territorial defense, the Gyr has fed on at least the following: N. Harrier, Rough-legged Hawk, and numerous Short-eared Owls. In Alaska lemmings and voles attract the Short-eared Owl, which, in turn, is taken by the Gyr; 3 adult owls were brought to an aerie in less than 24 hrs. (Cade 1960).

Carrion and immobilized prey   The latter includes ptarmigan entangled in snares set by Inuit children; furbearers caught in traps; various dead mammals, probably when normal prey is scarce. In Iceland: eyes of the heads of slaughtered sheep (Timmermann 1949); in Feb., 5 Gyrs seen feeding on dead codfish on the same day (in Cade 1960); in early June, a recently shot Glaucous Gull (*Larus hyperboreus*) (R. Palmer).

RALPH S. PALMER

PRAIRIE FALCON

Falco mexicanus Schlegel

Fairly large falcon, nearly of Peregrine size. Coloration mostly gray-browns dorsally; crown streaked; narrow black "mustache" mark; underparts whitish to creamy-buff with variable amount of dark markings, the flanks barred in Basic feathering; underwing with black extending from body out at least to beyond axillars, but varying with individual to extending beyond to bend of wing (almost all of lining). Sexes similar. Juvenal darker above than Basic, underparts more buffy and with more dark markings, the flanks streaked; tail barring more extensive and/or evident. Basic I is more completely bar tailed and more blue backed than later Basics.

These are useful diagnostic features of bird in hand when comparing with our other falcons: feathering very compact; outer toe (minus talon) slightly longer than inner; tarsus much longer than middle toe minus talon and less than upper ½ feathered with inner side almost naked; 2d primary from outer longest, or 2d and 3d about equal, as are 1st and 4th; the 2 outermost emarginated on inner web, and 2d and 3d with outer web narrowed; tail more than ½ length of wing chord and slightly rounded.

There is no overlap in size and wt. between larger ♀ and smaller ♂. Combined: length about 14½–18½ in. (37–47 cm.), wingspread 35–43 in. (89–119 cm.). Average wt. of ♂ about 20 oz. (570 gm.) and ♀ about 28½ (810 gm.).

No subspecies, but note under affinities, below.

NOTE **Type locality** "Mexico" (Schlegel 1850), "Monterrey, Mexico" (Schlegel 1862), and "Mexico = Monterrey" (Swann 1922), these from Friedmann (1950). It was "Mexico" in the 3d, 4th, and 5th editions of the AOU *Check-list*, then "Mexico = Monterrey, Nuevo León" in the 6th edition. The collector, Deppe, apparently never was in Nuevo León. In 1848 (after Deppe's time) California was ceded to the U.S. by

Mexico, and Stresemann (1954) stated that Deppe had "collected a number of interesting birds near Monterey, California." The type locality is not Monterrey (which is in Nuevo León), but Monterey, which is in California (formerly a part of Mexico).

DESCRIPTION   One Plumage/cycle with Basic II earliest definitive. There may be slight av. differences in the sexes in coloring or pattern, as distinctness of dorsal barring, but no useful information at hand.

▶♂ ♀ Def. Basic Plumage (entire feathering), renewed by molt of all feathering in warmer months. **Beak** bluish with dark tip, cere and eyelid yellow, **iris** very dark brownish. Head top variably gray-brown streaked dusky; part of cheek very pale (as throat) with conspicuous narrow black "mustache" mark from below forward edge of eye down side of chin. Many feathers of the **dorsum** and upper wing coverts light tan, internally patterned with large transverse dark brownish to sooty areas, and with pale tan margins, the general effect varying with individual from tan to rusty-brownish or same with bluish cast (more evident in Basic I). **Underparts** whitish or somewhat buffy, the breast light; going posteriorly, there is usually an increase in number of blackish spots, generally much enlarged and transverse along the sides, alos more or less on the flanks. Legs and **feet** yellow, talons black. **Tail** dorsally varies from grayish toward rusty (generally a pronounced brownish cast) with about 10 narrow dusky bars (often not complete across middle pair of feathers, but nearly always in Basic I—see below), and very tip white. Flight feathers of **wing** very dark with light tan to orange-rusty bars; underwing varies with individual from mostly light with black axillars and some adjoining feathers to same extending from body outward to include almost all coverts.

Prebasic II and later Prebasics—Colo. data (Enderson 1964). **Molting** "adults" trapped at aeries and postbreeding: molting begins "near early May" with wing, then body, then tail, with overlapping timing. Primaries, beginning late May–early June, are renewed in this sequence: 5 birds dropped #4 (counting from inner) first and 1 dropped #5; usual sequence was #4 5 6 3 7 2 1 9 10, with these exceptions—1 before 8, 8 before 2, 9 before 8, and 8 before 1. Primary #10 (outer) was last in 15 individuals for which it could be determined. Tail feathers (beginning about mid-June) begin to drop in this sequence: #1 (of central pair), #2 6 3 4 5 with no observed variability (the sequence as Gyr, not Peregrine). Body feathering is renewed late June into Oct. All new flight feathers are grown by early Oct. There was individual difference of up to 3–4 weeks in progress of molting.

AT HATCHING   The down is white; see also Reproduction, below.

▶♂ ♀ Juv. Plumage (entire feathering) fully developed at about 40 days posthatching and retained about a year. At first the **beak** is bluish with dusky tip, cere and eye-ring pale bluish, **iris** very dark. Feathering is somewhat softer than in Basics, pattern much the same but differs thus: pale **stripe over eye** often more prominent; crown and **dorsum** darker, more or less toward sooty; individual feathers tend to be plain dark internally (not clearly patterned) and narrowly edged medium brownish (it may wear off); **underparts** typically white on chin–throat and remainder toward a brownish buffy; there tend to be more dark markings, numerous even on upper breast, and larger (tend to coalesce into blackish area on sides); flanks heavily streaked. **Tail** darker

408

dorsally, the barring sometimes narrower and/or more numerous, and complete across all feathers except central pair, the tip white. Legs and **feet** pale bluish at first, talons black. Cere, eye ring, lores, and feet tend toward yellow while Juv. feathering is worn but (H. Webster 1944) still lack "adult" coloring. **Wing** about as Basic, with less patterned upper coverts.

Prebasic I molting (out of Juv.) begins much earlier in the year than later Prebasics (Enderson 1964).

▶ ♂ ♀ Basic I Plumage (entire feathering) acquired beginning in spring of 2d calendar year of life and retained about a year. Differs from later Basics mainly as follows: **head** superciliary line has brownish streaks; **dorsum** (especially of ♂ ♂) has slaty-bluish cast, the scapulars 4 or 5 dark bars; **tail** all feathers, including central pair, barred on both webs. This is the bluish-backed, barred-tailed "immature" of Friedmann (1950); the bluish persists to some extent in later Basics, where largely confined to ♂ ♂.

Color phases None. Bent (1938) stated that "adults" were of light and dark phases plus intermediates. H. Webster (1944) mentioned "very dark individuals" nearly impossible to distinguish from young Peregrines, which he saw in migrations. There is some individual variation, but the dark-appearing birds are 1st-fall young.

A cream-colored ♂ having some darkish markings, photographed in Weld Co., Colo., in 1931, was seen there for 9 years; the photograph appeared in A. Bailey and Niedrach (1933), pl. 10 in Bent (1938), and in H. Webster (1944).

Measurements Specimens from widely scattered parts of the range: 17 ♂ BEAK from cere 18–20 mm., av. 18.8, WING across chord 289–313, av. 299.4; and 18 ♀ BEAK from cere 20.5–26 mm., av. 22.2, and WING across chord 331–357, av. 342.8 (Freidmann 1950).

Weight Live "adults" with empty crops in Colo. in summer–fall: 15 ♂ 500–635 gm., av. 554, and 31 ♀ 760–975, av. 863; Juv.; 5 ♂ 515–570 gm., av. 539, and 12 ♀ 675–925, av. 824 (Enderson 1964).

These figures are the means (data probably from museum labels): 10 ♂ 495.7 gm., and 34 ♀ 810 (N. Snyder and Wiley 1976).

Live "adults" in sw. Idaho, dates and spreads not given; mean figures were 195 ♂ 570 gm., and 172 ♀ 810 (Steenhof 1983).

Hybrids In the wild in Sask. in 1985 a ♀ that had been released from captivity mated with a ♂ Peregrine that was captive-hatched in 1980 and released; they had 2 young in June (L. Oliphant). Effect of captive conditioning is unknown. (For 1986, see also Peregrine species account.)

The Prairie Falcon has bred in captivity, as has its captive-reared offspring. It can be crossed with other falcons by artificial means, but there is no available inclusive source of data on this subject. The technique of artificial insemination was described by L. Boyd et al. (1977). The usual goal, presumably, is to develop a stock having especially desirable characteristics for falconry, and commonest crosses have been with the Peregrine (either sex can be either parent). First generation hybrids vary from more or less resembling either parent species to birds almost exactly intermediate (a 4-egg clutch produced young resembling each parent plus 2 intermediate). An example of artificial crossing from the literature (I. Newton 1979): ♂ Shahin (Old World desert race of Peregrine) with ♀ Prairie Falcon, this hybrid then crossed with ♀ Merlin.

Details of parentage and sex and characteristics of crosses, back crosses, and so on, should be a matter of record, required internationally so far as possible, and such birds should wear distinctive permanent labeling.

Prairie Falcons have been fostered by the Peregrine and by Swainson's, Red-tailed, and Ferruginous Hawks (Olendorff et al. 1980).

Geographical variation   None (Browning 1978).

Affinities   The Prairie Falcon, a N. Am. inhabitant of arid lands, is apparently derived from the same ancestral stock as the Laggar Falcon (*F. jugger*) of s. Asia; it may have arrived during an interglacial, its known presence here dating back at least some 40,000 years. Friedmann (1950) was reluctant to maintain the Prairie as specifically distinct from the Laggar; he noted also that Prairie and Lanner (*F. biarmicus* of the Middle East and arid parts of Africa) ♂ ♂ are close except for head coloration. G. P. Dementiev, a lifelong raptor student (in Dementiev and Gladkov 1951, trans. 1966), regarded the Saker (*F. cherrug* of e. Asia and nw. Africa), the Laggar, and Prairie Falcon as "extremely closely allied," needing more study to determine their relative status. Speculation continues, and their treatment as species continues, as in L. Brown and Amadon (1968 **2**). Saker and Prairie Falcon seem less different (a subjective estimate) than do some recognized subspecies of Peregrine.   RALPH S. PALMER

FIELD IDENTIFICATION   Quite sizable pointed-winged falcon, length about 18 in., shape a bit more trim than the approximately similar-sized Peregrine—each can be mistaken for the other at a distance. Variably tan dorsally in all ages; the black facial "mustache" mark is about ½ as wide as when narrowest in the Peregrine. Tail proportionately longer and more squarish. Flight more buoyant and dashing (less heavy and direct). A notable field character of the Prairie is the black patch in underwing, extending from the body outward to an extent that varies with individual (Peregrine's underwing may appear dusky, not partly black).

Hardly to be confused with the larger Gyr and smaller Merlin, which also differ in pattern, coloring, and habitat. A possibility would be confusion with an escaped hybrid of more or less Prairie Falcon derivation or with some escaped imported Old World falcon (see affinities, above).

As with some other falcons (including Peregrine), whereabouts may be indicated by splashes of droppings below recesses in cliffs (aeries), on rock outcrops, and beneath other perch sites. At aeries, the ♂ is "less slim" than the ♀, is smaller, and has a relatively large head (Enderson 1964).   RALPH S. PALMER

VOICE   The usual alarm call is a series of *kik* notes, by both sexes, that varies somewhat in length and in rate of utterance. J. G. Tyler (1923) thought that there might be a sex difference in voice, some ♀ ♀ having "harsh cackling voices," ♂ ♂ having "rather pleasing high-pitched whistling calls." Other older literature uses such descriptive words as screaming, whining, yelping, whistling, screeching, cackling, and so on. Birds at an aerie can be very noisy; when not nesting they are usually silent.

Wrege and Cade (1977) studied displays and voices of 4 species of falcons in captivity but did not analyze their limited data on the Prairie Falcon. At least 75% of postures and displays were common to all (Gyr, Lanner, Prairie Falcon, Peregrine), and voices

410

were similar in basic structure and function. Structures of some vocalizations of Peregrines and Prairie Falcons are more complex than in the other species, and variability is in "degree of completeness of the basic unit and is associated with the motivational level of intensity of the behavior, not with specific contexts." In the Prairie Falcon, as intensity of motivation increases, "the sound unit is fragmented, with some parts repeated before a new unit is initiated." RALPH S. PALMER

HABITAT   Arid lands primarily. A cold-hardy and heat-tolerant raptor. Habitat includes vast deserts—Great Basin, Mojave, Sonoran, and Chihuahuan—and foothills and mountain valleys therein and elsewhere; also some semiforested areas plus plains and prairies, especially where there are rocky elevations or eroded banks of watercourses. Not an obligate breeder near water, hence uses areas unsuited to the Peregrine. A few breed high up in alpine areas and many hunt there in late summer–autumn. In winter much more frequent e. on the prairies to well into the Mississippi drainage, but present also in such desert areas as Death Valley. There is a correlation of winter wheat fields (agricultural land) with Horned Larks (foraging birds) and Prairie Falcon (it feeds on the larks).

Generally absent from forest, except overhead in passage; evidently nowhere a coastal dweller or traveler (as is the Peregrine). RALPH S. PALMER

DISTRIBUTION   (See map.) As a **breeder,** widespread from s. areas in w. Canada down into Mexico (where evidently rare); there is current hearsay evidence that this falcon breeds well down into Mexico, this from persons seeking Peregrines—that is, have little interest in any other species. Within its total range there are sizable areas

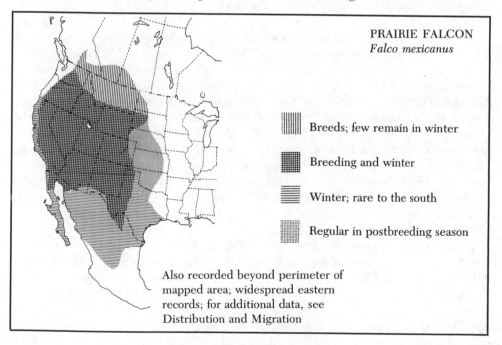

PRAIRIE FALCON
Falco mexicanus

▥ Breeds; few remain in winter

▦ Breeding and winter

▤ Winter; rare to the south

▨ Regular in postbreeding season

Also recorded beyond perimeter of
mapped area; widespread eastern
records; for additional data, see
Distribution and Migration

411

where the bird is absent or local because of human activity and ecological conditions. There are a few breeding records in the alpine zone, in Colo. (Marti and Braun 1975) to 3,688 m. elevation. Recorded breeding once long ago at Maryville in nw. Mo. (Goss 1891).

Late summer/fall Birds of breeding age evidently are not given to straggling any distance n. of known breeding places, but the young do this regularly, which extends known occurrence somewhat in Canada.

In winter some remain even at upper limits of breeding; others travel s. or se., so that rather few remain above the lat. of the Oreg.-Calif. boundary (42°N) except in Wash., Oreg., and a considerable number in s. Idaho. This is the season of occurrence out onto the plains and prairies to the se., limits of regular occurrence then being about to the e. ⅕ of Kans. and thence through w. Tex. This seasonal spread also includes fairly regular occurrence in such states as Minn., Mo., and Ill. Farther se. there are some scattered records into the Carolinas and down to the gulf coast—probably both natural occurrence and escapees.

Winter Southernmost records are in Mexico: Baja Calif., Sonora, Durango, across to include Tamaulipas, and reportedly seen in Veracruz.

Salt water Rare, a Dec. record for the Farallons (Calif.) and a few others for is. in and near Baja Calif.

Reintroduced There have been a few local reintroductions, by placing young in aeries or nests of other raptors, in Canada and the U.S. (at least Calif.). Range was extended in Canada along the n. Saskatchewan R. near where this falcon was fostered by 2 *Buteo* species (Olendorff et al. 1980).

History and prehistory The nearly cosmopolitan Peregrine has a N. Am. breeding range that completely encompasses that of the Prairie Falcon geographically but not ecologically. The fossil record suggests that both were rather widely distributed in the West during the late Pleistocene, the oldest applicable radiocarbon dating being 40,000± years of age for fossil wood in a pit in the Los Angeles area that also contained both of these falcons. Based on radiocarbon-dated material from 33,000 years BP. which included a bone from a young bird probably reared nearby (Brodkorb and Phillips 1970), it then bred in the Valley of Mexico. For summary of Pleistocene and later records, including much information relating specifically to environmental changes in Utah, see Porter and White (1973). After the Pleistocene, relative distribution and numbers of the 2 falcons were probably much the same as historically. That is, occurrence of one has not excluded the other, although the Prairie Falcon appears to have a marked advantage, for several reasons, in arid environments. It is reasonable to assume that, for a very long time down to the present, climatic shifts from cooler and wetter to warmer and drier have favored the Prairie Falcon and the opposite the Peregrine (Porter and White).

Recorded as **fossil** from the Pleistocene of Calif. (2 sites), Nev., N.Mex. (3), Tex., and Nuevo León in Mexico; and from **prehistoric sites** in Oreg., Calif. (2), Utah (2), Ariz. (2), Idaho, and S.D. (3)—based on Brodkorb (1964) with additions.

RALPH S. PALMER

MIGRATION From upper limits of breeding range in s. Canada to a considerable but unknown distance s., some birds of breeding age remain locally around the year;

others, plus the young, migrate. In warm parts of the range, seasonal travel any distance perhaps is primarily by prebreeders, if there is adequate year-round food locally for the birds that have established breeding territories. Young Prairie Falcons subsequently return to establish territories close to where they were reared.

Post nesting through winter   Data from 3 papers are given here. The 1st gives timing of movements plus some data on age and sex ratios of winterers; the other 2 pertain primarily to timing of movements and distances covered. All 3 are from within a rather limited portion of the breeding range.

N.-CENT. UTAH   Migrant falcons usually arrive in the valleys in late Oct., and the species remains through Mar., feeding on grassland birds. A few, however, are resident near aeries (theirs, presumably); most are transient. Although trapping and observing methods were not uniform, total captured in 3 winters were: "immatures" 23 ♀ and 2 ♂ and "adults" 9 ♂ and 2 ♀. Additionally, 22 ♀ (mostly "immature") and 12 ♂ were seen. In later work, 14 of 19 birds trapped were "immature," and only 4 of these were ♂. Thus "immatures" (64–73%) greatly outnumbered "adults," and ♀ ♀ greatly outnumbered ♂ ♂ (White and Roseneau 1970). On the other hand, in Enderson's study (given next) in Wyo. and cent. Colo., "adults" greatly outnumbered "immatures" in winter.

WYO.-COLO.   "Adults" moved to the Laramie Plains and became temporary residents where Horned Larks were numerous and other prey was present. Stay av. at least 31 days, with 13 birds probably averaging 44. In 1960, some birds were already there on July 4, the maximum was 9 on Aug. 9, then a decrease until all were gone on Oct. 15. In 1961 they first appeared the 2d week in June, a maximum of 13 later, and the last gone in mid-Oct. No birds banded within 150 mi. (240 km.) of the study area were known to have occurred on the plains; that is, the birds there came from elsewhere.

An analysis of banding records showed a strong tendency for the young to move e. to the plains provinces and states, with little w. movement. Young birds from Wyo. and Colo. moved ne., e., and se.; 4 of 5 banded in Calif. were recovered e. of the Continental Divide. When older, they still moved e., but one banded in Utah moved w. Four of 27 returned to their previous wintering area. (From Enderson 1964.)

SW. IDAHO   The Snake R. Birds of Prey Area has a very high concentration of breeding Prairie Falcons; many were banded, and 259 were also given patagial wing-markers. The birds scattered from the breeding area soon after the young were on the wing, since Townsend's ground squirrel (their principal prey locally) aestivates by mid-July and so is unavailable in late summer and early fall. The falcons seek localities where food is abundant temporarily; some even go to alpine areas. Of those going over 100 km. from their marking location, there were records of movement of individuals ne. (into Mont.), se. (Kans.; n. Coahuila in Mexico by mid-Sept. of year of hatching), and s. (Utah, Ariz.). In a small sample, birds in their year of hatching did not move significantly farther than older ones. (From Steenhof et al. 1984.)

Two nestlings were banded May 2, 1928, at Merrill, Oreg. Both were recovered that same year, 1 about Aug. 5 n. at Irvine, Alta., the other s. on Sept. 29 at Arbuckle, Calif. (in Bent 1938). One banded as a nestling in Calif. was recovered in Sask. after 5 years and 5 months; 1 banded as a nestling in Wyo. was recovered in S.D. in winter after 13 years and 6 months (Enderson 1964).

Spring Return is mainly in Feb.–Apr., with some back even at upper limits of breeding in Mar. In late Mar., 2 were seen flying so high that they were barely visible without binoculars (Enderson 1964). RALPH S. PALMER

BANDING STATUS From 1955 through 1972, the number banded was 2,717, with 3.8% recovered. More than ½ recoveries were of birds in their 1st year of life. Many of the falcons had been shot (Shor 1975). To Aug. 1981, the number banded was 8,980, with 480 recoveries (5.3%). (Clapp et al. 1982). Main places of banding: Alta., Colo., Idaho, Sask., Utah, Wyo., Oreg., Mont., and Calif. Banding data have been used in calculating survival rates (which see); there is also scattered mention of recoveries and notable migration studies by Enderson (1964) and Steenhof et al. (1984). RALPH S. PALMER

REPRODUCTION Usually **first breeds** when in Basic feathering, hence age at least 2 years. Some ♀ ♀ breed successfully as yearlings (H. Webster 1944). In ne. Colo. in 1976 and 1977, of 31 paired ♀ ♀, 7 were "juveniles" and all reared young to flight age (S. W. Platt 1977). In the latter year, foraging conditions were optimal for an expanding population. Yearling ♂ ♂ paired with older ♀ ♀ have attempted to breed without success (Enderson 1964), yet possibly they succeed on occasion. Sperm from a captive-reared 11-month-old bird (it had been given testosterone, probably unnecessarily) was used to inseminate a ♀, which then laid a "normal" 5-egg clutch (L. Boyd et al. 1977).

In sw. Idaho the birds are not near aeries until late Jan.; most known territories have pairs established by late Feb.; at some, the birds are not seen until Mar. (V. Ogden and Hornocker 1977). In Colo., the ♂ usually arrives at the aerie first, preceding the ♀ by a week or 10 days, with a "complete pair" at the cliff on or before Mar. 15; after a mild winter, however, they may occupy the aerie 3–4 weeks earlier (H. Webster 1944). Also in Colo., 2 ♀ were present Feb. 22, and 9 of 11 ♀ were the 1st arrivals (Enderson 1964—his major study cited simply as "Enderson" below).

Displays Mates seem not to be associated on wintering areas, although presumably those that remain near breeding areas may be in contact. Renewal of the pair bond, or formation of one if the birds are first breeding or one is new to the site, occurs after arrival (Enderson). Thus display occurs annually. Pairs spend long periods perched near the aerie; then there are spectacular activities lasting about a month that include much vocalizing and flying past the site where the clutch is later laid. This repertoire has not been described, but Wrege and Cade (1977), from study of captive falcons, stated that there is at least 75% overlap with the Gyr and Peregrine. Birds were banded at an aerie in 1960; in 1961 the ♂ did not return and was replaced by another, which was captured and banded; in 1962 the original ♀ and the new ♂ of 1961 were at the site (Enderson).

Laying site The ideal aerie is recessed in a cliff at any height where it is safe from mammalian predators, commonly above 30 ft. and not at the top. That is, a sheltered ledge having loose material such as gravel at the "scrape" site, overlooking treeless hunting country. In n. prairie regions, holes in eroded banks along watercourses. Directional orientation is not entirely random; in some areas those sites facing s. or e. would be snow-free and dry earlier.

414

Exceptional sites Include inactive cliff nests of sticks, of the N. Raven (quite frequently), Golden Eagle, and Red-tailed Hawk. Tree nests rarely—Mo. (Goss 1891), Wyo. (P. A. McLaren and Rinde 1983), and Nev. (M. Perkins 1982). At least 1 of these was alternative after failure on a ledge, and the Mo. site might have been a hole in the tree. Others reported: large holes in cliffs, wall of a cave (on an old stick nest), abandoned quarries, and on a building.

Territory A pair ordinarily needs about 10 sq. mi. in the breeding season for aerie plus hunting, with active aeries exceptionally as close as 200 ft. provided they are out of sight of one another (contact avoidance). There has been fatal combat between ♀ Prairie Falcons (Fyfe, in I. Newton 1979). Many Peregrine aeries, abandoned after long tradition of usage, have been taken over by the Prairie Falcon. When hunting, areas of different Prairie Falcons may overlap greatly, sometimes the distance from aerie to foraging area being so great that perhaps the latter is not defended except (the Craigheads) against other falcon species.

Occupancy rate Of traditional Prairie Falcon aeries, high, around 75%, in the 1960s to mid-1970s, based on summary of 9 studies (S. W. Platt 1981); may have improved subsequently. Specifically, in Enderson's study, less than ½ of the breeding birds failed to return to the same (or any observed) site of a previous year, only 14 of 25 sites were occupied 3 consecutive years, and yet some individuals were remarkably faithful. Of 56 occupied territories in sw. Idaho in 1970–1972, inclusive, 54 were occupied all 3 years (most pairs **changing sites** within a territory annually), and 2 were occupied 2 of the 3 years. Apparently only 5 pairs used identical sites 2 of the 3 years, and a single site was used 2 consecutive years (V. Ogden and Hornocker 1977). At Los Padres Natl. Forest in Calif., 3 territories were active 1977–1981, inclusive, 2 were active 4 of the 5 years, and the remaining 17 for 3 years or fewer (Eakle 1984). Failure at a site is not a deterrent to its use the next year (Enderson).

Enderson saw a ♂ investigating ledges of a cliff, "presumably" before scraping a depression for the eggs. The actual site is typically a mere "scrape" in the loose substrate. In Ariz. in late Mar., a ♂, carrying a stick in his talons, flew to a scrape (Barber 1979)—perhaps a substitute for prey delivery to the ♀. Although the substrate is manipulated or rearranged, no nest is built.

Copulation May occur without evident preliminaries; frequent—"certainly occurring several times each day" (Enderson).

Laying interval "A day or two" (Bendire 1982), perhaps supposition; no recent information other than that captives often lay daily for several days.

Clutch size Among various available data are the following. CALIF., OREG., and WASH. 100 clutches: 7 (of 3 eggs), 21 (4), 70 (5), and 2 (6) (Skinner, in Bent 1938), av. 4.67. This is on the high side, not unexpectedly, as collectors tend to accumulate larger clutches. SW. IDAHO 68 clutches in 1971–1972: 3 (of 2), 10 (3), 13 (4), 39 (5), and 3 (6), av. 4.4 (V. Ogden and Hornocker 1977). W.-CENT. ARIZ. in 1979–1981: for 26 clutches the mean was 3.32 ± 1.51 (Millsap 1984).

One **egg** each from 20 clutches in Calif. **size** length 52.15 ± 1.65 mm., breadth 39.52 ± 1.78, and radii of curvature of ends 15.98 ± 0.99 and 11.41 ± 1.11; **shape** av. between short elliptical and subelliptical, elongation 1.32 ± 0.051, bicone -0.083, and asymmetry $+0.153$ (F. W. Preston). A total of 331 eggs from "all sections" of range av. 52.3 × 40.5 mm. (Bent 1938). They av. smaller than those of the Peregrine and (Skinner, in Bent) av. lighter in **coloring** than those of any of our other falcons except the Am. Kestrel. The shell is finely granulated, often "pimpled," ground color white, creamy, or slightly pinkish. Over about ½ the surface there are fine, even dots; the other ½ has larger spots that may be concentrated at 1 end; sometimes there is a broad wash of color at 1 end; the overlying color may obscure the ground color, the former various browns. Very rarely an egg is uniformly colored, as a purplish shade. (Condensed from Bent 1938.)

Incubation In Colo., as determined by time-lapse photography: beginning the day the 1st egg was laid, "adults" incubated 15%, 22%, 64%, 90%, and 90% of daylight through the next 6 days. The ♀ was on the eggs at dusk and dawn 5 of the 6 nights, "suggesting that, even prior to steady incubation, the eggs are covered at night" (Enderson and Wrege 1973, Enderson et al. 1973). The ♂ perches nearby; he may spend some time on the eggs while the ♀ is off feeding on food he has brought her. From onset of laying or beforehand until the young are well grown, he does all the hunting under ordinary circumstances. **Incubation period** 31 days (H. Webster 1944, V. Ogden and Hornocker 1977), sometimes longer.

Dates for presumably viable clutches Calif. 134 records Mar. 1–May 25 (67 Apr. 6–15); Wash. and Oreg. 16 records Mar. 25–Apr. 28 (8 Apr. 5–14); Alta. and Sask. 7 records Apr. 22–June 14; Mont. and Wyo. 14 records Apr. 25–June 10 (7 May 4–19); Tex. and Mexico 10 records Feb. 18–May 25 (5 Apr. 22–May 10). (From Bent 1938.) In w.-cent. Ariz., earliest clutch date was Mar. 8, about 15 (of 26) pairs had clutches Mar. 25, and latest date eggs were seen in a successful aerie was May 18 (Millsap 1984).

Spread of clutch-completion dates is from early Mar. at lat. 25°–34°N to May 10 at lat. 43°N, and, in general, aeries are at lower elevation with increasing lat. (R. N. Williams 1985).

Replacement clutches Enderson noted 2 when the previous clutches were destroyed early in incubation. J. G. Tyler (1923) stated that if a clutch is taken, another is laid in 20–25 days, usually at the same aerie, otherwise at another aerie on the same cliff or not far away.

Nonlaying The number of pairs that occupy a territory and produce no clutch was 13.3% in w.-cent. Ariz. (Millsap 1984) and is about the same in studies to the n. Occasionally there is a lone bird at an aerie.

Density In Colo., 23 pairs on 16 mi. of cliffs (H. Webster 1944). Pawnee Natl. Grasslands in ne. Colo.—1.4 pairs/100 sq. mi. (Olendorff 1973). Snake R. Region in sw. Idaho—101 pairs in a 45-mi. stretch (V. T. Ogden 1973), a remarkable density.

Yearlings They return in spring to aeries where they were raised and, after attempts at display, are driven off by occupying pairs (H. Webster, 1944). (That some ♀ yearlings breed was mentioned above.)

Aerie defense Varies; some birds are extremely aggressive, others have little or no aggressiveness. This falcon is not as bold as the Peregrine (H. Webster 1944), and the ♀ often sits tight, flushing at the very last moment when the observer is close (Enderson); if a bird is startled on its clutch, it may "turn to fight" (Olendorff 1975). Both parents defend, the ♀ more aggressive but less persistent than the ♂. Once the observer was struck 3 times when there were small nestlings (Enderson); this has happened rarely to others. There have been various episodes in which the observer also flushed a nearby nesting Barn Owl, Great Horned Owl, or Redtail, which provoked an attack on them—usually immediate and fatal—summary in Evans (1982). The Golden Eagle and Great Horned Owl have been known to prey on Prairie Falcon nestlings, neither as a serious predator. Yet it is possible that the owl captures a considerable number of undefended older nestlings during the night.

Especially during the breeding cycle, the Prairie Falcon and Peregrine are antagonists, not occupying sites near one another amicably. For example, in Ariz., when they had aeries only about 200 m. apart, hostile encounters were frequent and serious; the Peregrines usually were the aggressors and dominated the combat. This and other evidence of conflict was reported by Ellis and Groat (1982), and there is relevant information in Porter and White (1973) and other sources. Yet if the 2 species are separated by some distance (and often an ecological difference), both breed successfully in the same general region. As for the N. Raven, which also nests early in the season, Dawson (1923) stated that "close association" with the falcon at "nesting time" is the "strangest element" in the lives of both. Decker and Bowles (1930) wrote of the "friendly relationship" when both are "nesting" along the same cliff as "nothing short of astounding." (See Bent 1938.) Yet the Raven has been known to eat falcon eggs (which must have been unguarded), and the falcon occasionally appropriates and uses disused Raven nests; then the Raven must build elsewhere. There is enmity between the 2 birds, but the Raven is extremely adept at self-preservation if attacked.

The ♀ slides her feet under the eggs to incubate (or under small nestlings to brood them), and they may be scattered if she is frightened off suddenly. Then she has a problem in gathering them, since she moves around with her toes closed (feet "balled"), which limits her actions (H. Webster 1944).

Rearing period The clutch hatches over a span of 2 to several days, and the ♀ stays close, brooding and feeding the young for about 4 weeks; by this time she begins hunting, and when the young are old enough to fly, she may be absent much of the time (Enderson). Early after hatching, unneeded prey may be cached near the aerie (1976 Snake R. Birds of Prey *Spec. Res. Rept.* for 1975), but the extent of such behavior is unknown. The falcons have been observed to remove prey remains from the aerie (F. H. Fowler 1931, later authors). Mammals may be torn and partly eaten before delivery to the aerie; larger birds, at least, may be more or less plucked beforehand. When a ♂ had a broken leg, the ♀ spent the majority of her time hunting, taking prey directly to the aerie, where all nestlings were reared to flight age (S. W. Platt 1981). In Colo., there was a "very abrupt change" in food from rodents to exclusively birds when the nestlings were beginning to show "ravenous" appetites (H. Webster 1944). This change occurred when nestlings of small birds were first out of the nest and easily captured.

Development of young Various data on growth and **development of nestlings** were recorded over a half-century ago by F. H. Fowler (1931), with important sections quoted in Bent (1938). The reader is referred to these sources. Recent data include a photographic guide for estimating age of nestlings, by Moritsch (1983b), the text abstracted here:

Days 5–7: the down is white; young huddle together much of the time; length about

417

13 cm. Days 9–11: they can sit up and hold up their heads; length about 15 cm. Days 13–15: sheathed primaries and secondaries begin to show; some bare areas of skin are very evident; length 20 cm. Days 17–19: flight feathers of wing begin to break from their sheaths; the 2d (white) down covers the bare areas; tail quills show, their tips out of sheaths; length 23 cm. Days 21–23: greater primary coverts out of sheaths; feathers show above eye, on crown, and in ear area; scapulars begin to show. Days 25–27: dark feathers around eyes; wings 50% feathered and scapulars distinct; upper tail coverts visible. Days 29–31: head now 50–75% feathered; streaked breast feathers conspicuous. Days 33–35: head and dorsal areas almost fully feathered; a scattering of down remains.

Age at first flight Enderson stated that 15 broods remained in aeries 36–41 days, and other observers report about the same. Where the young are undisturbed, they may spend several days hopping and flapping from ledge to ledge before actual departure. As soon as they are capable of sustained flight, they leave the area.

Sex ratio of nestlings 45 ♂ : 46 ♀ (Enderson).

Breeding success About a dozen papers have some information, the following being among the more useful:

SASK. In 1969 in 10 nests 38 young were reared at least to banding age (Houston 1970).

Sw. IDAHO At 30 aeries in 1971 and 38 in 1972, combined clutch size av. 4.4 eggs, and 81 were lost from infertility, disappearance, predation, breakage, and dead embryos. Of 221 falcons hatched, 36 (17%) died before attaining flight. An av. of 3.25 young were reared in 87 breeding attempts; when failed attempts are included, the figure drops to 3.1 (V. Ogden and Hornocker 1977).

COLO. Fifty-five clutches av. 4.5 eggs, producing 67 (av. 1.9) young/aerie, of which 1.2/aerie attained flight (Enderson). This is about the lowest reported success; see summation of 5 sources (Colo. 3, Mont. 1, Idaho 1) in V. Ogden and Hornocker (1977).

W.-CENT. ARIZ. In 1979–1981 in 30 territories, no eggs were laid in 4; in theothers, clutch size was 3.32 ± 1.51, brood size was 2.97 ± 1.56, and 2.80 ± 1.47 young/aerie attained flight (Millsap 1984).

In general, it would seem that, having larger clutch size than the Peregrine, the Prairie Falcon has greater reproductive potential that is often unachieved.

Many scores of Prairie Falcons and their progeny have been produced in captivity.

RALPH S. PALMER

SURVIVAL In Colo. there has been high nestling mortality from massive infestation of a tick (*Ornithodoros concanensis*) common to ground squirrels (*Citellus = Spermophilus*); H. Webster (1944) estimated it at 65%, and later authors have given various lower figures for other places and years down to a low of 10%.

Enderson (in Hickey 1969) gave a life table, based on banding data, with a calculated mortality in the 1st year of life of 74% and an av. annual figure thereafter of 25%—rates representative of a population then sharply declining but probably biased by several factors. There is a graph of "probability of survival" in S. W. Platt (1981) in which potential natural longevity, estimated as a function of observed mortality rate, is 9 years for ♀♀ and 32 for ♂♂ (!). An error is obvious. Average age of falcons that Platt trapped and released was 3.2 years.

The oldest bird reported by Clapp et al. (1982) was 9 years, 1 month, but Enderson (in Hickey 1969) gave 13 years as the longest period between banding and recovery. Twenty years is a reasonable estimate of potential maximum longevity (Enderson).

RALPH S. PALMER

HABITS   The Prairie Falcon is noted for its dashing flight, alternating a series of rapid strokes with short glides. Its speed, grace, and maneuverability are much admired, and, since much of its hunting is done within perhaps 30 m. of the ground, its actions are easy to observe. Generally it approaches a perch from below and, with great momentum, swings up rapidly to alight. Its activities are generally confined to the least possible radius necessary to secure required food, and when a favored prey species disappears or becomes so diminished in numbers as to require undue effort to capture it, the falcon switches to another. Regardless of this, it takes some prey opportunistically, and so the list of known quarry is quite extensive.

Hunting methods   There is an enormous amount of information in Bent (1938), including descriptions of capture of various quarry, and the reader is referred to this source. Since Bent's time, Rock Doves by the 1,000s have taken up residence among the high raptor population of the Snake R. Canyon in s. Idaho. The doves have their survival tactics and are not high on the raptor menu. If a Prairie Falcon stoops, an experienced dove uses what might be termed its anti-Peregrine strategy—it drops to the ground, then ducks low at the last instant so that the falcon misses its strike, then flees in the opposite direction to shelter before the falcon can come about and overtake it.

Perch-and-wait hunting   Much time is spent on lookout, this being a preferred method of sighting prey where elevated perches are available.

Low-level hunting style   Particularly suited to areas lacking such obstructions as trees. Flapping low over ground or water, the falcon flushes prey close up. A variant is flapping flight at some 10–30 m., then a sudden perpendicular stoop (Dekker 1982).

Hovering   Occasionally it hovers, perhaps 30 m. up or higher, then descends almost straight down on its quarry. A Juv. flew slowly and very low, occasionally hovering above clumps of brush like a harrier (White 1962).

Stoop from a soar   It may stoop from altitudes in excess of 1,000 m., descending at various angles, leveling off and flushing prey at close range (Dekker 1982). Or, from 10–150 m., it may make a sudden oblique descent, rapidly, to low over ground or water, to attack prey that flushed (Dekker).

Accipiter method   A ♀ dropped from about 100 ft. to just above sagebrush and fences, using these as a screen, then shot up into a European Starling flock. She missed the 1st time, perched, and then repeated with success (White 1962). This is typical of accipiters and is also used by the Gyr.

Merlin method   White-throated Swifts and Violet-green Swallows followed a ♂ falcon as it mounted high up; then, after some maneuvering, the tiercel made a downwind stoop, and accomplished the kill quickly. The Merlin is better known for this tactic.

A Prairie Falcon hunted in a "lowly manner" in Jan. in Calif.; it was **on the ground** in a large grainfield. It hopped about, checking bunches of stubble and hopping up onto small clumps of straw, which it scrutinized carefully, presumably in case some small prey was concealed. It covered ½-acre of ground but was not seen to make a capture (J. G. Tyler 1923). It perches on the ground near prairie dog colonies, on lookout for prey (A. K. Fisher 1893). Six authors, describing foraging habits from s. Canada to Ariz., list grasshoppers as food, 1 specifically commenting that these form a considerable portion of the diet of "immature" falcons. The so-called lowly manner is typical of Swainson's Hawk.

Using a beater In late Nov. 1867 in w. Nev., Ridgway (1877) watched these falcons following N. Harriers, compelling the latter to release quarry that the falcon then caught in midair. It was a "systematic habit." In Jan. in Calif. a N. Harrier captured an Am. Coot, was pursued by a falcon, and dropped it; the falcon alighted at it. Soon the harrier returned, accompanied by another, and they drove off the falcon (Parmenter 1941). In Jan.–Feb. 1980 in e. N.Mex., on 6 occasions S. Merchant (1982) saw Prairie Falcons apparently hunting close to actively hunting harriers. A falcon would fly above and behind a harrier, which seemed deliberate. Merchant saw no prey taken. Twice an "immature" Peregrine pursued a Rock Dove, and both times a Prairie Falcon captured it (Enderson 1964).

When flying a trained Prairie Falcon, if W. R. Spofford did not manage to flush quarry, the "impatient" bird overhead would stoop and strike at his hat. (It is recorded in the older falconry literature that, when dogs were used as beaters and no quarry was put up, the Peregrine, "waiting on" overhead, sometimes stooped and struck them.)

Some other raptor interrelationships Most daylight contacts with the Great Horned Owl occur where the 2 raptors breed along the same cliff; for example, in a single stoop the ♀ falcon killed the flying owl. When 1 of these owls was caught in a trap, a falcon struck at it repeatedly (Grinnell et al. 1930), and placing a live owl as decoy next to a mist net is a method of trapping this falcon (H. Webster 1944). Occasionally the Burrowing Owl is on the falcon's menu. In Mont., a Golden Eagle seemingly flustered a falcon, which then dropped a meadowlark (Cameron 1907). A Prairie Falcon was flushed from an Am. Kestrel carcass (1983 *Am. Birds* **37** 195). A young Prairie Falcon, newly on the wing, robbed prey from a Peregrine aerie (Ellis and Groat 1982). The Rough-legged Hawk, Golden Eagle, and N. Harrier rob the falcon of heavy prey and fly off with it; the falcon may leave its prey and fly to meet an approaching raptor in hope of driving it away (Enderson 1964). Trained Prairie Falcons wearing leg jesses often have these mistaken for captured prey by other Prairie Falcons and other raptors, which attempt to grasp them (S. W. Platt 1980).

The strike In a few experiments with falcons flown at flying quarry, the Prairie Falcon (a) stooped, struck briefly, and did not grip its prey or (b) approached it from low level and apparently tried to maintain grasp after contact. Once it was seen to strike with 1 foot (Goslow 1971).

Killing method The heavier Peregrine typically kills sizable prey by striking hard, knocking the prey to the earth; the lighter, more agile Prairie Falcon is more inclined to grip its prey. Prey seized is killed in the air or on the ground by biting through the neck vertebrae. The head and part of the neck are crushed and eaten, including the beak and some feathers. Larger flying birds may be struck so hard as to be killed by the blow, in Peregrine fashion. Then, although the quarry is already dead, it is frequently "killed" by breaking its neck. Breast muscles and bone, lungs, heart, and liver are consumed 1st, and when prey is plentiful, the remainder may be discarded. Ordinarily, it seizes a lizard "about the middle or just behind the forelegs" and crushes the head with its beak (R. Bond 1936). Small mammals are killed similarly—after the strike the skull is crushed and the neck bitten through. Larger mammals are hit by several stoops at the head and neck at such speed that the talons do not hold well; the prey is stunned or blinded, its skull fractured or neck dislocated (R. Bond). Thus the falcon can kill prey, such as jackrabbits, much too heavy for it to carry. It may have accidents, such as losing a talon or breaking a toe or leg.

Eating   Prey that can be transported is carried to an elevated site where the falcon can watch its surroundings, a precaution against robbery by some other raptor. Sometimes it crouches motionless on the ground with wings out, thus "mantling" over its quarry in hope of avoiding detection (R. Bond 1936, Enderson 1964).

Winter territory   These evidently are away from aeries. The av. area used by 4 marked ♂♂ was 3.8 mi. (6.1 km.) and for 6 marked ♀♀ 7.2 mi. (11.5 km.), perhaps suggesting that the latter use more area; meas. were between the 2 most distant points of observation (Enderson 1964).

Bathing   The only definite reference is Taverner's (1919) statement that in July–Aug. these falcons were usually seen bathing in shallows along the shore of the Red Deer R. in Alta. A ♀ drowned in a stock tank, having entered either to bathe or to get 1 of several floating dead meadowlarks (Enderson 1964). From the quantity of skeletal remains found it is evident that many died in open tar pits in Calif. during the late Pleistocene, the McKittrick pool especially (L. Miller, in Bent 1938); presumably they either were attempting to bathe or were attracted by potential quarry already trapped there.

Play   Near Kamloops, B.C., on Aug. 2 a falcon flew carrying a piece of cow dung and alighted with it. Soon it flew with another piece, dropping and retrieving it in midair. Then it alighted and repeatedly tossed the piece of dung ahead of it, fluttering after it to pounce on it. It would rise several ft. from the ground, flinging the dung ahead and above and attempting to catch it in the air. The tossing was done with both feet, and the bird was not consistently successful in recapturing it in the air (D. A. Munro 1954).

Temperament   Moody, peevish, whimsical (J. Tyler 1923). It has a "vile and unpredictable temper," calm one day and "wilder than a hurricane" the next. Its capacity for fasting for rather long periods renders it difficult for a falconer to get it into condition because of "seeming lack of any appreciable appetite" (H. Webster 1944).

Temperature regulation   In a study of temperatures of falcons in relation to ambient temperature, an index of tarsal surface area per unit of body wt. was correlated with temperature regimen—species from hottest climates having the greatest tarsal index values (Mosher and White 1978). The value was relatively high for the Prairie Falcon.

Numbers   Probably fewer than in prehistoric time. As for the immediate past, after the period of pesticide-related decline, this falcon has good production of young and stable or increasing numbers regionally to the extent that breeding habitat is essentially saturated in a few places. Many Prairie Falcons now find it convenient to use former traditional Peregrine aeries. It is estimated that 5,000–6,000 pairs attempt to breed annually (1979 Snake R. Birds of Prey *Spec. Res. Rept.*).

Artificial breeding sites Have been provided; digging holes in earthen banks and making recesses in cliffs (Olendorff et al. 1980, E. D. Smith 1985). Captive-hatched young have been reared in aeries of certain other raptors.

Indian usage Falcons were held in high esteem by the plains Indians, and their remains are associated with human burials. Ubelaker and Wedel (1975) described and illustrated the remains of a Prairie Falcon interred with an individual and representing the remains of a "medicine bird."

Past losses Shooting was formerly a very common cause of mortality, judging from banding recoveries. In the weeks after departure from the aerie, the young falcons have no fear and are easy targets. Human disturbance and the taking of eggs and nestlings has caused aeires to be abandoned. Falling rock has destroyed some sites. Environmental contaminants, notably DDE, have resulted in eggshell thinning and breakage (Fyfe et al. 1969, later authors). Mercury contributes to embryonic mortality (Fimreite et al. 1970). Where this falcon fed primarily on birds reproductive success was much lower than where prey was primarily mammalian (Fyfe 1972), the latter having lower levels of contaminants. In general, from lesser intake of pesticide residues, levels have been lower than in the Peregrine. The contaminant problem is now alleviated yet can recur where pesticides are used in agricultural areas.

In Calif., pest control operations eliminated an estimated 1,000,000 passerines from 1966 to 1972, perhaps 30% of them Horned Larks (Garrett and Mitchell 1973), which are a major winter prey of the Prairie Falcon.

Literature There is a long list of papers in D. Evans (1982); his text coverage includes parasites and diseases. RALPH S. PALMER

FOOD Birds and mammals, occasionally lizards and insects.

Sherrod (1978) listed many prey species in his summary of 10 published and 3 unpublished sources. To these add especially V. Ogden and Hornocker (1977) for sw. Idaho and Millsap (1984) for w.-cent. Ariz. Additional papers having some mention of food have been consulted. From papers on general habits, especially, it is evident that individuals or pairs tend to focus on a single prey species (bird or mammal) for a considerable time, then shift quite abruptly to another that becomes readily available. It might be said that mammals are favored in early summer and birds all winter, but the falcons are not bound by simplistic rules. Some breeding pairs concentrate on birds. Mammals that are abroad in any season, such as hares and rabbits, are taken opportunistically around the year.

Mammals Many authors emphasize a diet of largely to almost exclusively ground squirrels (*Spermophilus*) in the early warm months until they disappear (aestivate). See especially V. Ogden and Hornocker (1977) for sw. Idaho. At least 8 species are recorded. Far fewer, but heavier, are cottontails and jackrabbits; even though large for the falcon, the latter are taken readily. Other mammals consist of a few rodent species, in small numbers and not larger than pocket gophers and wood rats.

Birds Numerous species, as opportunity allows, in size from Mallard, Sharp-tailed Grouse, Ring-necked Pheasant, White-tailed Ptarmigan, and Rock Dove down to pipits and sparrows. Of the many examples of emphasis on a particular prey, these are typical: falcons at an aerie fed almost exclusively on homing pigeons, taking them at a nearby escarpment (H. Webster 1944); in Mont. in winter, a "relentless persecutor" of Sharp-tailed Grouse (Cameron 1907). As for quantity of individuals, especially in winter, emphasis is on open-country flocking species—Horned Lark (widely reported), meadowlarks, longspurs, European Starling, and Mourning Dove.

Domestic fowl (seldom fully grown?) are listed by 5 authors, but the falcon is a great menace to domestic and feral pigeons.

Reptiles At least 7 small common lizards are recorded, including the horned "toad" (*Phrynosoma*). In Calif. the only remains at an aerie were chuckwallas (*Sauromalus*), "large desert lizards that abound in the haunts of these birds" (Pierce 1935).

Insects Six authors list grasshoppers—see especially Taverner (1926) and R. B. Williams and Matteson (1948)—and 2 each list locusts and crickets.

Other invertebrates Scorpion (V. T. Ogden (1973).

NOTE It may be of interest that prey in alpine habitat in Colo. included: pika (*Ochotona*), Horned Lark, Mountain Bluebird, Water Pipit, and Rosy Finch (Marti and Braun 1975). RALPH S. PALMER

423

List of literature cited in this volume
is combined with that of vol. 4.

LITERATURE CITED IN VOLUMES 4 AND 5

Initials are omitted except when there is a need to distinguish among different authors having the same surname.

After an author's papers are listed chronologically, those of which he or she also is senior coauthor are listed chronologically rather than alphabetically by coauthor.

Abbors 1979 *Fledging, Local Dispersal and Roost-associated Behavior of the Turkey Vulture* Calif. State Univ., Hayward, M.S. thesis. Abbott 1911 *Home-life of the Osprey* London; 1933 *Condor* **35** 10–14. Abramson 1976 *Am. Birds* **30** 661–662. Adams and Scott 1979 *W. Birds* **10** 157–158. Aiken 1928 *Auk* **45** 373–374. Albuquerque 1978 *Rev. Brasil Biol.* **38** 727–737. 1982 *Raptor Res.* **16** 91–92. Alcott 1870 *Am. Nat.* **4** 376. Aldrich and Bole 1937 *Cleveland Mus. Nat. Hist. Sci. Publ.* **7** 5–196. Aleksiuk 1964 *Arctic* **17** 263–267. Alexander and Fitter 1955 *Brit. Birds* **48** 1–14. Alford and Bolen 1972 *Wilson Bull.* **84** 487–489. Ali and Ripley 1968 *Handb. of Birds of India and Pakistan* **1** London. Allan 1947 *Condor* **49** 88; Allan and Sime 1943a *Condor* **45** 110–112; 1943b *Wilson Bull* **55** 33–34. Allard 1934 *Auk* **51** 514–515. Allen, A. A. 1929 *Bird-Lore* **31** 356–368. Allen, C. S. 1892 *Auk* **9** 313–321. Allen, E. G. 1951 *Trans. Am. Phil. Soc.* n.s. **41**, pt. 3. Allen, J. A. 1868 *Mem. Boston Soc. Nat. Hist.* **1** 488–526. Allen, R. P., and Peterson 1936 *Auk* **53** 393–404. Allin 1941 *Can. Field-Nat.* **55** 110. Alvarez del Toro 1952 *Condor* **54** 112–114. Amadon 1961a *Auk* **78** 256–257; 1961b *Noved. Columbiana* **1** 358–360; 1964 Am. Mus. Nat. Hist. *Novitat.* no. 2166; 1975 *Auk* **92** 380–382; 1977 *Condor* **79** 413–416; 1982a *Jour. Yamashina Inst. Ornith.* **14** 108–121; 1982b Am. Mus. Nat. Hist. *Novitat.* no. 2741; Amadon and Phillips 1939 *Auk* **56** 183–184; 1947 *Auk* **64** 576–587; Amadon and Eckleberry 1955 *Condor* **57** 65–80. Ames 1964 *Atlantic Nat.* **19** 15–27. Ames and Mersereau 1964 *Auk* **81** 173–185. Anderle 1966 *Condor* **68** 177–184; 1967 *Wilson Bull.* **79** 163–197; 1982 *Ont. Field Biol.* **36** 43–44. Anderson, D. W., and Hickey 1972 *Proc. Intl. Ornith. Cong.* **15** 514–540. Anderson, R. M. 1907 *Proc. Davenport Acad. Sci.* **11** 125–417. Angell 1969 *Living Bird* **8** 225–241. Anthony 1893 *Zoe* **4** 228–247. Apanius 1977 *Auk* **94** 585. Apfelbaum and Seelbach 1983 *Raptor Res.* **17** 97–113. Arbib 1976 *Am. Birds* **30** 1031–1039. Armstrong 1944 *Bull. Mass. Audubon Soc.* **28** 255–256. Arnell 1971 *Prey Utilization by Nesting Golden Eagles in Cent. Utah* Brigham Young Univ., Provo, Utah, M.S. thesis. Arnold 1942 *Condor* **44** 280; 1948 *Audubon Mag.* **50** 256; 1954 USDI Fish & Wildl. Serv. *Circular* 27. Arredondo 1976 *Smithsonian Contrib. Paleobiol.* 27:179–187. Arvidsson 1980 *Vår Fågelvärld* **39** 385–392. Asay 1980 *Habitat, Biology, and Productivity of Cooper's Hawks Nesting in the Oak Woodlands of Calif.* Univ. of Calif., Davis, M.S. thesis. Audubon 1831 *Ornith. Biog.* **1**; 1838 **4**; 1839 **5**; 1840 *The Birds of*

America 1. Austin, E. S. 1976 *Auk* 93 202–203. Austin, O. L., Jr. 1948 Mus. Comp. Zool. Harvard *Bull.* 101 (1). Anon. 1971 *Audubon* 73 72. Aughey 1878 *First Ann. Rept. (for 1877) U.S. Entomol. Comm. relating to the Rocky Mt. Locust* App. 2. Azetegui 1975 *Hornero* 11 321.

Baars-Kleinenberg and Wattel 1964 *Ardea* 52 225–226. Bacon 1981 *Passenger Pigeon* 43 51. Bagg, A. C., and Eliot 1937 *Birds of Conn. Valley* Northampton, Mass. Bagg, A. M., and Parker 1951 *Auk* 68 315–333; 1953 *Auk* 70 490–491. Bagg, E. 1889 *Ornith. and Ool.* 14 73–74. Bahrmann 1974 *Zool. Abh. Mus. Tierk.* (Dresden) 33 1–7. Bailey, A. M. 1956 *Auk* 73 560; Bailey, A. M., and Wright 1931 *Wilson Bull.* 43 190–219; Bailey, A. M., and Niedrach 1933 *Am. Forests* 39 356–358, 384. Bailey, B. H. 1917 *Auk* 34 73–75; 1918 *Iowa Geol. Surv. Bull.* 6. Bailey, F. M. 1915 *Bird-Lore* 17 431–438; 1917 *Handb. of Birds of W. U.S.* rev. ed., Boston; 1928 *Birds of N.Mex.* Albuquerque. Bailey, H. H. 1925 *Birds of Fla.* Baltimore. Baillie 1953 *Audubon Field Notes* 7 270–272; 1963 *Ont. Field Biol.* 17 15–26. Baird, S. F., et al. 1874 *Hist. N. Am. Birds* 3 *Land Birds* Boston. Baker, B. W., and Walkinshaw 1946 *Can. Field-Nat.* 60 5–10. Baker, J. A., and Brooks 1981 *Condor* 83 42–47. Baker, J. K. 1962 *Condor* 64 500–504. Baker-Gabb 1981 *Breeding Behavior and Ecol. of Australasian Harrier* Massey Univ., Palmerston North, N.Z., M.S. thesis. Balch 1982 *Birding* 14 114–128. Baldwin 1940 *Auk* 57 413. Balfour 1957 *Bird Notes* 27 216–224; 1962 *Bird Notes* 30 69–73; Balfour and MacDonald 1970 *Scottish Birds* 6 157–166; Balfour and Cadbury 1975 *Natural Environment of Orkney* (ed. R. Goodier), 122–128, Edinburgh; 1979 *Ornis Scand.* 10 133–141. Balgooyen 1971 *Condor* 73 382–385; 1975 *Jack-Pine Warbler* 53 115–116; 1976 *Univ. Calif. Pub. Zool.* 103 1–83; Balgooyen and Moe 1973 *Am. Midland Nat.* 90 454–455. Bandy, L. and B. 1978 *Wilson Bull.* 90 133–134. Bang 1960 *Nature* 188 547–549; 1968 *Jour. Morphol.* 115 153–184. Bangs and Barbour 1922 Mus. Comp. Zool. Harvard *Bull.* 65 no. 6. Bannerman 1956 *Birds of the Brit. Isles* 6 Edinburgh. Barber 1979 *Raptor Res.* 13 16. Barbour 1923 *Birds of Cuba* Mem. Nuttall Ornith. Club no. 6; 1943 *Cuban Ornith.* Mem. Nuttall Ornith. Club no. 9. Barclay 1980 *Release of Captive-produced Peregrines in the E. U.S. 1975–1979* Mich. Tech. Univ., Houghton; M.S. thesis. Barlow 1897 *Auk* 14 14–21. Barrett and Mackey 1975 *Wilson Bull.* 87 514–519. Barrows 1912 *Mich. Bird Life* Mich. Ag. College, Dept. Zool. and Physiol. *Spec. Bull.* Barth 1964 *Sterna* 6 49–73. Bartholomew and Cade 1957 *Wilson Bull.* 69 149–154. Bartram 1791 *Travels through N. & S. Carolina, Ga., E. and W. Fla.* Philadelphia. Batchelder 1881 *Bull. Nuttall Ornith. Club* 6 58–60. Bauer 1982 *Raptor Res.* 16 10–13. Baumgras 1942 *Wilson Bull.* 54 50. Baynard 1909 *Oologist* 26 191–193; 1910 *Oologist* 27 112; 1913 *Auk* 30 240–247; 1914 *Bird-Lore* 16 471–477. Beal 1932 *Oologist* 48 128. Beaman 1979 *Brit. Birds* 72 288. Bebe 1886 *Forest and Stream* 27 [designated 26 in error] no. 17: 327. Bechard 1980 *Factors Affecting the Productivity of Swainson's Hawk Nesting in Se. Wash.* Wash. State Univ., Pullman, Ph.D. diss.; 1982 *Condor* 84 153–159; 1983 *Wilson Bull.* 95 233–242; Bechard and Houston 1984 *Condor* 86 348–352; Bechard et al. 1985 *Jour. Wildl. Mgmt.* 49 226–228. Beckel 1981 *Passenger Pigeon* 43 3–4. Becker 1985 *Wilson Bull.* 97 226–230; Becker and Sieg 1985 *Raptor Res.* 19 52–55. Bednarz and

Dinsmore 1981 *Jour. Wildl. Mgmt.* **45** 236–241; 1985 *Can. Field-Nat.* **99** 262–264.   Bee, J. W. 1958 *Univ. Kans. Mus. Nat. Hist. Pub.* **10** no. 5.   Bee, R. A. 1942 *Great Basin Nat.* **3** 61–85.   Beebe, F. L. 1960 *Condor* **62** 145–189; 1974 B.C. Prov. Mus. *Occas. Pap.* no. 17.   Beebe, W. 1947 *Zoologica* **32** 153–169.   Beecham and Kochert 1975 *Wilson Bull.* **87** 506–513.   Behle et al. 1944 Utah Acad. Sci., Arts and Letters *Proc.* **21** no. 4: 4, 1985 Utah Mus. Nat. Hist. *Occas. Bull.* no. 4.   Beissinger 1983 *Auk* **100** 84–92; 1984 *Mate Desertion and Reproduction Effort in Snail Kite* Univ. Mich., Ann Arbor, Ph.D. diss., Beissinger and Takakawa 1983 *Fla. Field Nat.* **11**   Beissinger et al. 1983 *Am. Birds* **37** 262–265.   Belcher and Smooker 1934 *Ibis* 13th ser. **4** 572–595.   Belknap 1960 *Kingbird* **10** 55.   Bellrose 1936 *Auk* **53** 348.   Belton 1973 *Auk* **90** 94–99.   Bendire 1882 *Ornith. and Ool.* **6** 88; 1887 *Proc. U.S. Nat. Mus.* **11** 551–558; 1892 U.S. Nat. Mus. *Spec. Bull.* 1 [*Smithsonian Contr. Knl.* **28**].   Bengtson 1971 *Ibis* **113** 468–476; 1975 *Fauna Flora* (Uppsala) **70** 8–12.   Benners 1887 *Ornith. and Ool.* **12** 65–69; 1889 *Ornith. and Ool.* **14** 83–85.   Benson, C. W. 1960 *Ibis* **103b** 5–106; 1971 *Birds of Zambia* London.   Benson, P. C. 1982 *Prevention of Golden Eagle Electrocution* Palo Alto, Calif.: Electric Power Res. Inst. EPRI EA-2680 Final Rep., 90pp.   Bent 1937 *U.S. Nat. Mus. Bull.* 167; 1938 *U.S. Nat. Mus. Bull.* 170.   Bente 1981 *Nesting Behavior and Hunting Activity of Gyrfalcon in s.-cent. Alaska* Univ. Alaska, Fairbanks, M.S. thesis.   Berger 1957 *Wilson Bull.* **69** 110–111; Berger et al. 1963 *Jour. Wildl. Mgmt.* **27** 778–791.   Bergstrom 1985 *Jour. Field Ornith.* **56** 415.   Bermuda Audubon Soc. 1959 *Check List and Guide to Birds . . . of Bermuda* (ed. D. Wingate) Hamilton, Bermuda.   Berry 1972 *Jour. Wildl. Mgmt.* **36** 1283–1288.   Bertelson 1983 *Vår Fågelvärld* **42** 98.   Bertoni 1924 *Hornero* **3** 279.   Beske 1978 *Harrier Radio-tagging Techniques . . .* Univ. Wis., Stevens Point, M.S. thesis; 1982 *Raptor Res.* **16** 39–53.   Besson 1969 *Alauda* **37** 258–260.   Beyer et al. 1908 *Auk* **25** 439–448.   Biederman and Lin 1982 *In Vitro* **18** 415–418.   Bierregaard 1974 *Auk* **91** 618–619.   Bijleveld 1974 *Birds of Prey of Europe* London.   Bildstein 1976 *Behavior of Wintering N. Harriers* Ohio State Univ., M.S. thesis; 1978 *Behavioral Ecology* [4 raptor spp.] *and Other Raptorial Birds Wintering in s.-cent. Ohio* Ohio State Univ., Columbus, Ph.D. diss.; 1979a *Inland Bird Banding* **51** 63–65; 1979b *Raptor Res.* **13** 40–46; 1979c *Chat* **43** 82–85; 1980 *Wilson Bull.* **92** 128–130; 1982a *Raptor Res.* **16** 83–88; 1982b *Jour. Field Ornith.* **53** 7–14; Bildstein and Ashby 1975 *Auk* **92** 807–808; Bildstein and Grubb 1980 *Raptor Res.* **14** 90–91; Bildstein and Hamerstrom 1980 *Jour. Field Ornith.* **51** 356–360.   Binford 1979 *W. Birds* **10** 1–16.   Bird, C. G. and E. G. 1941 *Ibis* **83** 118–161.   Bird, D. M. 1982 *Nature* **299** 300–301; Bird, D. M. (chief ed.) 1983 *Biol. and Mgmt. of Bald Eagles and Ospreys* McGill Univ., Ste. Anne de Bellevue, Que.; Bird, D. M., and Buckland 1976 *Can. Jour. Zool.* **54** 1595–1597; Bird, D. M., and Laguë *Raptor Res.* **10** 1–8; 1977 *Can. Jour. Zool.* **55** 1351–1358; 1980 *Can. Jour. Zool.* **58** 1022–1026; Bird, D. M., and Rehder **1981** *Avic. Mag.* **87** 208–212; Bird, D. M., and Laguë 1982a *Can. Jour. Zool.* **60** 71–79; 1982b *Can. Jour. Zool.* **60** 80–88; 1982c *Can. Jour. Zool.* **60** 89–96; Bird, D. M., and Aubry 1982 *Can. Field-Nat.* **96** 167–171; Bird, D. M., and Tinker 1982 *Raptor Res.* **16** 58–59; Bird, D. M., and Clark 1983 *Raptor Res.* **17** 77–84.   Bird, S. 1941 *Oologist* **58** 22.   Bishop, L. B. 1900 *N. Am. Fauna* no. 19.   Bishop, S. C. 1925 *Auk* **42** 268–269.   Black 1979 *Bull. Okla. Ornith. Soc.* **12** 29.   Blair 1978 *Breeding Biol. and*

Prey Selection of Ferruginous Hawks in Nw. S.D. S.D. State Univ., Brookings, M.S. thesis; 1981 *Raptor Res.* **15** 120; Blair and Schitoskey 1982 *Wilson Bull.* **94** 46–54.   Blake, C. H. 1948 *Condor* **50** 148–151; 1975 *Am. Birds* **29** 923–925.   Blake, E. R. 1977 *Manual of Neotropical Birds* **1** Chicago.   Blake, N. M. 1980 *Land into Water—Water into Land* Tallahassee, Fla.   Blohm et al. 1980 *Wilson Bull.* **92** 251–252.   Blood 1968 *Can. Field-Nat.* **82** 169–176.   Bloom 1973 *W. Bird Bander* **48** 17–19; 1980 *Status of Swainson's Hawk in Calif., 1979* Calif. Dept. Fish and Game, Nongame Wildl. Investig. Job II-8; Bloom and Hawks 1983 *Raptor Res.* **17** 9–14. Boardman 1875 *Forest and Stream* **4** no. 2; 22.   Bock and Lepthien 1976 *Condor* **78** 554–557.   Boeker 1972 *Powerlines and Bird Electrocutions* USDI Bur. Sport Fisheries and Wildl., 8pp.; 1974 *Wildl. Soc. Bull.* **2** 46–49; Boeker and Ray 1971 *Condor* **73** 463–467, Boeker and Bolen 1972 *Jour. Wildl. Mgmt.* **36** 477–484.   Boedeltje and Zijlstra 1981 *Limosa* **54** no. 3: 73–80.   Bohl 1957 *Condor* **59** 143.   Bohm 1978 *Loon* **50** 6–8.   Bolen 1975 *Jour. of Range Mgmt.* **28** 11–17; Bolen and Derden 1980 *Jour. Field Ornith.* **51** 174–175.   Bonaparte 1828 *Am. Ornith.* **2.**   Bond, J. 1941 *Auk* **58** 364–375; 1956 *Check-list of Birds of the W. Indies* Philadelphia; 1961 *Birds of W. Indies* Boston; 1965 *Tenth Suppl. Check-list of Birds of W. Indies* Philadelphia; 1971 *Birds of the W. Indies* 3d ed. Boston; 1973 *Eighteenth Suppl. Check-list Birds of W. Indies* Philadelphia; 1976 *Twentieth Suppl. Check-list Birds of W. Indies* Philadelphia; 1978 *Twenty-second Suppl. Check-list Birds of W. Indies;* 1979 *Proc. Acad. Nat. Sci. Phila.* **131** 89–103; 1980 *Twenty-third Suppl. Check-list Birds of W. Indies* Philadelphia.   Bond, R. M. 1936 *Condor* **38** 72–76; 1942 *Wilson Bull.* **54** 81–88; 1943 *Condor* **45** 168–185; 1946 *Condor* **48** 101–116; 1951 *Condor* **53** 256; Bond, R. M., and Stabler 1941 *Auk* **58** 346–349.   Bonney 1979 *Am. Birds* **33** 695–697.   Bonnot 1921 *Condor* **23** 136.   Borell 1937 *Condor* **39** 44.   Bortolotti 1984a *Jour. Field Ornith.* **55** 54–66; 1984b *Jour. Wildl. Mgmt.* **48** 1173–1179; 1984c *Jour. Wildl. Mgmt.* **48** 72–81; 1984d *Wilson Bull.* **96** 524–542; 1984e *Jour. Field Ornith.* **55** 467–481.   Bourne 1985 *Snail Kite Feeding Ecology* Univ. Mich., Ann Arbor, Ph.D. diss.; 1985 *Ibis* **127** 141–147.   Bowen 1980 *Jour. of Mammal.* **61** 376–377.   Bowles and Decker 1931 *Murrelet* **12** 65–70.   Boyce 1985 *Raptor Res.* **19** 94–96; Boyce et al. 1982 *Wildl. Soc. Bull.* **10** 380–381.   Boyd et al. 1977 *Jour. Wildl. Mgmt.* **41** 266–271.   Bradlee et al. 1931 *Proc. Boston Soc. Nat. Hist.* **39** 279–382.   Brandt 1924 *Auk* **41** 59–64; 1943 *Alaska Bird Trails* Cleveland; 1951 *Ariz. and Its Bird Life* Cleveland.   Brannon, J. D. 1980 *Reproductive Ecology of a Tex. Harris' Hawk Pop.* Univ. of Tex., Austin, M.S. thesis.   Brannon, P. A. 1921 *Auk* **38** 463–464. Braun (chm.) 1975 *Wilson Bull.* **87** 140–143; 1977 *Wilson Bull.* **89** 360–369. Breckenridge 1935 *Condor* **37** 268–276; Breckenridge and Errington 1938 *Auk* **55** 668–670. Brewster 1880 *Bull. Nuttall Ornith. Club* **5** 57–58; 1983 *Bull. Nuttall Ornith. Club* **8** 21–36; 1902 Mus. Comp. Zool. Harvard *Bull.* **41** 1–242; 1925 Mus. Comp. Zool. Harvard *Bull.* **66** 211–402.   Britton, ed. 1973 Arctic Inst. N. Am. *Tech. Paper* no. 25.   Brodkorb 1935 *Auk* **52** 183–184; 1944 *Pap. Mich. Acad. Sci., Arts and Letters* **29** (1943) 115–121; 1955 *Wilson Bull.* **67** 142; 1964 *Bull. Fla. State Mus., Biol. Sci.* **8** no. 3; Brodkorb and Phillips 1970 *XXXV Ann. Meeting Soc. Am. Archaeol.*, Mexico, D.F. pp. 16–19.   Broley 1947 *Wilson Bull.* **59** 3–20; 1950 *Audubon Mag.* **52** 43–49; 1958 *Audubon Mag.* **60** 162–163; 171.   Broley, M. J. 1952 *Eagle Man* Pellegrini and Cudahay, N.Y.   Brooke 1962 *Ostrich* **33** 23–25;

1965 *Ostrich* **36** 43.   Brooks 1922 *Auk* **39** 556–559; 1927a *Condor* **29** 112–114; 1927b *Condor* **29** 245–246; 1928 *Am. Game* **17** 88, 91; 1933 *Auk* **17** 31–34.   Broun 1939 *Auk* **56** 429–441; 1947 *Auk* **64** 317–318; 1949 *Hawks Aloft: The Story of Hawk Mt.* New York; Broun and Goodwin 1943 *Auk* **60** 487–492.   Brown, H. 1901 *Auk* **18** 392–393.   Brown, L. H. 1955 *Eagles* London; 1969 *Brit. Birds* **62** 345–363; 1976a *Brit. Birds of Prey* London; 1976b *Eagles of the World* New York; Brown, L. H., and Watson 1964 *Ibis* **106** 78–100; Brown, L. H., and Amadon 1968 *Eagles, Hawks and Falcons of World* **1** and **2** New York.   Brown, P. 1979 *Scottish Ospreys from Extinction to Survival* London.   Brown, W. H. 1971 *Am. Birds* **25** 813–817; 1973 *Am. Birds* **27** 6–7; 1975 *Am. Birds* **29** 12–14; 1976 *Am. Birds* **30** 909–912.   Browning 1974a Nw. Sci. **48** 166–171; 1974b *Am. Birds* **28** 865–867; 1978 *Proc. Biol. Soc. Wash.* **91** 85–122.   Bruce et al. 1982 *Raptor Res.* **16** 132–134.   Bruderer 1976 *Ornith. Beob.* **73** 29–30.   Bruns 1970 *Can. Field-Nat.* **84** 301–304.   Bryan 1984 *Raptor Res.* **18** 143–147.   Bryant 1887 *Bull. Calif. Acad. Sci.* **6** 269–318.   Bryens 1941 *Jack-Pine Warbler* **19** 38–42.   Buechner 1950 *Am. Midland Nat.* **43** 257–354.   Buhnerkempe and Westmeier 1984 *Wilson Bull.* **96** 495–496.   Bull 1964 *Birds of New York Area* New York.   Bullock 1956 *Auk* **73** 283–284.   Burke 1979 *Effect of Prey and Land Use on Mating Systems of Harriers* Univ. of Wis., Stevens Point, M.S. thesis.   Burky et al. 1972 *Biol. Bull.* (USA) **143** 304–316.   Burleigh 1944 La. State Univ. *Occas. Pap. Mus. Zool.* no. 20.   Burnham 1983 *Jour. Wildl. Mgmt.* **47** 158–168, Burnham and Mattox 1984 *Meddel. om Grøland, Bioscience* **14** 1–25; Burnham et al. 1984 *Auk* **101** 578–583.   Burns 1911 *Wilson Bull.* **23** 139–320; 1915 *Wilson Bull.* **27** 275–286.   Burrows 1917 *Oologist* **34** 78–81.   Burtch 1905 *Ooologist* **22** 42–43; 1927 *Auk* **44** 248–249.   Busch 1984 *Raptor Res.* **18** 74–77.   Bush and Gehlbach 1978 *Bull. Tex. Ornith. Soc.* **11** 41–43.   Buskirk and Lechner 1978 *Auk* **95** 767–768.   Bussjaeger et al. 1967 *Condor* **69** 425–426.   Butterfield 1954 *Brit. Birds* **47** 342–347.   Byers 1957 *Auk* **74** 265.   Byrd et al. 1974 *Condor* **76** 288–300.   Bystrak 1974 *Wintering Areas of Bird Species Potentially Hazardous to Aircraft* Natl. Audubon Soc., New York.

Cade 1953 *Wilson Bull.* **65** 26–31; 1955a *Wilson Bull.* **67** 5–17; 1955b *Condor* **57** 313–346; 1960 *Univ. Calif. Pub. Zool.* **63** 151–290; 1968 *Living Bird* **7** 237–240; 1973 *Peregrine Fund Newsletter* no. 1:1–6; 1982 *Falcons of the World* Ithaca, N.Y.; Cade and Greenwald 1966 *Condor* **68** 338–350; Cade et al. 1968 *Condor* **70** 170–178; Cade et al. 1971 *Science* **172** 955–957; Cade et al. 1977 *Raptor Res.* **11** 29–48.   Calef and Heard 1979 *Auk* **96** 662–674.   Call 1978 USDI Bur. Land Mgmt. *Tech. Note* no. 316.   Cameron 1905 *Auk* **22** 158–167; 1907 *Auk* **24** 241–270; 1908a *Auk* **25** 251–268; 1908b *Auk* **25** 468–471; 1913 *Auk* **30** 167–176, 381–394; 1914 *Auk* **31** 158–167.   Campbell, C. A. 1975 *Raptor Res.* **9** 12–17.   Campbell, H. 1950 *Jour. Wildl. Mgmt.* **14** 477–478.   Campbell, J. A., and Nelson 1975 N. Am. Falconry Assoc. *Jour.* **14** 24–31.   Campbell, J. M. 1960 *Condor* **62** 298.   Campbell, J. S. 1934 *Auk* **41** 370–371.   Campbell, M. J., and Walker 1977 *Jour. Royal Stat. Soc.* A **140** 411–431.   Campbell, R. W. 1985 *Condor* **87** 294; 1985 *Condor* **87** 294; Campbell, R. W., et al. 1977 *Condor* **79** 500–501.   Cantwell 1888 *Ornith. and Ool.* **13** 92.   Carnie 1954 *Condor* **56** 3–12.   Carpenter, F. H. 1882 *Ornith. and Ool.* **7** 141; 1887 *Ornith. and Ool.* **12** 167–168.   Carpenter, T. W. 1979 *Jack-Pine Warbler* **57** 109–110.   Carriker

1910 *Ann. Carnegie Mus.* **6** 314–915. Carruthers, D. *Beyond the Caspian* Edinburgh. Carson 1979 *Nat. Hist.* **88** no. 6: 30–32, 36. Carter, C. E. 1960 *Wilson Bull.* **72** 201–202. Carter, D. L., and Wauer 1965 *Condor* **67** 82–83. Carter, J. L. 1974 *Fla. Experience* Baltimore. Casement 1973 *Sea Swallow* **23** 33–65. Cash 1914 *Scot. Nat.* **25** 149–158. Casillo 1937 *Nature Mag.* **30** 171–172. Cawkell and Hamilton 1961 *Ibis* **103a** 1–27. Cely and Sorrow 1983 *Ann. Rep. 1983 S.C. Wildl. and Marine Resources Dept.:* Nongame Heritage Trust sec. Cereley 1955 *Gyr Falcon Adventure* London. Chancellor, R. D., ed. 1977 *World Conf. Birds of Prey, Vienna, Oct. 1–3, 1975* Intl. Coun. Bird Prot., London. Chandler and Anderson 1974 *Am. Birds* **28** 856–858. Chapman 1899 Am. Mus. Nat. Hist. *Bull.* **12** 219–244; 1908 *Camps and Cruises of an Ornithologist* New York; 1916 *Handb. Birds of E. N. Am.* New York; 1917 Am. Mus. Nat. His. *Bull* **36;** 1926 Am. Mus. Nat. Hist. *Bull.* **55;** 1933 *Auk* **50** 30–34. Chaplin et al. 1984 *Condor* **86** 175–181. Chernikin 1965 *Ornitologiya* **7** 272–275. Cherrie 1916 Mus. of Brooklyn Inst. Arts and Sci. *Sci. Bull.* **2** no. 6: 133–374. Chesser 1979 *Wilson Bull.* **91** 330–331. Choate 1972 *Wilson Bull.* **84** 340–341. Christy 1928 *Auk* **45** 285–289. Chubb 1916 *Birds of Brit. Guiana* **1** London. Chura and Stewart 1967 *Wilson Bull.* **79** 441–448. Cieslak 1980 *Przeglad Zoologiczny* **24** 123–135. Clapp and Woodward 1968 U.S. Nat. Mus. *Proc* **124** no. 3640: 1–39; Clapp et al. 1982 *Jour. Field Ornith.* **53** 81–124. Clark, A. H. 1905a *Proc. Biol. Soc. Wash.* **18** 61–63; 1905b Boston Soc. Nat. Hist. *Proc.* **32** 219–243; 1910 U.S. Nat. Mus. *Proc.* **38** 25–74. Clark, R. J. 1972a *Blue Jay* **30** 43–48; 1972b *Jour. Wildl. Mgmt.* **36** 962–964; 1975 *Wildl. Monogr.* no. 47; 1977 *Auk* **94** 142–143; Clark, R. J., and Ward 1974 *Proc. Pa. Acad. Sci.* **48** 79–87. Clark, W. S. 1974 *Auk* **91** 172; 1982 *Jour. Field Ornith.* **53** 49–51; 1984 *Birding* **16** no. 6: 251–263; 1985 *Raptor Res.* **19** 85–93. Clarke, A. 1977 *Jour. Zool.* (London) **181** 11–20. Clarke, R. G. 1984 *Sharp-shinned Hawk in Interior Alaska* Univ. of Alaska, Fairbanks, M.S. thesis. Clausen and Gudmundsson 1981 *Jour. Wildl. Diseases* **17** 105–109. Clement 1949 *Bull. Mass. Audubon Soc.* **33** no. 1: 371–374. Clunie 1972 *Notornis* **19** 302–322. Cochran 1975 *Hawk Chalk* **14** no. 2: 28–37. Cole 1954 *Jour. Wildl. Mgmt.* **15** 233–252. Coleman et al. 1985 *Condor* **87** 291–292. Coles, A. F. 1982 *Brit. Birds* **75** 588. Coles, V. C. 1938 *Studies Life Hist. of Turkey Vulture* Cornell Univ. Ithaca, N.Y. Ph.D. diss.; 1944 *Auk* **61** 219–228. Collar 1978 *Brit. Birds* **71** 398–412. Collett, R. 1921 *Norges Fugle,* . . . **2** Kristiana, Norway. Collett, S. F. 1977 *Auk* **94** 365–367. Collier 1982 *Yankee* **46** no. 8: 107–108, 111–112, 158–159. Collins and Bird 1979 *Blue Jay* **37** 229. Collopy 1973 *Raptor Res.* **7** 25–31; 1977 *Condor* **79** 63–68; 1983 *Jour. Wildl. Mgmt.* **47** 360–368; 1984 *Auk* **101** 753–760. Condon and Amadon 1954 *S. Australian Mus. Records* **11** 189–246. Connor 1985 *Eyas* **8** no. 3: 2. Cooke 1943 *Bird-Banding* **14** 67–74. Coomber 1977 *Brit. Birds* **70** 391–392. Cooper 1971 N. Am. Falconry Assoc. *Jour.* **10** 41–42; Cooper and Greenwood, eds. 1980 *Recent Advances in Study of Raptor Diseases* London. Cope 1949 *Jour. Mammal.* **30** 432. Cottam 1936 *Wilson Bull.* **48** 11–13; 1962 *Auk* **79** 463–478; Cottam and Knappen 1939 *Auk* **56** 138–169. 1981 Cottrell *Resource Partitioning and Reprod. Success of Three Species of Hawks (Buteo spp.) in an Oreg. Prairie* Oreg. State Univ., Corvallis, M.S. thesis. Compton 1938 *Univ. Calif. Pub. Zool.* **42** 173–212. Coon et al. 1969 *Jour. Wildl. Diseases* **6** 72–76. Cooper 1870 *Ornithology* [of California] **1**

Cambridge, Mass.; 1890 *Zoe* **1** no. 8: 248–249.   Coues 1861 *Proc. Acad. Nat. Sci. Phila.* 215–257; 1866 *Proc. Acad. Nat. Sci. Phila.* **18** 39–100; 1874a *Am. Nat.* **8** no. 5: 282–287; 1874b Dept. Interior, U.S. Geol. Surv. Terr. *Misc. Pub.* no. 3; 1874c *Am. Nat.* **8** 596–603; 1881 *Bull. Nuttall Ornith. Club* **6** 248; 1882 *Coues' Check List of N. Am. Birds* 2d ed. Boston; 1903 *Key to N. Am. Birds* 5th ed. **2** Boston; Covert 1949 *Ky. Warbler* **25** no. 2: 33.   Cowles, G. S. 1969 *Brit. Birds* **62** 542–543.   Cowles, R. B. 1928 *Condor* **30** 327; 1968 *Proc. Tall Timber Fire Ecol. Conf.* **7** 217–224.   Craddock and Carlson 1970 *Condor* **72** 375–376.   Crafts 1968 *Wilson Bull.* **80** 327–328.   Craig 1978 *Raptor Res.* **12** 40–45; Craig and Powers 1976 *Condor* **78** 412; Craig and Renn 1977 *Condor* **79** 392; Craig and Trost 1979 *Wilson Bull.* **91** 50–61; Craig, T. and E. 1984 *Auk* **101** 610–613.   Craighead, F. C., Jr., and J. J. 1939 *Hawks in the Hand* Boston; Craighead, F. C., and Mindell 1981 *Jour. Wildl. Mgmt.* **45** 865–872.   Craighead, J. J. and F. C., Jr. 1940 *Wilson Bull.* **52** 241–248; 1956 *Hawks, Owls and Wildlife* Harrisburg, Pa.   Cram 1899 *Bird-Lore* **1** 180–184.   Cramp and Simmons, eds. 1980 *Handb. Birds Europe, Middle East and North Africa* **2** London and New York.   Crandall 1915 *Auk* **32** 368; 1941 *Zoologica* **26** pt. 1: 7–8, 4 pls.   Cranson 1972 *Colo. Field Ornith.* **11** 5–10.   Criddle 1912 *Ottawa Nat.* **25** 147–151; 1917 *Ottawa Nat.* **31** 74–76.   Crocoll 1984 *Breeding Biol. of Broad-winged and Red-shouldered Hawks in W. N.Y.* State Univ. College, Fredonia, N.Y., M.S. thesis.   Crook 1935 *Auk* **52** 78–79.   Cruickshank, A. D. 1937 *Auk* **54** 385; 1939 *Auk* **56** 474–475; 1942 *Birds around New York City* New York; 1947 *Wings in the Wilderness* New York.   Cruickshank, H. 1977 *Fla. Nat.* **50** 21–23.   Cruttenden 1940 *Oologist* **57** 26–28.   Cruz 1976 *Condor* **78** 409–412.   Cupper, J. M. and L. 1981 *Hawks in Focus* Mildura, Australia.   Czech 1968 *N.Y. Conservationist* **23** no. 1: 10–12, 37.   Czechura 1984 *Raptor Res.* **18** 81–91.

Dale 1936 *Condor* **38** 208–210.   Dall 1874 *Proc. Calif. Acad. Sci.* **5** 270–281; Dall and Bannister 1869 *Trans. Chicago Acad. Sci.* **1** pt. 2: 267–310.   Danforth 1935 *Jour. Agric. Univ. of Puerto Rico* **19** no. 4.   Daniels, G. G. 1975 *Am. Birds* **29** 634–637.   Daniels, K., and Duke 1980 *Comp. Biochem. Physiol.* **66A** 703–706.   Darling 1934 *Nature* **134** 325–326.   Darrow 1983 *Fla. Field Nat.* **11** 35–39.   Davidson 1951 *Fla. Nat.* **24** 112.   Davis, D. 1979 *W. Birds* **10** 125–130. Davis, D. E. 1941 *Wilson Bull.* **53** 37–40; ed. 1982 *CRC Handb. of Census Methods for Terrestrial Vertebrates* Boca Raton, Fla.   Davis, J. 1953 *Condor* **55** 90–98.   Davis, L. I. 1954 *Audubon Field Notes* **10** 429.   Davis, M. 1946 *Auk* **63** 85; 1948 *Auk* **65** 298–299.   Davis, T. A. W. 1954 *Ibis* **96** 441–448.   Dawson 1923 *Birds of Calif.* **4** San Diego, Calif.; Dawson and Bowles 1909 *Birds of Wash.* **2** Seattle.   Dean and Tarboton 1983 *Ostrich* **54** 238–239.   Deane, C. D. 1962 *Brit. Birds* **55** no. 7: 272–274.   Deane, R. 1907 *Auk* **24** 182–186.   Decker and Bowles 1930 *Auk* **47** 25–31.   DeGrange and Nelson 1982 *Jour. Field Ornith.* **53** 407–409.   DeGroot 1928 *Condor* **30** 360–361.   Dekker 1979 *Can. Field-Nat.* **93** 296–302; 1980 *Can. Field-Nat.* **94** 371–382; 1982 *Can. Field-Nat.* **96** 477–478; 1984 *Raptor Res.* **18** 92–97; 1985 *Can. Field-Nat.* **99** 383–385.   Delamain 1932 *Why Birds Sing* London.   Delaney 1982 *Mem. 3d Simp. Sobre Fauna Puerto Rico* 136–140.   Delnicki 1978 *Auk* **95** 427.   Dementiev 1931 *Ornith. Monatsber.* **39** 54–55; 1951 [*Gyrfalcon*] Moscow Naturalists' Soc. [in German, rev. 1960

Neue Brehm-Bücherei no. 264], Dementiev and Gladkov, eds. 1951 [*Birds of Soviet Union*] 1 [English trans. 1966 Israel Program Sci. trans.]; Dementiev and Böhme 1970 *Beitr. Vogelkunde* **16** 67–71. Dennis 1983 *Brit. Birds* **76** 310–311. Deppe 1972 *Jour. für Ornith.* **113** 440–444. Des Granges 1978 *Bull. Orn.* (Que.) **23** 18–19. Devers 1982 *N.Y. Conservationist* **36** no 6: 2–7. DeVore 1977 *Bull. Okla. Ornith. Soc.* **10** 31–32. DeWitt Miller *see* Miller, Waldron DeW. Dickey and van Rossem 1938 *Field Mus. Nat. Hist. Pub.* **406** (**Zool. Ser. 23**). Dickson 1974 *Brit. Birds* **67** 511–513; 1982 *Brit. Birds* **75** 329–330; 1984 *Brit. Birds* **77** 481–482. Dijkstra et al. 1982 *Ibis* **124** 210–213. Dilley 1953 *Everglades Nat. Hist.* **1** no. 2: 79. Dillon 1961 *Wilson Bull.* **73** 387. Ditto 1983 *Raptor Res.* **17** 91. Dixon, J. B. 1928 *Condor* **30** 228–236; 1937 *Condor* **39** 49–56; Dixon, J. B. and R. E. 1938 *Condor* **40** 3–11; Dixon, J. B. et al. 1957 *Condor* **59** 156–165. Dixon, J. S. 1938 *Birds and Mammals of Mt. McKinley Natl. Park* Nat. Park Serv. Fauna Ser. no. 3. Dobbs and Benson 1984 *Proc. 2d Symp. African Predatory Birds*, Durban, 219–228. Natal Bird Club. Doherty 1982 *Smithsonian* **13** no. 2: 104–110, 112–113. Doran 1976 *Irish Nat. Jour.* **18** 261–264; 1977 *Irish Nat. Jour.* **19** 21–23. Douglas 1829 *Vogor's Zool. Jour.* **4** no. 1: 328–330. Dresser 1865 *Ibis* n.s. **1** no. 3: 312–330; 1878 *History of Birds of Europe* **5** London. Drinkwater 1953 *Auk* **70** 215. Duebbert and Lokemoen 1977 *Prairie Nat.* **9** 33–40. van Duin et al. 1984 *Limosa* **57** 97–103. DuMont 1934 *Univ. of Iowa Studies in Nat. Hist* **15** 1–171. Duncan, B. W. 1981 *Ont. Bird Banding* **14** 21–32. Duncan, S. 1980 *Jour. Field Ornith.* **51** 178. Dunkle 1977 *Auk* **94** 65–71. Dunlavy 1935 *Auk* **52** 425–431. Dunning 1984 W. Bird-Banding Assoc. *Mongr.* no. 1. Dunstan 1968 *Loon* **40** 109–112; 1974 *Wilson Bull.* **86** 74–76; 1975 *Survival and Food Habits of Nestling and Fledging Bald Eagles on the Chippewa Natl. Forest, Minn.* Final Research Rept. 39pp.; 1978 *Natl. Geog. Mag.* **153** no. 2: 186–199, Dunstan and Borth 1970 *Wilson Bull.* **82** 326–327. Durand 1972 *Brit. Birds* **65** 428–442. Dwight 1905 *Auk* **22** 34–38.

Eakle 1984 *Raptor Res.* **18** 31–33. Eanes 1928 *Oologist* **45** 140–141. Earl 1918 *Wilson Bull.* **30** 15. Eastgate 1944 *Blue Jay* **2** 11. Eaton 1914 *Birds of N.Y.* **2** N.Y. State Mus. *Mem.* 12, pt. 2; 1953 *Kingbird* **3** 52–55. Eck 1982 *Zool. Abh.* (Dresden) **38** 65–82. Eckstein et al. 1979 *Passenger Pigeon* **41** 145–148. Edscorn 1973 *Fla. Field Nat.* **1** 15; 1974 *Fla. Field Nat.* **2** 12–13. Edwards, C. C. 1969 *Winter Behavior and Pop. Dynamics of Am. Eagles in Utah* Brigham Young Univ., Provo, Utah; Ph.D. diss. Edwards, E. P., and Lea 1955 *Condor* **59** 31–34. Edwards, T. C., Jr., and Collopy 1983 *Auk* **100** 630–635. Egorov 1959 [Ecol. of the Yakutsk Falcon] *Zool. Zhurn.* (Moscow) **38** 112–122. Eisenmann 1963a *Auk* **80** 74–77; 1963b *Wilson Bull.* **75** 244–249; 1971 *Am. Birds* **25** 529–536. Eisentraut 1935 *Mitteil. Zool. Mus. Berlin* **20** 367–443. Eklund 1946 *Auk* **63** 89–90. Elliott 1941 Linn. Soc. N.Y. Proc. nos. 52–53: 127–128. Ellis, D. H. 1975 *Bird-Banding* **46** 217–219; 1979 *Wildl. Monogr.* no. 70; Ellis et al. 1969 *Great Basin Nat.* **29** 165–167; Ellis and Depner 1979 *Condor* **81** 219–220; Ellis and Powers 1982 *Raptor Res.* **16** 134–136; Ellis and Groat 1982 *Raptor Res.* **16** 89–91; Ellis and Garat 1983 *Auk* **100** 269–271. Ellis, J. B. 1918 *Oologist* **35** 11–12. Elst 1982 *Cormorant* **10** 46. Elwell et al. 1978 *Loon* **50** 31–34. Ely 1962 *Condor* **64** 34–39. Emison and Bren 1981 *Emu* **80** (suppl.) 288–

291. Emslie 1986 *Nat. Hist.* **95** no. 4: 10, 11–13. Enderson 1960 *Wilson Bull.* **72** 222–231; 1964 *Auk* **81** 332–352; 1965 *Wilson Bull.* **77** 327–329; Enderson et al. 1972 *Living Bird* **11** 113–128; Enderson and Wrege 1973 *Jour. Wildl. Mgmt.* **37** 476–478; Enderson and Kirven 1983 *Raptor Res.* **17** 33–37. Eng and Gullion 1962 *Wilson Bull.* **74** 227–242. Engel 1966 *Jour. of Mammal.* **47** 143. Engelmann 1928 *Die Raubvögel Europas* Neudamm. England 1963 *Brit. Birds* **56** 444–452. Engle 1980 *Bull. Okla. Ornith. Soc.* **13** 21–22. Ernst 1945 *Auk* **62** 452–453. Errington 1930 *Wilson Bull.* **42** 237–239; 1930 *Condor* **34** 75–86; 1932a *Wilson Bull.* **44** 189; 1932b *Condor* **34** 75–86; 1933 *Condor* **35** 19–29; 1938 *Bird-Lore* **40** 115–119; Errington and Breckenridge 1936 *Am. Midland Nat.* **7** 831–848. Eubanks 1971 *Bull. Okla. Ornith. Soc.* **4** 33. Evans, D. L. 1982 USDI Fish and Wildl. Serv., *Spec. Sci. Rept.— Wildlife* no. 238; Evans et al. 1985 *Jour. Field Ornith.* **56** 184–187. Evans, S. A. 1981 *Ecology and Behavior Miss. Kite in S. Ill.* S. Ill. Univ., M.A. thesis. Evenden, chm. 1968 *Auk* **85** 117–126.

Faanes 1981 *N. Am. Fauna* no. 93. Faccio and Russock 1984 *Raptor Res.* **18** 77–78. Fala et al. 1985 *Raptor Res.* **19** 1–7. Fannin 1894 *Auk* **11** 322. Farley 1923 *Auk* **40** 532–533; 1924 *Auk* **41** 154–155. Fay 1910 *Auk* **27** 453–454. Feldsine and Oliphant 1985 *Raptor Res.* **19** 60–67. Fellows 1876 *Forest and Stream* **6** no. 18: 276. Fenton and Kurath 1953 Bur. Am. Ethnol. *Bull.* 156. Ferguson, A. and H. 1922 *Auk* **39** 488–496. Ferguson-Lees 1957 *Brit. Birds* **50** 149–155; 1968a *Brit. Birds* **61** 465; 1968b *Brit. Birds* **61** 256–257. Fetterholf 1979 *Can. Field-Nat.* **93** 198. Fevold and Craighead 1958 *Auk* **75** 312–317. Fewkes 1900 *Am. Anthro.* n.s. **2** 690–707. ffrench 1973 *Guide to Birds of Trinidad and Tobago* Wynnewood, Pa. Field, M. and D. 1980 Hawk Cliff Raptor Banding Sta., *8th Ann. Rept.* Figgins 1923 *Auk* **40** 666–667. Fimreite et al. 1970 *Can. Field-Nat.* **84** 269–276. Finley 1906 *Condor* **8** 135–142; 1908 *Condor* **10** 59–65. Fischer, D. L. 1984 *Raptor Res.* **18** 155–156; 1985 *Condor* **87** 246–251. Fischer, W. 1959 *Die Seeadler* 1st ed. Neue Brehm-Bücherei no. 221 (3d rev. ed. 1982); 1963 *Die Geier* Neue Brehm-Bücherei no. 311; 1968 *Der Wanderfalk* Neue Brehm-Bücherei no. 380; 1982 *Beitr. Vogelkd.* **28** 289–315; Fischer, W., et al. 1980 *Beitr. Vogelkd.* **26** 295–297. Fisher, A. K. 1893 *Hawks and Owls of U.S. in Their Rel. to Agric.* USDA Div. Ornith. and Mammal. *Bull.* 3. Fisher, D. 1978 *Brit. Birds* **71** 461. Fisher, H. I. 1939 *Auk* **56** 407–410; 1943 *Condor* **45** 69–73; 1946 *Am. Midland Nat.* **35** 545–727; 1947 *Pacific Sci.* **1** 227–236. Fisk 1972 *Bird-Banding* **43** 288–289. Fitch 1958 *Univ. Kans. Pub., Mus. Nat. Hist.* **11** 63–326; 1963 *Univ. Kans. Publ., Mus. Nat. Hist.* **12** 503–519; 1974 *Condor* **76** 331–333; Fitch et al. 1946a *Calif. Fish and Game* **32** 144–154; 1946b *Condor* **48** 205–237, Fitch and Bare 1978 *Trans. Kans. Acad. Sci.* **81** 1–13. Fitzner 1978 *Behavioral Ecology of Swainson's Hawk in Se. Wash.* Wash. State Univ., Pullman, Ph.D. diss.; Fitzner et al. 1977 *Condor* **79** 245–249. Fitzpatrick 1979 *Ont. Field Biol.* **33** 55. Flath 1972 *Auk* **89** 446–447. Fleetwood and Hamilton 1967 *Auk* **84** 598–601. Fleming 1907 *Auk* **24** 71–89. Flook and Thomas 1962 *Can. Field-Nat.* **76** 123. Floyd 1982 *Bird Observer of Mass.* **10** no. 4: 183–185. Follen 1975 *Passenger Pigeon* **37** 91–92; 1976 *Passenger Pigeon* **38** 111. Foman 1969 *Nos Oiseaux* **30** 109–139. Forbush 1927 *Birds of Mass. and Other New Eng. States* **2** Mass. Dept. Agric. Ford, E. R. 1941 *Auk* **58** 254–255. Ford, H. S., and Alcorn, 1964 *Condor* **66** 76–77. Forsman 1980 [*Hawks and Eagles—Identification Guide*] (In Finnish) Helsinki. Forsythe and Ezell 1979 *Proc. First S.C. Endangered Species Symp.* (1976). Wildl. and Marine Res. Dept., Columbia, S.C. Foster 1959 *Mass. Audubon* **43** no. 3: 139. Fowler, D. and S. 1981 *Ont. Bird Banding* **14** no. 2: 3–14. Fowler, F. H. 1903 *Condor* **5** 68–71; 1931 *Condor* **33** 193–201. Fowler, S. 1981 *Ont. Bird Banding* **14** no. 2: 15–20. Fox, A. C. 1938 *Wilson Bull.* **50** 142. Fox, A. D., and Stroud, eds. 1981 *Rept. 1979 Greenland White-fronted Goose Study* Univ. College of Wales, Aberystwyth. Fox, G. A. 1971 *Jour. Wildl. Mgmt.* **35** 122–128. Fox, N. 1976 *Raptor Res.* **10** 61–64; 1977 *New Zealand Falcon* . . . Univ. Canterbury, Christchurch, N.Z., Ph.D. diss. Fox, R., et al. 1976 *Science* **192** 263–265. Fox, R. P. 1956 *Auk* **73** 281–282. Frank 1979 *Audubon* **81** no. 4: 82–87. Fraser 1981 *Breeding Biology and Status of Bald Eagle on Chippewa Natl. Forest* Univ. of Minn., Minneapolis, Ph.D. diss.; Fraser et al. 1983 *Raptor Res.* **17** 29–30. Freer 1973 *Wilson Bull.* **85** 231–233. Freycinet 1824 *Voyage autour du monde* . . . *zoologie* Paris. Friedmann 1933a *Proc. Biol. Soc. Wash.* **46** 187–190; 1933b *Proc. Biol. Soc. Wash.* **46** 199–200; 1934 *Jour. Wash. Acad. Sci.* **24** 310–318; 1935 *Jour. Wash. Acad. Sci.* **25** 44–51; 1950 U.S. Nat. Mus. *Bull.* **50** pt. 11, Friedmann et al. 1950 *Pacific Coast Avifauna* no. 29; Friedmann and Smith 1950 U.S. Nat. Mus. *Proc.* **100** 411–538; 1955 U.S. Nat. Mus. *Proc.* **104** 463–524. Fuertes 1920 *Natl. Geog. Mag.* **38** 430–467. Fuller 1979 *Spatiotemporal Ecology: Four Sympatric Raptor Species* Univ. of Minn., Minneapolis, Ph.D. diss.; Fuller et al. 1979 *Comp. Biochem. Physiol.* A *Comp. Physiol.* **62** 433–438. Funderberg 1967 *Fla. Nat.* **40** 65. Furniss 1938 *Wilson Bull.* **50** 17–27. Fyfe 1972 *Raptor Res.* **6** (suppl. C) 43–52; 1976a *Can. Field-Nat.* **90** 308–319; 1976b *Can. Field-Nat.* **90** 370–375; Fyfe et al. 1969 *Can. Field-Nat.* **83** 191–200; Fyfe and Banasch 1981 *Alta. Nat.*, spec. issue no. 2: 57–61.

Gabrielson and Lincoln 1959 *Birds of Alaska* Harrisburg, Pa. Gaby 1982 *Age-Specific Resource Utilization by Wintering Migrant Turkey Vultures in S. Fla.* Univ. of Miami, Fla. Ph.D. diss. Gaddis 1980 *Condor* **82** 348–349. Gallup 1927 *Oologist* **44** 181. Galushin 1981 *Raptor Res.* **15** 4–11. Gambel 1848 Acad. Nat. Sci. Phila. *Proc.* for 1846, 1847 [3] 44–48. Ganier 1902 *Osprey* **1** 85–90; 1940 *Migrant* **11** 99–102; 1953 *Migrant* **24** 83–84. Garber, D.P. 1972 *Breeding Ecology of Ospreys in Lassen and Plumas Counties, Calif.* Humboldt State Univ., Arcata, Calif., M.S. thesis: Garber and Koplin 1972 *Condor* **74** 201–202. Garber, S. D. 1977 *Bat Research News* **18** 37–38. Garcia 1978 *Brit. Birds* **71** 460–462. Gardner 1978 *Auk* **47** 367–369. Gargett 1978 *Ostrich* **49** 57–63. Garrett and Mitchell 1973 Calif. Fish and Game, Wildl. Mgmt. Branch, *Admin. Rept* 73–72. Garrott and Eberhardt 1982 *Jour. Mammal.* **63** 173–174. Garrido 1967 *Poeyana* Ser. A no. 50, 1976 Acad. Sci. Cuba, *Misc. Zoologica* no. 3: 1; Garrido and Montana 1975 *Catalogo de las Aves de Cuba* Acad. Cien. Cuba, Havana. Garsd and Howard 1981 *Ecology* **62** 930–937. Gaston et al. 1985 Can. Wildl. Serv. *Rept. Ser.* no. 46. Gates 1972 *Wilson Bull.* **84** 421–433. Geller and Temple 1983 *Wilson Bull.* **95** 492–495. Genter 1985 *Wilson Bull.* **97** 108–109. Gerig 1979 *Am. Birds* **33** 836–837. Geroudet 1965 *Les rapaces d'Europe* Neuchatel, Switzerland. Gerow 1943 *Murrelet* **24** 11. Gerrard, J. 1983

Charles Broley: An Extraordinary Naturalist Headingley, Man.; Gerrard, J. et al. 1974 *Blue Jay* **32** 218–226; 1976 *Blue Jay* **34** 240–246; 1978 *Can. Field-Nat.* **92** 375–382; 1980 *Can. Field-Nat.* **94** 391–397; Gerrard and Ingram 1985 *Bald Eagle in Canada* Headingley, Man. Gerrard, P. N., et al. 1979 *Raptor Res.* **13** 57–64. Gessaman 1979a *Raptor Res.* **13** 91–96; 1979b *Wilson Bull.* **91** 625–626; 1980 *Comp. Biochem. Physiol.* **64A** 273–289; Gessaman and Findell 1979 *Comp. Biochem. Physiol.* **63A** 57–62. Gianini 1917 *Auk* **36** 394–402. Gibson 1981 *Condor* **83** 65–77. Gilbert, H. A. 1927 *Brit. Birds* **21** 26–30. Gilbert, S., et al. 1981 *Intl. Zoo Yearbook* **21** 101–109. Gilbert, V. C. 1955 *Everglades Nat. Hist.* **3** no. 2: 116–117. Giles 1924 *Oologist* **41** 83. Gilmer and Wiehe 1977 *Prairie Nat.* **9** 1–10; Gilmer et al. 1983 *Prairie Nat.* **15** 133–143; Gilmer and Stewart 1983 *Jour. Wildl. Mgmt.* **47** 146–157; 1984 *Condor* **86** 12–18. Gilmore 1932 *Pap. Mich. Acad. Sci., Arts and Letters* **16** 33–52. Gilpin 1873 *Am. Nat.* **7** 429–430. Giraud 1844 *Birds of Long Island* New York. Glading et al. 1943 *Calif. Fish and Game* **29** 92–121; Glading, B. and C. 1970 *Condor* **72** 244–245. Glazener 1964 *Condor* **66** 162. Glinski 1982 *Am. Birds* **36** 801–803; Glinski and Ohmart 1983 *Condor* **85** 200–207. Gloyd 1925 *Wilson Bull.* **37** 133–149. Glutz von Blotzheim et al. 1971 *Handb. Vogel Mitteleuropas* **4** Frankfurt. Godfrey 1966 *Bird of Can.* Nat. Mus. Can. *Bull.* 203. Golsan 1939 *Auk* **56** 482–483. Gordon 1927 *Days with the Golden Eagle* London; 1955 *Golden Eagle: King of Birds* (1st Am. ed.) New York. Goslin 1955 *Ohio Jour. Sci.* **55** 358–362. Goslow 1971 *Auk* **88** 815–827. Goss 1878 *Bull. Nuttall Ornith. Club* **3** 32–34; 1886 *Ornith. and Ool.* **11** no. 12: 183; 1891 *Hist. of Birds of Kans.* Topeka. Gosse 1859 *Letters from Ala., Chiefly Relating to Natural History* London. Graber and Golden 1960 Ill. Nat. Hist. Survey, *Biol. Notes* no. 41. Grant, J. *Can. Field-Nat.* **71** 82. Grant, P. R. 1965 *Postilla* no. 90; Grant, P. R., and Cowan **1964** *Condor* **66** 221–228. Gray **1958** *Bird Hybrids* Commonwealth Agric. Bur. Farnham Royal, Bucks, England. Grayson **1871** Boston Soc. Nat. Hist. *Proc.* **14** 261–302. Green, C. 1949 *Ibis* **29** 117–118. Green, J. C., and Janssen 1975 *Minn. Birds* Minneapolis, Minn. Green, R. 1976 *Ibis* **118** 475–490. Greene 1944 *Auk* **61** 302–304; Greene, R., et al. 1945 *Birds of Ga: A Prelim. Check-list* Ga. Ornith. Soc. Pub. no. 2. Greenway 1958 *Extinct and Vanishing Birds of World* Am. Committee Intl. Wildl. Prot., *Spec. Pub.* no. 3. Greenwood 1980 *Anim. Behav.* **28** 1140–1162. Gregory 1981 Am. Assoc. Zool. Parks and Aquariums, *Regional Conf. Proc. 1981:* 407–418. Grier 1969 *Jour. Wildl. Mgmt.* **33** 961–966; 1980 *Wildl. Soc. Bull.* **8** 316–322. Griffee 1941 *Murrelet* **22** 40–41. Griffin 1976 *Raptor Res.* **10** 50–54; 1981 *Wilson Bull.* **93** 259–264; Griffin, C. R., and Elder 1980 *Trans. Mo. Acad. Sci.* **14** 5–7; Griffin, C. R., et al. 1980 *Trans. 45th N. Am. Wildl. and Nat. Res. Conf.* 252–262; 1982 USDI Fish and Wildl. Serv. *Spec. Sci. Rept.—Wildl.* no. 247. Griffiths et al. 1954 *Brit. Birds* **47** 25. Grimes 1944 *Fla. Nat.* **17** 22–31. Grinnell 1917 *Condor* **19** 70–71; 1921 *Univ. Calif. Chron.* **23** 392–396; Grinnell et al. 1930 *Univ. Calif. Pub. Zool.* **35** 1–594. Griscom 1927 Am. Mus. Nat. Hist. *Novitat.* no. 282; 1932 Am. Mus. Nat. Hist. *Bull.* **64;** Griscom and Crosby 1925 *Auk* **42** 432–440, 519–537; Griscom and Snyder 1955 *Birds of Mass.* Salem, Mass. Gromme 1935 *Auk* **52** 15–20. Gross 1928 *Progress Rept. New Eng. Ruffed Grouse Invest. Committee* Boston: 1958 *Auk* **75** 91. Grossman and Hamlet **1964** *Birds of Prey of the World* New York. Grover 1984

Condor **86** 489.   Grubb, T. C. 1977a *Auk* **94** 146–149; 1977b *Wilson Bull.* **89** 149–150; Grubb, T. C., and Shields 1977 *Auk* **94** 140.   Grubb, T. G. 1976 *Auk* **93** 842–843; Grubb, T. G., and Coffey 1982 *Wilson Bull.* **94** 84–85.   Gudmundsson 1970 *Proc. XV Intl. Ornith. Cong.* 649.   Gullion 1947 *Condor* **49** 244; 1957 *Condor* **59** 210–211; 1981a *Loon* **53** 82–84; 1981b *Loon* **53** 3–5; 1984 *Grouse of the N. Shore* Oskosh, Wis.; Gullion et al. 1959 *Condor* **61** 278–297.   Gundlach 1876 *Contribucion a la Ornitologia Cubana* Havana.

Hackman and Henny 1971 *Chesapeake Sci.* **12** 137–141.   Hafner, J. and M. 1977 *Auk* **94** 293–303.   Hagan 1986 *Condor* **88** 200–205.   Hagar, D. 1957 *Wilson Bull.* **69** 263–272.   von Hagen 1957 *Ancient Sun Kingdoms of the Americas* Cleveland and New York.   Hagen 1947 *Vår Fågelvärld* **6** 137–141; 1952a *Rovfluglene og Viltpleien* Oslo; 1952b *Skrifter Utgitt av Det Norske Videnskaps-Akademi* **1** *Math.-Naturv. Klasse* no. 4; 1969 *Fauna* **22** 73–126; 1976 *Havørn of Kongeørn i Norge* Viltrapport no. 1.   Hahn 1927 *Oologist* **44** 141–142.   Hailman and Emlen 1985 *Fla. Field Nat.* **13** 20.   Hakkinen and Häsänen 1980 *Ann. Zool. Fenn.* **17** 131–139.   Hall, E. M. 1947 *Condor* **49** 211–212.   Hall, G. H. 1958 *Brit. Birds* **51** 402–403; 1970 *Can. Field-Nat.* **84** 209–230 [reprint of 1955 *Story of Sun Life Falcons*, with addenda].   Haller 1982 *Ornith. Beob.* **79** 163–211.   Hallberg et al. 1983 *Vår Fågelvärld* **42** 73–80.   Hallinan 1924 *Auk* **41** 304–326.   Hamerstrom, Frances 1957 *Condor* **59** 192–194; 1963 *Proc. XIII Intl. Ornith. Cong.* 866–869; 1965 *Passenger Pigeon* **27** 3–8; 1968 *Inland Bird-Banding News* **40** 43–46; 1969 *Nat. Hist.* **78** no. 5: 62–69; 1970 *An Eagle to the Sky* Ames, Iowa; 1971 *Inland Bird-Banding News* **43** 9–11; 1974 *Proc. Hawk Migr. Conf.* 1974 103–105; 1979 *Auk* **96** 370–374; 1986 *Harrier: Hawk of the Marshes* Washington, D.C.; Hamerstrom, F. and F. 1971 *Die Vogelwarte* **26** 192–197 [in English: 1972 *Raptor Res.* **6** 144–149]; 1977 *Inland Bird-Banding News* **49** 4–8; 1978 *Raptor Res.* **12** 1–14; Hamerstrom and Weaver 1968 *Ont. Bird Banding* **4** 133–138; Hamerstrom and De La Ronde Wilde 1973 *Inland Bird-Banding News* **45** 123–128; Hamerstrom et al. 1973 *Jour. Wildl. Mgmt.* **37** 400–403; Hamerstrom and Kopeny 1981 *Raptor Res.* **15** 86–88.   Hamerstrom, F. N., Jr., and Hamerstrom 1951 *Wilson Bull.* **63** 16–25.   Hamilton, K. L. 1981 *Sw. Nat.* **26** 440.   Hamilton, W. J., Jr. 1941 *Auk* **58** 244–255.   Hammond and Henry 1949 *Auk* **66** 271–274.   Hancock 1964 *Wilson Bull.* **76** 111–120; 1970 *Adventure with Eagles* Sanichton, B.C.; 1973 *1973 Intl. Zoo Yearbook* **13** 244–249.   Hankinson 1925 *Auk* **42** 130.   Hanna 1924 *Condor* **26** 146–153; 1930 *Condor* **32** 121–123; 1940 *Condor* **42** 166–167.   Hanning 1978 *Aspects of Reproduction in Pomacea paludosa* Fla. State Univ., Tallahassee, M.S. thesis.   Hansen et al. 1984 *Bald Eagles of Chilkat Valley, Alaska* Natl. Audubon Soc. and Fish and Wildl. Serv.; 1985 Hansen and Hodges *Jour. Wildl. Mgmt.* **49** 454–458.   Hanson et al. 1956 *Arctic Inst. N. Am. Spec. Pub.* no. 3.   Hantzsch 1929 *Can. Field-Nat.* **43** 31–34 [trans., part].   Harden 1972 *Bull. Okla. Ornith. Soc.* **5** 4–5.   Hardin et al. 1977 *Trans. Ill. State Acad. Sci.* **70** 341–348.   Hardy, M. 1907 *Forest and Stream* **68** no. 15: 571.   Hardy, R. 1945 *Auk* **62** 523–542.   Harmata 1981 *North Am. Bird Bander* **6** 144–147; 1982 *Raptor Res.* **16** 103–109.   Harper 1936 *Auk* **53** 381–392; 1953 *Am. Midland Nat.* **49** 1–116.   Harper, F. 1942 *Proc. Rochester Acad. Sci.* **8**, 208–221.   Harris, H. 1941 *Condor* **43** 3–55.   Harris, J. T. 1979 *Peregrine Falcon in*

Greenland Columbia, Mo. Harrison, C. 1968 *Bull. Brit. Ornith. Club* **88** 138–139; 1982 *Atlas of Birds of W. Palaearctic* Princeton, N.J.; 1984 *Field Guide to Nests, Eggs and Nestlings of N. Am. Birds* Brattleboro, Vt. Harrison, E. N., and Kiff 1980 *Condor* **82** 351–352. Harrison, K. G. 1977 *Wilson Bull* **89** 486–487. Hart 1972 *Raptor Res.* **6** 1–3. Hartert 1922 *Vogel Paal. Fauna* **2** 1175–1181. Harting 1891 *Bibliotheca Accipitraria* London (rep. 1969 Boston); 1898 *Hints on Mgmt. of Hawks and Practical Falconry* 2d ed. London (rep. 1981 Vermillion, N.D.). Hartman 1955 *Condor* **57** 221–238; 1961 *Smithsonian Misc. Colls.* **143** 1–91. Harwood 1982 *Audubon* **84** no. 5: 8, 10–11; 1985 (ed.) *Proc. Hawk Migr. Conf. IV* Hawk Migr. Assoc. N. Am. Hatch, D. R. M. 1968 *Blue Jay* **26** 78–80. Hatch, D. E. 1970 *Auk* **87** 111–124. Hatch, P. L. 1892 *Notes on Birds of Minn.* 1st Rept. Minn. State Geologist. Hatler 1974 *Auk* **91** 825–827. Haucke 1971 *Condor* **73** 475. Haug 1985 *Raptor Res.* **19** 103. Haugh 1970 *Study of Hawk Migr. and Weather in E. N. Am.* Cornell Univ., Ithaca, N.Y., Ph.D. diss.; Haugh and Cade 1966 *Wilson Bull.* **78** 88–110. Haukioja, E. 1967 *Ornis Fennica* **44** 6–11; Haukioja, E. and M. 1970 *Finnish Game Res.* **31** 13–20. Haverschmidt 1947 *Condor* **49** 210; 1948 *Wilson Bull.* **68** 230–239; 1954 *Wilson Bull.* **66** 264–265; 1959 *Auk* **76** 526; 1962 *Condor* **64** 154–158; 1964 *Jour. f. Ornith.* **105** 64–66; 1968 *Birds of Surinam* Edinburgh and London; 1970 *Auk* **87** 580–584; 1977a *Auk* **94** 392; 1977b *Auk* **94** 392. Hawbecker 1940 *Condor* **42** 106–111; 1942 *Condor* **44** 267–276; 1958 *Condor* **60** 407–408. Hayes and Gessaman 1980 *J. Therm. Biol.* **5** 119–125. Hearne 1795 *Journey from the Prince of Wales's Fort in Hudson's Bay to the Northern Ocean* London. Heath 1962 *Condor* **64** 234–235. Hebard 1941 *Winter Birds of Okefinokee and Coleraine* Ga. Soc. Naturalists *Bull.* no. 3. Hecht 1951 *Wilson Bull.* **63** 167–176. Heck 1963 *Der Zool. Garten* **27** 295–297. Hector 1981 *Habitat, Diet, and Foraging Behavior of Aplomado Falcon* Okla. State Univ., Stillwater, M.S. thesis; 1985 *Condor* **87** 336–342. Heermann 1854 Acad. Nat. Sci. Phila. *Proc.* **7** 177–180; 1859 *Repts. Expl. and Surv. . . . Miss. R. and Pacific Ocean 1853–6* **10** pt. 4: 29–80; Washington, D.C. Hegner 1906 *Bird-Lore* **8** 151–157. Hehnke 1973 *Nesting Ecol. and Feeding Behavior of Bald Eagles on Alaska Pen.* Calif. State Univ., Humboldt, M.S. thesis. Heinroth, O. and M. 1927 *Vogel Mitteleuropas* **2** Berlin and Leipzig. Heintzelman 1964 *Wilson Bull.* **76** 323–330; 1966 *Auk* **82** 307; 1975 *Autumn Hawk Flights* New Brunswick, N.J.; 1981 *Am. Hawkwatcher* no. 1; 1982 *Am. Hawkwatcher* no. 2, Heintzelman and Nagy 1968 *Wilson Bull.* **80** 306–311. Heinzman 1963 *Fla. Nat.* **36** 77. Helander 1980 *Fauna Flora* **75** 183–187; 1981 *Bird Study* **28** 235–241. Hellmayr and Conover 1949 Field Mus. Nat. Hist. Zool. Ser. **13** pt. 1. no. 4. Henckel 1976 *North Am. Bird Bander* **1** 126. Henderson 1920 *Oologist* **37** 122. Hennessey 1978 *Ecological Relationships of Accipiters in N. Utah . . .* Utah State Univ., Logan, M.S. thesis. Henning 1896 *Iowa Ornith.* p. 85. Henny 1972 USDI Fish and Wildl. Serv. Wildl. *Res. Rept.* no. 1; 1977a *Bird-Banding* **48** 274; 1977b *Trans. N. Am. Wildl. and Nat. Resources Conf.* **42** 397–411; Henny and Wight 1969 *Auk* **86** 188–198; 1972 Henny and Van Velzen *Jour. Wildl. Mgmt.* **36** 1133–1141; Henny and Wight 1972 USDI Fish and Wildl. Serv. Wildl. *Res. Rept.* no. 2: 229–250; Henny et al. 1973 *Ecology* **54** 545–554; 1974 *Chesapeake Sci.* **15** 125–133; Henny and Noltemeier 1975 *Am. Birds* **29** 1073–1079; Henny et al. 1977 *Jour. Wildl. Mgmt.* **41** 254–265; 1978 *Murrelet* **59** 14–25; Henny and

Anderson 1979 *Bull. S. Calif. Acad. Sci.* **78** 89–106; Henny and Clark 1982 *Jour. Field Ornith.* **53** 326–332; Henny et al. 1984a *Raptor Res.* **18** 41–48; 1984b *Jour. Wildl. Mgmt.* **48** 1–13; 1985 *Jour. Field Ornith.* **56** 97–112.   Henry 1939 *Auk* **56** 75.   Hensel and Troyer 1964 *Condor* **66** 282–286.   Henshaw 1875 *Rept. upon Geogr. and Geol. Expl. and Surv. w. of 100th Meridian* **5** Washington, D.C.   Herbert and Hickey 1941 Linn. Soc. N.Y. *Proc.* **52/53** 128–129; Herbert and Spofford 1943 *Am. Falconer* **1** no. 4: 14–18; Herbert, R. and K. 1965 *Auk* **82** 62–94.   Heredia and Clark 1984 *Raptor Res.* **18** 30–31.   Herklots 1961 *Birds of Trinidad and Tobago* London.   Herrick 1924a *Auk* **41** 89–105; 1924b *Auk* **41** 213–231; 1924c *Auk* **41** 389–422; 1924d *Auk* **41** 517–541; 1929 *Natl. Geog. Mag.* **55** 635–660; 1932a *Auk* **49** 307–323; 1932b *Auk* **49** 428–435; 1933 *Auk* **50** 35–53; 1934 *American Eagle: A Study in Natural and Civil History* New York.   Hesse 1912 *Jour. f. Ornith.* **60** 481–494.   Heydweiller 1935 *Auk* **52** 203–204.   Hickey 1942 *Auk* **59** 176–204; 1952 USDI Fish and Wildl. Serv. *Spec. Sci. Rept.—Wildl.* no. 15; 1969 (ed.) *Peregrine Falcon Populations* Madison, Wis.; Hickey and Anderson 1968 *Science* **162** no. 3850: 271–273. Hickman 1971 *Auk* **88** 427.   Hicks, L. 1935 *Ohio State Univ. Studies* **40** no. 5: 125–190.   Hicks, T. 1955 *Wilson Bull.* **67** 63.   Hildén and Linkola 1955 *Suuri Lintukirja* Helsinki.   Hill 1945 *Condor* **47** 129.   Hills 1970 *Can. Field-Nat.* **84** 399–401.   Hirsch 1982 *Nature* **300** 57–58.   Hockey 1981 *Cormorant* **9** 44.   Hodge (ed.) 1907 *Handb. Am. Indians N. of Mexico, Pt. 1* Bur. Am. Ethnol. *Bull.* 30.   Hodges et al. 1979 *Jour. Wildl. Mgmt.* **43** 219–221; 1984 *Jour. Wildl. Mgmt.* **48** 993–998.   Hodgson and Wyatt 1979 *Brit Birds* **72** 288–289.   Hodson 1975 *Some Aspects of Nesting Ecology of Richardson's Merlin on Can. Prairies* Univ. of B.C., Vancouver, M.S. thesis; 1978 *Can. Field-Nat.* **92** 76–77.   Hoechlin 1976 *W. Birds* **7** 137–152.   Hofslund 1966 *Wilson Bull.* **78** 79–87, 1973 *Raptor Res.* **7** 107–108.   Hogan 1983 *Can. Field-Nat.* **97** 330–331.   Hoglund 1964 *Viltrevy* **2** no. 4: 195–270.   Höhn 1975 *Auk* **92** 566–575; 1983 *Blue Jay* **41** 208–210.   Holbøll 1842–1843 Ornith. Bidrag til den grønlandske Fauna *Naturhist Tidsskrift* **4** 361–457 (later printings listed in Salomonsen 1951).   Holroyd and Beaubien 1983 *Can. Field-Nat.* **97** 452.   Holstein 1942 *Duehogen—Astur gentilis* Copenhagen.   Holt, E. G., and Sutton 1926 *Ann. Carnegie Mus.* **16** 409–439.   Holt, J. B. 1959 *Mass. Audubon* **43** 239–242; Holt, J. B., and Frock 1980 *Hawk Mt. News* no. 54: 8–32.   Horel 1960 *Fla. Nat.* **33** 35–36.   Hornung 1978 *Am. Eagle in Art and Design* New York.   Housse 1940 *Bol. Mus. Hist. Nat. "J. Prado,"* Lima **4** no. 14: 373–386.   Houston, C. S. 1949 *Can. Field-Nat.* **53** 215–241; 1958 *Blue Jay* **16** 153–154; 1967 *Blue Jay* **25** 109–111; 1968a *Blue Jay* **26** 12–13; 1968b *Blue Jay* **26** 86–87; 1970 *Ring* **62** 5–8; 1975 *Auk* **92** 612–614; 1984 *Blue Jay* **42** 99–101; Houston, C. S., et al. 1977 *Blue Jay* **35** 38–41; Houston and Millar 1981 *Jour. Field Ornith.* **52** 238; Houston and Schmidt 1981 *Blue Jay* **39** 30–37; Houston and Bechard 1983 *Blue Jay* **41** 99–109; 1984 *Am. Birds* **38** 166–170.   Houston, D. C. 1984 *Ibis* **126** 67–69.   Hovingh and Ponshair 1951 *Jack-Pine Warbler* **29** 88.   Hovis et al. 1985 *Raptor Res.* **19** 15–19.   Howard, H. 1929 *Univ. Calif. Pub. Zool.* **32** 301–394; 1930 *Condor* **32** 81–88; 1932 Carnegie Inst., Wash. *Contr. Paleontol.* no. 429; 1962 Los Angeles Co. Mus. *Contrib. in Sci.* no. 58.   Howard R. 1975 *Breeding Ecology of Ferruginous Hawk in n. Utah and s. Idaho* Utah State Univ., Logan, M.S. thesis; Howard, R., and Powers 1973 *Animal Kingdom* **73** no. 3: 22–27; Howard, R., and Rolfe

1976 *Jour. Range Mgmt.* **29** 33–37; Howard R., and Gore (eds.) 1980 *Workshop on Raptors and Energy Developments* Bonneville Power Admin., U.S. Fish and Wildl. Serv., Idaho Power Serv., 125pp.   Howe and Allen 1901 *Birds of Mass.* Cambridge, Mass.   Howell, A. H. 1932 *Fla. Bird Life* Fla. Dept. Game and Freshwater Fish, Tallahassee.   Howell, J. C. 1937 *Auk* **54** 296–299; 1941 *Auk* **58** 402–403; 1949 *Auk* **66** 84; 1954 *Auk* **71** 306–309; 1958 *Auk* **75** 96–98; 1962 *Auk* **79** 716–718; 1968 *Auk* **85** 680–681; 1973 *Auk* **90** 678–680; Howell, J. C., and Heinzman 1967 *Auk* **84** 602–603.   Howell, T. R. 1957 *Condor* **59** 73–111; 1972 *Condor* **74** 316–340.   Howes 1926 *Bird-Lore* **28** 175–180.   Hoxie 1886 *Auk* **3** 245–247; 1888 *Ornith. and Ool.* **13** 77–78; 1910 *Auk* **47** 454.   Hubbard 1971 *Nemouria* (Del. Mus. Nat. Hist.) no. 2; 1972 *Nemouria* no. 5; 1973 *Living Bird* **12** 155–196; 1974a *Auk* **91** 163–166; 1974b *Condor* **76** 214–215.   Huber 1929 *Auk* **46** 544; 1932 Acad. Nat. Sci. Phila. *Proc.* **84** 205–249.   Hudson 1920 *Birds of La Plata* **2** New York.   Huey 1913 *Condor* **15** 228; 1933 *Condor* **35** 125–126; 1941 *Auk* **58** 270; 1962 *Auk* **79** 485.   Hughes, D. 1973 *Audubon* **75** no. 5: 78–85.   Hughes, J. 1882 *Forest and Stream* **18** no. 85.   Hughes, M. 1970 *Condor* **72** 164–168.   Hughes, R. 1941 *Auk* **58** 403.   Hulce 1886 *Forest and Stream* **26** [= **27**] no. 17: 327; 1887 *Forest and Stream* **28** 392.   Hull 1980 *Jack-Pine Warbler* **58** 30.   Humphrey et al. 1970 *Birds of Isla Grande (Tierra del Fuego)* Prelim. Smithsonian Manual.   Hundley 1967 *Fla. Nat.* **40** 29; Hundley and Hames 1960 *Fla. Nat.* **33** no. 3: 150–155.   Hunt, G. 1909 *History of the Seal of the United States* Washington, D.C.   Hunt, W. G., et al. 1975 *Can. Field-Nat.* **89** 111–123.   Husain 1959 *Condor* **61** 153–154.   Hyde 1953 *Condor* **55** 277.

Imhof 1962 *Alabama Birds* Tuscaloosa, Ala.   Imler 1937 *Bird-Banding* **8** 166–169; Imler and Kalmbach 1955 USDI Fish and Wildl. Serv. *Circular* no. 30.   Ingles 1940 *Condor* **42** 104–105.   Ingolfsson 1964 *Status, Food and Breeding Biol. of White-tailed Eagle in Iceland* [unpub. report] Reykjavik.   Irving 1960 U.S. Nat. Mus. *Bull.* **217**.   Isleib and Kessel 1973 Univ. of Alaska *Biol. Papers* no. 14.

J. M. W. 1882 *Ornith. and Ool.* **6** 89–91.   Jackson, A. 1945 *Tex. Game and Fish* **3** 6–7, 26.   Jackson, J. A. 1975 *Auk* **92** 802–803; Jackson, J. A., et al. 1972 *Mississippi Kite* **2** 25–32; 1977 *Raptor Res.* **11** 86; 1978 *Wilson Bull.* **90** 141–143.   Jackson, T. 1903 *Bird-Lore* **5** 184–187.   Jackson, V. 1941 *Can. Field-Nat.* **55** 129–130.   Jaksic et al. 1980 *Auk* **97** 196–198.   James 1970 *Ecology* **51** 365–390.   Jameson 1962 *Hawking of Japan* Davis, Calif.; Jameson and Peeters 1971 (rev. 1977) *Introduction to Hawking* Davis, Calif.; Jameson et al. 1982 *Condor* **84** 439–441; Jameson and Seymour 1983 *Can. Jour. Zool.* **61** 2199–2202; Jameson et al. 1983 *Can. Jour. Zool.* **61** 466–469.   Janes 1984a *Ecology* **65** 862–870; 1984b *Condor* **86** 200–203.   Janik and Mosher 1982 *Raptor Res.* **16** 18–24.   Jehl and Parkes 1982 *Wilson Bull.* **94** 1–19.   Jenkins, M. 1974 *Behavior of Gyrfalcon from Hatching to Fledging: A Time-Lapse Photog. Study* Brigham Young Univ., Provo, Utah, M.S. thesis; 1978 *Auk* **95** 122–127, 1984 *Raptor Res.* **18** 151–153.   Jenkins, M., and Joseph 1984 *Raptor Res.* **18** 111–113.   Jenkins, R. 1970 *Wilson Bull.* **82** 97–98.   Jensen, A. S., et al. (eds.) 1934 *Zool. of the Faroes* **3** pt. 2, Copenhagen.   Jensen, J. 1923 *Auk* **40** 452–469.   Jewett et al. 1953 *Birds of Wash. State* Seattle.   Johanesson 1975 *Vår*

Fågelvärld **34** 197–206.   Johansen 1956 Revision und Entstehung der Arktischen Vogelfauna Erster teil. *Acta Arctica* fasc. 8, Copenhagen; 1957 *Jour. f. Ornith.* **98** 155–171; 1961 *Auk* **78** 44–56.   Johansson 1958 *Vår Fågelvärld* **17** 351.   Johnson, A. 1936 *Auk* **53** 210.   Johnson, A. W. 1965 *Birds of Chile . . .* 1 Buenos Aires.   Johnson, D., and Melquist 1973 *Unique, Rare and Endangered Raptorial Birds of n. Idaho* Univ. of Idaho Dept. Biol. Sci. *Publ. R1-73-021.*   Johnson, E. 1980 *North Am. Bird Bander* **5** 14; Johnson, E., et al. 1983 *Am. Birds* **37** 941–945.   Johnson, N. K., and Peeters 1963 *Auk* **80** 417–446.   Johnson, R. 1961 *Auk* **78** 646; Johnson. R. and J. 1968 *Wilson Bull.* **80** 102–103.   Johnson, S. J. 1975 *Auk* **92** 732–736.   Johnson, W. J., and Coble.   1967 *Jack-Pine Warbler* **45** 97–98.   Johnston, R. 1960 Mus. Nat. Hist., Univ. of Kans., Misc. Pub. no. 23.   Jollie 1947 *Auk* **64** 549–576.   Jones, F. 1940 *Oologist* **57** no. 3: 28–31.   Jones, G. 1952 *Wilson Bull.* **64** 166–167.   Jones, L. 1907 Oberlin College, *Laboratory Bull.* no. 13.   Jones, S. 1979 USDI Bur. Land Mgmt. *Tech. Note* no. 335.   Jourdain 1933 *Auk* **50** 201–204.   Judge 1983 *Wilson Bull.* **95** 243–255.   Junge and Mees 1961 *Avifauna of Trinidad and Tobago* Leiden.

Kahl 1963 *Physiol. Zool.* **36** 141–151.   Kaiser et al. 1980 *Pesticide Monit. Jour.* **13** 145–149.   Kale (ed.) 1978 *Rare and Endangered Biota of Fla.* **2** Birds Gainesville, Fla.   Kalla 1979 *Dist., Habitat Pref., and Status of Mississippi Kite in Tenn., with Ref. to Other Populations* E. Tenn. State Univ., Johnson City, M.S. thesis; Kalla and Alsop 1983 *Am. Birds* **37** 146–149.   Kalmbach 1939 *Jour. Am. Veterinary Med. Assoc.* n.s. **47** no. 3: 187–191; Kalmbach et al. 1964 *Am. Eagles and Their Econ. Status* USDI Fish and Wildl. Serv., Bur Sport Fisheries and Wildl.   Karlsen 1978 [Eagles v. Sheep and Reindeer] *Viltrapport* no. 6.   Keast and Morton (eds.) 1980 *Migrant Birds in the Neotropics* Washington, D.C.   Keeler 1893 *Occas. Pap. Calif. Acad. Sci.* no. 3.   Keir and De la Ronde Wilde 1976 *Wilson Bull.* **88** 658–659.   Keister and Anthony 1983 *Jour. Wildl. Mgmt.* **47** 1072–1079.   Kemper and Eastman 1970 *Auk* **87** 814.   Kempton 1927 *Wilson Bull.* **39** 142–145.   Kennard 1894 *Auk* **11** 197–210.   Kennedy, P. D. 1980 *Prey Size Selection Patterns of Nesting Male and Female Cooper's Hawks* Univ. Idaho, Moscow, M.S. thesis; Kennedy, P., and Johnson 1986 *Wilson Bull.* **98** 111–115.   Kennedy, R. S. 1973 *Bird-Banding* **44** 180–186.   Kent 1978 *Iowa Bird Life* **48** no. 4: 143.   Kenyon 1942 *Auk* **59** 443–444; 1947 *Condor* **49** 152–158; 1961 *Auk* **78** 305–326.   Keran 1978 *Raptor Res.* **12** 15–20; 1981 *Raptor Res.* **15** 108–112.   Kerlinger et al. 1983 *Auk* **100** 488–490.   Kern 1978 *Audubon* **80** 10–17.   Kessel et al. 1953 *Study of Birds of Colville R. (Final Report)* Office of Naval Res./Univ. of Alaska, Nonr-768(00); Kessel and Springer 1966 *Condor* **68** 185–195.   Kewata 1973 *Intl. Zoo Yearbook* **13** 114–115.   Keyes 1907 *Warbler* **3** 41–45 (or see N. Wood 1932).   Kibbe 1975 *Am. Birds* **29** 968; 1982 *Am. Birds* **36** 291–293.   Kiff 1981 *Bull. Brit. Ornith. Club* **101** no. 3: 318–323; Kiff et al. 1978 *Proc. Intl. Ornith. Cong.* **17** 949–952; 1979 *Condor* **81** 166–172.   Kilham 1958 *Condor* **60** 141–142; 1964 *Condor* **66** 247–248; 1979 *Raptor Res.* **13** 17–19; 1980 *Raptor Res.* **14** 29–31; 1981 *Raptor Res.* **15** 123–124; 1982a *Wilson Bull.* **94** 566–567; 1982b *Fla. Field Nat.* **10** 23.   Kimmel and Fredrickson 1981 *Trans. Mo. Acad. Sci.* **15** 21–27.   King, B. 1982 *Fla. Field Nat.* **10** 19.   King, J. G., et al. 1972 *Jour. Wildl. Mgmt.* **36** 1292–1295.   King, W. B. 1978 *Endangered Birds of the World/The ICBP Bird Red Data*

Book Washington, D.C. Kirby, R. E., and Fuller 1978 *Auk* **95** 598–599. Kirby, R. P. 1959 *Wilson Bull.* **70** 382. Kirkpatrick 1980 *Bird-Banding* **52** 23. Kirtland 1883 *Bull. Nuttall Ornith. Club* **8** 126–127. Kish 1970 *Intl. Zoo Yearbook* **10** 26–29. Kistschinskii 1958 [*Biol. of Gyrfalcon on Kola Pen* (Murmansk region)] *Uchen. Zap.* **197** 61–76. Kitchin 1918 *Condor* **20** 91. Kjaran, B. 1967 [*The White-tailed Eagle*] Reykjavik. Klafs and Stubbs (eds.) 1977 *Die Vogelwelt Mecklenburgs* Jena. Kleiman 1966 *Wilson Bull.* **78** 122. Klem et al. 1985 *Wilson Bull.* **97** 230–231. Knight, C. 1976 *Fla. Field Nat.* **4** 14. Knight, C. W. R. 1930 *Nat. Hist.* **30** 339–348; 1932 *Natl. Geog. Mag.* **62** 247–260. Knight, O. W. 1908 *Birds of Maine* Bangor, Maine. Knight, R. L., et al. (eds.) 1980 *Proc. Wash. Bald Eagle Symp., June 14–15, 1980* Seattle; Knight, R. L., and Erickson 1976 *Raptor Res.* **10** 108–111. Kochert 1972 *Pop. Studies and Chem. Contamination in Golden Eagles in Sw. Idaho* Univ. of Idaho, Moscow, M.S. thesis; 1973 *Ann. Prog. Rept.* USDI Bur. Land Mgmt., 54pp.; Kochert et al. 1983 *Wildl. Soc. Bull.* **11** 271–281. Koehler, A. 1968 [Captive breeding of some raptors] *Der Falkner* **18** 28–33 (or see 1969 *Raptor Res. News* **3** 3–18). Koford 1953 *California Condor* Natl. Audubon Soc. Research Rept. no. 4. Koivusaari et al. 1972 *Ornis Fenn.* **49** 11–13; 1973 *Suomen Luonto 1973* no. 4: 147–177. Kokhanov 1970 [Weight Gyrfalcon can supposedly carry] *Trudy Kandalashkogo Gos. Zapov.* **8** 233–234. Konrad and Gilmer 1982 *Condor* **84** 343. Koplin 1973 *Raptor Res.* **7** 39–42; Koplin et al. 1980 *Auk* **97** 795–806. Krabbe 1934 *Vidensk. Medd. fra Dansk. Naturh. Foren.* **98** 49–108. Krebs 1964 Arctic Inst. N. Am. *Tech. Paper* no. 15. Kreuningen 1980 *Dutch Birding* **2** 10. Krider 1879 *Forty Years' Notes of a Field Ornithologist* Philadelphia. Kroeber 1902 *Arapaho* Am. Mus. Nat. Hist. *Bull.* **18** pt. 1. Krog 1953 *Condor* **55** 299–304. Kumlien and Hollister 1903 *Birds of Wisconsin* Bull. Wis. Nat. Hist. Soc. no. 3. Kunkle 1976 *Urner Field Observer* **16** 13–25. Kushlan 1973 *Auk* **90** 889–890; 1975 *Nautilus* **89** 21–23. Kussman and Frenzel 1972 [3pp. in] *Trans. 34th Ann. Midwest Fish and Wildl. Conf., Dec. 10–13, 1972* Des Moines, Iowa. Kuyava 1958 *Flicker* **30** 35. Kuyt 1962 *Condor* **64** 508–510; 1967 *Bird-Banding* **38** 78–79.

Lacey 1911 *Auk* **28** 200–219. Ladd and Schempf (eds.) 1982 *Proc. Symp. and Workshop Raptor Mgmt. and Biol. in W. Alaska and W. Canada* USDI Fish and Wildl. Serv., Alaska Regional Office (Anchorage). La Fontaine and Fowler 1976 *Auk* **93** 390. Laine 1928 *Can. Field-Nat.* **42** 47. Laing, H. M. 1938 *Auk* **55** 525–527; 1979 *Allan Brooks: Artist Naturalist* B. C. Prov. Mus. *Spec. Pub.* no. 3. Laing, K. 1985 *Raptor Res.* **19** 42–51. Lamont and Reichel 1970 *Auk* **87** 158–159. Lamore 1956 *Wilson Bull.* **68** 154; 1963 *Wilson Bull.* **75** 461. Lancaster 1886 *Am. Nat.* **20** 223–230. Land 1963 *Condor* **65** 49–65; 1970 *Birds of Guatemala* Wynnewood, Pa. Lang 1924 *Nautilus* **37** 73–77. Langille 1884 *Our Birds in Their Haunts* Boston. Lano 1922 *Auk* **39** 258–259. Lardy 1980 *Raptor Inventory and Ferruginous Hawk Biol. in se. Oreg.* Univ. of Idaho, Moscow, M.S. thesis. La Rivers 1941 *Condor* **43** 65–69. Larson 1980 *Am. Birds* **34** 689–690. Lascelles, G. 1892 *Art of Falconry* London (rep. 1980). Lasiewski and Dawson 1967 *Condor* **69** 13–23. Latham, R. 1959 *Kingbird* **8** 98–101. Latham, R. M. 1950 *Food of Predatory Animals in the Ne. U.S.* Pa. Game Comm., Final Rept., P-R proj. 36-R. Laval 1948

441

Murrelet **28** 41.   Law 1915 *Condor* **17** 131; 1919 *Condor* **21** 26–27.   Lawrence, G. N. 1874 Boston Soc. Nat. Hist. Mem. **2** 265–319; 1875 U.S. Nat. Mus. *Bull.* **4.**   Lawrence, L. de K. 1949 *Wilson Bull.* **61** 15–25.   Lawson 1977 *W. Birds* **8** 73–90.   Laycock 1982 *Audubon* **84** no. 4: 26, 28–29.   Layher 1984 *Wilson Bull.* **96** 469–470.   Layne 1980 *Fla. Field Nat.* **8** 1–10; 1982 *North Am. Bird Bander* **7** 94–99; Layne and Douglas 1976 *Fla. Field Nat.* **4** 19–21; Layne et al. 1977 *Fla. Field Nat.* **5** 1–4.   Lefebvre and Joly 1982 *Animal Behavior* **30** 1020–1028.   Leffler 1971 *Wilson Bull.* **83** 196.   LeFranc and Clark 1983 *Working Bibliog. of Golden Eagle and Genus Aquila.* Washington, D.C.   Lehmann V 1957 *Noved. Colombianas* no. 3: 101–156; Lehmann and Haffer 1960 *Noved. Colomb.* **1** 242–255.   Lehti 1947 *Jour. Wildl. Mgmt.* **11** 348–349.   Lemke 1979 *Condor* **81** 207–208.   Leopold, A. S. 1944 *Wilson Bul.* **56** 116.   Léotaud 1866 *Oiseaux de l'île de la Trinidad* Port d'Espagne.   Lister 1976 *Macro Polo's Travels in Xanadu with Kublai Khan* London.   Levenson 1979 *Condor* **81** 364–369; Levinson, H., and Koplin 1984 *Jour. Wildl. Mgmt.* **48** 1374–1377.   Levy 1961 *Auk* **78** 99; 1971 *Condor* **73** 476.   Lewis [= Vesey], E. 1938 *In Search of the Gyrfalcon* London.   Lewis, H. F., and Smith 1939 *Can. Field-Nat.* **53** 45–46.   Lien 1975 *Auk* **92** 584–585.   Ligon, J. D. 1967 Univ. Mich., Mus. Zool., *Occas. Pap.* no. 651.   Ligon, J. S. 1961 *N.Mex. Birds and Where to Find Them* Albuquerque, N.Mex.   Lilford, Lord [Thos. Littleton Powys] 1903 *Lord Lilford on Birds* (ed. Trevor-Battye) London.   Lincer 1975 *Jour. Appl. Ecol.* **12** 781–793; Lincer et al. 1970 *Can. Field-Nat.* **84** 255–263; Lincer and Sherburne 1974 *Jour. Wildl. Mgmt.* **38** 427–434; Lincer and Clark 1978 *N.Y. Fish and Game Jour.* **25** 121–128; Lincer et al. 1979 *Working Bibliog. of Bald Eagle* Washington, D.C.   Lind 1976 *Production, Nest Site Selection, and Food Habits of Ospreys in Deschutes Natl. Forest, Oreg.* Oreg. State Univ. Corvallis, M.S. thesis.   Lindberg 1981a *Vår Fågelvärld* **40** 217; 1981b *Vår Fågelvärld* **40** 327–340.   Linduska 1943 *Auk* **60** 597.   Linner 1980 *Resource Partitioning . . . Marsh Hawks and Short-eared Owls* Utah State Univ., Logan, M.S. thesis.   Linsdale 1938 *Am. Midland Nat.* **19** 1–206.   Littlefield 1973 *Sw. Nat.* **17** 433;   Littlefield et al. 1984 *Raptor Res.* **18** 1–5.   Lloyd, H. 1937 *Can. Field-Nat.* **51** 137.   Lloyd, W. 1887 *Auk* **4** 181–193.   Lobkov, E. G. 1978 [Steller's Sea Eagle in Kamchatka] *Zool. Zhurn.* (Moscow) **57** 1048–1052.   Locke 1961 *Condor* **63** 342; Locke et al. 1966 *Condor* **68** 497–502.   Lodge, G. E. 1946 *Memoirs of an Artist Naturalist* London.   Loetscher 1955 *Auk* **72** 14–54.   Lofberg 1935 *Condor* **37** 171–173.   Loftin 1963 *Caribbean Jour. Sci.* **3** 63–68; Loftin and Olson 1963 *Caribbean Jour. Sci.* **3** 191–195; Loftin and Tyson 1965 *Wilson Bull.* **77** 193.   Lohrer and Winegarner 1980 *Fla. Field Nat.* **8** 47–48; Lohrer, C. and F. 1984 *Fla. Field Nat.* **12** 42–43.   Lokemoen and Duebbert 1976 *Condor* **78** 464–470.   Long 1961 *Wilson Bull.* **73** 210.   Longhurst et al. 1952 Calif. Dept. Fish and Game, *Game Bull.* no. 6.   Looney 1972 *Bull. Okla. Ornith. Soc.* **5** 1–4.   Love, D. 1975 *Effect of Land Use on Nest Sites Selected by Mississippi Kites* Ohio State Univ., Columbus, M.S. thesis.   Love, J. A. 1883 *Return of the Sea Eagle* London.   Lovell 1941 *Auk* **64** 131–132; 1952 *Wilson Bull.* **64** 48–49.   Løvenskiold, H. 1963 *Avifauna Svalbardensis* Norsk Polar Inst. *Skrifter* **129.**   Lowe, C. 1978 *Certain Life History Aspects of the Red-tailed Hawk in Cent. Okla. and Interior Alaska* Univ. of Alaska, Fairbanks, M.S. thesis.   Lowery 1938 *Auk* **55** 280; 1955 *Birds* Baton Rouge, La.   Lowery and Dalquest 1951 *Univ.*

Kans. Pub., *Mus. Nat. Hist.* **3** no. 4: 531–649; Lowery and Newman 1954 *Birds of Gulf of Mexico* U.S. Fish and Wildl. Serv., *Fishery Bull.* **89** 518–540. Ludlow 1875 *Report of a Reconnaissance of the Black Hills of Dakota in Summer 1874* Washington, D.C. Lumsden 1981 *Raptor Res.* **15** 19–22. Lundevall and Rosenberg 1955 *Proc. 11th Intl. Ornith. Cong.* 599–603. Lundy 1957 *Animal Kingdom* **60** 117–121. Luttich et al. 1970 *Ecology* **51** 190–203; 1971 *Auk* **88** 75–87. Lyle and Tyler 1934 *Migrant* **5** 49–57. Lynch 1984 *Abstr. Pap. 1984 Raptor Res. Found. Ann. Meeting.* Lyon 1916 *Science* n.s. **48** no. 1098: 75–76. Lyons and Mosher 1982 *Ardea* **70** 217–219; 1983 *Wildl. Soc. Bull.* **11** 268–270.

MacDonald 1976 *Audubon* **78** no. 4: 76–79. MacFarlane 1891 U.S. Nat. Mus. *Proc.* **14** 413–446. MacGillivray 1836 *Descriptions of Rapacious Birds of G.B.* Edinburgh. Macpherson and Manning 1959 Nat. Mus. Can. *Bull.* 161. Mader 1975a *Living Bird* **14** 59–85; 1975b *Condor* **77** 482–485; 1977a *Auk* **94** 587–588; 1977b *Auk* **94** 370–371; 1978 *Auk* **95** 327–337; 1979 *Auk* **96** 776–788; 1981 *Condor* **83** 48–51; 1982 *Condor* **84** 261–271. Madsen 1970 [eagle item] *Desert News* (Salt Lake City, Utah), July 15, B1. Maestrelli and Wiemeyer 1975 *Wilson Bull.* **87** 45–53. Mahaffey 1981 *Territorial Behavior of Bald Eagle on Chippewa Natl. Forest* Univ. of Minn., Minneapolis, M.S. thesis. Mailliard 1908 *Condor* **10** 129; 1928 *Gull* **10** 1–2. Malherbe 1963 *Ostrich* **34** 95–96. Mallette and Bornemann 1966 *Calif. Fish and Game* **52** 185–203. Mank 1965 [Discovery of Am. Kestrel in the Cisbaltic] *Ornitologiya* **7** 479. Mann 1946 [Marsh Hawk nesting in willow; ref. missing, prob. in a local jour.]. Manniche 1910 *Meddel. om Grønland* **45** 1–199. Manning et al. 1956 Nat. Mus. Can. *Bull.* 143. Marakov 1966 [*Land Where Birds Have No Fear* = Commander Is.] Moscow. Marchant 1958 *Ibis* **100** 349–387; 1960 *Ibis* **102** 349–382, 584–599. Marion and Ryder 1975 *Condor* **77** 350–352. Marquiss 1980 *Brit. Birds* **73** 555–560, Marquiss and Newton 1982 *Brit. Birds* **75** 243–260. Marsh and Storer 1981 *Jour. Exper. Biol.* **91** 363–368. Marshall 1957 *Pac. Coast Avifauna* no. 32. Marti and Braun 1975 *Condor* **77** 213–214. Martin del Campo, R. 1945 *Animal Kingdom* **48** 14–16 [trans. "rather freely" and condensed from 1943 *An. del Inst. de Biol. Univ. Nat. de Mexico* **14** 635–643]. Maslowski 1934 *Auk* **51** 229–230. Mathisen 1970 *Loon* **42** 84–87. Matray 1974 *Auk* **91** 307–324; 1976 *N.Y. State Conservationist* **3** no. 2: 20–22. Matteson and Riley 1981 *Wilson Bull.* **93** 282–284. Mattox 1969 *Polar Notes* no. 9: 46–62; 1970 *Bird-Banding* **41** 31–37. Mattsson 1974 *Interaction of a Breeding Pair of Bald Eagles with Subadults at Sucker Lake, Mich.* St. Cloud Univ., St. Cloud, Mich., M.A. thesis. May 1935 (rev. ed. 1955) *Hawks of N. Am.* New York. Maynard 1881 *Birds of E. North Am.* 2d ed. Newtonville, Mass. Mayr 1941 Am. Mus. Nat. Hist. *Novitates* no. 1133; 1966 *Auk* **83** 664; Mayr and Cottrell (eds.) 1979 *Check-list of Birds of the World* **1** 2d rev. ed. Cambridge, Mass. McAtee 1917 *Auk* **34** 415–421; 1933 *Entomol. News* **44** 235; 1935 USDA *Circular* 370; 1955 *Chat* **19** 30–35. McBee 1969 *Auk* **86** 139. McCabe, T. and E. *Auk* **45** 374. McClary 1964 *Malacologia* **2** 87–104. McCollough 1986 *Post-fledging Ecology of Bald Eagles in Maine* Univ. of Maine, Orono, Ph.D. diss. McCrary 1982 *Raptor Res.* **16** 95; McCrary and Bloom 1984 *Condor* **86** 486. McDowell 1941a *Pa. Game News* **11** no. 11: 5, 31; 1941b *Pa. Game News* **12** no. 1: 4; 1949a *Pa. Game News* **20** no. 2: 14; 1949b *Pa.*

Game News **20** no. 4: 15. McElroy 1974 *Desert Hawking* Yuma, Ariz.; 1977 *Desert Hawking II* Yuma, Ariz. McEneaney and Jenkins 1983 *Wilson Bull.* **95** 694–695. McEwan and Hirth 1979 *Condor* **82** 229–231. McEwen 1957 *Can. Field-Nat.* **71** 109–115. McGahan 1967 *Jour. Wildl. Mgmt.* **31** 496–501; 1968 *Auk* **85** 1–12; McGahan, J. and L. 1971 *Natl. Geog. Mag.* **139** no. 5: 684–709. McGillivray and Brooks 1979 *Wilson Bull.* **91** 148. McGowan 1975 *Distribution, Density and Productivity of Goshawks in Interior Alaska* Rept. Alaska Dept. Fish and Game, Juneau. McHargue 1977a *Auk* **98** 182–185; 1977b *Wilson Bull.* **89** 328–329. McIlhenny 1937 *Auk* **54** 384; 1939 *Auk* **54** 472–474; 1940 *Bird-Banding* **11** 105–109; 1943 *Auk* **60** 541–549; 1945 *Auk* **62** 136–137. McIlwraith 1886 *Birds of Ont.* London. McInvaille and Keith 1974 *Can. Field-Nat.* **88** 1–20. McKelvey 1965 *Condor* **67** 265. McKay and Fischer 1972 *Bull. Tex. Ornith. Soc.* **5** no. 1: 10. "McL.," G. [prob. Guy MacLaughlin] 1887 [letter to ed.] *Oologist* **4** nos. 3–4: 91. McLachlan and Liversidge 1971 *Roberts' Birds of S. Africa* 3d ed., 2d impression, Cape Town. McLaren, I. A., and MacInnis 1977 *Can. Field-Nat.* **91** 310–311. McLaren, P. A., and Rinde 1983 *Jour. Colo.-Wyo. Acad. Sci.* **15** 56. McLean and Williamson 1958 *Brit. Birds* **51** 157–158. McNutt 1984 *Condor* **86** 378–382. Mead, C. J. 1973 *Bird Study* **20** 259–284. Mead, R. A. 1963 *Condor* **65** 167. Mearns, E. A. 1886 *Auk* **3** 60–73. Mearns, R. 1983a *Bird Study* **30** 81–90; 1983b *Bird Study* **30** 243–244; Mearns, R., and Newton 1984 *Ibis* **126** 347–355. Mebs 1956 *Die Vogelwelt* **77** 12–15; 1971 *Vogelwarte* **26** 98–105. Mees 1977 *Limosa* **50** 114–118. Meeth, P. and K. 1978 *Ardea* **66** 121. Mehner 1952 *Wilson Bull.* **64** 242. Meinertzhagen 1954 *Ibis* **96** 153–155; 1955 *Ibis* **97** 81–117; 1956 *Ibis* **98** 535; 1959 *Pirates and Predators* Edinburgh. Melo 1973 *Jour. of Forestry* **73** 724–725. Melquist and Johnson 1975 *Raptor Res. Rept.* no. 3: 121–123; Melquist et al. 1978 *Bird-Banding* **49** 234–236; Melquist and Johnson 1984 *Jour. Field Ornith.* **55** 483–485. Mendall 1944 *Jour. Wildl. Mgmt.* **8** 198–208. Mendelsohn 1983a *Ostrich* **54** 1–18; 1983b *Bokmakierie* **35** 11–14. Meng 1951 *Cooper's Hawk* Cornell Univ., Ithaca, N.Y., Ph.D. diss.; 1959 *Wilson Bull.* **71** 169–174. Mengel 1953 *Wilson Bull.* **65** 145–151; 1965 *Birds of Ky.* AOU *Ornith. Monogr.* no. 3. Merchant 1982 *Raptor Res.* **16** 26–27. Merriam, C. H. 1877 *Trans. Conn. Acad. Arts and Sci.* **4** 1–150. Merriam, F. A. 1896 *Auk* **13** 115–124. Merrill 1878 U.S. Nat. Mus. *Proc.* **1** 118–173. van der Merwe and Heunis 1980 *Ostrich* **51** 113–114. Meserve 1977 *Condor* **79** 263–265. Meslow and Keith 1966 *Can. Field-Nat.* **80** 98–100. Meyer de Schauensee 1964 *Birds of Colombia* Philadelphia; 1966 *Species of Birds of S. Am. and Their Distribution* Narberth, Pa.; 1970 *Guide to Birds of S. Am.* Wynnewood, Pa. Meyerriecks 1957 *Wilson Bull.* **69** 278–279. Michael 1925 *Condor* **27** 109–113. von Michaelis 1952 *Birds of the Gauntlet* London. Michener 1928 *Condor* **30** 169–175; 1930 *Condor* **32** 212; Michener, H. and J. 1938 *News from Bird-Banders* **13** 7–8. Millar 1964 *Blue Jay* **22** 148. Miller, A. H. 1932 *Condor* **34** 138–139; 1941 *Condor* **43** 113–115; 1946 *Auk* **64** 351–381; 1952 *Auk* **69** 450–457; Miller, A. H., and Fisher 1938 *Condor* **40** 248–256; Miller, A. H., et al. 1965 *Current Status and Welfare of the Calif. Condor* Natl. Audubon Soc. *Research Rept.* no. 6. Miller, B. W., and Tilson 1985 *Auk* **102** 170–171. Miller, J. R. 1978 *Auk* **95** 281–287. Miller, L. 1918 *Condor* **20** 212; 1926 *Condor* **28** 172–173; 1937 *Condor* **39** 160–162; 1952 *Condor* **54**

89–92; 1954 *Condor* **56** 230–231. Miller, R. F. 1905 *Oologist* **22** 60; Miller, W. DeW. 1924 Am. Mus. Nat. Hist. *Bull.* **50** 305–331. Mills 1975 *Wilson Bull.* **87** 241–247; 1976 *Auk* **93** 740–748; 1977 *Wilson Bull.* **89** 623. Millsap 1981 USDI Bur. Land Mgmt., *Tech. Note* no. 355; 1986 *Biosystematics of the Gray Hawk* Geo. Mason Univ., Fairfax, Va., M.S. thesis; Millsap and Vana 1984 *Wilson Bull.* **96** 692–701. Mindell 1983a *Auk* **100** 161–169; 1983b USDI Bur. Land Mgmt., *Tech. Rept.* no. 8 (Anchorage, Alaska); 1985 *Am. Birds* **39** 127–133. Minnemann 1976 *Zool. Garten* **46** nos. 1–2: 54–65. 1981 Minor, W. and M. 1981 *Kingbird* **31** 68–76. Miskimen 1957 *Auk* **74** 104–105. Mitchell, G. A. 1968 *Nebr. Bird Rev.* **36** No. 2: 33–35. Mitchell, M. H. 1957 *Observations on Birds of Se. Brazil* Toronto. Mockford 1951 *Ind. Audubon Qtly.* **29** 58–59. Mois 1975 *Aves* **12** 130–159. Monroe 1963 Mus. Zool., La. State Univ. *Occas. Pap.* no. 26; 1968 *Distr. Survey of Birds of Honduras* AOU *Ornith. Monogr.* no. 7. Monson 1934 *Wilson Bull.* **46** 37–58. Montagu 1802 *Ornith. Dict. of Brit. Birds* London. Monteil de la Garza 1978 *Estudios de Nidación del Gavilán Blanco . . . en Cadereyta Jiminéz Nuevo León* Univ. Autónoma de Nueovo León, Facultad de Ciencias Biol., thesis in Biol.: 8 + 117pp. Moon, L. and N. 1985 *Kingbird* **35** 7–31. Moore, B. J. 1968 *Bryologist* **71** 161–266. Moore, J. C. 1954 *Fla. Nat.* **27** 106; Moore, J. C., et al. 1953 *Auk* **70** 470–478. Moore, K. R., and Henny 1983 *Raptor Res.* **17** 65–76; 1984 *Nw. Science* **58** 290–299. Moore, R. A., and Barr 1941 *Auk* **58** 453–462. Moreau 1955 *Proc. Zool. Soc. London* **125** 253–295. Morgan-Davies 1965 *Bull. Brit. Ornith. Club* **85** 110–111. Mori 1980 *Tori* **29** nos. 2–3: 47–68. Moriarty 1966 *S. Dak. Bird Notes* **18** no. 4: 82. Morris, M. M. 1981 *Raptor Res.* **15** 124–125; Morris, M. M., and Lemon 1983 *Jour. Wildl. Mgmt.* **47** 138–145. Morris, R. O. 1895 *Auk* **12** 86–87; 1899 *Auk* **16** 85–86. Morrison, C. F. 1887 *Ornith. and Ool.* **12** 27–28; 1889 *Ornith. and Ool.* **14** 25. Morrison, M. L. 1978 *Bull. Tex. Ornith. Soc.* **11** no. 2: 35–40; Morrison, M. L., and Walton 1980 *Raptor Res.* **14** 79–85. Moritsch 1983a *Photographic Guide for Aging Nestling Red-tailed Hawks* USDI Bur. Land Mgmt., Boise (Idaho) Dist. 16pp.; 1983b *Photographic Guide for Aging Nestling Prairie Falcons* USDI Bur. Land Mgmt., Boise (Idaho) Dist. 20pp. Mosher and Matray 1974 *Auk* **91** 325–341; Mosher and White 1976 *Can. Field-Nat.* **90** 356–359; 1978 *Auk* **95** 80–84. Moss 1979 *Jour. Zool.* (London) **187** 297–314. Mossman 1976 *Passenger Pigeon* **38** 93–99. Mote 1969 *Auk* **86** 766–767. Mrosovsky 1971 *Auk* **88** 672–673. Mueller 1970 *Auk* **87** 580; 1971 *Wilson Bull.* **83** 249–254; 1973a *Animal Behavior* **21** 513–520; 1973b *Behaviour* **49** 313–324; 1976 *Condor* **78** 120–121; 1977 *Amer. Nat.* **111** 25–29; Mueller and Berger 1959 *Bird-Banding* **30** 182–183; Mueller et al. 1966 *Wilson Bull.* **78** 470; Mueller and Berger 1967a *Auk* **84** 183–191; 1967b *Auk* **84** 430–431; 1967c *Wilson Bull.* **79** 397–415; 1968 *Auk* **85** 431–436; 1970 *Auk* **87** 452–457; 1973 *Auk* **90** 591–596; 1976 *Bird-Banding* **47** 310–318; Mueller et al. 1977 *Auk* **94** 652–663; 1979a *Am. Birds* **33** 236–240; 1979b *Bird-Banding* **50** 34–44; 1981a *Wilson Bull.* **93** 85–92; 1981b *Wilson Bull.* **93** 491–499; 1981c *Jour. Field Ornith.* **52** 112–126. Muir 1974 *Study of Breeding Biology of Arctic Gryfalcons* Can. Wildl. Serv., e. region, Ottawa, MS 58pp.; Muir and Bird 1984 *Wilson Bull.* **96** 464–467. Mumford and Danner 1974 *Ind. Audubon Qtly.* **52** 96–98. Mundy 1982 *Comparative Biol. of S. African Vultures* Johannesburg. Munoff 1963 *Kingbird* **13** 67–74. Munro, D. A. 1954 *Auk* **71** 333–

334.   Munro, H. L., and Reid 1982 *Can. Field-Nat.* **96** 206–208.   Munro, J. A. 1929a *Condor* **31** 112–116; 1929b *Auk* **46** 387–388; 1940 *Condor* **42** 168–169.   Murdock 1877 *Bull. Nuttall Ornith. Club* **2** 79.   Murie, A. 1944 Nat. Park Service *Fauna Ser.* no. 5.   Murie, O. J. 1940 *Condor* **42** 198–202; 1951 *Elk of N. Am.* Washington, D.C.; 1959 *North Am. Fauna* no. 61.   Murphey 1937 *Contrib. Charleston Mus.* 9.   Murphy 1973 *Golden Eagle Critique* Conserv. Library, Denver, Colo., Pub. Library; 1973 *Raptor Res. Rept.* no. 3: 91–96; 1978 *Trans. N. Am. Wild. and Nat. Res. Conf.* **43** 241–251; Murphy, J. R., et al. 1969 Brigham Young Univ., *Sci. Bull., Biol. Ser.* **10** no. 4; 1973 *Raptor Res. Rept.* no. 3.   Murray, J. B. 1970 *Scottish Birds* **6** 34–37.   Murray, J. J. 1952 *Check-list of Birds of Va.* Va. Ornith. Soc.   Myers 1978 *Auk* **95** 419–420.

Nagy 1977 (*in* Chancellor 1977).   de Naurois 1969 *Alauda* **37** 301–314.   Neff 1947 *Condor* **49** 32–34.   Nehrling 1905 *Warbler* 2d ser. 1 no. 2: 36–41.   Nelson, E. W. 1876 *Bull. Essex Inst.* **8**; 1887 *Rept. Nat. Hist. Colls. Made in Alaska 1877–1881* Arctic Ser. Publ. issued in connection with Signal Serv., U.S. Army no. 3; 1899 *North Am. Fauna* no. 14: 21–62.   Nelson, R. W. 1968 *Auk* **85** 696–697; 1970 *Some Aspects of Breeding Behavior of Peregrine Falcons on Langara I., B.C.* Univ. of Calgary, Alta., M.S. thesis; 1972 *Raptor Res.* **6** 11–15; 1977 *Behav. Ecol. of Coastal Peregrines* Univ. of Calgary, Alta., Ph.D. diss.; Nelson, R. W., and Myres 1976 *Condor* **78** 281–293.   Nero 1963 Sask. Nat. Hist. Soc. *Spec. Publ.* no. 5.   Nesbitt 1974 *Fla. Field Nat.* **2** 45.   Nethersole-Thompson 1951 *Greenshank* London.   Nette 1984 *Can. Field-Nat.* **98** 252–254.   Newell 1950 *Nebr. Bird Review* **18** 16–17.   Newman 1958 *Jour. Exper. Biol.* **35** 280–285.   Newton, A., and Gadow 1896 *Dict. of Birds* London.   Newton, I. 1976a *Can. Field-Nat.* **90** 225–227; 1976b *Can. Field-Nat.* **90** 274–300; 1979 *Pop. Ecol. of Raptors* Vermillion, S.D.; Newton, I., et al. 1978 *Brit. Birds* **71** 376–398; Newton, I.. and Mearns 1981 *Ibis* **123** 578; Newton, I., and Chancellor (eds.) 1985 *Conservation Studies on Raptors Intl. Coun. for Bird Production Tech. Pub.* no. 5.   NG and Jesperson 1984 *Condor* **86** 214–215.   Nice 1954 *Condor* **56** 173–197; 1970 [in review no. 48] *Bird-Banding* **41** 57.   Nicholson 1926 *Auk* **43** 62–67; 1928a *Oologist* **45** 2–8; 1928b *Oologist* **45** 21–24; 1928c *Oologist* **45** 146–151; 1930 *Wilson Bull.* **42** 32–35; 1951 *Fla. Nat.* **24** 32–33; 1952 *Fla. Nat.* **25** 23–26.   Nickell 1967 *Jack-Pine Warbler* **45** 96–97.   Nieboer 1973 *Geog. and Ecol. Differentiation in the Genus Circus* Amsterdam Free Univ., Zool. Mus., Ph.D. diss.   Nielsen 1983 *Bliki* no. 2: 27 (Nat. Hist. Mus., Reykjavik).   Nordbakke 1980 Fauna norv., 3d serv., *Cinclus* **3** 1–8.   Norris, J. P. 1887 *Ornith. and Ool.* **12** 9–11; 1888a *Ornith. and Ool.* **13** 19–21; 1888b *Ornith. and Ool.* **13** 75–77; 1926 *Oologists' Record* **6** 25–41.   Norris, R. T. 1942 *Wilson Bull.* **54** 250.   Nunn et al. 1976 *Animal Behavior* **24** 759–763.   Nuttall 1832 *Manual of the Ornith. of U.S. and Can.: Land Birds* Cambridge, Mass.   Nutting 1882 U.S. Nat. Mus. *Proc.* **5** 382–409.   Nye and Suring 1978 *N.Y. Fish and Game Jour.* **25** no. 2: 91–107.

Oakley and Eltzroth 1980 *Raptor Res.* **14** 68–69.   Oberholser 1896 *A. Prelim. List of Birds of Wayne Co., Ohio* (priv. pub.); 1906 USDA Biol. Surv. *Bull.* no. 27; 1919 *Auk* **36** 81–85,   1938 *Bird Life of La.* La. Dept. Cons., New Orleans; Oberholser and

Kincaid 1974 *Bird Life of Tex.* 1 Austin, Tex.   Oeming 1958 *Blue Jay* 16 8–10.   Ofelt 1976 *Murrelet* 57 70.   O'Gara et al. 1983 *Wildl. Soc. Bull.* 11 253–264.   Ogden, J. C. 1967 *Fla. Nat.* 40 65; 1973 *Fla. Field Nat.* 1 30–33; 1974a *Fla. Field Nat.* 2 25–27; 1974b *Auk* 91 95–110; 1975 *Wilson Bull.* 87 496–505; 1977 (ed.) *Trans. N. Am. Osprey Conf., Coll. of Wm. and Mary, Williamsburg, Va.* U.S. Natl. Park Serv. *Trans. and Proc. Ser.* no. 2; 1983 *Bird Conservation* 1 87–102.   Ogden, V. T. 1973 *Nesting Density and Reprod. Success of Prairie Falcon in Sw. Idaho* Univ. of Idaho, Moscow, M.S. thesis; Ogden, V. T., and Hornocker 1977 *Jour. Wildl. Mgmt.* 41 1–11.   O'Kane 1953 *The Hopis* Norman, Okla. Olendorff 1968 *Raptor Res.* 2 77–92; 1973 *Ecol. of Nesting Birds of Prey of ne. Colo.* U.S. Intl. Biol. Program, Grassland Biome *Tech. Rept.* 211; 1974a *Condor* 76 215; 1974b *Condor* 76 466–468; 1975 *Golden Eagle Country* New York; 1976 *Am. Midland Nat.* 95 231–236; Olendorff, R. and S. 1968–1970 *An Extensive Bibliography of Falconry, Eagles, Hawks, Falcons* pts. 1–3 (priv. pub.); Olendorff and Stoddart 1974 *Raptor Res. Rept.* 2 47–87; Olendorff et al. 1980 USDI, Bur. Land Mgmt. *Tech. Note* no. 345; Olendorff and Fish 1985 *Wildl. Habitat on Managed Rangelands . . . Ferruginous Hawk Unpubl. MS.*   Oliphant 1974 *Blue Jay* 32 140–147; 1985 *Raptor Res.* 19 37–41; Oliphant and Thompson 1976 *Can. Field-Nat.* 90 364–365; Oliphant and McTaggart 1977 *Can. Field-Nat.* 91 190–192; Oliphant and Haug 1985 *Raptor Res.* 19 56–59; Oliphant and Tessaro 1985 *Raptor Res.* 19 79–84.   Olrog 1967 *Hornero* 10 292–298.   Olson 1965 *Fla. Nat.* 38 105; 1976 (ed.) *Smithsonian Contrib. Paleobiol.* no. 27; Olson et al. 1967 *Bird-Banding* 38 75–76; Olson and Hillgartner 1982 *Smithsonian Contrib. Paleobiol.* no. 48: 22–60; Olson and James 1982a *Smithsonian Contrib. Zool.* 365; 1982b *Science* 217 633–635.   d'Orbigny 1835 *Voyage dans l'Amérique méridionale . . .* 4 pt. 3 Paris.   Orians and Kuhlman 1956 *Condor* 58 371–385; Orians and Paulson 1969 *Condor* 71 426–431.   Osgood and Bishop 1900 *North Am. Fauna* no. 19.   Österlöf 1951 Fiskgjusens . . . flyttning *Vår Fågelvärld* 10 1–15; 1973 Fiskgjusen . . . i Sverige 1971 *Vår Fågelvärld* 32 100–106; 1977 *Ornis Scand.* 8 61–78.   Owen 1860 *Ibis* 1st ser. 2 240–243.   Owre and Northington 1961 *Am. Midland Nat.* 66 200–205.

Packard, F. M. 1949 *Fla. Nat.* 22 68.   Packard, R. L., et al. 1969 *Golden Eagle-Livestock Relationships: A Survey* Texas Tech. Coll., Intl. Center for Arid and Semiarid Land Studies *Spec. Rept.* no. 20.   Page, G., and Whitacre 1975 *Condor* 77 73–83.   Page, J. and S. 1982 *Natl. Geog. Mag* 162 no. 5: 607–629.   Page, S. and J. 1982 *Hopi* New York.   Palmer 1949 *Maine Birds* Mus. Comp. Zool. Harvard *Bull.* 102.   Parker, A. 1979 *Brit. Birds* 72 104–114.   Parker, J. W. 1974 *Breeding Biol. of Miss. Kite on Great Plains* Univ. of Kans., Lawrence, Ph.D. diss.; 1974 *Condor* 78 557–558; 1977a *Auk* 94 168–169; 1977b *Wilson Bull.* 89 176; 1981 *Jour. Field Ornith.* 52 159–162; 1985 *Kingbird* 35 159–162; Parker, J. W., and Ogden 1979 *Am. Birds* 33 119–129, Parker, J. W., and Ports 1982 *Raptor Res.* 16 14–17.   Parkes 1955 *Wilson Bull.* 67 194–199; 1958 *Condor* 60 139–140.   Parmalee 1954 *Auk* 71 443–453; 1958 *Auk* 75 169–176; 1967 *Wilson Bull.* 79 155–162; Parmalee and Jacobson 1959 *Jour. Mammal.* 40 401–405; Parmalee, P. and B. 1967 *Condor* 69 146–155.   Parmelee and MacDonald 1960 Nat. Mus. Can. *Bull.* no. 169; Parmelee and Stephens 1964 *Condor* 66 443–445; Parmelee et al. 1967 Natl. Mus. Can. *Bull.* no. 222.   Parmenter 1941

Condor **43** 157. Parrott 1970 *Jour. Exper. Biol.* **53** 363–374. Pasanen 1972 *Suomen Riista* **24** 10–18; Pasanen and Sulkava 1971 *Aquilo Ser. Zool.* **12** 53–63. Paterson 1984 *Wilson Bull.* **96** 467–469. Pattee et al. 1981 *Jour. Wildl. Mgmt.* **45** 806–810. Paulson 1983 *Auk* **100** 749; 1985 *Auk* **102** 637–639. Payne and Watson 1983 *Scottish Birds* **12** 159–162. Paynter *Ornithogeog. Yucatan Pen.* Yale Univ., Peabody Mus. *Nat. Hist. Bull.* no. 9. Peabody 1900 *Bird-Lore* **2** 43–49. Pearson 1919 *Bird-Lore* **21** 319–322; 1921 *Auk* **38** 513–523; 1933 *Bird-Lore* **35** 73–74; Pearson and Brimley 1919 *Birds of N.C.* Raleigh, N.C. Peck 1913 *Oologist* **30** 133–135; 1924 *Oologist* **41** 56. Peeters 1963 *Wilson Bull.* **75** 274. von Pelzeln 1871 *Zur Ornith. Brasiliens* Vienna. Pemberton 1925 *Condor* **27** 38. Pennie 1962 *Scottish Birds* **2** 167–192. Pennock 1890 *Auk* **7** 56–57. Pennycuick 1969 *Ibis* **111** 525–556. Pereyra 1937 *Mem. Jardin Zool.* **7** 198–321; 1942 *Hornero* **8** 218–222; 1950 *Hornero* **9** 178–241. Perez-Rivera 1980 *Am. Birds* **34** 935. Perkins, A. 1922 *Auk* **39** 566–567. Perkins, J. 1964 *Audubon Mag.* **66** no. 5: 294–299; 1975 *Proc. N. Am. Hawk Migr. Conf. 1974* 54. Perkins, M. 1982 *North Am. Bird Bander* **7** 105–106. Perine 1931 *Auk* **48** 117. Perry 1973 *Fla. Scientist* **36** 22–30. Pierce 1935 *Condor* **37** 226. Pitelka 1957 Oreg. State College 18th Ann. Biol. Colloq. 73–88. Petersen 1979 Wis. Dept. Nat. Res. (Madison) *Tech. Bull.* no. 111; Petersen and Thompson 1977 *Jour. Wildl. Mgmt.* **41** 587–590. Peterson 1961 *Audubon Mag.* **63** 72–75; 1969 *Natl. Geog. Mag.* **136** 52–67. Petrovic and Mills 1972 *Wilson Bull.* **84** 491. Pettengill 1976 *Jack-Pine Warbler* **54** 70–74. Peyton 1915 *Condor* **17** 230–232. Phelps, F. 1914 *Wilson Bull.* **26** 86–101. Phelps, W. H. and W. H., Jr. 1968 *Lista de las Aves de Venezuela con su Distribucion* Caracas. Phillips, A. 1968 *Pap. Archaeol. Soc. N.Mex.* **1** 129–155; Phillips, A., et al. 1964 *Birds of Ariz.* Tucson, Ariz. Phillips, C. 1939 *Oologist* **56** 48. Phillips, R., et al. 1984 *Wildl. Soc. Bull.* **12** 269–273. Pickwell 1930 *Condor* **32** 221–239. Picozzi 1978 *Ibis* **120** 498–509; 1980 *Ornis Scand.* **11** 1–11; 1981 *Bird Study* **28** 159–161; 1983a *Brit. Birds* **76** 123–128; 1983b *Ibis* **125** 377–382; 1984 *Ibis* **126** 356–365. Piechocki 1954 (rev. 1982) Der Turmfalke *Neue Brehm-Bücherei* no. 116. Pierce 1937 *Condor* **39** 137–143. Pierson and Donahue 1983 *Am. Birds* **37** 257–259. Pinchon and Vaurie 1961 *Auk* **78** 92–93. Pinel and Wallis 1972 *Blue Jay* **30** 30–31. Pinto 1965 *Hornero* **10** 276–277. Pitcher et al. 1979 *Raptor Res.* **13** 39–40. Platt, J. B. 1971 *Great Basin Nat.* **31** 51–65; 1973 *Habitat and Time Utilization by a Pair of Nesting Sharp-shinned Hawks* Brigham Young Univ., Provo, Utah, M.S. thesis; 1976a *Am. Birds* **30** 783–788; 1976b *Condor* **78** 102–103; 1976c *Can. Field-Nat.* **90** 338–345. Platt, J. B. 1977 *Breeding Behavior of Wild and Captive Gyrfalcons in Relation to Their Environment and Human Disturbance* Cornell Univ., Ithaca, N.Y., Ph.D. diss. Platt, S. W. 1977 *Raptor Res.* **11** 81–82; 1980 *Jour. Field Ornith.* **51** 281–282; 1981 *Prairie Falcon: Aspects of Population Dynamics . . .* Brigham Young Univ., Provo, Utah, Ph.D. diss. Ponton 1983 *Raptor Res.* **17** 27–28. Poole, A. 1979 *Auk* **96** 415–417; 1981 *Colonial Waterbirds* **4** 20–27; 1982a *Auk* **99** 781–784; 1982b *Oecologia* (Berlin) **53** 111–119; 1985 *Auk* **102** 479–492; Poole, A., and Spitzer 1983 *Oceanus* **26** 49–54. Poole, E. L. 1938 *Auk* **55** 511–517. Pope 1913 *Oologist* **30** 64–66. Porsild 1943 *Can. Field-Nat.* **57** 19–35. Portenko 1939 [*Fauna of Anadyr Region: Birds*] pt. 2; 1972 (trans. 1981) [*Birds of the Chukotsk Pen. and Wrangel I.*] **1** Leningrad. Porter

1975 *Ibis* **117** 510–515; Porter and Wiemeyer 1970 *Jour. Wildl. Mgmt.* **34** 594–604; 1972 *Condor* **74** 46–53; Porter and White 1973 *Peregrine Falcon in Utah* . . . Brigham Young Univ., Provo, Utah, *Sci. Bull., Biol. Ser.* **18** no. 1; Porter et al. 1987 *Working Bibliog. of Peregrine Falcon* Washington, D.C. Portnoy and Dodge 1979 *Wilson Bull.* **91** 104–117. Postvit and Grier 1982 *Jour. Wildl. Mgmt.* **46** 1045–1048. Postupalsky 1975 *Jack-Pine Warbler* **53** 76–77; Postupalsky and Stackpole 1974 *Raptor Res. Rept.* **2** 105–117. Pough 1951 *Audubon Water Bird Guide* New York. Powell, J. W. 1895 *Canyons of the Colorado* New York (rep. New York, 1961, with new title). Power (ed.) 1980 *Calif. Islands* Multidisciplinary Symp., Santa Barbara (Calif.) Mus. *Nat. Hist. Proc.* Powers, L. R. 1981 *Nesting Behavior of Ferruginous Hawk* Idaho State Univ., Pocatello, Ph.D. diss., Powers, L. R., et al. 1984 *Raptor Res.* **18** 78–79. Powers, W. L. 1905 *Jour. Maine Ornith. Soc.* **7** 1–7. Prather et al. 1976 *Wilson Bull.* **88** 667–668. Preble 1902 *North Am. Fauna* no. 22. Pregill and Olson 1981 *Ann. Rev. Ecol. Sys.* **12** 75–98. Preston, F. W. 1968 *Auk* **85** 454–463. Preston, J. W. 1885 *Ornith. and Ool.* **10** 35; 1886 *Ornith. and Ool.* **11** 181–183. Prestt et al. 1968 *Brit. Birds* **61** 457–465. Prestwich 1955 *Records of Birds of Prey Bred in Captivity* 2d ed., rev. and enl. (priv. pub.) London. Prévost 1979 *Auk* **96** 413–414; 1982 *Wintering Ecology of Ospreys in Senegambia* Univ. of Edinburgh; Ph.D. diss.; 1983 *Ardea* **71** 199–209; Prévost et al. 1978 *Can. Field-Nat.* **92** 294–297. Price, H. 1941 *Oologist* **58** 26–27. Price, P. 1981 Bald Eagle Mgmt. and Propagation at Dickerson Park Zoo [Springfield, Mo.] *Am. Assoc. Zool. Parks and Aquariums, Regional Conf.* 425–431. Prill 1931 *Oologist* **48** 150–152. Prins 1946 *Passenger Pigeon* **8** 124. Proctor 1973 *Wilson Bull.* **85** 332. Prouty et al. 1982 *Bull. Environ. Contam. Toxicol.* **28** 319–321. Pruett-Jones et al. 1980 *Am. Birds* **34** 682–688; 1981 *Emu* **80** suppl., 253–267. Pulliainen 1975 *Ornis Fenn.* **52** 19–22. Purdue et al. 1972 *Wilson Bull.* **84** 92–93.

Quinlan 1983 *Jour. Wildl. Mgmt.* **47** 1036–1043.

Rabenold 1986 *Auk* **103** 32–41. Racey 1922 *Murrelet* **3** 6. Ragsdale 1894 *Auk* **11** 251–252. Rand 1946 Nat. Mus. Can. *Bull.* no. 105; 1948a Nat. Mus. Can. *Bull.* no. 111; 1948b *Auk* **65** 416–432; 1960 *Auk* **77** 448–459. Randall 1940 *Wilson Bull.* **52** 165–172. Ramsden 1911 *Auk* **28** 485. Raphael 1985 *Condor* **87** 437–438. Rapp 1941a *Wilson Bull.* **53** 196; 1941b *Auk* **58** 572–573; 1943 *Auk* **60** 95; 1944 *Bird-Banding* **15** 156–160. Ratcliffe 1962 *Ibis* **104** 13–29; 1963 *Brit. Birds* **56** 457–460; 1967 *Nature* **215** no. 5097: 208–210; 1972 *Bird Study* **19** 117–156; 1980 *Peregrine Falcon* Vermillion, S.D.; 1984a *Bird Study* **31** 1–18; 1984b *Bird Study* **31** 232–233. Ravel 1981 *Alauda* **49** 230–231. Ray 1928 *Condor* **30** 250. Rea 1973 *Auk* **90** 209–210. Rearden 1984 *Audubon* **86** 40–54. Recher, H. and J. 1966 *Caribbean Jour. Sci.* **6** 151–161. Reese 1977 *Auk* **94** 201–221; 1981 *Estuaries* **4** 369–373. Reid 1884 U.S. Nat. Mus. *Bull.* **25** 163–279. Reindahl 1941 *Nature Mag.* **34** 191–194. Remedios 1980 *Proc. Bald Eagle Days 1980* 225–234. Remsen and Ridgley 1980 *Condor* **82** 69–75. Retfalvi 1965 *Breeding Behav. and Feeding Habits of Bald Eagle on San Juan I.,* *Wash.* Univ. of B.C., Vancouver, M.F[orestry]. thesis; 1970 *Condor* **72** 358–361. Reynolds, H. V. 1969 *Pop. Studies of Golden Eagle in S.-Cent. Montana* Univ.

of Mont., Missoula, M.S. thesis.   Reynolds, R. T. 1979 *Food and Habitat Partitioning in Two Groups of Coexisting Accipiter* Oreg. State Univ., Corvallis, Ph.D. diss., Reynolds, R. T., and Wight 1978 *Wilson Bull.* **90** 182–196; Reynolds, R. T., et al. 1982 *Jour. Wildl. Mgmt.* **46** 124–138; Reynolds, R. T., and Meslow 1984 *Auk* **101** 761–779.   Rhodes, L. 1972 *Jour. Wildl. Mgmt.* **36** 1296–1299.   Rhodes, R. 1979 *Brit. Birds* **72** 289–290.   Rice 1982 *Auk* **99** 403–413.   Richards 1967 *Condor* **69** 88; 1970 *Condor* **72** 476.   Richardson 1957 *Murrelet* **38** 37.   Richmond 1976 *Wilson Bull.* **88** 667.   Richter 1974 *Beitr. Vogelkunde* **20** 310–315.   Ricklefs 1967 *Ecology* **48** 978–983; 1968 *Ibis* **110** 419–451.   Ridgley 1976 *Guide to Birds of Panama* Princeton, N.J.   Ridgway 1873 *Am. Nat.* **7** 197–203; 1876 *U.S. Geog. Surv. Terr. Bull.* **2** no. 2: 183–195; 1877 *U.S. Geol. Expl. 40th Parallel* . . . 4 pt. 3 *Ornithology*, pp. 303–669, Washington, D.C.; 1883 U.S. Nat. Mus. *Proc.* **6** 90–96; 1889 *Descriptive Cat. of Birds of Ill.* Springfield, Ill.; 1890 *Auk* **7** 205; 1895 *Nidiologist* **3** nos. 4–5: 42–44, 1902 *Osprey* **6** 21–33; 1905 *Condor* **7** 151–160.   Riney 1951 *Condor* **53** 178–185.   Ringelman and Longcore 1983 *Can. Field-Nat.* **97** 62–75.   Ripley 1951 *Minn. Naturalist* **2** no. 1: 14–15; Ripley and Watson 1963 *Postilla* (Peabody Mus., Yale Univ.) no. 77.   Roalkvam 1985 *Raptor Res.* **19** 27–29.   "Roamer" [Everett Smith] 1875 *Forest and Stream* **3** no. 21: 324.   Roberts, J. L., and Green 1983 *Bird Study* **30** 193–200.   Roberts, J. O. L. 1967 *Ont. Bird-Banding* **3** no. 3: 95–106.   Roberts, R. E., and Kale 1978 *Fla. Field Nat.* **6** 49.   Roberts, T. S. 1932 *Birds of Minn.* **1** Minneapolis, Minn.; 1955 *Manual for Ident. of Birds of Minn. and Neighboring States* Minneapolis, Minn.   Robbins 1975 *Proc. N. Am. Hawk Migration Conf. 1974* 29–40; Robbins et al. 1966 *Guide to Field Ident. Birds of N. Am.* New York.   Robertson 1962 *Auk* **79** 44–76; 1978 *Am. Birds* **32** 1128–1136.   Robinson, C. S. 1940 *Notes on the Calif. Condor, Collected on Los Padres Natl. Forest, Calif.* U.S. Forest Serv. (Santa Barbara) 21pp. [cited as 1939 in Koford 1953].   Robinson, T. S. 1957 *Trans. Kans. Acad. Sci.* **60** 174–180.   Rockwell 1909 *Condor* **11** 90–92.   Roddy 1888 *Auk* **5** 244–248.   Roest 1957 *Auk* **74** 1–19.   Rogers, D. T., and Dauber 1977 *Bird-Banding* **48** 73.   Rogers, W., and Leatherwood 1981 *Condor* **83** 89–90.   Rolfe 1897 Nidiologist **4** 39–41.   Rolfs 1973 *Kans. Ornith. Soc. Bull.* **24** 9–11.   Rosen 1975 *Can. Field-Nat.* **89** 455.   Roseneau 1972 *Summer Dist., Numbers and Food Habits of Gyrfalcon on Seward Pen., Alaska* Univ. of Alaska, Fairbanks, M.S. thesis.   Rosenfield 1978 *Passenger Pigeon* **40** 419; 1979 *Passenger Pigeon* **41** 60; 1982 *Raptor Res.* **16** 63; 1984 *Raptor Res.* **18** 6–9; Rosenfield and Evans 1980 *Loon* **52** 66–69; Rosenfield et al. 1982 *Wilson Bull.* **94** 365–366; Rosenfield and Wilde 1982 *Wilson Bull.* **94** 213; Rosenfield and Anderson 1983 *Status of Cooper's Hawk in Wis.* Final Rep. Wis. Dept. Nat. Resources, 10pp.; Rosenfield et al. 1984 *Jour. Field Ornith.* **55** 246–247; 1985 *Wilson Bull.* **97** 113–115.   Ross 1974 *Can. Field-Nat.* **88** 492–493.   van Rossem 1936 *Trans. San Diego Soc. Nat. Hist.* **8** 121–148; 1938 *Proc. Biol. Soc. Wash.* **51** 99; 1939 *Ann. Mag. Nat. Hist.*, 11th ser. **4** 439–443; 1942 *Trans. San Diego Soc. Nat. Hist.* **9** 377–384; 1945 Mus. Zool., La. State Univ. *Occas. Pap.* no. 21; 1946 *Condor* **48** 180–181.   Rossman, G. and R. 1971 Bald Eagles of the Chippewa Natl. Forest *Grand Rapids (Minn.) Herald Review* 32pp.   Rothfels and Lein 1983 *Can. Jour. Zool.* **61** 60–64.   Rowan 1921–1922 *Brit. Birds* **15** 122–129, 194–202, 222–231, 246–253.   Rowlett 1980 *Jour. Hawk Migr. Assoc. N. Am.* **2** no. 1: 54.   Rowley 1984 *Proc.*

W. Foundation Vert. Zool. **2** no. 3: 73–224.   Rudolph 1982 *Ecology* **63** 1268–1276; 1983 *Condor* **85** 368–369.   Ruggiero and Cheney 1979 *Raptor Res.* **13** 33–36.   Rüppell 1981 *Jour. für Ornith.* **122** 285–305.   Rusch and Doerr 1972 *Auk* **89** 139–145; Rusch et al. 1972 *Jour. Wildl. Mgmt.* **36** 282–296.   Russell, K. B. 1981 *Differential Winter Distribution by Sex in Birds* Clemson Univ., Clemson, S.C., M.S. thesis.   Russell, S. M. 1964 *A Dist. Study of Birds of Brit. Honduras* AOU *Ornith. Monogr.* no. 1; Russell and Lamm 1978 *Wilson Bull.* **90** 123–131.   Russoch 1979 *Raptor Res.* **13** 112–115.   Rust 1971 *Ann. Ornith. Gesell. Bayern* **10** 83–91.   Ruttledge 1985 *Raptor Res.* **19** 68–78.

Saenger 1984 *Jour. Field Ornith.* **55** 387–388.   Saïller 1977 *Nos Oiseaux* **34** 65–72.   Salomonsen 1951 *Grønlands Fugle* pt. 3 Copenhagen; 1959 *Beretninger Vedrørende Grønland* no. 1: 55–58; 1967 *Fuglene pa Grønland* Copenhagen; 1979 *Meddel. om Grønland* **204** no. 6: 214pp.   Salt, W. 1939 *Bird-Banding* **10** 80–84 [rep. 1981 *Alta. Nat.* spec. issue no. 2: 33–37].   Salt, W. and J. 1976 *Birds of Alta.* Edmonton, Alta.   Sandermann 1956 *Sw. Nat.* **1** 80.   Santana et al. 1986a *Condor* **88** 109–110; 1986b *Jour. Field Ornith.* **57** 235–238.   Saul 1983 *Wilson Bull.* **95** 490–491.   Saunders, A. 1906 *Bird-Lore* **8** 165–167; 1913 *Condor* **15** 99–104.   Saunders, W. 1918 *Ottawa Nat.* **32** 20.   Saurola 1976 *Ornis Fenn.* **53** 135–139.   Savard 1982 Can. Wildl. Serv. *Progress Note* no. 131.   Schaldach 1963 *Proc. W. Found. Vert. Zool.* **1** no. 1.   Scharf and Balfour 1971 *Ibis* **113** 323–329; Scharf and Hamerstrom 1975 *Raptor Res.* **9** 27–32.   Schauensee *see* Meyer de Schauensee.   Schiemenz 1958 *Jour. für Ornith.* **99** 59–66.   Schibler 1981 *Some Aspects of Winter Ecol. of Harriers on Tex. High Plains* Tex. Tech. Univ., Lubbock, M.S. thesis.   Schiøler 1931 *Danmarks Fugle* **3** *Rovfugle* Copenhagen.   Schipper 1973 *Gerfaut* **63** 17–120; 1978 *Ardea* **66** 77–102; Schipper et al. 1975 *Ardea* **63** 1–29.   Schlatter et al. 1980 *Auk* **97** 186–190.   Schlegel and Verster de Wulverhorst 1844–1853 *Traité de Fauconnerie* Leiden and Dusseldorf (rep. and trans. 1973 Denver, Colo.).   Schmid 1963 *Bird-Banding* **34** 160.   Schmutz, J. 1977 *Rel. between Three Species of Buteo in Se. Alta.* Univ. of Alta., Calgary, M.S. thesis; 1984 *Jour. Wildl. Mgmt.* **48** 1180–1187; Schmutz, J. and S. 1975 *Auk* **92** 105–110; Schmutz, J., et al. 1980 *Can. Jour. Zool.* **58** 1075–1089; 1984 *Jour. Wildl. Mgmt.* **48** 1009–1013.   Schmutz, S. and J. 1975 *Raptor Res.* **9** 58–59; 1981 *Condor* **83** 187–189.   Schnell, G. 1967a *Audubon Bull. Qtly.* Ill. Audubon Soc. no. 143: 13–14; 1967b *Kans. Ornith. Soc. Bull.* **18** 21–28; 1968 *Condor* **70** 373–377; 1969 *Auk* **86** 682–690.   Schnell, J. 1958 *Condor* **60** 377–403; 1979 USDI Bur. Land Mgmt. *Tech. Note* no. 329.   Scholander 1955 *Auk* **72** 225–239.   Schönwetter 1961 *Handb. der Oologie* Lieferung 3 Berlin.   Schoonmaker et al. 1985 *Condor* **87** 423–424.   Schorger 1917 *Auk* **34** 209; 1929 *Trans. Wis. Acad. Sci.* **24** 457–499; 1954 *Food Habits of Dirunal Raptors* Typescript.   Schreiber, R. and E. 1977 *Fla. Field Nat.* **5** 5–7.   Schroeder and Melquist 1975 *Condor* **77** 99–100.   Schroder 1947 *Nat. Hist.* **56** no. 2: 84–85.   Schueler 1980 *Incident at Eagle Ranch* San Francisco.   Schultze 1904 *Condor* **6** 106–108.   Schüz 1942 *Der Vogelzug* **13** 2–17.   Schwabe 1940 *Am. Midland Nat.* **24** 209–212.   Schweigman 1941 *Ardea* **30** 269.   Sclater and Salvin 1859 *Ibis* **1** 213–234.   Scott, F., and Houston 1983 *Blue Jay* **41** 27–32.   Scott, J. 1942 *Auk* **59** 477–498.   Scott, O. 1956 *Audubon Field Notes* **10** 270–271; 1960 *Audubon Field*

Notes **14** 60. Scott, T. 1941 *Ecology* **22** 211–212. Scott, W. 1886 *Auk* **3** 421–432; 1889 *Auk* **6** 243–245; 1890 *Auk* **7** 301–314; 1892 *Auk* **9** 120–129. Sealy 1965 *Blue Jay* **23** 25; 1966 *Blue Jay* **24** 127–128; 1967 *Blue Jay* **25** 63–69. Seibel 1971 *Kans. Ornith. Soc. Bull.* **22** 6–7. Sefton 1934 *Condor* **36** 83–84. Seidensticker and Reynolds 1971 *Wilson Bull.* **83** 408–418. Selleck and Glading 1943 *Calif. Fish and Game* **29** 122–131. Sennett 1887 *Auk* **4** 24–28. Ser   veheen 1976 *Raptor Res.* **10** 58–60; 1985 *Raptor Res.* **19** 97–99. Sexton 1975 *Am. Midland Nat.* **93** 463–468; Sexton and Marion 1974 *Wilson Bull.* **86** 167–168. Sferna 1984 *Raptor Res.* **18** 148–150. Shapiro and Weathers 1913 *Comp. Biochem. Physiol.* **68A** 111–114. Sharp, C. 1902 *Condor* **4** 116–118; 1904 *Condor* **6** 165; 1906 *Condor* **8** 144–148. Sharp, W. 1951 *Jour. Wildl. Mgmt.* **15** 224–226. Shea et al. 1979 *Fla. Nat.* **7** 3–5. Sheldon 1965 *Jack-Pine Warbler* **43** 79–83. Shelley 1935 *Auk* **52** 287–299. Sherman 1913 *Auk* **30** 406–418. Sherrod 1978 *Raptor Res.* **12** 49–121; 1983 *Behavior of Fledgling Peregrines* Ithaca, N.Y.; Sherrod et al. 1975 *Jour. Mammal.* **56** 701–703; 1976 *Living Bird* **15** 143–182; 1982 *Hacking: A Method for Releasing Peregrine Falcons and Other Birds of Prey* 2d ed. Ithaca, N.Y. Shor 1975 *Raptor Res.* **9** 46–50. Short 1974 *Condor* **76** 21–32; Short and Crossin 1967 *Trans. San Diego Soc. Nat. Hist.* **14** no. 20. Shrubb 1983 *Brit. Birds* **76** 33–34. Shuster 1976 *W. Birds* **7** 108–110; 1977 *W. Birds* **8** 29; 1980 *W. Birds* **11** 89–96. Shy 1982 *Jour. Field Ornith.* **53** 370–393. Sibley, F. C. 1970 *Ann. Nesting of Calif. Condor* Paper presented ann. meeting Cooper Ornith. Soc., Ft. Collins, Colo. 3pp. Sibley, F. C., et al. 1968 *Calif. Fish and Game* **54** 297–303. Sick 1960 *Univ. Brasil Mus. Nac. Publ. Avulsas* no. 34; 1961 *Auk* **78** 646–648. Siegfried 1965 *Ostrich* **36** 224. Siewert 1941 *Jour. für Ornith., Erganzungsband* **3** 145–193. Silloway 1903 *Birds of Fergus Co., Mont.* (priv. pub.). Simmons, G. 1925 *Birds of Austin Region* Austin, Tex. Simmons, L. (ed.) 1942 *Sun Chief: The Autobiography of a Hopi Indian* New Haven, Conn. (rep. 1962). Simons 1977 *Fla. Field Nat.* **5** 43–44. Simpson, M. and S 1977 *N.C. Hist. Rev.* **54** 1–16. Simpson, R. 1909 *Oologist* **26** 85–87; 1911 *Oologist* **28** 54–56. Singley 1886a *Ornith. and Ool.* **11** 123–124; 1886b *Ornith. and Ool.* **11** 154–155; 1887a *Ornith. and Ool.* **12** 38–39; 1887b *Ornith. and Ool.* **12** 163–165. Skaggs 1974 *Inland Bird-Banding News* **46** 171–176; 1976 *Inland Bird-Banding News* **48** 132–134. Skinner 1962 *Auk* **79** 273–274. Skutch 1945a *Auk* **62** 8–37; 1945b *Nw. Sci.* **19** 80–89; 1947 *Condor* **49** 25–31; 1950 *Ibis* **92** 185–222; 1954 *Pacific Coast Avifauna* no. 31; 1965 *Condor* **67** 235–246; 1969 *Auk* **86** 726–731; 1981 *Nuttall Ornith. Club Pub.* no. 19. Slevin 1929 Calif. Acad. Sci. *Proc.* 4th ser. **18** 45–71. Slud 1964 *Birds of Costa Rica* Am. Mus. Nat. Hist. *Bull.* **128;** 1980 *Smithsonian Contrib. Zool.* no. 292. Smallwood et al. 1982 *Jour. Field Ornith.* **53** 171–172. Smiley, A. and D. 1930 *Bird-Banding* **1** 144–145. Smith, A. P. 1915 *Condor* **17** 41–57. Smith, A. R. 1981 *Alta. Nat.* spec. issue no. 2: 38–40. Smith, D., et al. 1972 *Sw. Nat.* **17** 73–83; Smith, D., and Murphy 1978 *Sociobiology* **3** 79–98; 1979 *Raptor Res.* **13** 1–14; Smith, D., et al. 1981 *Condor* **83** 171–178, Smith, D., and Knight 1981 *Winter Pop. Trends of Raptors in Wash. from Christmas Counts* Wash. Dept. Game, 76pp. Smith, E. 1985 *Wildl. Soc. Bull.* **13** 543–546. Smith, Everett, *see* "Roamer." Smith, F. 1936 *Auk* **53** 301–305. Smith, G., and Muir 1978 *Kingbird* **28** 5–25. Smith, H. 1963 *Wilson Bull.* **75** 88–89. Smith, N. 1973 *Am. Birds* **27** 3–5 (correction: 1976 *Auk* **93** 16A). Smith, S.

1982 *Murrelet* **63** 68–69.   Smith, T. B. 1982 *Biotropica* **14** 79–80; Smith, T. B., and Temple 1982a *Auk* **99** 197–207; 1982b *Condor* **84** 131.   Smith, T. G. 1975 *Can. Field-Nat.* **89** 190; 1981 *Can. Field-Nat.* **95** 366.   Smithe 1966 *Birds of Tikal* Garden City, N.Y.   *Snake R. Birds of Prey Spec. Res. Rept.* 1979 USDI Bur. Land Mgmt., Boise (Idaho) Dist.   Snelling 1972 *Jour. Wildl. Mgmt.* **36** 1299–1304.   Snow, C. 1973a USDI Bur. Land Mgmt. *Tech. Note* [unnumbered = Rept. no. 5], 1973b USDI Bur. Land Mgmt. *Tech. Note* 239.   Snow, W. 1974 *Codline's Child* Middletown, Conn.   Snyder, H. and N. 1974 *Condor* **76** 215–216.   Snyder, L. 1932 Royal Ont. Mus. Zool. *Handb.* 2; 1938 Royal Ont. Mus. Zool. *Occas. Pap.* no. 4; 1960 *Can. Field-Nat.* **74** 164; Snyder, L., and Logier 1931 *Trans. Royal Can. Inst.* **18** 117–236.   Snyder, N. 1974 *Living Bird* **13** 73–97; 1983 *Bird Conservation* **1**; Snyder, N. and H. 1969 *Living Bird* **8** 177–233; 1970 *Condor* **72** 492–493; 1971 *Behavior* **40** 175–215; Snyder, N., et al. 1973 *Bioscience* **23** 300–305; Snyder, N. and H. 1973 *Condor* **75** 461–463; 1974a *Condor* **76** 219–222; 1974b *Natl. Geog. Mag.* **145** 432–442; Snyder, H., and Wiley **1976** *Sexual Size Dimorphism* . . . AOU *Ornith. Monogr.* no. 20; Snyder, N. and H. 1979 *Natl. Geog. Soc. Res. Repts.* 1970 Proj.: 487–491; Snyder, N., and Kale 1983 *Auk* **100** 93–97; Snyder, N., et al. 1984 *Condor* **86** 170–174; Snyder, N., and Johnson 1985 *Condor* **87** 1–13; Snyder, N., and Hamber 1985 *Condor* **87** 374–378; Snyder, N., et al. 1986 *Condor* **88** 228–241.   van Someren 1956 *Fieldiana: Zoology* **38**.   Soper 1942 *Trans. Royal Can. Inst.* **24** 19–97.   Southern 1963 *Wilson Bull.* **75** 42–55; 1964 *Wilson Bull.* **76** 121–137; 1967 *Jack-Pine Warbler* **45** 70–80; 1974 *Auk* **86** 285.   Sparrowe 1972 *Jour. Wildl. Mgmt.* **36** 297–308.   Speirs 1939 *Auk* **56** 411–419; 1977 *Birds of Ont. Co.* (part) Fed. Ont. Nat.   Sperry 1957 *Wilson Bull.* **69** 107–108.   Spitzer 1980 *Dynamics of Discrete Breeding Pop. of Ospreys in the Ne. USA, 1969–1979* Cornell Univ., Ithaca, N.Y., Ph.D. diss.; Spitzer et al. 1978 *Science* **202** 333–335; Spitzer and Poole 1980 *Am. Birds* **34** 234–241.   Spofford 1943 *Migrant* **14** 57; 1946 *Auk* **63** 85–87; 1947a *Migrant* **18** 49–51; 1947b *Migrant* **18** 60; 1958a *Kingbird* **8** 6–7; 1958b *Kingbird* **8** 42; 1964 Natl. Aubudon Soc., *Audubon Cons. Rept.* no. 1; 1971 *Am. Birds* **25** 3–7.   Springer, A. M. 1975 *Condor* **77** 338–339.   Springer, M. A. 1979 *Raptor Res.* **13** 19; Springer, M., and Kirkley 1978 *Ohio Jour. Sci.* **78** 323–328; Springer, M. A., and Osborne 1983 *Ohio Jour. Sci.* **83** 13–19.   Sprunt, Jr. 1936 *Auk* **53** 102; 1937 *Auk* **54** 384–385; 1939 *Auk* **56** 330–331; 1940 *Auk* **57** 564–565; 1945 *Audubon Mag.* **47** 15–22; 1946 *Audubon Mag.* **48** 42–44; 1950 *Tex. Jour. Sci., 1950*: 463–470; 1954 *Fla. Bird Life* New York; 1955 *N. Am. Birds of Prey* (revision of J. B. May 1935) New York; Sprunt, Jr., and Chamberlain 1949 *S.C. Bird Life* Columbia, S.C.   Sprunt IV 1973 *Trans. 38th N. Am. Wildl. and Nat. Res. Conf.* 96–106.   Stabler 1943 *Am. Falconer* **2** no. 2: 9–12.   Stager 1941 *Condor* **43** 137–139; 1952 Los Angeles Co. Mus. *Contrib. in Sci.* no. 81.   Stahlecker 1979 *Wildl. Soc. Bull.* **7** 59–62; Stahlecker and Griese 1977 *Wilson Bull.* **89** 618–619; Stahlecker and Beach 1979 *Bird-Banding* **51** 56–57.   Stalmaster 1980 *Murrelet* **61** 43–44; 1981 *Ecol. Energetics and Foraging Behav. Wintering Bald Eagles* Utah State Univ., Logan, Ph.D. diss.; Stalmaster and Newman 1978 *Jour. Wildl. Mgmt.* **42** 506–513, Stalmaster and Gessaman 1982 *Jour. Wildl. Mgmt.* **46** 646–654.   Stauber 1984 *Raptor Res.* **18** 67–71.   Steadman et al. 1986 *Current Res. in the Pleistocene* **3** 22–23.   Stedman 1983 *Fla. Field Nat.* **11** 55.   Steenhof 1978 Mgmt. of Wintering Bald Eagles USDI Fish and Wildl.

Serv. *Biol. Services Program* 59pp.; 1983 *Raptor Res.* **17** 15–27; Steenhof et al. 1983 *Auk* **100** 743–747; 1984 *Jour. Field Ornith.* **55** 357–368; 1985 Steenhof and Kochert *Oecologia* **66** 1–16.　Steffee 1966 *Fla. Nat.* **39** 42–71.　Steffen 1957 *Auk* **94** 593–594.　Stegmann 1933 [Relation of S. Am. and N.Z. falcons] Acad. Sci. USSR, *Compt. Rendu* **4** 172–175; 1937 [*Fauna of USSR . . . Birds*] **1** no. 5 [*Falconiformes*] Moscow.　Steidl 1928 *Auk* **45** 503.　Stejneger 1885 U.S. Nat. Mus. *Bull.* **29**. Stemmler 1955 *Der Steinadler in den Sweisen Alpen* Schaffhausen, Switzerland.　Stendell and Waian 1968 *Condor* **70** 187; Stendell and Myers 1973 *Condor* **75** 359–360.　Stensrude 1965 *Condor* **67** 319–321.　Stephanic 1953 *Everglades Nat. Hist.* **1** no. 2: 78.　Stevenson, H. 1957 *Wilson Bull.* **69** 39–77; 1958 *Audubon Field Notes* **12** 344–348.　Stevenson and Meitzen 1946 *Wilson Bull.* **58** 198–205.　Stewart, P. 1970 *Bird-Banding* **41** 103–110; 1974 *Auk* **91** 595–600; 1977 *Bird-Banding* **48** 122–124; 1978 *Living Bird* **17** 79–84.　Stewart, R. 1949 *Wilson Bull.* **61** 26–35; Stewart, R. E., and Robbins 1958 *North Am. Fauna* no. 62.　Stieglitz and Thompson 1967 USDI Bur. Sport Fish and Wildl. *Spec. Sci. Rept.—Wildl.* no. 109.　Stinson 1976 *Raptor Res.* **10** 73; 1977a *Oikos* **28** 299–303; 1977b *Bird-Banding* **48** 72–73; 1978 *Oecologia* **36** 127–139; 1980 *Condor* **82** 76–80; Stinson et al. 1976 *Raptor Res.* **10** 90–91; 1981 *Jour. Field Ornith.* **52** 29–35.　Stjernberg, T. 1981 *Projekt Hausorn i Finland och Sverige Jord. och Skogsbruksinenisteriet* Helsinki.　Stocek and Pearce 1978 Bald Eagle and Osprey in Maritime Prov. Can. Wildl. Serv., Wildl. Toxicol. Div., *MS Repts.* no. 37.　Stoddard 1931 *Bobwhite Quail . . .* New York; 1978 *Birds of Grady Co., Ga.* Tall Timbers Res. Sta. *Bull.* **21**.　Stohn 1974 *Falke* **21** no. 11: 391.　Stone, C., and Porter 1979 *Raptor Res.* **13** 47–48.　Stone, W. 1937 *Bird Studies at Old Cape May* **1** Del. Valley Ornith. Club.　Stoner 1939a Univ. State of N.Y. *Bull. to the Schools* **25** 114–117; 1939b *Auk* **56** 474.　Stoner E. 1933 *Condor* **35** 121; 1936 *Condor* **38** 124.　Storer 1952 *Condor* **54** 283–289; 1962 *Condor* **64** 77–78; 1966 *Auk* **83** 423–436.　Stotts and Henny 1975 *Wilson Bull.* **87** 277–278.　Strecker 1930 *Contrib. Baylor Univ. Mus.* **22** 1–14.　Street 1955 *Cassinia* no. 41: 3–76.　Stresemann 1954 *Condor* **56** 86–92; 1959 *Jour. für Ornith.* **100** 337; Stresemann, V. and E. 1960 *Jour. für Ornith.* **101** 373–403.　Studer 1881 *Birds of N. Am.* New York.　Suchetet 1897 *Des hybrides a l'état sauvage* **1** pt. 4 [birds of prey] [this author is variously cited as 1893, 1896, and 1897].　Suetens and Groenendael 1976 *Gerfaut* **66** 44–62; 1977 *Gerfaut* **67** 54–72.　Sumner, E. 1929a *Auk* **46** 161–169; 1929b *Condor* **31** 85–111; 1931 *Condor* **33** 89–91; 1933 *Univ. Calif. Pub. Zool.* **40** 277–307; 1934 *Univ. Calif. Pub. Zool.*, **40** 331–362; 1930 *Condor* **42** 39–40.　Sumner, F. A. 1933 *Condor* **35** 231–232.　Suter and Joness 1981 *Raptor Res.* **15** 12–18.　Sutton, C. 1980 *Cassinia* no. 58: 19.　Sutton, G. 1925 *Wilson Bull.* **37** 1–7; 1927 *Cardinal* **2** no. 2: 35–41; 1928 *Wilson Bull.* **40** 84–95; 1929 *Auk* **46** 235–236; 1932 Carnegie Mus. Mem. **12**, pt. 2, sect. 2; 1934 *Ann. Carnegie Mus.* **24** 1–50; 1939 *Condor* **41** 41–53; 1942 *Auk* **59** 304–305; 1944 *Wilson Bull.* **56** 3–8; 1953 *Wilson Bull.* **65** 5–7; 1967 *Okla. Birds* Norman, Okla.; Sutton, G., and Burleigh 1940 *Condor* **42** 259–262; Sutton, G., and Pettingill 1942 *Auk* **59** 1–34, Sutton, G., and Parmalee 1956 *Arctic* **9** 202–207; Sutton, G., and Tyler 1979 *Bull. Okla. Ornith. Soc.* **12** 25–29.　Sutton, I. 1955 Everglades Nat. Hist. **3** no. 2: 72–84.　Swann 1921 *Auk* **38** 357–364; 1940 *Mongr. of Birds of Prey* **1** London.　Swanton 1946 *Indians of the Se. U.S.* Bur. Am. Ethnol. *Bull.* **137**.　Swarth 1905 *Condor* **7** 22–28, 47–50, 77–81; 1911

Univ. Calif. Pub. Zool. **7** 9–172; 1920 *Birds of Papago Saguaro Natl. Monument and Neighboring Regions* USDI Natl. Park Serv., 63pp.; 1934 *Pacific Coast Avifauna* no. 22; 1935 *Condor* **37** 199–204. Swartz et al. 1973 *Raptor Res. Rept.* no. 3: 71–75. Swenk 1935 *Wilson Bull.* **47** 74; 1939 *Nebr. Bird Review* **7** 10–11. Swenson 1979a *Jour. Wildl. Mgmt.* **43** 595–601; 1979b *Auk* **96** 408–412. Swisher 1964 *Wilson Bull.* **76** 186–187. Sykes 1979 *Wilson Bull.* **91** 495–511; 1983a *Fla. Field Nat.* **11** 73–88; 1983b *Jour. Field Ornith.* **54** 237–246; 1985 *Condor* **87** 438; Sykes and Chandler 1974 *Wilson Bull.* **86** 282–284, Sykes and Kale 1974 *Auk* **91** 818–820; Sykes and Forrester 1983 *Fla. Field Nat.* **11** 111–116. Sylvén 1978 *Ornis Scand.* **9** 197–206.

Tabb 1973 *EBBA News* suppl. **36** 11–29; 1977 *North Am. Bird-Bander* **2** 163. Takekawa and Beissinger 1983 *Fla. Field Nat.* **11** 107–108. Talbot 1882 *Bull. Nuttall Ornith. Club* **7** 59. Tamisier 1970 *Terre et Vie 1970:* 511–562. Tarboton 1978 *Condor* **80** 89–91. Tate 1981 *Am. Birds* **35** 3–10. Tatum 1981 *Brit. Birds* **74** 97. Taverner 1919 *Auk* **36** 1–21; 1921 *Can. Field-Nat.* **35** 135–140; 1926 *Birds of W. Can.* Ottawa; 1927 Can. Dept. Mines, Victoria Mem. Mus. *Bull.* 48; 1936 *Condor* **38** 66–71; 1940 *Condor* **42** 157–160. Taylor, G. 1860 *Ibis* **2** 222–228. Taylor, J. 1964 *Jour. Mammal.* **45** 300–301. Taylor, W., and Shaw 1927 *Mammals and Birds of Mt. Rainier Natl. Park* USDI, Natl. Park Serv. Tebeau 1971 *History of Fla.* Coral Gables, Fla. Temme 1969 *Ornith. Mitteil.* **21** 3–6. Temple 1969 *Wilson Bull.* **81** 94; 1970 *Systematics and Evolution of N. Am. Merlins* Cornell Univ., Ithaca, N.Y., M.S. thesis; 1972a *Bird-Banding* **43** 191–196; 1972b *Auk* **89** 325–338; 1978 (ed.) *Endangered Birds: Mgmt. Techniques for Preserving Threatened Species* Madison, Wis. Terres, J. K. (ed.) 1961 *Discovery: Great Moments in Lives of Outstanding Naturalists* Philadelphia. Tewes 1984 *Wilson Bull.* **96** 135–136. Thiel 1976 *Passenger Pigeon* **38** 137–143. Thiollay 1979 *Alauda* **47** 235–245; 1981 *Gerfaut* **71** 575–610. Thomas, E. 1928 *Ohio State Mus. Sci. Bull.* **1** 29–35. Thomas, G. 1908 *Condor* **10** 116–118. Thomas, J., et al. 1964 *Wilson Bull.* **76** 384–385. Thompson, B. 1975 *Auk* **92** 395. Thompson, M. 1962 *Wilson Bull.* **74** 173–176. Thompson, S. 1982 *Wilson Bull.* **94** 564–565. Thorsteinsson and Tozier 1957 *Arctic* **10** 2–31. Thurow et al. 1980 *Raptor Ecol. of Raft R. Valley* Idaho Falls, Idaho; Thurow and White 1983 *Jour. Field Ornith.* **54** 401–406. Timmermann 1949 *Die Vögel Islands* pt. 2 *Visindafelag Islendinga* **28** 282–524 (Reykjavik). Tinkham 1948 *Condor* **50** 274. Titus and Mosher 1981 *Auk* **98** 270–281. Tjernberg 1977 *Vår Fågelvärld* **36** 21–32; 1981 *Holarctic Ecol.* **4** 12–19; 1983a *Viltrevy* (Stockholm) **12** 131–163; 1983b *Holarctic Ecol.* **6** 17–23. Todd, C., et al. 1982 *Jour. Wildl. Mgmt.* **46** 636–645. Todd, F. 1974 *Intl. Zoo Yearbook* **14** 145–147; Todd, F., and Gale 1970 *Intl. Zoo Yearbook* **10** 15–17. Todd, H. 1938 *Migrant* **9** 23–24. Todd, W. 1947 *Ann. Carnegie Mus.* **30** 383–421; 1950 *Ann. Carnegie Mus.* **31** 289–296; 1963 *Birds of Labrador Pen.* Toronto, Ont.; Todd and Friedmann 1947 *Wilson Bull.* **59** 139–150. Toland 1984 *Raptor Res.* **18** 107–110; 1985a *Jour. Field Ornith.* **56** 419–422; 1985b *Condor* **87** 434–436. Tomback and Murphy 1981 *Wilson Bull.* **93** 92–97. Tomkins 1965 *Wilson Bull.* **77** 294. Tordoff 1955 *Wilson Bull.* **67** 139–140. Toro *see* Alvarez del Toro. Toups et al. 1985 *Am. Birds* **39** 865–867. Townsend, C. 1913 *Auk* **30** 1–10; 1920 *Suppl. to Birds of Essex Co., Mass.* Nuttall Ornith.

Club, Cambridge, Mass.; 1927 *Auk* **44** 549–554.   Townsend, W., et al. 1980 *Maine Bird Life* **2** no. 1: 9.   Tozer and Richards 1974 *Birds of Oshawa-Lake Scugog Region, Ont.* Oshawa, Ont.   Tozzer and Allen 1910 *Pap. Peabody Mus. Am. Archaeol. and Ethnol., Harvard* **4** no. 3: 273–372 + 39 pls.   Trautman 1940 Univ. Mich. Mus. Zool. *Misc. Pub.* no. 44; 1942 *Wilson Bull.* **54** 139; 1964 *Auk* **81** 435.   Traylor 1941 Field Mus. Nat. Hist., *Zool. Ser.* **24** no. 19: 195–225.   Treleaven 1977 *Peregrine: Private Life of Peregrine Falcon* Penzance, Cornwall; 1980 *Zeitschr. Tierpsychol.* **54** 339–345.   Trimm 1985 *The [N.Y.] Conservationist* **39** no. 4: 24–25, Jan.–Feb.   Truslow 1961 *Natl. Geog. Mag.* **119** 123–148.   Tuck, G. 1970 *Sea Swallow* **20** 36–38.   Tuck, L. 1968 *Auk* **85** 304–311.   Tufts 1962 *Birds of N.S.* N.S. Mus., Halifax.   Tuggle and Schmeling 1982 *Jour. Wildl. Diseases* **18** 501–506.   Turcotte 1933a *Oologist* **49** 21–22; 1933b *Oologist* **49** 63–64; 1885 U.S. Nat. Mus. *Proc.* **8** 233–254. Turner 1886 *Contrib. Nat. Hist. Alaska* Arctic Ser. Pub. no. 2, pt. 5, issued in connection with Signal Service, U.S. Army, Washington, D.C.   Twente 1954 *Wilson Bull.* **66** 135–136.   Tyler, H. 1979 *Pueblo Birds and Myths* Norman, Okla.   Tyler, J. 1913 *Pacific Coast Avifauna* no. 9; 1923 *Condor* **25** 90–97.   Tyrrell, J. B. (ed.) 1916 *David Thompson's Narrative, . . . 1784–1812* Champlain Soc., Toronto, Ont.; 1934 (ed.) *Journals of Samuel Hearne and Philip Turnor* Champlain Soc., Toronto, Ont.   Tyrrell, W. B. 1936 *Auk* **53** 261–268; 1938 *Auk* **55** 468–470.

Ubelaker and Wedel 1975 *Am. Antiquity* **40** 444–452.   Udall 1986 *Aubudon* **88** no. 1: 26–28, 30–31.   Ueoka and Koplin 1973 *Raptor Res.* **7** 32–38.   Urner 1925 *Auk* **42** 31–41.   Uspenskii 1963 [Birds and mammals of Bennett I.] *Trans. Arctic and Anarctic Inst.* (Leningrad) **224** 180–205.   Uttendorfer 1952 *Neue Ergebnisse uber die Ernahrung der Greifvogel und Eulen* Berlin.

Van Daele, L. and H. 1982 *Condor* **84** 292–299; Van Daele, L., et al. 1980 *Status and Mgmt. of Ospreys Nesting in Long Valley, Idaho* Univ. Idaho, Dept. Biol. Sci., 3 + 49 pp.   Van de Kraan and Van Strien 1969 *Limosa* **42** 34–35.   Van den Akker 1954 *Wilson Bull.* **66** 136.   Van Tyne 1935 Univ. Mich. Mus. Zool., *Misc. Pub.* no. 27; 1943 *Auk* **60** 267–268; 1950 Univ. Mich. Mus. Zool., Occas. Pap. no. 525; Van Tyne and Sutton 1937 Univ. Mich. Mus. *Zool. Misc.* Pub. no. 37; Van Tyne and Trautman 1945 *Wilson Bull.* **57** 203–204; Van Tyne and Mayfield 1952 Univ. Mich. Mus. Zool. *Occas. Pap.* no. 538.   Varona 1976 Inst. Zool., Acad. Sci. Cuba *Misc. Zool.* no. 3: 2–3.   Vasina 1975 *Hornero* **11** no. 4: 281–284; Vasina and Straneck 1984 *Raptor Res.* **18** 123–130.   Vaughn 1943 *Migrant* **14** 49–50.   Vaurie 1957 *Wilson Bull.* **69** 301–313; 1961a Am. Mus. Nat. Hist. *Novitat.* no. 2035; 1961b Am. Mus. Nat. Hist. *Novitat.* no. 2038; 1961c Am. Mus. Nat. Hist. *Novitat.* no. 2042; 1965 *Birds of Palearctic Fauna: Non-Passeriformes* London.   Vennor 1876 *Our Birds of Prey; or, Eagles, Hawks and Owls of Can.* Montreal.   Verbeek 1982 *Auk* **99** 347–352.   Vermeer et al. 1974 *Environ. Pollut.* **7** 217–236.   Verner 1978 *Calif. Condor: Status of Recovery Effort* U.S. Forest Serv., *Gen. Tech. Rept. PSW-28.*   Vesey, E., *see* "Lewis," E. = pseud. Vleugel 1950 *Ardea* **38** 96–97.   Vogel 1950 *Auk* **67** 210–216.   Voous 1955 *Birds of St. Martin, Saba and St. Eustatius* Studies Fauna Curaçao and Other Caribbean Is. **6** no. 25, 1957 *Birds of Aruba, Curaçao, and Bonaire* Studies Fauna Curaçao and Other Caribbean

Is. **7** no. 29; 1961 *Ardea* **49** 176–177; 1968 *Beaufortia* **15** 195–208; 1969 *Ardea* **57** 117–148; Voous and Wattel 1972 *Jour. für Ornith.* **113** 214–218; Voous and van Dijk 1973 *Ardea* **61** 179–185; Voous and de Vries 1978 *Gerfaut* **68** 245–252.   de Vos 1964 *Am. Midland Nat.* **71** 489–502.   Vuilleumier 1970 *Breviora* [Mus. Comp. Zool. Harvard] no. 355.

Waggener 1975 *Bull. Okla. Ornith. Soc.* **8** 27.   Wagner, G. 1933 *Bird-Banding* **4** 50–51.   Wagner, H. 1941 *Ornith. Monatsber.* **49** 162–166.   Waian 1976 *Nat. History* **85** no. 9: 40–47; Waian and Stendell 1970 *Calif. Fish and Game* **56** 188–198.   Wakeley 1974 *Raptor Res.* **8** 67–72; 1978a *Condor* **80** 316–326; 1978b *Condor* **80** 327–333; 1978c *Auk* **95** 667–676.   Walker, C., and Franks 1928 Ohio State Mus. *Sci. Bull.* **1** no. 1: 59–63.   Walker, L. and M. 1939 *Nat. Hist.* **43** no. 5: 284–289; 1940 *Nature Mag.* **33** 320–333; 1941 *Audubon Mag.* **43** 35–39.   Walker, M. 1974 *Oriole* **39** 13–14.   Walker, W. 1977 *Auk* **94** 442–447.   Waller, Renz 1937 *Der Wilde Falk ist Mein Gesell* Neudamm; 1939 *Deutscher Falkenorden* **1** 14–20.   Warburton 1952 *Auk* **69** 85.   Ward and Berry 1972 *Jour. Wildl. Mgmt.* **36** 484–492.   Warham 1956 *Emu* **56** 83–93.   Warkentin 1985 *Raptor Res.* **19** 104–105; Warkentin and Oliphant 1985 *Raptor Res.* **19** 100–101.   Warner and Rudd 1975 *Condor* **77** 226–230.   Warren 1890 *Report on Birds of Pa.* 2d ed. Harrisburg, Pa. Wassenich 1968 *Regulus* **9** 214–225.   Waters, F. 1963 *Book of Hopi* New York.   Waterston 1960–1961 *Bird Notes* **29** 130–135, 175–184; 1964 *Brit. Birds* **57** 458–467.   Watson, A., and Dickson 1972 *Scottish Birds* **7** 24–29.   Watson, D. 1977 *Hen Harrier* Berkhamsted, England.   Watson, F. 1940 *Condor* **42** 295–304.   Wattel 1973 *Geog. Differentiation in Genus Accipiter* Pub. Nuttall Ornith. Club no. 13, Cambridge, Mass.   Wauer 1969 *Condor* **71** 331–336; Wauer and Russell 1967 *Condor* **69** 420–423.   Wayne 1906 *Auk* **23** 56–57; 1910 *Birds of S.C.* Charleston Mus. Contrib. no. 1.   Wayre and Jolly 1958 *Brit. Birds* **51** 285–290.   Weaver and Cade 1985 *Falconry Propagation* rev. ed. Ithaca, N.Y.   Webster, F. 1969 *Audubon Field Notes* **23** 673–675.   Webster H. 1944 *Auk* **61** 609–616.   Webster, J. 1958 *Wilson Bull.* **70** 243–256; 1973 *Condor* **75** 239–241.   Wechsler 1971 *Minn. Volunteer* **34** no. 197: 50–58.   Weekes 1974 *Can. Field-Nat.* **88** 415–419; 1975 *Can. Field-Nat.* **89** 35–40.   Wegner 1976 *Wilson Bull.* **88** 670; 1981 *Jour. Wildl. Mgmt.* **45** 248–250.   Wehle 1984 *Sea Frontiers* **30** no. 1: 4–11.   Weigand 1967 *Auk* **84** 114.   Weir and Picozzi 1975 *Brit. Birds* **68** 125–141.   Weis 1923 *Life of Harrier in Denmark* London.   Welch 1980 *Newsletter of Hawk Migr. Assoc. N. Am.* **5** no. 2: 11–12.   Weller 1967 *Ibis* **109** 391–411; 1968 *Condor* **69** 133–145; Weller et al. 1955 *Wilson Bull.* **67** 189–193.   West, J. 1875 *Forest and Stream* **4** no. 14: 220.   West, S. 1975 *Condor* **77** 354.   Wetherbee, D. and N. 1961 *Bird-Banding* **32** 141–159.   Wetmore, A. 1914 *Proc. Biol. Soc. Wash.* **27** 119–122; 1920 *Auk* **37** 393–412; 1939 U.S. Nat. Mus. *Proc.* **86** 175–243; 1943 U.S. Nat. Mus. *Proc.* **93** 215–340; 1947 *Smithsonian Misc. Colls.* **106** no. 1; 1962 *Smithsonian Misc. Colls.* **145** no. 1; 1964 *Smithsonian Misc. Colls.* **146** no. 6; 1965 *Birds of Republic of Panama* pt. 1 (*Smithsonian Misc. Colls.* **150**) Washington, D.C.   Wetmore, S., and Gillespie 1976a *Can. Field-Nat.* **90** 330–337; 1976b *Can. Field Nat.* **90** 368–369.   Whaley 1979 *Ecol. and Status of Harris' Hawk in Ariz.* Univ. Ariz, Tucson, M.S. thesis; 1986 *Pop. Ecol. Harris' Hawk in Ariz.* In press.   Wheeler and Raile

1967 *Murrelet* **48** 20–21. Wheelock 1904 *Birds of Calif.* . . . Chicago. Whitacre et al. 1982 *Wilson Bull.* **94** 565–566. White 1962 *Condor* **64** 439–440; 1968a *Biosystematics of N. Am. Peregrine Falcons* Univ. of Utah, Salt Lake City, Ph.D. diss.; 1968b *Auk* **85** 179–191; 1969 *Wilson Bull.* **81** 339–340; 1974 *Trans. 39th N. Am. Wildl. and Nat. Res. Conf.* 301–312; 1975 *Raptor Res. Rept.* no. 3: 33–50; White and Springer 1965 *Auk* **82** 104–105; White and Weeden 1966 *Condor* **68** 517–519; White and Roseneau 1970 *Condor* **72** 113–115; White and Cade 1971 *Living Bird* **10** 107–150; 1975 *Raptor Studies along Proposed Susitna Powerline Corridors* . . . Alaska Rept. submitted to U.S. Fish and Wildl. Serv., Anchorage: 28pp.; White et al. 1983 *Great Basin Nat.* **43** 717–727; White and Thurow 1985 *Condor* **87** 14–22. Whitfield, D. P. 1985 *Ibis* **127** 544–558. Whitfield, D. W. A., et al. 1969 *Blue Jay* **27** 74–79; 1974 *Can. Field-Nat.* **88** 399–407. Widén 1982 *Symp. Zool. Soc. London* no. 49: 153–160; 1984 *Ornis Fenn.* **61** 109–112. Wilkinson and Debban 1980 *W. Birds* **11** 25–34. Williamson 1957 *Condor* **59** 317–388. Widmann 1907 *Prelim. Cat. of Birds of Mo.* St. Louis Acad. Sci. *Trans.* **17** 1–288. Wiemeyer 1981 *Raptor Res.* **15** 68–82; Wiemeyer et al. 1975 *Jour. Wildl. Mgmt.* **39** 124–139; 1978 *Bull. Environ. Contam. Toxicol.* **19** 56–63; 1980 *Estuaries* **3** 155–167. Wiggins 1969 *Proc. Calif. Acad. Sci.* **36** 317–346. Wiklund 1979 *Ibis* **121** 109–111. Wilbur 1973 *W. Birds* **4** 15–22; 1975 *Calif. Fish and Game* **61** 144–148; 1978a *North Am. Fauna* no. 72; 1978b *Wilson Bull.* **90** 642–643; 1980 *Calif. Fish and Game* **66** 40–48; Wilbur and Borneman 1972 *Auk* **89** 444–445; Wilbur and Jackson (eds.) 1983 *Vulture Biol. and Mgmt.* Berkeley and Los Angeles, Calif. Wilcox 1944 Univ. of State of N.Y., *Bull. to the Schools* **30** 262–264. Wiley, J. 1975a *Condor* **77** 133–139; 1975b *Condor* **77** 480–482; 1975c *Auk* **92** 157–159, Wiley, J., and Lohrer 1973, *Wilson Bull.* **85** 468–470. Wiley, R., and Bolen 1971 *Sw. Nat.* **16** 151–169. Wilhelm 1960 *Wilson Bull.* **72** 401–402. Wilkinson and Debban 1980 *W. Birds* **11** 25–34. Willard 1910 *Condor* **12** 110; 1916a *Condor* **18** 200–201; 1916b *Oologist* **33** 2–10. Willett 1912 *Pacific Coast Avifauna* no. 7. Willgohs 1961 *White-tailed Eagle in Norway* Arbok for Universitet I Bergen. Mat.-Naturv. serie no. 12. Williams, G. 1951 *Auk* **68** 372. "Williams," "John" [C. J. Pennock] 1916 *Wilson Bull.* **28** 38. Williams, R. B., et al. 1948 Wyo. Fish and Game Dept. (Cheyenne) *Bull.* **5.** Williams, R. N. 1985 *Raptor Res.* **19** 129–134. Williamson, E. 1913 *Auk* **30** 582–583. Williamson, F. 1957 *Condor* **59** 317–388. Willis 1963 *Condor* **65** 313–317; 1966 *Condor* **68** 104. Willoughby 1966 *Auk* **83** 201–206; Willoughby and Cade 1964 *Living Bird* **3** 75–96. Wilmers 1983 *Raptor Res.* **17** 94–95. Wilson, A., and Bonaparte (ed. Jardine) 1832 *Am. Ornith.* **1–3** London and Edinburgh. Wilson, F. 1927 *Bird-Lore* **29** 397–402. Wilson, G. 1928 *Hidatsa Eagle Trapping* Am. Mus. Nat. Hist. *Anthrop. Pap.* **39** pt. 4. Wilson, P., and Grigsby 1980 *Inland Bird Banding* **52** 35. Wimberger 1984 *Auk* **101** 614–618. Windigstad et al. 1981 *Auk* **98** 393–394. Windsor and Emlen 1975 *Condor* **77** 359–361. Wing, L. 1949 *Auk* **66** 38–41; Wing, L. and A. 1939 *Condor* **41** 168–170. Winge 1898 *Grønlands Fugle* Meddel. om Grønland **21.** Winship 1896 *Coronada Exped., 1540–1542* Bur. Am. Ethnol. *14th Ann. Rept.* pt. 1: 329–613. Wishart et al. 1981 *Prairie Naturalist* **13** 23–25. Witherby 1920 *Brit. Birds* **14** 154–155; 1924 (ed.) *Practical Handb. of Brit. Birds* **2** pt. 1 (pp. 81–256 actually pub. in 1921) London. 1939 Witherby (ed.) *Handb. of Brit. Birds* **3** (usually cited as 1941, but reviewed 1939 *Auk* **56** 485) London.   Witthoft 1946 *Jour. Wash. Acad. Sci.* **36** 372–384.   Woffinden 1977 *Great Basin Nat.* **37** 411–425; Woffinden and Mosher 1979 *Great Basin Nat.* **39** 253–254; Woffinden and Murphy 1982 *Raptor Res.* **16** 1–4; 1983 *North Am. Bird Bander* **8** 94–96.   Wolhuter and Kish 1970 *Wilson Bull.* **82** 96–97.   Wood, C. A., and Fyfe, F. M. 1943 *Art of Falconry by Frederick II of Hohenstaufen* Stanford, Calif. (reissued 1961; rep. 1969).   Wood, D. 1951 *Condor* **45** 159.   Wood, M. 1938 *Auk* **55** 123–124.   Wood, N. 1932 *Wilson Bull.* **44** 78–87.   Wood, W. 1871 *Am. Nat.* **5** 1–8.   Woodcock 1942 *Sci. Monthly*, Sept.: 226–232.   Woodford 1960 *Manual of Falconry* London.   Woodin, M. and C. 1981 *Fla. Field Nat.* **9** 64.   Woodman, *see* 1944 *Fla. Nat.* **17** 38.   Woods, R. S. 1929 *Auk* **46** 386.   Woods, R. W. 1975 *Birds of Falkland Is.* Oswestry.   Woodson and McClellan 1981 *Miss. Kite* **11** 13–14.   Worcester 1905 *Oologist* **22** 140.   Work and Wool 1942 *Condor* **44** 149–159; 1947 *Nat. Hist.* **56** 412–417, 428.   Worth 1939 *Bird-Lore* **41** 279–284.   Worthington and Todd 1926 *Wilson Bull.* **38** 204–229.   Wrakstraw 1972 *Wyo. Bald and Golden Eagle Survey* 1972 Wyo. Fed. Aid Proj. W-50, R-21, Job no. 31: 7pp.   Wray 1887 *Proc. Zool. Soc. London 1887* 343–357.   Wrege and Cade 1977 *Raptor Res.* **11** 1–27.   Wright, A., and Harper 1913 *Auk* **30** 477–505.   Wright, B. S. 1953 *Jour. Wildl. Mgmt.* **17** 55–62.   Wright, B. A. 1978 *Ecology of White-tailed Kite in San Diego Co.* (abstract *Raptor Res.* **13** 26–27) San Diego State Univ., Calif., M.S. thesis.   Wright, M. H., et al. 1970 *Coll. of Observations and Field Notes on Nesting Activities of Swallow-tailed Kite in Everglades Natl. Park* (priv. pub.).   Wynne-Edwards 1952 *Auk* **69** 353–391; 1981 *Ibis* **123** 250–251.

Yanez et al. 1980 *Auk* **97** 629–631.   Yapp 1982 *Birds in Medieval Manuscripts* 1st Am. ed. New York.   Yocom 1944 *Wilson Bull.* **56** 116–117.   Young and Blomme 1975 *Ont. Field Biol.* **29** 44–49.

Zimmermann 1965 *Audubon Field Notes* **19** 475–477; 1976a *Auk* **93** 650–655; 1976b *Condor* **78** 420–421; Zimmermann and Harry 1951 *Wilson Bull.* **63** 302–314.   Zirrer 1947 *Passenger Pigeon* **9** 79–94.   Zukowsky 1956 *Zool. Garten* (NF) **21** 365–371.

INDEX TO VOLUMES 4 AND 5

Volume numbers are in **boldface**

Accipiter
  cooperii, **4** 320–354
  gentilis, **4** 355–378
  nisus, **4** 303
  striatus, **4** 304–319
Accipitridae
  (part), **4** 71–247; (concluded), **5** 3–231
aequitoralis, Falco sparverius, **5** 258
aeruginosus, **4** 251
aesalon, Falco columbarius, **5** 295
alascensis, Buteo jamaicensis, **5** 103
albicaudatus
  Buteo, **5** 74–84
  Buteo albicaudatus, **5** 76
albicilla
  Haliaeetus, **4** 238–247
  Haliaeetus albicilla, **4** 241
albidus, Accipiter gentilis, **4** 360
albigula, Buteo brachyurus, **5** 36
albonotatus, **5** 85–95
alleni, Asturina lineata, **4** 415
amplus, Gymnogyps, **4** 50
anatum, Falco peregrinus, **5** 330
anthracinus
  Buteogallus, **4** 379–389
  Buteogallus anthracinus, **4** 381
antillarum, Buteo platypterus, **5** 8
Aquila chrysaetos, **5** 180–231
arrigonii, Accipiter gentilis, **4** 360
Asturina
  lineata, **4** 413–429
  plagiata, **4** 402–410
  magnirostris, **4** 411–412
atratus
  Coragyps, **4** 11–24
  Coragyps atratus, **4** 12
  Vultur, **4** 11
atricapillus, Accipiter gentilis, **4** 359
audubonii, Polyborus plancus, **5** 237
aura
  Cathartes, **4** 25–42
  Cathartes aura, **4** 27

babylonicus, Falco peregrinus, **5** 334
bangsi, Buteogallus anthracinus, **4** 381
"*barthelemyi,*" *Aquila chrysaetos,* **5** 182

Bartramian names, **4** 11, 132, 166
borealis, Buteo jamaicensis, **5** 101
brachyurus
  Buteo, **5** 34–47
  Buteo brachyurus, **5** 36
brasiliensis, Coragyps atratus, **4** 12
brevipennis, Falco sparverius, **5** 258
brookei, Falco peregrinus, **5** 334
brunnescens, Buteo platypterus, **5** 8
Buteo
  albicaudatus, **5** 74–84
  albonotatus, **5** 85–95
  brachyurus, **5** 34–47
  buteo, **5** 134
  jamaicensis, **5** 96–133
  lagopus, **5** 152–179
  lineatus (see *Asturina lineata*), **4** 413
  nitidus, **4** 402
  platypterus, **5** 3–33
  regalis, **5** 135–151
  solitarius, **4** 1
  swainsoni, **5** 48–73
Buteogallus anthracinus, **4** 379–389
buteoides, Accipiter gentilis, **4** 360
Buzzard, Common, **5** 134

caerae, Falco sparverius, **5** 258
caeruleus
  Elanus, **4** 132–147
  Elanus caeruleus, **4** 134
calidus, Falco peregrinus, **5** 334
californianus, Gymnogyps, **4** 43–66
calurus, Buteo jamaicensis, **5** 101
canadensis, Aquila chrysaetos, **5** 186
Caracara
  Common, **5** 235
  Crested, **5** 235–249
  Carancho, **5** 235
caribararum, Falco sparverius, **5** 258
carolinensis, Pandion haliaetus, **4** 76
cassini, Falco peregrinus, **5** 333
Cathartes aura, **4** 25–42
Cathartidae, **4** 9–69
caucae, Falco sparverius, **5** 258
cheriway, Polyborus plancus, **5** 238
chionogaster, Accipiter striatus, **4** 307

Chondrohierax uncinatus, 4 102–108
chrysaetos
    Aquila, 5 180–231
    Aquila chrysaetos, 5 186
cinereus, Circus cyaneus, 4 257
cinnamominus, Falco sparverius, 5 258
Circus
    aeruginosus, 4 251
    cyaneus, 4 251–303
Condor, California, 4 *frontispiece, 8, 43–66*
colonus, Buteo albicaudatus, 5 76
columbarius
    Falco, 5 291–314
    Falco columbarius, 5 294
Conversion tables, 4 4
cooperii, Accipiter, 4 320–354
Coragyps atratus, 4 11–24
costaricensis, Buteo jamaicensis, 5 105
cristatus, Pandion haliaetus, 4 77
Crow, Jim (or John), 4 31
cubanensis, Buteo platypterus, 5 8
cyaneus
    Circus, 4 251–303
    Circus cyaneus, 4 257

daphanea, Aquila chrysaetos, 5 186
dominicensis, Falco sparverius, 5 258

Eagle
    American, 4 187
    Bald, 4 187–237
    "black" (Juv. Golden), 5 225
    Fishing (Osprey), 4 73
    Golden, 5 180–231
    Mexican (Caracara), 5 235, 247
    Pacific, 4 248
    White-headed, 4 187
    White-shouldered, 4 248
    White-tailed, 4 238–247
Elanoides forficatus, 4 109–131
Elanus caeruleus, 4 132–147
elegans, Asturina lineata, 4 416
Erne, 4 238
ernesti, Falco peregrinus, 5 335
erythronemius, Accipiter striatus, 4 307
Eyass: defined, 5 378
extima, Asturina lineata, 4 415

Falco
    columbarius, 5 291–314
    femoralis, 5 315–322
    glaucus, 4 132
    "*kryenborgi*," 5 333
    mexicanus, 5 407–423

    misisippiensis, 4 167
    peregrinus, 5 324–380
    rusticolus, 5 381–406
    sparverius, 5 253–290
    subcerulius, 4 166
    tinnunculus, 5 250–252
Falcon
    Aplomado, 5 315–322
    Barbary, 5 334
    Big-footed, 5 324
    Peregrine, 5 *frontispiece*, 324–380
    Prairie, 5 407–423
Falcon: defined, 5 378
Falconidae, 5 233–423
Falconry, 5 376–378
falklandica, Cathartes aura, 4 28
femoralis
    Falco, 5 315–322
    Falco femoralis, 5 316
fernandensis, Falco sparverius, 5 258
Fish Hawk (Osprey), 4 73
foetens, Coragyps atratus, 4 12
forficatus
    Elanoides, 4 109–131
    Elanoides forficatus, 4 111
fringilloides, Accipiter striatus, 4 307
fuertesi, Buteo jamaicensis, 5 104
fujiyamae, Accipiter gentilis, 4 360
fuliginosus, Buteo brachyurus, 5 36
fumosus, Buteo jamaicensis, 5 105
furuitii, Falco peregrinus, 5 335

gallinarum, Accipiter gentilis, 4 360
gentilis
    Accipiter, 4 355–378
    Accipiter gentilis, 4 360
glaucus, Falco, 4 132
Goshawk
    Mexican (Gray Hawk), 4 402
    Northern, 4 355–378
griseocauda, Asturina magnirostris, 4 411
groenlandicus, Haliaeetus albicilla, 4 243
gryphus, Vultur, 4 43
gundlachi, Buteogallus anthracinus, 4 381
Gymnogyps
    amplus, 4 50
    californianus, 4 43–66
Gyrfalcon, 5 381–406

hadropus, Buteo jamaicensis, 5 104
Haggard: defined, 5 378
Haliaeetus
    albicilla, 4 238–247

leucocephalus, 4 187–237
pelagicus, 4 248–250
haliaetus
 Pandion, 4 73–101
 Pandion haliaetus, 4 77
Harrier
 Hen, 4 251
 Marsh, 4 251
 Northern, 4 251–303
harrisi, Parabuteo unicinctus, 4 392
Hawk
 Bay-winged, 4 390–401
 Black, 4 379
 Broad-winged, 5 3–33
 Common Black, 4 379
 Cooper's, 4 320–354
 Crab, 4 379
 Duck, 5 324
 Dusky, 4 390
 Ferruginous, 5 135–151
 Fish (Osprey), 4 73
 Gray, 4 402–410
 "Harlan's," 5 102, 132
 Harris's, 4 390
 Hawaiian, 4 1
 Insect, 4 411
 "Krider's," 5 103
 Lesser Black, 4 379–389
 Marsh, 4 251
 Mexican Black, 4 379
 partridge (Gyrfalcon), 5 381
 Pigeon, 5 291
 Red-bellied, 4 416
 Red-shouldered, 4 413–429
 Red-tailed, 5 96–133
 Roadside, 4 411–412
 Rough-legged, 5 152–179
 Sharp-shinned, 4 304–319
 Short-tailed, 5 34–47
 Swainson's, 5 48–73
 White-tailed, 5 74–84
 Zone-tailed, 5 85–95
homeyeri, Aquila chrysaetos, 5 186
hudsonius, Circus cyaneus, 4 257
hypoleucus, Elanus caeruleus, 4 134
hypospodius, Buteo albicaudatus, 5 76

Ictinia
 mississippiensis, 4 166–186
 plumbea, 4 168–169
 subcerulea, 4 166
insignis, Falco columbarius, 5 296
insulicola, Buteo platypterus, 5 8
intermedius, Elanus caeruleus, 4 134

interstictus, Falco tinnunculus, 5 251
isabellinus, Falco sparverius, 5 258

jamaicensis
 Buteo, 5 96–133
 Buteo jamaicensis, 5 104
japonensis, Falco peregrinus, 5 334
japonica, Aquila chrysaetos, 5 186
Jerfalcon, 5 381
Jim (or John) Crow. *See* Crow, Jim
jota, Cathartes aura, 4 28

kamtschatkensis, Buteo lagopus, 5 158
kemsiesi, Buteo jamaicensis, 5 105
Kestrel
 American, 5 253–290
 Eurasian, 5 250–252
Kite
 American Swallow-tailed, 4 109–131
 Black-shouldered, 4 132–147
 Black-winged, 4 132
 Everglade, 4 148
 Hook-billed, 4 102–108
 Mississippi, 4 166–186
 Snail, 4 148–165
 Swallow tailed, 4 109–131
 White-tailed, 4 132
"kryenborgi," Falco, 5 333

lagopus
 Buteo, 5 152–179
 Buteo lagopus, 5 159
laingi, Accipiter gentilis, 4 366
leucocephalus, Haliaeetus, 4 187–237
leucurus, Elanus caeruleus, 4 134
lineata
 Asturina, 4 413–429
 Asturina lineata, 4 415
lineatus, Buteo (see *Asturina lineata*), 4 413
lutosus, Polyborus plancus, 5 237
lymani, Falco columbarius, 5 296

macropus, Falco peregrinus, 5 334
madens, Falco peregrinus, 5 334
madrensis, Accipiter striatus, 4 307
magnirostris, Asturina, 4 411–412
major, Rostrhamus sociabilis, 4 150
majusculus, Elanus caeruleus, 4 134
Merlin, 5 291–314
mexicanus, Falco, 5 407–423
micra, Asturina plagiata, 4 404
minor, Falco peregrinus, 5 334
mirus, Chondrohierax uncinatus, 4 104

misisippiensis, Falco, 4 167
mississippiensis, Ictinia, 4 166–186

nesiotes, Falco peregrinus, 5 335
nicaraguensis, Falco sparverius, 5 258
nisus, Accipiter, 4 303
nitida
    Asturina, 4 404
    Asturina nitida, 4 404
nitidus, Buteo, 4 402
notatus, Elanus caeruleus, 4 134

occidentalis, Coragyps, 4 14, 22
ochraceus, Falco sparverius, 5 258
Osprey, 4 73–101

pacificus, Falco columbarius, 5 296
pallida, Asturina nitida, 4 404
pallidus
    Falco columbarius, 5 296
    Polyborus plancus, 5 238
Pandion haliaetus, 4 73–101
papa, Sarcoramphus, 4 67–69
Parabuteo unicinctus, 4 390–401
Passage bird: defined, 5 377
paulus, Falco sparverius, 5 257
pealei, Falco peregrinus, 5 330
pelagicus, Haliaeetus, 4 248–250
pelegrinoides, Falco peregrinus, 5 334
peninsularis, Falco sparverius, 5 257
peregrinator, Falco peregrinus, 5 334
Peregrine, **5** *frontispiece,* 324–380
peregrinus
    Falco, **5** *frontispiece,* 324–380
    Falco peregrinus, 5 333
perobscurus, Accipiter striatus, 4 307
peruvianus, Falco sparverius, 5 258
pinchinchae, Falco femoralis, 5 316
plagiata
    Asturina, 4 402–410
    Asturina plagiata, 4 414
plancus
    Polyborus, 5 235–249
    Polyborus plancus, 5 238
platypterus
    Buteo, 5 3–33
    Buteo platypterus, 5 8
plumbea, Ictinia, 4 168–169
plumbeus, Rostrhamus sociabilis, 4 150
Plumages/Molting: Schematic Diagram, 4 6–7
Polyborus plancus, 5 235–249

radama, Falco peregrinus, 5 334
regalis, Buteo, 5 135–152

richardsonii, Falco columbarius, 5 295
ridgwayi, Pandion haliaetus, 4 76
rivierei, Buteo playtpterus, 5 8
Rostrhamus sociabilis, 4 148–165
Roughleg, 5 152–179
    Ferruginous, 5 135–151
ruficollis, Cathartes aura, 4 28
rusticolus, Falco, 5 381–406

Sarcoramphus papa, 4 67–69
sanctijohannis, Buteo lagopus, 5 158
schedowi, Accipiter gentilis, 4 360
Sea-Eagle
    Gray, 4 238
    Pacific, 4 248
    Steller's, 4 248–250
    White-headed, 4 187
    White-shouldered, 4 248
    White-tailed, 4 238
septentrionalis
    Cathartes aura, 4 27
    Falco femoralis, 5 316
Shaheen
    Black, 5 334
    Red-naped, 5 334
sociabilis
    Rostrhamus, 4 148–165
    Rostrhamus sociabilis, 4 150
socorroensis, Buteo jamaicensis, 5 105
solitarius, Buteo, 4 1
solitudinis, Buteo jamaicensis, 5 104
Sparrowhawk, Eurasian, 4 303
sparverius
    Falco, 5 253–290
    Falco sparverius, 5 257
sparveroides, Falco sparverius, 5 258
striatus
    Accipiter, 4 304–319
    Accipiter striatus, 4 307
subaesalon, Falco columbarius, 5 295
subcerulia, Ictinia, 4 166
subcerulius, Falco, 4 166
submelanogenys, Falco peregrinus, 5 334
suckleyi, Falco columbarius, 5 295
sumatranus, Elanus caeruleus, 4 134
superior, Parabuteo unicinctus, 4 392
suttoni, Accipiter striatus, 4 307
swainsoni, Buteo, 5 48–73

Tercel, or tircel: defined, 5 377
texana, Asturina lineata, 4 415
tinnunculus
    Falco, 5 250–252
    Falco tinnunculus, 5 251

tropicalis, Falco sparverius, **5** 258
tundrius, Falco peregrinus, **5** 331

umbrinus, Buteo jamaicensis, **5** 104
uncinatus
   Chondrohierax, 4 102–108
   Chondrohierax uncinatus, 4 104
unicinctus
   Parabuteo, 4 390–401
   Parabuteo unicinctus, 4 393

velox, Accipiter striatus, 4 307
venator, Accipiter striatus, 4 307
ventralis, Accipiter striatus, 4 307

vociferus, Elanus caeruleus, 4 134
Vultur
   atratus, 4 11
   gryphus, 4 43
Vulture
   American Black, 4 11–24
   King, 4 67–69
   Turkey, 4 25–42

wahgiensis, Elanus caeruleus, 4 134
wilsonii, Chondrohierax uncinatus, 4 104

yetapa, Elanoides forficatus, 4 111